Spicer and Pegler's
Book-keeping and Accounts

To Helen

Spicer and Pegler's Book-keeping and Accounts

Twentieth Edition

Paul Gee, BA, FCA
Principal Lecturer, Bristol Business
School, Bristol Polytechnic

Butterworths
London
1988

United Kingdom	Butterworth & Co (Publishers) Ltd, 88 Kingsway, LONDON WC2B 6AB and 61A North Castle Street, EDINBURGH EH2 3LJ
Australia	Butterworths Pty Ltd, SYDNEY, MELBOURNE, BRISBANE, ADELAIDE, PERTH, CANBERRA and HOBART
Canada	Butterworth & Co (Canada) Ltd, TORONTO and VANCOUVER
New Zealand	Butterworths of New Zealand Ltd, WELLINGTON and AUCKLAND
Singapore	Butterworth & Co (Asia) Pte Ltd, SINGAPORE
USA	Butterworth Legal Publishers, ST PAUL, Minnesota, SEATTLE, Washington, BOSTON, Massachusetts, AUSTIN, Texas and D & S Publishers, CLEARWATER, Florida

© Butterworth & Co (Publishers) Ltd 1988

British Library Cataloguing in Publication Data
Spicer, E. E.
   Spicer and Pegler's Book-keeping and accounts.
   —20th ed.
   1. Accounting
   I. Title   II. Pegler, Ernest Charles
   III. Gee, Paul
   657

ISBN 0 406 67812X

Typeset by Latimer Trend & Company Ltd, Plymouth
Printed and bound in Great Britain by
Mackays of Chatham Ltd, Kent

PREFACE

Since its first appearance over 75 years ago, *Spicer and Pegler's Book-keeping and accounts* has enjoyed a reputation as one of the leading textbooks on financial accounting.

The nineteenth edition, whilst retaining the traditions and objectives of previous editions, was extensively rewritten to reflect developments in financial accounting over the previous decade.

This edition has been completely updated to cover recent developments in fixed asset accounting, including revaluations, goodwill, merger accounting, long-term contracts, deferred tax, off-balance sheet finance, extraordinary items and accounting for price changes. The chapters dealing with interpretation of accounts have been extended to give increased coverage to this key area.

One aspect is worth particular mention. The method of preparing group accounts has been completely revised. The previous method, based on 'T' accounts has been replaced by a method involving analysis of shareholders' equity schedules. This method has been successfully used at Bristol Business School for some years. From a student's viewpoint the method involves shorter workings and helps focus on the essential nature of consolidation adjustments. The method can also be easily adapted to spreadsheets. I very much hope that users of the book will also find the approach in this new edition helpful.

The present edition has been prepared with the examination needs of the student primarily in mind. The student should also find particularly useful for this purpose the new companion volume, *Spicer and Pegler's Book-keeping and Accounts Workbook*. However, I very much hope that the book will also be useful to practitioners and accountants in industry and commerce.

I would like to thank once again all those who have helped in various ways with the completion of this edition. I am particularly grateful to Debbie Thom and Jane Leonard for their invaluable assistance in preparing the manuscript. I would also like to express my thanks to my family for their patience, help and encouragement.

Paul Gee
Bristol Business School
March 1988

CONTENTS

LIST OF ABBREVIATIONS

ACT	Advance corporation tax
ASC	Accounting Standards Committee
AVCO	Average cost
B/S	Balance sheet
CA	Companies Act
CC	Current cost
CCA	Current cost accounting
CCAB	Consultative Committee of Accountancy Bodies
CCR	Current cost reserve
COSA	Cost of sales adjustment
CPP	Current (constant) purchasing power
CRC	Current replacement cost
CRR	Capital redemption reserve
DA	Depreciation adjustment
ED	Exposure draft
EEC	European Economic Community
EPS	Earnings per share
EV	Economic value
FCM	Financial capital maintenance
FIFO	First-in-first-out
GA	Gearing adjustment
HC	Historical cost
HCA	Historical cost accounting
IASC	International Accounting Standards Committee
IPM	Investment period method
IRR	Investment revaluation reserve
IT	Income tax
LIFO	Last-in-first-out
MCT	Mainstream corporation tax
MHC	Modified historical cost
MI	Minority interest
MWCA	Monetary working capital adjustment
NCI	Net cash investment
NCRC	Net current replacement cost
NI	National insurance
NPSR	New profit-sharing ratio

NRV	Net realisable value
OCM	Operating capital maintenance
OPSR	Old profit-sharing ratio
PAYE	Pay-as-you-earn
PER	Price/earnings ratio
P/L	Profit and loss account
R + D	Research and development
ROCE	Return on capital employed
SOI	Statement of interest
SORP	Statement of recommended practice
SSAP	Statement of standard accounting practice
UCPP	Units of consent purchasing power
VAT	Value added tax
WDV	Written down value

ACKNOWLEDGEMENTS

The following acknowledgements are gratefully made:

To the Institute of Chartered Accountants in England and Wales, the Accounting Standards Committee and the International Accounting Standards Committee for permission to reproduce extracts from exposure drafts, accounting standards and statements of recommended practice.

To the directors of the following companies for permission to reproduce extracts from their annual reports and accounts:
  Bass plc
  Beechams plc
  Cadbury Schweppes plc
  Crown House plc
  Scottish & Newcastle Breweries plc.

To the directors of The Peninsula & Oriental Steam Navigation Company for permission to reproduce Part V (Profit forecast of the SGT Group) from the Listing Particulars of P&O published in February 1985.

1 INCOMPLETE RECORDS

1.1 INCOMPLETE RECORDS

(a) Introduction

Chapters 1 to 4 deal with basic matters regarding the preparation of accounts of sole traders, clubs, partnerships and companies. Chapter 5 introduces the regulatory framework for the preparation of published accounts. Chapter 6, Modern Financial Accounting sets the scene for the rest of the book which deals with advanced aspects of the preparation and interpretation of financial statements and reports for companies and groups.

For the purpose of this section, the expression 'incomplete records' is intended to signify any accounting records which fall short of complete double entry. There are varying degrees of incompleteness and the procedure to be adopted in order to prepare final accounts must depend upon the nature of the records and data available. In extreme cases, it may be found that there are no records whatever of the day-to-day transactions, owing either to neglect on the part of the trader to keep them, or to the destruction of the books and vouchers by a fire on the trader's premises, or through some other cause. In such circumstances, accounts would have to be built up largely from estimates obtained by exhaustive enquiry and the careful sifting of whatever evidence can be found. In other instances, books may have been kept by 'single entry', or data may be available by means of which double entry can be constructed. A profit and loss account and balance sheet can then be extracted.

(b) Approach to be adopted

In order to prepare a profit and loss account and a balance sheet, the following procedure is recommended:

Stage 1

Construct a statement of the financial position at the beginning of the year. This requires assets and liabilities to be determined.

The values of any fixed assets can be obtained from such details as the trader is able to supply of their cost and the dates upon which they were acquired, provision for depreciation from the date of acquisition to the commencement of the current period being deducted. The trader must provide an estimate of the value of his stock and particulars of any book debts and liabilities. Accounts should be opened, and estimated asset values posted to the debit side. The total of the book debts should be debited to a total debtors account, and the total of the liabilities credited to a total creditors account (see below). The excess of the aggregate of the assets over the liabilities may be taken to represent the amount of the trader's capital at the commencement of the period and should be credited to his capital account.

Stage 2

A careful analysis should be made of the bank statement, and a cash summary (or receipts and payments account) prepared. For this purpose, analysis columns should be prepared for each of the principal headings of receipts and payments.

For example, the lodgments into the bank may be analysed under the headings of cash takings, income from investments, the sale of assets, new capital paid in and private income of the trader. Payments from bank should be analysed as between payments for goods purchased, rent, rates, insurances and other business expenses, cheques cashed for wages, petty cash and personal expenditure, and cheques drawn for the trader's private purposes.

Stage 3

Ascertain the amounts of any cash takings which have not been paid into the bank, but have been used by the trader for the payment of business expenses, goods purchased for cash and personal expenses. An estimate should also be obtained of the value of any stock which may have been withdrawn by the trader for his own personal use or for that of his family.

Stage 4

On completion of the above analysis, postings will be made as follows:

(1) from the debit side of the cash summary;

    (i) cash takings to the credit of total debtors account;

    (ii) income from investments (if any) to the credit of income from investments account;

    (iii) proceeds of sale of assets (if any) to the credit of the appropriate asset accounts;

    (iv) other items to the credit of the relevant accounts.

If a profit or loss on the sale of assets is disclosed, this should be transferred either to profit and loss account or to the proprietor's capital account.

(2) from the credit side of cash summary;

    (i) payments for goods purchased to the debit of total creditors account;

    (ii) payments of expenses to the debit of the relevant nominal accounts;

    (iii) cheques drawn for petty cash to the debit of petty cash account;

    (iv) the proprietor's personal drawings to the debit of his current account;

    (v) the purchase of assets (if any) to the debit of the respective asset accounts.

Stage 5

The amount of any cash takings used for business or private purposes should be noted, the appropriate account debited and total debitors account credited. Note, however, that in incomplete record questions, private drawings may need to be calculated as a balancing figure.

Stage 6

This involves calculating year end adjustments and balances.

A schedule should be compiled of the book debts outstanding, the total of which should be carried down in the total debtors account. The balance of this account will now represent the total sales for the period and should be transferred to the credit of trading account.

Similarly, a schedule should be made of liabilities outstanding to trade and other creditors. The total should be carried down in the total creditors account. The balance of this account will now represent the total purchases for the period and should be transferred to the debit of trading account.

Accruals and prepayments will be carried down as closing balances in the relevant expense accounts.

Stage 7

The whole of the transactions will now be recorded in total in double entry form and it will be possible to extract a trading profit and loss account and balance sheet in the usual way.

(c) Reliability of information

The gross profit percentage revealed by the trading account may afford some indication as to the accuracy or otherwise of the data and estimates used in compiling the accounts. If it is found that this percentage is substantially lower than the percentage of gross profit normally earned in the particular trade, doubt would be thrown on the accuracy of the opening or closing stocks, purchases or sales, and further enquiry would be necessary. In particular, information should be elicited as to the style in which the trader lives. It will often be found that the amount of cash takings alleged to be withdrawn for private use is wholly incompatible with the size and character of the trader's domestic establishment and mode of life, and re-estimation of the amount of the personal drawings might be necessary. (See also comments in (e).)

(d) An illustration

A is the proprietor of a grocery and general store. He has not previously engaged an accountant. He informs you that this year the Inspector of Taxes refuses to accept the account A has supplied of his trading results for the year ended March 31 19X6. That account is as follows:

	£		£
Payments for goods	9,495	Takings	10,930
Payments for expenses	1,130		
Profits	305		
	£10,930		£10,930

He instructs you to examine his records and prepare accounts.

From your examination of the records and from interviews with your client, you ascertain the following information:

(1) The takings are kept in a drawer under the counter; at the end of each day the cash is counted and recorded on a scrap of paper; at irregular intervals Mrs A transcribes the figures into a notebook; a batch of slips of paper was inadvertently destroyed before the figures had been written into the notebook, but Mr and Mrs A carefully estimated their takings for that period, and the estimated figure is included in the total of £10,930.

(2) The following balances can be accepted:

	March 31	
	19X5	*19X6*
	£	£
Cash in hand	45	87
Balance at bank	156	219
Good debts	458	491
Creditors for purchases of stock	279	243
Stock at cost	1,950	1,900

(3) Debts totalling £356 were abandoned during the year as bad; the takings included £25 recovered in respect of an old debt abandoned in a previous year.

(4) A rents the shop and living accommodation on a weekly tenancy for £3 per week including rates; the rent is included in expenses of £1,130. The living accommodation may be regarded as one-third of the whole.

(5) The expenses total also includes:

    (i) £35 running expenses of A's private car;

    (ii) £60 for exterior decoration of the whole premises, the landlord having refused to have this done;

    (iii) £160 for alterations to the premises to enlarge the storage accommodation.

(6) A takes £10 per week from the business and hands it over to his wife, who pays all the household and personal expenses except those referred to below.

(7) A pays for his own cigarettes and beer with cash taken from the drawer; this is estimated at £1·50 per week.

(8) A competed in a football pool for 30 weeks of the year, staking £1 each week, buying a postal order with cash taken from the drawer; his winnings totalled £59.

(9) During the year A bought a secondhand car (not used for business) from a friend; the price agreed was £350, but as the friend owed A £67 for goods supplied from the business the matter was settled by a cheque for the difference.

(10) An assurance policy for A's life matured and realised £641.

(11) A cashed a cheque for £100 for a friend; the cheque was dishonoured and the friend is repaying the £100 by instalments. He had paid £40 by March 31 19X6;

(12) Other private payments by cheque totalled £96 plus a further sum of £110 for income tax.

(13) You are to provide £42 for accountancy fees.

You are required to prepare:

(a) A balance sheet of the business as at March 31 19X5;
(b) A profit and loss account for the year ended March 31 19X6; and
(c) A balance sheet for the business as at March 31 19X6.

Solutions

(a) Balance sheet at 31 March 19X5

Current assets	£
Stock	1,950
Debtors	458
Cash at bank	156
Cash in hand	45
	2,609
Less creditors	279
	2,330
Capital account of A	2,330

(b) Trading and profit and loss account for the year ended 31 March 19X6

	£	£
Sales		11,638
Opening stock	1,950	
Purchases	9,459	
	11,409	
Less closing stock	1,900	
Cost of sales		9,509
Gross profit		2,129
Rent and rates ($\frac{2}{3} \times £3 \times 52$ weeks)	104	
Sundry expenses	719	
Cost of enlarging storage accommodation	160	
Repairs ($\frac{2}{3} \times £60$)	40	
Bad debts (356 − 25)	331	
Accountancy fees	42	
		1,396
Net profit for the year		733

NOTE
The cost of enlarging storage accommodation could be capitalised but it has been written off in the year in which incurred on prudence grounds.

(c) Balance sheet at 31 March 19X6

Current assets	£	£
Stock		1,900
Debtors		491
Cash at bank		219
Cash in hand		87
		2,697
Less current liabilities		
Trade creditors	243	
Accountancy fees	42	
	285	
		2,412
Capital account of A		
Balance at 1 April 19X5		2,330
Net profit		733
		3,063
Less drawings		651
		2,412

Workings

CASH SUMMARY

	£		£
Balances 1/4/X5 (cash £45; bank £156)	201	Expenses	1,130
		Purchases	9,495
Bad debt recovered	25	Cash drawings	520
Football pool winnings	59	Personal cigarettes etc.	78
Insurance policy	641	Football pools	30
Repaid by friend	40	Car (350–67)	283
Balance cash takings carried		Loan to friend	100
to total debtors account	11,182	Drawings by cheque	96
		Income tax	110
		Balance 31/3/X6 (cash £87; bank £219)	306
	£12,148		£12,148

TOTAL DEBTORS

	£		£
Debtors 1/4/X5	458	Cash takings	11,182
Balance = sales	11,638	Friend re car	67
		Bad debts w/o	356
		Debtors 31/3/X6	491
	£12,096		£12,096

TOTAL CREDITORS

	£		£
Cash	9,495	Creditors 1/4/X5	279
Creditors 31/3/X6	243	Balances = purchases	9,459
	£9,738		£9,738

SUNDRY EXPENSES

	£		£
Cash	1,130	Rent	156
		Car expenses	35
		Repairs to premises	60
		Alterations	160
		Balance sundry expenses	719
	£1,130		£1,130

DRAWINGS

	£		£
Cash	520	Football pool winnings	59
Cheques	96	Life policy money	641
Rent (private element)	52	Repayments by friend	40
Private car expenses	35	Balance net drawings	651
Decorations (house) (one-third of £60)	20		
Purchase of car	350		
Cash paid to friend	100		
Cigarettes etc	78		
Football pools	30		
Income tax	110		
	£1,391		£1,391

(e) Use of the gross profit percentage

In the above illustration there was sufficient information to enable the sales figure of £11,638 to be calculated from the total debtors account.

In some questions, however, such information is not always readily available. In cases such as these, it may be possible to calculate sales indirectly as long as a gross profit percentage is provided.

The approach is quite simple:

(1) Calculate cost of sales:

Opening stock + purchases – closing stock;

(2) Convert cost of sales to sales:

e g if gross profit percentage is 20%, sales $= \dfrac{100}{80}$ cost of sales.

Once sales for the year have been estimated, and opening and closing debtors taken into account, the figure of cash takings can be calculated as a balancing figure in the total debtors account.

(f) Deficient accounting records

Where the available records are so deficient that it is impossible to compile a reasonably complete cash summary, the only method of estimating the profit or loss for the period is to prepare statements of affairs showing the 'net worth' of the business at the beginning and at the end of the period respectively.

A statement of affairs for this purpose is a document in the form of a balance sheet, showing on one side the estimated amounts of the various assets, and on the other the liabilities, the difference between the two sides representing the proprietor's 'net worth' or capital at the date of the statement.

If a statement of affairs has been drawn up at the end of the preceding period, the opening capital for the current period would be shown thereby. It would then be necessary to prepare a similar statement at the end of the current period, and to find the difference between the opening and closing figures of capital, the amount of which, after adding back any sums withdrawn, and deducting any new capital introduced, would represent the profit or loss for the period.

Illustration

J's last statement of affairs prepared at January 1 was:

STATEMENT OF AFFAIRS

January 1	£		£
Creditors	6,000	Office furniture	500
Bills payable	500	Stock	2,000
Capital account—being		Debtors	4,500
excess of assets over		Bills receivable	1,000
liabilities at this date	3,000	Cash	1,500
	£9,500		£9,500

On December 31 he finds his liabilities to be: creditors £4,500, bills payable £700; and his assets: office furniture £450, stock £1,500, debtors, £5300, bills receivable £700, cash £800. His drawings during the period have amounted to £450. What profit has he made?

STATEMENT OF AFFAIRS

December 31	£		£
Creditors	4,500	Office furniture	450
Bills payable	700	Stock	1,500
Capital account—being		Debtors	5,300
excess of assets over		Bills receivable	700
liabilities at this date	3,550	Cash	800
	£8,750		£8,750

Calculation of profit	£
Capital, December 31	3,550
Drawings for the year	450
Capital, January 1	(3,000)
Estimated net profit for the year	1,000

No great difficulty should be experienced in estimating values of the assets and liabilities at the end of the period under review, provided that the work of preparing the statement is undertaken shortly after that date, since the necessary material for the valuation will probably be still accessible. The preparation of earlier statements may present more difficulty, and the most searching enquiries may have to be made. Needless to say, this method of ascertaining results is most unsatisfactory, and the trader should be advised to install double entry book-keeping without delay.

1.2   INCOME AND EXPENDITURE ACCOUNTS

(a) Introduction

An *income and expenditure account* is the profit and loss account of a non-trading concern. It contains only revenue items, being debited with all expenditure, and credited with all income of a period, whether or not it has actually been paid or received within that period. The final balance of an income and expenditure account represents the excess of income over expenditure, or the excess of expenditure over income, as the case may be, for the period. This balance is similar to the net profit or loss of a trading concern.

Receipts and payments accounts and income and expenditure accounts are used commonly by such non-trading concerns as social clubs, societies etc for the purpose of presenting their financial position to their members.

A receipts and payment account is *no* substitute for an income and expenditure account as the latter is prepared on an accruals basis.

(b) Contrast with receipts and payment accounts

The main differences between the two accounts are:

Receipts and payments	*Income and expenditure*
Cash transactions only	Includes accruals and prepayments
Includes capital receipts and capital payments	Excludes capital receipts and capital payments
Balance represents cash in hand, bank balance, or bank overdraft	Balance represents surplus/ deficiency of income over expenditure for a given period

(c) Basis of preparation

In order to prepare an income and expenditure account from a receipts and payments account, post all revenue items appearing in the receipts and payments account to the opposite sides of the income and expenditure account, and make adjustments for accruals and prepayments at the beginning and the end of the period.

Such items as subscriptions, entrance fees, income from investments etc which have been received in cash and debited to the receipts and payments account, must be credited to the income and expenditure account, whilst expenditure such as rent, wages, repairs etc appearing on the credit side of the receipts and payments account must be debited to the income and expenditure account. Capital items appearing in the receipts and payments account will be posted to the debit or credit, as the case may be, of the relevant asset or liability accounts, and will not affect the income and expenditure account.

The balance sheet of a non-trading concern is prepared in the usual way, and contains particulars of all the assets and liabilities at the date as at which it is made up. The excess of the assets over the liabilities is similar to the capital of a trader, but is usually called the accumulated fund, or general fund since it is normally made up of the excess of income over expenditure which has been accumulated within the concern.

Separate accounts should be kept for funds raised for special purposes e g building appeal funds and election funds.

Two problems on the solutions of which accountants are divided are:

(1) Should club entrance fees be credited in the income and expenditure account or be shown on the balance sheet of the club as an addition to the accumulated fund? Provided entrance fees are consistently treated, either method is correct; although it can be argued that revenue might be distorted if there were a large number of entrance fees in any one period, the benefit of which is to be spread over a number of accounting periods.

(2) Should club subscriptions in arrear be shown as debtors at the balance sheet date?

A large number of club subscriptions in arrear are never received and the balance sheet could be distorted by a fictitious asset of debtors should club subscriptions in arrear be included on the balance sheet and never received. In practice, subscriptions in arrears are often excluded from the balance sheet on prudence grounds. In theory examiners may require such arrears to be taken into account.

(d) Illustration

The Westminster Political Association prepared accounts for the year to December 31.

(1) They started the year with £470 in the bank and ended with an overdraft of £615, which was secured by the deposit of investments with the bank.

(2) They received subscriptions amounting to £835, of which £25 represented arrears, £760 current subscriptions and £50 in advance.

(3) They received £520 donations to the general fund and £850 to the election fund, which had £15 in hand at January 1, and out of which £720 was paid for election expenses. There was no separate bank account.

(4) They held government securities at January 1, which cost £2,000. Half were sold for £1,250 and the balance was valued at £1,200 at December 31. These investments produced interest of £35 during the year.

(5) Office premises were purchased during the year for £3,000 and a mortgage was arranged through a building society for £1,500. Legal expenses amounted to £105 and one instalment of £80 was paid to the society of which £45 was interest. Alterations and decorations of the premises cost £570, of which £150 was still owing.

(6) Office furniture was valued at £150 at January 1. £170 was paid for additions during the year and £70 was still owing. Depreciation is estimated at 10% per annum.

(7) The only other receipt was £75 for sale of literature, £60 worth was given away. The total cost of literature amounted to £120, and no stocks were left at the end of the year.

(8) Other payments were:

Agent's salary and expenses	£700 (of which £50 related to next year)
Office salaries	£350
Rent and rates	£170 (£50 owing at January 1)
Meetings and propaganda	£165 (£30 for a meeting to be held in the new year)
Stationery, postage and sundries	£150.

Prepare a receipts and payments account and an income and expenditure account for the year ended December 31, and a balance sheet as at that date. Subscriptions in arrear are to be brought into account. Ignore taxation.

THE WESTMINSTER POLITICAL ASSOCIATION
RECEIPTS AND PAYMENTS ACCOUNT

for the year ended December 31

		£			£	£	£
Jan 1	Balance bf	470	Dec 31	Election expenses			720
Dec 31	Subscriptions	835		Cost of premises	£3,000		
	Donations	520		Legal expenses	105		
	Election fund	850			———		
	Sale of securities	1,250			3,105		
	Interest received	35		*Less* mortgage	1,500		
	Sale of literature	75			———	1,605	
	Balance being			Building society			
	overdraft c/f	615		payments		80	
				Alterations and			
				decorations		420	
				Office furniture		170	
				Agent's salary		700	
				Office salaries		350	
				Rent and rates		170	
				Meetings etc		165	
				Stationery and			
				postage		150	
				Cost of literature		120	
		———					———
		£4,650					£4,650

NOTE
The above account has been presented in double-sided format as this would appear to give a clearer presentation to readers.

By contrast, the income and expenditure account is presented in the usual vertical format.

INCOME AND EXPENDITURE ACCOUNT

for the year ended December 31

	£	£	£
Income			
Subscriptions receivable			760
Interest on investments			35
			——
			795
Expenditure			
Agent's salary and expenses		650	
Office salaries		350	
Rent and rates		120	
Stationery, postage and sundries		150	
Meetings and propaganda		135	
Cost of literature distributed	60		
Less profit on sales	15		
	——		
		45	
Interest on mortgage		45	
Depreciation of office furniture		39	
		——	
			1,534
			——
Excess of expenditure over income			(739)
			——

BALANCE SHEET AS AT 31 DECEMBER

	Cost £	Depreciation	Net book value £
Fixed assets			
Office premises	3,675	—	3,675
Office furniture	390	39	351
	4,065	39	4,026
Investments at cost (market value £1,200)			1,000
			5,026
Current assets			
Payments in advance (50 + 30)		80	
Current liabilities			
Subscriptions in advance	50		
Creditors (150 + 70)	220		
Bank overdraft	615	(885)	(805)
			4,221
Long-term liability			
Mortgage (secured on office premises)			
(1,500 − 35)			(1,465)
			2,756
General fund			
Balance at January 1			2,580
Profit on sale of investments			250
Donations			520
			3,350
Less excess of expenditure over income for year			739
			2,611
Election fund			
Balance at January 1		15	
Add donations		850	
		865	
Less election expenses		720	
			145
			2,756

Workings

	£
(1) *Office premises*	
Cost	3,000
Alterations	570
Legal expenses	105
	3,675
(2) *Office furniture*	
Cost at January 1	150
Additions	240
	390
(3) *Election fund at January 1*	
Bank (excluding election fund)	455
Subscriptions in arrears	25
Investments	2,000
Office furniture	150
	2,630
Less rent accrued at January 1	50
	2,580

2 PARTNERSHIP ACCOUNTS—1

2.1 INTRODUCTION

Partnership is defined by the Partnership Act 1890 as 'the relation which subsists between persons carrying on a business in common with a view of profit'. The participation in profits is not, however, of itself alone conclusive evidence of the existence of a partnership, since the relationship rests upon mutual intention.

Detailed considerations of partnership law are outside the scope of this book so no further reference will be made to the question of whether or not a partnership actually exists. It is, however, important to discuss the significance of the partnership agreement.

As the essence of partnership is mutual agreement, it is desirable for the partners to come to some understanding before entering into partnership as to the conditions upon which the business is to be carried on, and as to their respective rights and powers.

The Partnership Act 1890 lays down certain rules to be observed in the absence of agreement. The circumstances must determine whether these rules are applicable in the particular case, and since many matters should be decided which are not included in these rules, it is desirable that a formal agreement be entered into with a view to preventing disputes in the future. The advantages of a written agreement need no emphasis, and it is preferable that it should be under seal, since the character of a deed precludes contradiction by any party of the terms which have been agreed.

Even though a formal agreement is made, this does not preclude subsequent variation where changing circumstances demand it; such variation can always be effected with the consent of all the partners, which may be evidenced by an amending agreement, or inferred from a course of dealing.

(a) Clauses relating to accounting matters

The general provisions affecting questions of accounts that should be contained in all partnership agreements, apart from any special circumstances, are as follows:

(1) As to capital; whether each partner should contribute a fixed amount or otherwise;
(2) As to the division of profits and losses between the partners, including capital profits and losses.
(3) Whether the capitals are to be fixed, drawings and profits being adjusted on current accounts, or whether they are to be adjusted on the capital accounts.
(4) Whether interest on capital or on drawings, or both, is to be allowed or charged before arriving at the profits divisible in the agreed proportions, and if so, at what rate.
(5) Whether current accounts (if any) are to bear interest, and if so, at what rate.
(6) Whether partners' drawings are to be limited in amount.
(7) Whether partners are to be allowed remuneration for their services before arriving at divisible profits, and if so, the amounts thereof.
(8) That proper accounts shall be prepared at least once a year so that these shall be audited.
(9) That such accounts when duly signed shall be binding on the partners, but

13

shall be capable of being reopened within a specified period on an error being discovered.

(10) The method by which the value of goodwill shall be determined in the event of the retirement or death of any of the partners.

(11) The method of determining the amount due to a deceased partner and the manner in which the liability to his personal representatives is to be settled e g by a lump sum payment within a specified period, by instalments of certain proportions etc, and the rate of interest to be allowed on outstanding balances.

(12) In the event of there being any partnership insurance policies, the method of treating the premiums thereon and the division of the policy money.

(b) Rights and duties of partners in the absence of a partnership agreement

The Partnership Act 1890 stipulates that the following rules apply in the absence of an agreement to the contrary (note that the rules are *not* mandatory).

The interests of partners in the partnership property, and their rights and duties in relation to the partnership shall be determined, subject to any agreement, express or implied, between the partners by the following rules:

(1) All the partners are entitled to share equally in the capital and profits of the business, and must contribute equally towards the losses, whether of capital or otherwise, sustained by the firm.

(2) The firm must indemnify every partner in respect of payments made and personal liabilities incurred by him:

(a) in the ordinary and proper conduct of the business of the firm; or

(b) in or about anything necessarily done for the preservation of the business or property of the firm.

(3) Whether the capitals are to be fixed, drawings and profits being adjusted on current accounts, or whether they are to be adjusted on the capital accounts.

(4) A partner is not entitled, before the ascertainment of profits, to interest on the capital subscribed by him.

(5) Every partner may take part in the management of the partnership business.

(6) No partner shall be entitled to remuneration for acting in the partnership business.

(7) No person may be introduced as a partner without the consent of all existing partners.

(8) Any difference arising as to ordinary matters connected with the partnership business may be decided by a majority of the partners, but no change may be made in the nature of the partnership business without the consent of all existing partners.

(9) The partnership books are to be kept at the place of business of the partnership (or the principal place, if there is more than one), and every partner may, when he thinks fit, have access to and inspect and copy any of them.

2.2   PARTNERS' ACCOUNTS (CAPITAL, CURRENT, LOAN)

(a) Capital and current accounts

Where, as is usual, the partnership agreement provides for a fixed amount of capital to be contributed by each partner, it is preferable for the amounts thereof to be credited to the respective partners' capital accounts, and for partners' drawings, salaries, interest on capital and shares of profit to be dealt with in current accounts (see illustration below—Duck, Drake, Cygnet).

This enables a clear distinction to be made in the accounts between fixed capital (no part of which should be withdrawn, except by agreement) and undrawn profits. If partners' drawings, salaries, interest and shares of profit are passed through the capital accounts, the balances on these accounts will be constantly fluctuating, and there may be a danger of a partner's capital being depleted by drawings in excess of his share of profits etc, without particular attention being drawn to the fact.

(b) Partners' loan accounts

Where a partner makes an advance to the firm as distinct from capital, the amount thereof should be credited to a separate loan account and not to the partner's capital account. This is important, since under the Partnership Act 1890, advances by partners are repayable on dissolution in priority to capital.

Moreover, even in the absence of agreement on the point, a partner is entitled, under the Partnership Act 1890, to interest at 5% per annum on advances made to the firm, whereas he is not entitled to interest on capital.

Interest on a partner's advance or loan at the agreed rate (or, in the absence of agreement, at 5% per annum) should be credited to his current account, and debited to profit and loss account as an expense of the business in arriving at net profit. Interest on a partner's loan is as much a charge against the profits of a business as a loan from a third partner. By contrast, interest on capital is an appropriation of profit, being in the nature of a preferential allocation of divisible profits.

2.3 ALLOCATION OF PARTNERSHIP PROFITS

The formula for allocation of partnership profits between the partners will usually be set out in the partnership agreement. The formula may take account of some or all of the following adjustments:

(a) Interest on capital.
(b) Interest on drawings.
(c) Partners' salaries.
(d) Profit-sharing ratios.

(a) Interest on capital

By making a notional charge against profits for interest at a fair commercial rate on the capital employed in a business, it can be seen whether the balance of profit remaining is sufficient to justify the continuance of the firm with unlimited liability, since the interest charged may be regarded as approximately the income the partners would have derived from the investment of their capital in securities involving little or no risk. Apart from this, however, where there are two or more partners with unequal capitals, the effect of charging interest on capital is to adjust the rights of the partners as between themselves as regards capital, giving each a reasonable return on his capital before dividing the balance of profit in the agreed proportions.

Where the capital is fixed, and the profits are shared in the same proportions as capital, the charging of interest makes no difference to the ultimate amount credited to each partner. Even in such cases, however, it may be desirable to charge interest for the first reason mentioned above.

Interest on capital should be calculated for the period during which the business has had the use of the capital, allowance being made for any additions or withdrawals during the period.

It may happen that the profits of the business in a particular year are less than the interest on capital credited to the partners. In such circumstances, unless the partnership agreement provides an alternative method, the interest should be charged in full, the resulting 'loss' being borne by the partners in the proportions in which they share profits. In this manner, the real result of the trading for the period is disclosed.

As already indicated, partners are not entitled to interest on capital unless the payment thereof is expressly authorised by the partnership agreement.

Illustration 1

A, B and C, sharing profits and losses equally, have capitals of £10,000, £5,000 and £2,000 respectively, on which they are entitled to interest at 5% per annum. The profits for the year, before charging interest on capital, amounted to £5,500. Show how the profits will be divided between the partners.

Statement of allocation of net profit (or appropriation account)

	Total	A	B	C
	£	£	£	£
Interest on capital	850	500	250	100
Balance of profits (shared equally)	4,650	1,550	1,550	1,550
Net profit, allocated between partners	5,500	2,050	1,800	1,650

(b) Interest on drawings

Frequently, partners make drawings in varying amounts and at irregular intervals, and in such cases, if interest is charged the rights of the partners are adjusted. In many cases, however, drawings are made by mutual agreement and no interest is charged at all.

Where interest is charged, it is usually calculated at a fixed rate per cent per annum from the date of each drawing to the date the accounts are closed and taken account of in the statement of allocation of net profit in a similar way to interest on capital.

(c) Partners' salaries

As already stated, in the absence of agreement no partner is entitled before arriving at the amount of divisible profits to remuneration for his services to the firm. In the following cases however, it may be desirable for the partnership agreement to provide for the payment of salaries to the partners:

(1) Where some of the partners take a greater or more effective part in the conduct and management of the business than others.
(2) Where there are junior partners, whom it is desired to remunerate by way of a fixed salary plus, perhaps, a small percentage of the profits.
(3) Where the partnership business is wholly managed by the partners, and it is desired to ascertain the true profit, after such a charge for managerial services had been made as would have been incurred had the business not been managed by the proprietors.

Where the agreement provides for the payment of salaries to partners, it should be appreciated that such payments, although designated salaries are, like interest on capital, merely in the nature of preferential shares of the divisible profit. The amounts of such salaries should therefore be taken into account in the statement of allocation of net profit.

Illustration 2

Duck, Drake and Cygnet carried on a retail business in partnership. The partnership agreement provides that:

(1) The partners are to be credited at the end of each year with salaries of £1,000 to Duck and £500 each to Drake and Cygnet, and with interest at the rate of 5% per annum on the balances at the credit of their respective capital accounts at the commencement of the year.

(2) No interest is to be charged on drawings.

(3) After charging partnership salaries and interest on capital, profits and losses are to be divided in the proportion: Duck, 50%; Drake, 30% and Cygnet, 20%; with the proviso, however, that Cygnet's share in any year (exclusive of salary and interest) shall not be less than £1,000, any deficiency to be borne in profit-sharing ratio by the other two partners.

The trial balance of the firm at December 31 19X8 was as follows:

	Dr £	Cr £
Partners' capital accounts:		
Duck—Balance January 1 19X8		8,000
Drake—Balance January 1 19X8		5,000
Cygnet—Balance January 1 19X8		3,000
Partners' current accounts:		
Duck—Balance January 1 19X8		1,600
Drake—Balance January 1 19X8		1,200
Cygnet—Balance January 1 19X8		800
Sales		46,500
Trade creditors		3,700
Shop fittings at cost	3,600	
Shop fittings—provision for depreciation, January 1 19X8		1,400
Freehold premises—cost	6,000	
Leasehold premises—purchased during year	4,500	
Leashold premises—additions and alterations	2,500	
Purchases	28,000	
Stock on hand, January 1 19X8	4,200	
Salaries and wages	6,400	
Office and trade expenses	4,520	
Rent, rates and insurance	1,050	
Professional charges	350	
Debtors	2,060	
Provision for doubtful debts, January 1 19X8		50
Balance at bank	4,370	
Drawings, other than monthly payments:		
Duck	1,700	
Drake	1,100	
Cygnet	900	
	71,250	71,250

You are given the following additional information:

(1) Stock on December 31 19X8 was valued at £3,600.

(2) A debt of £60 is to be written off, and the provision against the remaining debtors should be 5%.

(3) Salaries and wages include the following monthly drawings by the partners: Duck £50, Drake £30, Cygnet £25.

(4) Partners had during the year been supplied with goods from stock and it was agreed that these should be charged to them as follows: Duck £60 and Drake £40.

(5) On December 31, rates paid in advance and office and trade expenses owing were £250 and £240 respectively.

(6) Depreciation of shop fittings is to be provided at 5% per annum on cost.

(7) Professional charges include £250 fees paid in respect of the acquisition of the leasehold premises, which fees are to be capitalised.

(8) The cost of and the additions and alterations to the leasehold premises were to be written off over 25 years, commencing on January 1 in the year in which the premises were acquired:

You are required to prepare:

(a) the trading and profit and loss account for the year ended December 31 19X8;
(b) the balance sheet as on that date; and
(c) partners' current accounts in columnar form for the year ended December 31 19X8.

(a)   DUCK, DRAKE AND CYGNET TRADING PROFIT AND LOSS ACCOUNT
for the year ending 31 December 19X8

	£	£	£
Sales			46,500
Opening stock		4,200	
Purchases	28,000		
Goods supplied to partners	100		
	———	27,900	
		———	
		32,100	
Less closing stock		3,600	
		———	28,500
			———
Gross profit			18,000
Salaries and wages		5,140	
Office and trade expenses		4,760	
Rent, rates and insurance		800	
Professional charges		100	
Bad debts		110	
Amortisation of leasehold premises		290	
Depreciation of shop fittings		180	
		———	11,380
			———
Net profit			6,620
			———

Statement of allocation of net profit

	Total	Duck	Drake	Cygnet
	£	£	£	£
Interest on capital	800	400	250	150
Partners' salaries	2,000	1,000	500	500
Balance of profits (shared 50:30:20)	3,820	1,910	1,146	764
	———	———	———	———
Provisional allocation of net profit	6,620	3,310	1,896	1,414
Adjustment to bring Cygnet's share of 'balance' of profit up to £1,000 (i e adjustment of 1,000—764) borne by Duck and Drake in ratio 5:3	—	(147)	(89)	236
	———	———	———	———
Final allocation of net profit	6,620	3,163	1,807	1,650
	———	———	———	———

(b) Balance sheet as at 31 December 19X8

	Cost £	Accumulated depreciation £	Net book value £
Fixed assets			
Freehold premises	6,000	—	6,000
Leasehold premises	7,250	290	6,960
Shop fittings	3,600	1,580	2,020
	16,850	1,870	14,980
Current assets			
Stock		3,600	
Debtors	2,000		
Less provision for doubtful debts	100		
		1,900	
Prepayments		250	
Cash at bank		4,370	
		10,120	
Less: current liabilities			
Trade creditors	3,700		
Accrued expenses	240		
		3,940	
Net current assets			6,180
			21,160

Partners' accounts	Capital accounts £	Current accounts £	Total £
Duck	8,000	2,403	10,403
Drake	5,000	1,507	6,507
Cygnet	3,000	1,250	4,250
	16,000	5,160	21,160

(c) Partners' current accounts

	Duck £	Drake £	Cygnet £		Duck £	Drake £	Cygnet £
Drawings:							
Cash	2,300	1,460	1,200	Bal b/f	1,600	1,200	800
Goods	60	40	—	Share of net			
Bal c/f	2,403	1,507	1,250	profit	3,163	1,807	1,650
	4,763	3,007	2,450		4,763	3,007	2,450

2.4 GOODWILL

(a) Definition of goodwill

The following are some judicial definitions of goodwill:

(1) 'The goodwill of a business is the advantage, whatever it may be, which a person gets by continuing to carry on, and being entitled to represent to the outside world that he is carrying on a business, which has been carried on for some time previously.' (Warrington J, in *Hill v Fearis* [1905] 1 Ch 466.)

(2) '[Goodwill] is a thing very easy to describe, very difficult to define. It is the benefit and advantage of the good name, reputation and connection of a

business. It is the attractive force which brings in custom. It is the one thing which distinguishes an old established business from a new business at its first start ... Goodwill is composed of a variety of elements. It differs in its composition in different trades and in different businesses in the same trade. One element may preponderate here, and another there.' (Lord Macnaughten in *IRC v Muller* [1901] AC 217.)

From the accountant's viewpoint, goodwill, in the sense of attracting custom, has little significance unless it has a saleable value. To the accountant, therefore, goodwill may be said to be that element arising from the reputation, connection or other advantages possessed by a business which enables it to earn greater profits than the return normally to be expected on the capital represented by the net tangible assets employed in the business. In considering the return normally to be expected, regard must be had to the nature of the business, the risks involved, fair management remuneration and any other relevant circumstances.

The goodwill possessed by a firm may be due, inter alia, to the following:

(a) The location of the business premises.
(b) The nature of the firm's products or the reputation of its service.
(c) The possession of favourable contracts, complete or partial monopoly etc.
(d) The personal reputation of the partners.
(e) The possession of efficient and contented employees.
(f) The possession of trade marks, patents or a well-known business name.
(g) The continuance of advertising campaigns.
(h) The maintenance of the quality of the firm's product, and development of the business with changing conditions.
(i) Freedom from legislative restrictions.

Goodwill is defined in SSAP 22 as 'the difference between the value of a business as a whole and the aggregate of the fair value of its separable net assets'. (See chapter 7.)

(b) Goodwill in partnership accounts

Although a firm may possess goodwill, it is not customary to raise an account for it in the books except to the extent that cash or other assets of the firm have been used to pay for it. It follows, therefore, that when goodwill exists and is unrecorded in the books, the capitals of the partners of the firm are understated to the extent of the value of their respective shares of the goodwill.

Even though a goodwill account may at some time have been raised in the books, the goodwill account would not be adjusted to give effect to every variation in its value, and in most cases, therefore, the partners' capitals are at all times understated or overstated in the books to some extent by their shares of the unrecorded appreciation or depreciation in the value of goodwill.

As the amount by which goodwill is undervalued (or overvalued) in the books is a profit (or a loss) to be shared by the partners in their agreed profit-sharing ratio, any alteration in the proportions in which profits and losses are shared, without first making an adjustment in the book value of goodwill, will result in an advantage to one or more partners and a disadvantage to others.

(c) Situations requiring adjustments to respect of goodwill

In each of the following cases, a change in the profit-sharing ratio takes place and therefore, unless a goodwill account already stands in the books at its correct value, some adjustment must be made:

(1) Upon the introduction of a new partner.
(2) Upon the retirement or death of a partner.
(3) Upon an agreed change in profit-sharing ratio between the partners.

These are dealt with later in the chapter under the respective heading.

(d) Methods of valuing goodwill

Various methods are advocated for the valuation of goodwill. In many cases the method adopted is a purely arbitrary one and is often governed by the custom of the particular trade in which the business is engaged. The more usual bases of valuation are as follows:

(1) *The average profits of a given number of past years multiplied by an agreed number*

Thus, 'three years' purchase of net profits' is commonly spoken of as the basis upon which goodwill is valued. This method is purely arbitrary and will frequently produce a figure for goodwill out of all proportion to its true value.

Illustration 3

The average net profit made by A, B and Co for the past five years has been £2,000 per annum before charging interest on capital and partners' salaries. The average capital employed in the business has been £10,000.

On the basis of three years' purchase of net profits, £6,000 would be payable for the goodwill of the firm. It is apparent, however, that no goodwill actually exists; in fact, there is a negative goodwill since no one would be prepared to pay £16,000 for a business which produces only £2,000 per annum before making any provision for fair remuneration to the proprietors in respect of their services to the business.

Allowing as little as £1,500 per annum for the services of the proprietors, only £500 per annum remains for interest on capital invested and, therefore, at, say 10% per annum, such a business would be worth as an investment only £5,000, irrespective of the fact that £10,000 was invested in it.

(2) *The average gross income of the business for a number of past years multiplied by an agreed number*

This method is frequently adopted by professional firms, but is subject to the same disadvantages as those described above. In many cases the gross income of certain years will have been inflated by business of a non-recurring nature, and therefore the purchaser will be paying for goodwill calculated on income which he himself will not enjoy. Furthermore, it is quite conceivable that the expenses incurred in earning the gross income may be so great that there is actually a loss, in which case a sum will be payable for the 'goodwill' of a business from which a loss is to be expected.

(3) *The capital value of an annuity for an agreed number of years of an amount equal to the average super profits of the business*

Super profits are the profits in excess of the amount necessary to pay a fair return upon the capital invested in the business, having regard to the nature of the business and the risks involved and a reasonable remuneration for the services of the partners who work therein.

Illustration 4

The average net profits expected in the future by A, B and Co are £10,000 per annum. The average capital employed in the business is £50,000.

The rate of interest expected from capital invested in this class of business, having regard to the risk involved, is 10%.

Fair remuneration to the partners of the firm in respect of their services to the business is estimated to be £2,500 per annum.

Valuation of goodwill

	£	£
Average annual profits		10,000
Less interest on capital employed at 10%	5,000	
partner's remuneration (say)	2,500	
		7,500
Annual super profit		2,500

It is now necessary to ascertain the present value of an annuity of £2,500 per annum for a suitable number of years. Alternatively, 'x years' of purchase' of £2,500 may be taken as the value of goodwill, according to the number of years that could be regarded as necessary to build up such a goodwill, discounted by reference to the fact that any goodwill purchased is a wasting asset, since the influence of the vendor diminishes as that of the purchaser increases.

(4) *Excess of value of a business over value of tangible net assets*

The value of the business as a going concern is estimated by reference to the expected earnings and the yield required. From the figure arrived at the value of the net tangible assets is deducted, the difference being taken to represent the value of goodwill.

Illustration 5

	£
Estimated future annual profit	10,000
Less partners' remuneration	2,500
Available for interest on capital employed	7,500

Assuming a yield of 10% per annum is expected, the capital value of the business is £75,000. If the value of the net tangible assets of the business is £50,000, the goodwill is worth a maximum of £25,000. This figure may have to be discounted as the earning of super profits entails greater risks than the earnings of the smaller amount required to provide a fair return on money invested in tangible assets.

2.5   CHANGES IN PARTNERSHIP ARRANGEMENTS: NEW PARTNERS

This can raise two particular problems:

(a) Adjustment for goodwill.
(b) Apportionment of profit.

(a) Adjustment for goodwill

It was stated above that if the value of goodwill is unrecorded in the books, the capital accounts of the partners are understated by the value thereof.

Illustration 6

Assume that the following is the balance sheet of the firm of A and B, who share profits in the proportion of two-thirds and one-third respectively.

	£	£	£
Fixed assets			
Land and buildings			5,250
Plant and machinery			3,075
			8,325
Current assets			
Stock		4,500	
Debtors	3,000		
Less provision for doubtful debts	150		
		2,850	
Cash at bank		300	
		7,650	
Less creditors		3,975	
			3,675
			12,000
Capital accounts			
A			8,500
B			3,500
			12,000

The goodwill of the firm is valued at £6,000 and, therefore, the true capitals of A and B are £4,000 and £2,000 respectively more than the amounts standing to the credit of their capital accounts. As these increments arise from the fact that goodwill is not recorded in the books, it is apparent that some adjustment must be made in the event of the introduction of a new partner, in order that he shall not take a share of goodwill without payment.

There are two main methods of dealing with the goodwill.

Method 1—raise an account for goodwill

An account is raised in the old firm's books for the full value of goodwill, the old partners' capital accounts being credited therewith in the proportions in which they share profits or losses. The new partner may or may not bring in capital according to the agreement. In any event, whatever he brings in will be credited to his capital account. The effect of this method is to increase the old partners' capital accounts to the extent of the value of goodwill previously unrecorded.

In the example above, assume that A and B agree to admit C into partnership, giving him a one-fifth share of profits; C to bring in capital to the extent of one-quarter of the combined capitals of A and B after adjustment for goodwill. A's and B's proportions of profit in the new firm are to be in the same ratio between themselves as before.

Assuming C brings in the required amount of cash, the following journal entries are relevant:

JOURNAL

	Dr £	Cr £
(1) Goodwill account	6,000	
Capital account of A		4,000
Capital account of B		2,000
Creation of goodwill as agreed on admittance of C into partnership		
(2) Cash	4,500	
Capital account of C		4,500
Capital brought in by C ($\frac{1}{4}$ of 12,500 + 5,500)		

The balance sheet after the above transactions is:

		£
Fixed assets		
Goodwill		6,000
Land and buildings		5,250
Plant and machinery		3,075
		14,325
Current assets		
Stock	4,500	
Debtors (net)	2,850	
Cash at bank	4,800	
	12,150	
Less creditors	3,975	
		8,175
		22,500
Capital accounts		
A		12,500
B		5,500
C		4,500
		22,500

Method 2—no account retained for goodwill

No goodwill account is raised in the books, but the proportion of the agreed value of goodwill attributable to the incoming partner's share of profit is paid for by him in cash. The additional cash brought in by the new partner for the acquisition of a share of goodwill is credited to the capital accounts of the old partners in the proportions in which they shared profits before the introduction of the new partner, if the old partners continue to share profits as between themselves in the same proportions as they did before. The cash brought in by the new partner as his capital will be credited to his capital account in the normal manner.

Illustration 7

Assuming the same facts as for the previous example, but that no goodwill account is to be opened in the books on C's admission, the latter introducing £3,300 as his capital and £1,200 for his share of goodwill.

Show by journal entries the adjustments to be made on C's introduction, and the balance sheet of the new firm.

JOURNAL

	£	£
Cash	1,200	
Capital accounts:		
A ($\frac{2}{3}$)		800
B ($\frac{1}{3}$)		400

Payment by C for a one-fifth in the goodwill.

	£	£
Cash	3,300	
C Capital account		3,300

Capital introduced by C

Balance sheet after completion of transactions:

Fixed assets
Land and buildings	5,250
Plant and machinery	3,075
	8,325

Current assets
Stock	4,500	
Debtors	2,850	
Cash at bank	4,800	
	12,150	
Less creditors	3,975	
		8,175
		16,500

Capital accounts
A	9,300
B	3,900
C	3,300
	16,500

Workings

The simplest approach is to:

(1) Credit A and B with their goodwill shares in the old profit sharing ratios (OPSR).
(2) Debit A, B and C with their goodwill shares in the new profit sharing ratio (NPSR).

CAPITAL ACCOUNTS

	A £	B £	C £		A £	B £	C £
Goodwill				Balances b/f	8,500	3,500	
account	3,200	1,600	1,200	Goodwill a/c	4,000	2,000	
Balances c/f	9,300	3,900	3,300	Cash introduced:			
				For goodwill			1,200
				For capital			3,300
	12,500	5,500	4,500		12,500	5,500	4,500

GOODWILL ACCOUNT

	£		£
Capital accounts:		Capital accounts:	
A ($\frac{2}{3} \times$ £6,000)	4,000	A ($\frac{8}{15} \times$ £6,000)	3,200
B ($\frac{1}{3} \times$ £6,000)	2,000	B ($\frac{4}{15} \times$ £6,000)	1,600
		C ($\frac{3}{15} \times$ £6,000)	1,200
	6,000		6,000

(b) Apportionment of profit

In order to apportion the profits or losses between the partners upon a change of personnel, or where the existing partners vary as between themselves the profit-sharing ratio, unless the change takes place at the financial year end of the business, it will be necessary for stock to be taken and work in progress valued, or alternatively for the profits for the year to be apportioned. If the profits are to be apportioned, they will be apportioned either on a time basis, or in proportion to the turnover of the periods prior to and after the charge, or by a combination of these methods.

Illustration 8

Green and Blue were partners in a retail business sharing profits and losses: Green, two-thirds and Blue, one-third. Interest on fixed capitals was allowed at the rate of 6% per annum, but no interest was charged or allowed on current accounts. Accounts were made up to 31 March in each year.

The following was the partnership trial balance as on 31 March 19X9:

	£		£	£
Leasehold premises		Fixed capital accounts:		
purchased 1 April 19X8	6,000	Green	3,000	
Purchases	16,400	Blue	2,000	
				5,000
Motor vehicles at cost	3,400			
Balance at bank	9,280	Current accounts:		
Salaries, including		Green	1,600	
partners' drawings	5,200	Blue	1,200	
				2,800
Stock 31 March 19X8	4,800			
Shop fittings at cost	1,200	Cash introduced—Black		5,000
Debtors	900	Sales (£14,000 to 30		
Professional charges	420	September 19X8)		35,000
Shop wages	2,200	Provisions for depreciation		
Rent, rates, lighting		on 1 April 19X8:		
and heating	1,240	Motor vehicles	1,200	
General expenses		Shop fittings	400	
(£1,410 for six months				1,600
to 30 September 19X8)	2,640	Creditors		4,280
	53,680			53,680

You are given the following additional information:

(1) On 30 September 19X8, Black was admitted as a partner and from that date, profits and losses were shared: Green, two-fifths, Blue, two-fifths and Black, one-fifth. For the purpose of these changes, the value of the goodwill of the firm was agreed at £12,000. No account for goodwill was to be maintained in the books, adjusting entries for transactions between the parties being made in their current accounts. On 1 October 19X8, Black had introduced £5,000 into the firm of which it was agreed £1,500 should comprise his fixed capital and the balance should be credited to his current account.

Any apportionment of gross profit was to be made on the basis of sales; expenses, unless otherwise indicated, were to be apportioned on a time basis.

(2) On 31 March 19X9, the stock was valued at £5,100.

(3) Provision was to be made for depreciation on the motor vehicles and shop fittings at 20% and 5% per annum respectively, calculated on cost.

(4) Salaries included the following partners' drawings: Green £600, Blue £480 and Black £250.

(5) At 31 March 19X9, rates paid in advance amounted to £260 and a provision of £60 for electricity consumed was required.

(6) A difference on the books of £120 had been written off at 31 March 19X9 to general expenses, which was later found to be due to the following errors:

(i) sales returns of £80 had been debited to sales but had not been posted to the account of the customer concerned;

(ii) the purchase journal had been undercast by £200.

(7) Professional charges included £210 paid in respect of the acquisition of the leasehold premises. These fees are to be capitalised as part of the cost of the lease, the total cost of which was to be written off in 25 equal annual instalments. Other premises, owned by Blue, were leased by him to the partnership at £600 per annum, but no rent had been paid or credited to him for the year to 31 March 19X9.

(8) Doubtful debts (for which full provision was required) as of 30 September 19X8 amounted to £120 and as of 31 March 19X9 to £160.

You are required to prepare:

(a) the trading and profit and loss account for the year ended 31 March 19X9;
(b) the balance sheet as on that date; and
(c) partners' current accounts, in columnar form.

Solution

(a)   MESSRS GREEN, BLUE AND BLACK TRADING, PROFIT AND
LOSS ACCOUNT

for the year ended 31 March 19X9

	£	£
Sales		
1.4.X8 to 30.9.X8		14,000
1.10.X8 to 31.3.X9		21,000
		35,000
Stock 1.4.X8	4,800	
Purchases (16,400 + 200)	16,600	
	21,400	
Less stock 31.3.X9	5,100	
		16,300
Gross profit		18,700

	Period 1.4.X8 to 30.9.X8 £	Period 1.10.X8 to 31.3.X9 £
Gross profit (allocated ratio 14:21)	7,480	11,220
Salaries (5,200 − 1,330)	1,935	1,935
Rent, rates, lighting and heating (1,240 + 600 + 60 − 260)	820	820
Shop wages	1,100	1,100
Professional charges (420 − 210)	105	105
General expenses (2,640 − 120)	1,410	1,110
Depreciation:		
Motor vehicles 680		
Shop fittings 60		
740		
	370	370
Amortisation of lease $\frac{1}{25}$ of (6,000 + 210)	124	124
Provision for doubtful debts	120	40
Net profit c/d	1,496	5,616

Statement of allocation of net profit

	Total £	Green £	Blue £	Black £
Interest on capital				
6 m to 30.9.19X8	150	90	60	
6 m to 31.3.19X9	195	90	60	45
Balance of profits				
6 m to 30.9.19X8				
(1,486 – 150) in ratio 2:1:0	1,346	897	449	—
(5,616 – 195) in ratio 2:2:1	5,421	2,168	2,168	1,085
Totals	7,112	3,245	2,737	1,130

(b) Balance sheet as 31 March 19X9

	Cost £	Depreciation £	Net book value £
Fixed assets			
Leasehold premises	6,210	248	5,962
Motor vehicles	3,400	1,880	1,520
Shop fittings	1,200	460	740
	10,810	2,588	8,222

Current assets			
Stock			5,100
Debtors (900 – 80)	820		
Less provision for doubtful debts	160		
	—		660
Prepayments			260
Cash at bank			9,280
			15,300
Less creditors (4,280 + 60)			4,340
Net current assets			10,960
			19,182

	Capital accounts £	Current accounts £	Total £
Partners' accounts			
Green	3,000	7,445	10,445
Blue	2,000	3,257	5,257
Black ,	1,500	1,980	3,480
	6,500	12,682	19,182

(c) Partners' current accounts

	Green £	Blue £	Black £		Green £	Blue £	Black £
Goodwill				Bal b/f	1,600	1,200	—
written down				Share of profit	3,245	2,737	1,130
(NPSR)	4,800	4,800	2,400	Goodwill			
Drawings	600	480	250	written up			
Bal c/f	7,445	3,257	1,980	(OPSR)	8,000	4,000	—
				Rent	—	600	—
				Cash introduced	—	—	3,500
	12,845	8,537	4,630		12,845	8,537	4,630

OPSR = old profit sharing ratio (2:1)
NPSR = new profit sharing ratio (2:2:1)

2.6 CHANGES IN PARTNERSHIP ARRANGEMENTS: OUTGOING PARTNERS

(a) Introduction

In the absence of any agreement or uniform usage to the contrary, a partner, on retirement, or the representative of a deceased partner, is entitled to have the partnership assets, including goodwill, revalued on a proper basis as at the date of the retirement or death, and any appreciation or depreciation so revealed is taken into account in computing the sum due to him or them. The total amount so ascertained to be due is normally a debt due by the firm to the retired partner or the representatives of the deceased partner.

An agreement may, however, be made between the partners whereby, in the event of the death or retirement of a partner, the remaining partners shall assume, personally, the liability for the amount due. In such circumstances, the debt is no longer due by the firm but by the partners individually in the ratio agreed upon.

(b) Repayment of amounts owing by instalments

Upon the retirement or death of a partner, the value of his capital and share of the goodwill etc is ascertained, either in accordance with the provisions of the partnership agreement or by accounts taken at the date of the dissolution, and the amount so ascertained is paid out to him or his representatives forthwith, or credited to a loan account, and repaid by instalments, with interest running on the outstanding balance. It is important, where payment is not made at once, that the amount due should be credited to a loan account, and not retained in the books as capital, especially in the case of a retired partner, when retention of the amount due to him as capital might imply that he was still a partner.

Illustration 9

M, a partner in a firm, died on 31 March 19X8 and his share of capital and goodwill is ascertained to be £7,600. It was arranged that this should be paid out by annual instalments of £2,000 to include principal and interest on the outstanding balance at 5% per annum. The first payment is made one month after death, and succeeding payments are made on the anniversary of the date of death. Show the account in the firm's books relating thereto until completion. Ignore income tax, and make calculations to nearest £.

THE EXECUTORS OF M (DECEASED) ACCOUNT

		£			£
19X8			*19X8*		
30 April	Cash	2,000	31 March	Capital account	7,600
	Balance c/f	5,632	30 April	Interest, 1 month	32
		7,632			7,632
19X9			*19X8*		
31 March	Cash	2,000	1 May	Balance b/f	5,632
	Balance c/f	3,890	*19X9*		
			31 March	Interest, 11 mths	258
		5,890			5,890
19X10			*19X9*		
31 March	Cash	2,000	1 April	Balance b/f	3,890
	Balance b/f	2,085	*19X10*		
			31 March	Interest, 1 year	195
		4,085			4,085
19X11			*19X10*		
31 March	Cash	2,000	1 April	Balance b/f	2,085
	Balance c/f	189	*19X11*		
			31 March	Interest, 1 year	104
		2,189			2,189
19X12			*19X11*		
31 March	Cash	198	1 April	Balance b/f	189
			19X12		
			31 March	Interest, 1 year	9
		198			198

(c) Amount owing remains on as a loan to the firm

Where this course is adopted, the retired partner's capital must be transferred to a loan account. Usually, the rate of interest payable on this loan and the conditions of repayment are laid down in the partnership agreement or by a contract entered into at the date of retirement, but in the absence of agreement it is provided by s 42 of the Partnership Act 1890 that the retired partner is entitled to interest at 5% per annum, or such share of the profits as the court may determine to be attributable to the use of his share of the partnership assets. If a retired partner enforces his right to a share of profit in these circumstances, the court would deduct a reasonable sum for the services of the remaining partners for carrying on the business, before arriving at the profit to be divided.

Where an option is given to the continuing partners to purchase the share of the retired partner, and the option is exercised, the retired partner is not entitled to any further share of the profits. His capital is therefore transferred to the capital accounts of the continuing partners, who must pay him according to the terms of the agreement.

When it is agreed that the loan shall carry a rate of interest varying with the profits of the firm, or entitle the retired partner to a share of such profits, such an agreement will not of itself cause the retired partner to continue to be liable as a partner of the firm, provided that the contract is in writing and signed by or on behalf of all the parties thereto. If, however, the firm should become bankrupt, the retired partner will be a deferred creditor in respect of any loan made in such circumstances.

(d) Amount owing satisfied by way of an annuity

Where a partner retires or dies, the liability of the continuing partners for his capital and share of goodwill is sometimes discharged by an agreement to pay to him or to his widow, dependants or representatives an annuity, either for a certain term of years or for the lifetime of the retired partner, or his widow, or some named dependants.

In such a case, the most convenient method of dealing with the matter in the partnership books is to transfer the amount due to an annuity suspense account, which must be credited with interest at a fixed rate per annum on the diminishing balance (profit and loss account being debited), and debited annually with the annuity paid. If the credit balance on the annuity suspense account is exhausted during the lifetime of the annuitant, subsequent instalments of the annuity must be borne by the partners and debited to their current accounts (or to profit and loss account before arriving at divisible profits). In the event of the annuitant dying before the credit on the annuity suspense account is exhausted, the balance then remaining on the account is a profit to the continuing partners and should be transferred to their capital accounts in the proportion in which they share profits. Such a profit will not, normally, be represented by liquid resources available for distribution and, it might therefore be inadvisable to transfer it to profit and loss account or to the partners' current accounts.

The balance of the annuity suspense account at the commencement of the transaction and at the date of each balance sheet should, strictly, represent the present worth of the annuity, subject to variation in the expectation of life. An actuarial valuation for the adjustment of the suspense account might be made periodically, say, every five years, but as, with a single annuity, there is no scope for the law of average to apply, it is not usual to do this, the simpler procedure outlined above being adopted in preference.

Illustration 10

A, B and C are partners sharing profits in the ratio of 3, 2 and 1. A retires from the firm as from 31 December 19X8, the determined amount of his share being £10,000. It is agreed that this should be commuted by an annuity of £1,500, the first payment to be made on the following day, and subsequent payments on 1 January of each year. A dies after the receipt of the fifth annuity payment.

Show the annuity suspense account in the books of the firm, assuming that the amount outstanding is deemed to earn interest at the rate of 6%. Ignore income tax and make calculations to nearest £.

ANNUITY SUSPENSE ACCOUNT

		£			£
19X9			*19X9*		
1 Jan	Cash	1,500	1 Jan	Balance b/f	10,000
31 Dec	Balance c/f	9,010	31 Dec	Profit and loss account—interest (on £8,500)	510
		10,510			10,510
19X10			*19X10*		
1 Jan	Cash	1,500	1 Jan	Balance b/f	9,010
31 Dec	Balance c/f	7,961	31 Dec	Profit and loss account—interest (on £7,510)	451
		9,461			9,461
19X11			*19X11*		
1 Jan	Cash	1,500	1 Jan	Balance b/f	7,961
	Balance c/f	6,849	31 Dec	Profit and loss account—interest (on £6,461)	388
		8,349			8,349
19X12			*19X12*		
1 Jan	Cash	1,500	1 Jan	Balance b/f	6,849
31 Dec	Balance c/f	5,670	31 Dec	Profit and loss account—interest (on £5,349)	321
		7,170			7,170
19X13			*19X13*		
1 Jan	Cash	1,500	1 Jan	Balance b/f	5,670
31 Dec	Profit transferred to: B ⅔ 2,780 C ⅓ 1,390	4,170			
		5,670			5,670

It cannot be assumed that the business would be able to pay the amount of the annuity in all cases out of its liquid resources, as this might result in considerable embarrassment in the course of a few years. The remaining partners should, therefore, if necessary, introduce annually additional capital to the extent of the amount of the annuity less the amount of interest credited to the annuity suspense account. As this interest has been charged to profit and loss account before arriving at the amount of the divisible profits, cash to the extent thereof has been retained in the business and it is therefore only necessary for B and C to introduce the balance.

Alternatively, B and C could restrict their drawings each year by the amount required. For example, at the end of the first year the following entry could be made:

JOURNAL

	£	£
Current accounts:		
B	660	
C	330	
Capital accounts:		
B		660
C		330

Transfer from current accounts to capital accounts of amount necessary to restore the firm's working capital after the payment of annuity of £1,500 to A.

B $\frac{2}{3}$ of £(1,500 − 510) = £660
C $\frac{1}{3}$ of £(1,500 − 510) = £330

(e) Adjustments to asset values

When a partner retires, it does not follow that the balance of his capital account represents his true interest in the partnership, apart from the question of goodwill (to which reference has already been made), since some assets may have appreciated in value without any adjustment having been made in the books, whilst others may have been insufficiently depreciated, over-depreciated, or entirely written off. It will be necessary, therefore, to correct these values, in order that the outgoing partner shall receive his true share. A revaluation account should be opened, to which all differences in values should be debited or credited, as the case may be, the resultant balance being divided among the partners according to the ratio in which they share profits and losses.

Illustration 11

Brown, Jones and Robinson, sharing profits and losses equally, had been trading for many years and Robinson decided to retire as at 31 December 19X8 on which date the balance sheet of the firm was as under:

	£	£
Fixed assets		
Freehold premises		8,000
Plant and machinery		4,000
Patents		6,000
		18,000
Current assets		
Stock	5,000	
Debtors	6,000	
Cash at bank	3,000	
	14,000	
Less creditors	8,000	
		6,000
		24,000
Capital accounts		
Brown		10,000
Jones		8,000
Robinson		6,000
		24,000

The value of the goodwill was agreed at £8,000.

The freehold premises had increased in value as a result of general economic conditions, the value being agreed of £11,000. Plant and patents were respectively revalued at £3,600 and £5,300 and it was also agreed to provide 5% in respect of debtors, it having been the practice in the past only to write off bad debts actually incurred.

Show the adjusted balance sheet of the firm, and the amount to which Robinson would be entitled under the following alternative assumptions:

(1) The ongoing partners wish to retain the assets in the balance sheet at their revised valuations.
(2) The assets are to be reflected in the balance sheet at their previous valuations.

(1) Balance sheet reflecting revised valuations

	£	£
Fixed assets		
Freehold premises		11,000
Plant and machinery		3,600
Patents		5,300
Goodwill		8,000
		27,900
Current assets		
Stock		5,000
Debtors	6,000	
Less provision	300	
		5,700
Cash at bank		3,000
		13,700
Less creditors		8,000
		5,700
		33,600
Capital accounts		
Brown		13,200
Jones		11,200
		24,400
Loan account		
Robinson		9,200
		33,600

Workings

REVALUATION ACCOUNT

	£	£		£
Plant		400	Goodwill	8,000
Patents		700	Freehold premises	3,000
Provision for bad debts		300		
Balance transferred to capital accounts:				
Brown	3,200			
Jones	3,200			
Robinson	3,200			
	9,600			
		11,000		11,000

(2) Balance sheet retaining previous valuations

Although the above adjustments have been made in order to ascertain the amount due to Robinson, the remaining partners may not desire to disturb the existing book values, in which case the difference on revaluation (£9,600) would be written back to the capital accounts of Brown and Jones, in the proportions in which they will share profits and losses in future, the position then being:

	£	£
Fixed assets		
Freehold premises		8,000
Plant and machinery		4,000
Patents		6,000
		18,000
Current assets		
Stock	5,000	
Debtors	6,000	
Cash	3,000	
	14,000	
Less creditors	8,000	
		6,000
		24,000
Capital accounts		
Brown (13,200 – 4,800)		8,400
Jones (11,200 – 4,800)		6,400
		14,800
Loan account		
Robinson		9,200
		24,000

NOTE

Alternative (2) has been shown for illustration purposes. While the partners may wish to exclude goodwill from the partnership balance sheet, any assets which have suffered a diminution in value (such as debtors, in this example) should be stated at a prudent amount (e g debtors, £5,700).

(f) Life assurance policies to provide for repayment of share of a deceased partner

In some cases partners effect assurance on their lives, either jointly or severally, in order to provide the cash required to pay out the whole or part of the capital and goodwill of a partner who dies. Such an assurance is of particular advantage where the surviving partners have insufficient resources outside the business to purchase a deceased partner's interest in the partnership.

Partnership life assurance may be dealt with in the accounts by any of the following methods:

(1) The premiums paid on the policy are written off to profit and loss account, thereby reducing the profits divisible between, and available to be withdrawn from, the business by the partners. This has the effect of charging the partners with the cost of the assurance in the proportions in which they share profits. No account in respect of the policy appears in the books, so that the value of the policy at any time represents a secret reserve which belongs to the partners in profit-sharing ratio. Accordingly, on the death of a partner each partner's capital account must be credited with his proper share of the policy money received. The cash so made available can then be applied in or towards the sum due to the representative of the deceased partner.

The advantage of this method is that it avoids the danger of the working capital of the firm being depleted by the withdrawal of cash to pay the premiums, the cost of the assurance being borne by the partners out of their shares of profit.

(2) A life policy account is opened in the books, to which the premiums are debited as and when they are paid. The policy will thus appear in the books as

an asset at cost, and the amount receivable on the death of a partner will be credited to this account, any difference between the amount standing to the debit of the account and the sum received being divided between the partners in profit-sharing ratio, and credited to their respective capital accounts.

Although this method has the advantage of disclosing the existence of the asset acquired by the payment of the premiums, if (as is usually the case in early years of the policy) its surrender value is less than the total amount of the premiums paid, the policy will appear in the books at more than its current realisable value. Furthermore, as the profits disclosed by the accounts are not reduced by the premiums, if the whole of the profits are withdrawn, the premiums will, in effect, have been paid out of capital, and the liquid resources of the business may become unduly depleted.

(3) The premiums paid are debited to a life policy account, as in method (2), but the book value of the policy is adjusted each year to its surrender value by a transfer from profit and loss account. This overcomes the objection, referred to in method (2), to the policy appearing in the books at more than its realisable value. It does not, however, conserve the working capital by reducing the divisible profits by the premiums paid.

(4) The premiums paid are debited to a life policy account, and a sum equal to the annual premium is debited each year to profit and loss account and credited to a life policy fund account. The book value of the policy is then adjusted to surrender value by a transfer from the life policy fund account instead of from profit and loss account. On the death of a partner, the sum received under the policy will be credited to the life policy account, any profit disclosed by the account being transferred to the credit of the life policy fund account. The final balance on the latter account will now represent a reserve equal to the total sum received under the policy, and will be transferred to the credit of the partners' capital accounts in their profit-sharing proportions.

This method has the advantage of disclosing the existence of the asset at its realisable value and also of avoiding the danger of depleting the working capital of the firm.

Each of the above methods is exemplified by the following illustration.

Illustration 12

A, B and C are in partnership, sharing profits in the proportion of two-thirds, one-sixth, and one-sixth respectively, and in order to provide cash for the immediate payment of a portion of the amount due to any one of them in the event of death, in respect of both capital and goodwill, an assurance was effected on their lives jointly for £9,000 without profits, at an annual premium of £350.

A died on June 30 19X4, three months after the annual accounts had been prepared, and in accordance with the partnership agreement, his share of the profits to the date of death, was estimated on the exact basis of the profits for the preceding year. In addition to this, the agreement provided for interest in capital at 5% per annum on the balance standing to the credit of the capital account at the date of the last balance sheet, and also for goodwill, which was to be brought into account at two years' purchase of the average profits for the last three years, prior to charging the above-mentioned insurance premiums, but after charging interest on capital.

A's capital on March 31 19X4 stood at £12,000, and his drawings from then to the date of death amounted to £900.

The net profits of the business for the three preceding years amounted to £3,350, £4,150 and £4,050 respectively, after charging interest on capital but before charging insurance premiums, or adjustments of the policy account to surrender value (as the case may be).

The total premiums paid on the life policy to March 31 preceding A's death amounted to £4,500, and the surrender value at that date was £4,000. In that year it became necessary to debit profit and loss account with £250 in order to adjust the policy account to the surrender value of the policy.

You are instructed to adjust A's capital account as at the date of death, for a settlement with his executors.

Method (1)

A's CAPITAL ACCOUNT

	£		£
Drawings	900	Balance b/f	12,000
Balance c/d	23,000	Interest on capital 5% for	
		three months	150
		Profit to date of death	617
		Goodwill	5,133
		Insurance policy, ⅔ of £9,000	6,000
	23,900		23,900
		Balance b/d	23,000

NOTES

(1) The value of goodwill is arrived at as follows:

	£
Profit first year	3,350
Profit second year	4,150
Profit third year	4,050
	3) 11,550
Three years' average profit	£3,850
Total amount of goodwill	£7,700

A's share = ⅔ of £7,700 = £5,133

(2) A's share of profit for the three months to the date of death, based on the profit of the previous year is $\frac{1}{4} \times \frac{2}{3}$ £(4,050 − 350) = £617.

Method (2)

A's CAPITAL ACCOUNT

	£		£
Drawings	900	Balance b/f	12,000
Balance c/d	20,058	Interest on capital—	
		three months	150
		Profit to date of death	675
		Goodwill	5,133
		Life policy account—	
		share of profit	3,000
	£20,958		£20,958
		Balance b/d	20,058

NOTE

A's share of profit is $\frac{1}{4} \times \frac{2}{3}$ × £4,050 = £675.

LIFE POLICY ACCOUNT

	£		£
Balance (premiums paid		Cash	9,000
to date) b/f	4,500		
Profit:			
A (⅔)	£3,000		
B (⅙)	750		
C (⅙)	750		
	4,500		
	£9,000		£9,000

Method (3)

A's CAPITAL ACCOUNT

	£		£
Drawings	900	Balance b/f	12,000
Balance c/d	20,350	Interest on capital	150
		Profit to date of death	633
		Goodwill	5,133
		Life policy account—	
		share of profit	3,334
	£21,250		£21,250
		Balance b/d	20,350

NOTE
The divisible profit for the previous year was £4,050 less £250 charged to profit and loss account and credited to policy account to adjust it to surrender value = £3,800. A's share is $\frac{1}{4} \times \frac{2}{3} \times £3,800 = £633$.

LIFE POLICY ACCOUNT

		£		£
Balance (surrender			Cash	9,000
value) b/f		4,000		
Profit:				
A ($\frac{2}{3}$)	£3,334			
B ($\frac{1}{6}$)	833			
C ($\frac{1}{6}$)	833			
		5,000		
		£9,000		£9,000

Method (4)

A's CAPITAL ACCOUNT

	£		£
Drawings	900	Balance b/f	12,000
Balance c/d	23,000	Interest on capital	150
		Profit to date of death	617
		Goodwill	5,133
		Life policy fund account	6,000
	£23,900		£23,900
		Balance b/d	23,000

NOTE
A's share of profit is as in method (1).

LIFE POLICY ACCOUNT

	£		£
Balance b/f	4,000	Cash	9,000
Life policy fund—			
profit transferred	5,000		
	9,000		9,000

LIFE POLICY FUND ACCOUNT

	£		£
Balance transferred to		Balance b/f	4,000
partners:		Life policy account—	
A ($\frac{2}{3}$)	6,000	profit transferred	5,000
B ($\frac{1}{6}$)	1,500		
C ($\frac{1}{6}$)	1,500		
	9,000		9,000

3 PARTNERSHIP ACCOUNTS—2

3.1 DISSOLUTION OF PARTNERSHIPS—GENERAL CONSIDERATIONS

(a) Basic principles

Upon the dissolution of a partnership, s 44 of the Partnership Act 1890 provides that the assets of the firm, including the sums (if any) contributed by the partners to make up losses or deficiencies of capital, must be applied in the following manner and order:

(1) In paying the debts and liabilities of the firm to persons who are not partners therein.
(2) In paying to each partner rateably what is due from the firm to him for advances as distinguished from capital.
(3) In paying to each partner the amount due to him in respect of his capital and current account balances.

In the absence of agreement to the contrary, the Partnership Act 1890 provides that the following shall be grounds for the dissolution of a partnership:

(1) The expiration of the term for which the partnership was entered into, if a fixed term was agreed upon.
(2) The termination of the adventure or undertaking, when a single adventure or undertaking was the purpose of the partnership.
(3) When one partner gives notice to the others of his intention to dissolve the firm.
(4) The death of a partner.
(5) The bankruptcy of a partner.
(6) The happening of an event which causes the partnership to become illegal.
(7) When a partner allows his share of the partnership to be charged for his separate debt.

(b) Formula for closing partnership books on dissolution

Apart from special circumstances, the following outline of the steps necessary to close the books of a partnership when the assets are sold en bloc, may be found useful:

(1) Open a realisation account, and debit thereto the book value of the assets, crediting the various asset accounts. The realisation account will also be debited with any expenses of realisation, and cash credited.
(2) Debit cash and credit realisation account with the amount realised on the sale of the assets.
   Note
   Should any of the assets be taken over at a valuation by any of the partners, debit such partners' capital accounts, and credit realisation account with the agreed price.
(3) Pay off the liabilities, crediting cash and debiting sundry creditors. Any discount allowed by creditors on discharging liabilities should be debited to the creditors' accounts and credited to realisation account.
(4) The balance of the realisation account will be the amount of the profit or loss

on realisation, which will be divided between the partners in the proportion in which they share profits and losses and transferred to their capital accounts.
(5) Pay off any partners' advances as distinct from capital, first setting off any *debit* balance on the capital account of a partner against his loan account.
(6) The balance of the cash book will now be exactly equal to the balances on the capital accounts, provided they are in credit; credit cash and debit the partners' capital accounts with the amounts paid to them to close their accounts.

Should the capital loss of any partner be in debit after being debited with his share of the loss, or credited with his share of the profit on realisation, the cash will be insufficient by the amount of such debit balance to pay the other partners the amounts due to them. If the partner whose account is in debit pays to the firm the amount of his indebtedness, the other partners' capital accounts can then be closed by the payment of cash. If, however, he is unable to do so, the deficiency must, according to the decision in *Garner v Murray*, be borne by the solvent partners, in proportion to their capitals, and not in the proportion in which they share profits and losses. The application of this rule is illustrated in section 3.2 below.

The following illustrations show the closing of the books on the dissolution of partnerships in varying circumstances:

(1) *Where, on dissolution, there is a profit on the realisation of the assets*

Illustration 1

X and Y are in partnership sharing profits—five-eighths and three-eighths. They agree to dissolve partnership, and their abridged balance sheet at the date of dissolution, 30 June 19X2, is as follows:

X AND Y BALANCE SHEET

June 30 19X2

	£			£
Capital accounts:			Premises	1,200
X	£1,500		Stock	1,400
Y	1,300	2,800	Debtors	1,100
			Cash	600
Creditors		1,500		
		£4,300		£4,300

The dissolution is completed by December 31 19X2, the assets, other than cash, being sold en bloc and realising £4,500. Close the books of the firm.

REALISATION ACCOUNT

19X2			£	19X2		£
June 30	Sundry assets		3,700	Dec 31	Cash	4,500
Dec 31	Profit transferred					
	to capital accounts:					
	X($\frac{5}{8}$)	£500				
	Y($\frac{3}{8}$)	300				
			800			
			£4,500			£4,500

SUNDRY CREDITORS

19X2		£	19X2		£
Dec 31	Cash	1,500	June 30	Balance b/f	1,500

X CAPITAL ACCOUNT

19X2		£	19X2		£
Dec 31	Cash	2,000	June 30	Balance b/f	1,500
			Dec 31	Realisation account:	
				profit	500
		£2,000			£2,000

Y CAPITAL ACCOUNT

		£			£
Dec 31	Cash	1,600	June 30	Balance b/f	1,300
			Dec 31	Realisation account:	
				profit	300
		1,600			1,600

CASH

		£				£
June 30	Balance b/f	600	Dec 31	Creditors		1,500
Dec 31	Realisation account	4,500		Capital accounts:		
				X	£2,000	
				Y	1,600	
						3,600
		£5,100				£5,100

(2) *Where, on dissolution, the liabilities are paid in full, but there is a loss on the realisation of the assets*

Illustration 2

D, E and F, sharing profits and losses, one-half, one-third, and one-sixth respectively, dissolve partnership. At the date of dissolution their creditors amount to £2,300, and in the course of winding up a contingent liability of £200, not brought into the accounts, matured and had to be met. The capitals stood at £6,000, £4,000 and £1,500, respectively. D had lent to the firm as distinct from capital £2,000. The assets realised £10,000. Close the books of the firm.

REALISATION ACCOUNT

	£			£
Sundry assets	15,800	Cash		10,000
Contingent liability matured	200	Loss transferred to capital accounts:		
		D $(\frac{1}{2})$	£3,000	
		E $(\frac{1}{3})$	2,000	
		F $(\frac{1}{6})$	1,000	
				6,000
	£16,000			£16,000

SUNDRY CREDITORS

	£		£
Cash	2,500	Balance b/f	2,300
		Realisation account:	
		Contingent liability matured	200
	————		————
	£2,500		£2,500
	════		════

D LOAN ACCOUNT

	£		£
Cash	2,000	Balance b/f	2,000
	════		════

D CAPITAL ACCOUNT

	£		£
Realisation account: loss	3,000	Balance b/f	6,000
Cash	3,000		
	————		————
	£6,000		£6,000
	════		════

E CAPITAL ACCOUNT

	£		£
Realisation account: loss	2,000	Balance b/f	4,000
Cash	2,000		
	————		————
	£4,000		£4,000
	════		════

F CAPITAL ACCOUNT

	£		£
Realisation account: loss	1,000	Balance b/f	1,500
Cash	500		
	————		————
	£1,500		£1,500
	════		════

CASH

	£		£
Realisation account	10,000	Creditors	2,500
		D loan account	2,000
		D capital account	3,000
		E capital account	2,000
		F capital account	500
	————		————
	£10,000		£10,000
	════		════

NOTE
The book value of the assets is equal to the sum of the capitals plus the creditors, viz
£6,000 + £4,000 + £1,500 + £2,300 + £2,000 = £15,800.

(3) *Where, on dissolution, there is a loss on the realisation of the assets, placing one partner's capital account in debit, which amount he pays into the firm's account in cash*

Illustration 3

J and P are in partnership, with capitals of £700 and £100. The creditors are £2,300. The assets realise £1,900. Partners share profits and losses equally. Close the books of the firm, P having brought in the amount due by him.

REALISATION ACCOUNT

	£		£
Sundry assets	3,100	Cash	1,900
		Loss to capital accounts	
		J ($\frac{1}{2}$)	600
		P ($\frac{1}{2}$)	600
	£3,100		£3,100

J CAPITAL ACCOUNT

	£		£
Realisation account: loss	600	Balance b/f	700
Cash	100		
	£700		£700

P CAPITAL ACCOUNT

	£		£
Realisation account: loss	600	Balance b/f	100
		Cash	500
	£600		£600

CREDITORS

	£		£
Cash	2,300	Balance b/f	2,300

CASH

	£		£
Realisation account	1,900	Creditors	2,300
P capital account	500	J capital account	100
	£2,400		£2,400

Where, on dissolution, the assets are not sold en bloc, but are realised separately, or certain assets are taken over by partners on account of the sums due to them, it may be preferable, instead of transferring all the assets to a realisation account and crediting that account with the total proceeds, to credit each separate asset account with the amount at which it is sold or taken over, transferring the resultant profit or loss to a realisation profit and loss account, the ultimate balance of which will represent the net profit or loss on the dissolution.

Illustration 4

G and T, having carried on business as drapers and household furnishers at the same premises for a number of years, sharing profits and losses equally, decide to dissolve partnership.

At the date of dissolution, their abridged balance sheet was as follows:

	£	£		£	£
Capital accounts:			Goodwill		1,000
G	7,000		Freehold premises		8,000
T	8,000		Fixtures:		
		15,000	Drapery department	750	
Creditors		3,200	Furnishing department	400	
					1,150
			Debtors		1,050
			Stock:		
			Drapery department	1,600	
			Furnishing department	1,400	
					3,000
			Cash at bank		4,000
		£18,200			£18,200

The agreed terms were:

G was to take over the premises at £7,000, the drapery stock at £1,700, and drapery fixtures at £500.

T, having rented another shop nearby, was to take over the furniture stock at £1,500 and the fixtures of that department at £300.

Goodwill was to be written off.

Any loss on debtors was to be shared as to G, three-fifths, and T, two-fifths.

The creditors were to be paid by G.

The debtors relaised £950, the proceeds being retained by G.

Prepare accounts, showing the final settlement between the partners.

REALISATION PROFIT AND LOSS ACCOUNT

	£	£		£	£
Goodwill written off		1,000	Profit on transfer of stock		200
Bad debts		100	Loss on debtors shared by agreement:		
Loss on transfer of:			G ($\frac{3}{5}$)	60	
Freehold premises	1,000		T ($\frac{2}{5}$)	40	
Fixtures	350	1,350			100
			Loss on realisation of other assets:		
			G, capital account	1,075	
			T, capital account	1,075	
					2,150
		£2,450			£2,450

CASH ACCOUNT

	£		£
Balance b/f	4,000	T, capital account	5,085
G, capital account	1,085		
	£5,085		£5,085

DEBTORS

	£		£
Balance b/f	1,050	G, proceeds of realisation	950
		Realisation profit and loss account	100
	£1,050		£1,050

FREEHOLD PREMISES

	£		£
Balance b/f	8,000	G, capital account	7,000
		Realisation profit and loss account	1,000
	£8,000		£8,000

FIXTURES

	£		£
Balance b/f		G, capital account	500
Drapery	750	T, capital account	300
Furnishings	400	Realisation profit and loss account	350
	£1,150		£1,150

STOCK

	£		£
Balance b/f		G, capital account	1,700
Drapery	1,600	T, capital account	1,500
Furnishings	1,400		
Realisation profit and loss account	200		
	£3,200		£3,200

CAPITAL ACCOUNTS

	G £	T £		G £	T £
Freehold premises	7,000	—	Balances b/f	7,000	8,000
Stock	1,700	1,500	Creditors taken over	3,200	—
Fixtures	500	300	Cash	1,085	—
Debtors	950	—			
Bad debts	60	40			
Loss on realisation	1,075	1,075			
Cash	—	5,085			
	£11,285	£8,000		£11,285	£8,000

3.2 DISSOLUTION OF PARTNERSHIPS—THE RULE IN GARNER V MURRAY [1904] 1 CH 57

(a) Background

This is the situation where, on dissolution, a partner's capital account is in debit and he is unable to discharge his indebtedness. (Contrast with the situation in section 3.1(b) above.)

Prior to the decision in *Garner v Murray* it was generally supposed that any loss occasioned by one of the partners of a firm being unable to make good a debit balance on his account should be borne by the remaining partners in the proportions in which they shared profits and losses.

In this case, however, it was held that a deficiency of assets occasioned through the default of one of the partners must be distinguished from an ordinary trading loss, and should be regarded as a debt due to the remaining partners individually and not to the firm.

The decision of the case gave rise to considerable controversy. The circumstances were as follows: Garner, Murray and Wilkins were in partnership under a parole agreement by the terms of which capital was to be contributed by them in unequal shares, but profits and losses were to be divided equally. On the dissolution of the partnership, after payment of the creditors and of advances made by two of the partners, there was a deficiency of assets of £635, in addition to which Wilkins' capital account was overdrawn by £263, which he was unable to pay. There was thus a total deficiency of £898, and the plaintiff claimed that this should be borne by the solvent partners, Garner and Murray, in their agreed profit-sharing ratio viz equally. Mr Justice Joyce held, however, that each of the three partners was liable to make good his share of the £635 deficiency of assets, after which the available assets should be applied in repaying to each partner what was due to him on account of capital. Since, however, one of the 'assets' was the debit balance on Wilkins' account, which was valueless, the remaining assets were to be applied in paying to Garner and Murray rateably what was due to them in respect of capital, with the result that Wilkins' deficiency was borne by them in proportion to their capitals.

The effect of the decision is shown in the following illustration.

(b) Illustration 5

A, B and C, with unequal capitals, share profits and losses equally. They decide to dissolve partnership, and the following balance sheet shows the position of affairs after the assets have been realised and the liabilities discharged.

ABRIDGED BALANCE SHEET

	£		£
Capitals:		Cash	500
A	600	Capital C overdrawn	200
B	400	Deficiency of assets	300
	£1,000		£1,000

C is insolvent and is unable to contribute anything towards either his overdraft on capital or his share of the loss on realisation.

The loss on realisation of £300 should first be debited in profit-sharing ratio to the partners' accounts, thus reducing A's capital to £500 and B's to £300, and increasing C's deficit to £300.

If the ruling in *Garner v Murray* were followed strictly, A and B would introduce cash of £100 each to make good their shares of the deficiency and thus restore their capitals to £600 and £400 respectively. The balances then remaining in the books would be as shown by the reconstructed balance sheet given below.

BALANCE SHEET

	£		£
Capitals:		Cash	700
A	600	C's capital overdrawn	300
B	400		
	£1,000		£1,000

The only true asset, viz cash of £700, would now be divided between the solvent partners, A and B, in proportion to their capitals, viz:

	£
A ($\frac{6}{10}$ of £700)	= 420
B ($\frac{4}{10}$ of £700)	= 280
	£700

The only balances then remaining in the books would be the debit balance on C's capital account, £300, and the credit balances on the capital accounts of A and B, £180 and £120 respectively. As C is insolvent, the debit balance on his account will be written off against A and B, in the ratio of their respective capitals, viz £180 to A and £120 to B, thus closing their accounts.

As has been shown the net effect of the above treatment is to cause A and B to bear C's deficiency in proportion to their respective capitals. The introduction of cash by A and B to meet their share of the loss on realisation is unnecessary, as the balances on their capital account are sufficient to meet this loss. C's deficiency should be written off against the capital accounts of A and B in *capital* ratio, viz 6:4, after which the cash in hand will be exactly sufficient to repay to A and B the balances due to them on capital account, as shown hereunder.

CAPITAL ACCOUNTS

	A £	B £	C £		A £	B £	C £
Balance b/f			200	Balances b/f	600	400	
Realisation account–				A and B – C's			
loss	100	100	100	deficiency trans-			
C	180	120		ferred:			
Cash	320	180		A ($\frac{6}{10}$)			180
				B ($\frac{4}{10}$)			120
	£600	£400	£300		£600	£400	£300

3.3 DISSOLUTION OF PARTNERSHIPS—PIECEMEAL REALISATION AND INTERIM DISTRIBUTIONS

When assets are realised piecemeal, the partners may desire, as soon as all liabilities have been discharged, to withdraw immediately such cash as is available for division between them rather than wait until all the assets have been sold. In such circumstances, subject to any contrary agreement between the partners, the interim payments to the partners should be of such amounts that even though the remaining assets prove to be worthless no partner will receive more than the amount to which he is ultimately found to be entitled after being debited with his proper share of the total loss sustained on realisation of all the assets. To enable this to be done the proceeds of realisation of assets must first be applied in repaying to partners any sums necessary to reduce their capitals to amounts which will bear the same proportion to the total capital as those in which profits and losses are shared. Further realisations will then be shared in that ratio.

Illustration 6

A, B, C and D are in partnership, sharing profits in the ratio 3:2:1:4. It is decided to dissolve the firm on 1 January 19XX, on which date the balance sheet was as below:

	£	£
Fixed assets		
Land and buildings		8,500
Plant and machinery		7,921
Goodwill		3,000
Investments		2,000
		21,421
Current assets		
Stock	6,348	
Debtors	3,841	
Cash at bank	313	
	10,502	
Less creditors	6,923	
		3,579
		25,000
Capital accounts		
A		7,000
B		4,000
C		3,000
D		4,000
		18,000
Leasehold redemption fund		2,000
General reserve		5,000
		25,000

The assets are realised piecemeal as under:

			£
January	10	Stock (part)	3,500
	14	Debtors (part)	2,932
	28	Investments	2,420
February	3	Goodwill	2,000
	21	Land and buildings	7,000
	21	Debtors (part)	500
	21	Stock (balance)	2,750
March	15	Plant and Machinery	6,560
	15	Debtors (balance)	351

Subject to providing £500 to meet the probable expenses of realisation, the partners decide that after the creditors have been paid, all cash received shall be divided between them immediately.

The expenses of realisation, which are paid on March 15, amount to £400.

Prepare a statement showing how the distributions should be made, and show the realisation profit and loss account, cash account and partners' capital accounts. Calculations are to be made to the nearest £.

After transferring the general reserve to the partners' capital accounts in profit-sharing ratio the capitals of the partners will be:

	A	B	C	D	Total
	£	£	£	£	£
Balances, January 1	7,000	4,000	3,000	4,000	18,000
General reserve	1,500	1,000	500	2,000	5,000
	£8,500	£5,000	£3,500	£6,000	£23,000
The profit-sharing ratio is	3	2	1	4	10
The capital per unit of profit is	£2,833	£2,500	£3,500	£1,500	

D has the smallest capital in relation to his share of profit viz £1,500 capital per unit of profit. If the capitals of the other partners were held on the same basis, A's capital would be £4,500, B's £3,000 and C's £1,500. A, B and C, therefore, have surplus capital over that of D of £4,000, £2,000 and £2,000 respectively, which surplus must be repaid to them before any payments are made to D.

| | A | B | C | D | Total |
	£	£	£	£	£
Balances as above	8,500	5,000	3,500	6,000	23,000
Capitals in profit-sharing ratio	4,500	3,000	1,500	6,000	15,000
Surplus capitals	£4,000	£2,000	£2,000	–	£8,000
The profit-sharing ratio between A, B and C is	3	2	1		
The surplus capital per unit of profit is	£1,333	£1,000	£2,000		

As between A, B and C, B has the smallest surplus capital in relation to his share of profit. If B's surplus capital of £2,000 were in the same proportion to the total surplus capital as his share of profit, the total surplus capital would be £6,000, of which A's share would be £3,000, B's £2,000 and C's £1,000. A and C therefore have surplus capital over B of £1,000 each, which must be repaid to them before any payment is made to B.

| | A | B | C | D | Total |
	£	£	£	£	£
Surplus capital as above	4,000	2,000	2,000	–	8,000
Surplus capitals in profit-sharing ratio (A,3; B,2; C,1)	3,000	2,000	1,000	–	6,000
Further surplus capital	£1,000	–	£1,000	–	£2,000

As between A and C, the profit-sharing ratio is 3:1 so that the further surplus capital per unit of profit is A, £333 and C, £1,000. If A's surplus of £1,000 represented three-quarters of the total surplus, C's share would be £333. C, therefore has a further surplus over A of £667 as shown hereunder.

| | A | B | C | D | Total |
	£	£	£	£	£
Surplus capital as above	1,000	–	1,000	–	2,000
Surplus capital in profit-sharing ratio (A,3; C,1)	1,000	–	333	–	1,333
Ultimate surplus capital	–	–	£667	–	£667

The amounts becoming available for distribution should accordingly be paid to the partners in the order of priority shown in the following statement.

| | A | B | C | D | Total |
	£	£	£	£	£
The first £667			667		667
The next £1,333 (A,3; C,1)	1,000		333		1,333
	1,000		1,000		2,000
The next £6,000 (A,3; B,2; C,1)	3,000	2,000	1,000		6,000
	£4,000	£2,000	£2,000	–	£8,000

After repayment of the above £8,000, the balances remaining on the capital accounts will be A £4,500, B £3,000, C, £1,500 and D £6,000, these amounts being in the same proportion as that in which profits and losses are shared. By dividing all further realisations in this ratio, therefore, each partner will receive his proper share of the profit or bear his proper share of the loss.

STATEMENT OF ACTUAL DISTRIBUTIONS

19XX		Cash available	A	B	C	D	Total
		£	£	£	£	£	£
	Balance b/f	313					
Jan 10	Realisation	3,500					
14	Realisation	2,932					
28	Realisation	2,420					
		9,165					
	Less creditors	6,923					
		2,242					
Jan 28	*Less* provided for expenses	500					
		1,742					
	Less to C	667	–	–	667	–	667
	Divisible between A and C in proportion of A,3; C,1	£1,075	806	–	269	–	1,075
			£806	–	£936	–	£1,742
19XX							
Feb 3	Realisations	2,000					
	Less balance of £1,333 to A and C in proportion of A,3; C,1	258	194	–	64	–	258
	Divisible between A, B and C in proportion of A,3; B,2; C1	£1,742	871	581	290	–	1,742
			£1,065	£581	£354	–	£2,000
19XX							
Feb 21	Realisations	10,250					
	Less balance of £6,000 to A, B and C in proportion of A,3; B,2; C,1	4,258	2,129	1,419	710	–	4,258
	Divisible between A, B, C and D in profit-sharing ratio of A,3; B,2; C,1; D,4	£5,992	1,798	1,198	599	2,397	5,992
			3,927	2,617	1,309	2,397	10,250
19XX							
Mar 15	Realisations	6,911					
	Add overprovision for expenses	100					
	Divisible between A, B, C and D in profit-sharing ratio A,3; B,2; C,1; D,4	£7,011	£2,103	£1,403	£701	£2,804	£7,011

The accounts will be closed as follows:

CASH ACCOUNT

		£				£
Jan 1	Balance b/f	313	Jan 2	Creditors		6,923
15	Stock account	3,500		Capital accounts:		
14	Debtors	2,932		A		806
28	Investments	2,420		C		936
Feb 3	Goodwill	2,000	Feb 3	Capital accounts:		
21	Land and buildings	7,000		A		1,065
	Debtors	500		B		581
	Stock	2,750		C		354
Mar 15	Plant and machinery	6,560	21	Capital accounts:		
	Debtors	351		A		3,927
				B		2,617
				C		1,309
				D		2,397
			Mar 15	Realisation profit and loss account: expenses		400
				Capital accounts:		
				A		2,103
				B		1,403
				C		701
				D		2,804
		£28,326				£28,326

REALISATION PROFIT AND LOSS ACCOUNT

		£				£
Feb 3	Goodwill	1,000	Jan 28	Investments		420
21	Land and buildings	1,500	Feb 21	Leasehold redemption fund		2,000
	Stock	98				
	Plant and machinery	1,361	Mar 15	Loss transferred to capital accounts:		
	Debtors	58		A $(\frac{3}{10})$	£599	
	Cash—expenses of realisation	400		B $(\frac{2}{10})$	399	
				C $(\frac{1}{10})$	200	
				D $(\frac{4}{10})$	799	
						1,997
		£4,417				£4,417

CAPITAL ACCOUNTS

	A	B	C	D		A	B	C	D
	£	£	£	£		£	£	£	£
Jan 28 Cash	806	–	936		Jan 1 Balances b/f	7,000	4,000	3,000	4,000
Feb 3 Cash	1,065	581	354	–	General				
21 Cash	3,927	2,617	1,309	2,397	reserve	1,500	1,000	500	2,000
Mar 15 Loss on realis-									
ation	599	399	200	799					
Cash	2,103	1,403	701	2,804					
	8,500	5,000	3,500	6,000		8,500	5,000	3,500	6,000

Another, and more cautious method, is to treat the assets remaining unrealised after each realisation as completely valueless, and to charge each partner with his share of the notional loss in the agreed profit-sharing ratio. If a partner's capital is thereby thrown into debit, the amount thereof is charged to the other partners in proportion to their capitals, in accordance with the rule in *Garner v Murray*. The aggregate of the balances of the partners' capital accounts, after deducting the amounts of any previous distributions, will then equal the sum available for distribution. This process will be repeated on each realisation, with the result that after the final distribution, each partner will have borne his proper share of the ultimate loss and in no circumstances will any partner be required to repay anything.

Illustration 7

A, B, and C share profits in the proportion of one-half, one-third and one-sixth. Their balance sheet is as follows:

	£		£
A Capital account	3,000	Assets, *less* liabilities	8,000
B Capital account	3,000		
C Capital account	2,000		
	£8,000		£8,000

The partnership is dissolved, and the assets are realised as follows:

	£
First realisation	1,000
Second realisation	1,500
Third and final realisation	2,500
	£5,000

	£	A £	B £	C £	Total Distributions £
Capitals		3,000	3,000	2,000	
First realisation	1,000				
Balance of assets treated as loss	7,000 ($\frac{1}{2}$) 3,500	($\frac{1}{3}$) 2,333	($\frac{1}{6}$) 1,167		
	£8,000	*Dr* £500	667	833	
A's debit balance divided between B and C in *capital* ratio (*Garner v Murray*)			($\frac{3}{5}$) 300	($\frac{2}{5}$) 200	
Distribution of first realisation			£367	£633	1,000
Capitals		3,000	3,000	2,000	
Second realisation	1,500				
Balance of assets treated as loss	5,500 ($\frac{1}{2}$) 2,750	($\frac{1}{3}$) 1,833	($\frac{2}{6}$) 917		
	£7,000	250	1,167	1,083	
Less first distribution		–	367	633	
Distribution of second realisation		£250	£800	£450	1,500

	£	£	£	£
Capitals		3,000	3,000	2,000
Final realisation	2,500			
Balance of assets, being ultimate loss	3,000 ($\frac{1}{2}$)	1,500 ($\frac{1}{3}$)	1,000 ($\frac{1}{6}$) 500	
	£5,500	1,500	2,000	1,500
Less first and second distributions		250	1,167	1,083
Distribution of final realisation		£1,250	£833	£417 2,500

The ultimate loss of £3,000 has thus been borne by the partners in the correct proportions. The accounts will be closed as follows:

REALISATION ACCOUNT

	£			£
Net assets	8,000	Cash:		
		1st realisation		1,000
		2nd		1,500
		3rd		2,500
		Loss transferred to capital accounts:		
		A ($\frac{1}{2}$)	£1,500	
		B ($\frac{1}{3}$)	1,000	
		C ($\frac{1}{6}$)	500	3,000
	£8,000			£8,000

CASH ACCOUNT

	£		£
1st realisation	1,000	Capital accounts:	
		B	367
		C	633
2nd realisation	1,500	Capital accounts:	
		A	250
		B	800
		C	450
3rd realisation	2,500	Capital accounts:	
		A	1,250
		B	833
		C	417

CAPITAL ACCOUNTS

	A £	B £	C £		A £	B £	C £
Cash 1st realisation		367	633	b/f	3,000	3,000	2,000
2nd realisation	250	800	450				
3rd reliisation	1,250	833	417				
Realisation account: loss	1,500	1,000	500				
	3,000	3,000	2,000		3,000	3,000	2,000

The partners may, of course, agree between themselves on some other basis of distribution. One or other of the above methods should be used in the absence of agreement.

3.4 AMALGAMATION OF FIRMS

Where members of two or more partnerships decide to amalgamate, the transaction resolves itself into the dissolution of the existing partnerships and the formation of a new one. For the purposes of the amalgamation, it is probable that the goodwill and other assets of the original firms will be revalued, and the capitals of the respective partners adjusted by reference to the profit or loss arising on such revaluation, before arriving at the amount of capital introduced by each partner into the new firm. Where the capital of the new firm is a fixed amount, to be provided by the partners in specified proportions or sums, it may be necessary, after giving effect to the agreed revaluations of assets, for cash to be withdrawn or paid in by one or more of the partners in order to adjust the capitals to the agreed amounts.

Illustration 8

In similar type businesses, R and Y are in partnership as R, Y and Co, and V and B as V, B & Co. It was mutually agreed that as on January 1 19X9, the partnerships be amalgamated into one firm, Tints Co. The profit-sharing ratios in the various firms were and are to be as follows:

	R	Y	V	B
Old firms	4	3	3	2
New firms	6	5	4	3

As on December 31 19X8, the balance sheets of the firms were as follows:

	R, Y & Co £	V, B & Co £		R, Y & Co £	V, B & Co £
Capital accounts:			Property	7,400	10,000
R	15,300	–	Fixtures	1,800	1,400
Y	11,000	–	Vehicles	3,000	1,800
V	–	11,300	Stock	8,300	6,600
B	–	7,400	Investment	800	–
Creditors	5,200	6,000	Debtors	6,800	5,800
Bank overdraft	–	900	Bank balance	3,400	–
	£31,500	£25,600		£31,500	£25,600

The agreement to amalgamate contains the following provisions:

(1) Provision for doubtful debts at the rate of 5% be made in respect of debtors, and a provision for discount receivable at the rate of $2\frac{1}{2}$% be made in respect of creditors.

(2) Tints Co to take over the old partnership assets at the following values:

	R, Y & Co £	V, B & Co £
Stock	8,450	6,390
Vehicles	2,800	1,300
Fixtures	1,600	—
Property	10,000	—
Goodwill	6,300	4,500

(3) The property and fixtures of V, B & Co not to be taken over by Tints Co. (These assets were sold for £13,500 cash on January 1 19X9.)

(4) Y to take over his firm's investment at a value of £760.

(5) The capital of Tints Co to be £54,000 and to be contributed by the partners in profit-sharing ratios, any adjustments to be made in cash.

Close the books of R, Y & Co and of V, B & Co and prepare the opening balance sheet of Tints Co.

R, Y & CO AND V, B & CO REALISATION ACCOUNTS

	R, Y & Co £	V, B & Co £		R, Y & Co £	£	V, B & Co £
Assets (at book values)			Creditors	5,200		6,000
Property	7,400	10,000	Partners' capital account:			
Fixtures	1,800	1,400	Y — investment	760		
Vehicles	3,000	1,800	Tints Co:			
Stock	8,300	6,600	Assets taken over (at agreed values)			
Investment	800		Stock	£8,450	6,390	
Debtors	6,800	5,800	Vehicles	2,800	1,300	
	28,100	25,600	Fixtures	1,600	–	
			Property	10,000	–	
Partners' capital accounts:			Goodwill	6,300	4,500	
Profit on realisation:			Debtors	6,460	5,510	
R ($\frac{4}{7}$) £4,800				35,610	17,700	
Y ($\frac{3}{7}$) 3,600	8,400		Less creditors	5,070	5,850	
				30,540		11,850
V ($\frac{3}{5}$) 3,450			Cash — sale of property and fixtures			13,500
B ($\frac{2}{5}$) 2,300		5,750				
	£36,500	£31,350		£36,500		£31,350

PARTNERS' CAPITAL ACCOUNTS

	R £	Y £	V £	B £		R £	Y £	V £	B £
Realisation account:					Balances b/f	15,300	11,000	11,300	7,400
Investment taken over		760			Realisation account	4,800	3,600	3,450	2,300
Cash	2,100		2,750	700	Cash		1,160		
Transferred to Tints Co	18,000	15,000	12,000	9,000					
	£20,100	£15,760	£14,750	£9,700		£20,100	£15,760	£14,750	£9,700

CASH ACCOUNTS

	R, Y & Co £	V, B & Co £		R, Y & Co £	V, B & Co £
Balance brought forward	3,400		Balances brought forward		900
Realisation account—sale of property and fixtures		13,500	Tints Co	2,460	9,150
Y	1,160		R	2,100	
			V		2,750
			B		700
	£4,560	£13,500		£4,560	£13,500

TINTS CO

	R, Y & Co £	V, B & Co £		R, Y & Co £	V, B & Co £
Realisation account	30,540	11,850	Capital accounts:		
Cash	2,460	9,150	R $\frac{6}{18}$ of 54,000	18,000	
			Y $\frac{5}{18}$ of	15,000	
			V $\frac{4}{18}$ of		12,000
			B $\frac{3}{18}$ of		9,000
	£33,000	£21,000		£33,000	£21,000

TINTS & CO BALANCE SHEET

as at 1 January 19X9

	£	£	£
Fixed assets (at cost)			
Goodwill			10,800
Property			10,000
Fixtures			1,600
Vehicles			4,100
			26,500
Current assets			
Stock		14,840	
Debtors	12,600		
Less provision for doubtful debts	630		
		11,970	
Cash at bank		11,610	
		38,420	
Less current liabilities			
Creditors	11,200		
Less provision for discounts receivable	280		
		10,920	
Net current assets			27,500
			54,000
Capital accounts			
R			18,000
Y			15,000
V			12,000
B			9,000
			54,000

3.5 CONVERSION OF A PARTNERSHIP INTO A LIMITED COMPANY

(a) Introduction

Frequently a private business is 'converted' into a limited company. The partners give up their partnership stakes in exchange for shares in the company. This conversion is usually seen as a necessary stage of development of the growth of the business. A later stage may see the conversion of the private company into a public limited company (plc).

(b) Accounting entries

Such a transaction will necessitate the books of the firm being closed, and new books being opened for the company. The following will be the procedure for closing the firm's books:

(1) Open a realisation account, and transfer to the debit thereof the book value of the assets taken over by the purchasing company, crediting the various asset accounts.

(2) Transfer to the credit of the realisation account the liabilities assumed by the company, debiting the respective liability accounts.

(3) Debit the purchasing company's account, and credit realisation account with the agreed purchase price of the net assets taken over by the company.
Note
The term 'net assets' means the assets less the liabilities.

(4) The balance on the realisation account, after debiting expenses (if any), will represent the profit or loss on realisation of the net assets, and will be transferred to the partners' capital accounts in the proportions in which they share profits and losses.

(5) Debit the accounts of the assets (e g cash, shares, debentures etc) received as purchase consideration, and credit the purchasing company's account.

(6) Pay off any liabilities not taken over by the new company, crediting cash and debiting the liability accounts.

(7) Distribute between the partners the shares, debentures etc received from the company in the proportions agreed between them, debiting their capital accounts and crediting the accounts of the shares, debentures etc.

(8) Any balances remaining on capital accounts must now be cleared by the withdrawal or payment in of cash.

(c) Illustration 9

The firm of J, S and R decide to form a limited company, J, S & R Ltd, and transfer business thereto. Their balance sheet is as follows:

J, S & R

Abridged balance sheet as at 30 June

	£	£		£	£
Capital accounts:			Freehold property		30,000
J	£25,000		Plant		10,900
S	15,000		Fixtures, fittings		
R	10,000		and furniture		1,500
		50,000	Stock-in-trade		19,500
			Debtors	£68,830	
Creditors		63,300	*Less* provision	2,000	
Loan on mortgage		20,000			66,830
			Cash at bank	4,500	
			Cash in hand	70	
					4,570
		£133,300			£133,300

They share profits—J, four-ninths, S, three-ninths, R, two-ninths. The purchase consideration was £85,000 (the company taking over all the assets and liabilities except the loan on mortgage) and was payable as to £25,000 in cash, £20,000 in 5% mortgage debentures, and £40,000 in ordinary shares. Expenses amounting to £600 were payable by the firm.

Assuming the transactions to have been carried through, and the loan on mortgage repaid, close the books of the firm, the debentures and shares being divided between the partners in the following proportions: J one-half, S one-quarter, R one-quarter.

REALISATION ACCOUNT

	£		£
Sundry assets	135,300	Provision for bad debts	2,000
Expenses	600	Creditors	63,300
Capital accounts, being profit:		J, S & R Ltd purchase	
		consideration	85,000
J ($\frac{4}{9}$) £6,400			
S ($\frac{3}{9}$) £4,800			
R ($\frac{2}{9}$) £3,200			
	14,400		
	£150,300		£150,300

LOAN ON MORTGAGE

	£		£
Cash	20,000	Balance b/f	20,000

J, S & R LTD

	£		£
Realisation account purchase		Cash	25,000
consideration	85,000	Debentures in J, S & R Ltd	20,000
		Ordinary shares in J, S & R Ltd	40,000
	£85,000		£85,000

DEBENTURES IN J, S & R LTD

	£		£
J, S & R Ltd	20,000	J capital account	10,000
		S	5,000
		R	5,000
	£20,000		£20,000

ORDINARY SHARES IN J, S & R LTD

	£		£
J, S & R Ltd	40,000	J Capital account, ($\frac{1}{2}$)	20,000
		S Capital account, ($\frac{1}{4}$)	10,000
		R Capital account, ($\frac{1}{4}$)	10,000
	£40,000		£40,000

J CAPITAL ACCOUNT

	£		£
Debentures in J, S & R Ltd	10,000	Balance b/f	25,000
Ordinary shares in J, S & R Ltd	20,000	Realisation account, profit	6,400
Cash	1,400		
	£31,400		£31,400

S CAPITAL ACCOUNT

	£	£		£
Debentures in J, S & R Ltd		5,000	Balance b/f	15,000
Ordinary shares in J, S & R Ltd		10,000	Realisation account, profit	4,800
Cash		4,800		
		£19,800		£19,800

R CAPITAL ACCOUNT

	£		£
Debentures in J, S & R Ltd	5,000	Balance b/f	10,000
Ordinary shares in J, S & R Ltd	10,000	Realisation account, profit	3,200
		Cash	1,800
	£15,000		£15,000

CASH ACCOUNT

	£			£
J, S & R Ltd	25,000	Loan on mortgage		20,000
Capital account: R	1,800	Expenses		600
		Capital accounts:		
		J	£1,400	
		S	4,800	6,200
	£26,800			£26,800

Normally, where a partnership is converted into a limited company, the partners of the firm will agree as to the manner in which the shares, debentures etc of the company, received as purchase consideration, are to be divided between them. Where, however, the partners cannot agree upon such proportions, an independent valuation of the shares, debentures etc should be obtained and the profit or loss disclosed thereby divided between the partners in their profit-sharing ratio. The shares, debentures etc at their agreed valuation will then be divided between the partners in proportion to the adjusted balances on their capital accounts. If it is desired by the partners to share the profits of the company in the proportions in which the profits of the partnership were formerly divided, the shares, debentures etc should be allocated to the partners in their profit-sharing ratio, a cash adjustment being made between the partners in respect of any balances remaining due to or by them individually.

The accounting entries in the books of the company are discussed in chapter 4.

3.6   JOINT VENTURE ACCOUNTS

(a) Definition

'Joint venture' is defined in *Bell's Principles*, art 392 as follows:

> Joint adventure or joint trade is a partnership confined to a particular adventure, speculation, course of trade or voyage, and in which the partners, either latent or known, use no firm or social name, and incur no responsibility beyond the limits of the adventure.

A joint venture cannot be distinguished in any way from an ordinary partnership, beyond the fact that the agreement is of a specially limited character.

In actual practice ventures resolve themselves broadly into two classes:

(1) Where a separate set of books is opened for the joint venture transactions.
(2) Where no separate set of books is opened.

(b) Separate set of books opened for the transactions of the joint venture

In such a case, a joint banking account may be opened and the transactions recorded in a manner precisely similar to those of ordinary partnerships, each partner's capital account being credited with the amount which he pays into the joint account. Interest on capital is usually taken into consideration, and the profits or losses are divided according to the shares agreed upon.

Illustration 10

A and B were partners in a joint venture in timber, sharing profits two-thirds and one-third respectively. A banking account in their joint names is opened on January 1, A paying in £700, and B, £850.

The transactions were as follows:

			£
Jan 8	Purchased from F Daponta cargo of timber valued at		665
	Accepted draft for same at one month		665
Jan 11	Paid freight and expenses to Liverpool		142
Feb 20	Sold T Stephens & Sons logs		180
Feb 21	Received cash *less* 5%		171
Feb 26	Bought for cash from Lehman & Co, cargo of timber, net		800
Mar 17	Paid freight and expenses to Hull		125
	Sold M White & Co deals, net		300
	Received their acceptance at one month		300
April 21	Sold for cash to M Black & Co, cargo purchased from Lehman & Co		1,400
April 30	Stock balance of Daponta's cargo valued at		320

The venture was closed on April 30 by B taking over the unsold stock at an agreed valuation of £320, less 10%.

Adjust the accounts as between the partners at April 30, allowing interest on capital (calculated to the nearest £) at 5% per annum, and show:

(1) The joint venture account.
(2) The partners' capital accounts.
(3) The joint cash account.
(4) The joint bills receivable and bills payable accounts.

JOINT VENTURE ACCOUNT

		£			£	
Purchases:				Sales:		
F Daponta	£665			T Stephens & Sons	£180	
Lehman & Co	800			M White & Co	300	
		1,465		M Black & Co	1,400	
Freight and expenses:						1,880
Liverpool	142					
Hull	125			B capital account: value of stock		
		267		taken over, £320 *less* 10%		288
Discount		9				
Interest on capital:						
A	12					
B	14					
		26				
Balance, being profit:						
A (⅔)	267					
B (⅓)	134					
		401				
		£2,168				£2,168

A CAPITAL ACCOUNT

		£				£
April 30	Cash	979	Jan 1	Cash		700
			April 30	Interest on capital		12
			April 30	Profit		267
		£979				£979

B CAPITAL ACCOUNT

		£			£
April 30	Stock taken over	288	Jan 1	Cash	850
April 30	Cash	710	April 30	Interest on capital	14
			April 30	Profit	134
		£998			£998

CASH BOOK

		£			£
Jan 1	A Capital account	700	Jan 11	Freight and expenses	142
	B Capital account	850	Feb 8	Bills payable	665
Feb 21	T Stephens & Sons	171	Feb 26	Cash purchases:	
April 17	Bills receivable	300		Lehman & Co	800
April 21	Cash sales:		Mar 17	Freight and expenses	125
	M Black & Co	1,400	April 30	Balance c/d	1,689
		£3,421			£3,421
April 30	Balance b/d	1,689	April 30	A	979
				B	710
		£1,689			£1,689

BILLS RECEIVABLE ACCOUNT

		£			£
Mar 17	M White & Co	300	April 17	Cash	300

BILLS PAYABLE ACCOUNT

		£			£
Feb 8	Cash	665	Jan 8	F Daponta	665

In some cases, although a separate set of books is kept for the joint venture, it is not considered necessary to open a special banking account therefor. In these circumstances, each party to the venture will disburse sums on behalf of the joint account from his own banking account, into which he will also pay cash received by him from time to time. In the books of the joint venture, the capital accounts of the parties concerned will be credited with the sums paid out on behalf of the venture and debited with the cash collected.

Illustration 11

A and B are partners in a joint venture in produce, sharing profits in the ratio 2:1. A separate set of books is opened for the venture, but all cash transactions are dealt with by the partners through their own banking accounts.
    The transactions of the venture were as under:

			£
Jan	1	Purchased produce from J Smith	1,000
		Freight and expenses thereon paid by A	120
Feb	1	J Smith's account met by A subject to 10% cash discount	
Feb	13	Sold to A Brown produce for	860
Feb	15	Sold to T Jones produce for	620
March	1	Cash purchase by B for	600
April	1	Payment to B by A Brown in settlement of his account	
May	1	Payment to A by T Jones in settlement of his account	
June	1	Sundry expenses paid by A	61
		Balance of produce sold by A for £700 cash	

The accounts of the venture are to be made up to June 30, on which date a settlement is effected between the parties. Interest is to be calculated to the nearest £ at 5% per annum.

A CAPITAL ACCOUNT

		Mos	Int £	£				Mos	Int £	£
May 1	Cash from T Jones	2	5	620	Jan 1	Freight and expenses	6	3	120
June 1	Cash sales	1	3	700	Feb 1	J Smith	5	19	900
June 30	Balance of interest to contra		14		June 1	Sundry expenses	1		61
					June 30	Balance of interest			14
			£22					£22	
	Cheque from B in settlement			99		Profit			324
				£1,419					£1,419

B CAPITAL ACCOUNT

		Mos	Int £	£				Mos	Int £	£
April 1	Cash from A Brown	3	11	860	Mar 1	Cash purchase	4	10	600
June 30	Balance of interest			1	June 30	Balance of interest to contra		1	
			£11					£11	
						Profit			162
						Cheque to A in settlement			99
				£861					£861

JOINT VENTURE ACCOUNT

	£				£
Purchases:			Sales:		
J Smith	£1,000		A Brown	£860	
Cash	600		T Jones	620	
		1,600	Cash	700	
Freight and expenses		120			2,180
Sundry expenses		61	Discount		100
Interest: A		14	Interest: B		1
Profit:					
A ($\frac{2}{3}$)	324				
B ($\frac{1}{3}$)	162				
		486			
		£2,281			£2,281

In their respective books A and B will keep accounts to record the payments made by them on behalf of the venture and the cash received therefrom. These accounts will appear as under:

A'S BOOKS
JOINT VENTURE WITH B

		£			£
Jan 1	Cash—Freight and		May 1	Cash—T Jones	620
	expenses	120	June 1	Cash sales	700
Feb 1	Cash—J Smith	900	June 30	Cheque from B	99
June 1	Cash—Sundry expenses	61			
June 30	Interest account	14			
	Profit and loss account —two-thirds of profit on venture	324			
		£1,419			£1,419

B'S BOOKS
JOINT VENTURE WITH A

		£			£
Mar 1	Cash purchase	600	April 1	Cash—A Brown	860
June 30	Profit and loss account —one-third of profit on venture	162	June 30	Interest account	1
	Cheque to A	99			
		£861			£861

(c) No separate set of books opened for the transactions of the joint venture

In such a case, each party will record his own transactions on behalf of the joint venture in his own books, and no joint banking account will normally be opened. In order to ascertain the profit or loss, each party must render to the other a complete statement of all transactions entered into by him, and these must then be combined into a *memorandum* joint venture account. This account, which does not appear in the books of either party, but is raised from material supplied by both, is in the nature of a profit and loss account. As soon as the result is ascertained, each partner will debit or credit the account for the joint venture in his books with his share of the result, and the balance of this account, if the venture has been completed, will then represent the amount due to or by the other party.

Illustration 12

M and R were partners in an underwriting venture, sharing profits and losses: M, three-fifths and R, two-fifths. They agree to guarantee the subscription at par of 100,000 shares of £1 each in a company, and to pay all expenses up to allotment, in consideration of a commission of 6% in cash and 10% in fully-paid shares of the company.

M provided cash for the following expenses: registration fees, £620; advertising, £2,700; printing and prospectuses, £270. R provided the cash for the remainder viz rent of offices, £45; petty cash, £20; stamps, £90; law costs, £250. The whole of the commission was received by M.

The public having subscribed for only 70,000 shares, the underwriters had to take up 30,000, the cash being provided by and shares allotted to them in the proportions of: M, three-fifths and R, two-fifths.

In due course they sold all the shares except 5,000, including those received for commission, at an average price of 80p, less brokerage of 5p per share, the remaining 5,000 being taken over by M at 65p per share. The sales were effected as to 21,000 by M and 14,000 by R.

Prepare a joint venture account, and the separate accounts of the partners in their own books, showing the final balance payable by the one to the other, the shares taken over by M being brought into account, and no interest being taken into consideration.

M'S BOOKS JOINT ACCOUNT WITH R

	Shares	£		Shares	£
Cash—expenses		3,590	Cash—commission		6,000
—shares taken up	18,000	18,000	—proceeds of shares sold	21,000	15,750
Shares received as commission	10,000	—	Own investment account—shares taken over	5,000	3,250
Profit and loss account: $\frac{3}{5}$ of £1,505		903	Shares sold by R	2,000	—
Balance due to R c/d		2,507			
	28,000	25,000		28,000	£25,000
			Balance due to R b/d		2,507

R'S BOOKS JOINT ACCOUNT WITH M

	Shares	£		Shares	£
Cash—expenses		405	Cash—proceeds of shares sold	14,000	10,500
—shares taken up	12,000	12,000	Balance due from M c/d		2,507
Shares drawn from M	2,000	—			
Profit and loss account: $\frac{2}{5}$ of £1,505		602			
	14,000	13,007		14,000	£13,007
Balance due from M b/d		2,507			

MEMORANDUM JOINT VENTURE ACCOUNT

	£	£		£	£
Expenses paid by M:			Cash—underwriting commission		6,000
Registration fees	620		Sale of 35,000 shares at 75p net:		
Advertising	2,700		M	15,750	
Printing etc	270		R	10,500	
		3,590			26,250
Expenses paid by R:					
Rent	45				
Petty cash	20		Shares taken over by M,		
Stamps	90		5,000 @ 65p		3,250
Law costs	250				
		405			
Cost of shares taken up:					
M	18,000				
R	12,000				
		30,000			
Balance, being profit:					
M ($\frac{3}{5}$)	903				
R ($\frac{2}{5}$)	602				
		1,505			
		£35,500			£35,500

NOTES TO ILLUSTRATION

(1) It is preferable to place no value on the shares received as commission until they are sold, when the proceeds are credited to the joint account. As these shares were received by M, the receipt and sale thereof appear in the joint account in his books.

(2) The shares allotted to M and R respectively are the property of the partnership, not of the individual partners; they represent the stock-in-trade of the venture, part of which is in the custody of M and part of R. Where it is necessary for one partner to draw on stock held by the other for the purpose of effecting delivery of shares sold, this involves no payment of cash between the partners, but each partner must account to the venture for the proceeds of the sales effected by him. Thus, R must credit his joint account with the proceeds of the 14,000 shares sold by him, although delivery of 2,000 of these shares must be made out of the shares held by M.

(3) The 5,000 shares taken over by M represent a purchase by him from the venture, the agreed price being credited to the joint account in his books as the proceeds of a sale by the venture, and debited to M's personal investment account.

Alternative approach

An alternative method is for one (or each) of the partners to record the *whole* of the transactions in his own books, in which, in addition to the joint venture account, a personal account for the other partner will be opened. The joint venture account will be debited with all the payments made, and credited with all the sums received, by *both* partners, the cash being credited with the payments made and debited with the receipts of the partner in whose books the transactions are being recorded, and the personal account of the other partner credited and debited respectively with the payments and receipts made by him. Any stock taken over by the partners will be credited to the joint venture account, and debited, in the case of the first-named partner, to his purchases or other appropriate account, and in the case of the other partner to his personal account.

The profit disclosed by the joint venture account will be divided between the partners according to the agreement between them, the first-named partner's share being credited to his profit and loss account or capital account, and the other partner's share to his personal account. A loss will be treated in the converse manner. The balance remaining on the personal account of the other partner will now represent the sum due to or from him to close the venture.

Illustration 13

Bear and Bull agreed to deal in stocks and shares on joint account and to share any profits or losses equally.

The following transactions took place:

(1) January 4. Bear purchased 2,000 £1 shares in Washers Ltd at 175p per share, expenses amounting to £35.

(2) January 10. Bull purchased 1,000 £1 ordinary stock units in Assurances Ltd at 210p cum div, expenses amounting to £32.

(3) March 30. Bull purchased a further 500 £1 ordinary stock units in Assurances Ltd at 200p ex div. expenses amounting to £16.

(4) April 15. A dividend of £100 for the year ended the previous December 31, on 1,000 Assurances Ltd £1 ordinary stock units, was received by Bull.

(5) April 30. A fully-paid allotment letter was received by Bear from Washers Ltd in respect of an issue in the proportion of one new £1 share credited as fully paid for every two shares held. These shares ranked for dividend pari passu with the old shares as from May 1. Bear sold the new shares for 115p each, less a brokerage of 5p per share.

(6) April 30. A dividend of £220 for the year ended the previous December 31, was received by Bear from Washers Ltd.

(7) June 25. Bull purchases £250 (1,000 units of 25p) ordinary stock in Showers Ltd at 50p per unit, expenses amounting to £25.

(8) July 31. A capital distribution of 5p per unit was received by Bull on the Showers Ltd ordinary stock.

(9) August 30. Bear sold the shares in Washers Ltd at 125p per share, expenses amounting to £32.

On September 30, it was agreed to terminate the venture, Bull taking over the Assurances Ltd stock at a valuation of 250p per £1 unit, and Bear the Showers Ltd stock at a valuation of 75p per 25p unit, the balance between them being settled by cash.

You are required to prepare:

(a) The joint venture account; and
(b) Bear's account;

as they would appear in Bull's books.
Ignore taxation.

JOINT VENTURE ACCOUNT

		£				£
Jan 4	Bear, purchase 2,000 £1 shares in Washers Ltd at 175p a share plus expenses of £35	3,535	Apr 15	Cash dividend on 1,000 £1 ordinary stock units in Assurances Ltd	100	
10	Cash 1,000 £1 ordinary stock units in Assurances Ltd at 210p each plus expenses of £32	2,132	Apr 30	Bear, sale of 1,000 shares in Washers Ltd at 110p net	1,100	
				Bear, dividend on 2,000 £1 shares in Washers Ltd	220	
Mar 30	Cash 500 £1 ordinary stock units in Assurances Ltd at 200p ex div plus expenses of £16	1,016	July 3	Cash capital distribution on Showers Ltd stock	50	
June 25	Cash 1,000 stock units of 25p in Showers Ltd at 50p a unit plus expenses £25	525	Aug 30	Bear, sale of 2,000 £1 shares in Washers Ltd at 125p a share less expenses £32	2,468	
Sept 30	Bear, half share of profit on venture £615		Sept 3	Investment account, 1,500 £1 ordinary stock units in Assurances Ltd taken over at 250p each	3,750	
	Profit and loss account, half share of profit on venture 615			Bear, 1,000 stock units of 25p in Showers Ltd taken over at 75p each	750	
		1,230				
		£8,438			£8,438	

BEAR'S ACCOUNT

		£			£
Apr 30	Joint venture account, sale of 1,000 £1 shares in Washers Ltd received as bonus shares at 110p net	1,100	Jan 4	Joint venture account, purchase of shares in Washers Ltd	3,535
	Joint venture account, dividend on 2,000 shares in Washers Ltd	220	Sept 30	Joint venture account, half share of profit on venture	615
				Cash	388
Aug 30	Joint venture account, sale of 2,000 shares in Washers Ltd at 125p less expenses £32	2,468			
Sept 30	Joint venture account, stock units in Showers Ltd taken over	750			
		£4,538			£4,538

Where the venture is not completed at the time the accounts of one or both parties are normally closed, and it is desired to ascertain the profit or loss to date, the unsold stock must be valued and brought into account.

It is suggested that the basis of valuation should be similar to that adopted in the case of unsold stock on consignment viz cost plus a proportion of the expenses which have been incurred (reduced if necessary to the net realisable value). The proportions in which the parties provided the stock or bore expenses in connection therewith are, at this stage, irrelevant. As already stated, the stock is the property of the partnership, not of the individual partners, and for the purpose of an interim settlement of account, each party should carry forward in his joint account his proportion of the value of the stock in the ratio in which he shares profits. By carrying down the unsold stock in the profit-sharing ratio, the profit or loss earned to date will automatically be divided between the partners in the correct proportions.

If an immediate settlement between the parties is not required it will be sufficient for each partner to balance his joint venture account, bringing down the balance disclosed thereon and deferring settlement until the completion of the venture.

Illustration 14

On January 1 A and B entered into a joint venture, agreeing to share profits and losses in the ratio of 3:2. A supplied goods to the value of £3,000 and incurred expenses amounting to £400. B supplied £1,000 in goods and paid £500 expenses. Their agent sold three-quarters of the goods for £5,500, and remitted the proceeds to B after deducting 5% commission on sales, on March 31, on which date accounts were prepared, and an interim settlement was effected between A and B.

On June 30 the agent reported that he had sold the remainder of the goods of £2,000, and remitted the proceeds to B, less 5% commission. A final settlement was then effected between the partners.

A's BOOKS JOINT ACCOUNT WITH B

		£			£
Jan 1	Goods	3,000	Mar 31	Balance c/d—pro-	
	Cash—expenses	400		portion of unsold	
Mar 31	Profit to date	930		stock	735
				Cash from B	3,595
		£4,330			£4,330
Apr 1	Balance b/d	735			
June 30	Profit	405	June 30	Cash from B in	
				settlement	1,140
		£1,140			£1,140

B's BOOKS JOINT ACCOUNT WITH A

		£			£
Jan 1	Goods	1,000	Mar 31	Agent—sales	5,500
	Cash—expenses	500		Balance c/d—pro-	
Mar 31	Agent's commission	275		portion of unsold	
	Profit to date	620		stock	490
	Cash to A	3,595			
		£5,990			£5,990
June 30	Balance b/d	490	June 30	Agent—sales	2,000
	Agent's commission	100			
	Profit	270			
	Cash to A in settlement	1,140			
		£2,000			£2,000

MEMORANDUM JOINT VENTURE ACCOUNT

		£	£			£
Jan 1	Goods sup-plied, A	3,000		Mar 31	Sales	5,500
	Goods sup-plied, B	1,000	4,000		Balance c/d—stock unsold	1,225
		400				
		500				
			900			
Mar 31	Agent's commission		275			
	Profit—A ($\frac{3}{5}$)	930				
	Profit—B ($\frac{2}{5}$)	620				
			1,550			
			£6,725			£6,725
Apr 1	Balance—stock b/d		1,225	June 30	Sales	2,000
	Agent's commission		100			
	Profit—A ($\frac{3}{5}$)	405				
	Profit—B ($\frac{2}{5}$)	270				
			675			
			£2,000			£2,000

NOTE

The unsold stock at March 31 is valued as follows:

One-quarter of £4,000, cost of goods	£1,000		
One-quarter of £900, expenses	225		
	£1,225-apportioned	A ($\frac{3}{5}$)	£735
		B ($\frac{2}{5}$)	490
			£1,225

At the conclusion of the venture, A has received from B a total of £4,735, being the amount of his expenditure on the venture, £3,400, plus his share of the profit, £1,335. B has received back his expenditure of £1,500 plus his share of the profit £890 = £2,390, represented by:

	£
Remittances received from agent	7,125
Less paid to A	4,735
	£2,390

3.7   FOREIGN JOINT VENTURES

Where the ventures operate in different countries, the aforementioned principles still apply except that each party will record his transactions in his own currency, and profits and losses on foreign exchange will be shared in profit-sharing ratio. As mentioned above, for purposes of an interim settlement or at their respective accounting dates, each venturer should credit his account and bring down his share of the unsold stock regardless of which party acquired it, since otherwise the venturer holding the greater share of stock will, in effect, pay or show the other venturer as a creditor for an amount in respect of the excess proportion of stock held when, in fact, any residual stock belongs to each venturer in profit-sharing ratio and the intention would normally be to dispose of the whole of the stock to third parties.

Illustration 15

Bubble and Squeak, who are brothers, each received £25,000 from the estate of a deceased aunt. Bubble is resident in Soresia and Squeak in Antesia, the relevant currencies being Sorics and Antics.

Bubble and Squeak agreed to deal on their respective stock exchanges with the two inheritances as a joint venture, sharing profits and losses equally as from January 1 19X8. At the end of each year, any balance due between them to be cleared by payment.

There was concern regarding the stability of the exchange rates of the Soric and the Antic. It was therefore agreed that in the event of any fluctuation in the exchange rate, after the year end but prior to the remittance of any balance, the amount of the remittance should be adjusted by reference to the Doly. Any adjustments so arising to be written off in the accounts of the following year. The Doly is the unit of currency of Dolysia, which it was felt had a stable currency. It would be assumed that on the last day of each year, the amount remittable had been used to purchase Dolys to be held on behalf of the recipient.

Throughout 19X8 the relevant rates of exchange were:
£ sterling = 8 Sorics = 10 Antics = 5 Dolys.

No separate set of books was kept but each party undertook to keep an account recording his transactions.

The following transactions took place in 19X8:

January 1. The inheritances are remitted to the brothers, subject to bank commission of £10 on the transfer to Soresia, and £12 to Antesia.

January 15. Bubble buys 12,000 shares in Ace Ltd at a cost of 90,000 Sorics.

January 18. Squeak buys 15,000 shares in Leas Ltd for 150,000 Antics.

March 1. Bubble takes up a three months' option to purchase 50,000 shares in Thames Ltd at a price of 15 Sorics each. The option money payable was 50,000 Sorics.

March 15. Squeak sells 80,000 shares in Lawrus Ltd for 168,000 Antics for delivery on April 6. On April 6 he arranges for this bargain to be kept open until May 6, subject to interest at the rate of 12% per annum. On May 6 Squeak purchased 80,000 shares in Lawrus Ltd for 160,000 Antics and completed his bargain.

June 1. Bubble exercises his option in respect of the shares in Thames Ltd.

June 20. Bubble sells 45,000 shares in Thames Ltd for 825,000 Sorics.

June 30. Squeak is credited with bank deposit interest of 2,500 Antics and Bubble is debited with overdraft interest of 2,100 Sorics.

August 31. Bubble received a dividend of 3,600 Sorics from Ace Ltd.

September 15. Squeak received a dividend of 4,800 Sorics from Leas Ltd, and paid 360 Antics to an investment advisory service.

October 1. Squeak transferred 60,000 Antics to Bubble who was credited, after bank charges, with 47,900 Sorics.

October 5. Bubble purchased 20,000 shares in Salps Ltd for 98,000 Sorics.

As on December 31, 19X8, the mid-market prices of the various securities were:

Ace Ltd   —   7 Sorics
Thames Ltd —20 Sorics
Salps Ltd   —   4.75 Sorics
Leas Ltd   — 11 Antics

On January 15 19X9, there was a general realignment of currencies, and the following position emerged:

4 Sorics = 6 Antics = 2 Dolys

On January 31 19X9, the difference shown on the two accounts of Bubble and Squeak was settled by payment.

You are required:

(a) to prepare the accounts kept by Bubble and Squeak in respect of the transactions during 19X8 and the memorandum joint venture account; and
(b) to compute the amount of the payment to be made on January 15 19X9.

In the books of Bubble:

(a)
JOINT VENTURE WITH SQUEAK

19X8		*Sorics*	19X8		*Sorics*
Jan 1	Bank charges (£10 at £1 = S8)	80	June 20	Sale of 45,000 shares in Thames Ltd	825,000
Jan 15	Purchase of 12,000 shares in Ace Ltd	90,000	Aug 31	Dividend—Ace Ltd	3,600
Mar 1	Option on 50,000 shares in Thames Ltd	50,000	Oct 1	Squeak— A60,000	48,000
June 1	50,000 shares in Thames Ltd taken at S15 per share	750,000			876,600
June 30	Interest on overdraft	2,100	Dec 31	Share of invest-ments held, carried down	189,500
Oct 1	Bank charges	100			
Oct 5	Purchase of 20,000 shares in Salps Ltd	98,000			
		990,280			
Dec 31	Share of profit	53,916			
	Balance due to Squeak, carried down	21,904			
		S1,066,100			S1,066,100
19X9		*Sorics*	19X9		*Sorics*
Jan 1	Balance, brought down	189,500	Jan 1	Balance, brought down	21,904
(Jan 15	Bank—remit-tance to Squeak at new rate	27,380)			

JOINT VENTURE WITH BUBBLE

19X8		Antics	19X8		Antics
Jan 1	Bank charges (£12 at £1 = A10)	120	May 6	Sale of 80,000 shares in Lawrus Ltd	168,000
18	Purchase of 15,000 shares in Leas Ltd	150,000	June 30	Deposit interest	2,500
			Sept 15	Dividend—Leas Ltd	4,800
Apr 6	Backwardation— 1% on A168,000	1,680			———
May 6	Purchase of 80,000 shares				175,300
	in Lawrus Ltd	160,000	Dec 31	Share of invest- ments held,	
Sept 15	Investment advisory			carried down	236,875
	service	360		Balance due from	
Oct 1	Bubble	60,000		Bubble, carried down	27,380
		———			
		372,160			
Dec 31	Share of profit	67,395			
		———			———
		A439,555			A439,555
		═══			═══

19X9		Antics	19X9		Antics
Jan 1	Balance, brought down	236,875	(Jan 15	Bank—proceeds of remittance from Bubble at	
	Balance, brought down	27,380		new rate	41,070)

MEMORANDUM JOINT VENTURE ACCOUNT

Bubble's transactions:	Cost	Proceeds	On hand 31/12/X8	Profit	Loss
	S	S	S	S	S
12,000 shares in Ace Ltd	90,000		84,000		6,000
45,000 shares in Thames Ltd	720,000	825,000		105,000	
5,000 shares in Thames Ltd	80,000		80,000		
20,000 shares in Salps Ltd	98,000		95,000		3,000
	S988,000	S825,000	S259,000	105,000	9,000
				9,000	

Dealing profit		96,000
Dividend received		3,600
		99,600
Less bank charges and interest		2,280
Net profit		S97,320

Equivalent to Dolys	D60,825

Squeak's transactions:	A	A	A	A
15,000 shares in Leas Ltd	150,000		150,000	
80,000 shares in Lawrus Ltd	160,000	168,000		8,000
	A310,000	A168,000	A150,000	

Dealing profit		8,000
Dividend and interest received		7,300
		15,300
	A	
Less bank charges and interest	1,800	
Investment advisory fee	360	
		2,160
		A13,140

Equivalent to Dolys	D6,570

Total profit D60,825 + D6,570 = D67,395	S107,832 = A134,790
Half shares	S53,916 = A67,395

(b) Computation of payment to be made by Bubble on January 15 19X9:

On December 31 19X8, S21,904 would have purchased D13,690 at S8 = D5.

On January 15 19X9, D13,690 will cost Bubble S27,380 at S4 = D2. and Squeak will receive A41,070 at S4 = SA6. as opposed to A27,380 due to him at December 31 19X8.

Note The differences between the amounts remitted and received as compared with the balances carried down on the individual joint venture accounts will be adjusted in the following year, in accordance with the terms of the question.

WORKINGS

Shares held on December 31 19X8, at lower of cost or market value

		Sorics	Antics
12,000	Ace Ltd at 7 Sorics (market value)	84,000	
5,000	Thames Ltd at cost $\frac{5,000}{50,000} \times 800,000$	80,000	
20,000	Salps Ltd at 4.75 Sorics (market value)	95,000	
		259,000	
	259,000 Sorics converted into Antics at 8 Sorics = 10 Antics		323,750
15,000	Leas Ltd at 10 Antics (cost)		150,000
	150,000 Antics converted into Sorics at 10 Antics = 8 Sorics	120,000	
		379,000	473,750
	Bubble—half-share	S189,500	
	Squeak—half-share		A236,875

NOTES TO ILLUSTRATION

(1) Each venturer prepares his joint venture account with the other party in his own currency. It is unnecessary to prepare accounts in Dolys.

(2) No distinction need be made between capital and income transactions.

(3) Profits and losses on exchange arising from the final remittance are to be accounted for in the 19X9 accounts as per the question.

4 COMPANY ACCOUNTS—BASIC CONSIDERATIONS

4.1 DISTINCTIONS BETWEEN PARTNERSHIPS AND LIMITED COMPANIES

Company law today is embodied in the Companies Act 1985. In the future, further pieces of legislation can be expected as a result of membership of the European Community.

The majority of companies in the UK are limited liability companies, where the liability of each shareholder is limited to the amount unpaid on shares allotted. By contrast, the majority of partnerships in the UK are unlimited. The principal distinctions between unlimited partnerships and limited companies are set out in the table below:

	Unlimited partnerships	Limited companies
1	No separate legal entity apart from its members.	Separate legal entity which is not affected by changes in its membership. A company may contract, sue and be sued in its own name and capacity.
2	Liability of each member for debts of the firm is unlimited.	If the company is limited by shares, each shareholder is limited to the amount he has agreed to pay to the company for shares allotted. If his shares are fully paid, he has no further liability.
3	Number of partners limited to 20 except for firms of solicitors, accountants, stockbrokers and certain other specified exceptions.	A limited company must have at least two members. The maximum number of shares is restricted to the company's authorised share capital.
4	Every partner can normally take part in the management of the business; he can legally bind the firm by his action with the outside world within the scope of his real or apparent authority.	Rights of management are delegated to directors who alone can act on behalf of and bind the company.
5	Copies of accounts need not be filed with the Registrar of Companies.	Copies of accounts must be filed with the Registrar of Companies. Exemptions on amount of information to be filed are available to small and medium-sized companies (see chapter 5, at 5.14)

6 Although a written partnership agreement is desirable, it is not mandatory.	A company is required to have a memorandum and articles of association which define powers and duties of directors.
7 A partnership is subject to the Partnership Act 1890, which can be varied by mutual agreement.	A company is subject to the Companies Act 1985, the provisions of which cannot be varied.
8 The capital is contributed by the partners by agreement. The amount need not be fixed.	The authorised capital is fixed by the memorandum of association. It can be increased by passing ordinary resolution. It can only be reduced by special resolution and sanction of the court.
9 A share in a partnership cannot be transferred except by the consent of all partners.	In public companies, shares are freely transferable. In private companies share transfers are subject to any restrictions imposed by the articles of association.
10 A partnership is not obliged to keep statutory books of account and an audit is not compulsory.	A company is required to keep specified accounting records and is subject to compulsory audit.
11 Profits are subject to income tax.	Profits are subject to corporation tax.

4.2 TYPES OF COMPANIES

The principal categories of companies are summarised in the diagram below:

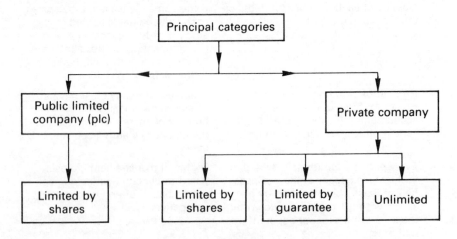

NOTES
(a) A public limited company (plc) must be registered as such and have an authorised share capital in excess of £50,000. The title of the company must include the words public limited company or the abbreviation plc.
(b) A private company is any company which is not a plc i e it is a residual category. A private company is not permitted to offer securities to the public.
(c) All companies are liable without limit for their debts. A company limited by shares is the most important category of company. In such a company, a shareholder is liable to pay

to the company the amount (if any) which is due on the shares and which has not already been paid.

(d) A company limited by guarantee must be a private company except in the rare situation that it also has share capital. In the usual situation, a shareholder is liable, when the company is wound up to contribute to the company's assets if needed for the purpose of discharging debts. The amount involved is limited to that specified in the memorandum of association.

(e) For an unlimited company, the liability of a shareholder arises only when the company goes into liquidation. In such an event, there is no limit on the shareholder to provide money towards the payment of debts.

4.3 FINANCIAL STATEMENTS OF COMPANIES

Special features of company financial statements include:

(a) Profit and loss account

The profit and loss account will be charged with directors' remuneration and auditors' remuneration. If the company has borrowings in the form of loan or debenture stock (see section 4.7 below), the profit and loss account will be charged with interest. Company profits are assessable to corporation tax and the profit and loss account thus includes a charge for tax on profits. Finally, the profit and loss account will show appropriations of profit, for example, dividends paid and proposed.

(b) Balance sheet

The balance sheet will include liabilities for tax and proposed dividends. It may also include long-term liabilities in the form of loan or debenture stock (see section 4.8 below). Finally, the 'capital' section of the balance sheet will include share capital and reserves.

Company financial statements to be presented to shareholders are subject to detailed disclosure requirements. These are dealt with in detail in chapter 5. The illustration below shows the preparation of accounts in a form suitable for presentation internally (e g to the directors). It is intended as a gentle introduction to chapter 5!

Illustration 1

The following trial balance for Hughes Ltd relates to the year ended 31 December 19X9:

	£'000	£'000
Sales		1,850
Purchases	940	
Wages and salaries	196	
Directors' remuneration	84	
Rent, rates and insurance	35	
Heat, light and water	42	
Auditors' remuneration	9	
Telephone, stationery and advertising	31	
Debenture interest	16	
Interest on bank overdraft	7	
Sundry expenses	24	
Dividend paid	30	
Freehold land and buildings		
—cost	1,094	
—accumulated depreciation		41
Plant and machinery		
—cost	193	
—accumulated depreciation		23
Stock at 1.1.X9	175	
Debtors and prepayments	273	
Cash in hand	18	
Creditors and accrued expenses		137
Bank overdraft		86
8% debenture stock 19X36		200
Called up share capital		
(50p ordinary shares)		100
Profit and loss account at 1.1.X9		730
	3,167	3,167

Additional information

(1) Depreciation for the year is to be provided as follows:

Plant and machinery	£16
Buildings	£11

(2) £123,000 is to be provided for the year in respect of corporation tax.
(3) Closing stock has been valued at £154,000 for accounts purposes.
(4) The directors propose a dividend of 25 pence per share.

Required
A profit and loss account for the year ended 31 December 19X9 and a balance sheet as at that date. Ignore the specific disclosure requirements of the Companies Act 1985.

Solution

PROFIT AND LOSS ACCOUNTS OF HUGHES LTD

for the year ended 31 December 19X9

	£'000	£'000
Sales		1,850
Opening stock	175	
Purchases	940	
	1,115	
Less closing stock	154	
Cost of sales		961
Gross profit		889
Depreciation (16 + 11)	27	
Wages and salaries	196	
Directors' remuneration	84	
Rent, rates and insurance	35	
Heat, light and water	42	
Telephone, stationery and advertising	31	
Auditors' remuneration	9	
Debenture interest	16	
Interest on bank overdraft	7	
Sundry expenses	24	
		471
Profit before tax		418
Taxation—corporation tax		123
Profit after tax		295
Dividends on ordinary shares		
Paid	30	
Proposed (25p × 200,000)	50	
		80
Retained profit		215
Balance brought forward		730
Balance carried forward		945

Balance sheet of Hughes Ltd as at 31 December 19X9

	£'000 Cost	£'000 Accumulated depreciation	£'000 Net book value
Tangible fixed assets			
Freehold land and buildings	1,094	52	1,042
Plant and machinery	193	39	154
	1,287	91	1,196
Current assets			
Stock		154	
Debtors and prepayments		273	
Cash in hand		18	
		445	
Current liabilities			
Creditors and accrued expenses		137	
Taxation		123	
Dividend		50	
Overdraft		86	
		396	
Net current assets			49
			1,245
Creditors due in more than one year			
—8% debenture stock 19X36			(200)
			1,045
Capital and reserves			
Ordinary share capital			100
Profit and loss account			945
			1,045

Workings

Accumulated depreciation:

Buildings	$41 + 11 = 52$
Plant and machinery	$23 + 16 = 39$

4.4   SHARE CAPITAL OF A COMPANY

The most common class of share capital is ordinary shares which carry votes. In principle a company may have more than one class of shares, including:

(a) Voting ordinary shares which carry the right to vote on all matters and to participate in surplus profits (on a distribution) or surplus assets (on a liquidation).

(b) Non-voting ordinary shares (occasionally referred to as 'A' ordinary shares) which have similar rights as for (a) above except that the ability to vote is restricted.

(c) Preference shares, which are entitled to a fixed amount of dividend in priority over ordinary shares, provided that there are profits available for distribution. Two further points are relevant:

   (1) preference shares are deemed to be cumulative unless they are designated as non-cumulative. Cumulative means that should a company be unable to pay a preference dividend in a particular year (because of lack of available profits), the entitlement is carried forward as a memorandum note outside the double entry system. Should available profits arise in a subsequent year, such arrears of preference dividends must be paid in priority to ordinary dividends; and

   (2) participating preference shares are a special type of share. They may have a prior entitlement to a fixed amount of dividend, and then a further entitlement, once ordinary shareholders have received a particular amount.

(d) Deferred or founders' shares—such shares carry votes but shareholders are not entitled to dividends until holders of ordinary shares have received a specified dividend. Such shares are fairly rare.

4.5   ISSUE OF SHARES

(a) Journal entries relating to the issue of shares

Upon each occasion on which an allotment of shares is made, an entry should be made in the journal, debiting an application and allotment account with the amount payable on application and allotment in respect of the shares so allotted, and (assuming the shares are issued at par) crediting share capital account, reference being made to the minutes of allotment and to the pages in the application and allotment book, where the details are shown. If more than one class of capital is being issued, separate accounts must be opened in the ledger for each class.

Similar entries must be made debiting the vendor or other persons, and crediting share capital account, in respect of all shares issued for a consideration other than cash, reference being made to the minutes of allotment and to the contract under which the shares are issued.

When calls are made, an entry must be made debiting call account and crediting share capital account with the total amount due in respect of the call.

(b) Shares issued at a premium

A company may issue shares at a premium i e for an amount in excess of their nominal value. Such an issue might be made by a successful company which has paid high dividends on its existing capital and where shares, as a result, already stand at a premium on the market. When shares are issued at a premium, whether for cash or otherwise, the premium must be credited to an account called 'the share premium account'. The amount credited to share premium account can only be applied as follows:

(1) subject to the confirmation of the court, in a scheme for reduction of capital, as if it were paid-up share capital of the company;

(2) in paying up unissued shares of the company to be issued to the members as fully paid bonus shares;

(3) in writing off:

   (a) preliminary expenses; or

   (b) the expenses of, or commission paid or discount allowed on, any issue of shares or debentures of the company; and

(4) in providing for the premium payable on the redemption of debentures of the company. (The special application of the share premium account for the purchase or redemption of shares is dealt with in chapter 25.)

The premium is usually payable with the instalment due on allotment, and where this is so, the journal entry for allotment must show the amount payable for the premium, which must be credited direct to the share premium account, only the proportion of the amount due representing a payment on account of the nominal value of the shares being credited to share capital account.

Illustration 2

On April 30, a company goes to allotment, and the following shares are allotted:

(a) 80,000 ordinary shares of £1 each issued at 113p per share;
(b) 50,000 7% preference shares of £1 each, issued at par.

The ordinary shares are payable 13p on application, 25p (including the premium) on allotment; 25p one month after allotment and 50p three months after allotment. The preference shares are payable 13p on application, 12p on allotment, 25p one month after allotment, and 50p three months after allotment. Make the journal entries to record these transactions, and show the cash book and ledger accounts.

JOURNAL

		£	£
April 30			
Application and allotment account (ordinary shares)	Dr	30,400	
Ordinary share capital account			20,000
Share premium account			10,400
13p on application and 25p on allotment (13p thereof being premium) on 80,000 ordinary shares of £1 each, each, allotted as per minute of this date.		£30,400	£30,400
April 30 Application and allotment account (preference shares)	Dr	12,500	
Preference share capital account			12,500
13p on application and 12p on allotment of 50,000 preference shares of £1 each allotment as per minute of this date			
May 31 First call account (ordinary shares)	Dr	20,000	
Ordinary share capital account			20,000
First call of 25p on 80,000 ordinary shares of £1 each			
May 31 First call account (preference shares)	Dr	12,500	
Preference share capital account			12,500
First call of 25p on 50,000 preference shares of £1 each			
July 31 Final call account (ordinary shares)	Dr	40,000	
Ordinary share capital account			40,000
Final call of 50p on 80,000 ordinary shares			
July 31 Final call account (preference shares)	Dr	25,000	
Preference share capital account			25,000
Final call of 50p on 50,000 preference shares			

It will be noted that a single journal entry is made combining the amounts payable on application and allotment. Some accountants prefer to make these entries separately, but the above course is advocated on two grounds, viz (1) the contract to take shares is not complete until allotment, and the offer may be withdrawn at any time prior to that date, and (2) applications may not be accepted, or accepted only for a portion of the shares applied for.

APPLICATION AND ALLOTMENT ACCOUNT ORDINARY SHARES

		£				£
April 30	Ordinary share capital account	20,000	April 30	Cash		10,400
	Share premium account	10,400	May 2	Cash		20,000
		£30,400				£30,400

FIRST CALL ACCOUNT: ORDINARY SHARES

		£			£
May 31	Ordinary share capital account	20,000	June 2	Cash	20,000

FINAL CALL ACCOUNT: ORDINARY SHARES

		£			£
July 31	Ordinary share capital account	40,000	Aug 1	Cash	40,000

ORDINARY SHARE CAPITAL ACCOUNT

		£
April 30	Application and allotment account	20,000
May 31	First call account	20,000
July 31	Final call account	40,000
		£80,000

SHARE PREMIUM ACCOUNT

		£
April 30	Application and allotment account (ordinary shares)	10,400

APPLICATION AND ALLOTMENT ACCOUNT PREFERENCE SHARES

		£			£
April 30	Preference share capital account	12,500	April 30	Cash	6,500
			May 2	Cash	6,000
		£12,500			£12,500

FIRST CALL ACCOUNT: PREFERENCE SHARES

		£			£
May 31	Preference share capital account	12,500	June 2	Cash	12,500

FINAL CALL ACCOUNT: PREFERENCE SHARES

		£			£
July 31	Preference share capital account	25,000	Aug 1	Cash	25,000

PREFERENCE SHARE CAPITAL ACCOUNT

			£
April 30	Application and allot-ment account		12,500
May 31	First call account		12,500
July 31	Final call account		25,000
			£50,000

CASH BOOK

			£
April 30	Application and allot-ment accounts: 13p per share on application for		
		80,000 ordinary shares	10,400
		50,000 preference shares	6,500
May 2	Application and allot-ment accounts: Ordinary shares— 25p per share due on allotment on 80,000 shares		20,000
	Preference shares— 12p per share due on allotment on 50,000 shares		6,000
June 2	First call accounts: Ordinary shares— 25p per share on 80,000 shares		20,000
	Preference shares— 25p per share on 50,000 shares		12,500
Aug 1	Final call accounts: Ordinary shares— 50p per share on 80,000 shares		40,000
	Preference shares— 50p per share on 50,000 shares		25,000

(c) Redeemable preference shares

The subject of redeemable preference shares in particular, and purchase and redemption of shares in general is dealt with in chapter 25.

4.6   FORFEITURE OF SHARES

The articles of a company usually give power to the directors to forfeit shares on which calls are unpaid and overdue, proper notice having been given to the defaulting shareholder that, unless the calls are paid, his shares will be forfeited.

Until the shares are reissued, the balance on forfeited shares account should appear in the balance sheet as a separate item under the heading, 'Reserves'.

Forfeited shares can be reissued as fully paid at any price, so long as the sum received on reissue, plus the amount received from the original allottee before forfeiture, make up together at least the nominal value of the shares forfeited. If, after the reissue of the shares, there still remains a credit balance on the forfeited shares account, this would represent an amount received by the company on those shares in excess of their nominal value which, it is submitted, should be regarded as a premium on the issue of such shares and transferred to share premium account.

If the forfeited shares were originally issued at a premium which had been paid before forfeiture, the share premium account need not be disturbed as the premium is not a payment for the shares themselves, but is a payment for the right to acquire the shares. Where, however, shares are forfeited for non-payment of instalments which include the premium, so that the premium has not been received by the company, share premium account should be debited and forfeited shares account credited.

The book-keeping entries can be summarised as follows:

Debit	Credit	Remarks
On forfeiture		
Share capital	Forfeited shares	Total *nominal* amount payable to date of forfeiture
	Calls	
Forfeited shares	Application and allotment	Amounts unpaid on shares
Share premium	Forfeited shares	Any unpaid premium
On reissue		
Forfeited shares	Share capital	Nominal amount called up to date of reissue
Cash	Forfeited shares	Cash received on reissue
Forfeited shares	Share premium	Any balance on forfeited shares account must be transferred to share premium account

Illustration 3

A company has an issued capital of £20,000 in shares of £1 each, fully paid with the exception of 200 shares on which only 50p has been paid, forfeited for non-payment of calls, and subsequently reissued as fully paid at the price of 75p per share. Show the entries in the company's journal including cash and ledger recording these transactions.

JOURNAL

	£	£
Share capital account	Dr 200	
Forfeited shares account		200
200 shares of £1 each forfeited for non-payment of calls as per minute dated		
Forfeited shares account	Dr 100	
Call account		100
Calls in arrear, 50p per share on 200 shares forfeited, now transferred		
Forfeited shares account .	Dr 200	
Share capital account		200
Reissue of 200 forfeited shares of £1 each		
Cash	Dr 150	
Forfeited shares account		150
Cash received: 75p per share on 200 shares reissued		
Forfeited shares account	Dr 50	
Share premium account		50
Transfer of balance		

LEDGER SHARE CAPITAL ACCOUNT

	£		£
Forfeited shares account	200	Balance b/f	20,000
Balance c/d	20,000	Forfeited shares account	200
	20,200		20,200

CALL ACCOUNT

	£		£
Balance b/f	100	Forfeited shares account	100

FORFEITED SHARES ACCOUNT

	£		£
Call account	100	Share capital account	200
Share capital account	200	Cash	150
Share premium account	50		
	£350		£350

SHARE PREMIUM ACCOUNT

		£
	Forfeited shares account	50

NOTE

As all the shares have been reissued, the balance of the forfeited shares account, after transferring 25p per share (the amount necessary to make the price of reissue up to par), is a premium on the issue of the shares and should be transferred to the share premium account.

It may happen that forfeiture takes place upon failure of the allottee to pay the amount due upon allotment, subsequent calls being due prior to the reissue of the shares.

4.7   RESERVES AND PROVISIONS

(a) Reserves

The term reserves may include the following:

(1) Reserves created by means of appropriation from profit and loss account. The reserves referred to below are voluntary reserves, i e the amounts transferred

are at the discretion of the directors. These reserves may include the following:

(i)   general reserve;
(ii) fixed asset replacement reserve;
(iii) stock replacement reserve;
(iv) debenture reserve.

There is no legal restriction on the use of any of these reserves to pay a dividend to the shareholders. However, the fact that a particular company has any of these reserves implies that the directors wish funds to be kept within the business for a future purpose (e g redemption of debentures) rather than be distributed as dividends.

(2) Share premium account (see section 4.5(b)).
(3) Revaluation reserve (see chapter 7).
(4) Capital redemption reserve (see chapter 25).
(5) Merger reserve (see chapter 16).
(6) Reserves provided for by the articles of association.

(b) Provisions

This term is defined by the Companies Act 1985 and includes:

(1) Provision for depreciation or diminution in value of assets—this includes provision for depreciation, stock and doubtful debts. Such provisions are deducted from the asset heading to which they relate. Whether separate disclosure is required is dealt with in chapter 5.
(2) Provisions for liabilities or charges—amounts retained as reasonably neces-sary for the purpose of providing for any liability or loss which is either:

(i) likely to be incurred, or
(ii) certain to be incurred but uncertain as to amount or date on which it will arise.

This includes provisions for redundancy and reorganisation, repairs and mainten-ance, warranty expenditure and deferred taxation.

4.8   ISSUE OF DEBENTURES

(a) Definition of a debenture

A debenture is a written acknowledgment of a debt by a company, usually under seal and generally containing provision for payment of interest and repayment of capital; a simple or naked debenture carries no charge on assets; a secured debenture carries either a fixed charge on a specific asset or a floating charge on all or some of the assets. All forms of loan stock are debentures.

A fixed charge is a mortgage on specific assets, under which the company loses the right to deal with the assets charged, except with the consent of the mortgagee. A floating charge is not a mortgage at all, since the charge is such that so long as the company continues to carry on its business and observe the terms of the charge, the directors are entitled to deal in any way they please in the ordinary course of business with the assets of the company, and may even make specific charges on property which, subject to the terms of the floating charge given, will have priority to the floating charge. The floating charge is a charge on a class of assets, present and future, which in the ordinary course of business is changing from time to time, and attaches to the property included therein in priority to the general liabilities of the company. The floating charge hovers overs or 'floats' with the assets, until some event happens (e g default in repaying principal or interest) which crystallises or fixes the charge.

A company may make more than one issue of debentures; issues subsequent to the first may rank pari passu (i e on an equal footing) with the original issue, or may confer a charge, subject to and following the first, according to whether the original debentures contained clauses allowing or forbidding subsequent pari passu issues. Where the debentures carry different priorities, they are usually designated first debentures, second debentures etc—a higher rate of interest usually being payable on those of lower rank to compensate for the lower degree of security.

A company can issue debentures within the limits of its borrowing powers, as set out in its memorandum and/or articles of association. A trading company's borrowing powers are implied unless there are provisions to the contrary in the memorandum or articles.

Interest at the agreed rate is payable on the debentures whether the company makes profits or not, since the charge given covers both principal and interest. Income tax is deductible from the interest payable.

In a liquidation, the debenture holders are entitled to the proceeds of their securities, if any, otherwise they rank equally with the unsecured creditors; if the proceeds of a security are insufficient to repay the debentures, the debenture holders rank as unsecured creditors for the balance still due to them.

The entries in the books of a company for an issue of debentures are similar to those on an issue of shares, instalment accounts being debited with the various instalments as they become due, and debentures account credited. If debentures are issued to the vendor as part of the consideration for a business acquired by the company, the vendor's account is debited and the debentures account credited. The appropriate entry must also be made in the register of charges kept by the company.

(b) Debentures issued at a premium

When debentures are issued at a premium, debenture account is credited with the nominal amount and debenture premium account with the premium. Debenture premium account can be shown in the balance sheet as a (revenue) reserve. The Companies Act does not specify the uses of the debenture premium account.

(c) Debentures issued at a discount

Debentures can be issued at a discount, but must be redeemed at par or a premium; since a capital profit (which is subject to tax) is made on redemption, a lower rate of interest can be paid than if the debentures were issued at their redeemable price.

The effect of issuing debentures at a discount can be seen from the following example.

Illustration 4

A company issued debentures of £100 at 95, interest at 5% repayable at the end of 20 years at par.

Over the 20 years, ignoring tax, the holder receives £100 as interest, and at the end of that period is repaid £100 for £95 advanced. The average return is therefore £200 − 95/20 = £5·25 on his investment of £95, or 5·5%. (This rate is not accurate, as it ignores compound interest, but it is sufficiently accurate to show the effect.)

Where debentures are issued at a discount, cash is debited with the net sum received and discount on debentures account with the amount of the discount; debentures account being credited with the full nominal value of the debentures, at which value they must appear as a liability in the balance sheet. The discount on debentures, or so much as has not been written off, must be shown separately in the balance sheet.

The discount on the issue is, in effect, deferred interest, and should accordingly be written off over the period having the use of the money raised by the debentures, unless a sinking fund is created to accumulate the full redemption price, including the discount. Where the debentures are redeemable at the end of a specified period, the discount should be written off by equal annual instalments over that period. If, however, the debentures are to be redeemed by annual drawings, the discount should be written off by proportionately reducing instalments, since each succeeding year has the use of a reducing amount of principal.

Illustration 5

A company issued on January 1 19XX £3,000 debentures at 90% repayable by instalments of £1,000 at the end of the first, second, and third years respectively. Show the discount account, assuming the discount to be written off over the period proportionately.

DISCOUNT ON ISSUE OF DEBENTURES ACCOUNT

1st year		£	1st year		£
Jan 1	Debenture account	300	Dec 31	Profit and loss account:	
				$\frac{3}{6}$ of £300	150
				Balance c/d	150
		£300			£300
2nd year			2nd year		
Jan 1	Balance b/d	150	Dec 31	Profit and loss account:	
				$\frac{2}{6}$ of £300	100
				Balance c/d	50
		£150			£150
3rd year			3rd year		
Jan 1	Balance b/d	50	Dec 31	Profit and loss account:	
				$\frac{1}{6}$ of £300	50
		£50			£50

NOTE
The discount has been written off against the profits of the respective years in the proportions of 3:2:1, since the first year has the use of £3,000, the second year £2,000 and the third year £1,000 of the capital provided by the debentures.

Where the redemption of the nominal amount of the debentures repayable is provided for by charges against profit and loss account, the charges should include the provision for discount, so that the discount can be written off against the credit balance on the redemption account.

(d) Debentures repayable at a premium

These debentures will stand in the balance sheet as a liability at their nominal amount, with a note of the amount at which they are repayable, any discount or premium on issue being treated as described above.

If a sinking fund is raised to provide for repayment, it should include provision for the payment of the premium on redemption. If no sinking fund is created, the premium should be provided for out of profits over the period of the debentures.

Debentures may even be issued at a discount and repayable at a premium.

Illustration 6

A company issued £10,000 debentures, at a discount of 5%, repayable at 102% at the end of ten years.

Over the ten years, in addition to the interest payable, profit and loss account must be charged with £7 per £100 debenture i e £700 in all, by yearly amounts of £70. Of this £50 is credited to discount on debentures acount, and £20 to a provision for premium on the redemption of debentures account.

If the debentures were repayable by equal annual drawings, the £700 would be charged in the ratio of 10, 9, 8, 7, 6, 5, 4, 3, 2, 1 i e $\frac{10}{55}$ of £700 = £127·27 would be charged to profit and loss account in the first year, $\frac{9}{55}$ of £700 = £114·55 in the second year, and so on. The premium paid on redemption would be debited to the provision account, and the balance carried forward until the last year, when it would be closed by the last redemption.

4.9   REDEMPTION OF DEBENTURES

Debentures may be irredeemable (i e the company may be under no obligation to repay the debentures at any specified date); but this is unusual, except in companies formed under special Act of Parliament.

Debentures may either be redeemed at the end of a given period or by annual drawings. The trust deed, or if there is no trust deed, then the debentures themselves, will contain provision for redemption and will usually stipulate the establishment of a sinking fund for repayment out of profits—see illustration given below.

Alternatively a company may take out a sinking fund policy with an insurance company for the amount of the debentures.

Section 194 empowers a company which has redeemed debentures to reissue them, either by reissuing the same debentures, or by issuing other debentures in lieu; unless provision, express or implied, is contained in the articles or the conditions of issue, or unless the company has, by passing a resolution, or by some other act, shown its intention that the debentures shall be cancelled. Where a company has redeemed debentures, every balance sheet must show particulars of debentures that may be redeemed. On reissue the debentures must be stamped as an original issue; they retain, however, the same priorities as the original debentures.

The company can purchase its own debentures; when debentures are purchased at below the issued price a capital profit will result from the purchase. Strict accounting demands appropriate adjustments for accrued interest included in the purchase price. In practice this would frequently be ignored.

Illustration 7

A company issued £100,000 8% debenture stock at 98% on January 1, Year 1. The interest is payable half-yearly on June 30 and December 31. The stock is redeemable at the end of 20 years, at 102½, but the company has power to redeem at any time after the first year at 105, if it gives six months' written notice. Provision is made for the establishment of a sinking fund, and the annual contribution of £2,000, together with the interest received during the preceding year, is invested on January 1 in each year, the first investment being made at the beginning of the second year. The trustees are empowered to purchase debentures in the open market should they be below par with the proceeds of the sinking fund investments. Investments were realised as follows to purchase debenture stock:

	Original cost	Proceeds	Nominal value of debenture stock purchased
April 30, Year 2	£1,050	£1,060	£1,100
September 30, Year 3	2,000	2,100	2,150

Interest received on the sinking fund investments was, for Year 2, Year 3 and Year 4, £40, £80 and £120, respectively.

Prepare accounts showing the transactions up to December 31, Year 4. Ignore taxation and calculate to the nearest £.

DEBENTURE STOCK ACCOUNT

Year 2		£	*Year 1*		£
Dec 31	Debenture redemption account, cancellation of £1,100 debenture stock	1,100	Jan 1	Cash	98,000
				Debenture discount account	2,000
	Balance c/d	98,900			
		£100,000			£100,000
Year 3			*Year 3*		
Dec 31	Debenture redemption account, cancellation of £2,150 debenture stock	2,150	Jan 1	Balance b/d	98,900
	Balance c/d	96,750			
		£98,900			£98,900
			Year 4		
			Jan 1	Balance b/d	96,750

DISCOUNT ON DEBENTURES ACCOUNT

Year 1		£	*Year 2*		£
Jan 1	Debenture stock account	2,000	Dec 31	General reserve account (see note 4)	1,100
				Balance c/d	900
		£2,000			£2,000
Year 3			*Year 3*		
Jan 1	Balance b/d	900	Dec 31	General reserve account (see note 4)	900

SINKING FUND ACCOUNT

		£			£
Year 2			*Year 1*		
Dec 31	General reserve account	1,100	Dec 31	Profit and loss account	2,000
	Balance c/d	3,019			
			Year 2		
			Dec 31	Sinking fund investments account — profit on sale	10
				Debenture redemption account — profit on purchase	69
				Interest on investments	40
				Profit and loss account	2,000
		£4,119			£4,119
Year 3			*Year 3*		
Dec 31	General reserve account	2,150	Jan 1	Balance b/d	3,019
	Balance c/d	3,142	Dec 31	Sinking fund investments account — profit on sale	100
				Debenture redemption account — profit on purchase	93
				Interest on investments	80
				Profit and loss account	2,000
		£5,292			£5,292
Year 4			*Year 4*		
Dec 31	Balance c/d	5,262	Jan 1	Balance b/d	3,142
			Dec 31	Interest on investments	120
				Profit and loss account	2,000
		£5,262			£5,262
			Year 5		
			Jan 1	Balance b/d	5,262

SINKING FUND INVESTMENTS ACCOUNT

		£			£
Year 2			*Year 2*		
Jan 1	Cash	2,000	Apr 30	Cash	1,060
Dec 31	Sinking fund account — profit on sale of investments	10	Dec 31	Balance c/d	950
		£2,010			£2,010
Year 3			*Year 3*		
Jan 1	Balance b/d	950	Sept 30	Cash	2,100
	Cash	2,069	Dec 31	Balance c/d	1,019
Dec 31	Sinking fund account — profit on sale of investments	100			
		£3,119			£3,119
Year 4			*Year 4*		
Jan 1	Balance b/d	1,019	Dec 31	Balance c/d	3,142
	Cash	2,123			
		£3,142			£3,142
Year 5					
Jan 1	Balance b/d	3,142			

DEBENTURE REDEMPTION ACCOUNT

Year 2		£	Year 2		£
Apr 30	Cash, purchase of £1,100 debentures cum div	1,060	Apr 30	Debenture interest account, four months accrued interest on £1,100 debentures purchased cum div	29
Dec 31	Sinking fund account — profit on debentures purchased for cancellation	69	Dec 31	Debentures account, debentures cancelled	1,100
		£1,129			£1,129
Year 3			Year 3		
Sept 30	Cash, purchase of £2,150 debentures cum div	2,100	Sept 30	Debenture interest account, three months accrued interest on £2,150 debentures purchased cum div	43
Dec 31	Sinking fund account — profit on debentures purchased for cancellation	93	Dec 31	Debentures account, debentures cancelled	2,150
		£2,193			£2,193

DEBENTURE INTEREST ACCOUNT

Year 1		£	Year 1		£
June 30	Cash: $\frac{1}{2}$ year's interest on £100,000	4,000	Dec 31	Profit and loss account	8,000
Dec 31	Interest on £100,000	4,000			
		£8,000			£8,000
Year 2			Year 2		
Apr 30	Debenture redemption account— four months' interest on £1,100 debentures purchased cum div	29	Dec 31	Profit and loss account	7,941
June 30	Cash: $\frac{1}{2}$ year's interest on £98,900	3,956			
	interest on £98,900	3,956			
		£7,941			£7,941
Year 3			Year 3		
June 30	Cash: $\frac{1}{2}$ year's interest on £98,900	3,956	Dec 31	Profit and loss account	7,869
Sept 30	Debenture redemption account— 3 months' interest on £2,150 debentures purchased cum div	43			
Dec 31	Cash: $\frac{1}{2}$ year's interest on £96,750	3,870			
		£7,869			£7,869

Year 4			Year 4		
June 30	Cash: ½ year's interest on £96,750	3,870	Dec 31	Profit and loss account	7,740
Dec 31	½ year's interest on £96,750	3,870			
		£7,740			£7,740

SINKING FUND CASH ACCOUNT

Year 1		£	Year 2		£
Dec 31	General cash — annual instalment	2,000	Jan 1	Sinking fund invest- ment account	2,000
Year 2			Apr 30	Debenture redemption account debentures	
Apr 30	Sinking fund invest- ments account, proceeds of sale	1,060	Dec 31	purchased Balance c/d	1,060 2,069
Dec 31	Interest on investments	40			
	General cash — annual instalment	2,000			
	General cash refund of interest on deben- tures cancelled	29			
		£5,129			£5,129
Year 3			Year 3		
Jan 1	Balance b/d	2,069	Jan 1	Sinking fund invest- ments account	2,069
Sept 30	Sinking fund invest- ments account, proceeds of sale	2,100	Sept 30	Debenture redemption account, debentures purchased	2,100
Dec 31	Interest on investments	80	Dec 31	Balance c/d	2,123
	General cash — annual instalment	2,000			
	General cash — refund of interest on deben- tures cancelled	43			
		£6,292			£6,292
Year 4			Year 4		
Jan 1	Balance b/d	2,123	Jan 1	Sinking fund invest- ments account	2,123
Dec 31	Interest on investments	120	Dec 31	Balance c/d	2,120
	General cash — annual instalment	2,000			
		£4,243			£4,243
Year 5					
Jan 1	Balance b/d	2,120			

GENERAL RESERVE ACCOUNT

Year 2		£	Year 2		£
Dec 31	Discount on deben- tures account	1,100	Dec 31	Sinking fund account	1,100
Year 3			Year 3		
Dec 31	Discount on deben- tures account	900	Dec 31	Sinking fund account	2,150
	Balance c/d	1,250			
		£2,150			£2,150
			Year 4		
			Jan 1	Balance b/d	1,250

NOTES

(1) The profit or loss on redemption of debentures, disclosed in the debenture redemption account, is the difference between the price paid on redemption and the nominal value. As the price paid on redemption includes accrued debenture interest, an adjustment has been made debiting debenture interest account and crediting debenture redemption account with the accrued interest. The amount of such interest, having been paid out of sinking fund cash, must be reimbursed thereto out of general cash, and reinvested.

If debentures are purchased or redeemed when they are *ex*-interest, the price paid will exclude interest from the date of purchase to the interest payment date; an adjustment can be made debiting debenture redemption account and crediting debenture interest account with interest on the debentures purchased or redeemed from the date of purchase to the interest payment date; general cash will be debited and sinking fund cash credited.

(2) No purpose is served by apportioning the proceeds of sale of the investments between capital and income, as both the interest earned and any profit or loss on realisation of the investments must be transferred to the sinking fund account.

(3) An amount equal to the nominal amount of the debenture stock cancelled has been transferred from the sinking fund account to general reserve, as the assets representing it are now part of the general assets and are not included in the sinking fund investment account.

(4) The discount allowed on the issue should be written off as soon as possible. The discount allowed on the issue of cancelled stock *must* be written off, as the debentures are no longer outstanding. As, however, the general reserve is available, it has been thought advisable to write off the whole discount against it immediately.

4.10 PURCHASE OF A BUSINESS BY A LIMITED COMPANY

(a) Introduction

Several advantages may stem from the 'conversion' of a private business into a limited company e g perpetual succession, whereby a member of a company can transfer his shares, or bequeath them by will at death, without disturbing the constitution of the company or its financial resources.

The 'conversion' may take the form of the transfer to a private company of the assets and goodwill of the business in consideration of the allotment of shares in the company, which the sellers of the business will continue to hold, and through which they will retain the control of the business. Alternatively, a public company may be formed to acquire the business; a promoter or syndicate purchases the business from the original owners, and resells it to the company at a profit, the capital of the company being raised by public subscriptions. Or a public company may be formed to take over the business of a private company, the shareholders of the private company receiving shares or other interests in the public company in exchange for their existing holdings.

(b) Accounting entries in the purchasing company's books

In the purchasing company's books, the assets acquired must be debited at acquisition values, which are often different from the book values shown in the vendor business's books; when a business is sold, assets are frequently revalued. Sometimes the purchasing company assumes trade liabilities as part of the purchase consideration; sometimes the company discharges the trade liabilities and collects the book debts as agent for the sellers; interest may be allowed or charged until final settlement between the purchasing company and the sellers is effected. Book debts are usually acquired at book values less an agreed provision for bad or doubtful debts; any excess received over the book values less the provision for doubtful debts is a capital profit in the purchasing company's books.

In addition to the purchase price of the tangible assets, a further sum is usually payable for goodwill. A company making a public issue for the purpose of acquiring a business must state in the prospectus the amount of the purchase consideration attributable to goodwill.

Goodwill is the excess of the total purchase consideration over the value of the other assets acquired, less the amount of any liabilities assumed by the company.

Summary of entries

The entries in the company's books necessary to record the purchase of the business are as follows:

Debit	Credit	Notes
Assets	Vendor's account	Assets acquired at acquisition values
Vendor's account	Liabilities	Liabilities acquired at acquisition values
Vendor's account	Share capital Share premium Debentures Cash	Purchase consideration
Goodwill	Vendor's account	Excess of purchase consideration over net assets required
Vendor's account	Capital reserve	Excess of net assets acquired over purchase consideration.

Note Any debtors taken over should be debited at book values and any provision for doubtful or bad debts should be credited to a provision for bad debts account.

Some accountants prefer to pass the purchase of a business through a purchase of business account, which replaces the vendor's account, being credited with the assets acquired and debited with the liabilities taken over and with the purchase consideration.

Illustration 8

A company takes over the following assets and liabilities of a private business:

	£
Leasehold property	7,000
Plant and machinery	3,000
Stock-in-trade	4,600
Sundry debtors	3,000
Cash	1,500
	19,100
Less trade creditors	2,100
	£17,000

The purchase consideration is £20,000 payable to the vendor as follows: £10,000 in ordinary shares of £1 each fully paid, £5,000 in 5% preference shares of £1 each fully paid, all issued at par, and the balance in cash. Show the opening journal entries in the books of the company.

JOURNAL

		£	£
Leasehold property	Dr	7,000	
Plant and machinery		3,000	
Stock-in-trade		4,600	
Sundry debtors		3,000	
Cash		1,500	
Goodwill		3,000	
Sundry creditors			2,100
Vendor (or purchase of business account)			20,000
Sundry assets and liabilities taken over as per contract dated		£22,100	£22,100

		£	£
Vendor (or purchase of business account)	Dr	20,000	
Ordinary share capital—10,000 shares of £1 each fully paid			10,000
Preference share capital—5,000 shares of £1 each fully paid			5,000
Cash			5,000
Discharge of purchase consideration as per contract dated		£20,000	£20,000

NOTE

The amount debited to goodwill acount is the excess of the amount of the purchase consideration, £20,000, over the total amount of the assets acquired, less the amount of the liabilities assumed, £17,000.

Where the purchase consideration is less than the value at which the net assets stood in the books of the vendor, but the values of the assets taken over are correctly stated (as ascertained by revaluation), the surplus, instead of being treated in the company's books as a capital reserve, may be applied in writing down fixed assets to the level of the consideration. The surplus is not available for distribution to shareholders and cannot be credited to a revenue reserve account.

The absence of a goodwill account indicates that no payment has been made for goodwill; it does not indicate that it is nonexistent.

Where a partnership business is transferred to a limited company some difficulty may be experienced in capitalising the company so as to ensure that the rights of the partners are preserved. If the capitals of the partners are in the same ratio as that in which profits are shared, the problem is simplified, as the allotment to the partners of ordinary shares in that ratio will preserve the relationship as nearly as possible. Often, where the capitals are not held in profit-sharing ratio, the problem is complicated, particularly when taxation is considered.

The following illustration shows the effect on the books of a firm of the conversion of a private firm into a limited company, and also the entries in the books of the company:

Illustration 9

The X Company Ltd, was formed to purchase the business of A and B, who share profits, two-thirds and one-third respectively, and whose balance sheet was as follows:

BALANCE SHEET A and B

	£			£
Creditors	2,700	Goodwill		1,000
Bills payable	900	Freehold property		5,000
Loan account	400	Plant and machinery		2,500
Capitals—		Stock		3,000
A	£8,000	Debtors	£3,100	
B	5,000	*Less* provision for bad		
		debts	200	
	13,000			2,900
		Bills receivable		800
		Investments		600
		Cash		1,200
	£17,000			£17,000

The company takes over the assets at book value, with the exception of the freehold property, which is taken over at £6,000. The investments are retained by the firm, and sold by them for £450. They also discharge the loan of £400, but the company takes over the remaining liabilities.

The purchase consideration for the net assets taken over is fixed at £18,950, payable as follows: £9,500 5% debentures 7,600 fully paid ordinary shares of £1 each, both at par, and the balance in cash. A and B agree to divide the assets forming the purchase consideration in proportion to the balances standing to the credit of their respective capital accounts, after the adjustments caused by the sale of the business and investments have been completed.

Show the ledger accounts closing the firm's books, and the journal entries opening the company's books.

FIRM'S BOOKS REALISATION ACCOUNT

	£		£
Freehold property	5,000	Creditors	2,700
Plant and machinery	2,500	Bills payable	900
Goodwill	1,000		
		Provision for bad debts	200
Stock	3,000	X Co Ltd	18,950
Debtors	3,100		
Bills receivable	800		
Cash	1,200		
Loss on investments	150		
Balance, being profit on			
realisation c/d	6,000		
	£22,750		£22,750

	£		£
Capital accounts:		Balance b/d	6,000
A ($\frac{2}{3}$)	4,000		
B ($\frac{1}{3}$)	2,000		
	£6,000		£6,000

X COMPANY LTD

	£		£
Realisation account	18,950	Debentures	9,500
		Ordinary shares	7,600
		Cash	1,850
	18,950		18,950

DEBENTURES IN X CO LTD

	£		£
X Co Ltd	9,500	A capital account $\frac{12}{19} \times$ £9,500	6,000
		B capital account $\frac{7}{19} \times$ £9,500	3,500
	£9,500		£9,500

ORDINARY SHARES IN X CO LTD

	£		£
X Co Ltd	7,600	A capital account $\frac{12}{19} \times$ £7,600	4,800
		B capital accounts $\frac{7}{19} \times$ £7,600	2,800
	£7,600		£7,600

CAPITAL ACCOUNTS

	A	B		A	B
	£	£		£	£
Balances c/d	12,000	7,000	Balances b/f	8,000	5,000
			Profit on realisation	4,000	2,000
	£12,000	£7,000		£12,000	£7,000
Debentures in X Co Ltd	6,000	3,500	Balances b/d	12,000	7,000
Shares in X Co Ltd	4,800	2,800			
Cash	1,200	700			
	£12,000	£7,000		£12,000	£7,000

CASH BOOK

	£		£
X Co Ltd	1,850	Loan account	400
Investments	450	Balance c/d	1,900
	£2,300		£2,300
	£		£
Balance b/d	1,900	A capital account $\frac{12}{19} \times$ £1,900	1,200
		B capital account $\frac{7}{19} \times$ £1,900	700
	£1,900		£1,900

INVESTMENTS

	£		£
Balance b/f	600	Cash	450
		Realisation account — loss	150
	£600		£600

LOAN

	£		£
Cash	400	Balance b/f	400

X COMPANY LTD'S BOOKS: JOURNAL

		£	£
Freehold property	Dr	6,000	
Plant and machinery		2,500	
Stock		3,000	
Debtors		3,100	
Bills receivable		800	
Cash		1,200	
Goodwill		6,150	
Creditors			2,700
Bills payable			900
Provision for bad debts			200
Vendors (or purchase of business account)			18,950
Assets and liabilities taken over as per contract dated		£22,750	£22,750

NOTE

The amount debited to goodwill account is the difference between the total of the assets, less the liabilities taken over, and the purchase consideration payable to the vendors.

		£	£
Vendors (or purchase of business account)	Dr	18,950	
Ordinary share capital			7,600
Debentures			9,500
Cash			1,850
		£18,950	£18,950

7,600 ordinary shares of £1 each, and £9,500 5% debentures issued fully paid, and cash paid in settlement of purchase consideration as per contract dated

Sometimes a company on acquiring a business does not take over the book debts and liabilities of the vendor, but collects as agent the book debts and pays the liabilities out of the proceeds, accounting to the vendor for the balance; the company should provide special columns in its cash book, into which receipts from debtors and payments to creditors made on behalf of the vendor are entered, and from which they are posted to the personal accounts of the vendor's debtors and creditors. These postings, however, form no part of the double entry from the point of view of the company, since the accounts to which the amounts are posted are not in the company's ledgers. The double entry in the company's books for these transactions is completed by posting periodically the *totals* of the receipts and payments made on behalf of the vendor to the credit and debit respectively of the vendor's account. If the company wishes to continue to use the old debtors and creditors accounts, a line should be ruled across each account some distance below the last entry prior to the transfer, and the company's own transactions should be entered below this line, in order that the debts owing to and by the company may not be confused with those owing to and by the vendor.

If the company carries on the old debtors and old creditors accounts without a break, it has acquired debtors which it has debited to total debtors account. These must be credited to debtors suspense account since from the company's standpoint they are valueless. Similarly creditors are credited to total creditors account and debited to creditors suspense account. In the illustration below, by continuing to operate upon the vendor's debtors and creditors accounts, the ledger contains assets, £5,400, and liabilities, £3,700, which do not belong to the company, debtors suspense account is credited with £5,400, and creditors suspense account debited with £3,700. At the end of the accounting period, all transactions relating to these debtors and creditors are transferred in total from the sales ledger to the debtors suspense account and from the bought ledger to the creditors suspense account. Payments made to the vendor for debts collected or receipts from the vendor for liabilities met are passed through the current account with the vendor in the normal way.

Any balances remaining on the suspense accounts when the company prepares its balance sheet represent the amounts of the debtors and creditors of the vendor still appearing in the company's books, and must be deducted from the totals of the debtors and creditors respectively to arrive at the figures to be shown in the company's balance sheet.

Illustration 10

On January 1 YZ Ltd acquired the business of X, taking over all the assets with the exception of the book debts, which it undertook to collect on behalf of X, and out of the proceeds pay the liabilities owing at the date of the transfer. At that date the book debts amounted to £5,400 and the liabilities to £3,700.

The company continued to operate on the old debtors and creditors accounts without a break, and at the following December 31 the total of the book debts amounted to £6,200, of which £400 represented debts owing to X, whilst the total creditors were £5,300, the whole of X's liabilities having been discharged. During the year, the company had written off £700 debts as bad, of which £300 was for X's debtors. Discounts allowed by the company during the year amounted to £680, of which £185 was allowed to X's debtors. Discounts allowed to the company amounted to £1,400 of which £104 was for pre-transfer liabilities.

Show the relevant ledger accounts in the company's books.

TOTAL DEBTORS ACCOUNT

		£
Dec 31	Balance	6,200

TOTAL CREDITORS ACCOUNT

		£
Dec 31	Balance	5,300

X's DEBTORS SUSPENSE ACCOUNT

		£				£
Dec 31	Bad debts account	300	Jan 1	Total debtors account—		
	Discounts allowed			—debts not taken over		
	account	185		from X		5,400
	X's account—cash					
	collected	4,515				
	Balance c/d	400				
		———				———
		£5,400				£5,400
			Jan 1	Balance b/d		400

X's CREDITORS SUSPENSE ACCOUNT

		£				£
Jan 1	Total creditors account—		Dec 31	Discounts received		
	liabilities not taken over			account		104
	from X	3,700		X's account—cash paid		3,596
		———				———
		£3,700				£3,700

X's ACCOUNT

		£				£
Dec 31	X's creditors suspense account — cash paid to creditors	3,596	Dec 31	X's debtors suspense account — cash received from debtors		4,515
	Balance c/d	919				
		£4,515				£4,515
			Jan 1	Balance b/d		919

BAD DEBTS ACCOUNT

		£			£
Dec 31 Sundry debtors — debts written off		700	Dec 31	X's debtors suspense account — amounts applicable to X's debtors	300
				Profit and loss account	400
		£700			£700

DISCOUNTS ALLOWED ACCOUNT

		£			£
Dec 31 Sundry debtors — discounts allowed		680	Dec 31	X's debtors suspense account — discounts allowed to X's debtors	185
				Profit and loss account	495
		£680			£680

DISCOUNTS RECEIVED ACCOUNT

		£			£
Dec 31	X's creditors suspense account — discounts received in respect of X's liabilities	104	Dec 31	Sundry creditors account — discounts received	1,400
	Profit and loss account	1,296			
		£1,400			£1,400

NOTE

As a result of the above entries, there will appear in the company's balance sheet a liability to X of £919, whilst the sundry debtors will be £5,800, viz £6,200, less the credit balance of £400 carried down in the debtors suspense account. The bad debts and discounts transferred to the company's profit and loss account are reduced by the amounts transferred to the suspense accounts, and thus borne by the vendor.

5 COMPANY ACCOUNTS—THE REGULATORY FRAMEWORK

5.1 INTRODUCTION

The previous chapter dealt with the preparation of financial statements for internal use. We must now consider the preparation of financial statements for presentation to the shareholders in accordance with the requirements of the Companies Act 1985.

This chapter refers also to Statements of Standard Accounting Practice (SSAPs) and Stock Exchange disclosure requirements as well as the important topics of realised profits and distributable profits.

The overall regulatory framework relating to UK financial reporting and the role of SSAPs is dealt with in the following chapter (Modern Financial Accounting).

5.2 THE IMPACT OF THE COMPANIES ACT 1985

The Companies Act 1985 introduced several important changes regarding financial reporting requirements for companies. Most of these changes resulted from the government's implementation of the EEC Fourth Directive. The changes affected both (a) accounts presented to shareholders and (b) accounts filed with the Registrar of Companies.

As regards (a), all companies are treated in the same way, quite irrespective of size. The 1985 Act specifies balance sheet and profit and loss account formats, as well as minimum contents to be provided in notes. A source and application of funds statement is not required by law, but is mandatory under SSAP 10 for companies with an annual turnover in excess of £25,000.

As regards (b), special concessions are available for certain small and medium-sized companies (as defined) as regards the amount of information required to be filed by law with the Registrar of Companies. This separate aspect is covered in section 5.14 of this chapter.

5.3 THE PROFIT AND LOSS ACCOUNT AND BALANCE SHEET FORMATS

The formats are set out below. The following comments are relevant:

(a) The numbers and letters against items are for reference purposes in interpreting the requirements of the Act. They need not (and should not) be used in published company accounts.
(b) As vertical form accounts are almost universal in the UK, other possible layouts are not referred to.
(c) In the balance sheet and profit and loss account, any item identified by an arabic number may be shown on the face of the statement or relegated to the notes. All other items must be shown on the face of the balance sheet or profit and loss account.
(d) For the profit and loss account, two formats are possible. Both are used in practice, and examiners may specify the use of a particular method. Of the two, format 1 (analysis by purpose) is more popular with larger companies than format 2. Both formats are illustrated in an example later in the chapter.
(e) The balance sheet and profit and loss should include items (provided they

apply to the particular company) under the headings and in the sequence indicated in the formats. However, items indicated by arabic numbers may be shown in greater detail. Furthermore, the Act requires the directors to adapt arabic number items where the special circumstances of the business require such adaptation.

(f) A change in format (from one year to another) is only permitted if there are special reasons for a change e g a single company is taken over by a group which uses a different format for its profit and loss account. In such circumstances, disclosure is required of particulars and reasons for the change.

(g) Comparative figures are required for all items with the exception of the following:
(1) movement on fixed assets;
(2) details of substantial investments (shareholding in excess of 10%);
(3) movement on provisions;
(4) movement on reserves;
(5) disclosure of transactions involving directors and others.

Companies Act 1985 formats

(1) *Profit and loss account* (analysis by purpose)

	£	£
FORMAT 1		
1 Turnover		X
2 Cost of sales		(X)
3 Gross profit or loss		X
4 Distribution costs		(X)
5 Administrative expenses		(X)
6 Other operating income		X
7 Income from shares in group companies	X	X
8 Income from shares in related companies	X	
9 Income from other fixed asset investments	X	
10 Other interest receivable and similar income	X	X
11 Amounts written off investments		(X)
12 Interest payable and similar charges		(X)
– Profit or loss on ordinary activities before taxation		X
13 Tax on profit or loss on ordinary activites		(X)
14 Profit or loss on ordinary activities after taxation		X
15 Extraordinary income	X	
16 Extraordinary charges	(X)	
17 Extraordinary profit or loss	X	
18 Tax on extraordinary profit or loss	(X)	X
19 Other taxes not shown under the above items		(X)
20 Profit or loss for the financial year		X
– Dividends	X	
– Transfer to (from) reserves	X	(X)
		X
Profit and loss account brought forward		X
Profit and loss account carried forward		£XX

(2) *Profit and loss account* (analysis by type)

FORMAT 2	£	£
1 Turnover		X
2 Change in stocks of finished goods and in work in progress		(X)
3 Own work capitalised		X
4 Other operating income		X
5 (a) Raw materials and consumables	X	
(b) Other external charges	X	(X)
6 Staff costs:		
(a) wages and salaries	X	
(b) social security costs	X	
(c) other pension costs	X	(X)
7 (a) Depreciation and other amounts written off tangible and intangible fixed assets	X	
(b) Exceptional amounts written off current assets	X	(X)
8 Other operating charges		(X)
9 Income from shares in group companies	X	
10 Income from shares in related companies	X	
11 Income from other fixed asset investments	X	
12 Other interest receivable and similar income	X	X
13 Amounts written off investments		(X)
14 Interest payable and similar charges		(X)
– Profit or loss on ordinary activities before taxation		X
15 Tax on profit or loss on ordinary activities		(X)
16 Profit or loss on ordinary activities after taxation		X
17 Extraordinary income	X	
18 Extraordinary charges	(X)	
19 Extraordinary profit or loss	X	
20 Tax on extraordinary profit or loss	(X)	X
21 Other taxes not shown under the above items		(X)
22 Profit or loss for the financial year		X
– Dividends	X	
– Transfer to (from) reserves	X	
		(X)
		X
Profit and loss account brought forward		X
Profit and loss account carried forward		£XX

(3) *Balance sheet* (vertical form)

			£	£	£
A	Called up share capital not paid				X
B	Fixed assets				
	I	Intangible assets			
		1 Development costs	X		
		2 Concessions, patents, licences, trade marks and similar rights and assets	X		
		3 Goodwill	X		
		4 Payments on account	X		
			—	X	
	II	Tangible assets			
		1 Land and buildings	X		
		2 Plant and machinery	X		
		3 Fixtures, fittings, tools and equipment	X		
		4 Payments on account and assets in course of construction	X		
			—	X	
	III	Investments			
		1 Shares in group companies	X		
		2 Loans to group companies	X		
		3 Shares in related companies	X		
		4 Loans to related companies	X		
		5 Other investments other than loans	X		
		6 Other loans	X		
		7 Own shares	X		
			—	X	
	(Total of B)				X
C	Current assets				
	I	Stocks			
		1 Raw materials and consumables	X		
		2 Work in progress	X		
		3 Finished goods and goods for resale	X		
		4 Payments on account	X		
			—		
			X		
			—		
	II	Debtors			
		1 Trade debtors	X		
		2 Amounts owed by group companies	X		
		3 Amounts owed by related companies	X		
		4 Other debtors	X		
		5 Called up share capital not paid	X		
		6 Prepayments and accrued income	X		
			—		
			X		
			—		
	III	Investments			
		1 Shares in group companies	X		
		2 Own shares	X		
		3 Other investments	X		
			—		
			X		
			—		
	IV	Cash at bank and in hand	X		
	(Total of C)			X	

D   Prepayments and accrued income   X

    (Total of C and D)   X

E   Creditors: amounts falling due within one year
   1 Debenture loans   X
   2 Bank loans and overdrafts   X
   3 Payments received on account   X
   4 Trade creditors   X
   5 Bills of exchange payable   X
   6 Amounts owed to group companies   X
   7 Amounts owed to related companies   X
   8 Other creditors including taxation and social security   X
   9 Accruals and deferred income   X

    (Total of E)   X

F   Net current assets (liabilities) $C + D - E$ X

G   Total assets less current liabilities $(A + B + F)$ X

H   Creditors: amounts falling due after more than one year
   1 Debenture loans   X
   2 Bank loans and overdrafts   X
   3 Prepayments received on account   X
   4 Trade creditors   X
   5 Bills of exchange payable   X
   6 Amounts owed to group companies   X
   7 Amounts owed to related companies   X
   8 Other creditors including taxation and social security   X
   9 Accruals and deferred income   X   (X)

I   Provisions for liabilities and charges
   1 Pensions and similar obligations   X
   2 Taxation, including deferred taxation   X
   3 Other provisions   X   (X)

J   Accruals and deferred income   (X)

     £XX

K   Capital and reserves
   I   Called up share capital   X
   II   Share premium account   X
   III   Revaluation reserve   X
   IV   Other reserves
      1 Capital redemption reserve   X
      2 Reserve for own shares   X
      3 Reserves provided for by the articles of association   X
      4 Other reserves   X   X

   V   Profit and loss account   X

     £XX

5.4   A SUMMARY OF THE PRINCIPAL DISCLOSURE REQUIREMENTS (COMPANIES ACT 1985 AND SSAPs)

(a) Accounting policies

(1) *General*

Disclosure requirement for significant accounting policies.

(2) *Depreciation*

For each major class of depreciable asset:

(i)   Methods used.
(ii) Useful lives or depreciation rates.

(3) *Development expenditure*

(i)   Accounting policy followed.
(ii) Where costs capitalised:
    (a) period over which costs to be written off;
    (b) reasons for capitalising the development costs in question.

(4) *Goodwill*

If capitalised as intangible fixed asset:

(i)   Write-off period.
(ii) Reasons for choosing that write-off period.

(5) *Stocks and work-in-progress*

(i)   Cost.
(ii) Net realisable value.
(iii) Attributable profit and foreseeable losses.

(6) *Deferred taxation*

Description of method of calculation.

(7) *Foreign currency translation*

(i)   Method used to translate financial statements of foreign enterprises.
(ii) Treatment of exchange differences.

(8) *Leasing—lessees*

Policies for accounting for operating leases and finance leases.

(9) *Leasing—lessors*

Policies for accounting for operating leases, finance leases and lease income.

(b) Profit and loss items requiring disclosure

(1) *Turnover*

(i)   Analysis of turnover over:

    (a) substantially different business activities;
    (b) substantially different geographical markets.

(ii) Analysis of profit before tax between substantially different business activities.

(2) *Depreciation*

(i) Total depreciation provided (including amortisation of intangibles).
(ii) Additional provisions for depreciation:

    (a) temporary diminution in value of fixed asset investment;
    (b) permanent diminution in value of any fixed asset;
    (c) write back of provision considered no longer necessary;
    Any of the above items not shown in P/L must be shown by note.

(iii) Where assets revalued during current year, disclose the effect, if material, on the depreciation charge.

(3) *Expense items*

(i)   Charges for hire of plant and machinery.
(ii) Auditor's remuneration.
(iii) Interest payable:

    (a) bank loans, overdrafts and other loans:

        (1) repayable (other than by instalments) and due within five years of B/S date;
        (2) repayable by instalments all of which are repayable within five years of B/S date.

    (b) Loans of any other kind.

(4) *Particulars of staff*

(i)   Staff includes directors.
(ii) Average number of persons employed during year (determined on a weekly basis) and analysed within categories according to organisation of company's activities.
(iii) Staff costs disclosing:

    (a) wages;
    (b) social security costs;
    (c) other pension costs.

(5) *Directors' emoluments*

(i) Aggregate of:

    (a) directors' emoluments;
    (b) directors' or past directors' pensions;
    (c) compensation to directors or past directors for loss of office.

(ii) Each item above to distinguish between:

    (a) amounts receivable in respect of services as director;
    (b) other emoluments (e g management remuneration)

(iii) Emoluments of chairman.
(iv) Emoluments of highest paid director (if in excess of chairman).
(v)   Numbers of directors who emoluments fall in bands:

0–£ 5,000
£ 5,001–£10,000
£10,000–£15,000 etc

Note: For purposes of (iii), (iv) and (v), emoluments should exclude employer's part of pension contributions.

(vi) Number of directors who have waived rights to emoluments and aggregate amount waived in year.

NOTES
(1) If aggregate emoluments (as per (i) above) do not exceed £60,000, items (iii)–(vi) above need not be disclosed provided company is not part of a group.
(2) Items (iii), (iv) and (v) do not apply to directors whose duties were wholly or mainly outside UK during the year.

(6) *Highly-paid employees*

(i) For employees earning in excess of £30,000 (excluding employer's pension contributions) disclose numbers falling within bands:

> £30,000–£35,000
> £35,001–£40,000
> £40,001–£45,000 etc

(ii) Information need not be disclosed for persons who worked wholly or mainly outside the UK during the year.

(7) *Income items*

(i) Income from listed investments.
(ii) If a substantial part of company's revenue, rents from lands.

(8) *Exceptional and extraordinary items*

(i) Effect of transactions that are exceptional by virtue of size or incidence, though they fall within the ordinary activities of the company.
(ii) Particulars of extraordinary income or charges (disclose tax separately).
(iii) Prior year adjustments.

(9) *Taxation*

(i) Basis of calculation of UK tax.
(ii) Particulars of special circumstances affecting tax liability; indication of extent to which tax charge is reduced by accelerated capital allowances.
(iii) State amounts for:

(a) charge for UK corporation tax;
(b) if greater than (a), charge for tax had double tax relief not been obtained;
(c) charge for UK income tax;
(d) amount of overseas tax;
(e) tax attributable to franked investment income;
(f) deferred taxation;
(g) irrecoverable ACT;
(h) relief for overseas taxation.

(iv) Amounts for (a)–(d) above to be stated separately in respect of tax on ordinary activities and tax on extraordinary items.

(10) *Other matters*

Amounts provided for the redemption of:

(i) share capital.
(ii) loans.

(c) Balance sheet disclosures

(1) *Fixed assets—general points*

Unless indicated otherwise, the points below relate also to fixed asset investments and intangibles.

(i) Cost or valuation: for each fixed asset category disclose:

    (a) aggregate at beginning of year;
    (b) revisions to valuation;
    (c) acquisitions;
    (d) disposals;
    (e) transfers between asset categories;
    (f) aggregate at end of year.

(ii) Cumulative depreciation: for each fixed asset category disclose:

    (a) cumulative amount at beginning of year;
    (b) amounts provided during the year;
    (c) adjustments in respect of disposals;
    (d) amount of any other adjustments during year;
    (e) cumulative amount at end of year.

(iii) For fixed assets (other than listed investments) included on a valuation basis, state:

    (a) the years and values involved (effectively analysis of aggregate cost or valuation at B/S date);
    (b) for assets valued during financial year:

        (1) names of valuers or particulars of their qualification;
        (2) bases of valuation.

(iv) Land and buildings—analysis of NBV between:

    (a) freehold;
    (b) long leasehold; and
    (c) short leasehold.

(v) For fixed assets included at a valuation state, either:

    (a) aggregate cost and aggregate depreciation as would have been determined under historical cost rules; or
    (b) difference between (a) and amounts actually included in B/S under modified historical cost.

(vi) If no record of original purchase price or production cost of asset:

    (a) use value ascribed in earliest available record of its value after acquisition or production; or
    (b) disclose particulars of such cases.

(vii) For investment properties, see below.

(2) *Investments*

(i) Disclosure rules (ii)–(iv) below apply whether fixed or current asset.
(ii) Disclose amount relating to listed investments (distinguishing between listed on recognised stock exchange and other listed investments).
(iii) The aggregate market value of the listed investments.
(iv) The market value of the listed investments and the stock exchange value in situation where market value is the higher of the two.
(v) Fixed asset investments included at a value determined on a basis that the directors consider appropriate: disclose particulars of the method of valuation and reasons for adopting it.

(vi) Nominal value of own shares held.

(3) *Significant shareholdings* (in excess of 10%)

(i) Situations:

    (a) nominal value (NV) held exceeds NV of equity share capital of investee;
    (b) NV held exceeds 10% of allotted share capital of investee;
    (c) book value of investment exceeds 10% of assets of investor company.

(ii) Disclosure:

    (a) name of the company;
    (b) country in which incorporated if outside GB;
    (c) its country of registration (England or Scotland) if different from the investing company;
    (d) identity and proportion of nominal value of each class of share held.

(iii) Comparatives not required.

(4) *Significant shareholdings* (in excess of 20%)

(i) Situations: NV of shares held exceed 20% in NV of allotted share capital of investee.

(ii) Disclosure (additional to 10% plus requirements above):

    (a) aggregate amount of capital and reserves of investee as at B/S ending with or prior to that of investor;
    (b) profit or loss of investee.

(iii) Disclosure not required if investment accounted for by equity method of valuation.

(iv) Comparatives not required.

(5) *Intangible fixed assets*

(i) Development costs:

    (a) period over which costs are to be written off;
    (b) reasons for capitalising development costs;
    (c) movement on deferred development expenditure;
    (d) separate disclosures—not under current assets.

(ii) Goodwill (acquired for valuable consideration):

    (a) write-off period;
    (b) reasons for choosing that write-off period.

(6) *Stocks and work-in-progress*

(i) Accounting policies for determining:

    (a) cost;
    (b) net realisable value;
    (c) attributable profit and foreseeable losses.

(ii) Sub-classification of balance sheet figure into main appropriate categories.

(iii) For long-term contract work-in-progress:

    (a) cost plus attributable profit less foreseeable losses;
    (b) cash received and receivable as progress payments on account.

(iv) If anticipated losses on individual contracts exceed cost incurred to date less progress payments received and receivable, such excesses should be shown separately as provisions.

(v) If materially different, disclosure of difference between:

    (a) purchase price or production cost of stock in company's balance sheet using one of the specified methods such as FIFO, average cost etc; and

    (b) replacement cost at balance sheet date (or, if considered more appropriate by directors, the most recent actual purchase price or production cost).

(vi) Payments on account of orders to be shown in positions E3 or H3 of the format to the extent that they are not shown as deductions from stock.

(7) *Debtors*

For each item included under debtors: show separately amounts falling due after more than one year.

(8) *Creditors*

(i)   For each item shown under creditors, disclose:

    (a) aggregate amount of debts repayable (other than by instalments) more than five years after B/S date;

    (b) aggregate amount of debts repayable by instalments any of which fall due more than five years after the B/S date;

    (c) for each item in (b), the aggregate amount of instalments falling due after the five years.

(ii) For each debt required to be disclosed within, disclose:

    (a) terms of payment or repayment and rate of interest payable; or

    (b) if above statement would be of excessive length, a general indication of the terms of payment or repayment and rates of interest payable.

(iii) For each item under creditors, supply:

    (a) aggregate amount of any debts in respect of which security has been given;

    (b) indication of nature of securities given.

(iv) Issues of debentures during the year—disclose:

    (a) reason for making issue;

    (b) classes of debentures issued;

    (c) for each class, amount issued and consideration received by company.

(v) Particulars of redeemed debentures which company has power to reissue.

(vi) Where any of company's debentures are held by a nominee of or trustee for the company: state nominal amount of debentures and amount at which stated in the accounting records.

(vii) Convertible debenture loans:

    (a) amount of any convertible loans is required to be shown separately;

    (b) see share capital section (right to require allotment of shares to any person).

(9) *Taxation*

(i)   Other creditors including taxation and social security (balance sheet items E8 and H8): show separate amount for taxation and social security.

(ii) State amount of any provisions for taxation other than deferred taxation.

(iii) Disclose date of payment of corporation tax unless included as a current liability.

(iv) Include ACT on proposed dividends as a current tax liability.

(v) Deferred tax account balances to be shown separately in B/S:

    (a) indicate nature and amount of major elements;

    (b) description of method of calculation adopted.

(vi) For each principal category of deferred taxation show:

(a) potential amount of deferred tax;
(b) amount provided within the account.

(vii) Recoverable ACT relating to proposed dividends:

(a) deduct from deferred tax account if available; failing which
(b) show ACT recoverable as a deferred asset.

(viii) Value of asset shown by way of note and differing from book value: disclose, if material, tax implications of realisation at valuation figure.

(ix) Deferred tax relating to movements on reserve: show separately; disclose treatment.

(10) *Dividends*

(i) State aggregate amount recommended for distribution as dividend.

(ii) If arrears of fixed cumulative dividends, memorandum note of:

(a) amount of arrears;
(b) period for which dividends (or each class of dividends) are in arrear.

(11) *Provisions*

(i) Where amounts transferred to any provision for liabilities and charges, disclose:

(a) amount of provision at beginning of year;
(b) amount transferred to the provision during the year;
(c) source and application of amounts so transferred;
(d) amount of provision at end of year.

(ii) Where amounts are transferred from any provision for liabilities and charges except for purpose for which provision was established, disclose similar information as for (i) above.

(iii) Other provisions (B/S item I3): where amount of a provision is material, give particulars of each provision included under this heading.

(iv) Comparatives not required.

(12) *Guaranteed and other financial commitments*

(i) Particulars of any charge on the assets of the company to secure the liabilities of any other person, including, where practicable, the amount secured.

(ii) Any other contingent liability not provided for:

(a) amount or estimated amount of that liability (as at date on which financial statements are approved by board of directors);
(b) its legal nature;
(c) whether any valuable security has been provided by the company in connection with the liability and if so, what;
(d) the uncertainties which are expected to affect the ultimate outcome;
(e) explain taxation implications of a contingency, where necessary for a proper understanding.

(iii) Capital commitments:

(a) contracts for capital expenditure not provided for;
(b) capital expenditure authorised by directors but not yet contracted for.

(iv) Pension commitment particulars:

(a) pension commitments included under any provision shown in the B/S;
(b) pension commitments for which no provision made;
(c) where applicable, separate particulars of pension commitments relating wholly or partly to pensions payable to past directors.

(v) Particulars of any other financial commitments which:

    (a) have not been provided for; and

    (b) are relevant to assessing the company's state of affairs.

(13) *Share capital*

(i) Authorised share capital.

(ii) Allotted share capital:

    (a) where more than one class of shares allotted, number and aggregate nominal value of each class;

    (b) amount of allotted share capital;

    (c) amount of called-up share capital which has been paid up.

(iii) Allotted redeemable shares:

    (a) earliest and latest dates on which company has power to redeem;

    (b) whether redemption is mandatory or at option of company;

    (c) premium, if any, payable on redemption.

(iv) Shares allotted during the financial year:

    (a) reasons for making the allotment;

    (b) classes of shares allotted;

    (c) for each class of share;

        (1) number allotted,

        (2) aggregate nominal value,

        (3) consideration received by company.

(v) Options to subscribe for shares and any other rights to require allotment of shares to any person (including convertible loan stock):

    (a) number, description and amount of shares in relation to which right is exercisable;

    (b) period during which it is exercisable;

    (c) price to be paid for the shares allotted.

(14) *Reserves*

(i) Where any amount is transferred to or from any reserves, disclose:

    (a) amount of reserves at beginning of year;

    (b) any amounts transferred to or from the reserves during the year.

(15) *Loans for acquisition of own shares*

Loans under the Companies Act 1985, s 153(4)(b) or (c) or s 155: where included under any B/S item, disclose aggregate amount of loans for each such item.

(16) *Government grants*

Capital-based government grants: where deferred credit method is selected.

(i) Show deferred credit separately in B/S quite distinct from share-holders' funds.

(ii) Suitable position would be B/S item J (deferred income).

(17) *Investment properties*

(i) Valuation:

    (a) name of valuer or particulars of qualifications;

    (b) bases of valuation used;

    (c) if appropriate, fact that valuer is employee or officer of the company.

(ii) Investment revaluation reserve:

  (a) disclose prominently in financial statements;
  (b) disclose movements during year.

(iii) Carrying value of investment properties: disclose prominently in financial statements.

(18) *Leasing and hire purchase*

The specific disclosure requirements are dealt with in chapter 10.

(d) Directors' report—summary of matters to be disclosed

(1) Principal activities of the company and any significant changes.
(2) A fair review of the development of the business of the company during the financial year and of its position at the end of it.
(3) Names of persons who were directors at any time during the year.
(4) Significant changes in the fixed assets of the company during the year.
(5) The difference, as precisely as is practicable, between the market value and the book value of land and buildings, where such difference is substantial.
(6) Director's interest in shares or debentures of this company or any other group company both at the beginning of the financial year (or date of appointment as director, if later) and at the end of the year.
(7) Particulars of any important events which have occurred since the balance sheet date.
(8) An indication of likely future developments in the business of the company.
(9) An indication of the activities (if any) of the company in the field of research and development.
(10) Amount recommended to be paid by way of dividend.
(11) Amount to be carried to reserve.
(12) Charitable and political donations:

  (i) if combined amount exceeds £200, the split between charitable and political;
  (ii) details of any individual amount for political purposes where amount exceeds £200; name of recipient and amount given.

(13) Disabled persons—statement describing policies for:

  (i) employment;
  (ii) training;
  (iii) career development;
  (iv) promotion.

  (Not applicable to companies which employ fewer than 250 persons within the UK.)
(14) Particulars of acquisitions of company's own shares.

5.5 PUBLISHED ACCOUNTS ILLUSTRATION—VENEERING MANUFACTURERS PLC

(a) Basic data

The year end of Veneering Manufacturers plc is 30 June. The trial balance at 30 June 19X9 was as follows:

	£	£
100,000 8% (now 5.6% plus tax credit) cumulative preference shares of £1 each fully paid, redeemable at the company's option on January 1 19X30 at a premium of 25p per share (authorised £100,000)		100,000
400,000 ordinary shares of £1 each (authorised £500,000)		400,000
Freehold land and buildings, July 1 19X8 cost	414,900	
Additions during the year	20,000	
Plant and equipment (cost, £240,000)—see note	120,000	
Office furniture (cost, £30,000)	22,000	
Stock of raw materials, July 1 19X8	93,200	
Stock of finished goods, July 1 19X8	12,700	
Work-in-progress, July 1 19X8	9,200	
Debtors	107,600	
4% debenture (repayable at par, January 1 19X22) (secured by a floating charge)		150,000
Debenture interest, half-year to December 19X8 (gross), paid on January 1 19X9	3,000	
Dividends and interest:		
From unquoted investments received May 1 19X9 (cash received)		700
From quoted investments received June 20 19X9 (gross)		3,000
Share premium account		136,400
Unquoted investments at cost	32,000	
Quoted investments at cost (British government securities) (market value £71,000)	60,200	
Profit and loss account—balance July 1 19X8		30,900
Cash at bank and in hand	182,920	
Creditors		78,580
Sales		791,000
Purchases	319,600	
Carriage inwards	16,000	
Bank interest	2,900	
Wages and national insurance (factory)	137,900	
Plant hire (internal telephone system)	1,300	
Rates	5,000	
Repairs to premises	600	
Administrative salaries (including director's, £30,000)	61,300	
Salesmen's salaries (including director's, £40,000)	100,000	
Postage and telephone	1,800	
Printing and stationery	400	
Legal and professional charges	800	
Advertising	500	
Directors' fees	600	
Bank charges	100	
Salesmen's commissions	5,200	
Power and lighting (factory)	6,700	
Insurances—factory	7,200	
Insurances—office	400	
Repairs to plant	8,500	
Preference share dividend for half-year, due and paid on January 1 19X9	2,800	
Income tax account	900	
Provision for corporation tax, payable January 1 19X0		30,240
ACT account	1,200	
Deposit interest received		38,600
	1,759,420	1,759,420

The following adjustments are required:

		£
(1)	Accruals:	
	Power and lighting	2,400
	Salesmen's commissions	1,600
	Auditor's remuneration, including expenses	1,000
(2)	Doubtful debts provision	2,500

(3) Depreciation:

    Plant and equipment　10% straight-line on cost
    Office furniture　　　10% on reducing balance

(4) Corporation tax on profits for the year estimated at £67,000.
(5) Half-year's preference dividend (payable 1.7.19X9) is to be provided for.
(6) A final ordinary dividend of 5% (payable 31.7.19X9) is to be provided for.
(7) Closing stocks:

Raw materials	76,400
Work-in progress	12,800
Finished goods	40,100

(8) Prepayments:

Factory insurances	1,100
Rates	1,200

The following additional information is provided:

(9) The income tax position is:

INCOME TAX ACCOUNT

19X9		£	19X9			£
April 14	Bank	900	Jan	1	Debenture interest (tax deducted)	900
June 20	Quoted investment income account (tax deducted from unfranked investment income)	900	June 30		Corporation tax account	900
		1,800				1,800

(10) Corporation tax payable on 1 January 19X10, has been agreed at £28,840.
(11) At June 30 19X9, the company had placed contracts for heavy machinery for £80,000 and the Board has authorised, but not yet placed, a contract for a new storeroom for £30,000.
(12) During the year, the company acquired new plant for £10,000 and sold obsolete plant at written-down value (cost, £5,000; accumulated depreciation, £4,000). There were no acquisitions or disposals of office furniture.
(13) The unlisted investments relate to a 3% shareholding in a private company.
(14) There is no substantial difference between the purchase price or production costs of closing stocks, and their replacement cost or most recent prices at the balance sheet date.
(15) The historical cost of land and buildings at 1 July 19X8 was £200,000.
(16) The company acquired the business of G Huyton & Co on 18 August 19X9 for consideration in cash amounting to £139,500.

(17) *Staff details*
These details include relevant information relating to directors.

(i) Administrative salaries include £4,017 in respect of social security costs and £3,675 in respect of other pension costs. Respective figures for salesmens' salaries are in £7,095 and £6,042; for factory wages and national insurance, £10,538 and £8,473.
(ii) Details of numbers of staff employed are:

Office and management	6
Selling and marketing	12
Manufacturing	21
	39

(18) *Director's emoluments*
Details of director's emoluments, exclusive of pension contributions are:

Williams (Chairman)	£5,500
Pace	£2,750
Slow	£15,930
Ruslow	£19,760
Harris	£12,750

(b) Required

(1) A detailed manufacturing, trading and profit and loss account for the year ended 30 June 19X9, in a form suitable for presentation to the directors.
(2) A profit and loss account in a form suitable for presentation to the shareholders using both formats permitted by the revised Sch 4 of the Companies Act 1985.
(3) A balance sheet as at 30 June 19X9, in a form suitable for presentation to the shareholders.
(4) Notes for the profit and loss account and the balance sheet, including accounting policies.

NOTES
(1) Ignore comparative figures and the requirements of SSAP 3 (earnings per share).
(2) Income tax should be taken at 30%, corporation tax at 50% and ACT at $\frac{3}{7}$. Deferred tax should be ignored.
(3) A directors' report and a source and application of funds statement are not required.

(c) Veneering Manufacturers plc

MANUFACTURING, TRADING AND PROFIT AND LOSS ACCOUNT

for the year ended 30 June 19X9 for presentation to the directors

	£	£
Materials:		
Stock at 1.7.19X8		93,200
Purchases		319,600
Carriage inwards		16,000
		428,800
Less stock at 30.6.19X9		76,400
		352,400
Wages and national insurance		137,900
Prime cost		490,300
Factory overheads:		
Power and lighting	9,100	
Insurance	6,100	
Repairs to plant	8,500	
Depreciation of plant	24,000	
		47,700
Factory cost of production		538,000
Work-in-progress, 30.6.19X9	12,800	
Work-in-progress, 30.6.19X8	9,200	
		(3,600)
Factory cost of finished goods produced		534,400

	£	£
Sales:		791,000
Stock of finished goods at 1.7.X8	12,700	
Factory cost of finished goods produced	534,400	
	547,100	
Less stock of finished goods at 30.6.X9	40,100	
Cost of sales		507,000
Gross profit		284,000
Deposit interest received		38,600
Income from investments—quoted		3,000
—unquoted		1,000
		326,600
Administrative expenses:		
Rates	3,800	
Plant hire (internal telephones)	1,300	
Repairs to premises	600	
Insurances	400	
Depreciation of office furniture	2,200	
Directors' emoluments	30,600	
Salaries	31,300	
Auditors' remuneration	1,000	
Postage and telephone	1,800	
Printing and stationery	400	
Legal and professional charges	800	
	74,200	

	£	£
Selling and distribution expenses:		
Salesmen's salaries	100,000	
Commissions	6,800	
Advertising	500	
	107,300	
Finance expenses:		
Debenture interest	6,000	
Bank interest	2,900	
Bank charges	100	
Provision for doubtful debts	2,500	
	11,500	
		193,000
Profit before tax		133,600
Taxation:		
Corporation tax		
Provided for the year	67,000	
Overprovided in previous year	(1,400)	
	65,600	
Tax credit on dividends received	300	
		65,900
Profit after tax		67,700
Dividends:		
Preference shares		
Paid	2,800	
Proposed	2,800	
Ordinary shares		
Proposed	20,000	
		25,600
Retained profit		42,100
Balance at 1.7.X8		30,900
Balance at 30.6.X9		73,000

(d) Veneering Manufacturers plc

PROFIT AND LOSS ACCOUNT

for the year ended 30 June 19X9
for presentation to the shareholders (format 1)

	£	£
Turnover		791,000
Cost of sales		507,000
Gross profit		284,000
Distribution costs	107,300	
Administrative expenses	76,800	184,100
		99,900
Income from fixed asset investments	1,000	
Other interest receivable	41,600	
		42,600
Interest payable		(8,900)
Profit on ordinary activities before taxation		133,600
Tax on profit on ordinary activities		65,900
Profit on ordinary activities after taxation		67,700
Dividends		25,600
Retained profit		42,100
Profit and loss account brought forward		30,900
Profit and loss account carried forward		73,000

Workings

(1) *Cost of sales and distribution costs*
Per detailed manufacturing account.

(2) *Administrative expenses*

	£
Per manufacturing account	74,200
Bank charges	100
Doubtful debts	2,500
	76,800

(e) Veneering Manufacturers plc

PROFIT AND LOSS ACCOUNT

for the year ended 30 June 19X9
for presentation to the shareholders (format 2)

	£	£
Turnover		791,000
Deduct operating costs (see note)		691,100
Trading profit		99,900
Income from fixed asset investments	1,000	
Other interest receivable	41,600	
		42,600
Interest payable		(8,900)
Profit on ordinary activities before taxation		133,600
Tax on profit on ordinary activities		65,900
Profit on ordinary activities after taxation		67,700
Dividends		25,600
Retained profit		42,100
Profit and loss account brought forward		30,900
Profit and loss account carried forward		73,000

NOTES—OPERATING COSTS

	£
Change in stocks of finished goods and work in progress	(31,000)
Raw materials and consumables	336,400
Other external charges	16,000
Staff costs	306,600
Depreciation	26,200
Other operating charges	34,600
Hire of plant and machinery	1,300
Auditors' remuneration	1,000
	691,100

Workings

(1) *Change in stocks*

	£
Finished goods	27,400
Work in progress	3,600
	31,000

(2) *Raw materials and consumables*

Opening stock	93,200
Purchases	319,600
Closing stock	(76,400)
	336,400

(3) *Other external charges*

Carriage	16,000

(4) *Staff costs*

Factory wages and NI	137,900
Directors' emoluments (admin)	30,600
Salaries (admin)	31,300
Salesmen's salaries and commission	106,800
	306,600

(5) *Depreciation*

Plant	24,000
Office furniture	2,200
	26,200

(6) *Other operating charges*

Power and lighting	9,100
Insurance	6,100
Repairs to plant	8,500
Rates	3,800
Repairs to premises	600
Insurances	400
Postage and telephone	1,800
Printing and stationery	400
Legal and professional	800
Advertising	500
Bank charges	100
Doubtful debts	2,500
	34,600

(f)   VENEERING MANUFACTURERS PLC—BALANCE SHEET
as at 30 June 19X9

	£	£	£
Fixed assets			
Intangible assets			550,700
Investments			32,000
			582,700
Current assets			
Stocks		129,300	
Debtors		116,870	
Investments		60,200	
Cash at bank and in hand		182,920	
		489,290	
Creditors: amounts falling due within one year			
Trade creditors	78,580		
Taxation and social security	38,310		
Proposed dividends	22,800		
Accruals and deferred income	8,000		
		147,690	
Net current assets			341,600
Total assets less current liabilities			924,300
Creditors: amounts falling due after more than one year			
Debenture loans		150,000	
Taxation and social security		64,900	
			(214,900)
			709,400

Capital and reserves	£	£
Called-up share capital		500,000
Share premium account		136,400
Profit and loss account		73,000
		709,400

(g) Notes to the accounts (part of the financial statements)

(1) *Accounting policies*
The accounts are prepared under the historical cost convention, modified to include the revaluation of freehold land and buildings.

(2) *Depreciation*
Depreciation is provided on all tangible assets, other than freehold land and buildings, at rates calculated to write off the cost or valuation, less estimated residual value, of each asset evenly over its expected useful life as follows:

Plant and machinery—10% pa on a straight-line basis
Office furniture   —10% pa on a reducing balance basis

(3) *Stocks and work-in-progress*
Stocks are stated at the lower of cost and net realisable value as follows:

Costs include all cost incurred in bringing each product to its present location and condition and is determined as follows:
Raw materials—purchase costs on a first-in-first-out basis.
Work in progress and finished goods—cost of direct materials and labour, plus attributable overheads based on the normal level of activity.

Net realisable value is based on estimated selling price, less further costs expected to be incurred to completion and disposal.

(4) *Turnover*
Turnover represents the invoiced amount of goods sold and services provided, stated net of credits and allowances and value added tax.

(5) *Profit on ordinary activities before tax*
This is stated after charging or crediting:

	£	£
Staff costs (see notes 6 and 7 below)		306,600
Auditors' remuneration		1,000
Depreciation		26,200
Hire of plant and machinery		1,300
Interest payable:		
Bank loans and overdrafts, wholly repayable within five years		2,900
Other loans		6,000
Interest receivable on deposit accounts		38,600
Income from investments:		
Listed		3,000
Unlisted		1,000

(6) *Staff costs*
Staff costs (including directors) were as follows:

	£
Wages and salaries	266,760
Social security costs	21,650
Other pension costs	18,190
	306,600

The average weekly number of employees, including directors, during the year was made up as follows:

	No
Office and management	6
Selling and marketing	12
Manufacturing	21
	39

(7) *Directors' remuneration*

	£
Fees	600
Other emoluments (including pension (contributions))	70,000
	70,600

The emoluments of the chairman, excluding pension contributions, were £5,500 and of the highest paid director, excluding pension contributions, £19,760.

Other directors' emoluments, excluding pension contributions, fell within the following ranges:

	No
£ Nil–£ 5,000	1
£ 5,001–£10,000	—
£10,001–£15,000	1
£15,001–£20,000	1

(8) *Tax on profit on ordinary activities*

Based on the profit for the year:

Corporation tax at 50%	67,000
Tax credits attributable to dividends received	300
Corporation tax overprovided in previous years	(1,400)
	65,900

(9) *Tangible fixed assets*

	Total	Freehold land and buildings	Plant and machinery	Fixtures, fittings and equipment
	£	£	£	£
Cost or valuation				
At 1 July 19X8	679,900	414,900	235,000	30,000
Additions	30,000	20,000	10,000	—
Disposals	(5,000)	—	(5,000)	—
At 30 June 19X9	704,900	434,900	240,000	30,000
Depreciation				
At 1 July 19X8	132,000	—	124,000	8,000
Provided during the year	26,200	—	24,000	2,200
Eliminated on disposals	(4,000)	—	(4,000)	—
At 30 June 19X9	154,200	—	144,000	10,200
Net book amounts at:				
30 June 19X9	550,700	434,900	96,000	19,800
30 June 19X9	547,900	414,900	111,000	22,000

For the freehold land and buildings included at valuation, comparable historical cost figures are:

At 1 July 19X9	£200,000
At 30 June 19X9	£220,000

(10) *Investments*

	£
Cost at 1 July 19X9 and at 30 June 19X9	
Listed investments (market value £71,000)	60,200
Unlisted investments	32,000
	92,200

(11) *Stocks*

Raw materials	76,400
Work in progress	12,800
Finished goods	40,100
	129,300

(12) *Debtors*

Trade debtors	105,100
Other debtors	9,470
Prepayments	2,300
	116,870

Other debtors includes a deferred asset—ACT recoverable.

(13) *Debenture loan*
The debenture loan bears interest at 4% and is repayable in 19X22.
   The loan is secured by a floating charge on the assets of the company.

(14) *Taxation and social security*
This relates to corporation tax payable on 1 January 19X11.

(15) *Called-up share capital*

	Authorised	Allotted, issued and fully paid
	£	£
Ordinary shares of £1 each	500,000	400,000
8% now (5.6% plus tax credit) Cumulative preference shares at £1 each	100,000	100,000
	600,000	500,000

The preference shares are redeemable at the company's option on 1 January 19X30 at a premium of 25p per share.

(16) *Post-balance sheet event*
On 18 August 19X9, the company acquired the business of G Huyton & Co for cash consideration of £139,500.

(17) *Capital commitments*

	£
Contracted	80,000
Authorised but not contracted	30,000

(18) *Contingent liabilities*

Guarantee of the bank overdraft of a supplier	£95,000

(19) *Pension commitments*
There is insufficient information for the purposes of a meaningful note.

Workings

(1) *Staff costs*

	Total	Wages and salaries	Social security costs	Other pension costs
	£	£	£	£
Administrative salaries	61,300	53,608	4,017	3,675
Salesmen's salaries	100,000	86,863	7,095	6,042
Salesmen's commissions	6,800	6,800		
Factory wages and national insurance	137,900	118,889	10,538	8,473
Directors' fees	600	600	—	—
	306,600	266,760	21,650	18,190

(2) *Directors' remuneration*

	Fees	Other emoluments
	£	£
Administrative salaries	400	45,000
Salesmen's salaries	200	25,000
	600	70,000

(3) *Debtors*

	£	£
Trade debtors		107,600
Less provision for doubtful debts		2,500
		105,100
Other debtors—ACT recoverable		9,470
Prepayments:		
Factory insurances	1,100	
Rates	1,200	
		2,300
		116,870

(4)   MAINSTREAM CORPORATION TAX ACCOUNT (MCT)

	£		£
P/L (over-provided last year)	1,400	Bal b/d	30,240
Bal c/d	28,840	P/L (this year charge)	67,000
IT a/c	900		
ACT a/c	1,200		
Bal c/d (67,000 − 900 − 1,200)	64,900		
	97,240		97,240

(5)   ADVANCE CORPORATION TAX ACCOUNT (ACT)

	£		£
Per trial balance ($\frac{3}{7}$ × 2,800 pref div)	1,200	MCT a/c	1,200
Bal c/d	9,470	Bal c/d	9,470
(see working below)			
	10,670		10,670

EXPLANATION OF CALCULATIONS

(i) *ACT asset and liability*

Proposed dividends	22,800
Dividends received	700
	22,100
ACT $\frac{3}{7}$ × 22,100	9,470

(ii) *ACT set-off*

Corporation tax on 19X9 profits		67,000
ACT paid (relating to dividends paid in 19X9)	1,200	
Income tax	900	
		2,100
Mainstream corporation tax liability		64,900

(This is explained in some detail in Chapter 8).

(iii) *Tax and social security payable within one year*

ACT	9,470
MCT	28,840
	38,310

5.6 OVERRIDING TRUE AND FAIR VIEW

The Companies Act 1985 introduces an important concept—that of overriding true and fair view.

There are two aspects of this concept:

(a) If compliance with the detailed requirements of the Companies Act accounts provisions would not provide sufficient information for purposes of a true and fair view, any necessary additional information must be provided.

An example of this could be the disclosure of distributable profits. There is no specific legal requirement for a company to distinguish in its balance sheet between distributable and non-distributable reserves. However, CCAB has referred to situations where material non-distributable profits are included in the profit and loss account or in other reserves which a reader of the accounts might assume to be distributable.

It may be necessary to disclose and quantify the non-distributability in order for the accounts to give a true and fair view.

(b) If, because of the special circumstances of a company, compliance with any detailed requirement would prevent the financial statements from giving a true and fair view, the directors are required to depart from the detailed requirements.

Disclose:

(1) particulars of the departure;
(2) reasons for the departure;
(3) effect of the departure.

Examples include investment properties (see 7.4) and long-term contracts (see 8.3).

5.7 EXTRAORDINARY ITEMS AND PRIOR YEAR ADJUSTMENTS

(a) Background

Prior to the issue in 1974 of SSAP 6 (Extraordinary items and prior year adjustments) some companies adopted the practice referred to as 'reserve accounting'. An example of this was where items of an extraordinary nature, such as costs relating to discontinued activities, were dealt with through reserves as opposed to profit and loss account. A principal aim of SSAP 6 was to limit reserve accounting to specified situations.

Following a review of SSAP 6, ED 36 was issued in 1985. A revised version of SSAP 6 was subsequently issued in 1986.

(b) Basis of SSAP 6

Two viewpoints have been expressed concerning the inclusion of certain revenue items in the profit and loss account:

(1) under the current operating performance concept, the profit and loss account should reflect only the normal recurring activities of the business (i e excluding extraordinary items);
(2) under the all-inclusive concept, the profit and loss account should reflect all profits and losses including extraordinary items.

SSAP 6 and Companies Act 1985 support the all-inclusive concept for the following reasons:

(i) different users of financial statements are interested in different profit figures. SSAP 6 requires extraordinary items to be presented separately from the profit on ordinary activities before tax. This enables profit on ordinary activities to be shown as a separate element of the profit for the financial year.

Companies Act 1985 terminology

| Current operating performance profit | Profit on ordinary activities |

Plus
↓

| Extraordinary items | Extraordinary income less charges |

Equals
↓

| All inclusive profit | Profit for the financial year |

(ii) the above presentation enables the profit and loss account to give a better view of a company's profitability and progress;

(iii) the dividing line between extraordinary items and profit on ordinary activities is sometimes subjective and a matter of judgement. Exclusion of identified extraordinary items could result in a loss of comparability between the reported results of companies;

(iv) exclusion of extraordinary items could result in significant revenue items being overlooked when five-year (or ten-year) results were being considered.

(c) Terminology

The following definitions are important:

(1) *Ordinary activities*

Ordinary activities are any activities which are usually, frequently or regularly undertaken by the company and any related activities in which the company engages in furtherance of, incidental to, or arising from those activities. They include, but are not confined to, the trading activities of the company.

(2) *Exceptional items*

Exceptional items are material items which derive from events or transactions that fall within the ordinary activities of the company, and which need to be disclosed separately by virtue of their size or incidence if the financial statements are to give a true and fair view.

(3) *Extraordinary items*

Extraordinary items are material items which derive from events or transactions that are outside the ordinary activities of the company and which are therefore expected not to recur frequently or regularly. They do not include exceptional items nor do they include prior year items merely because they relate to a prior year.

(4) *Prior year adjustments*

Prior year adjustments are those material adjustments applicable to prior years arising from changes in accounting policies or from the correction of fundamental errors. They do not include normal recurring corrections or adjustments of accounting estimates made in prior years.

(5) *Business segment*

A business segment is a material and separately identifiable component of the business operations of a company or group whose activities, assets and results can be clearly distinguished from the remainder of the company's activities. A business segment will normally have its own separate product lines or markets.

(d) Examples of exceptional items

Subject to the nature of the business and the circumstances of the transaction, the following are examples of items which would normally be treated as exceptional:

(1) redundancy costs relating to continuing business segments;
(2) reorganisation costs unrelated to the discontinuance of a business segment;
(3) previously capitalised expenditure on intangible fixed assets written off other than as part of a process of amortisation;
(4) amounts transferred to employee share schemes;
(5) profits or losses on the disposal of fixed assets;
(6) abnormal charges for bad debts and write-offs of stock and work-in-progress;
(7) abnormal provisions for losses on long-term contracts;
(8) surpluses arising on the settlement of insurance claims;
(9) amounts received in settlement of insurance claims for consequential loss of profits.

(e) Examples of extraordinary items

Subject to the nature of the business and the circumstances of the transactions, the following are examples of items that would normally be treated as extraordinary:

(1) the discontinuance of a business segment, either through termination or disposal;
(2) the sale of an investment not acquired with the intention of resale, such as investments in subsidiary and associated companies;
(3) profits or losses on the disposal of fixed assets;
(4) provision made for the permanent diminution in value of a fixed asset because of extraordinary events during the period;
(5) the expropriation of assets;
(6) a change in the basis of taxation, or a significant change in Government fiscal policy.

Illustration 1

The following information relates to the accounts of DW plc:

	£
Sales	1,860,000
Cost of sales (excluding abnormal stock write-off)	840,000
Abnormal stock write-off	150,000
Redundancy costs relating to discontinued activity	240,000
Tax	
Operating profit	300,000
Redundancy costs	(84,000)
	216,000
Dividends proposed	120,000

Required

Prepare a summarised profit and loss account reflecting the above information.

Solution

PROFIT AND LOSS ACCOUNT OF DW plc for . . .

	£	£
Turnover		1,860,000
Cost of sales (including exceptional item of £150,000)		990,000
Profit on ordinary activities before tax		870,000
Tax on profit on ordinary activities		300,000
Profit on ordinary activities after tax		470,000
Extraordinary charge—redundancy costs on discontinued activity	240,000	
less taxation	(84,000)	
		156,000
Profit for the financial year		214,000
Dividends proposed		120,000
Retained profit for the year		94,000

(f) Prior year adjustments

These include the financial effects of changes in accounting policies and corrections of fundamental errors.

(1) *Changes in accounting policy*

Examples could include policy changes by a company regarding depreciation of buildings (SSAP 12), deferred tax (SSAP 15), goodwill (SSAP 22) or finance leases (SSAP 21).

Illustration 2

In previous years, Hawkshead Ltd has included purchased goodwill in the balance sheet at original cost of purchase. With effect from the current year, goodwill will be amortised on a straight-line basis over ten years.
    Relevant information is:

(i)   Cost of purchased goodwill £80,000, date of acquisition 1.1.19X2.
(ii) Profit and loss account balance at 1.1.19X7 and 19X8 £777,000 and £852,000 respectively.
(iii) Retained profit as reported for 19X7 was £75,000.
(iv) Retained profit for 19X8 allowing for goodwill amortisation of £8,000 (i e $\frac{1}{10}$ × £80,000) was £93,000.

Requirements
Show the statement of retained profit for 19X8. Comparative figures should be shown.

Calculations required
(i)   Prior year adjustments:

At 1.1.X7: 5 years × £8,000	£40,000
At 1.1.X8: 6 years × £8,000	£48,000

(ii) Retained profit for 19X7 (restated) £75,000 less £8,000 £67,000

Presentation

MOVEMENT ON RESERVES—PROFIT AND LOSS ACCOUNT

	19X8 £	19X7 £
At 1 January		
—as previously reported	852,000	777,000
—prior year adjustment	48,000	40,000
—as restated	804,000	737,000
Retained profit for the year	93,000	67,000
At 31 December	897,000	804,000

(2) *Correction of fundamental errors*

This refers to errors which are of such fundamental importance as to affect the true and fair view. Had the errors been recognised at the time they occur the financial statements would have been withdrawn and subsequently amended.

Illustration 3

During 19X7 a breakdown occurred in part of the company's system. The breakdown was undetected at the date of approval of the 19X7 accounts. Had the company been aware of the situation the accounts would have been withdrawn and revised accounts issued. During the preparation of the 19X8 accounts the system breakdown is detected and it becomes apparent that the 19X7 figures were incorrect.

When the 19X8 accounts are prepared, the reserves at the beginning of 19X8 should be restated to adjust for the effects of errors discovered. Comparative figures for 19X7 should also be restated for the effects of the fundamental error.

(g) Terminated activities

(1) Once a decision has been made to discontinue a business segment, a provision will be required in respect of the consequence of decisions taken up to the balance sheet date. The provision will usually be treated as an extraordinary item.

(2) The provision may consist of the following:

    (i) redundancy costs (net of government contributions);
    (ii) costs of retaining key personnel during the run-down period;
    (iii) profits or losses arising from the disposal of assets, including anticipated ongoing costs such as rent, rates, and security;
    (iv) pension costs;
    (v) bad and doubtful debts arising from the decision to close;
    (vi) all debits and credits arising from trading after the commencement of implementation;
    (vii) any losses due to penalty clauses in contracts.

(3) Reorganisation programmes which involve redundancies and a reduction in the level of activities, do not amount to the discontinuance of a business segment and will therefore normally be treated as exceptional rather than extraordinary.

(h) Reserve movements

These may be required or permitted in the following circumstances:

(1) changes in value of investment properties (required by SSAP 19);
(2) certain exchange differences required to be taken direct to reserves by SSAP 20;

(3) immediate write-off against reserves (required by SSAP 22 where the write-off option is selected);
(4) amounts required by law to be charged direct to share premium account:
  (i) preliminary expenses
  (ii) commission or discount on shares or debentures
  (iii) premium on redemption of shares or debentures (if permitted by CA 85)
  (iv) purchase by company of own shares (other than out of proceeds of new issue of shares).

(i) Reasons given for revision of SSAP 6

(1) to achieve greater consistency between different companies of similar transactions;
(2) to give clarification of acceptable treatment of redundancy and reorganisation costs as well as terminated activities;
(3) to clarify the position regarding the treatment of reserve movements (see (j) below);
(4) to consider implications of the Companies Act 1985;
(5) to consider the accounting implications of incorporating fixed asset revaluations into the balance sheet. A particular problem is the determination of profit on the sale of a fixed asset previously carried in the balance sheet at a revaluation. In the end this matter was not dealt with in the revised version of SSAP 6. Fixed asset revaluations are under separate consideration by ASC (see chapter 7).

(j) Disclosure requirements of SSAP 6

SSAP 6 makes it very clear that the following items should be separately disclosed in the profit and loss account and dealt with in the following order:

(1) profit or loss on ordinary activities;
(2) extraordinary profit or loss;
(3) profit or loss for the financial year;
(4) dividends and other appropriations.

Note the following:

(i) Exceptional items—must be taken into account in determining profit on ordinary activities. In some cases it will be necessary to disclose exceptional items separately on the face of the P/L in order that the accounts give a true and fair view. In other cases it will be sufficient to refer to them by way of note.
(ii) Extraordinary items—disclose separately tax on extraordinary items and minority interest in extraordinary items.
(iii) Movement on reserves—need not necessarily follow profit and loss account but P/L should cross refer to where reserves statement can be found.
(iv) Prior year adjustments should be accounted for by:
  (1) restating P/L and B/S figures for previous years
  (2) adjusting opening balance of retained profit.

5.8 ACCOUNTING FOR POST-BALANCE SHEET EVENTS (SSAP 17)

(a) Terminology

(1) Post-balance sheet events are those events, both favourable and unfavourable, which occur between the balance sheet date and the date on which the financial statements are approved by the board of directors.

(2) Adjusting events are post-balance sheet events which provide additional evidence of conditions existing at the balance sheet date. They include events which because of statutory or conventional requirements are reflected in financial statements.

(3) Non-adjusting events are post-balance sheet events which concern conditions which did not exist at the balance sheet date.

(b) Adjusting events

These include two main categories:

(1) Events which provide additional evidence of conditions existing at the balance sheet date e g post-balance sheet proceeds of sale of obsolete and slow-moving stocks would help substantiate year-end stock provisions.

(2) Events which because of statutory or conventional requirements are reflected in financial statements. An example is dividends receivable from associated companies.

The financial effects of adjusting events should be reflected in the financial statements for the year under review.

In addition to the above, SSAP 17 requires adjustment of year-end amounts where a post-balance sheet event indicates that the application of the going concern concept is not appropriate.

(c) Non-adjusting events

The most common types of non-adjusting events are acquisitions or sales of subsidiaries, trading divisions or major investments. Share issues made or announced after the year end are a further possibility.

SSAP 17 also requires disclosure of a material post-balance sheet event where 'it is the reversal or maturity after the year end of a transaction entered into before the year end, the substance of which was primarily to alter the appearance of the company's balance sheet' (i e 'window dressing' transactions).

(d) Further examples

The following extract is taken from the appendix to SSAP 17:

This appendix is for general guidance and does not form part of the statement of standard accounting practice. The examples are merely illustrative and the lists are not exhaustive.

The examples listed distinguish between those normally classified as adjusting events and as non-adjusting events. However, in exceptional circumstances, to accord with the prudence concept, an adverse event which would normally be classified as non-adjusting may need to be reclassified as adjusting. In such circumstances, full disclosure of the adjustment would be required.

Adjusting events

The following are examples of post-balance sheet events which normally should be classified as adjusting events:

(1) FIXED ASSETS. The subsequent determination of the purchase price or of the proceeds of sale of assets purchased or sold before the year end.

(2) PROPERTY. A valuation which provides evidence of a permanent diminution in value.

(3) INVESTMENTS. The receipt of a copy of the financial statements or other information in respect of an unlisted company which provides evidence of a permanent diminution in the value of a long-term investment.

(4) STOCKS AND WORK-IN-PROGRESS

(i)　The receipt of proceeds of sales after the balance sheet date or other evidence concerning the net realisable value of stocks;

(ii)　The receipt of evidence that was the previous estimate of accrued profit on a long-term contract was materially inaccurate.

(5) DEBTORS. The renegotiation of amounts owing by debtors, or the insolvency of a debtor.

(6) DIVIDENDS RECEIVABLE. The declaration of dividends by subsidiaries and associated companies relating to periods prior to the balance sheet date of the holding company.

(7) TAXATION. The receipt of information regarding rates of taxation.

(8) CLAIMS. Amounts received or receivable in respect of insurance claims which were in the course of negotiation at the balance sheet date.

(9) DISCOVERIES. The discovery of errors or frauds which show that the financial statements were incorrect.

Non-adjusting events

The following are examples of post-balance sheets events which normally should be classified as non-adjusting events:

(1) Mergers and acquisitions.

(2) Reconstructions and proposed reconstructions.

(3) Issues of shares and debentures.

(4) Purchases and sales of fixed assets and investments.

(5) Losses of fixed assets or stocks as a result of a catastrophe such as fire or flood.

(6) Opening new trade activities or extending existing trading activities.

(7) Closing a significant part of the trading activities if this was not anticipated at the year end.

(8) Decline in the value of property and investments held as fixed assets, if it can be demonstrated that the decline occurred after the year end.

(9) Changes in rates of foreign exchange.

(10) Government action, such as nationalisation.

(11) Strikes and other labour disputes.

(12) Augmentation of pension benefits.

(e) Disclosure in financial statements

As a general rule, adjusting events will not normally require separate disclosure, unless they fall within the scope of SSAP 6 (for example, abnormal charges for bad debts and write-offs of stock and work in progress).

However, the appendix to SSAP 17 makes a reference to the prudence concept (see (d) above). A possible example, in the present economic climate, could be the closing of a significant part of the trading activities where a final decision was made after the year end but detailed reviews were still taking place up to the end of the year.

In deciding which non-adjusting events warrant disclosure, the guiding principle is to consider matters which are necessary to enable users of financial statements to assess the financial position.

Disclosure for non-adjusting events is required to be given in a note to the accounts (and therefore within the scope of the audit opinion) and includes:

(1) the nature of the event;

(2) an estimate of the financial effect, or a statement that it is not practicable to make such an estimate;

(3) where necessary, an explanation of the taxation implications.

In addition, disclosure is required of the date on which the board of directors formally approve the financial statements.

Finally, the Companies Act 1985 requires particulars of any important post-balance sheet events to be disclosed in the directors' report.

5.9 ACCOUNTING FOR CONTINGENCIES (SSAP 18)

(a) Terminology

A contingency is a condition which exists at the balance sheet date where the outcome will be confirmed only on the occurrence or non-occurrence of one or more uncertain future events. A contingent gain or loss is a gain or loss dependent on a contingency.

(b) Contingent losses

Contingent losses may fall into any one of three categories, depending on the expected outcome:

(1) Those which will be accrued in financial statements. This will apply where it is 'probable that a future event will confirm a loss which can be estimated with reasonable accuracy at the date on which the financial statements are approved by the board of directors'.
(2) Those which are disclosed by way of memorandum note (this will include material contingent losses not falling within (1)).
(3) Those contingent losses where the possibility of the loss is remote, and where no disclosure is required.

(c) Post-balance sheet information

Estimates of the outcome and of financial effect of contingencies should take account of information available up to the date of approval of the financial statements. This may be particularly important, say, in the case of a substantial legal claim against the company.

(d) Contingent gains

Contingent gains should not be accrued. If material, such gains should be disclosed if it is probable that a gain will be realised.

(e) Disclosure in financial statements

Where disclosure is required, the following information should be stated by way of note:

(1) the nature of the contingency;
(2) the uncertainties which are expected to affect the ultimate outcome;
(3) a prudent estimate of the financial effect, made at the date on which the financial statements are approved by the board of directors (or alternatively a statement that it is not practicable to make such an estimate);
(4) where appropriate, possible tax implications should be indicated.

Note: the amount disclosed, above, should be reduced by any amounts accrued and any components where the possibility of loss is remote.

(f) Companies Act 1985 disclosure requirements

The following should be disclosed regarding contingent liabilities:

(1) the amount or estimated amount of the contingent liability;

(2) its legal nature;
(3) whether any valuable security has been provided by the company in connection with that contingent liability and if so, what.

Disclosure is also required of:

(1) contracts for capital expenditure;
(2) pension commitments;
(3) any other commitments for which no provision is made in the accounts.

(g) Typical disclosure items

The most common contingencies, apart from those resulting from SSAP 15, relate to guarantees given by the holding company e g in relation to borrowings from subsidiaries, and associated companies and house purchase schemes.
    Other examples include:

(1) discounted bills of exchange;
(2) partly paid investments in other companies;
(3) law suits or claims pending.

5.10 STOCK EXCHANGE DISCLOSURE REQUIREMENTS

The Stock Exchange requires the annual report and accounts of a listed company to disclose a large number of matters including the following:

(a) A statement by the directors as to the reasons for any significant departures from applicable standard accounting practices.
(b) An explanation, should trading results shown by the current period's accounts differ materially from any published forecast made by the company.
(c) A geographical analysis of net turnover and of contribution to trading results of those trading operations carried on outside the UK and Ireland.
(d) The name of the principal country in which each subsidiary operates.
(e) The following particulars regarding each company in which the group interest exceeds 20% of the equity capital:

(1) the principal country of operation;
(2) particulars of its issued capital and debt securities;
(3) the percentage of each class of debt securities attributable to the company's interest.

(f) A statement at the end of the financial year showing as regards:

(1) bank loans and overdrafts; and
(2) other borrowings of the company/group, the aggregate amounts repayable, analysed:

(i)   in one year or less or on demand;
(ii) between one and two years;
(iii) between two and five years;
(iv) in five years or more.

(g) A statement of the amount of interest capitalised during the year, together with an indication of the amount and treatment of any related tax relief.
(h) A statement showing whether, so far as the directors are aware, the company is a close company for taxation purposes and whether there has been any change in that respect since the end of the financial year.

5.11   SEGMENT ANALYSIS

(a) Terminology

Alternative terms with similar meaning include:

(1) reporting financial information by segments;
(2) reporting diversified activities;
(3) disaggregated information;
(4) analysed reporting.

(b) The need for segmental analysis

In the words of International Accounting Standard 14 (reporting financial information by segment):

> Rates of profitability, opportunities for growth, future prospects and risks to investments may vary greatly among industry and geographical segments. Thus, users of financial statements need segment information to assess the prospects and risks of a diversified enterprise which may not be determinable from the aggregated date. The objective of presenting information by segments is to provide users of financial statements with information on the relative size, profit contribution, and growth trend of the different industries and different geographical areas in which a diversified enterprise operates, to enable them to make more informed judgements about the enterprise as a whole. [IAS 14, para 5.]

IAS 14 deals with the topic in some detail (see chapter 24 for principal requirements) but is not mandatory in the UK. There is no UK standard or exposure draft, although ASC have a current project on segmental reporting.
   Relevant UK regulations are summarised below.

(c) Companies Act 1985 requirements

CA 85 requires notes to accounts to give the following analyses:

(1) analysis of turnover between substantially different classes of business;
(2) analysis of profit or loss before tax between substantially different classes of business;
(3) analysis of turnover between substantially different geographical markets (determined by location of customers).

(d) Stock Exchange requirements

The Stock Exchange requires the annual accounts to provide a geographical analysis of turnover and of contribution to trading results of those trading operations carried on by the company (or group) outside the UK and Eire.

5.12   THE DETERMINATION OF REALISED PROFITS

(a) Background

The term 'realised profits' was introduced into statute comparatively recently by the Companies Act 1985.
   It is important in two separate contexts:

(1) Under the Companies Act 1985, in the determination of a company's distributable profits;
(2) Under the Companies Act 1985, in the context of the prudence concept i e

deciding whether a particular profit is realised and may therefore be included in the profit and loss account.

(b) Definition of realised profits

The Companies Act 1985 refers to such profits as fall to be treated as realised profits in accordance with generally accepted accounting principles at the date the accounts are prepared.

The CCAB have indicated that SSAPs must be considered to be highly persuasive in determining principles generally accepted in determining realised profits.

(c) SSAP—disclosure of accounting policies

SSAP 2 states that revenues and profits are not anticipated but are recognised by inclusion in the profit and loss account only when realised in the form of cash or of other assets (such as debtors) whose cash realisation can be assessed with reasonable certainty.

(d) Post-balance sheet events

The Companies Act 1985 requires all liabilities and losses which have arisen or are likely to arise in respect of the current financial year, or a previous year, to be taken into account. This should include those which have only become apparent between the balance sheet date and the date on which the financial statements are approved by the board of directors.

(e) Departures from the prudence concept

There may be special circumstances where a true and fair view could not be given without the inclusion of unrealised profits in the profit and loss account. The Companies Act 1985 allows the directors to include unrealised profits where there are special reasons for doing so, in which case disclosure is required of the departure from the prudence concept, the reason for it and its effect.

Such situations are likely to be rare. A particular example is the treatment of translation differences on long-term foreign loans (see chapter 18)

(f) Long-term contracts

In their October 1982 technical release (the determination of realised profits and the disclosure of distributable profits in the context of the Companies Act 1948 to 1981), the CCAB referred to the point that there was initially some confusion as to whether profits recognised in advance of completion of long-term contracts could be regarded as 'realised' in the context of the Companies Acts.

However, the CCAB concluded that since the profit recognition concepts of SSAP 9 were based on the concept of reasonable certainty as to eventual outcome, there was no conflict with the statutory accounting principles and the profits could be regarded as realised.

5.13   THE DETERMINATION OF DISTRIBUTABLE PROFITS

(a) Background

The Companies Act 1985 sets out conditions that must be satisfied before a company may make a distribution to its members. There are general rules which apply to all companies plus additional rules which apply only to public companies. Special rules apply to investment companies and insurance companies.

(b) Definition of distribution

A distribution is defined as any distribution in cash or otherwise except:

(1) An issue of fully or partly paid bonus shares;
(2) Redemption of preference shares out of the proceeds of a fresh issue of shares, plus payment of premium on redemption out of the share premium account;
(3) Reduction of share capital;
(4) Distribution of assets in a winding up.

(c) Restriction for all companies (plc and private)

(1) A distribution can only be made out of profits available for the purpose—namely, the aggregate of accumulated realised profits (not previously distributed or capitalised), less accumulated realised losses (so far as not previously written off by a reduction or reorganisation of capital).
(2) A profit is realised, provided it is treated as such under generally accepted accounting principles at the time when the accounts are prepared.

(d) Additional restriction for public companies

(1) A public company may not pay a dividend unless its net assets exceed its share capital plus undistributable reserves. The dividend must not reduce its net assets below this aggregate amount.
(2) Undistributable reserves are defined as:

   (i) share premium account;
   (ii) capital redemption reserve;
   (iii) the excess of accumulated unrealised profits over accumulated unrealised losses not previously written off by a reduction or reorganisation of capital;
   (iv) any other reserve which the company is prevented from distributing, as a result of statute, or by its memorandum or articles of association.

(e) Illustration—4

Balance sheet prior to distribution

	£'000
Ordinary share capital	500
Share premium	250
Revaluation reserve	160
Retained profits	290
	1,200

Whether the company is public or private, its distributable reserves are restricted to £290,000.

(f) The treatment of provisions

(1) Any provision, other than one relating to a diminution in value of a fixed asset appearing on a revaluation of all the fixed assets, or of all the fixed assets other than goodwill, of a company, shall be treated as a realised loss.
   Provisions for stock, debtors and depreciation of fixed assets are treated as realised losses thus reducing amounts available for distribution as dividends.
(2) The 'revaluation of all the fixed assets ...' referred to above need not necessarily be an actual valuation. As regards particular assets, a consideration of their value at a point in time will be regarded as a revaluation for these purposes. However, in this situation the exception will only apply if the

directors are satisfied that the aggregate value of the particular assets is not less than the aggregate amounts at which they are stated in the accounts.

(3) Where valuations are 'considered' rather than actual, and this is important in considering the relevant accounts, a note to the accounts must state:

(i) that the directors have considered the value of certain fixed assets without actually revaluing them; and

(ii) that the directors are satisfied that the aggregate value of those assets is or was not less than the aggregate amount at which they are/were stated in the accounts.

Note

In view of the stringent conditions referred to above, it follows that a loss for diminution in value recognised in the profit and loss account will usually be regarded as a realised loss.

(g) Effect of the above rules

They may be summarised as follows:

Figure 1—determination of whether a revaluation deficit is to be regarded as realised or unrealised

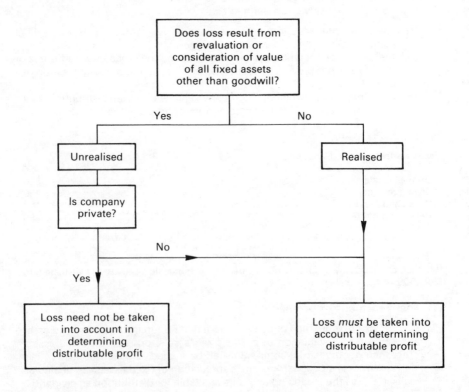

(h) Illustration—5

Balance sheet prior to distribution

	£'000
Ordinary share capital	500
Share premium	250
Revaluation deficits (net)	(120)
Retained profits	290
Net assets	920

Provided that the revaluation deficit results from the 'diminution in value of a fixed asset appearing on a revaluation of all the fixed assets ...' a private company may distribute up to £290,000.

However a public company's distributable profit is restricted to £170,000 (£290,000 less £120,000) since the dividend must not have the effect of reducing its net asset below its share capital plus undistributable reserves (i e a total of 500 + 250 = 750). The maximum reduction is thus (920 – 750) = £170,000.

(i) Specific points

(1) *Fixed asset revaluations incorporated into the balance sheet*

(i) When a fixed asset is revalued and the revaluation is incorporated in the accounts, SSAP 12 requires the depreciation charge to be based on the revalued amount.

(ii) The difference between the depreciation charge based on the revalued amount compared with that which would have applied had the asset not been revalued, may be regarded as a realised profit.

Illustration

The figure for an item of plant and machinery in a company's balance sheet was arrived at as follows:

	£
Historical cost	100,000
Accumulated depreciation (three years at 10%)	30,000
Net book value	70,000

The asset was revalued at £84,000 and the revaluation incorporated into the balance sheet. The surplus on revaluation of £14,000 was taken direct to revaluation reserve.

In subsequent years, the depreciation charge would be £12,000 (£84,000 divided by 7 years) as opposed to the previous £10,000 based on historical cost. For each subsequent year of the asset's remaining life, £2,000 of the revaluation reserve may be regarded as realised and hence distributable.

(2) *Development costs*

Development costs capitalised in accordance with SSAP 13 must in normal circumstances be regarded as a realised loss. The directors may in special circumstances depart from this principle; the special circumstances must be disclosed in the accounts.

It is generally assumed that the special circumstances are equivalent to the stringent conditions required to be satisfied by SSAP 13 in order to justify capitalisation of development costs.

(3) *Statutory current cost accounts*

The Companies Act 1985 permits a company, should it so choose, to adopt current cost accounting as its main accounting convention. This situation is likely to be rare.

Part of the current cost reserve will relate to realised items, such as depreciation adjustment, cost of sales adjustment, monetary working capital adjustment etc which were taken into account over a number of years in determining current cost profit.

The realised part of the current cost reserve is legally distributable under the Companies Act 1985 even though the effect of distributing this amount might be to impair the operating capability of the business.

(j) Investment companies

Companies Act 1985 contains special rules regarding investment companies. These rules are detailed and complex and the notes below are intended to emphasise certain key points.

(1) *Definition*

An investment company is a public company which has given notice to the registrar of companies of its intention to carry on business as an investment company. An investment company must also comply with certain specific requirements including the prohibition by its memorandum or articles of the distribution of *capital* profits.

(2) *Distribution of profits*

Investment companies may base their distributions on two alternative sets of rules (i e choose whichever is more favourable in the circumstances)—either:

(i)   usual PLC rules (as above); or
(ii) a distribution out of accumulated realised revenue profits less *revenue* losses (realised or unrealised). This alternative is subject to the proviso that at the time of the distribution the amount of the company's assets is at least equal to one and a half times the aggregate of its liabilities (clearly no part of the distribution must take the assets below that figure).

(k) Other areas

The effect of elimination of purchased goodwill on the distributable profits of individual companies is dealt with in chapter 7. The treatment of dividends paid out of pre-combination profits is discussed in chapter 16.

5.14   CONCESSIONS FOR SMALLER COMPANIES

(a) Introduction

All companies whether very small or listed on The Stock Exchange, must present their shareholders with the following:

(1) balance sheet;
(2) profit and loss account;
(3) notes;
(4) directors' report.

In addition, SSAP 10 requires companies whose annual turnover exceeds £25,000 to include a statement of source and application of funds.

(b) Smaller companies

The only concessions offered by the Companies Act 1985 are that smaller companies (as defined) may file less information with the Registrar of Companies than larger companies.

Smaller companies fall into two categories, each with a separate set of concessions. These categories are small and medium-sized respectively.

To qualify as small or medium-sized, two conditions must be satisfied:

(1) *Condition 1 — size*

The company must fall within two of the following three size criteria:

	Small	*Medium*
Gross assets	£975,000	£3,900,000
Turnover	£2,000,000	£8,000,000
Average number of employees	50	250

For groups and holding companies, the criteria apply to relevant consolidated totals.

(2) *Condition 2 — Status*

Whatever its size, a company cannot be regarded as small or medium-sized for these purposes if it falls within one of the following categories:

(i) public company;
(ii) banking, insurance or shipping company;
(iii) a member of a group which includes a public company or a banking, insurance or shipping company.

(c) Concessions for small companies

The minimum information which may be filed by a small company is as follows:

(1) A balance sheet in abbreviated form, containing only items designated in the formats by letters or roman numerals;
(2) Notes relating to the following matters:

(i) accounting policies;
(ii) share capital;
(iii) particulars of allotments of shares and debentures;
(iv) particulars of debts, including amounts payable in more than five years and fixed and floating charges;
(v) basis of translation of foreign currency amounts into sterling;
(vi) corresponding figure.

Note that a small company need not file a profit and loss account, a directors' report and information regarding directors' emoluments.

(d) Concessions for medium-sized companies

The concessions are restricted to the following:

(1) The profit and loss account may be presented in abbreviated form:

(i) In format 1, the items of turnover, cost of sales, gross profit and other operating income may be combined into a single figure described as gross profit;
(ii) In format 2, the items turnover, change in stocks of finished goods and work in progress, own work capitalised, other operating income, raw

materials and consumables and other operating charges may be combined into a single figure described as gross profit.

(2) Neither the total turnover, nor its analysis between different business activities and different geographical markets need be disclosed.

(3) Analysis of profit between different business activities is not required.

(e) Special auditors' report

Any small or medium-sized company which files modified accounts (i e accounts which fall short in any respect of those presented to shareholders) must include also a special auditors' report, as well as the appropriate statutory declaration by the directors.

6 MODERN FINANCIAL ACCOUNTING

6.1 INTRODUCTION

Financial accounting deals principally with the accumulation and classification of information for the preparation and analysis of financial statements and reports. Financial accounting is concerned with external reporting to investors, potential investors, creditors and other users of financial statements. By contrast, management accounting is concerned with the role of accounting information in the decision-making processes of management, and the preparation of internal reports.

The scope of financial accounting is summarised in Figure 1. The fact that financial statements are essentially historical records based on historical cost principles inevitably restricts their usefulness. It is important however to recognise that annual reports of companies are widely used by analysts and other users. For example, these reports convey information in special cases such as when a company proposes to make an issue of shares by an offer for sale, or when a company wishes to acquire the business of another company.

The last ten to fifteen years have seen significant developments in the field of financial accounting. Company reports have become both more detailed and more sophisticated. Unfortunately there have been occasions when improvements in information to one user group have been at the expense of clear communication to less sophisticated users. This period has also seen long-running controversies such as the most appropriate method of accounting for price changes and appropriate methods of accounting for business combinations. The pace of development shows little sign of slackening.

The remaining chapters of this book attempt to review the current financial accounting scene, referring to developments in recent years. Much of the book is concerned with the regulatory framework relating to single companies and groups, including the impact of international accounting standards, as well as the analysis of accounts and presentation of reports for special purposes.

Figure 1

External reporting—the scope of financial accounting

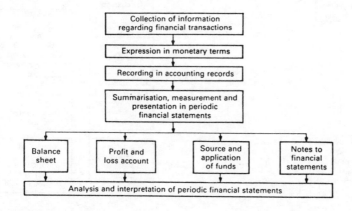

6.2   REGULATIONS AND INFLUENCES ON FINANCIAL REPORTING

UK companies have to comply with a wide range of regulations concerning financial reporting. To start with, all companies, irrespective of size, must comply with the requirements of the Companies Act 1985 as well as those contained in statements of standard accounting practice. Listed companies must also comply with Stock Exchange regulations contained in the Admission of Securities to Listing (Yellow Book), and those listed in the US have Financial Accounting Standards Board requirements to consider.

Apart from these regulations, there are a considerable number of influences on financial reporting (see Figure 2). These are important in practice as several prominent UK companies present far more information than the minimum required. Examples of such information include statistical summaries, ratios over a five-year period and value added statements.

The regulations and influences referred to in Figure 2 are considered under the relevant chapter headings. In particular, statutory regulations were considered in the previous chapter.

Figure 2

External reporting for a listed company

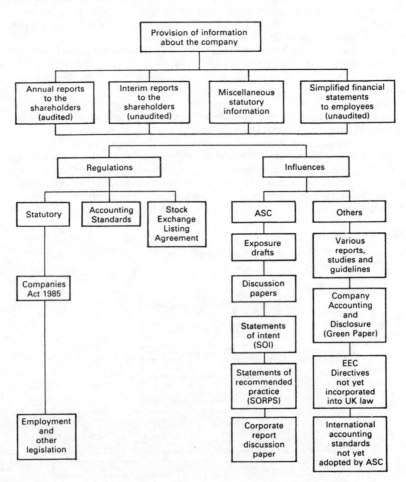

6.3 THE WORK OF THE ACCOUNTING STANDARDS COMMITTEE (ASC)

(a) Background

Accounting standards are prepared by ASC but are issued and enforced by the six members of the Consultative Committee of Accountancy Bodies (ICAEW, ICAS, ICAI, CACA, ICMA and CIPFA). ASC was set up in 1970 with the specific objective of developing definitive standards for financial reporting.

(b) Objectives of ASC

ASC's objects are to define accounting concepts, to narrow differences of financial accounting and reporting treatment, and to codify generally accepted best practice in the public interest. These objects encompass:

(1) fundamentals of financial accounting and the application to financial statements;
(2) definition of terms used;
(3) questions of measurement of reported results and financial position; and
(4) the content and form of financial statements.

(c) Terms of reference of ASC

ASC's terms of reference were set out as follows:

Bearing in mind the intention of the governing bodies to advance accounting standards and to narrow the areas of difference and variety in accounting practice by publishing authoritative statements in the public interest on best accounting practice which will wherever possible be definitive, the Committee shall:

(1) keep under review standards of financial accounting and reporting;
(2) propose to the Councils of the governing bodies statements of standard accounting practice and interpretations of such statements;
(3) publish consultative documents, discussion papers and exposure drafts and submit to the governing bodies non-mandatory guidance notes with the object of maintaining and advancing accounting standards;
(4) consult as appropriate with representatives of finance, commerce, industry and government, and other bodies and persons concerned with financial reporting; and
(5) maintain close links with the International Accounting Standards Committee and the accountancy profession in Europe and throughout the world.

(d) Review of the Standard Setting Process

In 1983, the Accounting Standards Committee published its report on the Review of the Standard Setting Process. Its principal conclusions were as follows:

(1) it was agreed that the standard setting process was in need of review and was capable of improvement;
(2) in future, accounting standards would deal only with matters of major and fundamental importance affecting the generality of companies. Standards would therefore be few in number. Standards would not be restricted to accounts of companies but would apply to all accounts intended to give a true and fair view;
(3) ASC would introduce a new form of consultative document called a statement of intent (SOI). A statement of intent would enable ASC to indicate at an early stage how it intended to deal with particular matters. SOIs have been

issued on deferred tax, accounting for price changes, acquisitions and mergers and goodwill;

(4) interpretations of accounting standards would not be issued. (This policy became clear when ASC was considering the implications for disclosure of long-term contracts of the Companies Act 1985); and

(5) ASC would issue a new category of final pronouncement, a Statement of Recommended Practice (SORP). SORPs would be issued when a need could be identified for a pronouncement on a specific topic, but where that topic did not meet all the requirements for an accounting standard. SORPs are further referred to in chapter 12.

(e) Stages in the identification and development of a standard

The ASC report identified the following stages:

Identification of topics
↓
Planning sub-committee
↓
Research study
↓
Formation of a working party
↓
Consultative documents:
(1) Discussion papers (optional)
(2) Statements of intent (optional)
(3) Exposure drafts (mandatory)
↓
Initial feedback to ASC
↓
The consultation plan/public exposure
↓
Technical drafting and consultation by working party
↓
Involvement of CCAB
↓
Consideration by ASC/publication of ED
↓
Exposure period (normally six months)
↓
Comments and reactions
↓
Finalisation and issue of a standard
↓
Guidance notes, appendices, technical releases
↓
Review and revision of standards

(f) Current accounting standards

Accounting standards in existence at 31 December 1987 included:

(1) Accounting for the results of associated companies.
(2) Disclosure of accounting policies.
(3) Earnings per share.
(4) The accounting treatment of government grants.
(5) Accounting for value added tax.
(6) Extraordinary items and prior year adjustments.

(8) The treatment of taxation under the imputation system in the accounts of companies.
(9) Stocks and work in progress.
(10) Statements of source and application of funds.
(12) Accounting for depreciation.
(13) Accounting for research and development.
(14) Group accounts.
(15) Accounting for deferred taxation.
(17) Accounting for post-balance sheet events.
(18) Accounting for contingencies.
(19) Accounting for investment properties.
(20) Foreign currency translation.
(21) Accounting for leases and hire purchase contracts.
(22) Accounting for goodwill.
(23) Accounting for acquisitions and mergers.

(g) ED 39 Accounting for pension costs
    ED 40 Stocks and long-term contracts
    ED 41 Accounting for research and development

(h) Current statements of recommended practice (SORPs)

SORPI Pension Scheme accounts.
ED 38 Accounting by charities.

6.4 SSAPS AND A TRUE AND FAIR VIEW

(a) Introduction

Towards the end of 1983, ASC obtained a written opinion from Counsel on the meaning of 'true and fair' with particular reference to the role of accounting standards.

It was pointed out in the introduction that the opinion needed to be read in its entirety and that any attempt to summarise the opinion would be misleading.

Subject to this proviso, the points below are extracted from the text of the opinion, together with paragraph references.

(b) The role of accounting standards

(1) An SSAP is a declaration by ASC that, save for exceptional circumstances, accounts which do not comply with the standard will not give a true and fair view (para 2).
(2) The question of whether accounts give a true and fair view in compliance with the Companies Act must be decided by a judge (para 8).
(3) The value of an SSAP to a court which has to decide whether accounts are true and fair is twofold:

   (i) An SSAP represents an important statement of professional opinion which readers may reasonably expect in accounts which are intended to be true and fair;
   (ii) An SSAP creates in readers of accounts an expectation that the accounts will be in conformity with prescribed standards (para 10).

(4) An SSAP has no direct legal effect. However, counsel expects an SSAP to have an indirect effect on the content, which the courts will give to the true and fair concept (para 11).
(5) Counsel sees no conflict between the functions of the ASC in formulating standards which it declares to be essential to true and fair accounts, and the function of the courts in deciding whether the accounts satisfy the law.

6.5   THE INTERNATIONAL ACCOUNTING STANDARDS COMMITTEE (IASC)

(a) Background

IASC was founded in 1973 with the objectives of formulating, publishing and promoting, in the public interest, international standards for financial statements. IASC seeks to improve the quality, reliability and comparability of financial reporting on a worldwide basis. Current international accounting standards (IASs) are listed below, together with their relationship with equivalent UK standards.

The subject of international standards is dealt with in some detail in chapter 24.

(b) Current international standards

The table opposite sets out the current position. The right-hand column indicates, where appropriate, the number of the UK standard which incorporates the international standard.

Items marked (1) indicate topics where there is no corresponding UK and Irish standard. Items marked (2) indicate topics where there is no specific UK SSAP but where compliance with UK law and SSAPs ensures general compliance with the international standard. International standards come into effect when their provisions are incorporated into SSAPs issued by the Councils of the CCAB bodies.

6.6   THE IMPACT OF EEC DIRECTIVES

EEC (European Economic Community) Directives do not become mandatory until implemented by the individual member states of the EEC. For example, the Fourth Directive on Company Accounts was adopted by the Council of Ministers in July 1978. This Directive dealt with the preparation, content and publication of accounts of individual companies. This Directive was eventually implemented by the Companies Act 1985 which is now mandatory for companies other than bank, insurance and shipping companies.

The Seventh Directive on Group Accounts specifies the preparation, content and publication of group accounts. The Directive was adopted by the Council of Ministers in June 1983. Member states have until the end of 1987 to implement the provisions of the Seventh Directive. When enacted the Directive will apply to group financial statements for years beginning on or after 1 January 1990.

However, member states need not apply it to undertakings for financial years commencing before 1990.

There are several other directives which will eventually become applicable in the UK, such as the Eighth Directive on qualification of auditors and a directive on prospectuses. These are not referred to further in this book.

6.7   THE CORPORATE REPORT

(a) Background

The 'Corporate Report' was the title given to a discussion paper published in 1975 by the Accounting Standards Committee. The term 'corporate report' may also be taken to mean the 'comprehensive package of information of all kinds which most completely describes an organisation's economic activity'.

(b) The main issues

The paper deals with three main issues:

	Notes
1 Disclosures of accounting policies	SSAP 2
2 Valuation and presentation of inventories in the context of the historical cost system	SSAP 9
3 Consolidated financial statements	SSAPs 1 & 14
4 Depreciation accounting	SSAP 12
5 Information to be disclosed in financial statements	(2)
7 Statement of changes in financial position	SSAP 10
8 Unusual and prior period items and changes in accounting policies	SSAP 6
9 Accounting for research and development activities	SSAP 13
10 Contingencies and events occurring after the balance sheet date	SSAPs 17 & 18
11 Accounting for construction contracts	SSAP 9
12 Accounting for taxes on income	SSAPs 8 & 15
13 Presentation of current assets and current liabilities	(2)
14 Reporting financial information by segment	(1)
16 Accounting for property, plant and equipment	(2)
17 Accounting for leases	SSAP 21
18 Revenue recognition	(1)
19 Accounting for retirement benefits in the financial statements of employers	(1)
20 Accounting for government grants and disclosure of government assistance	SSAP 4
21 Accounting for the effects of changes in foreign exchange rates	SSAP 20
22 Accounting for business combinations	SSAP 23
23 Capitalisation of borrowing costs	(1)
24 Related party disclosures	(1)

(1) the types of organisation which should be expected to publish regular financial information;
(2) the main users of such information and their particular needs;
(3) the form of report which would best meet those needs.

(c) Types of organisation

Economic entities of significant size or format have a public accountability to provide specified information. In the words of the Corporate Report:

In our view there is an implicit responsibility to report publicly (whether or not required by law or regulation) incumbent on every economic entity whose size or format renders it significant. By economic entity we mean every sort of organisation in modern society, whether a department of central government, a local authority, a co-operative society, an unincorporated firm, a limited company, or a non-profit-seeking organisation, such as a trade or professional association, a trade union or a charity. By significant we mean that the organisation commands human or material resources on such a scale that the results of its activities have significant economic implications for the community as a whole ...

(d) Rights and needs of user groups

Whenever possible, corporate reports should attempt to satisfy the needs of different user groups.

Users of corporate reports are defined as those having a reasonable right to information concerning the reporting entity. Such rights arise from public accountability, irrespective of whether or not the rights are supported by statutory powers to obtain information.

The user groups identified are:

(1) the equity investor group (including existing and potential shareholders);
(2) the loan creditor group (including existing and potential creditors);
(3) the employee group;
(4) the analyst-adviser group;
(5) the business contact group (customers, trade creditors and suppliers);
(6) the government;
(7) the public.

(e) Users and their information needs

The report considers each user group in turn, and discusses in detail their respective information needs. In general terms, corporate reports may be able to contribute to user needs in the following areas:

(1) Evaluating the performance of the entity.
(2) Assessing the effectiveness of the entity in achieving objectives established previously by its management, its members or owners or by society. This includes, but is by no means limited to, compliance with stewardship obligations.
(3) Evaluating managerial performance, efficiency and objectives, including employment, investment and profit distribution plans.
(4) Ascertaining the experience and background of company directors and officials including details of other directorships or official positions.
(5) Assessing the economic stability and vulnerability of the reporting entity.
(6) Assessing the liquidity of the entity, its present or future requirements for additional fixed and working capital, and its ability to raise long and short-term finance.
(7) Assessing the capacity of the entity to make future reallocations of its resources, for either economic or social purposes, or for both.
(8) Estimating the future prospects of the entity, including its capacity to pay dividends, remuneration and other cash outflows and predicting future levels of investment, production and employment.
(9) Assessing the performance, position and prospects of individual establishments and companies within a group.
(10) Evaluating the economic function and performance of the entity in relation to society and the national interest and the social costs and benefits attributable to the entity.
(11) Attesting to compliance with taxation regulations, company law, contractual and other legal obligations and requirements (particularly when independently verified).
(12) Ascertaining the nature of the entity's business and products.
(13) Making economic comparisons, either for the given entity over a period of time or with other entities.
(14) Estimating the value of users' own or other users' present or prospective interests in or claims on the entity.

(15) Ascertaining the ownership and control of the entity.

(f) The objective of corporate reports

The paper states that the fundamental objective of corporate reports is to communicate economic measurements of, and information about, the resources and performance of the reporting entity useful to those having reasonable rights to such information.

To achieve this, corporate reports should have the following characteristics:

Characteristic	General comments
Relevant	Reports should be relevant to the information needs of users.
Understandable	A careful balance must be kept between the need for comprehensive disclosure and the possible danger of confusion through excessive detail. Less sophisticated users may be assisted by the additional presentation of simplified financial statements.
Reliable	The confidence of users will be increased if information in corporate reports is independently verified.
Complete	The information should provide users with a rounded picture of the economic activities of the reporting entity.
Objective	Information should be objective and not biased towards the interest of a particular user group.
Timely	The date of publication of the report should be soon after the end of the period to which the report relates.
Comparable	Users should be able to compare the results of the entity with those of previous periods and with similar entities.

(g) Features of company reports in the early 1970s

Several principal features were identified:

(1) Published financial statements consisted principally of:

    (i) directors' report (strictly, not part of the financial statements);
    (ii) balance sheet;
    (iii) profit and loss account;
    (iv) funds flow statements;
    (v) notes.

(2) The statements were based on historical cost figures. It was noted that some companies periodically updated the balance sheet value of fixed assets. This practice (sometimes referred to as modified historical cost) is now common in the UK.

(3) The statements were concerned almost wholly with items and events which could be financially quantified.

(4) The statements concentrated on quantifying and highlighting distributable profit as one identifiable and absolute account.

(5) The statements were concerned primarily with the financial claims of shareholders and creditors.

(6) Reports were produced in many forms with varying quantities of information such as chairman's report, summarised financial information and statistical information. Apart from areas regulated by the Companies Act, there were few rules regarding presentation.

(7) Reports contained both audited and unaudited information. In some cases, the amount of unaudited information was significant.

(h) Criticisms of conventional reporting

As indicated above, it was felt that reports were principally concerned with providing measurements and information of use to shareholders and creditors. Clearly, this results from the legal framework within which many entities operate. However, it was felt that entities had responsibilities to other user groups and that the range of disclosures of corporate reports should be extended.

Conventional financial reporting information may be criticised on the following grounds:

(1) Profit is highlighted as a 'keynote' figure. This may lead users of statements to believe that maximisation of short-term profit is the sole aim of modern business enterprises when this is not so. This may also cause management to concentrate on short-term results.
(2) Audited profit is often presented as a definitive figure when it is in fact subject to many uncertainties.
(3) The format of financial statements (and in particular, the profit and loss account) implies that proprietors are the dominant interest group. This fails to acknowledge responsibilities to other user groups such as employees.

(i) The need for additional statements

In order to meet some of the above criticisms, it was felt that 'additional information and statements were needed which would assist the understanding of financial statements and reveal more fully how resources had been utilised'.

At the date of publication of the Corporate Report, source and application of funds statements were not mandatory. SSAP 10 became compulsory for accounts periods beginning on or after 1 January 1976. However, the likely effects of SSAP 10 could be predicted.

The Survey of Published Accounts published by the English Institute indicates the increase in the number of companies publishing such statements. The survey covers a total of 300 leading companies each year.

Year of survey	Number of companies publishing source and application of funds statements
1972/73	117
1973/74	153
1975	219
1976	256
1977	289

The Corporate Report recommended the following additional statements:

Name of statement	Objective?
(1) Statement of value added	To show how benefits of the efforts of an enterprise are shared between: (1) employees (2) providers of capital (3) the state (4) reinvestment
(2) Employment report	To show: (1) size and composition of workforce (2) work contribution of employees (3) benefits earned
(3) Statement of money exchanges with government	To show financial relationship between the enterprise and the state
(4) Statement of transactions in foreign currency	To show direct cash dealings of the reporting entity between this country and abroad
(5) Statement of future objectives	To show likely levels of: (1) future profit (2) employment (3) investment levels
(6) Statement of corporate objectives	To show: (1) management policy (2) medium term strategic targets

These statements are considered in further detail in chapter 21.

(j) Profit concepts and bases of measurement

The paper considered several possible bases including:

(1) *Historical cost bases*

   (i)   Pure historical cost.
   (ii) Modified historical cost.
   (iii) Current purchasing power.

(2) *Current value bases*

   (i)   Replacement cost.
   (ii) Net realisable value.
   (iii) Net present value.
   (iv) Value to the firm.

These are considered in detail in chapters 19 and 20.

(k) Objectives of financial statements

These may be summarised as follows:

Statement	Objectives
Income statement (profit and loss account)	Primary: measurement of performance Secondary: measurement of capital maintenance and income distributability
Position statement (balance sheet)	Measurement of resources owned by the entity
Flow of funds statement (source and application of funds statement)	Generation and disposition of funds

The following table summarises the way in which the individual financial statements may assist particular needs of users.

Need of user	Profit and loss account	Balance sheet	Source and application of funds statement
Evaluating performance of reporting entity	√	√	—
Assessing effectiveness of entity in achieving previously established objectives	√	√	√
Evaluating managerial performance, efficiency and objectives	√	√	—
Assessing economic stability and vulnerability of entity	√	√	√
Estimating capacity of entity to pay dividends	√	—	√
Making economic comparisons	√	√	—
Assessing liquidity and solvency of enterprise	—	√	—
Assessing capacity of entity to make future reallocations of resources	—	√	—
Estimating value of present and prospective interests in, or claims on, the entity	√	√	√

(I) Impact on current reporting

The Corporate Report has had some impact on the reporting by larger companies, particularly with regard to presentation of additional statements such as value added statements and employment reports (see chapter 21). However, the enthusiasm of some companies has not been shared by the majority of companies. By contrast, the reporting requirements of the Companies Act 1985 had an immediate impact. So, while the discussion paper has brought many issues into the area of public debate, it will require a new initiative to revive some of its issues.

6.8 FINANCIAL STATEMENTS

Financial statements are defined by ASC as follows:

> ... balance sheets, profit and loss accounts, statements of source and application of funds, notes and other statements, which collectively are intended to give a true and fair view of the financial position and profit or loss.

Financial statements of UK companies are usually prepared on the basis of historical cost. This is taken to mean the monetary amount sacrificed or laid out at the date of acquisition. This basis is used both for asset measurement (e g fixed assets at historical cost less depreciation) and profit measurement (e g depreciation charge and cost of sales).

Several companies incorporate fixed asset valuations into their balance sheets, in which case the depreciation charge in the profit and loss account is based on the revalued amount.

Some companies draw up their financial statements on a current cost basis, but this is rare compared with the use of historical cost or modified historical cost.

6.9 FUNDAMENTAL ACCOUNTING CONCEPTS

SSAP 2 (disclosure of accounting policies) refers to four basic assumptions underlying the periodic financial statements of enterprises. The term used to describe these broad assumptions is fundamental accounting concepts.

The concepts are:

(a) Going concern concept

This assumes that the enterprise will continue in operational existence for the foreseeable future. This means that there is no intention or necessity to either liquidate the entity or to curtail significantly its activities.

(b) Accruals concepts

Revenue is included in accounts when earned rather than when money is received. Costs are included when incurred rather than when paid. Revenues dealt with in the profit and loss account are then matched with associated costs in order to determine profit.

Should the accruals concept conflict with the prudence concept (see below), the prudence concept prevails.

(c) Consistency concept

This assumes consistency of treatment of similar items within a particular accounting period as well as from one period to the next.

(d) Prudence concept

Revenues and profits are not anticipated. They are recognised in the profit and loss account only when realised either in the form of cash or of other assets (e g debtors) whose cash realisation can be determined with reasonable certainty.

Provision should be made for all known liabilities whether the amount of these is known with certainty or is a best estimate in the light of the information available. (Reference should also be made to SSAP 18, Accounting for contingencies.)

If financial statements are not drawn up on the basis of the above assumptions, the facts should be disclosed.

6.10   FURTHER ASSUMPTIONS AND PRINCIPLES

These include:

(a) Entity assumption

This assumes that for accounting measurement purposes, the business is regarded as a separate entity quite apart from its owners or proprietors. A business is regarded as owning the resources (assets) which it uses and as owing the claims (liabilities) against those assets. The assets and liabilities of the business are kept completely separate from those relating to the owners.

(b) Money measurement assumption

This assumes that all assets, liabilities and transactions can be quantified in monetary terms.

(c) Stable standard of measurement assumption

Following on from (b), historical cost accounting assumes that transactions occurring over a period of time can be measured in terms of a single stable measuring unit, £ sterling. The obvious weaknesses of this assumption have led to calls for some form of system of accounting for price changes.

(d) Objectivity principle

This principle requires accounting to be carried out on an objective and factual basis. However, subjective opinions and estimates play an important part in historical cost accounting. Examples of subjectivity include estimated lives of fixed assets and net realisable value of stock items.

(e) Dual aspect principle

Every change in one element of an entity (assets, liabilities, equity) is accompanied by another change of a similar amount, but in an opposite direction. This principle underlies the basis of double-entry book-keeping.

(f) Substance over form

Transactions should be accounted for and presented in accordance with their substance and financial reality and not merely with their legal form. This principle is further discussed below (see section 6.12).

6.11   SSAP 2—DISCLOSURE OF ACCOUNTING POLICIES

This is probably the most important statement of standard accounting practice in that it deals with fundamental assumptions underlying the preparation of financial statements. Various aspects of the standard are dealt with below.

(a) Terminology

Three important terms are referred to:

Fundamental accounting concepts	Broad basic assumptions underlying the periodic financial statements of business enterprises. SSAP 2 names and defines four concepts (see section above); (1) going concern; (2) accruals; (3) consistency; (4) prudence.
Accounting bases	Methods developed for applying fundamental accounting concepts to financial transactions and items e g stock valuation methods, first-in-first-out, average cost.
Accounting policies	Specific accounting bases used by a particular business and regarded as appropriate to the circumstances of the business and suitable for the fair presentation of its results and financial position (see Bass plc accounts, below, p. 164).

(b) Problems in applying fundamental concepts

A particular problem is caused by the fact that the financial effects of certain business transactions are spread over a number of years.
Examples include:

(1) Expenditure on the acquisition of tangible fixed assets: in order to apply the accruals concept, it is necessary to arrive at an estimate of the asset's useful economic life to the present owner. An element of commercial judgement is thus necessary to decide how much to charge as depreciation expense in the current period, and how much to carry forward in the balance sheet as unamortised cost.
(2) Sales of goods subject to warranties or guarantees: what, if anything, should be provided at the balance sheet date for the estimated expenditure likely to be incurred by the company in remedying defective goods?
(3) Long-term contracts: if the contract extends over several years, future events may cause an apparently profitable contract to turn into a loss-making contract.

Other such areas include deferred development expenditure and deferred taxation. All the above situations require consideration of future events of uncertain financial effect. Thus an element of commercial judgement is inevitable.

(c) Problems with the consistency concept

Two particular accounting standards have come in for particular criticism. These are SSAP 22 on Accounting for Goodwill (see chapter 7) and SSAP 23 on Accounting for Acquisitions and Mergers (see chapter 16).

(1) SSAP 22 states that purchased goodwill should normally be eliminated from the accounts immediately on acquisition against reserves. However, the standard offers an alternative treatment—namely to regard goodwill as an intangible fixed asset subject to annual amortisation through the profit and loss account. Not only does the standard offer this choice of policies to a company but also permits a company to treat goodwill relating to different acquisitions in different ways. This is hardly consistent!
(2) Under SSAP 23 a business combination which is capable of satisfying four specified conditions may be accounted for in two quite different ways— merger accounting or acquisition accounting (see chapter 16). Again this is hardly consistent!

(d) Purposes and limitations of accounting bases

The accounting bases available to particular companies should provide:

(1) consistent, fair and (as far as is possible) objective solutions to situations where fundamental concepts are difficult to apply;
(2) an orderly framework within which to report the results and financial position of a business;
(3) limits to particular areas which are subject to the exercise of judgement.

It should be appreciated that:

(1) accounting bases are not intended as a substitute for the exercise of commercial judgement;
(2) generalised rules for the exercise of judgement are difficult (if not impossible) to develop. However, it may be possible to develop pragmatic rules for use in specific circumstances.

(e) Disclosure of accounting policies

In some areas of accounting, there may be more than one acceptable basis, for example, depreciation on a straight-line basis or depreciation on a reducing balance basis. Clear disclosure of accounting policies is essential to fair presentation since the choice of policy could have a significant effect on a company's reported results and position.

Since the issue of SSAP 2 in November 1971, a large number of exposure drafts and standards have been issued. These have had a significant effect in reducing the range of acceptable accounting bases. However, SSAP 2 reminds readers that 'the complexity and diversity of business renders total and rigid uniformity of bases impracticable'.

An illustration of disclosure taken from the accounts of Bass plc is shown in section (g) below.

(f) Standard accounting practice

(1) Any departures from the four fundamental accounting concepts should be fully disclosed. Unless such a disclosure is made, it will be assumed that the four concepts have been followed.
(2) Accounting policies used to deal with material or critical items should be disclosed.

(g) Extract from published accounts

Extract from annual report and accounts of Bass plc for the year ended 30 September 1986:

Accounting policies

The accounting policies are consistent with those adopted previously.

(A) BASIS OF ACCOUNTING

(i) The accounts have been prepared under the historical cost convention except that certain fixed assets are included at valuation.
(ii) The Group accounts deal with the state of affairs and profit of the Company and its subsidiaries, of which the principal are listed on page 43. The results of the United Kingdom trading subsidiaries are for the 52 week period ended 27th September 1986. Where local legislation or practice prevents overseas subsidiaries from complying with the Group's accounting policies, adjustments are made on consolidation to comply with those policies.
(iii) On acquisition of a business, the purchase consideration is allocated

between the underlying assets and liabilities on the basis of a fair value to Bass plc in accordance with its accounting policies. Any difference between the purchase consideration and the value attributed to the assets and liabilities represents discount or premium on acquisition. Any discount is taken to undistributable reserves. Premiums are taken to undistributable reserves (if available) or retained earnings (note 18b) in the year of acquisition.

(iv) The shares in the two subsidiaries which merged to form Bass plc are stated at the nominal value of the shares and unsecured loan stock issued in exchange therefor. Shares in all other subsidiaries are stated at cost less any appropriate provision.

(v) The Group regards those companies in which it owns not less than 20% of the allotted share capital as related companies. These companies are also regarded as associated companies in accordance with SSAP1. However, the Group does not account for its attributable share of profits in these companies as they are not material to the Group's results.

(B) DEFERRED TAXATION

(i) Deferred taxation is provided at projected future rates on taxation liabilities arising from timing differences other than those which are not expected to reverse. Where this policy gives rise to a balance which will be offset against future corporation tax liabilities this balance is carried forward as a debtor.

The contingent liability in respect of timing differences which are not expected to reverse, calculated using the liability method, is set out in note 6.

(ii) No contingent liability is considered to arise either for deferred taxation in respect of industrial buildings allowances as the properties are expected to be used in the business for periods longer than that for which the allowances could be reclaimed on disposal, or for taxation deferred by roll-over relief.

(iii) No account is taken of any taxation which might arise on the subsequent receipt in the United Kingdom of the Group's unremitted overseas earnings.

(C) FIXED ASSETS AND DEPRECIATION

(i) Intangible assets

(a) These comprise betting and bingo licences and are valued annually by the Group's professional staff at their current value to the business. Surpluses arising from such valuations are taken direct to revaluation reserve.

(b) These licenses are not depreciated.

(c) No value is attributed to concessions, patents, other licences, trade-marks and similar rights and assets.

(ii) Tangible assets

(a) Expenditure on additions and improvements to tangible fixed assets is capitalised for major projects on the basis of measured work completed, for other property projects on the basis of orders placed, and for all other expenditure as incurred.

(b) Surpluses arising from time to time from professional valuations of properties are taken direct to revaluation reserve. Valuation surpluses realised on sale are transferred from revaluation reserve to profit and loss account.

(c) Freehold land is not depreciated.

(d) Freehold properties comprising hotels and United Kingdom public houses are maintained, as a matter of company policy, by a programme of repair and refurbishment such that the residual values of these properties taken as a whole are at least equal to their book values. Having regard to this, it is the opinion of the directors that depreciation of any such property as required by the Companies Act 1985 and standard accounting practice would not be material.

(e) Other freehold properties are written off over 50 years, except breweries and maltings which are written off over 25 years, from the later of the date of acquisition or latest valuation.

(f) Leasehold hotels and United Kingdom public houses are amortised over the unexpired term of the lease when less than 100 years.

(g) Other leasehold properties are written off either over the periods as in (e) above or the term of the lease, whichever is the shorter.

(h) Cost of plant, machinery, fixtures, fittings, tools and equipment is spread, by equal annual instalments, over the estimated useful lives of the relevant assets, namely:

	Years
Plant and machinery	5–20
Equipment in retail outlets	8–20
Vehicles	3–10

The life of moveable plant and machinery is pro-rated for double-shift working.

(iii) Investments

Fixed asset investments are stated at cost less any provision for diminution in value.

(D) FOREIGN CURRENCIES

Assets and liabilities in foreign currencies together with the trading results of overseas subsidiaries are translated into sterling at the relevant rates of exchange ruling at the balance sheet date.

Exchange differences whether realised or unrealised:

(i) On overseas net assets are taken to retained earnings. (Note 18b)

(ii) On foreign currency borrowings of the investing company are taken to retained earnings to the extent that these differences match those in (i) above but are included as part of cost of borrowing where these differences are unmatched.

All other exchange differences are dealt with in arriving at the trading profit.

The Company's investment in overseas subsidiaries is translated into sterling at the rate of exchange ruling at the date of acquisition.

(E) GOVERNMENT GRANTS

Grants receivable are taken to a deferred income account and credited to profit over the estimated useful lives of the relevant assets.

(F) LEASES

The costs of operating leases are written off to profit as incurred.

(G) REPAIRS AND MAINTENANCE

Expenditure on repairs and maintenance carried out by Group companies is charged to profit as incurred. Work undertaken by outside contractors is charged to profit on the basis of orders placed.

(H) RESEARCH AND DEVELOPMENT

Expenditure on research and development is charged to profit as incurred.

(I) RETIREMENT AND DEATH BENEFITS

Contributions to group pension schemes are charged to profit as incurred. They are based on consistent percentages of members' pensionable pay as recommended by actuaries.

(J) STOCKS

The basis of valuation is as follows:

(i) Raw materials, bought-in goods, bottles, cases, pallets and consumable stores at the lower of cost and net realisable value.
(ii) Work in progress and finished stocks at the lower of cost, which includes an appropriate element of production overhead costs, and net realisable value.

(K) TURNOVER

Turnover is exclusive of VAT and comprises sales, rents, betting stake-monies and other trading income of the Group.

6.12 SUBSTANCE OVER FORM

The principle of substance over form was introduced in International Accounting Standard number 1 (IAS 1).

IAS 1 refers to three fundamental accounting assumptions—going concern, consistency and accrual. IAS 1 further refers to three considerations that should govern the selection and application by management of appropriate accounting policies—prudence, substance over form and materiality.

Substance over form is defined as follows: transactions and other events should be accounted for and presented in accordance with their substance and financial reality and not merely with their legal form.

Examples of substance over form include:

(a) Goods sold subject to reservation of title: legal title does not pass to the purchaser until the goods have been paid for. Nevertheless accounts are drawn up including the goods in stock with a corresponding creditor, i e in accordance with the commercial substance of the transaction.
(b) Fixed assets acquired under hire purchase contracts. Legal title does not pass until the final instalment is paid. Nevertheless the fixed asset is included in the balance sheet right from the start together with a corresponding creditor. Again this reflects the commercial substance of the transaction.
(c) Finance leases (see chapter 10). A lessee may obtain the use of a fixed asset over its useful economic life by means of a finance lease contract. Although the lessee never actually obtains legal title the lessee has rights and obligations similar to those of an outright purchaser.

    SSAP 21 requires a lessee to bring an asset into the balance sheet together with corresponding obligations. SSAP 21 states:

    > Conceptually, what is capitalised in the lessee's accounts is not the asset itself but his rights in the asset (together with an obligation to pay rentals). However, the definition of a finance lease is such that a lessee's rights are for practical purposes little different from those of an outright purchaser. Hence it is appropriate that lessees should include these assets in their financial statements, but they should describe them as 'leased assets' to distinguish them from owned assets.

(Note that the leased assets are usually included under the overall heading of tangible fixed assets—reflecting the commercial substance of the transaction as opposed to the legal form.)

(d) Further references to substances under form include:

    (1) off-balance sheet finance (see section 6.13(a));

    (2) long-term contract balances under ED 40 (see section 8.4(h)).

6.13 OFF-BALANCE SHEET FINANCE

(a) Introduction

Prior to the issue of SSAP 21, Accounting for leases and hire purchase contracts (see chapter 10), many companies found finance leasing to be a useful way of obtaining the use of fixed assets over their useful lives without being required to bring the related assets and obligations on to the face of the balance sheet. Obligations were effectively kept 'off-balance sheet'.

SSAP 21 has attempted to remove this aspect of off-balance sheet finance. In 1987, however, this subject has been one of the most widely-referred to and controversial topics in financial reporting. The English Institute issued a technical release TR 603 in December 1985 in order to provide guidance to accountants in the face of an ever increasing number of off-balance sheet schemes. It is the intention of the Accounting Standards Committee to issue an exposure draft on the topic. Although it is possible that a future ED may differ in important respects from TR 603 the subject is regarded as sufficiently important to warrant mention below. The notes below, based on TR 603, refer mainly to off-balance sheet finance as opposed to window-dressing.

(b) TR 603—Off-balance sheet finance and window-dressing

TR 603 makes the following key points:

(1) In order for financial statements to give a true and fair view it is necessary for a reader to be provided with sufficient information about a company to assess overall performance, full extent of its liabilities and its exposure to risks. The problem with off-balance sheet finance and window-dressing is that they may result in financial statements failing to present properly the full information required for such an assessment.

(2) Off-balance sheet finance is defined as: the funding or refinancing of a company's operatings in such a way that, under legal requirements and existing accounting conventions, some or all of the finance may not be shown on its balance sheet.

(3) The problem could be tackled by either an accounting solution or a disclosure solution. A disclosure solution would require disclosure of the transactions or arrangements required. An accounting solution could involve the inclusion of assets and liabilities in the balance sheet (see, for example, SSAP 21 on accounting for finance leases in the accounts of lessees).

(4) A view expressed by some accountants is that an accounting solution would be preferable because 'it is a well established principle that there are circumstances in which no amount of additional disclosure can take the place of appropriate accounting'. An accounting solution would 'reflect in the accounts the economic substance of the transaction rather than simply its legal form'. Not everyone would agree with this proposition!

(c) Examples of off-balance sheet finance

(1) *Non-subsidiary dependent company*

A company is set up in such a way that although it is effectively under the control of another company it is not legally a subsidiary and need not therefore be included in group accounts.

Illustration

The equity share capital of company X consists of 500 A shares and 500 B shares. Company P holds all the A shares, company Q holds all the B shares. Each shareholder is entitled to appoint an equal number of directors. P need not regard X as a subsidiary because P neither holds more than 50% of the equity share capital nor does it control the composition of the board of directors (see chapter 13). However, suppose that the articles of the company give those directors appointed by the A shareholders twice as many votes as those directors appointed by the B shareholders.

Company P has effective control of company X without having to regard X as a subsidiary. Assets transferred from P to X need not be included in the consolidated accounts of the P group.

(2) *Sale and purchase of stock*

Stock is sold with the option to buy back. The option is constructed in such a way that it is reasonably certain to be exercised.

Illustration

PQR Ltd sells goods to AB Ltd on 3 March 19X4 for proceeds of £120, banking the cash proceeds and recording a profit of £25 (being proceeds of £120 less cost of goods £95). PQR Ltd has a repurchase obligation to buy back at a future date. PQR Ltd uses the sale proceeds of £120 as a source of finance.

PQR's year end is 31 December 19X4 at which date the goods have not yet been repurchased. The stock and the related repurchase obligation are excluded from PQR's balance sheet.

The goods are repurchased on 1 February 19X5 at a cost of £140 (the £20 difference between the original selling price of £120 and the buy-back price of £140 is effectively a finance charge and is 18% × £120 for 11 months from 3.3.X4 to 1.2.X5). If the goods are subsequently sold by PQR to an independent third party for £180 the recorded profit would be £40 (£180 − £140).

(3) *Consignment stock*

A dealer (e g a garage selling cars) may obtain stock on consignment from a manufacturer. Instead of paying for the goods on normal trade terms it is agreed that the purchase price is payable to the manufacturer either immediately on sale to a third party or after a set period of time. The purchase price will be calculated by reference to the length of time for which the stock has been held. The substance of the transaction is that the manufacturer is effectively financing the trading stocks of the dealer. The advantage of the arrangement from the dealer's point of view is that neither the stock nor the effective loan from the dealer is reflected in the dealer's balance sheet.

6.14 ACCOUNTING CONVENTIONS AND PROFIT MEASUREMENT

Traditionally, financial statements have been based on the historical cost convention. The implications as far as the balance sheet and profit and loss account are concerned are:

(a) In the balance sheet, stock is stated at historical cost (unless it exceeds net realisable value) and fixed assets at historical cost less depreciation (unless fixed asset revaluations are incorporated into the balance sheet).
(b) In the profit and loss account, cost of sales is based on historical cost even

though sales are expressed in current terms. Depreciation charges are based on historical costs of fixed assets possibly acquired several years ago.

A frequently quoted defence of historical cost accounting is that it is essentially factual and objective. However, it should be remembered that subjectivity does play an important role. For example:

(1) Calculation of depreciation of fixed assets requires subjective estimates of useful life and residual value (chapter 7).
(2) Calculation of profits on long-term contracts requires estimation of future costs, contract outcome and so on (chapter 8).
(3) Deferred tax provisions depend for their calculation on estimates of future capital expenditure (chapter 9).

Criticisms of historical cost accounting over the past ten to fifteen years have led to the consideration of modifications to historical cost or to alternative accounting conventions. Central to these considerations have been the concepts of profit measurement and capital maintenance.

The development of accounting thinking on this vitally important subject is covered in chapters 17 and 18. However, weaknesses of historical cost accounting are inevitably referred to in certain of the intervening chapters.

7 ACCOUNTING FOR FIXED ASSETS

7.1 FIXED ASSETS AND DEPRECIATION

(a) Classification of fixed assets

Fixed assets may be classified under three main headings:

(1) tangible fixed assets—land and buildings, plant and machinery, fixtures and equipment;
(2) intangible fixed assets—goodwill, patents, licenses, trademarks, development costs etc;
(3) investments.

Sections 7.1 to 7.4 of this chapter are principally concerned with tangible fixed assets. Sections 7.5 and 7.6 are concerned with intangible fixed assets. Companies Act 1985 requirements regarding fixed asset investments were referred to in chapter 5 (section 5.4c(2)).

(b) SSAP 12—Accounting for depreciation

SSAP 12 was issued in revised form in January 1987. The standard applies to all fixed assets except for investment properties (see section 7.4), goodwill (see section 7.6), development costs (see section 7.5) and fixed asset investments. Note that the standard applies to all intangibles other than goodwill and development costs and so includes patents, licences, trademarks, publishing titles and so on.

(c) Definition of depreciation

Depreciation is defined in SSAP 12 as: the measure of the wearing out, consumption or other reduction in the useful economic life of a fixed asset, whether arising from use, effluxion of time or obsolescence through technology and market changes.

(d) Purpose of depreciation

The primary purpose of depreciation is to allocate a fair proportion of the cost of a fixed asset over the asset's expected useful life.

More specifically, SSAP 12 requires that provision for depreciation of fixed assets with finite useful lives should be made as follows: allocate cost (or revalued amount) less estimated residual value as fairly as possible over the number of years expected to benefit from the use of the asset.

A further aspect referred to by some accountants is replacement of fixed assets at the end of their useful lives. By making a depreciation charge, funds which might otherwise be distributed as dividend are retained within the business. Note, however that the standard does not regard adequacy of funds for asset replacement as a main purpose of providing depreciation. The guidance notes to SSAP 16 (subsequently withdrawn) stated:

> ... As with historical cost, the provision of cash to replace individual assets in the future is a matter for financial management and remains outside the ambit of the accounting system.

The conclusion, therefore, is that depreciation is concerned primarily with cost allocation in accordance with the accruals concept.

(e) Calculating depreciation

The following three factors need to be taken into account:

(1) cost (or valuation when an asset has been revalued in the financial statements);
(2) the nature of the asset and the length of its expected useful life to the business having due regard to the incidence of obsolescence;
(3) estimated residual value.

(f) Cost of valuation of an asset

The carrying amount of a fixed asset may be based on either historical cost or valuation.

(1) Historical cost—where an asset is purchased from an outside supplier, historical cost is an objective figure. Where a company constructs fixed assets for continuing use in the business historical cost includes all those costs incurred in bringing the assets to their present location and conditions and thus includes a proportion of production overheads as well as direct material and labour costs. In some circumstances a proportion of borrowing costs may also be included (see section 7.1 (p)).
(2) Valuation—a company may revalue fixed assets at a subsequent date and substitute a revaluation figure in place of historical cost.

(g) Residual value

SSAP 12 defines this as the realisable value of the asset at the end of its useful economic life based on prices prevailing at the date of acquisition or revaluation, where this has taken place. Realisation costs should be deducted in arriving at the residual value.

(h) Useful life

Useful life may be:

(1) predetermined, as in leaseholds;
(2) directly governed by extraction or consumption (e g mineral deposits);
(3) dependent on the extent of use;
(4) reduced by economic or technological obsolescence (e g specialised machinery manufacturing products for which there is no longer demand).

Useful life refers to useful economic life as far as the present owner is concerned and not the asset's total economic useful life.

Determination of useful life inevitably involves the exercise of judgement by management and should be reviewed annually. Where management considers that an original estimate of useful life needs to be revised, the unamortised cost of the asset should be charged to profit and loss account over the revised remaining useful life.

(i) Depreciation methods

The method selected should be the one most appropriate to the type of asset and its use in the business. The principal methods are set out below:

(1) *Straight-line (fixed instalment) methods*
    Under this method, cost (or valuation) less estimated residual value is allocated over the asset's estimated useful life on a straight-line basis.

Illustration 1

Plant and machinery was acquired on 1.1.19X6 at a cost of £70,000. Estimated useful life and residual value were four years and £5,000 respectively.
Annual depreciation charge

$$=\frac{£70,000-£5,000}{4}=£16,250$$

(2) *Reducing balancing method*
The depreciation charge is calculated by applying a percentage rate to the accounts written down-value of the asset.

In examination questions, the depreciation rate is given. However, the rate may be calculated by applying the following formula:

$R = C(1 - D)^L$
R = residual value
C = cost
D = depreciation rate
L = economic useful life

Applying the formula to the figures in the above illustration:

$£5,000 = £70,000 (1 - D)^4$
$(1 - D)^4 = 0.0714285$
$1 - D = 0.516973$
$D = 0.483027$

		£
Check	Cost at 1.1.19X6	70,000
	Depreciation charge 19X6	
	48.3027% × 70,000	33,812
	Acs WDV at 31.12.X6	36,188
	Depreciation charge 19X7	
	48.3027% × £36,188	17,480
	Acs WDV at 31.12.X7	18,708
	Depreciation charge 19X8	
	48.3027% × £18,708	9,036
	Acs WDV at 31.12.X8	9,672
	Depreciation charge 19X9	
	48.3027% × £9,672	4,672
	Acs WDV at 31.12.X10	5,000

NOTE
At the end of its useful life, the accounts written-down value equals the estimated residual value.

Advantages claimed for the reducing balance method include the following:

(1) the method reflects the more rapid fall in value of particular assets (e g cars) in their earlier years;
(2) the higher charge for depreciation in the early years of an asset's life balances out with lower repair charges. Correspondingly, as an asset becomes old, the lower depreciation charges balance out with higher repair charges.

(3) *Output or usage method*

This method apportions the cost of a fixed asset in relation to the output or usage each year. The method may be useful where the output or usage varies significantly from one year to another.

Illustration 2

A machine which cost £20,000 on 1.1.19X5 has an estimated life of three years. Its total life in machine hours is 2,700 hours, expected to arise as follows:

19X5	1500
19X6	800
19X7	400
	2700

Depreciation charges under this method (ignoring residual values) would be:

£

$19X5 \dfrac{1500}{2700} \times £20,000$ 11,111

$19X6 \dfrac{800}{2700} \times £20,000$ 5,926

$19X7 \dfrac{400}{2700} \times £20,000$ 2,963

20,000

(4) *Annuity or rising charges method*

The capital locked up in the asset is regarded as earning interest; a constant annual charge for depreciation is credited to the asset account, so calculated that during the life of the asset it will write off its cost (less any scrap value) plus the interest earned. The interest earned is debited to the asset account; it is calculated at a fixed rate per cent, but on the reducing balance. Actuarially, the cost of the asset is regarded as providing an annuity during its life, the value of the annuity being the annual charge to depreciation.

This is the most scientific system when investment is not desired outside the business, but may be criticised from the viewpoint that it introduces an uncertain element i e the rate of interest, which is bound to be arbitrarily arrived at, and also that it is not sufficiently conservative in the early years, so that if obsolescence supervenes, the true depreciation will not have been provided; but the latter objection can be met by shortening the estimated life on which the calculations are based. The annuity system is particularly applicable to long leases, where no additions are made to the asset during its life. It is not generally used for plant, since, when additions are made from time to time, these would at once necessitate further calculations.

Illustration 3

A lease costs £6,000 for a term of seven years. Depreciation by the Annuity Method at $6\frac{1}{2}\%$ per annum, calculations being taken to the nearest £, would be:

Workings

(i) *Notional depreciation charge*

The annual amount of depreciation under this system is calculated from actuarial tables compiled for the purpose employing the formula:

$$\frac{i}{1-(1+i)^n} = \text{Periodic rest of annuity whose present value is 1}$$

where i is the annual rate of interest and ^{n} is the number of years of the term.

Consequently, the annual depreciation is:

$$£6,000 \times \frac{6.5/100}{1-(1+6.5/100)^7}$$

$$= 6,000 \times \frac{6.5}{100\,(1-1/1.554)}$$

$$= 6,000 \times 0.1823 = £1,094 \text{ to the nearest £.}$$

(ii) Notional interest credit

	B/F	Notional interest $6\frac{1}{2}\%$	Notional depreciation (working (i))	C/F
19X1	6,000	390	(1,094)	5,296
19X2	5,296	344	(1,094)	4,546
19X3	4,546	295	(1,094)	3,747
19X4	3,747	244	(1,094)	2,897
19X5	2,897	188	(1,094)	1,991
19X6	1,991	129	(1,094)	1,026
19X7	1,026	68	(1,094)	—

(iii) Summary—depreciation charge in profit and loss account

	Total £
19X1	704
19X2	750
19X3	799
19X4	850
19X5	906
19X6	965
19X7	1026
	6000

(5) *Choice of method*

ED 37 issued in March 1985, stated:

> ... management should select the method regarded as most appropriate to the type of asset and its use in the business, so as to allocate depreciation as fairly as possible to the periods expected to benefit from the use of the asset. Although the straight-line method is the simplest to apply it may not always be the most appropriate.

(j) Change in method

A change in method is only allowed if the new method will give a fairer presentation of results and financial position.

Where the depreciation method is changed, the unamortised cost (i e cost less depreciation to date) should be written off over the remaining number of years' useful life.

If the change in method has a material effect on the profit for the year, the effect of the change should be disclosed.

(k) Supplementary depreciation

If a company wishes to provide depreciation in excess of that based on the carrying amount of the asset, the excess should not be charged to profit and loss account. It may, however, be treated as an appropriation of profit and credited to a specified fixed asset replacement reserve.

(l) Permanent diminution in value

There may be situations where the unamortised cost of a fixed asset is unlikely to be recovered in full. This may be due to the fact that the asset has become technologically obsolete.

Alternatively, the permanent diminution in value may be due to a fall in demand for the produce which the machine produces.

Illustration 4

The net book value at 31.12.19X6 of a group of fixed assets was arrived at as follows:

	£
Cost	280,000
Accumulated depreciation (Four years at 10%)	112,000
Net book value at 31.12.19X6	168,000

During 19X7, it has become apparent that the machines will only be used for a further two years, as the goods produced by the machines have suffered a permanent fall in demand.

At 31.12.19X7, an assessment was made of anticipated future net cash inflows expected to be generated. These were as follows:

19X8	30,000
19X9	15,000
	45,000

No further goods will be produced after this date, and the machinery is expected to be worthless on account of its specialised nature.

The effect on the financial statements will be as follows:

Year ended 31.12.X7
Profit and loss account: depreciation charge
(£168,000–£45,000)   £123,000
Balance sheet (net book value)   £45,000

Years ending 31.12.X8 and 19X9
Depreciation charge £22,500 per annum
(assuming straight-line depreciation is appropriate)

If subsequently the reasons for making the provision no longer apply, the provision should be written back to profit and loss account to the extent that it is no longer necessary.

(m) Importance of judgement

Several subjective estimates enter into the calculation of the depreciation charge. For example:

(a) original estimation of the useful life of a fixed asset;
(b) annual review of useful life;
(c) estimate of residual value;
(d) recognition of permanent diminution in value.

(n) Impact of rising prices

The incorporation into the accounts of fixed asset revaluations is covered in section 7.2. The more general problem of accounting for price changes is covered in chapters 19 and 20.

(o) Depreciation of buildings

The requirement to depreciate applies just as much to buildings as to other categories of fixed assets. SSAP 12 points out that buildings have a limited economic life. For example, although the physical life of a building may be extended almost indefinitely, its economic life may be restricted by reference to technological and environmental changes. A building may become technologically obsolete and therefore may need to be replaced by a more modern building.

The fact that the market value of a building exceeds the net book value does not remove the need to record a depreciation charge in the profit and loss account. Only if estimated residual value (measured at current price levels) is expected to equal or exceed existing net book value is no depreciation charge required.

Two points are worth mentioning:

(1) Investment properties, as defined in SSAP 19, should not be depreciated (see section 7.4).
(2) Depreciation is not necessary if failure to depreciate would not have a material effect on the accounts. For example, if a brewery group had a comprehensive and systematic programme to carry out maintenance work on its licensed houses, it might be able to argue that such maintenance expenditure kept estimated residual value very close to existing net book value. Several companies have successfully advanced this argument, particularly those in the licensed and hotel trades. (See 6.11 (g).)

(p) Capitalisation of borrowing costs

In certain circumstances, the interest cost of borrowed funds may be included in the production cost of an asset (e g a fixed asset or long-term contract work in progress).

The necessary conditions and disclosure requirements are set out in the Companies Act 1985.

(1) *Conditions*

(i) The interest must relate to capital borrowed to finance the production (i e to a specific source of finance).
(ii) The interest cost must accrue in respect of the production period.

(2) *Disclosure*

(i) The fact that such interest is capitalised.
(ii) The amount of capitalised interest.

(3) *Illustration of accounting policy note*
Interest costs incurred during the construction period on major fixed asset additions are capitalised and form part of the total asset cost. Depreciation is charged on the total cost including such interest.

(q) Companies Act 1985 requirements

Two particular aspects are worth noting:

(1) The Act requires fixed assets with a limited useful life to be depreciated. The Act does not specify a particular method but requires that the amount of the asset less any estimated residual value should be reduced systematically over its useful life.
(2) Provision should be made for any diminution in value which is considered to be permanent.

(r) Disclosure requirements of SSAP 12

The following should be disclosed in the financial statements for each major class of depreciable asset:

(1) the depreciation methods used;
(2) the useful lives or the depreciation rates used;
(3) total depreciation allocated for the period;
(4) the gross amount of depreciable assets and the related accumulated depreciation.

Other disclosure requirements, where material:

(1) in the event of a change in depreciation method, the effect on profit in the year of change as well as reasons for the change;
(2) in the event of fixed asset revaluations, the effect of the revaluation on the depreciation charge for the year of revaluation.

7.2   REVALUATION OF FIXED ASSETS

(a) Background

UK accounting practice has always permitted companies to incorporate fixed asset revaluations into their balance sheets. This practice, sometimes referred to as 'modified historical cost' is permitted by the Companies Act 1985 under the alternative accounting rules.

(b) Revaluation policy

UK companies may therefore carry assets in the balance sheet at either:

(1) historical cost less accumulated depreciation; or
(2) revaluation less accumulated depreciation since the date of revaluation.

However, companies are unlikely to revalue *all* assets annually (except for investment properties, see section 7.4) and may not extend revaluation to all categories of fixed assets. Companies are therefore given considerable discretion as to how they may apply modified historical cost. Companies are required to disclose in the directors' report significant differences between market values and book values of property assets.

(c) The viewpoint of ASC

The explanatory note to SSAP 12 states:

> It has, however, become increasingly common for enterprises to revalue their fixed assets, in particular freehold and leasehold property, and to incorporate these revalued amounts in their financial statements. This gives useful and relevant information to users of accounts. This statement does not prescribe how frequently assets should be revalued but, where a policy of revaluing assets is adopted, the valuations should be kept up to date.

Note that in August 1986, ASC referred to the starting of a new project on fixed assets and revaluations.

(d) The requirements of SSAP 12

Where assets are revalued, and the revaluation is reflected in the balance sheet, SSAP 12 requires the depreciation charge to be based on the revalued amount.
    In the year of change, disclosure by way of note is required of the breakdown of the new charge between that applicable to historical cost (or historical revaluation) and that applicable to the current change in valuation).

Illustration 5

A company acquired an asset on 1.1.19X2 at a cost of £100,000. The useful life of the asset was estimated as 10 years with a nil residual value at the end of that period. Depreciation is provided on a straight-line basis.

At 31.12.X4, the net book value of the asset is £70,000 (cost £100,000 less accumulated depreciation of £30,000). Suppose the asset is revalued at £84,000 and the remaining useful life still assumed to be seven years.

Revaluation surplus should be credited with £14,000 and the depreciation charge for 19X5 onwards should be £12,000 per annum (i e £84,000 ÷ 7).

Several important points may be made:

(1) The depreciation charge in the profit and loss account should be related to the carrying amount in the balance sheet. Once a revaluation is incorporated in the balance sheet, depreciation charges relating to periods after this date should be based on revalued amount. In particular, no part of the depreciation charge should be set directly against reserves. In the above illustration, profit and loss account should be debited with £12,000. It would not be acceptable to debit £10,000 to profit and loss account and the remaining £2,000 to revaluation reserve (the so-called split depreciation method).

(2) The effect of the revaluation has been to increase the annual depreciation charge by £2,000 (i e £12,000 less £10,000).

(3) Each year (from 19X5 onwards) the company should make a transfer within reserves of £2,000 i e taking £2,000 out of revaluation reserves and into profit and loss reserves as follows:

	Profit and loss account £	Revaluation reserve £
Balance 1.1.X5	X	14,000
Transfer within reserves	2,000	(2,000)
Retained profit 19X5	X	X
Balance 31.12.X5	X	X

Each year £2,000 of the revaluation reserve becomes realised and thus forms part of distributable profit (see chapter 5). At the end of the asset's useful life the part of the revaluation reserve relating to that asset should no longer exist.

(4) Depreciation charged prior to the revaluation should not be written back to profit and loss account except to the extent that it relates to a provision for permanent diminution in value which is subsequently found to be unnecessary, i e £14,000 must be credited to revaluation reserve (as indicated above) and not profit and loss account.

(e) Further illustration

(1) The details

A company owns a freehold building. The building is used by the company for its own operations and is therefore not to be treated as an investment property under SSAP 19.

At 1.1.X2, the relevant balances and the breakdown between land and buildings were:

	£	£
Land		150,000
Buildings:		
Cost	75,000	
Depreciation (8 years at 2%)	12,000	63,000
Net book value		213,000

The building was revalued on the last day of the year for £320,000. The valuer allocated the valuation as follows:

	£
Land	230,000
Buildings	90,000
	320,000

This revaluation was to be incorporated into the balance sheet at 31.12.X2. The remaining useful life of the building was left unchanged at 41 years.

Required: show the effect of the above information on the financial statements for the year.

(2) Working for required figures

(i) Calculation of surplus on revaluation
Since the revaluation takes place on the last day of the year, the depreciation charge for the whole year is based on historical cost i e 2% × £75,000 = £1,500.

For 19X3 and subsequent years, the depreciation charge will be $\frac{£90,000}{41}$ i e £2,195.

The surplus on revaluation may be calculated as follows:

	£
Net book value at 31.12.X2	211,500
(213,000 – 1,500)	
Revaluation figure	320,000
So surplus on revaluation	108,500

Attributable:	
Land (230,000 – 150,000)	80,000
Buildings (90,000 – (63,000 – 1,500))	28,500
	108,500

(ii) Effect on revaluation on depreciation charge of subsequent years

	£
Part of charge applicable to:	
Historical cost	1,500
$\frac{1}{41}$ × £28,500	695
Total charge	2,195

(3) Effect on financial statements

(i) Fixed asset schedule (extract)
Cost or revaluation

	£
Cost at 1.1.X2	225,000
Adjustment on revaluation	95,000
Revaluation at 31.12.X2	320,000

Depreciation	
At 1.1.X2	12,000
Provided during the year	1,500
Adjustment on revaluation (13,500)	(13,500)
At 31.12.X2	–

Net book value	
31.12.X2	320,000
31.12.X1	213,000

(iii) Profit and loss account (extract)
Depreciation charge   1,500

(iii) Revaluation reserve account
Movement on account   108,500

(iv) Comparable historical cost figures (Companies Act 85 disclosure)
Cost   225,000
Depreciation   13,500
                                                                                                     ─────────
                                                                                                       211,500
                                                                                                     ═════════

Additional comments

(1) The Companies Act 1985 requires information to be given regarding details of revaluations which took place during the year (e g name of valuer or qualification, basis of valuation).
(2) The part of the total revaluation reserve attributable to buildings (£28,500) may be amortised over the remaining life of the buildings (41 years) and dealt with each year as a transfer within reserves (as previously discussed).

(f) Sale of revalued assets

Neither SSAP 6 (see chapter 5) nor SSAP 12 deal with the determination of profit on the sale of a fixed asset previously carried in the accounts at a revaluation figure. This particular matter is under review within the context of a separate Accounting Standards Committee project on the operation and implications of fixed asset revaluations.

In the meantime, profit on sale may be determined in one of two ways:

(1) by comparing proceeds of sale with net book value (derived from a previous revaluation) at the date of sale, or
(2) by comparing proceeds of sale with depreciated original cost.

Illustration 6

A company acquired a building in 19X2 at a cost of £120,000. The building was revalued in 19X6 at £250,000. The revaluation was reflected in the accounts and £130,000 credited to revaluation reserve as an unrealised surplus. The building was subsequently sold in 19X8 for proceeds of £400,000. Ignore depreciation.

The profit on sale may be calculated as either:

(1) £400,000 − £250,000, i e £150,000. Assuming the profit on sale is to be regarded as an exceptional item, the profit and loss account would disclose an exceptional profit of £150,000. The amount of £130,000 hitherto included in revaluation reserve would then be transferred by means of a movement within reserves (i e no entry would be made in the actual profit and loss account) to profit and loss reserves.
(2) £400,000 − £120,000 = £280,000. The profit and loss account would disclose an exceptional profit of £280,000. It would be important to state clearly that the profit of £280,000 included an amount of £130,000 previously held in revaluation reserve.

NOTE

In either case, cumulative realised profit (the basis for distributable profits—see chapter 5) would include £280,000. However the two approaches reveal markedly differing reported profits for the year in the profit and loss account and hence differing earnings per share figures.

Until a new accounting standard is issued, either approach is acceptable provided the accounting policy is clearly stated and provided that, in the case of method 2, the company states clearly how much of the reported profit on sale was an amount held previously in revaluation reserve.

(g) Revaluation deficits

This again is a topic covered neither by SSAP 6 nor SSAP 12 but is part of the ASC's fixed asset revaluation project.

ED 36 on extraordinary items and prior year adjustments, now withdrawn, stated:

> deficits on the revaluation of fixed assets should be debited to the profit and loss account for the year to the extent that they exceed any surplus held in the reserves and identified as relating to previous revaluations of the same assets.

The treatment of revaluation deficits is far from clear. One view is that it is necessary to consider the position for each individual asset and not to consider a class of assets (the portfolio approach). The position will need to be clarified in a future accounting standard.

(h) The desirability of modified historical cost (MHC)

An advantage claimed for MHC is that the inclusion in the balance sheet of up-to-date property values helps to overcome a major limitation of historical cost accounts during a period of rising prices.

However, the practice of MHC creates several problems including:

(1) Lack of comparability between companies as regards revaluation policies. Some companies may extend MHC to several classes of fixed assets while others restrict revaluation to particular asset classes such as property assets. Some companies may state all their fixed assets at historical cost less depreciation. Frequency of revaluation is also likely to differ as between companies.

(2) Two companies may be identical in all respects and experience the same transactions and cash flows. Because one company adopts MHC and the other does not, they could report markedly differing profit figures because of different figures for depreciation charges and profit on sale of assets. Earnings per share could also look quite different. Would company analysts be able to allow for this and come to the correct conclusion that both companies had performed identically? There is evidence to show that this is a particular problem area. Difficulties caused by MHC are now becoming apparent. The ASC project will hopefully provide the opportunity for a critical review of the practice of MHC.

7.3   ACCOUNTING FOR GOVERNMENT GRANTS (SSAP 4)

(a) Revenue-based grants

Such grants should be credited to the profit and loss account of the period in which the related expenditure is incurred. Where a grant has not been received at the balance sheet date, it is acceptable to bring in as a debtor a reasonable estimate of the amount expected to be received provided it is clear beyond doubt that the grant will be received.

(b) Capital-based grants

Several methods are possible, but only methods 1 and 2 are permitted by SSAP 4.

(1) *Method 1 — credit grant to a deferred credit account*

This method, permitted by SSAP 4, shows the deferred credit as a separate item in the balance sheet. The deferred credit is credited to profit and loss account over the number of years corresponding to the related asset's useful life. This method has several advantages:

(i) It follows the accruals concept.
(ii) It treats fixed assets acquired at different times and in different locations in a comparable and consistent way.
(iii) The gross cost of the fixed asset is kept intact. This figure is useful for management purposes.

(2) *Method 2—credit grant to cost of fixed asset*

Under this method, depreciation charge is calculated on net cost. However, the overall effect on profit and loss account is the same as for method 1.

This method, also acceptable under SSAP 4, follows the accruals concept. However, it does not have the advantages (ii) and (iii) possessed by method 1.

(3) *Method 3—credit grant to profit and loss account in the year of receipt of grant*

This method is not acceptable. It fails to follow the accruals concept. The grant and the related fixed asset are not treated consistently.

7.4 ACCOUNTING FOR INVESTMENT PROPERTIES (SSAP 19)

(a) Background

The general principle established by SSAP 12, and confirmed by the Companies Act 1985, is that fixed assets with a restricted useful life should be subject to a depreciation charge.

The majority of fixed assets are used by the company for its own use in its business operations. However, certain types of property assets, referred to as investment properties, are held for their investment potential. Such properties have not usually been depreciated and have been excluded from the requirements of SSAP 12.

The definition and accounting treatment of investment properties is covered by SSAP 19.

(b) Definition

An investment property:

(1) *is* an interest in land and/or buildings in respect of which construction work and development work has been completed *and* which is held for its investment potential. It must be shown that the disposal of such a property would not materially affect any manufacturing or trading operations of the enterprise; and
(2) does *not* include:

    (i) property owned and occupied by the company for its own purposes;
    (ii) property let to, and occupied by, another group company. (*Note:* this does not exclude property let to an associated company provided that rental income is determined on an arms' length basis.)

(c) Accounting treatment

The main features are as follows:

(1) A current value accounting system which reflects the fact that the main interest is in the current values of properties and changes therein.
(2) Investment properties should not be subject to periodic depreciation charges.

There is an important exception to this. Investment properties held on leases with less than 20 years to run at the balance sheet date should be depreciated. This is to avoid a situation which might otherwise occur whereby a company purchased a short lease, charged the amortisation direct to reserves (Investment Revaluation Reserve) but credited any rentals received on the letting to profit and loss account.

(3) Investment properties (including those held on leases with less than 20 years to run) should be included in the balance sheet at their open market value.

(4) Changes in valuation from one balance sheet date to the next should be credited or debited to investment revaluation reserve (IRR). If the total balance on IRR is insufficient to cover an overall deficit on all investment properties, the excess should be charged to profit and loss account.

(d) Disclosure

The following should be disclosed in the financial statements:

(1) names of valuers or particulars of their qualifications;
(2) basis of valuation;
(3) whether valuations have been made by employees or officers;
(4) prominent disclosure of investment properties, IRR and movements thereon;
(5) historical cost information relating to revalued assets.

(e) Companies Act 1985 implications

Under the Act, fixed assets with a limited useful economic life should be subject to periodic depreciation charges.

However, the Act also has a true and fair view requirement which overrides specific requirements. Should this apply (as it does with SSAP 19), a note to the accounts should give 'particulars of that departure, the reasons for it, and its effect'. ASC give guidance on this in the statement accompanying SSAP 19.

The following is an example of a note to the accounts which would be acceptable:

INVESTMENT PROPERTIES
In accordance with SSAP 19, (i) investment properties are revalued annually and the aggregate surplus or deficit is transferred to a revaluation reserve, and (ii) no depreciation or amortisation is provided in respect of freehold investment properties and leasehold investment properties with over 20 years to run. The directors consider that this accounting policy results in the accounts giving a true and fair view. Depreciation or amortisation is only one of many factors reflected in the annual valuation and the amount which might otherwise have been shown cannot be separately identified or quantified.

Accordingly, where the above note is included, it will not be necessary for the accounts to show the effects of depreciation or amortisation, even on an arbitrary basis.

7.5   ACCOUNTING FOR RESEARCH AND DEVELOPMENT EXPENDITURE (SSAP 13)

(a) Background

The accounting treatment of research and development expenditure illustrates possible conflict between the accruals and prudence concept.

On the one hand, R + D expenditure in the current period may lead to higher revenues (or lower costs) in subsequent periods than would otherwise have been the case.

On the other hand, there are considerable uncertainties regarding the amount of benefits (let alone whether such benefits will actually materialise) and the timing of benefits.

A general principle has been established which effectively requires expenditure to be written off as it arises unless its relationship to revenue of a future period can be established with reasonable certainty.

(b) Definitions

Pure research	Original investigation undertaken in order to gain new scientific or technical knowledge and understanding. Not primarily directed towards any specific practical aim or application.
Applied research	Original investigation undertaken in order to gain new scientific or technical knowledge and directed towards a specific practical aim or objective.
Development	Use of scientific or technical knowledge in order to produce new or substantially improved materials, devices, products, processes, systems or services — *prior to the commencement of commercial production.*

(c) Accounting treatment—pure and applied research expenditure

This expenditure should be written off as incurred since any possible future benefits are difficult to assess.

(d) Accounting treatment—development expenditure

Development expenditure *may* (*not* must) be capitalised as an intangible asset and amortised over a period of time if *all* of the following conditions can be satisfied:

(1) There is a clearly defined project.
(2) The related expenditure is separately identifiable.
(3) The outcome of such a project has been assessed with reasonable certainty as to:

    (i) its technical feasibility; and
    (ii) its ultimate commercial viability considered in the light of factors such as likely market conditions (including competing products), public opinion, consumer and environmental legislation.

(4) If further development costs are to be incurred on the same project the aggregate of such costs together with related production, selling and administration costs are reasonably expected to be more than covered by related future revenues.
(5) Adequate resources exist, or are reasonably expected to be available, to enable the project to be completed and to provide any consequential increases in working capital.

The basic principle is that development expenditure may be deferred to the extent that its recovery can reasonably be regarded as assured. It is also important to carry out an annual balance sheet date review of unamortised expenditure to ensure that the conditions referred to above are still capable of being satisfied. Irrecoverable expenditure should be written off immediately. Finally, consistency of accounting treatment should be paramount.

(e) Capitalised development costs—basis of amortisation

Amortisation should start in the period in which commercial production of the product or process commences.

Development costs should be allocated over accounting periods by reference to:

(1) the sale or use of the product or process; *or*
(2) the period over which the product or process is expected to be sold or used.

(f) Further considerations

(1) The cost of fixed assets used for R + D purposes should be capitalised and depreciated.
(2) Market research expenditure may be treated in a similar way to R + D expenditure.
(3) Expenditure in locating and exploiting mineral deposits does not come within the scope of SSAP 13.
(4) Where companies enter into a firm contract to carry out development work on behalf of third parties, or to develop and manufacture at an agreed price calculated to reimburse development expenditure, such expenditure should be included in work in progress.

(g) Disclosure requirements

The disclosure requirements of SSAP 13 are that:

(1) movements on deferred development expenditure and the amount carried forward at the beginning and end of the period should be disclosed;
(2) deferred development expenditure should be separately disclosed and should not be included in current assets; and
(3) the accounting policy followed should be clearly explained.

(h) Companies Act 1985 implications

(1) Development costs may be capitalised in special circumstances (presumably those specified in SSAP 13). Disclosure is required of:

    (i) the period over which the costs are to be written off;
    (ii) the reasons for capitalising the development costs.

(2) Costs of research may not be capitalised under any circumstances.

(i) Review of SSAP 13

SSAP 13 is currently under review by ASC. An exposure draft (ED 41) was issued in June 1987.

The exposure draft gives further guidance on the type of activities that could be included under the heading 'research and development'. If a revised standard was based on the proposals of the ED it is unlikely that it would result in a different profit figure compared with the existing SSAP 13.

However, ED 41 proposes disclosure of expenditure on research and development and this goes further than the present SSAP 13.

7.6 ACCOUNTING FOR GOODWILL (SSAP 22)

(a) Background

The Accounting Standards Committee set up a working party in 1974. The members of the working party were unable to agree on a recommended approach and so the result was two sub-committees issuing contrasting recommendations.

The EEC Fourth Directive and the consequent Companies Bill 1981, and Companies Acts 1981 and 1985 re-activated the search to find an approach acceptable to a majority of accountants. ASC published a discussion paper in 1980, ED 30 in October 1982 and SSAP 22 in December 1984.

(b) Factors contributing to goodwill

An established business may possess advantages such as the following:

(1) superior management team;
(2) effective advertising;
(3) market dominance;
(4) established list of customers;
(5) experienced work-force;
(6) good relations with suppliers;
(7) reputation of products;
(8) strategic location, and so on.

(c) Definitions

Goodwill is defined by SSAP 22 as the difference between the value of a business as a whole and the aggregate of the fair values of its separable net assets.

Fair value is the amount for which an asset or liability could be exchanged in an arms' length transaction. Separable net assets are essentially those assets which can be sold or disposed of separately from the rest of the business.

(d) Classification of goodwill

Possible types of goodwill may be illustrated diagrammatically as follows:

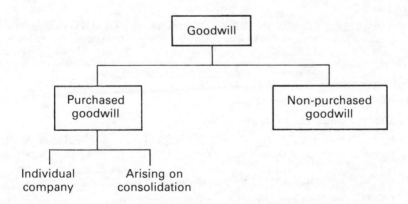

Non-purchased goodwill is sometimes referred to as inherent goodwill or internally generated goodwill.

(e) Special characteristics of goodwill

Several features distinguish goodwill from other assets, including:

(1) goodwill cannot be sold as a separate asset apart from the rest of the business;
(2) the value of goodwill may fluctuate from day to day;
(3) the value and existence of goodwill are subjective;
(4) the value of goodwill has no reliable relationship to costs which may have been incurred in this creation.

(f) Measurement problems

(1) *Purchased goodwill*

Purchased goodwill results from a definitive market transaction. Consequently, it is capable of objective and consistent appraisal. However, the value of goodwill reflects the valuation at the valuation date only. As mentioned above, the value of goodwill may subsequently fluctuate.

(2) *Non-purchased goodwill*

This presents considerable valuation problems. Such goodwill does not result from a definitive market transaction and cannot be appraised objectively and consistently. This is one important reason why non-purchased goodwill is not recognised in financial statements of companies.

(g) Measurement of purchased goodwill

Goodwill is defined as the difference between:

(1) the fair value of a business as a whole, and
(2) the aggregate of the fair values of its separable net assets. Thus it is important to consider fair values of property assets. In addition the fair value of intangibles other than goodwill (such as patents, licenses and trademarks), should be taken account of even if they do not appear in the balance sheet of the purchased company.

A final point is that in some cases the purchase price for a business may allow for anticipated future losses or reorganisation costs. It may be necessary to set up a provision.

Illustration 7

A Ltd paid £230,000 to acquire the business of B Ltd. The fair value of B Ltd's assets (on a going concern basis) amounted to £270,000. However, the purchase price reflected the fact that A Ltd had allowed £80,000 for anticipated losses and reorganisation costs. In this case A Ltd should set up a provision in its balance sheet amounting to £80,000 and record purchased goodwill at £40,000 (i e £230,000 − £270,000 + £80,000).

(h) Main requirements of SSAP 22

The principal requirements are as follows:

(1) Non-purchased goodwill should not be recognised in financial statements.
(2) Purchased goodwill should not be carried in the balance sheet as a permanent item.
(3) Purchased goodwill should be treated in one of the following ways:

 (i) The preferred method is that goodwill should be eliminated on acquisition by immediate write-off against reserves, without any entry in the profit and loss account.
 (ii) A permitted alternatives to treat purchased goodwill as an intangible fixed asset and to amortise it through the profit and loss account over its useful economic life.

SSAP 22 permits different methods to be used for different acquisitions.

(i) Immediate write-off against reserves

The standard does not specify which particular reserves may be used. The following is a guide to what may be regarded as acceptable:

(1) profit and loss reserves;
(2) capital reserve arising on consolidation;
(3) merger reserve under CA 85, s. 131 (see chapter 16).

Goodwill should not be written off against revaluation or share premium account (unless the permission of the court is obtained).

(j) SSAP 22 and the amortisation method

(1) *Balance sheet*

(i) Goodwill should be classified as an intangible fixed asset.
(ii) Goodwill should not be revalued upwards.
(iii) Goodwill should be reduced for any permanent diminution in value.

(2) *Profit and loss account*

The annual amortisation charge should be taken into account in arriving at the profit on ordinary activities before tax.

(3) *Amortisation basis*

Under this method, goodwill should be amortised in a systematic basis over the useful life of the goodwill. No maximum period is specified.

The useful life should be estimated at the time of acquisition and should take account of:

(i) expected changes in products, markets or technology;
(ii) expected period of future service of certain employees;
(iii) expected future demand, competition or other economic factors which may affect current advantages.

Guidance is given in appendix 1 of SSAP 22. Note that useful life may be subsequently shortened but should not be lengthened.

(k) Negative goodwill

Any excess of the aggregate of the fair values of the separable net assets acquired over the fair value of the consideration given should be credited direct to reserves.

SSAP 22 points out that the amounts allocated to the relevant separable net asset will need to be reviewed particularly carefully to ensure that fair values attributed to them are not overstated.

(I) Arguments for and against the two main approaches

	Method	Arguments for	Arguments against
(1)	Immediate write off direct to reserves.	(1) Goodwill is not like any other asset—it cannot be realised separately and to show it in the balance sheet is of little value to users of accounts. (2) To exclude goodwill from the balance sheet is to treat purchased and non-purchased goodwill in a consistent way. (3) Permitted by Companies Act 1985. (4) This method is more widely used than any other by large companies.	(1) If a purchaser paid valuable consider-ation for the good-will, it is difficult to dispute that it is an asset. (2) Inconsistent treat-ment in the P/L between purchased goodwill (no effect) and non-purchased goodwill (where expenditures are charges to P/L).
(2)	Intangible fixed assets—with amortisation.	(1) Goodwill is an asset on which capital has beeen expended in exchange for a number of years future earnings — this cost should be allocated to the periods expected to benefit (accruals concept). (2) Approach of EEC Fourth Directive and permitted by Companies Act 1985. (3) Recognises that purchased goodwill is eventually replaced by non-purchased goodwill.	(1) Possible double-charge to P/L —amortisation of purchased goodwill —expenditures incurred in building up non-purchased goodwill. (2) Economic useful life is difficult to determine — amortisation period is subjective.

(m) Other approaches to accounting for goodwill

These include:

(1) Intangible fixed asset with no amortisation—it is often argued that purchased goodwill does not fall in value as it is maintained by the on-going operations of the business. Against this it is argued that the value of purchased goodwill diminishes over time and is replaced by internally generated goodwill. Internally generated goodwill is never recognised in financial statements. This method is not permitted by SSAP 22 or Companies Act 1985.
(2) Permanent deduction from shareholders' funds (the dangling debit)—this method is prohibited by Companies Act 1985 as it involves offsetting assets against shareholders' funds. The goodwill is carried forward indefinitely in successive balance sheets.
(3) Negative goodwill write-off reserve—a reserve is created with an initial value of zero and goodwill is written off against it. This method is regarded by many accountants as artificial but it is not illegal.

Illustration 8

Profit of Appleton Ltd for 19X8 is £200. Balance brought forward is £600 so carried forward is £800. Revaluation reserve is £350 and share capital is £500.

Purchased goodwill arising during the year is £100. Useful life is regarded as 10 years.

The effect of the various methods on reported profits and balance sheets may be summarised as follows:

P/L	Amortisation through profit and loss account	Fixed asset without amortisation	Write off against reserves	Dangling debit	Negative goodwill write-off reserve
	£	£	£	£	£
Reported profit	190	200	200	200	200
Balance b/f	600	600	600	600	600
Balance c/f	790	800	800	800	800

B/S EXTRACTS					
Intangible fixed assets					
Goodwill	90	100	—	—	—
Capital and reserves					
Share capital	500	500	500	500	500
Profit and loss	790	800	700	800	800
Goodwill write off reserve	—	—	—	—	(100)
Revaluation reserve	350	350	350	350	350
	1,640	1,650	1,550	1,650	1,550
Goodwill	—	—	—	(100)	—
	1,640	1,650	1,550	1,550	1,550

The distinction between the dangling debit and the goodwill write-off reserve is a very fine one!

(n) Disclosure requirements

SSAP 22 requires disclosure of:

(1) accounting policy;
(2) for each material acquisition during the year, the amount of the goodwill;
(3) where the amortisation method is selected:

(i)   classification as an intangible fixed asset;
(ii) movement on goodwill account during the year (cost, accumulated amortisation, net book value etc);
(iii) amortisation period for each major acquisition.

(o) Companies Act 1985 implications

(1) Goodwill may only be treated as an intangible fixed asset if the goodwill was acquired for valuable consideration.
(2) As regards goodwill in the accounts of an individual company, it may only be treated as an asset if it is systematically written off over a period not exceeding its useful economic life. In this event, disclosure is required of:

(i)   the write-off period;
(ii) the reason for choosing that period.

This restriction does not apply to consolidation goodwill as this is covered by the EEC Seventh Directive on group accounts.
(3) The dangling debit treatment is effectively outlawed, but the Companies Act 1985 does not appear to prohibit immediate write-off of goodwill against reserves (the goodwill would have to be written off as it arose so that no asset ever appeared in the balance sheet).
(4) Any asset figure would require to be written down in the event of permanent diminution in value.

(p) Effect on distributable profits

The concept of distributable profits can only be related to individual companies. The accounting treatment of goodwill arising on consolidation has no effect on the distributable profits of individual companies.

Purchased goodwill in the accounts of an individual company has a limited useful economic life. As regards the Companies Act 1985 the elimination of this goodwill must ultimately constitute a realised loss.

The appendix to SSAP 22 suggests that the calculation of distributable profits should reflect the concept of amortisation of goodwill over a number of years. Where a company adopts an amortisation policy the profit and loss account balance for the year automatically achieves this (see the figure of £790 in the example above).

Where, however, goodwill is written off against reserves in the year of acquisition, the profit and loss account in the balance sheet will differ from that which would result from the use of the amortisation method. Despite this the distributable profits should be the same irrespective of the different accounting treatments of goodwill.

(q) Criticisms of SSAP 22

As indicated in section 7.6(a) accounting for goodwill has proved to be a major problem area for ASC.

SSAP 22 indicates a clear preference for the immediate write-off against reserves method. Nevertheless the standard is open to criticism in permitting two radically different approaches to accounting for goodwill. Furthermore, while companies are required to follow the consistency concept set out in SSAP 2 they are permitted to use different accounting treatments for the goodwill arising on purchase at different times in the year.

8 STOCKS AND WORK-IN-PROGRESS

8.1 BACKGROUND

(a) Principal objectives of SSAP 9

SSAP 9 (stocks and work-in-progress) was issued in 1975. Its main objectives were:

(1) to define practices of stock valuation;
(2) to narrow the differences and variations as between different companies;
(3) to ensure adequate disclosure in financial statements.

To a large extent, the standard has succeeded in achieving these aims. Aspects (2) and (3) are also covered by the Companies Act 1985.

(b) Stock categories

SSAP 9 stock categories may be illustrated diagrammatically as follows:

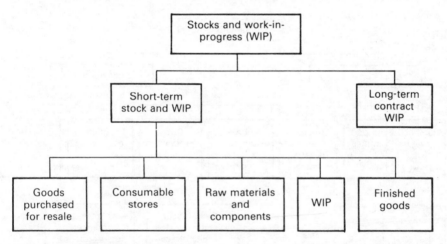

Section 8.2 of this chapter is concerned principally with short-term stocks while 8.3 deals with long-term contract work-in-progress.
   The Companies Act 1985 balance sheet formats refer to:

(1) raw materials and consumables;
(2) work-in-progress;
(3) finished goods and goods for resale;

but do not refer specifically to long-term WIP.

8.2 SHORT-TERM STOCKS AND WORK-IN-PROGRESS

(a) Basic concepts

The fundamental accounting concepts of SSAP 2 apply to stock valuation as follows:

(1) Going concern—the stock figure in the balance sheet implicitly assumes that the business will continue in operational existence in the foreseeable future, and that stock will be used or realised in an orderly manner in the operations of the business.

(2) Accruals—cost of sales (based as far as possible on actual costs incurred) are matched against sales revenues of the year in which the revenue arises, in order to determine business income.

(3) Prudence—stock should be stated in the balance sheet at net realisable value (NRV) in those specific cases where NRV is expected to be less than historical cost.

(4) Consistency—stock valuation bases should be consistently applied as between different stock categories and from one accounting period to the next.

The basis of stock valuation under both SSAP 9 and the Companies Act 1985 is that individual stock items (or groups of similar items) should be valued for accounts purposes at the lower of cost and net realisable value.

(b) Elements of cost

The overriding principle is that costs to be included in the stock valuation should relate to expenditure which has been incurred in the normal course of business bringing the product or service to its present location and condition.

These costs will include both purchase costs and conversion costs. Relevant cost elements are illustrated below:

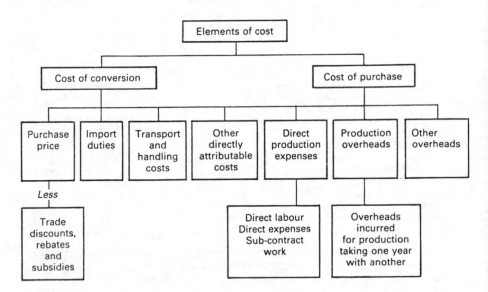

(c) Net realisable value (NRV)

NRV is defined as actual or estimated selling price, net of any trade discount and after deducting any further costs expected to be incurred in completing, marketing, selling or distributing the product. Problems in determining NRV are discussed below in (e).

(d) Cost flow assumptions

In a perfect world, when an item is sold the actual purchase or production costs of that item should be matched against sales in order to determine profit. This might be feasible for a garage selling cars but it is hardly practicable for a manufacturer of Widgets!

In the frequent situations where it is not practicable to relate actual expenditure incurred to specific stock items, an approximate method must be used. However, the standard requires management to ensure that whatever method is chosen provides the fairest practicable approximation to actual costs incurred in bringing the product to its present location and condition.

Possible approaches are discussed below and their acceptability or otherwise under SSAP 9 and the Companies Act 1985 referred to.

(1) First-in-first-out (FIFO)

Under FIFO, cost of stocks and work-in-progress is calculated on the basis that the quantities in closing stock represent the latest purchases or production.

Illustration

A trader's purchases and sales for the six months ended 30 June 19X8 were as follows:

		Purchases			Sales		
19X8	Q	P	T	Q	P	T	Stock level
		£	£		£	£	(quantity)
January	20	10	200	16	12	192	4
February	15	11	165	17	13	221	2
March	30	12	360	25	14	350	7
April	18	13	234	20	15	300	5
May	20	14	280	17	16	272	8
June	25	15	375	22	17	374	11
	128		1,614	117		1,709	

KEY
Q = Quantity (units)
P = Price per unit
T = Total (P × Q)

Closing stock calculation

Under FIFO, the closing stock of 11 units is deemed to result from the most recent purchases. As the June purchases were 25 units, the closing stock is assumed to relate to June purchases at £15 per unit, giving closing stock of 11 × £15 = £165.

Trading accounting FIFO

	£	£
Sales		1,709
Purchases	1,614	
Less closing stock	165	
Cost of sales		1,449
Gross profit		260

FIFO is a widely used stock valuation base and is acceptable under both SSAP 9 and the Companies Act 1985.

(2) Last-in-first-out (LIFO)

Under LIFO, cost of stocks and work-in-progress is calculated on the basis that the quantities in closing stock represent the earliest purchases or production.

Illustration

Using the same data as for the FIFO illustration, closing stock is calculated as follows:

COMPUTATION OF COST OF SALES AND CLOSING
STOCK FIGURES UNDER THE LIFO ASSUMPTION

19X8	Cost of sales		£	Closing stock at month end (memorandum note)	
January	16 at £10		160	4 at £10 = £40	
February	17	15 at £11 = 165 2 at £10 = 20	185	2 at £10 = £20	
March	25 at £12		300	2 at £10 5 at £12	£80
April	20	18 at £13 = 234 2 at £12 = 24	258	2 at £10 3 at £12	£56
May	17 at £14		238	2 at £10 3 at £12 3 at £14	£98
June	22 at £15		330	2 at £10 3 at £12 3 at £14 3 at £15	£143

Total cost of sales   £1,471

Trading account — LIFO

	£	£
Sales		1709
Purchases	1614	
Less closing stock	143	
Cost of sales		1471
Gross profit		238

NOTE: CALCULATIONS

LIFO calculations are rather detailed compared with FIFO. The main problem from a computational viewpoint is that in certain months, physical stock levels fall (e g February and April). In these months, costs of sales draws in purchase prices of earlier months.

COMMENTS ON ACCEPTABILITY OF LIFO

SSAP 9 states that LIFO cost of sales does not bear a reasonable relationship to actual costs obtaining during the period. For this reason, SSAP 9 does not usually regard LIFO as an acceptable valuation basis. However, the Companies Act 1985 permits the use of LIFO, as long as the directors consider it to be appropriate to the circumstances of the company. In practice, this provision has little practical importance in view of the restrictive terms of SSAP 9.

(3) *Average cost (AVCO)*

Under AVCO, cost of stocks and work-in-progress is calculated by applying an average price to the number of units on hand.

The average price may be computed in various ways, each of which may result in differing figures for closing stock. Possible approaches include:

(i)   a continuous calculation (e g every month, by means of computer program);
(ii) a periodic calculation (e g six-monthly or yearly);
(iii) a moving period calculation.

Illustration

Using the above figures and using an average for the six-month period:

$$\text{Average purchase cost per unit} = \frac{£1,614}{128} = £12.60$$

Closing stock = 11 × £12.60 = £139

Trading account—average cost

	£	£
Sales		1,709
Purchases	1,614	
Less closing stock	139	
Cost of sales		1,475
Gross profit		234

(4) *Comments on the usefulness of the above three methods*

Both FIFO and AVCO are widely used in the UK and are regarded as acceptable by both SSAP 9 and the Companies Act 1985. Although LIFO is permitted in certain cases by the Companies Act 1985, it is not considered generally acceptable under SSAP 9.

During periods of rising prices, FIFO may give an exaggerated impression of profitability, in that sales revenues (measured in current price terms) are matched with cost of sales (measured in terms of price levels possibly several months previously). However, FIFO may give a balance sheet stock figure which reflects current prices.

LIFO, on the other hand may give a balance sheet stock figure which is misleading as it could relate to prices of earlier periods (e g in the earlier illustration, two units of stock are valued at £10 per unit). When it comes to profit measurement, in some situations, LIFO may give a measure of profit which is a fair reflection of the capability of a business to make a distribution without impairing its future earning capacity. LIFO may result in the matching together of sales and cost of sales both in terms of current price levels. However, a drawback of LIFO is that where stock levels fall (as in the earlier illustration), cost of sales will reflect some items measured at price levels of earlier periods.

AVCO is acceptable from a practical viewpoint although it suffers from theoretical drawbacks during inflationary periods as regards profit measurement.

(5) *Other methods of stock valuation*

These include:

(i) UNIT COST

Unit cost is the cost of purchasing or manufacturing identifiable units of stock. This method is acceptable because it goes directly to actual costs rather than some approximation thereof. This method is appropriate for stock items such as jewellery and motor vehicles.

(ii) BASE STOCK

Certain types of businesses e g sugar refiners, require a certain minimum physical quantity of stock for continuous operations. This stock must be identified in terms of a predetermined number of units of stock which are then valued for balance sheet purposes at a fixed unit value. Such stock may be classified under tangible fixed asset.

Any excess of physical quantities over this number are valued on the basis of some other method such as FIFO or AVCO. Should the number of stock units fall below the predetermined minimum, stocks are valued on the basis of fixed unit value.

The base stock method is permitted by the Companies Act 1985 provided that:

(a) the overall value is not material to assessing the company's state of affairs; and
(b) the quantity, value and composition are not subject to material variation.

SSAP 9 does not regard base stock as a generally acceptable basis, although base stock has been used by companies such as Tate and Lyle.

(iii) REPLACEMENT COST

Replacement cost is the cost at which an identical asset could be purchased or manufactured. Replacement cost is not acceptable under the historical cost convention, as it does not derive from actual costs incurred. However, some companies have drawn up their statutory accounts on a current cost basis. Fixed asset and stock figures are then derived from replacement costs.

(iv) STANDARD COST

SSAP 9, App 2 states that cost is calculated on the basis of periodically predetermined costs calculated from management's estimates of expected levels of costs and of operations and operational efficiency and the related expenditure.

Where standard costs are used they should be reviewed frequently to ensure they bear a reasonable relationship to actual costs obtained during the period, in which case the approach is acceptable under both SSAP 9 and the Companies Act 1985.

(v) SELLING PRICE LESS MARGIN

Some retail stores use selling price less an estimated profit margin as a means of valuing stocks. This is acceptable, provided it can be shown that the method gives a reasonable approximation to actual cost.

(e) Problem areas

Two particular problem areas regarding stock valuation are allocation of production overheads and determination of net realisable value.

(1) *Allocation of production overheads*

Stock and work-in-progress should be valued for accounts purposes at the lower of cost and net realisable value. Cost should include all expenditure incurred in the normal course of business in bringing the product or service to its present location and condition.

These costs will include production overheads such as factory rent and rates and depreciation of plant and machinery, even though such costs accrue on a time basis.

Production overheads are defined in SSAP 9 as overheads incurred in respect of materials, labour or services, based on the normal level of activity taking one year with another.

In determining the normal level of activity SSAP 9, App 1 suggests that the following factors should be taken into account:

(i) the volume of production which the facilities are intended to achieve;
(ii) the budgeted level of activity for the current and following year;
(iii) the level of activity actually achieved in the current and previous years.

The following points may be added:

(a) It can be argued that in the present climate, key factors must be actual activity levels in current and previous years.
(b) The cost of unused capacity should be written off in the current year if the reduction in activity or trade of a company is considered to be permanent.
(c) Abnormal conversion costs (e g exceptional spoilage, idle capacity and other losses) should be excluded from stock valuation and should be charged to the profit and loss account of the period in which they are incurred.

Problems may also arise in determining whether particular overheads relate to the production, selling or administration function. Any arbitrary apportionment should reasonably have regard to the materiality of the amounts involved.

(2) *Determination of net realisable value*

(i) SITUATIONS WHERE APPLICABLE

SSAP 9 refers to the following situations where net realisable value is likely to be below cost:

(a) increase in cost or fall in selling price;
(b) physical deterioration of stocks;
(c) marketing decisions to manufacture and sell at a loss;
(d) errors in production or purchasing.

In addition, SSAP 9 refers to the situation of stock held which is unlikely to be sold within the usual turnover period. The likely delay in realising the stocks increases the possibility of situations (a) to (c) occurring. This should be borne in mind when considering net realisable value.

(ii) CONSIDERATION IN DETERMINING NRV

(a) *Formula approach*. It may be possible to determine NRV by using a formula and applying it to cost of items. The formula should be based on predetermined criteria which take account of age and movements of stock and estimated scrap values. The provision should then be reviewed in the light of any special circumstances which cannot be built into the formula.
(b) *Effect of finished goods valuation on raw materials*. If it is decided that finished goods stocks should be written down below cost, it is important that related raw material and sub-assembly stocks should be reviewed for possible write-down.
(c) *Post-balance sheet events*. Events between the balance sheet date and the date of approval of the financial statements by the directors should be taken into account in determining whether NRV is below cost.

   In certain cases, it may not be necessary to reduce cost of raw materials to a lower figure of realisable value. These would be cases where the finished product could be sold at a profit after allowing for inclusion of raw materials at cost price.

(f) Disclosure in financial statements

Disclosure requirements in the financial statements are specified in SSAP 9 and the Companies Act 1985. The disclosure requirements below relate to all stock categories with the exception of long-term contract work-in-progress.

(1) *Accounting policies*

The accounting policies used to determine cost and net realisable value should be disclosed.

(2) *Analysis of stocks total*

SSAP 9 requires that stocks and work-in-progress should be sub-classified in balance sheets or in notes to the financial statements in a manner which is appropriate to the business and so as to indicate the amounts held in each of the main categories. This is also effectively required by the Companies Act 1985 (see balance sheet formats).

(3) *Further disclosure*

In addition to the above disclosures, the Companies Act 1985 requires a note to the accounts disclosing the difference if material between:

(i)   the balance sheet value of stock;
(ii) the comparable figure determined either on replacement costs at the balance sheet date or on the most recent actual purchase price or production cost (but purchase price or production cost may only be used if they appear to the directors to constitute the more appropriate standard of comparison).

8.3   LONG-TERM CONTRACT WORK-IN-PROGRESS

(a) Definition

A long-term contract is defined in SSAP 9 as a contract entered into for manufacture or building of a single substantial entity or the provision of a service, where the time taken to manufacture, build or provide is such that a substantial proportion of all such contract work will extend for a period exceeding one year.

(b) Fundamental accounting concepts

The four concepts specified in SSAP 2 are particularly relevant. Also of particular interest is the possible conflict between the accruals concept and the prudence concept.

(1) *Going concern concept*

In view of the time period for completion of the contract, adequacy of financial resources is particularly important.

(2) *Accruals concept*

Such a long-term contract may extend over several accounting periods: the accruals concept would require profits to be allocated over these periods.

The method described below (see (e)), which achieves this, is sometimes referred to as the percentage of completion method. The alternative view, that profit should not be included in profit and loss account until the contract is complete, is not considered appropriate for long-term contracts, as it could distort comparison of profits as between successive accounting periods. This latter approach is sometimes referred to as the completed contract method and in normal circumstances may only be used for short-term work-in-progress.

(3) *Prudence concept*

In view of the considerable uncertainties surrounding the outcome of the contract, no profits should be recognised until such outcome can be assessed with reasonable certainty.

Clearly, the trade-off between the accruals concept and the prudence concept relies to a large extent on subjective judgement. Two companies may take significantly differing viewpoints!

(4) *Consistency concept*

In view of possible conflicts between accruals and prudence, it is essential that a company is consistent as between different contracts, and between successive accounting periods.

(c) Principal requirements of SSAP 9

The amount at which long-term contract work-in-progress is stated in periodic financial statements should be cost, plus any attributable profit, less any foreseeable losses and progress payments received and receivable.

(d) Specific points

The following points are referred to in the main part of SSAP 9 and in App 1. Certain of them reflect once again possible conflict between accruals and prudence.

(1) The profit taken up in a particular period should reflect the proportion of work carried out at the accounting date (accruals).
(2) Attributable profit is that part of total profit estimated to arise over the life of the contract which fairly reflects the proportion of work completed to date (accruals).
(3) There can be no attributable profit until the outcome of the contract can be assessed with reasonable certainty. SSAP 9 suggests that a company should define the earliest point for each particular contract before any attributable profit is taken up (prudence).
(4) If a company considers that the contract outcome can be assessed with reasonable certainty before the contract is completed, attributable profit should be taken up, but judgement should be exercised with prudence (accruals/prudence).
(5) SSAP 9 recognises that there are certain businesses which carry out contracts where the outcome cannot reasonably be assessed before completion. In these situations, profit should not be taken up prior to completion (prudence).
(6) Once it is expected that a contract will turn in a loss, full provision for the loss should be reflected in the current period financial statements (prudence).

(e) Calculating profits on long-term contracts

The non-mandatory appendix to SSAP 9 suggests the following approach:

Total sales value of contract		X
Total costs (including overheads) to date	X	
Total estimated further costs required to complete contract	X	
Estimated further costs of guarantee and rectification work	X	X
(1) Total estimated profit on contract		X

NOTE
This procedure should be followed even if there is no intention of taking any profit to the credit of profit and loss account, since it may indicate the possibility of a contract turning in a loss. In this event, further investigation of figures is required.

(2) Attributable profit (AP) = degree of completion % × total estimated profit.
(3) Degree of completion—possible acceptable approaches:

(a) costs incurred as proportion of total costs;
(b) surveys which measure work performed;
(c) completion of physical portion of contract work.

(4) Profit this year = AP − profit taken up in previous years.

NOTES
(1) The profit recognised this year will not necessarily represent the proportion of the total profit on the contract which corresponds with the amount of work carried out in the period. It is also likely to reflect the effect of changes in circumstances during the year which affect the total profit estimated to accrue on completion. (SSAP 9, App 1, para 27.)
(2) The above approach is not contained in the main body of the standard and consequently is not mandatory.

Alternative approaches may equally comply with the main requirements of the standard. An example of such an approach would be the traditional method of calculating profit to date by comparing value of work to date with cost of work to date. This latter approach has sometimes been modified by multiplying such profit by an arbitrary fraction (e g two-thirds) to reflect prudence. Such practice could hardly be described as scientifically based!

(f) Loss-making contracts

The principal requirements of SSAP 9 are:

(1) If a particular contract is expected to result in a loss, immediate provision should be made for the whole of the loss. In this situation, the particular contract will be stated at cost less foreseeable losses (i e effectively, net realisable values).
(2) If a particular contract is likely to absorb a considerable part of the company's capacity for a substantial period, then related overheads should be included in the loss calculations.
(3) If anticipated losses on individual contracts exceed costs incurred to date, less progress payments received and receivable, such excesses should be shown separately as provisions.

(g) Illustration 1

Contractors PLC are engaged in a number of long-term contracts. The following summarised details refer to three particular long-term contracts which were in progress at 31 December 19X6.

	Contract A £'000	Contract B £'000	Contract C £'000
Total contract price	700	400	800
Cost incurred to 31.12.X6	400	30	500
Estimated total costs to complete (allowing for contingencies)	790	300	570
Progress payments invoiced	390	40	600
Amounts received relating to above progress payments invoiced	350	20	450

How should each of these contracts be valued at 31.12.X6 in accordance with SSAP 9?

Contract A
This contract indicates a foreseeable loss of £90,000. SSAP 9 requires the full amount of the loss to be reflected in the 19X6 financial statements. Clearly it is important to ensure that estimated total costs of £790,000 have been determined on a prudent basis.

A further point is that the foreseeable loss of £90,000 exceeds cost to date, less progress payments received and receivable (£400,000 − £390,000 = £10,000) by £80,000. SSAP 9 requires this excess to be shown separately as a provision.

Contract B

This contract is expected to make a total profit of £100,000 (i e £400,000 less £300,000). However, since the contract is at a relatively early stage, it can be argued that the outcome of the contract cannot be assessed with reasonable certainty. On prudence grounds, therefore, the contract should be included in the balance sheet at cost of £30,000 less progress payments invoiced of £40,000. The £10,000 excess may be regarded as a creditor.

Contract C

This contract is expected to produce a total profit of £230,000. The contract is well advanced and it can be argued that its profitable outcome can be assessed with reasonable certainty. Once again, it is important to establish that estimated total costs of £570,000 have been arrived at on a prudent basis and allow for contingencies.

With the limited information available, the best way of determining attributable profit may be to use cost to date divided by expected total costs as an indicator of progress.

On this basis, attributable profit would be calculated as:

$$\frac{£500,000}{£570,000} \times £230,000 = £201,755$$

say, £201,000

Clearly, given more information, other indicators of progress might be available. A useful approach might be to use more than one method, each method providing a cross-check on the other.

Summary of effect of the three contracts on the balance sheet at 31.12.X6

	Contract A £'000	Contract B £'000	Contract C £'000	Total £'000
Cost to date	400	30	500	930
Attributable profits	—	—	201	201
Foreseeable losses	(90)	—	—	(90)
	310	30	701	1,041
Less progress payments:				
Received	(350)	(20)	(450)	(820)
Receivable	(40)	(20)	(150)	(210)
	(80)	(10)	101	11

Suggested disclosure of balance sheet figures

Current assets

	£'000
(1) Work-in-progress at cost plus attributable profit (W1)	731
Less progress payments received and receivable (W2)	640
	91

(2) Debtors: Progress payments receivable (W3)	210

PROVISION FOR LIABILITIES AND CHARGES Foreseeable losses in excess of costs to date, less progress payments	80

WORKINGS
W1 30 + 500 + 201   = 731
W2 20 + 20 + 450 + 150 = 640
W3 40 + 20 + 150   = 210

(h) Profit and loss account disclosures

The revenue (and hence reported turnover) earned in a period should be the cost incurred plus the attributable profit.

Illustration 2

A long-term contract extends over three accounting periods. A summary of the relevant figures for the three years are as follows:

	Year 1 £	Year 2 £	Year 3 £	Total £
Costs incurred	100	700	550	1350
Attributable profit	—	350	250	600
	100	1,050	800	1,950
Progress payments invoiced	(130)	(810)	(650)	(1,590)
Net amount	(30)	240	150	360

Note: Contract price is £1,950 and total (final) profit on contract is £600.

Extracts from profit and loss accounts (format 1)

	Year 1 £	Year 2 £	Year 3 £	Total £
Turnover	100	1,050	800	1,950
Cost of sales	100	700	550	1,350
Gross profit	—	350	250	600

(i) Further considerations

The appendix to SSAP 9 makes the following suggestions:

Aspect	*Suggested approach*
Variations (additional work).	Make conservative estimate of effect on sales value.
Foreseen claims or penalties against contractor.	Ensure allowed for in further costs of guarantee and rectification.
Settlement of claims by contractor arising from circumstances not envisaged in the contract or arising as an indirect consequence of approved variations.	Only provide for in sales value if negotiations in advanced stage *and* written evidence of acceptability and amount.

(j) Disclosure requirements

SSAP 9 requires disclosure of:

(1) The amount of work-in-progress at cost plus attributable profit, less foreseeable losses.
(2) Cash received and receivable at the balance sheet date as progress payments on account of contracts in progress.

A further possible disclosure arises from the Companies Act 1985 overriding true and fair requirements. The treatment of long-term contracts per SSAP 9 is a departure from the statutory valuation rule of lower of cost and net realisable value. This departure is justified by the overriding requirement for the accounts to give a true and fair view—the Companies Act 1985 would then require the effect of the departure to be quantified.

There were differences of opinion as to how this requirement should be interpreted. Consequently some companies disclosed attributable profit whilst others did not.

The matter was of concern to ASC who took Counsel's opinion. An exposure draft, ED 40 (see below), was issued in November 1986. ED 40 proposed important changes in the way that long-term contract balances are presented in the balance sheet. ED 40 is dealt with below.

8.4   ED 40—STOCKS AND LONG-TERM CONTRACTS

(a) Introduction

Following a revision of SSAP 9, ASC published ED 40 in November 1986. If eventually adopted as a standard, ED 40 will have little effect on the treatment of short-term stocks. The exposure draft does propose a change in the definition of a long-term contract as well as the presentation of long-term contract information in the profit and loss account and balance sheet. This will not affect the amount of profit reported in the profit and loss account.

(b) Definition

ED 40 defines a long-term contract as a contract entered into for the manufacture or the building of a single substantial entity or the provision of a service where the time taken to manufacture, build or provide is such that the contract activity falls into different acounting periods and normally is expected to extend for a period exceeding one year. However, the specific duration of performance may not be the sole distinguishing feature of such a contract and where the reporting entity is substantially engaged in contracts which extend for more than one year, it may not be appropriate to adopt a separate accounting policy for shorter term contracts.

(c) Determination of profit

Profit for a particular year should be determined by matching together an appropriate proportion of total contract value with the costs increased in reaching that stage of completion.

(d) Classification of balances

Under ED 40 contract balances could be classified under the following headings:

Assets

(1) costs not yet traded—disclosed within stocks;
(2) amounts receivable (the amount by which progress payments invoiced exceeds cash received)—disclosed within debtors;
(3) other balances which represent the excess of cumulative turnover recognised over progress payments invoiced—disclosed separately within debtors under the sub-heading 'amounts recoverable on contracts'.

Note that under SSAP 9, segments (1) and (3) are included under stocks while (2) is included under debtors. ED 40 therefore proposes an important change in classification of (3) from stock to debtors.

Liabilities

Where progress payments invoiced exceed cumulative turnover, the excess is referred to as applicable payments on account. Applicable payments on account should be deducted from costs not yet traded, any residual amount being classified within creditors.

(e) Worked example

Hayseed plc is a construction company. The following details relate to contract 467. The contract extended over four years. All figures are £'000.

	Year			
	1	*2*	*3*	*4*
Degree of completion at end of year	25%	60%	85%	100%
Contract price (as updated)	800	850	900	980
Estimated cost (as updated)	500	560	650	730
Estimated total profits	300	290	250	250
Costs to date (actual)	135	350	570	730
Progress payments invoiced (cumulative)	160	490	790	980
Progress payments received (cumulative)	130	480	720	980

Assumption: Attributable profit at the end of each year is calculated by applying the degree of completion percentage to the estimated total profit (for alternative approaches, see section 8.3(e)(3)).

(1) *SSAP 9 approach*

(i)   Reported profit each year is calculated as follows:

Year 1—no profit (assume contract not sufficiently advanced to assess
          outcome of contract with reasonable certainty)
Year 2—60%   £290,000   =£174,000
Year 3—(85% × £250,000 = £213,000) − £174,000   = £39,000
Year 4—£250,000 − £213,000   = £37,000
                                                                 ─────────
                                                                 £250,000

The preface to ED 40 points out that SSAP 9 does not deal with the method of recording turnover and related costs in the profit and loss account. ED 40 points out that a variety of methods have been used to determine the turnover disclosed in each accounting period.
Assume for this example that Hayseed's accounting policy is to determine reported turnover by adding together attributed contract costs and reported profit (as calculated above).
The respective profit and loss account extracts may now be completed as follows:

Year	*1*		*2*		*3*		*4*	£
	£'000		*£'000*		*£'000*		*£'000*	*£'000*
Turnover	135		389		259		197	980
Cost of sales	135	(350 −	215	(570 −	220	(730 −	160	730
		135)		350)		570)		
Gross profit	—		174		39		37	250

Note: The actual contract profit of £250,000 is recognised as follows:

Year	£'000	%	Degree of completion
1	—	—	25
2	174	69.6	35
3	39	15.6	25
4	37	14.8	15
	250	100.0	100

Hayseed does not recognise profit in the early stages of a contract on the grounds that the contract outcome cannot be assessed with reasonable certainty. This results in the recognition of a disproportionate amount of profit in year 2. In addition in year 3 the company has revised its estimate of expected total profit downwards from £290,000 to £250,000. This has resulted in the recognition of a relatively low proportion of profit in year 3 to the benefit of year 2.

(ii)   Balance sheet extracts under SSAP 9 are as follows:

Stocks and work-in-progress—long-term contract balances

	£'000	£'000	£'000
Year	1	2	3
Cost	135	350	570
Attributable profit	—	174	213
	135	524	783
Progress payments invoiced	160	490	790
	(25)	34	(7)

Note: figures in brackets would be aggregated with positive balances relating to other contracts, failing which they would be included under creditors.

Debtors

These relate to progress payments receivable:

Year	£
1 (160,000–130,000)	30,000
2 (490,000–480,000)	10,000
3 (790,000–720,000)	70,000

(2) *ED 40 approach*

(i)   Cost of sales calculations

Year		£
1	(25% × 500,000)	125,000
2	(60% × 560,000 = 336,000) – 125,000	211,000
3	(85% × 650,000 = 552,000) – 336,000	216,000
4	(730,000 – 552,000)	178,000
	Total	730,000

(ii)   Stocks at year end (costs not traded)

Year		£'000
1	Cost incurred	135
	Transfer cost of sales	125
		___
	Closing stock	10
2	Costs incurred	215
		___
		225
	Transfer cost of sales	211
		___
	Closing stock	14
3	Costs incurred	220
		___
		234
	Transfer cost of sales	216
		___
	Closing stock	18
4	Costs incurred	160
		___
		178
	Transfer cost of sales	178
		___
	Closing stock	–
		___

(iii)   Turnover calculations

Year		£'000	
1	No profit recognised, so based on cost of sales		125
2	Cumulative turnover		
	60% × 850,000	510	
	less recognised in year 1	125	385
		___	
3	Cumulative turnover		
	85% × 900	765	
	less recognised in years 1 & 2	510	255
		___	
4	Cumulative turnover (= contract price)	980	
	less recognised in years 1, 2 and 3	765	215
		___	___
	Total		980
			___

(iv)   Profit and loss acount summary

Year	1	2	3	4	Total
	£'000	£'000	£'000	£'000	£'000
Turnover	125	385	255	215	980
Cost of sales	125	211	216	178	730
	___	___	___	___	___
Gross profit	–	174	39	37	250
	___	___	___	___	___

(v)   Balance sheet information

Year	1	2	3
	£'000	£'000	£'000
Stock (costs not traded)	10	14	18
Debtors—amounts recoverable (510 – 490)		20	
Creditors—applicable payments on account			
(160 – 125)	(35)	—	
(790–765)			(25)
Net total to reconcile with SSAP 9 total	(25)	34	(7)

The above amounts would be presented each year as follows:

Year

1   £25,000 (excess of payments on accounts over stock) in creditors

2   £14,000 in stock, £20,000 in debtors under sub-heading 'amount recoverable on contracts'

3   £7,000   in creditors (as under 1 above)

Note that progress payments receivable each year would be classified under debtors as per SSAP 9 (above).

(f) Contracts expected to result in losses

Where it is expected that the contract as a whole will result in a loss, the whole amount of the loss should be accounted for as soon as it is recognised.

ED 40 also repeats the point in SSAP 9 that where unprofitable contracts are of such a magnitude that they can be expected to absorb a considerable part of the company's capacity for a considerable period, then the loss calculation should also reflect related overhead expenses expected to be incurred during the period to completion.

Illustration

A company commenced work at the beginning of the year on a long-term contract. At the end of year 1 the following information is available:

	£
Total contract price	650,000
Estimated costs to completion	850,000
Degree of completion	40%
Costs to date	350,000
Progress payments invoiced	290,000

Required: Extracts from financial statements for year 1.

(1) Profit and loss account for year 1

Turnover (40% × 650,000)	260,000
Cost of sales (see working)	460,000
Loss	200,000

Note: The foreseeable loss over the duration of the contract is £200,000 (£850,000 – £650,000). The full amount of this loss should be reflected in the profit and loss account in accordance with the accruals concept. The above results would be the same under either SSAP 9 or ED 40.

Working—cost of sales

	£	£
Costs incurred		350,000
Provision for future losses		
Future revenues 60% × 650,000	390,000	
Future costs (850,000 − 350,000)	500,000	110,000
		460,000

(2) Balance sheet extract (year 1)—SSAP 9

	£
Cost less foreseeable losses	
(350,000 − 200,000)	150,000
Progress payments invoiced	290,000
Net balance to be included under	
provisions (SSAP 9, para 27)	(140,000)

Note: This balance effectively incorporates two figures—the provision for future losses of £110,000 (see above) and the excess of progress payments invoiced over revenue recognised of £30,000 (£290,000 − £260,000).

(3) Balance sheet extract (year 1)—ED 40

	£
Balance of payments on account (290,000 − 260,000) to be included within creditors	£30,000
Provision (cost of sales 460,000 − costs to date 350,000)	£110,000
Total	140,000

Note: If the contract was completed in year 2 without any further loss, the profit and loss for the two years would appear as follows:

	1	2	Total
	£'000	£'000	£'000
Turnover	260	390	650
Cost of sales	460	390*	850
Profit (loss)	(200)	—	(200)

* Costs incurred (850,000 − 350,000) less release of provision of £110,000.

(g) Balance sheet presentation

Long-term contracts should be classified under stocks and separately disclosed. The amount should be determined by taking costs incurred (net of amounts transferred to cost of sales) and after deducting:

(1) foreseeable losses;
(2) applicable payments on account.

Separate disclosure is proposed of:

(1) net costs less foreseeable losses; and
(2) applicable payments on account.

(h) Substance over form

Appendix 3, ED 40, para 3 states:

An amount recoverable on contracts may not have the contractual status of a debtor in strict legal form. However, it is well established under the accruals concept of revenue and cost recognition that this should not preclude debtors and creditors from being recorded, where this is necessary to reflect the substance of a transaction.

A key feature of the ED 40 proposals is that long-term contract work in progress balances are regarded in substance as debts and not as work-in-progress.

9 ACCOUNTING FOR TAXATION

9.1 ACCOUNTING FOR TAX UNDER THE IMPUTATION SYSTEM

(a) Assumptions re tax rates

Unless otherwise indicated, the following tax rates are assumed to apply:

Corporation tax	35%
Advance corporation tax	$\frac{3}{7}$
Income tax	30%

(b) The payment of corporation tax

Companies are assessed to corporation tax on their profits. Where no dividends are paid during the year, a single payment of corporation tax will be paid at some time after the year end (payment dates are referred to in (c) below).

In general terms, ignoring special situations, the payment of dividends will not affect the total amount of corporation tax paid over. However, the payment of dividends will affect the *timing* of the tax payments.

The payment of a dividend triggers off a payment of advance corporation tax (ACT). ACT is regarded as an on account payment of gross corporation tax. The residual balance owing is referred to as mainstream corporation tax (MCT).

(c) Tax payment dates

(1) *ACT*

ACT is paid on a quarterly basis by reference to the account period in which the dividend is paid. For example if a dividend is paid in February, this falls in the quarter to 31 March and ACT is payable two weeks after the end of the quarter i e by 14 April.

(2) *MCT*

The payment date for MCT depends on whether the company was formed prior to 1965 when the corporation tax system was first introduced.

(i) PRE-1965 COMPANY
MCT is payable on 1 January following the 5 April following the company's year end. This applies provided that the company has not changed its accounting reference period.

Year end	MCT due	
31.1.19X2	1.1.19X3	(11 months later)
30.4.19X2	1.1.19X4	(20 months)
31.12.19X2	1.1.19X4	(12 months)
31.3.19X3	1.1.19X4	(9 months)

Where applicable, the illustrations in this chapter are based on the above legislation. However, new rules will come into operation for accounting periods beginning after 16 March 1987. These rules will have the effect of reducing the length of the long payment periods until eventually all tax payments will be made 9 months after the year end. The new rules are briefly referred to below.

212

Consider a company's first accounting period beginning after 16.3.87—suppose a company has a 30 April year end and MCT is payable 20 months after the year end:

YE 30.4.88 (accounting period 1)

Normal payment date	20 months
Less period of reduction	
$\dfrac{20-9}{3} = 3$ (whole number)	3
∴ Revised payment date	17 months

∴ Tax payable 30.4.88 + 17 months = 30.9.90

YE 30.4.89 (accounting period 2)

Start with revised payment date for period 1, i e	17 months
Less period of reduction—as above	3 months
Revised payment date	14 months

∴ Tax payable 30.4.89 + 14 months = 30.6.91

YE 30.4.90 (accounting period 3)
Tax payable 9 months after year end (same as for a post-1965 company) i e 31.1.92.

(ii) POST-1965 COMPANY
MCT is payable nine months after the end of the year.

(d) Offset of ACT paid

ACT relating to dividends paid in a particular accounting year may be offset against the corporation tax on the profits of that period.

Illustration 1

A post-1965 company paid a dividend of £14,700 on 3.8.X4. ACT of £6,300 (i e $\frac{3}{7} \times$ £14,700) was paid over on 14.10.X4 (i e 14 days after quarter to 30.9.X4).

Corporation tax for the year ended 31 December 19X4 was estimated at £39,500. Show relevant extracts from financial statements.

Balance sheet	£
Other creditors including tax and social security—corporation tax payable 1.10.X5 (39,500–6,300)	33,200

Profit and loss account	
Tax on profit on ordinary activities	39,500
Dividends paid	14,700

(e) ACT on proposed dividends

Dividends proposed at the year end will not give rise to payment of ACT until the dividends are actually paid. However, since proposed dividends are accrued in the balance sheet, SSAP 8 requires ACT on proposed dividends to be included within creditors: amounts falling due within one year.

When ACT is paid, it will become available for offset against the corporation tax on the profits of the following year (i e the year in which the dividend payment is made).

Provided the ACT on proposed dividends is regarded as recoverable (i e against tax on the following year profits), the ACT debit should be deducted from deferred tax account. In the absence of a deferred tax account, the ACT should be regarded as a deferred asset.

Illustration 2

In the previous example, the dividend of £14,700 was proposed at the year end. What difference would this have made?

First of all, no ACT offset could be made against the corporation tax of £39,500. The reason is that the *dividend* is paid in the year following that to which the corporation tax relates. ACT paid may be offset against the corporation tax for 19X5.

Secondly, a creditor for ACT of £6,300 should be made. Also, in the absence of a deferred tax account, a deferred asset of £6,300 should be set up.

The relevant extracts are then:

(1) Balance sheet

Debtors
Deferred asset—ACT recoverable   £6,300

Creditors—due within one year
   ACT   6,300   disclosed as ⎤
   MCT   39,500   single figure ⎦   45,800
Proposed dividends   14,700

(2) Profit and loss account

Tax on profit on ordinary activities   39,500
Dividends proposed   14,700

(f) Dividends received

Where dividends are paid and received in a period, ACT will be paid on the net amount.

Illustration 3

A company paid a dividend of £8,400 on 5.6.X2 and received a dividend of £2,100 on 18.9.X2. Corporation tax on the profits for the year to 31.12.X2 was estimated at £54,100.

Tax payments and receipts would be as follows:

	£
14.7.X2 ACT payment $\frac{3}{7} \times$ £8,400	£3,600
18.9.X2 ACT reclaim $\frac{3}{7} \times$ £2,100	(900)
1.10.X3 MCT paid (54,100 − 2,700)	51,400
Total tax paid	54,100

For presentation purposes, SSAP 8 requires dividends received to be shown gross inclusive of tax credit. Thus, in the above illustration, dividends received would be included at £3,000. The tax credit of £900 should be shown as a separate part of the tax charge.

Note that this grossing-up is purely for presentation purposes. It has no effect on ACT set-off.

Illustration 4

Profit and loss extracts for the above illustration:

		£
Dividends received		3,000
Tax on profit on ordinary activities		
Corporation tax	54,100	
Tax credits on dividends received	900	55,000
Dividends paid		8,400

(g) Income tax

The law requires companies to deduct income tax at the basic rate at source when paying loan interest, royalties etc.

A knowledge of the following terms is necessary to understand the treatment of income tax in accounts:

(1) Charges i e payments from which income tax must be deducted at source e g debenture interest, loan interest, mortgage interest, royalties.
(2) Unfranked investment income received i e income paid out of profits not subject to UK corporation tax e g loan interest received and income received from British government securities (from which income tax is deducted at source), local authority loans, and building society interest received.

The charge for royalties, debenture interest and annual charges in the profit and loss account is shown gross. Unfranked investment income is also shown gross. The double entry recording the payment of annual charges etc is: debit debenture interest etc, with the gross amount and credit cash with the cash paid to the debenture holder etc, and credit income tax account with the income tax deducted.

When unfranked investment income is received, debit cash with the cash received, debit income tax account with the income tax deducted by the payer at source, and credit unfranked investment income (UII) account with the gross amount.

In the balance sheet, an income tax account credit balance will be included in creditors. Accrued debenture and loan interest will be included in creditors, gross, and need not be disclosed separately on the balance sheet. Likewise, unfranked investment income receivable will be included in debtors at the gross amount.

Illustration 5

Company has year end of 31.12.X6. Debenture interest of £20,000 (gross) is paid net of tax on 23.6.X6. Debenture interest of £12,000 (gross) is received net of tax on 23.9.X6.

DEBENTURE INTEREST PAID

		£			£
23.6.X6	Cash	£14,000	31.12.X6	P/L	20,000
23.6X6	Income tax account (to gross up)	6,000 △			
		20,000			20,000

DEBENTURE INTEREST RECEIVED

		£			£
31.12.X6	P/L	12,000	23.9.X6	Cash	8,400
			23.9.X6	Income tax account (to gross up)	3,600
		12,000			12,000

INCOME TAX ACCOUNT

		£			£
14.7.X6	Cash (tax paid over)	6,000	23.6.X6	Debenture interest paid	6,000 △
23.9.X6	Debenture interest received	3,600	14.10.X6	Cash (tax reclaimed)	3,600
		9,600			9,600

Illustration 6

Company has year end of 31.12.X7. Debenture interest of £12,000 (gross) is paid net of tax on 23.6.X6. Debenture interest of £20,000 (gross) is received net of tax on 23.9.X6.
   The relevant ledger accounts are:

DEBENTURE INTEREST PAID

		£			£
23.6.X6	Cash	8,400	31.12.X6	P/L	12,000
23.6.X6	Income tax account				
	(to gross up)	3,600			
		12,000			12,000

DEBENTURE INTEREST RECEIVED

		£			£
31.12.X6	P/L	20,000	23.9.X6	Cash	14,000
			23.9.X6	Income tax account	6,000
		20,000			20,000

INCOME TAX ACCOUNT

		£			£
14.7.X6	Cash (tax		23.6.X6	Debenture interest	
	paid over)	3,600		paid	3,600
23.9.X6	Debenture interest		14.10.X6	Cash (tax	
	received	6,000		reclaimed)	3,600
			31.12.X6	Corporation tax account	
				(6,000 − 3,600)	2,400
		9,600			9,600

Note: The unrecovered income tax of £2,400 is offset against corporation tax thus reducing the corporation tax payment.

(h) Requirements of SSAP 8

SSAP 8 (the treatment of taxation under the imputation system in the accounts of companies) requires the following:

(1) *Profit and loss account*

(i) TAX CHARGE
The tax charge in the profit and loss account should include the following items. Where items are material, they should be disclosed separately.

(a) The amount of UK corporation tax. The following elements should be specified:

   (1) corporation tax;
   (2) deferred tax;
   (3) tax attributable to franked investment income (i e tax credits on dividends received);
   (4) irrecoverable ACT;
   (5) relief for overseas taxation.

   (Points (4) and (5) are referred to later in this chapter.)
(b) Total overseas taxation, relieved and unrelieved. Disclosure is required of the amount of unrelieved overseas taxation which results from the payment or proposed payment of dividends.

(ii) CORPORATION TAX RATE

If the rate of corporation tax is not known for either the whole of the period or part of the period, the latest known rate of corporation tax should be used and disclosed. Prior to the Finance Act 1984, the corporation tax rate was specified in the budget on a retrospective basis. However, in the 1984 budget, corporation tax rates for future years were specified.

(iii) DIVIDENDS PAID AND PROPOSED

These should be included in the profit and loss account at the amount of cash payable to the shareholders, without the inclusion of ACT or tax credits.

(iv) DIVIDEND INCOME

Dividend income should be included at the amount of cash received or receivable plus tax credit. For example, suppose a company receives a dividend of £2,800 from a UK resident company. In theory, dividend income could be presented in two possible ways, only one of which is permitted by SSAP 8:

	Net approach £		Gross approach £
Investment income	2,800		4,000
Tax on profit on ordinary activities			
Tax credit on dividends received	—	(1,200)	
Profit after tax	2,800		2,800

The difference between the two approaches is simply one of presentation. It can have no effect on tax payable or net profit. SSAP 8 requires the gross approach on the grounds of consistency i e all items which appear in the profit and loss account above the tax line should be included on a before-tax basis.

(2) *Balance sheet*

(i) DIVIDEND LIABILITY

Proposed dividends should be included in creditors (amounts payable within one year of the balance sheet date) without the addition of related ACT.

(ii) ACT ON PROPOSED DIVIDENDS

Whether or not this ACT is recoverable by offset against gross corporation tax, ACT payable should be included within creditors.

(iii) ACT RECOVERABLE ON PROPOSED DIVIDENDS

(a) ACT on proposed dividends is due for payment 14 days after the end of the quarter in which the payment is actually made.
(b) This ACT may be offset against the corporation tax on the profits of the accounting year in which the dividend is paid.

Illustration 7

Suppose a dividend is declared for the year ended 31 December 19X4. The dividend is paid on 15 April 19X5 so ACT is paid over 14 days after the quarter to 30 June 19X5 i e by 14 July 19X5.

ACT paid may be offset against the corporation tax on the profits for the year ending 31 December 19X5. The critical factor is the date when the dividend is paid. If the dividend payment falls in the year to 31 December 19X5, it may be offset against the corporation tax on the profits of that year. It may *not* be offset against the corporation tax on the profits for the year to 31 December 19X4.

If the company is, for example, a post-1965 company the MCT for 19X5 will be due on 1 October 19X6. The ACT offset thus reduces a payment 21 months after the 31 December 19X4 balance sheet. The right of set-off is therefore in the nature of a deferred asset.

SSAP 8 requires the recoverable ACT either:

(1) to be deducted from the deferred tax balance if a deferred tax account exists; failing which
(2) to be treated as a deferred asset (under the heading of debtors).

Irrecoverable ACT is discussed below.

(iv) PREFERENCE SHARES

Where divided rights on preference shares were established before 6 April 1973 at a particular gross rate, this was subsequently reduced to $\frac{7}{10}$ of its former rate.

Such preference share would be described as, for example:

100,000 10% (now 7% + tax credit) preference shares of £1   £100,00

(i) Illustrations

In each of the illustrations below, corporation tax is to be taken at 35% and income tax at 30%. Company accounting period is year ended 31 December 19X8. No deferred tax account is maintained. Ledger account entries are numbered for sequence of entries.

Illustration 8

Dividend paid on 8.9.X6 of £42,000. ACT paid on 14.10.X6 is £18,000 ($\frac{3}{7}$ × £42,000). Corporation tax for the year ended 31 December 19X6 is estimated at £203,000 and a dividend is proposed of £63,000. The company is a post-1965 company.
Required: (a) ledger accounts;
(b) extracts from financial statements.

ACT ACCOUNT

	£		£
14.10.X6		31.12.X6	
(1) Cash	18,000	(4) Corporation tax a/c (ACT set-off)	18,000
31.12.X6			
Bal c/d	27,000	(5) ACT recoverable account	27,000
	45,000		45,000
		Bal b/d	27,000

MCT ACCOUNT

	£		£
31.12.X6		31.12.X6	
(3) ACT a/c	18,000	(2) P/L	203,000
MCT c/d	185,000		
	203,000		203,000

DEFERRED ASSET A/C—ACT RECOVERABLE

	£
(5) ACT a/c ($\frac{3}{7}$ × 63,000)	27,000

Profit and loss account (extracts)

		£
Tax on profit on ordinary activities corporation tax at 35%		203,000
Dividends on ordinary shares		
Paid	42,000	
Proposed	63,000	105,000

Balance sheet extracts

Debtors—Deferred asset:
ACT recoverable 27,000
Creditors—Amounts falling
due within one year
Tax and social security 212,000
Proposed dividends 63,000

Working—tax and social security

	£
ACT payable	27,000
MCT payable	185,000
	212,000

Illustration 9

The company is a pre-1965 company.
The following details relate to tax and dividend matters:

(1) The balances brought forward at 1 January 19X8 relating to corporation tax balances
were:

	£
19X6 profits	460,000
19X7 profits	527,000

The amount owing for 19X7 was agreed during the year at £560,000.
(2) Dividends relating to 19X8 were as follows:

	£
Interim paid (8.8X8)	21,000
Final proposed	84,000

ACT amounting to £9,000 was paid
on 14.10.X8.
(3) Corporation tax on the profits for 19X8 has been estimated at £610,000. Required:

(a) ledger accounts;
(b) extracts from financial statements.

ADVANCE CORPORATION TAX

	£		£
19X8		*19X8*	
14 Oct		31 Dec	
(2) Cash	9,000	(5) Corporation tax (a/c)	
		(ACT set-off)	9,000
31 Dec			
Bal c/f	36,000	(6) ACT recoverable account	36,000
	45,000		45,000
		19X9	
		1 Jan	
		Bal b/d	36,000

MAINSTREAM CORPORATION TAX

19X8	£	19X8	£
1 Jan		1 Jan	
(1) Cash	460,000	Bal b/d (19X6)	460,000
31 Dec		Bal b/d (19X7)	527,000
(5) ACT a/c	9,000	31 Dec	
Bal c/d (19X7)	560,000	P/L	
(19X8) (610−9)	601,000	(3) Tax underprovided	
		(560,000−527,000)	33,000
		(4) Corporation tax charge	610,000
	1,630,000		1,630,000

DEFERRED ASSET ACCOUNT—ACT RECOVERABLE

	£		£
(6) ACT a/c			
($\frac{3}{7}$ × 84,000)	36,000		

Profit and loss account (extracts)

	£
Tax on profit on ordinary activities:	
Corporation tax at 35%	610,000
Corporation tax underprovided in previous years	33,000
	643,000

Dividends on ordinary shares:		
Paid	21,000	
Proposed	84,000	105,000

Balance sheet extracts

Debtors—deferred asset: ACT recoverable	36,000
Creditors—amounts falling due within one year:	
Tax and social security	596,000
Proposed dividends	84,000
Creditors—amounts falling due after more than one year:	
corporation tax payable	
1.1.X10	601,000

Working—tax and social security

ACT payable	36,000
MCT (19X7) payable	560,000
	596,000

Illustration 10

The company is a post-1965 company. The following details relate to tax and dividends matters:

(1) Dividends relating to 19X8 were as follows:

Interim paid (2.10.X8)	14,000
Final proposed	21,000

(2) Dividends received on 3.8.X8 amounted to £7,700.
(3) Corporation tax on the profits for 19X8 has been estimated at £220,000.

(4) ACT payable at 31.12.X8 is £2,700 (i e $\frac{3}{7}$ 14,000 − 7,700)
Required:
(a) ledger accounts;
(b) extracts from financial statements.

ADVANCE CORPORATION TAX

	£		£
19X8		*19X8*	
31 Dec		31 Dec	
Bal c/d	11,700	(2) Corporation tax a/c	
		(ACT set-off)	2,700
		(3) ACT recoverable account	
		($\frac{3}{7}$ × 21,000)	9,000
	11,700		11,700
		19X9	
		1 Jan	
		Bal b/d	11,700

MAINSTREAM CORPORATION TAX

	£		£
19X8		*19X8*	
31 Dec		31 Dec	
(2) ACT a/c	2,700	(1) P/L—tax charge	220,000
Bal c/d (MCT)	217,300		
	220,000		220,000
		19X9	
		1 Jan	
		Bal b/d	217,300

DEFERRED ASSET ACCOUNT—ACT RECOVERABLE

(3) ACT a/c	9,000

Comments on the above

(1) The receipt of dividend on 3.8.X8 has no immediate effect on ACT receipts or payments. No ACT can be claimed back as there were no ACT payments in previous accounting quarters.
(2) However, the above receipt does affect the ACT position as regards the dividend which is paid prior to the year end (i e the dividend of £14,000 paid on 2.10.X8).
    ACT payable by reference to the dividend payment is $\frac{3}{7}$ (14,000 − 7,700), i e £2,700.
    Thus, ACT is payable on 14.1.X9, and so is a creditor at the end of the year. Since the dividend to which the ACT relates was paid in 19X8, the £2,700 may be offset against the corporation tax on 19X8 profits of £220,000.
(3) ACT of £9,000 on the proposed dividend can only be offset against the corporation tax on 19X9 profits and so must be regarded as a deferred asset.
(4) The total ACT liability of £11,700 is payable as follows:

	£
14.1.X9	2,700
14.4.X9 (assuming dividend paid prior to 31.3.X9)	9,000
	11,700

Profit and loss extracts

		£
Income from investments		11,000
Tax on profit on ordinary activities:		
Corporation tax at 35%		220,000
Tax credit on UK dividends received		3,300
		223,300
Dividends on ordinary shares:		
Paid	14,000	
Proposed	21,000	35,000

Balance sheet extracts

	£
Debtors—deferred asset: ACT recoverable	9,000
Creditors—amounts falling due within one year:	
Tax and social security	229,000
Proposed dividends	21,000

Workings

	£
(1) *Tax and social security*	
ACT payable	11,700
MCT payable	217,300
	229,000

(2) *Income from investments*

$$£7,700 \times \frac{100}{70} = £11,000$$

NOTE
It is recommended that the grossing up of dividend income is done on the face of the profit and loss account without any entry in the ledger accounts.

Illustration 11

At 30 June 19X8, the balance sheet of Jones Ltd showed a provision for corporation tax payable 1 January 19X9 of £22,000 and a provision for corporation tax payable 1 January 19X10 of £23,200.

During the year ended 30 June 19X9:

(1) Corporation tax on profits for the year ended 30 June 19X7 was finally agreed at £21,500 and paid. Corporation tax on profits for the year ended 30 June 19X8 was finally agreed at £24,000.
(2) Debenture interest of £560 (net) was paid on both 31 December 19X8 and 30 June 19X9.
(3) Interest on government securities of £5,600 (net) was received on 31 March 19X9.
(4) Preference dividends of £700 (cash) were received on both 1 December 19X8 and 1 June 19X9 from quoted companies.
(5) An interim of ordinary dividend of £14,000 (cash) was paid on 23 March 19X9.
    Corporation tax based on profits for the year at 35% is estimated at £31,000. The directors propose a final ordinary dividend payable on 1 September 19X9 of £28,000. Assume income tax at basic rate of 30% and ACT at $\frac{3}{7}$ of the qualifying distributions, less tax credits.
    Required for the year ended 30 June 19X9:

(a) corporation tax account;
(b) income tax account;
(c) advance corporation tax account;
(d) unfranked investment income account.
(e) debenture interest account;
(f) deferred asset account;
(g) extracts from financial statements.

MAINSTREAM CORPORATION TAX

	£		£
19X9		*19X8*	
1 Jan		1 July	
Cash	21,500	Bal b/d (19X7)	22,000
		Bal b/d (19X8)	23,200
30 June			
P/L (22,000 – 21,500)	500		
Income tax	1,920		
ACT	5,400	*19X9*	
Bal c/d (19X8)	24,000	30 June	
Bal c/d (19X9)		P/L (24,000 – 23,200)	800
(31,000 – 5,400 – 1,920)	23,680	P/L	31,000
	———		———
	77,000		77,000
	═══		═══

INCOME TAX ACCOUNT

	£		£
19X9		*19X8*	
14 Jan		31 Dec	
Cash	240	Interest paid	240
31 March		*19X9*	
Interest received	2,400	14 April	
		Cash (refund)	240
		30 June	
		Interest paid	240
		Corporation tax account	
		(2,400 – 480)	1,920
	———		———
	2,640		2,640
	═══		═══

ADVANCE CORPORATION TAX

	£		£
19X9		*19X9*	
14 April		30 June	
Cash $\frac{3}{7}$ (14,000 – 700)	5,700	Bal c/d—ACT reclaim (payable	
30 June		14 July) $\frac{3}{7}$ × 700	300
Bal c/d	12,000	Corporation tax a/c	
		(5,700 – 300)	5,400
		Deferred asset $\frac{3}{7}$ × 28,000	12,000
	———		———
	17,700		17,700
	═══		═══

UNFRANKED INVESTMENT INCOME ACCOUNT

	£		£
19X9		*19X9*	
30 June		31 March	
P/L	8,000	Cash	5,600
		Income tax	2,400
	———		———
	8,000		8,000
	═══		═══

DEBENTURE INTEREST ACCOUNT

	£		£
19X8		*19X9*	
31 December		30 June	
Cash	560	P/L	1,600
Income tax	240		
19X9			
30 June			
Cash	560		
Income tax	240		
	_____		_____
	1,600		1,600
	=====		=====

DEFERRED ASSET ACCOUNT

	£		£
19X9			
30 June ACT a/c	12,000		

Profit and loss extracts

		£
Loan interest paid		1,600
Income from investments:		
Dividends	2,000	
Interest	8,000	10,000
	_____	
Tax on profit on ordinary activities:		
Corporation tax at 35%	31,000	
Tax underprovided in previous years	300	
Tax credit on UK dividends received	600	31,900
	_____	
Dividends on ordinary shares:		
Paid	14,000	
Proposed	28,000	42,000
	_____	

Balance sheet extracts

Debtors—deferred asset:	
ACT recoverable	12,000
ACT reclaimable	300
Creditors—amounts falling due within one year:	
Tax and social security	36,000
Proposed dividends	28,000
Creditors—amounts falling due after more than one year:	
Corporation tax payable 1.1.X11	23,680

(j) Recoverability of ACT

It has been assumed that any ACT paid may be offset in full in arriving at MCT. This is so provided that the net ACT paid over does not exceed 30% (at basic rate income of tax of 30%) of the corporation tax income.

For tax purposes, any ACT not relieved in this way may be carried back for six years or carried forward indefinitely.

For accounting purposes, it is necessary to decide whether the recovery of the ACT is reasonably certain and foreseeable. If this is not so, ACT should be written off in the profit and loss account. The amount written off forms part of the tax charge, but has no effect on the possible future availability of loss relief for tax purposes.

ACT may be regarded as recoverable in the following circumstances:

(1) where current year or preceding year income is sufficient for set-off purposes;

(2) where a deferred tax account of sufficient size exists (ACT must not exceed 30% of the income timing differences on which deferred tax is calculated);

(3) where income of the next accounting period is expected to be sufficient for set-off purposes.

Illustration 12

The following details related to Wilson Ltd.
Assume corporation tax rate is 35% and ACT $\frac{3}{7}$.

	Chargeable income £	Dividend paid £	ACT paid £
19X6	600,000	235,000	100,714
19X7	150,000	165,000	70,714

	£
Gross corporation tax is 35% × £600,000	210,000
Less ACT	100,714
So MCT =	109,286

(No restriction applies as ACT paid is below 30% of corporation tax income of £600,000. Unused set-off is £180,000, less £100,714 i e £79,286.)

19X7

	£
Gross corporation tax is 35% × £150,000	52,500
Less ACT set-off: restricted to 30% × 150,000	45,000
So MCT =	7,500

Surplus ACT is £70,714 − £45,000 = £25,714. As this is below the unused set-off of £79,286, the £25,714 may be reclaimed from the Inland Revenue.

Illustration 13

Suppose the facts as in the previous illustration, but the dividend paid in 19X7 amounted to £320,000 (ACT $\frac{3}{7}$ × 320,000 = £137,143). MCT would be the same, but surplus ACT would amount to £137,143 − £45,000 = £92,143. The maximum repayment would be £79,286, so £12,857 would remain unrelieved. Unless evidence could be produced to demonstrate its recovery within the following year, £12,857 should be written off to profit and loss account and included as a separate part of the tax charge.

(k) Unrelieved overseas tax

There may be two possible causes of unrelieved overseas taxation:

(1) The rate of overseas tax on overseas profits exceeds the rate of UK corporation tax applied to those profits.

Illustration 14

	£
UK profits	700,000 (35%)
Overseas profits	200,000 (60%)
Total	900,000

Overseas tax is 60% × £200,000 i e £120,000.
Relief is restricted to 35% × £200,000 i e £70,000.

Profit and loss account (extract)

	£
UK corporation tax on profits at 35%	315,000
Less relief for overseas tax	70,000
	245,000
Overseas tax	120,000
	365,000

(2) Payment of a large UK dividend so as to restrict relief for overseas tax.

9.2 DEFERRED TAXATION

(a) Introduction

In the UK, corporation tax is assessed on a company's tax-adjusted profit. It is unlikely that this will be the same as its accounting or reported profit.

Illustration 15

The tax computation of Gardens plc is as follows:

		£'000
Accounting profit (= reported profit)		800
Add depreciation	260	
Interest payable	90	
Entertaining	40	390
		1,190
Less capital allowances	440	
Interest paid	70	510
Taxable profit		680

Assuming a corporation tax rate of 35%, corporation tax payable amounts to 35% of £680,000 i e £238,000.

(b) Timing differences and permanent differences

The difference between the two profit figures can be analysed between timing differences and permanent differences.

Timing differences reflect the fact that some items are recorded in different periods for tax as opposed to accounts purposes.

For example:

(1) Interest payable is treated for accounts purposes on an accruals basis. For tax purposes, interest payable is dealt with on a purely cash basis.
(2) Depreciation charges are allocated over accounting periods over the asset's useful life on an accruals basis. For tax purposes, the Inland Revenue allow capital allowances rather than depreciation. Ignoring transitional provisions following the Finance Act 1984, capital allowances for most assets are calculated as 25% of the original expenditure, on a reducing balance basis. Again, the difference is one of timing.

Permanent differences are usually items which are reflected in the accounts but which are totally disregarded for tax purposes. For example, entertaining expenditure relating to UK customers is charged in the accounts but is never ever allowed for tax purposes.

Deferred tax is concerned with timing differences. Permanent differences are outside the scope of deferred tax.

Illustration 16

In the above illustration, accounting and taxable profit figures may be reconciled as follows:

		£'000
Accounting profit		800
Timing differences:		
Depreciation (440 – 260)	180	
Interest (90 – 70)	(20)	(160)
		640
Permanent differences:		
Entertaining		40
Taxable profit		680

(c) Examples of timing and permanent differences

(1) *Timing differences: short-term*

(i)   Interest payable.
(ii) Interest receivable.
(iii) Royalties payable
(iv) General bad debt provisions—not allowed for tax purposes until they become specific.
(v)   Pension costs accrued.
(vi) Provisions for repairs and maintenance.

(2) *Timing differences: other*

(i)   Capital allowances/depreciation.
(ii) Revaluation surpluses reflected in the accounts but not taxable until the related fixed asset is disposed of.
(iii) Disposal of fixed assets where payment of tax is postponed as a result of roll-over relief.

(3) *Permanent differences*

(i)   Disallowable entertaining expenditure.
(ii) Depreciation on buildings which do not rank for tax allowances.
(iii) Disallowable fines.

(d) The full provision approach to deferred taxation

Under a previous standard (subsequently withdrawn), deferred tax had to be provided in full in company accounts irrespective of the circumstances of a company. Deferred tax was calculated by applying the corporation tax rate applicable to the company to the timing differences. The calculation is illustrated below, using for simplicity a company with a single fixed asset.

Illustration 17

A company acquired a fixed asset on 1.1.X1 at a cost of £80,000. The company's depreciation policy is to depreciate over ten years on a straight-line basis, ignoring residual value. The profit after depreciation is £100,000 in each of the years 19X1 to 19X4. Assume the corporation tax rate is 30% and 25% writing-down allowances are available for tax purposes. No first year allowances are available.

   Required: show the relevant extracts for both profit and loss account and balance sheet for each of the years 19X1 to 19X4 assuming deferred tax is provided in full on all timing differences.

(1) Calculations

(i) Deferred tax

	(1) Accounts NBV £	(2) Tax WDV £	Deferred tax account (1) − (2) times 30%
Cost of asset 19X1	80,000	80,000	0
Depreciation (Dep)/writing-down allowance (WDA) 19X1	8,000	20,000	3,600
A/cs NBV/tax WDV 31.12.X1	72,000	60,000	3,600
Dep/WDA 19X2	8,000	15,000	2,100
A/cs NBV/tax WDV 31.12.X2	64,000	45,000	5,700
Dep/WDA 19X3	8,000	11,250	975
A/cs NBV/tax WDV 31.12.X3	56,000	33,750	6,675
Dep/WDA 19X4	8,000	8,437	131
A/cs NBV/tax WDV 31.12.X4	48,000	25,313	6,806
Dep/WDV 19X5	8,000	6,328	(502)
A/cs NBV/tax WDV 31.12.X5	40,000	18,985	6,304

(ii) Corporation tax

	19X1 £	19X2 £	19X3 £	19X4 £	19X5 £
Accounting profit	100,000	100,000	100,000	100,000	100,000
Add depreciation	8,000	8,000	8,000	8,000	8,000
Less capital allowances	(20,000)	(15,000)	(11,250)	(8,437)	(6,328)
Taxable profit	88,000	93,000	96,750	99,563	101,672
Corporation tax at 30%	26,400	27,900	29,025	29,869	30,502

(2) Extracts from financial statements

(i) Profit and loss account

	19X1 £	19X2 £	19X3 £	19X4 £	19X5 £
Profit on ordinary activities before tax	100,000	100,000	100,000	100,000	100,000
Taxation:					
Corporation tax	26,400	27,900	29,025	29,869	30,502
Deferred tax	3,600	2,100	975	131	(502)
	30,000	30,000	30,000	30,000	30,000
Total tax charge as percentage of accounting profit	30%	30%	30%	30%	30%

COMMENT

Assuming no permanent differences, then if deferred tax is provided in full, irrespective of the circumstances of the company, then the tax charge bears a relationship to reported profit.

(ii) Balance sheet

	19X1 £	19X2 £	19X3 £	19X4 £
Creditors—amounts falling due within one year:				
Corporation tax	26,400	27,900	29,025	29,869
Provisions for liabilities and charges:				
Deferred tax	3,600	5,700	6,675	6,806

Illustration 18

A company's only short-term timing differences relate to interest receivable. Relevant details are as follows:

	19X2 £	19X3 £	19X4 £	19X5 £
Debtors—interest receivable at 31 December	10,000	12,000	8,000	8,000
Profit before interest	50,000	50,000	50,000	50,000
Investment income	10,000	30,000	40,000	42,000
Cash received	Nil	28,000	44,000	42,000
Corporation tax rate	30%	30%	30%	30%
Taxable income	50,000	78,000	94,000	92,000
Corporation tax	15,000	23,400	28,200	27,600

Required: relevant extracts from financial statements.

Calculation of deferred tax

	£ Timing differences	£ Deferred tax (=timing differences × 30%)
Interest debtor at 31.12.X1	Nil	Nil
19X2		
Excess of income in P/L over cash received	10,000	3,000
Interest debtor at 31.12.X2	10,000	3,000
19X3		
Excess of income over cash	2,000	600
Interest debtor at 31.12.X3	12,000	3,600
19X4		
Excess of cash over income	(4,000)	(1,200)
Interest debtor at 31.12.X4	8,000	2,400
19X5		
Excess of income over cash	—	—
Interest debtor at 31.12.X5	8,000	2,400

Extracts from financial statements

(i) Profit and loss account

	19X2 £	19X3 £	19X4 £	19X5 £
Operating profit	50,000	50,000	50,000	50,000
Investment income	10,000	30,000	40,000	42,000
Profit on ordinary activities before tax	60,000	80,000	90,000	92,000
Taxation:				
Corporation tax	15,000	23,400	28,200	27,600
Deferred tax	3,000	600	(1,200)	—
	18,000	24,000	27,000	27,600
Total tax charge as percentage of accounting profit	30%	30%	30%	30%

(e) The need for deferred tax

For many years, most accountants have recognised the need for deferred tax even if they have not agreed upon the basis on which it should be computed.

Two principal reasons have been given to underline the importance of deferred tax:

(1) The fact that profit after tax is regarded as an important indicator of performance. This figure enters into the earnings per share calculation for listed companies, from which is computed the price/earnings ratio.
(2) The importance from the balance sheet viewpoint of the relationship between shareholders' funds and other sources of funds.

The implications of these two points are considered below under discussion of the possible approaches to deferred tax.

(f) Criticisms of the full provision approach

The full provision approach is sometimes referred to as the full deferral approach or comprehensive tax allocation approach. This approach was at one time mandatory for all companies under the requirements of the subsequently withdrawn standard SSAP 11.

The full provision approach considers individual timing differences relating to individual fixed assets, specific loans receivable, and so on. For example, referring back to the two illustrations in section (d):

(1) As regards the fixed asset purchase in 19X1, an originating timing difference of £12,000 (i e £20,000 less £8,000) comes about in 19X1. A further originating timing difference of £7,000 (i e £15,000 less £8,000) occurs in 19X2. These timing differences will not reverse until those subsequent years such as 19X5 where depreciations exceed capital allowances.

The reversal of these timing differences will result in a taxable income in excess of reported income, thus giving rise to larger than might be expected corporation tax liabilities in such years. The build-up of the deferred tax liability over the years 19X1 to 19X4 is then in anticipation of these liabilities.
(2) As regards loan interest receivable, the interest is recognised for accounts (reporting) purposes in the year of accrual, but not taxed until the subsequent year of receipt. The deferred tax liability is a provision for the tax that will eventually become assessable.

Why did the full deferral approach become subject to widespread criticism and eventually be replaced by an alternative approach? In order to appreciate the reasons, it is necessary to go back to years of 100% first year allowances and stock appreciation relief. Many companies investing in plant and machinery and stocks found that they were paying little or no corporation tax. This was not just a question of isolated years, but an annual occurrence. Effectively, any depreciation in the tax computation was more than out-weighed by capital allowances and stock relief.

In theory, if individual fixed assets were considered, then individual timing differences could be regarded as eventually reversing. In practice, if the company was looked at as a going concern, the directors of the company could often provide reasonable grounds to show that for the foreseeable future the aggregate of capital allowances each year would exceed the total depreciation charge for that year. In situations such as these, full deferral could be said to have two particular unfortunate consequences.

(i) As regards the tax charge in the profit and loss account, the effect of debiting deferred tax each year and adding this to corporation tax was to create an artificially high tax charge which had little meaning. This total charge was said to distort earnings per share, and possibly to counteract some of the fiscal aims of accelerated capital allowances.
(ii) As regards the deferred tax provision in the balance sheet, full deferral combined with a recurring annual situation of capital allowances in excess of depreciation resulted in an ever-increasing deferred tax balance. Such a liability was regarded by many accountants as fictitious and remote, possibly only ever becoming payable if the company went into liquidation. Users of financial statements might misunderstand the nature and effect of a deferred tax provision.

(g) Alternative approaches to deferred taxation

Two alternatives to full deferral have been advocated:

(1) Partial deferral—the approach in SSAP 15 and regarded as consistent with the Companies Act 1985. This approach is discussed in detail in section (h) below.
(2) Flow-through approach, whereby the total tax charge in the profit and loss account is based on the estimated corporation tax assessment for the year in question. Deferred tax is effectively ignored. The main argument in favour of the flow-through approach is that it removes the need for subjective judgement (which is an important aspect of partial deferral) and the possible calculation of unrealistic charges and provisions.

However, in some instances, the use of the flow-through approach could result in an imprudent approach to taxation. For example, a year in which substantial tax allowances were received might give an over-optimistic impression, only to be followed by a year of high tax charge. Such fluctuations would not assist users of accounts.

The flow-through approach has been rejected by the Accounting Standards Committee and is incompatible with the requirements of the Companies Act 1985. The Companies Act 1985 requires provision to be made for amounts retained as reasonably necessary for the purpose of providing for any liability which is either likely to be incurred or certain to be incurred, but uncertain as to amount or date of payment.

(h) Partial deferral

Under the partial deferral approach, provision is made for the tax effects of all timing differences expected to arise within the foreseeable future. Under the partial deferral approach, timing differences are considered on an overall rather than individual basis.

Illustration 19

The following information relates to Redbank plc. The only timing differences relate to capital allowances/depreciation.

(1) Historical information

Year	Capital allowances £m	Depreciation £m	Excess of capital allowances over depreciation £m
19X0	40	30	10
19X1	48	41	7
19X2	52	43	9
19X3	57	45	12

(2) Projections at balance sheet date (31.12.X3)

19X4	56	46	10
19X5	55	48	7
19X6	59	50	9

Assume, that at 31.12.X3, the excess of accounts net book value of the fixed assets over the tax written down value amounted to £110 million and that the relevant corporation tax rate is 35%.

When timing differences are considered in aggregate, it appears that looking ahead 3 years (19X4, 19X5, 19X6) no reversal of timing differences are anticipated (since there is no expectation in any year that depreciation will exceed capital allowances).

Under the partial deferral approach, *no* deferred tax provision would be required. The total potential deferred tax of £38.5 million (i e 35% × 110) would be dealt with as follows:

	£m
(a) provided in the balance sheet	Nil
(b) unprovided (referred to in a memorandum note	38.5
Total:	38.5

Illustration 20

Waterhead plc has always adopted the partial deferral approach to deferred taxation. However, in previous years, it has always been able to demonstrate that no provision is required for deferred tax.

The company is presently drafting its financial statements for the year ended 31 December 19X2. The projections for the next three years are as follows:

Year	Capital allowances £m	Depreciation £m	Capital allowance less depreciation £m
19X3	62	50	12
19X4	60	70	(10)
19X5	58	65	(7)

Should a deferred tax provision be set up in the balance sheet at 31 December 19X2? The main problem is that the company can foresee an overall reversal in timing differences in 19X4. In the 19X4 tax computation, it is predicted that taxable income will exceed accounting income by £10m thus giving rise to a correspondingly large payment of corporation tax. The question is should the company pick up the liability in 19X4 (flow-through approach), or set up a provision as soon as the need is foreseen? Under the Companies Act 1985, a provision is required for a liability which is likely to be incurred.

In order to determine whether a provision should be set up at 31.12.X2 (as opposed to waiting until, say, 31.12.X3), it is recommended that the following table is set up. Corporation tax is taken as 35%.

Projections at 31.12.X2

Year	Capital allowances £m	Depreciation £m	Originating (reversing) timing differences £m	Cumulative originating (reversing) timing differences £m
19X3	62	50	12	12
19X4	60	70	(10)	2
19X5	58	65	(7)	(5) ←

The final column is the cumulative total of column 3. A maximum cumulative reversal of £5 million can be foreseen. A deferred tax provision should therefore be set up in the balance sheet. The amount required is 35% × £5m i e £1.75m. Since the provision at the beginning of the year is nil, a charge should be made to profit and loss account of £1.75m. At the subsequent balance sheet date, a similar exercise should be repeated. Assume this shows the following and that no revision is made for the 19X5 and 19X6 projections.

Projections at 31.12.X4

Year	Capital allowances £m	Depreciation £m	Originating (reversing) timing differences £m	Cumulative originating (reversing) timing differences £m
19X4	60	70	(10)	(10)
19X5	58	65	(7)	(17) ←
19X6	85	70	15	(2)

The maximum cumulative reversal which can be foreseen is £17m. A deferred tax provision at 31.12.X3 of 35% × £17m i e £5.95m is required.

A deferred tax charge of (5.95 less 1.75) i e 4.20 should be made in the profit and loss account.

Projections at 31.12.X4

Year	Capital allowances £m	Depreciation £m	Originating (reversing) timing differences £m	Cumulative originating (reversing) timing differences £m
19X5	58	65	(7)	(7) ←
19X6	85	70	15	8
19X7	82	73	9	17

Deferred tax provision required at 31.12.X6 is 35% i e £2.45m.
  Credit to profit and loss account in respect of deferred tax (5.95 less 2.45) i e £3.50m.

Projections at 31.12.X5
No reversals are foreseen, so no provision is required. The opening provision of £2.45m is no longer required and so may be credited to profit and loss account.

Summary of effect on financial statements

	19X1 £m	19X2 £m	19X3 £m	19X4 £m	19X5 £m
Balance sheet (31 Dec)					
Provision for deferred tax	Nil	1.75	5.95	2.45	Nil
Profit and loss account (tax charge)					
Corporation tax	X	X	X	X	X
Deferred tax	Nil	1.75	4.20	(3.5)	(2.45)
Total tax charge	X	X	X	X	X

At each balance sheet date a memorandum note would be required stating any unprovided deferred tax. This would be calculated as follows:

	£m
Total potential deferred tax	
35% (acs NBV – tax WDV)	X
less deferred tax provision (as calculated above)	X
∴unprovided deferred tax (i e calculated as a balancing figure)	X

COMMENTS
(1) The deferred tax balance is built up to £5.95m by 31.12.X3. In 19X4, the net add back in the tax computation is £10m i e a substantial corporation tax payment will become due nine months after the end of the year (30 September 19X5). The deferred tax provision is the amount retained to provide for the 19X4 and 19X5 liabilities.
(2) Had no deferred tax provision been established prior to 19X4, the tax charge for 19X4 would have been substantial. The effect of deferred tax is to achieve a total tax charge in 19X4 equivalent to approximately 35% of the reporting accounting profit.

(i) The three approaches—an overview

The three approaches may be compared as follows:

	Full deferral approach	*Partial deferral approach*	*Flow-through approach*
ED/SSAP	ED 11/SSAP 11	ED 19/SSAP 15/ ED 33/SSAP 15 revised	N/A
Objective or subjective	Objective	Subjective	Objective
Acceptability (SSAPs, Companies Act 1985)	Unacceptable — unrealistic tax charge and liability	Acceptable — although dependent on subjective estimates, approach is generally regarded as realistic	Unacceptable — approach is imprudent and incompatible with Companies Act 1985

Note that all statements other than SSAP 15 revised have now been withdrawn.

(j) Principal requirements of SSAP 15 (Accounting for deferred taxation)

These requirements may be divided into two parts: accounting requirements and disclosure requirements.

(1) *Accounting requirements*

(i) *Approach*
SSAP 15 requires a partial deferred approach. Both full deferral and flow-through approaches are rejected. Deferred tax should be accounted for to the extent that it is probable that a liability or asset will crystallise. Undue prudence is discouraged in that SSAP 15 specifies that deferred tax should not be accounted for to the extent that it is probable that a liability or asset will not crystallise. The basis of calculation was covered in Illustration 20.

(ii) *Method*
Deferred tax should be computed under the liability method (see (k) below). The deferral method is thus unacceptable.

More detailed accounting requirements are referred under the relevant headings below.

(2) *Disclosure requirements*

(i) *Profit and loss account—disclosure:*

—deferred tax component of total tax charge on profit on ordinary activities;
—deferred tax relating to extraordinary items;
—unprovided deferred tax in a memorandum note analysing the amount into its major components;
—adjustments to deferred tax account. If they result from changes in tax rates they should form part of the total tax charge on profit on ordinary activities (separately disclosed if material). If the adjustments result from changes in the basis of tax or government fiscal policy they should be treated as extraordinary items.

(ii) *Balance sheet—disclosure:*

—deferred tax provided in B/S analysed into its major components;
—unprovided (i e memorandum only) deferred tax analysed into its major components;
—transfers to/from deferred tax account.

Illustration 21

Beckmire plc has summarised the following information relating to taxation matters:

(1) Deferred tax is provided for all timing differences on a partial deferral basis. At the present time, the only material timing differences relate to capital allowances and depreciation.
(2) The deferred tax balance at 1.1.X6 amounted to £875,200. During the year ended 31.12.X6, a transfer of £132,000 relating to the excess of capital allowances over depreciation is to be made to deferred tax account.
(3) At 31.12.X6, the excess of accounts net book value over tax written-down value amounts to £4,200,000. Corporation tax is 35%.
(4) Corporation tax on the profits for the year is estimated at £596,000.
(5) The total tax charge (corporation tax and deferred tax) has been reduced by £173,000 as a result of capital allowances.
(6) No dividends were paid during the year. A dividend amounting to £140,000 is proposed. ACT is to be taken as $\frac{3}{7}$.

Required: extracts from financial statements for the year ended 31 December 19X6.

Balance sheet extracts

Creditors: amount falling due within one year

	£
Proposed dividends	140,000
Tax and social security	656,000

(Workings: £596,000 + $\frac{3}{7}$ × £140,000 = £656,000)

Provision for liabilities and charges

Deferred taxation	947,200

(Workings: £875,200 + £132,000 − $\frac{3}{7}$ × £140,000 = £947,200)

Profit and loss account extracts

Tax on profit on ordinary activities:

	£
Corporation tax	596,000
Deferred tax	132,000
	728,000

Note: the tax charge has been reduced by £173,000 as a result of capital allowances.

NOTES TO THE ACCOUNTS:

(1) *Accounting policy note*
Provision is made for deferred taxation using the liability method on all timing differences except to the extent that these amounts are not regarded as likely to become payable in the foreseeable future.

(2) *Deferred tax*

	£
Balance at 1.1.19X6	875,200
Transfer during the year	132,000
	1,007,200
ACT on proposed dividends	60,000
	947,200

	Provided £	Unprovided £
Capital allowances	1,007,200	462,800
Other timing differences	X	X
	1,007,200	462,800
Advance corporation tax recoverable	60,000	
	947,200	

Working

Total potential deferred tax	
35% × £4,200,000	1,470,000
Provided in the accounts	1,007,200
∴ Unprovided	462,800

(k) Methods of computing deferred tax balances

In theory two methods of computing deferred tax balances are available. Where corporation tax rates fluctuate over a period of years, these two methods will give different results.

(i) The liability method—whereby the deferred tax balance is revised to take account of changes in the rate of corporation tax. This is the method which is compatible with the overall requirements of the Companies Act 1985. The advantage of this approach is that deferred tax balances in the balance sheet represent the best estimates of amounts which would be payable or receivable if the particular timing differences reversed. Any adjustments to deferred tax as a result of tax rate changes should be treated as part of the tax charge or credit in the profit and loss account.

As stated above, this is the method required by SSAP 15.

(ii) The deferral method—whereby the tax effects of timing differences are calculated using tax rates applicable when the timing differences arise. No adjustment to deferred tax balance is made as a result of subsequent changes in the rate of corporation tax. This approach regards the deferred tax balance as a deferred charge or credit rather than an asset or liability. This appears to be inconsistent with the requirements of the Companies Act 1985 and is not accepted under SSAP 15.

Illustration 22

A company acquired an asset on 1 January 19X2 at a cost of £50,000. The company's depreciation policy is to depreciate on a straight-line basis over ten years. The asset ranks for a writing-down allowance (WDA) of 25% but no first year allowance. Assume that deferred tax is provided in full, and the corporation rate is 35% in 19X2, 33% in 19X3 and 34% in 19X4. Calculate the relevant amounts for the deferred tax under the two approaches for the years 19X2, 19X3 and 19X4.

Depreciation and WDA calculations

	Accounts NBV £	Tax WDV £
Cost of asset 19X2	50,000	50,000
Depreciation/WDA 19X2	5,000	12,500
NBV/WDV 31.12.X2	45,000	37,500
Depreciation/WDA 19X3	5,000	9,375
NBV/WDV 31.12.X3	40,000	28,125
Depreciation/WDV 19X4	5,000	7,031
NBV/WDV 31.12.X4	35,000	21,094

Deferred tax calculations

	Liability method £	£	Deferral method £	£
Balance 1.1.X2		0		0
P/L 19X2				
35% (12,500 − 5,000)		2,625		2,625
Balance 31.12.X2		2,625		2,625
P/L 19X3				
35% (9,375 − 5,000)	1,531		1,531	
Tax rate adjustment				
(21,875 − 10,000) × 2%	(237)		—	
		1,294		1,531
Balance 31.12.X3		3,919		4,156
P/L 19X4				
35% (7,031 − 5,000)	711		711	
Tax rate adjustment				
1% × 11,875 = 119				
1% × 2,031 = (20)	99			
		810		711
Balance 31.12.X4		4,729		4,867

Note: In any subsequent year where timing differences reversed, under the deferral method, deferred credits to profit and loss account would be evaluated at 35%.

(I) Assessing the amount to be provided

The assessment should be based on reasonable assumptions. These should take account of:

(1) post-balance sheet events and management intentions;
(2) financial plans and projections—usually covering a 3 to 5 year period;
(3) prudence—a prudent view should be taken when financial plans or projections are susceptible to a high degree of uncertainty or are not fully developed for the appropriate period. (Note reference to prudence concept.)

(m) Separate consideration of deferred tax assets and deferred tax liabilities

The standard requires separate consideration of assets and liabilities. The procedures may be summarised as follows:

(1) Assess deferred tax liabilities. In determining the amount to be provided, short-term and other timing differences should be considered together.

(2) Consider each deferred tax asset category separately in order to determine whether an asset will crystallise. The standard is not specific on this matter but deferred tax assets could include the tax effects of losses, interest payable, provisions for repairs and maintenance etc. Such assets should only be regarded as crystallising if they are expected to be recoverable without replacement by equivalent debit balances.

(3) Those deferred tax liabilities required to be recognised in the accounts should be reduced by any deferred tax debit balances arising from any separate categories of timing differences and any advance corporation tax available for offset against those liabilities.

Illustration

Woodvale plc is preparing its accounts for the year ended 31 December 19X6. The following information is available regarding deferred tax.

(i) *Capital allowances*
   At 31.12.X6 the accounts net book value of fixed assets exceeds the tax written down value by £170,000. Projections at 31.12.X6 show the following position:

	Capital allowances £'000	Depreciation £'000	Timing differences £'000
19X7	120	100	20
19X8	140	110	30
19X9	70	130	(60)
19X10	110	125	15

(ii) *Interest receivable*
   At 31.12.X6, the relevant total of interest receivable in the balance sheet is £80,000. The loan to which this relates falls due for repayment in 19X7. No further investment by Woodvale is anticipated.

(iii) *Interest payable*
   Woodvale took out a loan some years ago repayable in 19X35. The interest payable amounted at 31.12.X6 to £60,000. No further loans are foreseen within the next five to seven years.

(iv) The balance sheet at 31.12.X6 included a provision for repairs and maintenance amounting to £40,000. The expenditure is expected to be incurred during 19X7.

Required

The deferred tax to be provided at 31.12.X6 assuming the rate of corporation tax is 35%. The memorandum amount of unprovided deferred tax should also be shown.

Solution

(1) Deferred tax liabilities—taking all categories of timing differences together:

	Capital allowances £'000	*Interest receivable £'000*	*Originating (reversing) £'000*	*Cumulative £'000*
19X7	20	(80)	(60)	(60)
19X8	30	—	30	(30)
19X9	(60)	—	(60)	(90)
19X10	15	—	15	(75)

Maximum cumulative reversal foreseen is £90,000
∴ provision required is 35% × £90,000   =   £31,500

Capital allowances 35% × £10,000   =   3,500
Interest receivable 35% × £80,000   =   28,000

                                                                                  31,500

Memo note—unprovided deferred tax
Capital allowances
Total potential 35% × 170,000   59,500
Provided (above)   3,500

Unprovided   56,000

Interest receivable unprovided   Nil

(2) Deferred tax assets:

                                                                                       £
  (i) *interest payable*   21,000
       —unprovided note
          35% × £60,000 =
  (ii) *provision for repairs*
       —provided 35% × £40,000 =   14,000
       —unprovided   Nil

Summary of disclosures—balance sheet

	Provided £'000	*Unprovided £'000*
Capital allowances	3,500	56,000
Short-term timing differences		
—liabilities	28,000	Nil
—assets	(14,000)	(21,000)
	7,500	35,000

(n) Deferred tax debit balances

(1) Deferred tax net debit balances—should not be carried forward as assets except to the extent that they are expected to be recoverable without replacement by equivalent debit balances.

(2) Deferred tax debit balances relating to advance corporation tax on dividends.

  (i) ACT on dividends payable or proposed—carry forward as assets provided that such ACT can be foreseen to be recoverable against tax on profits of the following year.

  (ii) ACT on dividends other than those payable or proposed at the year end—write off to P/L unless their recovery is assured beyond reasonable doubt.

9.3   PRESENTATION IN FINANCIAL STATEMENTS

(a) Introduction

Disclosure requirements for tax are set out in:

SSAP 8 The treatment of taxation under the imputation system in the accounts of companies.
SSAP 15 Accounting for deferred taxation.
Companies Act 1985 (Fourth Schedule).

The overall effect of these requirements is summarised below.

(b) Profit and loss account

P/L item	*Comments*
Income from fixed asset investments.	(1) Dividends to be included gross i e cash received plus tax credit.
	(2) Interest to be included gross of income tax.
Tax on profit on ordinary activities.	Disclose separately:
	(1) UK corporation tax: (i) corporation tax; (ii) deferred tax; (iii) tax attributable to franked investment income (tax credits); (iv) irrecoverable ACT; (v) relief for overseas taxation.
	(2) Total overseas tax: (i) relieved and unrelieved; (ii) specify the part of unrelieved tax arising from payment of dividends.
	(3) Latest known rate of corporation tax.
Tax on extraordinary profit or loss.	
Dividends paid/proposed.	State at cash paid/payable to shareholders — do not include related ACT.

(c) Balance sheet

B/S item	Comments
Debtors	
ACT recoverable.	⎫ Indicate any part not
	⎬ recoverable within 12 months
Deferred tax.	⎭ of balance sheet date.
Creditors: amounts falling due within one year	
Other creditors including tax and social security.	(1) Disclose tax and social security total separately.
	(2) This will include ACT, MCT, PAYE, NI, VAT.
Proposed dividends.	State at cash paid/payable to shareholders — do not include related ACT.
Creditors: amounts falling due after more than one year	
Other creditors including tax and security.	(1) Disclose tax and social security separately.
	(2) This will include MCT if payable in more than 12 months' time.
	(3) Disclose payment date.
Provisions for liabilities and charges	
Taxation, including deferred taxation.	Will usually relate to deferred tax only.
Capital and reserves Revaluation reserve.	Disclose deferred tax relating to movements on reserve.

(d) Other disclosure requirements

(1) Accounting policies statement.
(2) Particulars of special circumstances affecting the tax liability.
(3) Extent to which the tax charge for the period has been reduced by capital allowances and other timing differences.
(4) Where fixed asset valuation is disclosed by way of note, indicate tax implications if asset were to be realised at the balance sheet date at the valuation amount.

9.4   SSAP 5 (ACCOUNTING FOR VALUE ADDED TAX)

Value added tax (VAT) is a tax on the final consumer and, therefore, the trader is normally merely acting as a collector on behalf of the Revenue. Amounts due to and from the Revenue will be included in creditors and debtors, and need not be disclosed separately.

Turnover shown in the profit and loss account should exclude VAT.

Irrecoverable VAT attributable to fixed assets should be treated as part of their cost. Capital commitments should also include irrecoverable VAT.

Irrecoverable VAT should be included in costs e g where the trader suffers VAT on his inputs but is exempted, either in whole or in part, on his outputs.

10 LEASING AND HIRE-PURCHASE ACCOUNTING

10.1 BACKGROUND

(a) Financing of fixed assets

A company may acquire the right to use a fixed asset over its useful life in one of a number of ways. These include:

(1) outright purchase for cash;
(2) outright purchase using the proceeds of a secured or unsecured loan;
(3) hire-purchase (or lease purchase);
(4) finance leasing.

In the case of (1) and (2), legal title to the fixed asset is obtained at the date of purchase. In the case of (3), title is obtained when the final instalment has been paid and the option to purchase exercised. In the case of an agreement under a finance lease, as far as the UK is concerned legal title can never pass to the lessee.

(b) Hire-purchase accounting

Traditional assets acquired under hire-purchase agreements are brought into the balance sheet at cash price and depreciated over their useful economic life to the hiree. A corresponding obligation or liability is shown in the balance sheet. Payments to the hirer are allocated between capital and interest using some suitable basis. The capital part is used to reduce the balance sheet obligation, while the income part is debited to profit and loss account.

The justification for this treatment has been the substance over form argument: transactions and other events should be accounted for and presented in accordance with their substance and financial reality, and not merely with their legal form. Rights under hire-purchase agreements, prior to the obtaining of legal title, are for more practical purposes equivalent to those of immediate legal ownership.

(c) Lessee accounting

A lease is a contract between a lessor and a lessee for the hire of a specific asset.

Traditional practice has been to charge lease payments to profit and loss accounts as incurred. While this treatment may be justified for operating leases, it is not appropriate for those types of leases referred to as finance leases.

Operating leases usually involve the lessee paying a rental for the hire of an asset for a period of time which is substantially less than the asset's useful economic life. With an operating lessee, the lessor retains most of the risks and rewards of ownership.

By contrast, finance leases usually involve payment by the lessee to the lessor of the full cost of the asset together with a return on finance provided. Although the lessee never obtains legal title, the lessee has substantially all the risks and rewards which are usually associated with ownership.

(d) Typical characteristics of a finance lease

Characteristics will vary between different leases. The following characteristics are provided by way of illustration:

(1) Lessor retains title to asset. At the end of the lease, the asset is returned to the lessor *or* the asset is disposed of by the lessee as agent for the lessor. The lease may specify that the lessee obtains a substantial part (e g 95%) of the proceeds as a rebate of rentals.
(2) Payments to the lessor during the primary period are substantial and non-cancellable.
(3) Payments to the lessor during the secondary period are nominal in amount ('peppercorn rent'). The lessee may be given the option during the secondary period to renew on an annual basis.
(4) Lessee has uninterrupted use of the asset as long as leasing payments are made (rewards of ownership).
(5) Lessee is responsible for insurance and maintenance (risks of ownership).
(6) Lessee indemnifies lessor for claims.
(7) Lessee cannot dispose of asset.

(e) Arguments in favour of capitalisation of finance leases

SSAP 21 (accounting for leases and hire-purchase contracts) accepts the traditional treatment of operating leases since it reflects both the economic substance and the legal form of the transaction.

However both SSAP 21 and the exposure draft which preceded it (ED 29) have rejected the traditional treatment of finance leases and instead opted for capitalisation. The effect of capitalisation is to account for finance lease assets in a similar way to hire-purchase assets.

There are two main arguments in favour of capitalisation: substance over form, and the analysis of accounts argument.

(1) *Substance over form*

Substance over form recognises that a lessee's rights are for practical purposes little different from those of an outright purchaser. These rights represent an economic resource which is required in the business.

(2) *Analysis of accounts argument*

The traditional treatment of finance leases charges the lease payments to profit and loss account as such payments are made. The finance for such leasing arrangements is excluded from the balance sheet, a practice usually referred to as off-balance sheet finance. This practice may materially distort the view given by the following ratios:

(i) Fixed assets as a proportion of total assets—since leased assets are excluded from the balance sheet.
(ii) Debt/equity (or gearing)—since potentially large liabilities are built up off balance sheet.
(iii) Return on capital employed (profit before interest and tax as a percentage of fixed assets plus net current assets).

SSAP 21 makes it clear that capitalisation of finance leases should assist both external and internal users. External users may be assisted in making investment or credit decisions. Internal users such as managers may be in a better position to appraise divisional performance.

(f) Arguments against capitalisation

The principal argument against is the rejection of the substance over form concept. It is argued that legal form should not be ignored. Proponents of this viewpoint maintain that leased assets and the corresponding obligations thereunder should not be reflected in the balance sheet. However detailed memorandum information should be presented in the notes outside the double entry system. This argument has been rejected by the Accounting Standards Committee for the reasons outlined in (e) above.

Other more minor arguments have been put up but have all been effectively rejected.

(g) Problems of capitalisation concept

Although the theoretical arguments have been forcibly advocated, certain problems remain. For example, the problem of distinguishing between finance leases and operating leases. Secondly, in some cases (such as where an asset could not be alternatively purchased for cash) it is not always clear how much should be capitalised at the outset of the lease.

(h) Companies Act implications

Two aspects should be considered:

(1) accounting treatment;
(2) disclosure requirements.

(1) *Accounting treatment*

The Companies Act 1985 does not define or distinguish between operating leases and finance leases. Thus, no accounting requirements are set out in the Companies Act. However, once SSAP 21 becomes mandatory for particular accounting periods, the overriding true and fair view requirement will effectively add force to the requirements of SSAP 21.

(2) *Disclosure requirements*

Disclosure is required of:

(i)   plant hire charges;
(ii) financial commitments which have not been provided for and which are relevant to assessing the company's state of affairs.

Note that non-cancellable operating leases of land and buildings are included here. Also included are finance lease commitments in so far as not reflected in the balance sheet (e g in the periods before which capitalisation becomes mandatory under SSAP 21).

Finally, the overriding true and fair view requirements (see chapter 5) should always be borne in mind.

10.2   LESSEE ACCOUNTING—CLASSIFICATION

(a) Hire-purchase contracts

The accounting and disclosure requirements for finance leases generally apply equally to hire-purchase contracts. Special points which relate to hire-purchase contracts only will, however, be referred to separately.

(b) Finance leases

(1) *Definition*

A finance lease is a lease that transfers substantially all the risks and rewards of ownership of an asset to the lessee. This transfer is presumed to take place if, at the start of the lease, it can be shown that the present value of the minimum lease payments amounts to 90% or more of the fair value of the leased asset.

These terms are explained immediately below. However, it should be appreciated that the majority of exam questions are unlikely to require elaborate calculations relating to this point.

(2) *Explanation of terms*

(i) PRESENT VALUE

This is obtained by discounting the minimum lease payment using the interest rate implicit in the lease as a discount factor.

(ii) MINIMUM LEASE PAYMENTS

(a) Minimum payments over the remaining part of the lease term. These will relate essentially to the non-cancellable payments during the primary period.
(b) If applicable, any residual amounts (at the end of the lease) which have been guaranteed by the lessee.

(iii) INTEREST RATE IMPLICIT IN THE LEASE

This is the discount rate, which when applied at the outset of the lease, equates the following:

(a) the present value of the amounts which the lessor expects to receive and retain. These amounts will include the minimum payments in (ii) above together with any unguaranteed residual value not accountable to the lessee;
(b) the fair value of the asset.

(iv) FAIR VALUE OF ASSET

This is the price for which an asset could be exchanged in an arms' length transaction. This amount should be reduced by the amount of capital-based grants that such an asset would normally be entitled to.

(3) *Illustration*

Langdale Ltd wishes to acquire the use of a new item of machinery. The company could purchase outright for cash of £16,200 or alternatively enter into a finance lease. The asset has an estimated useful life of ten years with a residual value of £800.
    The terms of the finance lease are as follows:

(i)   Primary period of five years—five rentals of £4,000 p a payable on the first day of each year.
(ii) Secondary period—renewable on an annual basis for an indefinite period. Ignore secondary rentals.
(iii) Lessee responsible for insurance and maintenance.
(iv) At end of lease term, lessee entitled to 80% of proceeds of sale of asset as rebate of rentals.

Step 1
Calculate interest rate implicit in lease using a programmed calculator. To start with, identify the amounts which the lessor expects to receive and retain. These comprise:

(1) the lessee's minimum lease payments i e five lots of £4,000;
(2) unguaranteed residual value, less proportion accountable to the lessee i e 20% × £800 = £160.

It is then a question of determining what interest rate when applied to these amounts equates with a fair value of £16,200. This rate is determined as 12%.

	£
Check £4,000 × 1.0	4,000
£4,000 × 3.037 (annuity tables)	12,148
£160 × 0.322 (present value tables, year 10)	52
	16,200

Step 2

Calculate present value of minimum lease payments using a discount rate of 12%.

	£
£4,000 × 1.0 (payment now)	4,000
£4,000 × 3.037 (annuity, four years)	12,148
	16,148

Step 3

Compare with 90% of fair value of leased asset, i e

90% × £16,200 = £14,580

Conclusion

There is a presumption that the lease is a finance lease. It is unlikely that this presumption could be rebutted since the lease does transfer substantially all the risks and rewards of ownership to the lessee.

(c) Operating leases

An operating lease is defined as a lease other than a finance lease.

(d) Unusual situations

In exceptional circumstances, the above presumptions may be rebutted. For example in very unusual circumstances, a lease that would otherwise be classified as finance may instead be classified as operating. This could be so if it could be shown that the lease did not transfer to the lessee substantially all the risks and rewards of ownership. The converse might in exceptional circumstances also be true.

10.3   LESSEE ACCOUNTING—FINANCE LEASES AND HIRE-PURCHASE CONTRACTS

(a) The concept of capitalisation

Although a lessee never obtains legal title, in the case of finance leases the lessee's rights and obligations are such that the risks and rewards from the use of the asset are substantially (not, of course, identically) similar to those of an outright purchaser.

SSAP 21 makes it quite clear that what is capitalised (and included in the balance sheet as an asset) is *not* the asset itself but the lessee's rights in the asset. Also capitalised is the corresponding obligation to pay rentals. This point is intended to overcome certain criticisms made of ED 29.

However, the standard points out that from a practical viewpoint, these rights are substantially similar to those of an outright purchaser. The outcome of this is that these rights are effectively classified as finance lease assets and are included together with owned assets under the general balance sheet heading of tangible fixed assets. However, the leased assets should be distinguished from owned assets and the amount disclosed (see under lessee accounting disclosures).

(b) Accounting treatment

(1) *Calculation of initial amount to be recorded as asset and obligation*

(i) THEORETICAL APPROACH

The amount to be capitalised should be the present value of the minimum lease rentals, discounted at the rate of interest implicit in the lease.

ILLUSTRATION
Using the above example of Langdale Ltd, the amount to be capitalised would be £16,148.

(ii) PRACTICAL APPROXIMATION

In many cases, the fair value of the asset will provide a reasonable approximation to the above. Clearly, in the example of Langdale, it would be acceptable to capitalise £16,200.

In the subsequent illustrations, the amount to be capitalised will be taken as the fair value of the asset.

(2) *Depreciation of finance lease asset*

The asset should be depreciated over the shorter of:

(i)   Lease term—this includes:

  (a) the period for which the lessee has contracted to lease the asset (i e the non-cancellable primary period); plus
  (b) any further secondary periods under which the lessee has an option to continue leasing the asset (possibly renewing on an annual basis) and where it is reasonably certain at the start of the lease that the lessee will exercise the option; or

(ii) the asset's useful life.

The guidance notes point out that in most cases residual value will be small, and so for the purpose of depreciation, calculations may be taken as nil. In the case of Langdale, the straight-line depreciation would be 10% (12,400 − 80% × 800) i e £1,176 taking account of residual value or £1,240 ignoring it. The difference of £64 is clearly not material.

(3) *Allocation of rentals*

Rentals paid to the lessor should be apportioned between financial charge and repayment of obligation. Possible approaches to allocation of finance charges are explained below.

(c) Allocation of finance charges

The key principle is that the total finance charge should be allocated to accounting periods during the lease terms so as to produce a constant periodic rate of charge on the remaining obligation outstanding.

  Possible approaches include:

(1) Actuarial method—this accords exactly with the above requirement.
(2) Sum of the digits (rule of 78)—this is an approximation to the actuarial method. The sum of the digits method is regarded as a reasonable approximation provided that the lease term is not very long (say, a primary period of less than seven years) and interest rates are not very high.
(3) Straight-line method—this does not produce a constant periodic rate of

charge and is thus not normally regarded as acceptable. However, it may be used in practice in those situations where the total finance charges are not material.

Underlying calculations for each method are illustrated below.

(d) Illustration of calculations

(1) *Basic data*

An item of plant and machinery with a useful life of ten years may be purchased outright for cash for £21,400. Alternatively, use of the asset may be obtained by means of a finance lease. Under this arrangement, the lessee would be responsible for insurance and maintenance and would be required to make five annual payments of £5,800 all payable in advance. After the primary period of five years, the lessee would have the option to continue leasing the asset for an indefinite period for a nominal ('peppercorn') rental. The amount of the rental may be ignored.

It is assumed that the fair value of £21,400 provides an acceptable approxima-tion to the present value of the minimum lease payments discounted at the rate of interest implicit in the lease.

(2) *Depreciation calculation*

If the straight-line method is used, and if residual value is ignored, the annual depreciation charge will be £2,140.

(3) *Finance charge—actuarial method*

Total finance charge to be allocated to periods = excess of rentals paid over amount capitalised (i e £29,000 – 21,400 = £7,600).

The interest rate applicable is 18%. This may be calculated from annuity tables remembering that these tables assume the annuity is paid on the last day of each period.

Present value (21,400 – 5,800) = £15,600
Annuity—four amounts of £5,800

$$\text{Annuity factor} = \frac{£15,600}{£5,800} = 2.69$$

From actuarial tables, interest rate is 18%.

The following table may then be constructed:

Year	B/F £	Rentals (in advance) £	Finance charge at 18% £	C/F £
1	21,400	(5,800)	2,808	18,408
2	18,408	(5,800)	2,269	14,877
3	14,877	(5,800)	1,634	10,711
4	10,711	(5,800)	889	5,800
5	5,800	(5,800)	—	—
		29,000	7,600	

The column headed finance charge gives the debit to profit and loss account for each period (e g 18% (21,400 – 5,800) = 2,808).

The carry forward column gives the balance sheet liability (obligation) at each year end.

For example, at the end of year 1 the total obligation is £18,408 of which £14,877 is non-current and the balance of £3,531 is current.

(4) *Finance charge—sum of the digits method*

The sum of the digits may be calculated by the formula $\dfrac{N(N+1)}{2}$

where N is the number of periods over which the finance charge is to be allocated. For example, in the above illustration, the obligation is deemed to be reduced to nil by the first day of year 5. Consequently, the finance charge is to be allocated over four periods.

The sum of the digits is $(1+2+3+4)$ i e 10.

Alternatively, it may be calculated as $\dfrac{4(4+1)}{2} = 10$.

The finance charge allocation is as follows:

Year		£
1	$\frac{4}{10} \times £7,600$	3,040
2	$\frac{3}{10} \times £7,600$	2,280
3	$\frac{2}{10} \times £7,600$	1,520
4	$\frac{1}{10} \times £7,600$	760
Total		7,600

The obligation at each year end may be calculated by completing a table similar to that in (3) above.

(5) *Finance charge—straight-line method*

Annual finance charge $= \dfrac{£7,600}{4}$ i e £1,900.

10.4   LESSEE ACCOUNTING—OPERATING LEASES

Rentals under operating leases should be charged on a straight-line basis. This applies even if the payments are not made on this basis. No entry should be made in the balance sheet for either the right to use the asset or the obligation to pay rentals.

The standard requires the straight-line basis to be used unless 'another systematic and rational basis is more appropriate'. This could cover situations of rentals holidays where no payment is made during the first year in which the asset is in use. In such a situation, the guidance notes recommend that the rentals are charged over the period in which the asset is in use.

10.5   LESSEE ACCOUNTING DISCLOSURES—FINANCE LEASES

(a) Fixed assets

Two types of disclosure are possible:

(1) To disclose assets held under finance leases for each major class of asset, and to show:

  (i)   gross amounts of assets;
  (ii) accumulated depreciation;
  (iii) depreciation for the period.

(2) To integrate amounts for finance lease assets with those for owned assets. The only balance sheet information for leased assets would be the overall net book value.

Illustration of (2)

Using figures at the end of year 1 from the illustration above, the following note would appear at the foot of the fixed asset note:

The net book value of fixed assets of £x includes an amount of £19,260 in respect of assets held under finance leases and hire-purchase contracts.

(b) Obligations under finance leases

(1) Amounts of obligations related to finance leases (net of finance charges allocated to future periods) should be disclosed separately from other obligations and liabilities.
(2) The above information may be shown either on the face of the balance sheet or in the notes to the accounts.
(3) Net obligations under finance leases should be analysed between:

(i) amounts payable in the next year;
(ii) amounts payable in the second to fifth years inclusive from balance sheet date;
(iii) the aggregate amounts payable thereafter.

(4) The analysis above may be presented, either:

(i) separately for obligations under finance leases.

In this case, two alternatives are possible:

(a) analysing the net obligations;
(b) analysing the gross obligations and then deducting the future finance charges from the total;

or

(ii) where the total of finance lease obligations is combined on the balance sheet with other obligations and liabilities, by giving the equivalent analysis of the total in which it is included.

Note that whichever alternative is adopted, the obligation must be split between current and non-current for balance sheet presentation purposes.

In the above illustration, using figures from the actuarial method at the end of year 1, the total obligation of £18,408 would be included as follows:

Creditors: amounts falling due within one year £3,531
Creditors: amounts falling due after more than one year £14,877.

(c) Profit and loss disclosures

The following amounts should be disclosed. For illustration purposes, figures have been taken from year 1 calculations from the earlier illustration of the actuarial method:

Profit is stated after charging:

	£
Depreciation of assets held under finance leases and hire-purchase contracts	2,140
Finance charges payable—finance leases and hire-purchase contracts	2,808

An additional note is required to comply with the Companies Act 1985:

Amounts charged to revenue in respect of finance leases and hire-purchase contracts are shown separately under the headings of depreciation (£2,140) and finance charges (£2,808) (total £4,948).

(d) Additional notes

(1) Disclosure is required for commitments existing at the balance sheet date for finance leases which have been entered into but whose inception occurs after the year end. (Inception of a lease is when the asset is brought into use or when the rentals first accrue, whichever is the earlier.)
(2) Accounting policies should also be disclosed. A suitable disclosure would be:

Fixed assets held under leases
Where assets are financed by leasing agreements that give rights approximating to ownership ('finance leases') the assets are treated as if they had been purchased outright and the corresponding liability to the leasing company is included as an obligation under finance leases.

Depreciation on leased assets is charged to profit and loss account on the same basis as shown above.

Leasing payments are treated as consisting of capital and interest elements and the interest is charged to profit and loss account using the actuarial method.

All other leases are 'operating leases' and the relevant annual rentals are charged to profit and loss account on a straight-line basis over the lease term.

10.6   LESSEE ACCOUNTING DISCLOSURES—OPERATING LEASES

(a) The total of operating lease rentals charged as an expense in the profit and loss account should be disclosed and analysed between:

(1) amounts payable in respect of hire of plant and machinery; and
(2) other operating leases.

(b) The lessee should disclose operating lease payments which he is committed to make during the next year, analysed between those in which the commitment expires:

(1) within that year;
(2) in the second to fifth years, inclusive; or
(3) over five years from the balance sheet date.

Commitments in respect of leases of land and buildings should be shown separately from those for other operating leases.

Illustration

This is taken from the guidance notes to SSAP 21.
At 31 December 1987 the company had annual commitments under non-cancellable operating leases as set out below.

£000's	1987		1986	
	Land and other		Land and other	
	buildings		buildings	
Operating leases which expire:				
Within one year	30	100	25	90
In the second to fifth years inclusive	80	50	75	40
Over five years	120	20	110	10
	230	170	210	140

The majority of leases of land and buildings are subject to rent reviews.

10.7 LESSOR ACCOUNTING—BACKGROUND

(a) Categories of lessors

Lessors may fall into any one of three categories:

(1) Companies such as finance houses which provide finance under lease contracts so as to enable a single customer to acquire the use of an asset for the greater part of its useful life. These leases will usually be finance leases.
(2) Companies which operate a business which involves the renting-out of assets for varying periods of time, usually to more than one customer (operating leases).
(3) Companies which are manufacturers or dealer lessors who use leasing to market their products. This could relate to either a finance lease or operating lease.

(b) Accounting approach

(1) In the case of an operating lease, lessor retains both the legal title and the risks and rewards of ownership of the asset. The risks of ownership include the possibility of reduced demand for the lease of the asset as well as the risk of obsolescence. An operating lease asset should be capitalised and depreciated.
(2) In the case of a finance lease, the substance of the transaction is similar to that of a secured loan receivable. Consequently, the asset is treated as finance lease receivable.

10.8 LESSOR ACCOUNTING—OPERATING LEASES

(a) Accounting treatment

(1) Assets held for use in operating leases should be classified as fixed assets, being depreciated over their useful lives.
(2) Rental income should be recognised on a straight-line basis over the period of the lease. This applies even if the payments are not made on a straight-line basis. However, the standard does permit another systematic and rational basis to be used if this is more representative of the time pattern in which the benefits are receivable.

   Turnover should comprise the aggregate rentals receivable in respect of the accounting period.

(b) Lessor profit and loss account

Using format 2, the relevant profit and loss extract would appear as follows:

	£	£
Turnover		X
Staff costs	X	
Depreciation	X	
Other operating charges	X	
Interest payable	X	(X)
Profit on ordinary activities before tax		X

(c) Manufacturer/dealer lessor

Suppose a manufacturer/dealer enters into an operating lease. No sale has been made and so no immediate profit should be recognised.

If the asset has been manufactured, all reasonable manufacturing costs may be capitalised. If the asset has been acquired from a supplier, the purchased cost will be capitalised. The asset will be classified as a tangible fixed asset and depreciated over its useful life as far as the lessor is concerned.

Rental income will be credited to profit and loss account in the usual way.

10.9   LESSOR ACCOUNTING—FINANCE LEASES

(a) Introduction to accounting treatment

(1) *Profit and loss account*

The gross earnings from a finance lease comprise the excess of rentals received over the fair value of the asset. The way in which these earnings should be allocated over accounting periods is discussed below.

Illustration

The relevant extract from a profit and loss account prepared under format 2 would be:

	£	£
Gross earnings under finance leases		X
Staff costs	X	
Depreciation	X	
Other operating charges	X	
Interest payable	X	(X)
Profit on ordinary activities before tax		X

Note: The guidance notes to SSAP 21 suggest that the term 'turnover' should not be used in view of the special nature of the company's business. A term such as 'gross earnings under financial leases' may be appropriate.

However, it is considered that simply to disclose gross earnings would provide an incomplete measure of a lessor's activity. It is recommended that note disclosure should also be made of:

(i) aggregate rentals receivable under finance leases;
(ii) cost of assets acquired for letting under finance leases.

(2) *Balance sheet*

The relevant asset should be described as finance lease receivables and included under the general heading of debtors. It will also be necessary to disclose by way of note the split of this total between amounts receivable within one year and those amounts receivable thereafter.

(b) Methods of allocating gross earnings: before-tax methods

(1) *Introduction*

The mechanism of each of the before-tax methods are described below.
  The three methods are:

(i)   actuarial before-tax;
(ii) sum of the digits;
(iii) straight-line.

These methods are the mirror image of those previously considered for lessee accounting.

(2) *Actuarial before-tax*

Using the data in section 10.3(d):

Total gross earnings are £7,600
Allocation under actuarial method

Year	£
1	2,808
2	2,269
3	1,634
4	889

The lessor's profit and loss account extracts for the relevant years would appear:

Year	1	2	3	4
	£	£	£	£
Gross earnings under finance leases	2,808	2,269	1,634	889
Staff costs	(X)	(X)	(X)	(X)
Depreciation	(X)	(X)	(X)	(X)
Other operating charges	(X)	(X)	(X)	(X)
Profit on ordinary activities after tax	X	X	X	X
Dividends	(X)	(X)	(X)	(X)
Retained profit	X	X	X	X

NOTES
(1) For each year in question, gross earnings under finance leases must be calculated for each individual lease (or group of similar leases) and the results then aggregated.
(2) All other items, such as staff costs and taxation, must be calculated directly for the company as a whole.

In the balance sheet, current assets/debtors would include the caption finance lease receivables. At the end of year 1, this would amount to £18,408. A note to the debtors figure should disclose the non-current amount of £14,877.

(3) *Sum of the digits method*

Gross earnings would be allocated as previously calculated:

Year	£
1	3,040
2	2,280
3	1,520
4	760
	7,600

The sum of the digits method is usually regarded as a reasonable approximation to the actuarial method.

(4) *Straight-line method*

Gross earnings would be allocated £1,900 p a for four years.

(5) *Comment on the above approaches*

Both the actuarial before-tax, and the sum of the digits methods allocate gross earnings so as to give a constant periodic rate of return on the company's net investment in the lease.
   Net investment is defined by SSAP 21 as:

(i) gross investment in lease (minimum lease payments plus any unguaranteed residual value accruing to the lessor); *less*

(ii) gross earnings allocated to future periods.

However, the above approaches do not take account of the funds which the lessor has invested in the lease. For example, tax cash flows are ignored.

The net cash investment approaches (see below) take account of all relevant cash flows and thus are generally to be preferred.

(c) Methods of allocating gross earnings: after-tax methods

(1) *Introduction*

These methods base their approach on the funds invested in the lease by the lessor. The earnings allocation is related to the net cash investment (NCI).

NCI is defined as the net effect of the following:

(i)   cost of asset;
(ii)   government grants;
(iii)   rentals received;
(iv)   taxation payments and receipts (including the effect of capital allowances);
(v)   residual values at the end of the lease term;
(vi)   interest payments;
(vii)   interest received on cash surplus;
(viii) profit taken out of the lease.

The before-tax methods assume that the cash received by way of rentals is applied exclusively towards payment of notional interest on borrowings and repayment of capital.

The after-tax methods recognise that cash received has many 'calls' placed upon it. The following diagram ilustrates some of the possibilities:

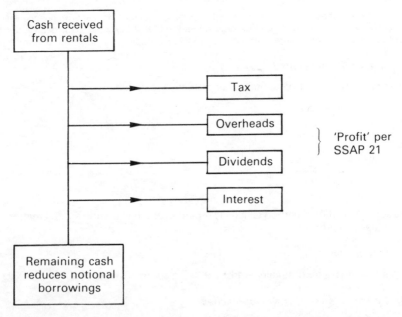

Cash is thus 'diverted'—for example, each lease must make some notional contribution towards payment of general overheads and dividends to shareholders.

(2) *Possible approaches*

There are two main approaches, each consisting of several variants:

(i)   actuarial after-tax method;
(ii) investment period method (IPM).

(3) *Actuarial after-tax method*

This method is illustrated by means of a detailed example taken from the guidance notes to SSAP 21.

(i) BASIC INFORMATION

A lessor leases out an asset on a non-cancellable lease contract with a primary term of five years from 1 January 1987. The rental is £650 per quarter payable in advance. The lessee has the right to continue to lease the asset after the end of the primary period for as long as he wishes at a peppercorn rent. In addition, the lessee is required to pay all maintenance and insurance costs as they arise. The leased asset could have been purchased for cash at the start of the lease for £10,000.

The lessor obtains writing-down allowances on the leased asset at the rate of 25%. The rate of corporation tax is 35%. The lessor's year end is 31 December and he pays or recovers tax nine months after the year end.

(ii) STAGE 1—SET UP HYPOTHETICAL CASH FLOWS SHOWING NET CASH INVESTMENT (NCI) AT END OF EACH QUARTER

The table below appears in the guidance notes to SSAP 21. The comments following the table relate to certain of the figures and calculations:

TABLE   ACTUARIAL METHOD AFTER TAX-BUILDING IN INTEREST PAYMENTS

Period (three months)	Net cash investment at start of period £	Cash flows in period (Note 1) £	Cash flows in period (Note 2) £	Average net cash investment in period £	Interest paid (Note 3) £	Profit taken out of lease (Note 4) £	Net cash investment at end of period £
1/87		(10,000)	650	(9,350)	(234)	(33)	(9,617)
2/87	(9,617)		650	(8,967)	(224)	(32)	(9,223)
3/87	(9,223)		650	(8,573)	(214)	(30)	(8,817)
4/87	(8,817)		650	(8,167)	(204)	(29)	(8,400)
			2,600		(876)	(124)	
1/88	(8,400)		650	(7,750)	(194)	(28)	(7,972)
2/88	(7,972)		650	(7,322)	(183)	(26)	(7,531)
3/88	(7,531)		650	(6,881)	(172)	(25)	(7,078)
4/88	(7,078)	272	650	(6,156)	(154)	(22)	(6,332)
			2,600		(703)	(101)	
1/89	(6,332)		650	(5,682)	(142)	(20)	(5,844)
2/89	(5,844)		650	(5,194)	(130)	(18)	(5,342)
3/89	(5,342)		650	(4,692)	(117)	(17)	(4,826)
4/89	(4,826)	(8)	650	(4,184)	(105)	(15)	(4,304)
			2,600		(494)	(70)	
1/90	(4,304)		650	(3,654)	(91)	(13)	(3,758)
2/90	(3,758)		650	(3,108)	(78)	(11)	(3,197)
3/90	(3,197)		650	(2,547)	(64)	(9)	(2,620)
4/90	(2,620)	(245)	650	(2,215)	(55)	(8)	(2,278)
			2,600		(288)	(41)	
1/91	(2,278)		650	(1,628)	(41)	(6)	(1,675)
2/91	(1,675)		650	(1,025)	(26)	(4)	(1,055)
3/91	(1,055)		650	(405)	(10)	(1)	(416)
4/91	(416)	(440)	650	(206)	(5)	(1)	(212)
			2,600		(82)	(12)	
1/92	(212)			(212)	(5)	(1)	(218)
2/92	(218)			(218)	(5)	(1)	(224)
3/92	(224)			(224)	(6)	(1)	(231)
4/92	(231)	226		1	(1)	—	—
		6					
		(10,000)	13,000		(17)	(3)	
	(189)				(2,460)	(351)	

(a) The fair value of asset is £10,000—at the outset, this is the NCI in the lease.

(b) Tax at the rate of 35% is payable at the beginning of period 4 in each year. It is calculated on rentals less interest paid and capital allowances, for example:

$$35\% \ (2,600 - 876 - 2,500) = \ £272$$
$$35\% \ (2,600 - 703 - 1,875) = \ £(8)$$
$$35\% \ (2,600 - 494 - 1,406) = \ £(245)$$

The figure at the bottom of the table of £(189) is the total of tax payments less recoveries.

(c) Rentals of £650 per quarter are payable in advance.

(d) Interest paid is calculated at 2.5% per quarter on the average net cash investment in each period.

(e) The profit taken out of the lease is determined on a trial and error basis. It is explained as follows.

The profit taken out of the lease is calculated at 0.36% on the average net cash invested in each period until period 3/92, after which point the lessor no longer has funds invested in the lease. The calculations made to arrive at 0.36% will normally be carried out by financial institutions by computer program, but it can be attained by trial and error. The calculation is, initially, carried out ignoring the profit taken out of the lease and this will then leave a balance of surplus cash left over at the end which represents the approximate profit on the transaction.

By dividing the total profit by the total average net cash investment in the period, an approximate percentage is obtained. As the profit taken out of the lease each quarter affects the average net cash investment in the following quarter, the net cash investment at the end of the whole transaction will not be zero until the percentage used is refined as in the above example to 0.36%. Note that NCI at end of 4/92 is nil.

Finally, profit referred to above is not profit in the sense of net profit. It is effectively profit after charging notional interest and notional tax but before deducting overheads.

(f) Calculations for 1/87:

$$2.05\% \times 9350 = £234$$
$$0.36\% \times 9350 = \quad £33$$

(ii) STAGE 2—GROSS UP NOTIONAL PROFIT FIGURES TO DETERMINE ALLOCATING OF GROSS EARNINGS

	1987 £	1988 £	1989 £	1990 £	1991 £	1992 £	Total £
'Profit' (per table)	124	101	70	41	12	3	351
Gross up at 35% corporation tax	191	155	108	63	18	5	540
Interest (per table)	876	703	494	288	82	17	2,460
Gross earnings	1,067	858	602	351	100	22	3,000

Note that the *actual* gross earnings on the lease are £3,000 (rentals £13,000 less fair value of £10,000).

The *actual* allocation of gross earnings under this method is as follows:

	£
1987	1,067
1988	858
1989	602
1990	351
1991	100
1992	22
	3,000

To determine the company's gross earnings for a particular year, it is necessary to carry out the above calculations for each lease (or group of similar leases) and aggregate for the company as a whole.

(iv) PROFIT AND LOSS ACCOUNT FOR EACH YEAR

Once gross earnings have been determined, other items such as depreciation, staff costs, operating charges, interest payable, tax and dividends will be calculated on a global basis for the company as a whole.

(v) BALANCE SHEET ITEMS—DEBTORS: FINANCE LEASE RECEIVABLE

Once the gross earnings allocation has been completed, the balance sheet debtors may be calculated as follows:

Year	B/F £	P/L £	Cash £	Bal C/F £
1987	10,000	1,067	(2,600)	8,467
1988	8,467	858	(2,600)	6,725
1989	6,725	602	(2,600)	4,727
1990	4,727	351	(2,600)	2,478
1991	2,478	100	(2,600)	(22)
1992	(22)	22	—	—

NOTES
(1) The non-current part of the balance sheet debtor must be disclosed separately (e g £6,725 at the end of 1987).
(2) The NCI figures in the previous table are purely hypothetical figures. They do not appear as actual balances in the balance sheet. The notional NCI figures are used to calculate the gross earnings allocation.

(4) *Investment period method (IPM)*

The approach of this method is similar to that of the actuarial after tax.

Under the IPM method, gross earnings of £3,000 are allocated between periods in proportion to the net cash investment for each period. The calculations are set out in the table below:

TABLE   ALLOCATION OF GROSS EARNINGS UNDER IPM

Period	Net cash investment at end of period £	Gross earnings allocation £	Total gross earnings for year £
1/87	9,617	285	
2/87	9,223	274	1,070
3/87	8,817	262	
4/87	8,400	249	
1/88	7,972	236	
2/88	7,531	223	857
3/88	7,078	210	
4/88	6,332	188	
1/89	5,844	173	
2/89	5,342	158	602
3/89	4,826	143	
4/89	4,304	128	
1/90	3,758	111	
2/90	3,197	95	352
3/90	2,620	78	
4/90	2,278	68	
1/91	1,675	50	
2/91	1,055	31	99
3/91	416	12	
4/91	212	6	
1/92	218	6	
2/92	224	7	20
3/92	231	7	
4/92	–	–	
	£101,170	£3,000	£3,000

Note: The sum of the NCI 'weights' is £101,170. The NCI for quarter 1 of 1987 is £9,617. Thus the finance charge allocation is:

$$\frac{£9,617}{£101,170} \times £3,000 = £285$$

Once the finance charge allocations have been completed, the balance sheet debtors figures may be calculated.

(d) The acceptability of the various approaches

(1) Hire-purchase transactions

In principle, earnings allocations should be based on net cash investment (NCI). However, under a hire-purchase agreement, the capital allowances accrue to the hiree (unlike the position of a lease where the allowances accrue to the lessor). Consequently, it is perfectly possible that the finance company's NCI is not significantly different from its net investment.

So for hire-purchase transactions, either of the before-tax methods (actuarial before-tax, sum of the digits) will be acceptable. The straight-line method, however, would not be acceptable.

(2) Finance leases

Because of the significance of cash flows other than net investment, only one of the after-tax methods should be used.

(e) Manufacturer/dealer lessor

Selling profit may be taken in full to profit and loss account in the period in which the agreement is entered into.

However, profit taken is restricted to the excess of the fair value of the asset over the manufacturer's or dealer's costs less any grants receivable by the manufacturer or dealer.

Illustration

A manufacturer constructs a machine at a cost of £20,000. He normally sells the machine for £25,000, giving a profit on sale of £5,000.

The manufacturer also offers the machine on a five year finance lease with a rental of £5,800 per annum (the lessee accounting example). This is equivalent to a capital cost of £21,400.

Profit on sale should be restricted to £1,400 (i e £21,400 less £20,000). The remainder of the profit is gross earnings and will be allocated over the lease term.

10.10 LESSOR ACCOUNTING—DISCLOSURE REQUIREMENTS

(a) Introduction

Certain aspects of disclosure have already been referred to. For completeness, all the principal disclosure requirements of SSAP 21 are referred to below.

(b) Operating leases

Disclosure is required of:

(1) accounting policy for operating leases;
(2) aggregate rentals receivable in respect of an accounting period in relation to operating leases;
(3) gross amounts of assets held for use in operating leases and related accumulated depreciation charges.

(c) Finance leases and hire-purchase contracts

Disclosure is required of:

(1) net investment, at each balance sheet date, in:

    (i)   finance leases;
    (ii) hire-purchase contracts;

(2) accounting policy for finance leases;
(3) aggregate rentals receivable in respect of an accounting period in relation to finance leases;
(4) cost of assets acquired for the purpose of letting under finance leases.

11 ACCOUNTING FOR PENSION COSTS

11.1 BACKGROUND

For a considerable time, the Accounting Standards Committee have attempted to issue a statement of standard accounting practice on the subject of Accounting for Pension Costs.

An exposure draft (ED 32) published in 1983 dealt with disclosure (as opposed to accounting) of pension information. In 1986 ED 32 was withdrawn and replaced by ED 39, Accounting for Pension Costs.

11.2 COMPANIES ACT 1985 IMPLICATIONS

Disclosure is required of:

(a) The amount of 'other pension costs so incurred' which forms part of the total of staff costs. Pension costs is defined as including:

(1) contributions paid by the company to a pension fund or insurance company;
(2) amounts set aside to a provision for employee benefits;
(3) any amounts paid by the company in respect of pension payments without being set aside as under (2).

Note that 'staff' includes directors provided that they are employed under contracts of employment.

(b) Pension commitments:

(1) any pension commitments included under any provision shown in the company's balance sheet; and
(2) any such commitment for which no provision has been made.

Note that particulars are also required of commitments relating to pensions payable to past directors of the company.

11.3 FUNDING OF PENSION ARRANGEMENTS

Some of the main possibilities may be illustrated diagrammatically as follows:

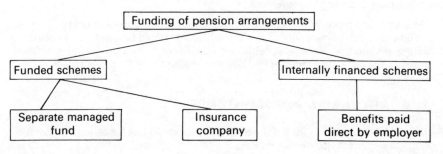

11.4 MAIN TYPES OF CONTRACTUAL SCHEMES

Two main groups of such schemes include defined contribution schemes and defined benefit schemes. Particular aspects of each may be contrasted as follows:

Aspect	Defined contribution schemes	Defined benefit schemes
(a) Benefit to employee?	Depends on funds available and performance of investments	May depend on employee's final pay prior to retirement
(b) Cost to employer?	Contributions payable in period (cost is easily measured)	Commitment is open-ended, final cost is often subject to considerable uncertainty
(c) Actuarial assumptions?	Not required	Crucial to calculation of pension costs in P/L ac
(d) Disclosures in annual accounts?	Relatively few	Extensive

11.5 ACTUARIAL APPROACHES AND METHODS

(a) Actuarial approaches

ED 39 refers to two main approaches:

(1) Discontinuance actuarial valuation—this is concerned with whether the existing assets are sufficient to secure the benefits of existing pensioners and members on the assumption that the scheme is to be wound up on the valuation date (this approach is often used to test the solvency of a pension scheme).
(2) Ongoing actuarial valuation—this assumes that contributions will continue to be paid by the employer and members.

(b) Actuarial valuation methods

The two main methods referred to in ED 39 are:

(1) accrued benefits method—this considers benefits attributable to members' service to a given date (which may be a current or future date);
(2) prospective benefits method—this considers benefits attributable to total expected service to retirement.

Note that for a discontinuance actuarial valuation a particular form of the accrued benefit method (namely service to a current date) should be used. For an ongoing actuarial valuation either a suitable accrued benefits method (using service to some future date) or a prospective benefits method may be applicable.

11.6 ACTUARIAL ASSUMPTIONS

The actuarial valuation for a defined benefit scheme must be based on assumptions regarding the following matters:

(a) future rates of inflation;
(b) future pay increases;
(c) increases to pensions in payment;
(d) earnings on investments;
(e) numbers of employees joining the scheme;
(f) probability that employees will die or leave before they reach retiring age.

11.7 ACCOUNTING AND FUNDING—AN IMPORTANT DISTINCTION

Traditionally the amount funded (ie the amounts paid by the employer company to the trustees of a pension fund or to an insurance company) has formed the basis of the charge to profit and loss account.

ED 39 proposes that a distinction be made between accounting and funding. Accounting should be concerned with the allocation of the total pension costs as between the profit and loss accounts of particular periods. Funding should be concerned with financial management and the availability of cash.

ED 39 points out that the funding amount may not always provide a satisfactory basis for determining the pension charge in the accounts. For example, three identical companies may have identical pension fund deficiencies following an actuarial valuation. Company A may increase the future ongoing contributions, Company B may make a single lump sum payment while Company C may spread the additional contribution over three years.

Current reporting methods may result in different figures of reported profit for each of the three companies for the same year.

11.8 ACCOUNTING OBJECTIVES

(a) *General objectives:* to charge the cost of pensions against profits on a systematic basis over the service lives of employees in the scheme. This objective may be satisfied by different actuarial methods with different sets of assumptions.

(b) *Specific objectives:*

(1) defined contribution schemes—profit and loss account should be charged with contributions payable in respect of the period;
(2) defined benefit schemes—the charge to the profit and loss account should consist of the following two elements. Each should be separately calculated and disclosed:

(i) regular cost (which provides a substantially level percentage of current and expected future pensionable payroll in the light of current actuarial assumptions);
(ii) variations from regular costs to be charged over the expected average remaining service lives of employees.

(c) Balance sheet implications: where the cumulative pensions cost charged to the profit and loss account differs from cumulative payments to date, the difference should be treated as a net pension liability or prepayment as appropriate.

11.9 VARIATIONS FROM REGULAR COSTS

These may arise in the following situations:

(a) experience deficiencies or surpluses;
(b) retroactive effects of changes in assumptions or method;
(c) retroactive changes in benefits or conditions for membership;

(d) increases to pensions in payment or deferred pensions not previously provided for.

11.10   EXPERIENCE DEFICIENCY OR SURPLUS

(a) *Definitions*
This is defined as the deficiency or surplus of the actuarial value of assets over the actuarial value of liabilities, on the basis of the valuation method used, which arises because events have not coincided with the actuarial assumptions made for the last valuation.

(b) *Accounting*
The surplus or deficiency should be spread over the expected average remaining service lives of employees (after allowing for future withdrawals). The exposure draft indicates that a period of ten to twelve years may be appropriate. A possible exception is where a material deficiency may require to be recognised over a shorter period on prudence grounds.

(c) *Extraordinary event*
Where the material surplus or deficiency is directly caused by an extraordinary event (such as closure of a major division) the surplus or deficiency should be recognised immediately and treated as an extraordinary item.

11.11   OTHER SITUATIONS

(a) Retroactive effects of changes in assumptions or methods—these should be accounted for in a similar way to an experience deficiency or surplus (see above).

(b) Retroactive changes in benefits or conditions for membership—past service costs relate to services to be provided in the future. An improvement in pension benefits should help an employer to attract and retain employees. The cost should be written off over the average remaining service lives of employees.

(c) Increases to pensions in payment or deferred pensions—increases to pensions which are specified in the pension scheme rules or by law should be taken into account in the actuarial assumptions. The cost of such an increase should be charged over the service lives of the employees.

11.12   DISCLOSURE IMPLICATIONS

(a) General requirements—sufficient information should be disclosed to give the user of the financial statements a broad understanding of the significance of the pension arrangements.

(b) Defined contribution schemes—disclose:

   (1) the nature of the scheme (ie defined contribution);
   (2) the pension cost charge for the period;
   (3) any outstanding or prepaid contributions at the balance sheet date.

Illustration

The company operates a defined contribution pension scheme. The assets of the scheme are held separately from those of the company in an independently administered fund. The pension cost charge represents contributions payable by the company to the fund and amounted to £500,000 (19X4 £450,000). Contributions totalling £25,000 (19X4 £15,000) were payable to the fund at the year end and are included in creditors.

(c) Defined benefit schemes—disclose:

(1) the nature of the scheme (ie defined benefit);
(2) whether the scheme is funded or unfunded;
(3) accounting policy (and if different, funding policy);
(4) whether pension cost and liability (or asset) are assessed in accordance with the advice of a professionally qualified actuary and if so disclose:

   (i) date of most recent formal actuarial valuation or later review used for this purpose;
   (ii) actuarial valuation method used;

(5) the pension cost charge for the period, distinguishing between:

   (i) regular cost, and
   (ii) variations from regular cost.

   Disclose:

   (i) explanation of variations/material changes in the regular cost;
   (ii) number of years over which the variations are to be spread

(6) provision or prepayments (difference between costs recognised and funding amounts);
(7) expected effects on financial statements or commitments to make additional payments over a limited number of years;
(8) amount of deficiency on a discontinuance actuarial valuation. Indicate action, if any, being taken to deal with the deficiency in the current and future financial statements;
(9) outline of results of most recent formal actuarial valuation for later review of funding of scheme on an ongoing basis:

   (i) relationship in percentage terms between the scheme assets as valued for actuarial purposes and actuarial value of accrued benefits. Account should be taken of future salary increases;
   (ii) where a material deficiency or surplus is so identified, an explanation of future intentions regarding the deficiency or surplus;
   (iii) contributions rate needed to maintain or achieve the target level of funding;
   (iv) whether experience since the last valuation has resulted in any material changes in the contribution rate.

Illustration

This is taken from the appendix to ED 39 and may be suitable for a small company:

> The company operates a pension scheme providing benefits based on final pay. The assets of the scheme are held separately from those of the company, being invested through insurance companies. Contributions to the scheme are charged against profits in the period in which they are payable to the scheme. The contributions are determined by a qualified actuary on the basis of triennial valuations using the projected unit method. The most recent valuation was as at 31 December 19X4. The pension charge for the period of £50,000 (19X4 £48,000) consisted of £55,000 in respect of the regular cost less £5,000 in respect of the amortisation of experience surpluses which are being recognised over ten years, the average remaining service lives of employees. The most recent actuarial valuation showed that the scheme's assets covered 120% of the benefits allowing for future increases in earnings, which had accrued to members. It is considered that this level of funding is not excessively high. The contributions of the company and employees will, therefore, remain at 11% and 5% of earnings respectively.

11.13 ILLUSTRATION—CROWN HOUSE (31.3.86)

(a) Pension commitments

All United Kingdom trading companies participate in the Crown House Staff Pension Fund which is administered by trustees for the benefit of employees. The assets of the fund are independent of the group. Benefits at retirement are determined by an employee's earnings and years of pensionable service. Independent actuaries carry out a valuation of the fund normally every three years and the valuation at 30 September 1983 showed that accrued liabilities were adequately funded on continuing and discontinued bases. The level of contributions made by employees and group companies has been maintained in accordance with the recommendation of the actuaries. There is no reason to believe that any significant adjustment to the level of group company contributions will be required in respect of the current benefits under the pension scheme.

(b) Pension fund

The Crown House Staff Pension Fund provides a pension scheme for all the permanent staff employed in the group who are eligible to join the scheme after a short qualifying period.

The fund is self administered and invests directly in property, Stock Exchange securities and bank deposits. A valuation of the assets and liabilities is made every three years by the actuaries to the fund. The last valuation was in September 1983 and the fund was found to be in surplus.

The assets of the fund are entirely divorced from the assets of the group and are vested in three trustees who register their ownership through a company—Crown House Pension Trustees Limited. The trustees administer the fund in accordance with rules jointly laid down by the board of Crown House plc and the trustees.

The fund provides benefits on retirement and on death in service. The principal benefits on retirement are a pension of 1/60th of final pensionable salary for each year of pensionable service and a widow's pension of half the member's pension on death after retirement. The main benefits on death in service are a sum equal to three times pensionable salary, repayment of the member's contributions and a widow's pension of half the member's prospective pension based on current pensionable salary.

The fund is not index-linked but pensions are reviewed each year. In recent years the increases have kept close to the rate of inflation.

The members of the fund make contributions of $5\frac{1}{2}\%$ of their pensionable salaries and group companies currently pay 10%. In the year ended 31 March 1986 the members' contributions amounted to £586,000 and group companies' contributions were £1,249,000. Members are contracted out of the State earnings related pension scheme.

The financial position of the pension fund at 31 March 1986 was as shown below:

	£000	£000
Investments at market value		
Listed securities (cost £15.0m)	18,483	
Properties (cost £4.8m)	5,415	
		23,898
Debtors and accrued interest	135	
Creditors	(101)	
Bank deposits and cash	288	
		322
Net assets		24,220
Accumulated fund at 1 April 1985		18,865
Surplus for year		5,355
Accumulated fund at 31 March 1986		24,220

11.14 ACCOUNTING FOR PENSION SCHEME DEFICITS

(a) Means of dealing with an experience deficiency (see section 11.10(a))—this may be dealt with in a number of ways:

   (i) by an increase to the future ongoing contribution;

    (ii) by the payment of additional special contributions (single sum or spread over a relatively short period).

(b) Determining the pension charge in the profit and loss account—although (a)(ii) may be satisfactory for funding purposes, ED 39 does not regard such payments as providing a satisfactory basis for determining the pension charge in the profit and loss account. The approach proposed by ED 39 is illustrated in the example below (this example is included in the appendix to ED 39).

Illustration
The actuarial valuation at 31.12.X4 of a pension scheme showed a deficiency of £90m. The actuary recommended that the company eliminate the deficiency by three lump sum payments of £30m in addition to the standard contributions of £10m per annum. The contributions would continue at £10m per annum thereafter. The average remaining service life of employees in the scheme at 31.12.X4 was ten years. The charge in the profit and loss account for the years 19X5 to 19X14 will be:

	£m
Regular cost	10
Variation from regular cost $\dfrac{3 \times £30m}{10}$	9
Total charge	19

This ignores interest and assumes no changes in circumstances over the above period. In practice it is likely that valuations will occur at three year intervals. These valuations may reveal a deficiency or surplus which would then require an adjustment to the profit and loss account charge in subsequent periods.

The effect on the financial statements may be summarised as follows:

	Funding £m	P/L charge £m	B/S (prepayment) £m
19X5	10 + 30 = 40	19	21
19X6	10 + 30 = 40	19	42
19X7	10 + 30 = 40	19	63
19X8	10	19	54
19X9	10	19	45
19X10	10	19	36
19X11	10	19	27
19X12	10	19	28
19X13	10	19	9
19X14	10	19	–
Total over 10 years	190	190	

COMMENTS
The estimate of average remaining service life of employees in the scheme is inevitably somewhat arbitrary and may not be applied consistently as between different companies. Additionally, some commentators do not regard the accounting treatment of deficits as prudent.

11.15 ACCOUNTING FOR PENSION SCHEME SURPLUSES

(a) Means of dealing with an experience surplus—these include:

    (i) by a reduction in the ongoing contribution rate;

    (ii) a contribution holiday (the employer ceases making contributions to the pension fund for a specified period, eg 2 years);

    (iii) withdrawing some of the surplus from the pension scheme (subject to agreement of trustees and Inland Revenue).

(b) Determining the pension charge in the profit and loss account—although (a)(ii) and (a)(iii) may be acceptable from a funding viewpoint, the payments concerned may not provide a satisfactory basis for determining the pension charge in the profit and loss account.

The approach proposed by ED 39 is illustrated in the example below (taken from the appendix to ED 39).

Illustration

The actuarial valuation at 31.12.X4 of a pension scheme showed a surplus of £260m. The actuary recommended that the company eliminate the surplus by taking a contribution holiday in 19X5 and 19X6 and then paying contributions of £30m per annum for 8 years. After 8 years, the standard contribution would be £50m per annum. The average remaining service life of employees in the scheme at 31.12.X4 was 10 years.

The annual charge in the profit and loss account for the years 19X5 to 19X14 will be:

	£
Regular cost	50
Variation from regular cost	
$\dfrac{260m}{10}$	(26)
Total charge	24

Again, interest is ignored and it is assumed that there are no changes in circumstances over the above period. Triennial valuations may reveal a deficiency or surplus which could then require an adjustment to the profit and loss account charge in subsequent periods.

The effect on the financial statements may be summarised as follows:

	Funding £m	P/L charge £m	B/S (provision) £m
19X5	–	24	24
19X6	–	24	48
19X7	30	24	42
19X8	30	24	36
19X9	30	24	30
19X10	30	24	24
19X11	30	24	18
19X12	30	24	12
19X13	30	24	6
19X14	30	24	–
Total over 10 years	240	240	
19X15	50	50	–
19X16	50	50	–

Note that in the above circumstances some companies would respond to the situation in 19X5 and 19X6 by making no charge in the profit and loss account. ED 39 clearly wishes to change this approach!

12 STATEMENTS OF RECOMMENDED PRACTICE

12.1 INTRODUCTION

A statement of recommended practice (SORP) is a new form of pronouncement issued by the Accounting Standards Committee. In 1986 ASC issued an explanatory foreword which set out the aims and status of SORPs.

12.2 AIMS

SORPs attempt to set out best accounting practice, and to narrow areas of difference and variety of treatment in the areas with which they are concerned.

12.3 SCOPE

SORPs will attempt to deal with areas not considered appropriate for an SSAP. These may include areas not considered essential in arriving at a true and fair view as well as areas which may be considered to be 'industry-specific'.

12.4 COMPARISON WITH SSAPS

Three areas of contrast may be identified:

(a) Scope (see above)—areas not considered appropriate for an SSAP;
(b) authority—SORPs are usually issued by ASC. SSAPs can only be issued with the approval of and through the Councils of the individual member bodies of CCAB;
(c) status—SSAPs are intended to be mandatory whereas SORPs are generally non-mandatory.

12.5 TERMINOLOGY

Ordinary SORPs are developed and issued by ASC. Franked SORPs however, are developed by a particular industry group and after approval and 'franking' by ASC are subsequently issued by the industry group.

12.6 CURRENT SORPS

ASC has issued the following SORPs:

(a) SORP 1—Pension scheme accounts
(b) ED 38—Accounting by charities

Further SORPs have been developed by specific industries (e g insurance and oil).

12.7   PENSION SCHEME ACCOUNTS

(a) Introduction

SORP 1 was issued in May 1986. The SORP was followed by the Occupational Pension Schemes (Disclosure of Information) Regulations 1986 which was laid before Parliament in June 1986 and which came into operation on 1 November 1986.

Although SORP 1 is not in itself mandatory it is special in that it is backed up by Government legislation.

Both the government's regulations and SORP 1 are very detailed. The aim of this part of the chapter is to outline the principal requirements.

(b) Effect of the new legislation

(1) The Occupational Pension Schemes (Disclosure of Information Regulations) 1986 will require trustees to make available to beneficiaries and members a report containing audited accounts, an actuarial statement and an investment report.

(2) The new legislation is mandatory for scheme years starting on or after 1 November 1986. Trustees will be required to state in a note to the accounts whether or not the accounts have been prepared in accordance with SORP 1. Compliance with the SORP (which is more detailed than the regulations) will ensure compliance with the law.

(c) Objectives of a pension scheme's annual report

The report should inform members and other users regarding:

(1) general activity, history and development of the scheme;
(2) transactions of the scheme and size of its fund;
(3) progress of the scheme towards meeting its potential liabilities and obligations to members;
(4) investment policy and performance of scheme.

(d) Contents of annual report

The main contents should comprise:

(1) trustees' report;
(2) accounts;
(3) actuary's statement;
(4) investment report.

(e) Trustees' report

This is mainly a review or comment on:

(1) membership statistics;
(2) major changes in benefits, constitution or legal requirements;
(3) financial development of the scheme (as disclosed in the accounts);
(4) actuarial position of the scheme (as disclosed in the actuary's statement) (see (g));
(5) investment policy and performance of scheme.

(f) Accounts of the pension scheme

The accounts are historical statements concerning the stewardship of the scheme. The accounts are designed to give a true and fair view of the financial transactions of the scheme during the accounting period and of the disposition of its net assets at the end of the period.

(g) Statement of actuary

The statement is based on the actuary's investigation into and report on (1) the ability of the current fund of the pension scheme to meet accrued benefits and (2) the adequacy of the fund and future contribution levels to meet promised benefits when due.

(h) Investment report

The report should include appended additional information on investments held and investment income and contents on investment policy and performance. The SORP suggests an analysis of investments which may be relevant to an investment report.

(i) Content of the accounts

The accounts should include:

(1) revenue account;
(2) net assets statement;
(3) reconciliation of movement in net assets of the scheme to the revenue account (this may be incorporated into (1) and (2));
(4) notes to the accounts.

Detailed guidance on possible formats is provided in Part 4 of the SORP.

(j) Revenue account

The main headings might include:

	£	£
Contributions receivable		X
—from employers		
—from members		X
—transfer in		X
		—
		X
Investment income		X
(distinguishing different categories)		X
Other income		X
		—
Total income		XX
		=
Benefits payable		
—pensions		X
—lump sum benefits		X
—death benefits		X
—payment to leavers		X
		—
		X
Other payments		X
Administrative and other expenses		X
		—
		XX
		=
Amount available for investment		XX
		=

(k) Net asset statement

This statement might include the following main headings (each main heading would be broken down into sub-headings detailed by way of note).

Investment assets		X
Fixed assets		X
Current assets	X	
Current liabilities	X	X
	—	
Long-term borrowings		(X)
		—
Balance of fund		XX
		==

Investments should be included in the net assets statement at their market value (or, if this is not available, at the trustees valuation). SORP 1 provides detailed guidance on valuation methods appropriate for particular types of assets.

(l) Reconciliation of the movement in the net assets of the scheme

As previously mentioned, this reconciliation may be incorporated into the revenue account or net assets statement. Alternatively it may be shown as a separate statement. An example of an acceptable format is shown below:

	£	£
Opening net assets of the scheme		X
Net new money invested (per revenue account)		X
Changes in market value of investments		
—realised	X	
—unrealised	X	X
	—	—
Closing net assets of the scheme		XX
		==

Changes in market value of investments—realised refers to profits and losses on sale of investments sold during the year. Unrealised changes refers to unrealised gains and losses on investments which have changed in value during the year and which are held at the year end.

(m) Notes to the accounts

These could include:

(1) information about capital commitments;
(2) information about post-balance sheet events and contingencies (but *not* future liabilities to pay pension and related outgoings);
(3) accounting policies:

   (i) policies adopted in applying the accruals concept to significant categories of income and expenditure for example:
      (a) contributions
      (b) investment income
      (c) transfer values
      (d) benefits.
   (ii) reference to the actuary's statement. A suitably worded note is:

      The accounts summarise the transactions and net assets of the scheme. They do not take account of liabilities to pay pensions and other benefits in the future. The actuarial position of the fund, which does account for such liabilities, is dealt with in the statement by the actuary on pages ..... to ..... of the annual report and these accounts should be read in conjunction therewith.

(iii) bases adopted for valuation of assets;
(iv) basis of foreign currency translation;
(v) treatment of interest on property developments;
(vi) bases adopted for accounting for investments in subsidiary and associated companies.

12.8 ACCOUNTING BY CHARITIES

(a) Introduction

'Accounting by charities: a discussion paper' was published by ASC in February 1984. Following comments received in the discussion period, ED 38 was published in November 1985. ED 38 is an exposure draft of a proposed statement of recommended practice.

(b) Regulatory factors

These could include the Charities Act 1960 and the Companies Act 1985. It should, however, be noted that many charities are not subject to detailed requirements regarding form and content of accounts nor to a statutory requirement to produce an annual report.

(c) Applicability of SORP to different-sized charities

The proposed SORP is applicable in principle to *all* charities irrespective of size or constitution. However, subject to relevant legal requirements, the proposed SORP leaves discretion to the trustees of each charity to apply the provisions of ED 38 in the manner they consider fit. No doubt trustees of smaller charities will welcome this flexibility!

(d) Purposes of the proposed SORP

Its main purposes are to:

(1) improve the quality of reporting by charities;
(2) reduce the number of diverse accounting practices presently adopted;
(3) provide assistance to those responsible for the preparation of charities annual reports.

(e) Annual report—general objectives

These include:

(1) objectives of charity;
(2) achievements of charity;
(3) resources entrusted to the charity;
(4) relationship between, and analyses of, the above information.

(f) Annual report—content

Charities will usually be required to present an annual report comprising:

(1) legal and administrative details;
(2) trustees' report (or equivalent statement);
(3) accounts;
(4) audit report (if accounts have been audited).

(g) Legal and administrative details

This could include:

(1) charity registration nurnber;
(2) company registration number (if applicable);
(3) registered address;
(4) governing instrument or legal status;
(5) origin, aims and objectives of charity;
(6) names of trustees etc;
(7) bankers, solicitors, auditors.

(h) Trustees' report

Minimum information could include:

(1) description of organisation and policies adopted in pursuance of charity's aims and objectives;
(2) review of developments, activities and achievements during the year;
(3) explanation of surpluses/deficits;
(4) review of financial position;
(5) outline of plans and commitments.

(i) Financial reporting

The aim is to provide a report setting out activities and resources in financial terms. The distinction between reporting objectives of charities as compared with commercial organisations should always be borne in mind. Information reported might usefully include:

(1) income and other resources made available during period;
(2) expenses and other expenditure incurred during year showing separately:

    (i) expenses relating directly to charitable activities;
    (ii) expenses relating to fund-raising, administration, public relations and information activities;

(3) assets, liabilities and funds of the charity including indication of how funds:

    (i) must be utilised (because of restrictions imposed);
    (ii) may be utilised;

(4) relationship between, and analyses of, the above information.

(j) Accounting statements

These should usually include:

(1) one or more income and expenditure accounts;
(2) one or more statements of source and application of funds (such statements may not always be appropriate or necessary);
(3) one or more balance sheets;
(4) notes.

(k) Basis of accounting

ED 38 proposes the following:

(1) accounts should be prepared on the basis of the accruals concept;
(2) incoming resources:

    (i) resources received for permanent endowment and unrealised gains on revaluations of fixed assets and investments should be taken direct to the relevant fund account;
    (ii) other resources should be included in the income and expenditure account as soon as is prudent and practicable.

(3) expenditure should be included as incurred;

(4) provision should be made for all known liabilities;

(5) expenditure on fixed assets (acquisition, production or installation) should be capitalised and depreciated through income and expenditure account over the asset's expected useful life.

A similar principle to (5) applies to receipts of fixed assets received by way of gift.

(l) Income and expenditure account

An overriding consideration is that the analysis of income and expenditure should be appropriate to the charity and enable the user to gain a proper appreciation of the activities of the charity.

With this aim in mind, it is proposed that the following items should be disclosed separately:

(1) realised gains and losses on disposal of fixed assets;

(2) realised gains and losses on disposal of investments;

(3) fund-raising expenses;

(4) public relations and information expenses;

(5) administration expenses;

(6) expenses relating directly to charitable activities.

Investment income and income received by deed of covenant should be included at a figure grossed up for tax recoverable.

(m) Balance sheet

(1) Particular items should be included on the following bases of valuation:

    (i) fixed assets—at depreciated cost or revalued amount;

    (ii) investments at cost or market value (if cost is adopted, market value should be disclosed);

    (iii) current assets—at lower of cost and net realisable value;

    (iv) liabilities—at settlement value.

(2) The following would be an acceptable categorisation of assets and liabilities:

	£	£
Fixed assets		
—land and buildings		
—freehold		X
—long lease		X
—short lease		X
		X
—Plant, machinery and vehicles		X
—Fixtures, fittings, tools and equipment		X
		X
Current assets	X	
less current liabilities	(X)	
		X
Total assets less current liabilities		X
Long-term liabilities		(X)
Accumulated fund		X

(n) Accounting policies

Examples of policies requiring disclosure could include:

(1) administration expenses;
(2) capitalisation and depreciation of fixed assets;
(3) commitments not yet met;
(4) donations and legacies (including those other than for cash);
(5) endowments;
(6) fund-raising expenses;
(7) grants payable and receivable;
(8) netting-off of expenses and related income;
(9) public relations and information expenses;
(10) restricted income and restricted assets;
(11) subscriptions for life membership;
(12) valuation of investments and recognition of investment income.

12.9   ILLUSTRATION—THE WESTDALE CHARITY

The Westdale Charity is a national charity concerned primarily with relief of poverty amongst specified sections of the community.

One of the charity's trustees has provided you with the following information related to the charity's two most recent financial statements:

INCOME AND EXPENDITURE ACCOUNTS

for the year ended 31 December 19X6

	19X6 *£'000*	*19X5* *£'000*
Income		
Donations	95	84
Investment income	21	18
Sundry income	2	3
	118	105
Expenditure		
Administration expenses	18	17
Purchase of equipment	10	—
Fund raising expenses	9	8
Charitable expenditure	125	110
	162	135
Excess of expenditure over income	(44)	(30)

Extract from balance sheet at 31 December

General fund	*19X6* *£'000*	*19X5* *£'000*
Balance at 1 January	147	82
Legacies received	25	92
Surplus on sale of investments	8	3
Excess of expenditure over income	(44)	(30)
Balance at 31 December	136	147

Additional information

(1) Legacies referred to above relate solely to pecuniary legacies. Occasionally legacies are received in the form of quoted investments. These are included in the accounts at nil cost although the description of the investments and their market values are disclosed in the notes to the accounts.
(2) Many years ago, a freehold property (currently valued at £145,000) was bequeathed to the charity. The property is occupied by the charity and used for administrative purposes. The notes to the accounts refer to a recent valuation of the property but the property is not included in the balance sheet.
(3) Tax repayments relating to investment income are included in the financial statements when the amounts are recovered from the Inland Revenue.

Required
Comment on the presentation of accounts and accounting policies of the charity, recommending any changes in policies or reporting which you would regard as desirable.

12.10 SUGGESTED SOLUTION TO THE WESTDALE CHARITY

(a) The income and expenditure account should highlight:

   (1) money raised and any associated costs;
   (2) amounts spent on charitable purposes (the primary aim of the charity);
   (3) amounts spent on administration;

(b) The income and expenditure account should also include the following:

   (1) pecuniary (cash) legacies;
   (2) surplus on sale of investments;
   (3) legacies of quoted investments (included in income at valuation of date of gift).

   In addition, investment income should be inclusive of tax credits.
(c) Fixed assets should be depreciated over useful life to the present owner, the annual charge being included in P/L.
(d) The fixed asset buildings might be included in the accounts at valuation at the date of transfer. A buildings fund could be credited.
(e) A suitable format for the income and expenditure account would be as follows:

	£	£
Income		
Donations		X
Investment income		X
Surplus on sale of investments		X
Legacies		X
		—
		X
Expenses		
Administration expenses	X	
Fund-raising expenses	X	
Charitable expenditure	X	
Depreciation	X	
	—	X
		—
Excess of income over expenditure		X
		—

13 GROUP ACCOUNTS—1

13.1 BACKGROUND

Most large organisations start in modest ways. A sole trader or partnership may decide to incorporate. The company which subsequently comes into being may initially expand through internal growth. At some stage, however, further expansion is often achieved by purchasing another business.

In some cases, such as the purchase of an unincorporated business, it is simply a question of introducing assets (including goodwill) into the company balance sheet. In other cases, the purchase involves the acquisition of a controlling shareholding in another company. Where one company owns a controlling interest in one or more other companies, a group comes into being.

13.2 THE NEED FOR GROUP ACCOUNTS

Suppose Elterwater has just paid £400 to acquire the entire shareholding (100 £1 shares) in Langdale Ltd.

Elterwater's summarised balance sheet immediately after the purchase is as follows:

	£	£
Fixed assets		
Tangible		890
Investments—shares in Langdale Ltd		400
Current assets		
Stocks	290	
Debtors	160	
Cash	30	
	480	
Creditors payable within one year		
Trade creditors	215	
		265
		1,555
Called-up share capital		1,000
Profit and loss account		555
		1,555

The balance sheet of Elterwater, although accurate is hardly informative! While it reveals the cost of the investment in Langdale Ltd, it says nothing about the underlying assets of the economic entity, the group. The group consists of Elterwater (referred to as the holding company) and Langdale Ltd (referred to as a subsidiary of Elterwater).

Suppose the summarised balance sheet of Langdale immediately prior to acquisition by Elterwater was as follows:

	£	£
Tangible fixed assets		260
Stocks	70	
Debtors	125	
Cash	5	
	200	
Trade creditors	150	
		50
		310

	£
Called-up share capital	100
Profit and loss account	210
	310

In order to reveal the assets (less liabilities) under the control of the group, a consolidated balance sheet may be prepared.

In the consolidated balance sheet, items for tangible fixed assets, stock, debtors and creditors would consist of combined totals for the two companies.

The difference between the cost of the investment in Langdale (£400) and the net assets of Langdale (£310) is usually referred to as goodwill arising on consolidation and amounts to £90. In line with SSAP 22 (see chapter 7), goodwill is usually eliminated as soon as it arises against reserves.

Share capital and reserves of Elterwater as at the date of acquisition are eliminated on consolidation.

The consolidated balance sheet is as follows:

CONSOLIDATED BALANCE SHEET OF ELTERWATER LTD AND ITS SUBSIDIARY

	£	£
Fixed assets		
Tangible assets (890 + 260)		1,150
Current assets		
Stocks (290 + 70)	360	
Debtors (160 + 125)	285	
Cash (30 + 5)	35	
	680	
Less Creditors: amounts falling due within one year:		
Trade creditors (215 + 150)	365	
Net current assets		315
Total assets less current liabilities		1,465
Called-up share capital		1,000
Profit and loss account (555 − 90)		465
		1,465

Points to note

(a) An acceptable alternative treatment for goodwill on consolidation would be to treat it as an intangible fixed asset amortised over its economic useful life (see chapter 7).
(b) Share capital relates only to share capital of the holding company.
(c) Profit and loss account relates only to that of the holding company. Profits made by Langdale prior to acquisition by Elterwater are referred to as 'pre-acquisition' profits and from the company viewpoint are regarded as capital in nature. However, any profits which Langdale makes in the future (post-acquisition profits) would be regarded as revenue and included in the group profit and loss account in the consolidated balance sheet. This is discussed further below.

The usual form of group accounts is described in SSAP 14, para 1 (group accounts) in the following terms:

In practice the group accounts usually take the form of consolidated financial statements which present the information contained in the separate financial statements of the holding company and its subsidiaries as if they were the financial statements of a single entity. . . .

The presentation of group accounts (consisting usually of a consolidated profit and loss account and a consolidated balance sheet) enables users of accounts to apply ratio analysis and other interpretative techniques to the results and financial position of the economic entity, the group.

13.3   LEGAL REQUIREMENTS

The Companies Act 1985 contains several definitions and requirements relating to the accounts of groups. Some of these are referred to immediately below, while others of a more complex nature are referred to in later chapters.

(a) Definitions

(1) The term group refers to a holding company together with its subsidiaries.
(2) A holding company/subsidiary relationship may be established in one of three ways:

   (i)   company A holds more than half of the nominal value of the equity share capital of company B. The term equity capital includes non-voting ordinary shares as well as participating preference shares. Fixed dividend preference shares (the usual situation) are irrelevant in determining whether one company is a subsidiary of another;
   (ii) company A is a member of (ie holds some shares in) company B and controls the composition of the board of directors of company B;
   (iii) company B is a subsidiary of company A, and company C is a subsidiary of company B.

   A   Holding company
   ↑
   B   Subsidiary
   ↑
   C   Sub-subsidiary

Situations (ii) and (iii) are discussed in detail in chapter 15.

(b) Obligation to lay group accounts before the holding company

A company which, at the end of its financial year, has one or more subsidiary companies must present group accounts at the general meeting at which its (the holding company's) own accounts are presented. There is a specific exemption where the company is itself a wholly owned subsidiary of another company incorporated in Great Britain.

(c) Form of group accounts

In principle, group accounts may take several possible forms. In practice, group accounts usually take the form of a single consolidated balance sheet and consolidated profit and loss account. This will be assumed to be the case throughout this chapter. In chapter 16, alternative forms of group accounts will be referred to.

13.4 THE MECHANICS OF CONSOLIDATED ACCOUNTS

A company which has subsidiaries is required to present:

(a) Its own (ie holding company) accounts, comprising:

    (i) holding company balance sheet; and

    (ii) holding company profit and loss account ((ii) is not required provided the consolidated profit and loss account is presented in a certain way and provides certain information).

(b) Group accounts, usually comprising:

    (i) consolidated balance sheet; and

    (ii) consolidated profit and loss account.

In this chapter, the preparation of both the consolidated profit and loss account, and the consolidated balance sheet will be considered together. Complications will be introduced gradually so that by the end of the chapter you should have a sound understanding of the mechanics of producing consolidated accounts.

For the purpose of illustration, format 1 of the Companies Act 1985 profit and loss account formats will be adopted.

13.5 A BASIC ILLUSTRATION

H Ltd acquired the entire share capital of S Ltd several years ago. At the date of acquisition by H, the reserves of S Ltd amounted to £110. The final accounts for the current year to 31 December 19X2 are as follows:

PROFIT AND LOSS ACCOUNTS

year ended 31.12.X2

	S Ltd £	H Ltd £
Turnover	2,900	1,200
Cost of sales	1,800	880
Gross profit	1,100	320
Distribution costs	(200)	(90)
Administrative expenses	(300)	(80)
Profit on ordinary activities before tax	600	150
Corporation tax	300	75
Profit after tax	300	75
Balance brought forward	930	215
Balance carried forward	1,230	290

BALANCE SHEETS

at 31.12.X2

	S Ltd £	H Ltd £
Tangible fixed assets	3,030	865
Investment in S Ltd	700	–
Stocks	570	155
Debtors	330	120
Cash at bank	160	30
	4,790	1,170
Ordinary share capital	2,000	500
Profit and loss account	1,230	290
Loan stock	1,000	200
Current taxation	300	75
Creditors	260	105
	4,790	1,170

(a) Preparing the consolidated balance sheet

Compared with previous editions, the approach to consolidation working papers been changed. The 'T' accounts approach is no longer used in this book. The approach now preferred is the analysis of equity method. This method is more compact than the 'T' accounts approach and has the advantage of highlighting the key purposes of the main adjustments.

Items such as fixed assets, stock, debtors, cash, taxation, trade creditors and loan stock present few problems—it is simply a matter of combining together the respective items for H and S.

Share capital and reserves of the subsidiary and cost of investment in S are dealt with in the analysis of equity schedule and are eliminated on consolidation.

Before considering the approach in detail, it is worth noting three particular points:

(1) As S Ltd is a wholly owned subsidiary of H Ltd, the question of outside (or minority) interests does not arise.
(2) The holding company balance sheet includes an asset 'investment in S Ltd'. This does not appear in the consolidated balance sheet of the group—instead the individual assets and liabilities of S Ltd are included under their respective headings (stock, debtors etc).

However, as mentioned in section 13.2 above it is necessary also to take account of goodwill arising on consolidation. This is the amount by which cost of investment exceeds net assets of subsidiary as at date of acquisition. An acceptable treatment under SSAP 22 is to write off goodwill against reserves in the year in which the acquisition takes place.

Net assets at acquisition also equal shareholders' funds at acquisition, ie:

Assets – Liabilities = Net assets = Shareholders' funds = Share capital plus reserves.

So goodwill arising on consolidation is:

	£	£
Investment in S Ltd		700
Net assets of S Ltd at acquisition = OSC + reserves at acquisition (500 + 110)		610
Therefore, goodwill on consolidation written off against reserves		90

(3) The reserves of the holding company amount to £1,230.
However, group reserves in the consolidated balance sheet include:

	£	£
(i) the reserves of the holding company;		1,230
(ii) the post-acquisition reserves of the subsidiary (ie the amount by which the subsidiary's reserves have increased since the date of acquisition);		
Reserves at 31.12.X2	290	
Less reserves at acquisition	110	
So post-acquisition increase		180
Less goodwill written off		(90)
Reserves in consolidated balance sheet		1,320

Recommended approach

Prepare a schedule of analysis of equity as follows:

	Total £	Group share (100%) pre-acquisition £	Group share (100%) post-acquisition £
Ordinary share capital	500	500	–
P/L reserves at acquisition	110	110	–
P/L reserves since acquisition	180	–	180
	790	610	
Cost of		700	
Goodwill on consolidation (see below)		90	
Reserves of H			1,230
Goodwill w/o against reserves			(90)
Consolidated P/L reserves			1,320

TUTORIAL NOTES
(1) P/L reserves since acquisition amounting to £180 has been calculated as a balancing figure (290 – 110).
(2) It has been assumed that the group's policy for goodwill on consolidation is to write it off against reserves as soon as it arises (see chapter 7).

CONSOLIDATED BALANCE SHEET

at 31.12.X2

	£	£	£
Fixed assets			
Tangible assets (3,030 + 865)			3,895
Current assets			
Stocks (570 + 155)		725	
Debtors (330 + 120)		450	
Cash at bank (160 + 30)		190	
		1,365	
Less creditors: amounts falling due within one year			
Creditors (260 + 105)	365		
Taxation (300 + 75)	375	740	
Net current assets			625
Total assets less current liabilities			4,520
Creditors: amounts falling due after more than one year—loan stock (1,000 + 200)			(1,200)
			3,320
Called-up share capital			2,000
Profit and loss account			1,320
			3,320

(b) Preparing the consolidated profit and loss account

Perhaps the most important point to remember is what we are aiming for—ie a completed profit and loss account. A good start is to draft a 'pro forma' with headings but leaving spaces for the numbers to be added later.

Using 'format 1', the headings are as follows:

CONSOLIDATED PROFIT AND LOSS ACCOUNT OF H LTD AND ITS SUBSIDIARIES

for the year ended 31 December 19X2

	£	£
Turnover		X
Cost of sales		X
Gross profit		X
Distribution costs	X	
Administrative expenses	X	
Profit on ordinary activities before tax		X
Taxation		X
Profit on ordinary activities after tax		X
Balance brought forward		X
Balance carried forward		X

Before filling in the figures, the following points should be borne in mind:

(1) The subsidiary is wholly owned. The complication of minority interest will be introduced later in the chapter.
(2) The subsidiary was owned throughout the year. Again, complications arising when a subsidiary is acquired during the current year will be dealt with later. (See chapter 14.)
(3) The consolidated profit and loss account does not deal with any profits of the subsidiary earned before acquisition by the holding company. Consequently the pre-acquisition reserves of S Ltd (£110) should *not* be included in either the brought forward or carried forward figures. This is most important!
(4) Finally, the balance carried forward should agree with the profit and loss account balance in the consolidated balance sheet!

In this simple example, the lines in the profit and loss account up to and including profit on ordinary activities after tax are arrived at by combining the respective amounts for H Ltd and S Ltd.

The balance brought forward is calculated as follows:

	£	£
H Ltd—full amount of b/f figure		930
S Ltd—post-acquisition part of b/f figure		
Reserves b/f	215	
Less reserves at acquisition (pre-acquisition)	110	
		105
		1,035
Less goodwill w/o in previous year (adjusted against opening reserves)		90
So figure for consolidated P/L is		945

The last line in the consolidated profit and loss account is arrived at simply by adding together the profit for the year and the brought forward figure.

Completing the consolidated profit and loss account:

CONSOLIDATED PROFIT AND LOSS ACCOUNT

for the year ended 31 December 19X2

	£	£
Turnover (2,900 + 1,200)		4,100
Cost of sales (1,800 + 880)		2,680
Gross profit		1,420
Distribution costs (200 + 90)	290	
Administrative expenses (300 + 80)	380	
		670
Profit on ordinary activities before tax		750
Taxation (300 + 75)		375
Profit on ordinary activities after tax		375
Balance brought forward (see above)		945
Balance carried forward		1,320

13.6 INTER-COMPANY DIVIDENDS

A subsidiary company is likely to make dividend payments to its shareholders. If the subsidiary is wholly owned, the full amount of the dividend will go to the holding company. As with any company, a subsidiary may pay its dividend in two parts—an interim and a final.

Illustration

Suppose H Ltd acquired the entire shareholding of S Ltd several years ago at a cost of £700 when the reserves of S Ltd amounted to £110.

The profit and loss accounts of the two companies for the year ended 31 December 19X2 are as follows:

	H Ltd £	S Ltd £
Turnover	2,900	1,200
Cost of sales	1,800	880
Gross profit	1,100	320
Distribution costs	(200)	(90)
Administrative expenses	(300)	(80)
Operating profit	600	150
Income from investments in group companies:		
Dividends received	10	–
Dividends receivable	20	–
Profit on ordinary activities before tax	630	150
Taxation	300	75
Profit on ordinary activities after tax	330	75
Dividends—paid	(70)	(10)
—proposed	(130)	(20)
Retained profit	130	45
Balance brought forward	930	215
Balance carried forward	1,060	260

Note carefully the relationship between:

(1) dividends paid and proposed by S Ltd; and
(2) dividends received (in cash) and receivable (in debtors) by H Ltd.

The balance sheets of the two companies are as follows:

	H Ltd £	S Ltd £
Tangible fixed assets	3,030	865
Investment in S Ltd	700	–
Stocks	570	155
Debtors	330	120
Dividends receivable	20	–
Cash at bank	100	20
	4,750	1,160
Ordinary share capital	2,000	500
Profit and loss account	1,060	260
Loan stock	1,000	200
Taxation	300	75
Creditors	260	105
Proposed dividends	130	20
	4,750	1,160

(a) Consolidated balance sheet workings

Note that dividends received and paid do not show up on the balance sheet—it is assumed that the respective companies' cash accounts have been adjusted.

The only additional complication is the dividend proposed and receivable amounting to £20. Their treatment in the analysis schedule is shown below:

ANALYSIS OF EQUITY OF S LTD

	Total £	Group share (100%) pre-acquisition £	Group share (100%) post-acquisition £
Ordinary share capital	500	500	–
P/L reserves at acquisition	110	110	–
P/L reserves since acquisition			
(260 – 110)	150	–	150
	760	610	
Cost of investment in S		700	
Goodwill on consolidation		90	
(see below)			
Reserves of H			1,060
Goodwill written off against			
reserves			(90)
Consolidated P/L reserves			1,120

TUTORIAL NOTE

It is important to pay particular attention to the treatment of inter-company dividends. S has provided in its accounts for a proposed final dividend of £20. In the above example H has accrued its share of the dividend receivable—H's reserves of £1,060 clearly include the £20.

An alternative possibility could have been that H had not accrued for the dividend and so H's reserves would have appeared as £1,040. In this situation it would have been necessary to increase H's reserves by £20, thus giving an adjusted figure of £1,060. Consolidated reserves would still have amounted to £1,120.

CONSOLIDATED BALANCE SHEET

at 31.12.X2

	£	£	£
Fixed assets			
Tangible assets			3,895
Current assets			
Stocks		725	
Debtors		450	
Cash at bank		120	
		1,295	
Less creditors: amounts falling due within one year			
Creditors	365		
Taxation	375		
Dividends	130		
Net current assets		870	425
Total assets less current liabilities			4,320
Less creditors: amounts falling due after more than one year—loan stock			1,200
			3,120
Called-up share capital			2,000
Profit and loss account			1,120
			3,120

TUTORIAL NOTE
The dividend proposed of £130 relates to the amount payable to the holding company shareholders.

(b) Consolidated profit and loss account workings

The only income from the subsidiary which is included in the holding company's profit and loss account is that relating to dividends received and receivable (ie £10 + £20 = £30).

While this reflects a fair situation for the holding company as a separate legal entity, it does not provide useful information for the group as a whole.

For the group accounts, it is far more useful to bring in the profit on ordinary activities after tax of £75, rather than simply include that part of the £75 which happens to be paid over (now or in the near future) as dividend (ie £30).

The essential point, therefore, is that the investment income of £30 is replaced by the various items which go to make up S's profit of £75.

This means that H's reserves in its own individual balance sheet will be smaller than the reserves in the consolidated balance sheet. The reason for this, of course, is that over a period of years, H's reserves include only dividends received from subsidiaries.

On the other hand, consolidated reserves include all attributable profits of subsidiaries irrespective of whether they are paid across as dividends (ie £30 in the above example) or ploughed back as retained profit (ie £45 above).

The consolidated profit and loss account should be tackled in the same way as before ie by drawing up a blank pro forma. Figures can then be slotted in as soon as they are calculated. This should save time and avoid unnecessary workings.

The completed consolidated profit and loss account is as follows:

	£	£
Turnover		4,100
Cost of sales		2,680
		———
Gross profit		1,420
Distribution costs	290	
Administrative expenses	380	
	———	
		670
		———
Profit on ordinary activities before tax		750
Taxation		375
		———
Profit on ordinary activities after tax		375
Dividends—paid	70	
—proposed	130	200
	———	———
Retained profit		175
Balance brought forward (W1)		945
		———
Balance carried forward		1,120
		———

W1	£	£
H Ltd—full amount		930
S Ltd—post-acquisition part		
at 31.12.X2	215	
at acquisition	110	
	———	105
		———
		1,035
Less goodwill w/o		90
		———
Group P/L balance b/f		945
		———

13.7 MINORITY INTERESTS

(a) Background

Suppose H Ltd purchased only 80% of the shares in S Ltd; the remaining shares (20%) continuing to be held by outsiders.

$$H$$
$$\uparrow \quad 80\%$$
$$S$$

S Ltd is now a partly owned (as opposed to wholly owned) subsidiary with a minority interest of 20%. As S Ltd is a subsidiary, it must be reflected in the group's accounts.

In theory two possible approaches could be:

(1) to include 80% of the respective items (stock, debtors, turnover, cost of sales etc) relating to S; or
(2) to include 100% of all such items but make a compensating adjustment to reflect 20% outside ownership.

The first approach has been used only on very rare occasions. Partly owned subsidiaries are normally consolidated using the second approach, in which items for minority interest appear in both the consolidated balance sheet and consolidated profit and loss account. Special situations are discussed later.

(b) Consolidated balance sheet procedures

The analysis schedule will now require an additional column for minority interest.

(c) Illustration

The basic data in section 13.5 will be used, the only difference being that £700 represents the cost of an 80% shareholding in S Ltd.

ANALYSIS OF EQUITY OF S LTD

	Total £	Group share pre-acquisition (80%) £	Group share post-acquisition (80%) £	MI (20%) £
Ordinary share capital	500	400	–	100
P/L reserves at acquisition	110	88	–	22
P/L reserves since acquisition (290 – 110)	180	–	144	36
	790	488		
Cost of investment in S		700		
Goodwill on consolidation		212		
Reserves of H			1,230	
Goodwill w/o against reserves			(212)	
Consolidated B/S totals			1,162	158

CONSOLIDATED BALANCE SHEET

at 31 December 19X2

	£	£	£
Fixed assets			
Tangible assets			3,895
Current assets			
Stocks		725	
Debtors		450	
Cash		190	
		1,365	
Less creditors: amounts falling due within one year			
Creditors	365		
Taxation	375		
		740	
Net current assets			625
Total assets less current liabilities			4,520
Less creditors: amounts falling due after more than one year—loan stock			1,200
			3,320
Called-up share capital			2,000
Profit and loss account			1,162
			3,162
Minority interest			158
			3,320

Note: All of the assets of S Ltd have been consolidated, even though H's ownership is only 80%. This provides a more meaningful indication of assets employed within the group than would be the case if only 80% of the relevant amounts were included. The minority interest of £158 (equal to 20% of the net assets of S Ltd £790—see balance sheet in section 13.5) indicates to holding company shareholders the extent of outside ownership.

(d) Consolidated profit and loss procedures

The basic approach is the same as that outlined earlier in the chapter. For all items up to and including profit on ordinary activities after taxation, the relevant consolidated profit and loss account line will include 100% of the respective item for S Ltd.

However, immediately after this line will appear a line for minority interest. This is calculated as 20% (in the above example) of the profit after tax of S Ltd ie 20% × £75 = £15.

Using the figures in section 13.5, the consolidated profit and loss account will appear as follows:

CONSOLIDATED PROFIT AND LOSS ACCOUNT
for the year ended 31 December 19X2

	£	£
Turnover		4,100
Cost of sales		2,680
Gross profit		1,420
Distribution costs	290	
Administrative expenses	380	
		670
Profit on ordinary activities before tax		750
Taxation		375
Profit on ordinary activities after tax		375
Minority interest		15
Profit attributable to members of H Ltd		360
Balance brought forward (W1)		802
Balance carried forward		1,162

W1	£	£
H Ltd—full amount		930
S Ltd–H's share of post-acquisition part		
—at 31.12.X2	215	
—at acquisition	110	
	105	
H's share 80%×£105		84
		1,014
Goodwill w/o		212
Group balance b/f		802

13.8 INTER-COMPANY DIVIDENDS AND PARTLY-OWNED SUBSIDIARIES

At this stage, it would be useful to consider the combined effects of the two previous sections. This will be developed by means of a further example using much of the data from the previous sections.

Illustration

H Ltd acquired 80% of the share capital of S Ltd at a cost of £700 when S's reserves amounted to £110. The draft final accounts for the year are as follows:

PROFIT AND LOSS ACCOUNTS
year ended 31 December 19X2

	H Ltd £	S Ltd £
Turnover	2,900	1,200
Cost of sales	1,800	880
Gross profit	1,100	320
Distribution costs	(200)	(90)
Administrative expenses	(300)	(80)
	600	150
Income from investments in group companies		
Dividends received	8	–
Dividends receivable	16	–
Profit on ordinary activities before tax	624	150
Taxation	300	75
	×80%	
Profit on ordinary activities after tax	324	75
Dividends—paid	(70)	(10)
—proposed	130	(20)
Retained profit	124	45
Balance brought forward	930	215
Balance carried forward	1,054	260

(Note relationship between dividends paid/proposed and dividends received/receivable.)

BALANCE SHEETS
at 31 December 19X2

	H Ltd £	S Ltd £
Tangible fixed assets	3,030	865
Investment in S Ltd	700	–
Stocks	570	155
Debtors	330	120
Dividends receivable	16	–
Cash at bank	98	20
	4,744	1,160
Ordinary share capital	2,000	500
Profit and loss account	1,054	260
Loan stock	1,000	200
Taxation	300	75
Creditors	260	105
Proposed dividends	130	20
	4,744	1,160

ANALYSIS OF EQUITY OF S LTD

	Total £	Group share (80%) pre-acquisition £	Group share (80%) post-acquisition £	MI (20%) £
Ordinary share capital	500	400		100
P/L reserves at acquisition	110	88		22
P/L reserves since acquisition	150		120	30
	760	488		
Cost of investment in S		700		
Goodwill on consolidation		212		
Reserves of H			1,054	
Goodwill w/o against reserves			(212)	
Consolidated B/S totals			962	152

TUTORIAL NOTES

(1) The reserves of H (£1,054) include H's share of dividend receivable from S (80% × £20 = £16).

(2) The proposed final dividend of S will be distributed as follows:

Payable to H   80% × 20 = 16
Payable to MI   20% × 20 = 4
                           ──
                           20
                           ──

The inter-company dividend of £16 has already been taken into account. The dividend payable to MI of £4 will result in a payment outside the group and should be included as a separate item under creditors—amounts due within one year.

Consolidated balance sheet as at 31 December 19X2

	£	£	£
Fixed assets			
Tangible assets			3,895
Current assets			
Stocks		725	
Debtors		450	
Cash		118	
		1,293	
Less creditors: amounts falling due within one year			
Creditors	365		
Taxation	375		
Proposed dividends			
Holding company	130		
Minority	4		
		874	

Net current assets	419
Total assets *less* current liabilities	4,314
Creditors: amounts falling due after more than	
one year—loan stock	1,200
	3,114
Capital and reserves	
Called-up share capital	2,000
Profit and loss account	962
	2,962
Minority interest	152
	3,114

Consolidated profit and loss account procedures

Once again, it is useful to start with a pro forma consolidated profit and loss account. This should contain a 'slot' for minority interest.

It is important (as always) to appreciate the difference between the holding company's own profit and loss and the consolidated profit and loss account.

The holding company's profit and loss account should include dividends received or receivable from subsidiaries ie 80% × £30 = £24 in the above example.

However, simply to include dividends received does not give a meaningful view of group profitability. So in the consolidated profit and loss account, profits are substituted for dividends.

All lines down to and including profit on ordinary activities after tax include 100% of the respective items (sales, cost of sales etc) of S Ltd.

The consolidated profit and loss account may be completed:

CONSOLIDATED PROFIT AND LOSS ACCOUNT

for the year ended 31 December 19X2

	£	£
Turnover		4,100
Cost of sales		2,680
Gross profit		1,420
Distribution costs	290	
Administrative expenses	380	
		670
Profit on ordinary activities before tax		750
Taxation		375
Profit on ordinary activities after tax		375
Minority interest		15
Profit attributable to members of H Ltd		360
Dividends—paid	70	
—proposed	130	
		200
Retained profit		160
Balance brought forward		802
Balance carried forward		962

(1) Minority interest is *always* calculated as the minority interest percentage of the subsidiary's profit after tax but before deducting dividends paid and proposed.
(2) The only dividends paid and proposed in the consolidated profit and loss account are those relating to the holding company.
(3) The balance brought forward is the same figure as calculated in the example in section 13.7.

13.9 MORE THAN ONE SUBSIDIARY

If the holding company has more than one subsidiary, it is useful to have a separate analysis of equity schedule for each subsidiary. However, for convenience, all minority items may be dealt with in a single account.

As regards presentation, only one item is shown for minority interest in the consolidated balance sheet and profit and loss account, even though the MI figures may relate to several groups of individuals owning shares in different companies.

13.10 GOODWILL ON CONSOLIDATION

The accounting treatment of goodwill on consolidation was discussed in detail in chapter 7.

For clarity, it is assumed for all group accounts illustrations, that the group policy is to eliminate goodwill on consolidation immediately on acquisition of a subsidiary, by means of a charge against reserves.

Under this policy, no entry is made in the profit and loss account. The amount written off will only be disclosed in the year of write-off. This approach is adopted by the majority of UK companies.

The amortisation alternative, although not illustrated here, would be acceptable provided it was consistent with the provisions of SSAP 22.

14 GROUP ACCOUNTS—2

14.1 SUBSIDIARIES ACQUIRED DURING THE CURRENT YEAR

(a) Introduction

First of all, what will be the effect of an acquisition during the year of a new subsidiary? The assets and liabilities of the new subsidiary should be included in the consolidated balance sheet as it is a member of the group at the year end.

As regards the consolidated profit and loss account, any profits earned by the subsidiary prior to acquisition should be excluded. The consolidated profit and loss account should include only post-acquisition profits.

(b) Possible approaches

Illustration

The profit and loss accounts of Fell and Tarn for the year ended 31 December 19X6 are as follows:

	Fell £	Tarn £
Turnover	900	600
Cost of sales	400	360
Gross profit	500	240
Distribution costs	(100)	(36)
Administrative expenses	(200)	(48)
Operating profit	200	156
Tax	90	72
Profit after tax	110	84

Fell acquired the entire share capital of Tarn on 30 September 19X6. How should the consolidated profit and loss account be presented?

In theory there are two possible methods:

Method 1: In the first part of the profit and loss account include the full year's figures for Tarn, but later eliminate the pre-acquisition part of the profit after tax, i e $\frac{9}{12}$ (9 months) × £84 = £63.

Method 2: Include only the proportionate ($\frac{3}{12}$) amounts of turnover, cost of sales etc.

The effect of the two methods may be compared:

CONSOLIDATED PROFIT AND LOSS ACCOUNT

for the year ended 31 December 19X6

	Method 1 £	Method 2 £
Turnover	1,500	1,050
Cost of sales	760	490
Gross profit	740	560
Distribution costs	(136)	(109)
Administrative expenses	(248)	(212)
Profit on ordinary activities before tax	356	239
Taxation	162	108
Profit on ordinary activities after tax	194	131
Group share of pre-acquisition profit of new subsidiary	63	N/A
Profit attributable to the members of Fell Ltd	131	131

TUTORIAL NOTE
All figures for method 2 include three months for Tarn e g turnover is $(900 + \frac{3}{12} \times 600)$.

COMMENT

Method 1 has the advantage of enabling a full year's group profit to be related to capital employed. Its main disadvantage is that a somewhat confusing item appears on the face of the profit and loss account. The method has declined in popularity and is now only rarely used in practice. Method 1 is not recommended for examination purposes.

Method 2 is widely used in practice by large companies and is recommended for examination purposes. On subsequent occasions in this book, only method 2 will be used.

(c) Pre-acquisition dividends received during the year

The holding company may well receive a dividend from a new subsidiary, shortly after its acquisition date. The problem is that this dividend may have been paid either wholly or partly out of pre-acquisition profits.

On receipt of the dividend, the holding company should apportion the dividend between:

(1) The pre-acquisition part—this should be credited to (i e effectively deducted from) cost of investment in subsidiary.
(2) The post-acquisition part—this should be credited to the holding company's profit and loss accounts.

The basis of apportionment is the date of acquisition in relation to the accounting year of the company paying the dividend.

Two short examples will be given: first, where only one dividend is paid for the year; secondly, where an interim and final dividend are paid. Note that recent developments in this area are discussed in chapter 16 (see section 16.22).

Illustration 1—one dividend only

H Ltd acquired 100% of the share capital of S Ltd on 31.8.19X3. The year end of both companies is 31 December. In its accounts for the year ended 31 December 19X3, S Ltd proposes a dividend of £3,600. How should this be treated in the final accounts of S?

Diagramatically

Pre-acquisition (8m)	Post acquisition (4m)
1.1.X3 31.8.X3	31.12.X3

The date of payment of the dividend (possibly in March or April of 19X4) is irrelevant. The only dates that matter are:

(1) the date of acquisition (31.8.X3);
(2) the year for which the dividend is declared (YE 31.12.X3).

So the post-acquisition part of the dividend is £1,200 ($\frac{4}{12} \times £3,600$) and the pre-acquisition part £2,400 ($\frac{8}{12} \times £3,600$).

The required journal entry in the books of H is:

	£		£
Debit dividend receivable *(debtor)*	3,600	*Credit* cost of investment in S	2,400
		Profit and loss account of H	1,200
	£3,600		£3,600

Illustration 2 — interim and final

H Ltd acquired 100% of the share capital of S Ltd on 31.8.19X3. The year end of both companies is 31 December. S paid an interim dividend of £1,000 on 7.7.19X3, and proposes a final dividend of £2,600. How should this be treated in the final accounts of S Ltd?

The crucial point is that both elements of the dividend (totalling £3,600) relate to the year ended 31 December 19X3.

H does not receive £1,000 since it was paid to the previous shareholders of the company before H obtained control.

But H must set up a debtor for dividend receivable of £2,600. The maximum amount of this which may be regarded as post-acquisition is:

Four months' proportion of the total of the interim and the final dividend i e: $\frac{4}{12} \times (£1,000 + £2,600) = £1,200$.

The balance of the final dividend (amounting to £2,600 − £1,200 = £1,400) must be regarded as capital.

The required journal entry is thus:

	£		£
Debit dividend receivable	2,600	Credit cost of investment in S Ltd	1,400
		Profit and loss	
		account of H	1,200
	2,600		2,600

Illustration 3—acquisitions of a wholly owned subsidiary

Easedale acquired the entire share capital of Loughrigg on 30 September 19X3. The draft final accounts of the two companies are as follows:

PROFIT AND LOSS ACCOUNTS

for the year ended 31 December 19X3

	Easedale £	Loughrigg £
Turnover	900	200
Cost of sales	500	112
Gross profit	400	88
Distribution costs	(90)	(16)
Administrative expenses	(150)	(32)
Operating profit	160	40
Dividends receivable (note 1)	2	—
	162	40
Taxation	80	20
Profit after tax	82	20
Proposed dividends	30	8
Retained profit	52	12
Balance b/f	120	40
Balance c/f	172	52

NOTE 1
Dividend receivable from Loughrigg is the post-acquisition part i e $\frac{3}{12} \times £8 = £2$. The balance of £6 has been deducted from the cost of investment of £175 (see balance sheet below).

BALANCE SHEETS
at 31 December 19X3

		Easedale	*Loughrigg*
		£	£
Tangible fixed assets		200	90
Investment in S Ltd	175		
Less pre-acq div	6	169	—
Stocks		105	45
Cash		120	25
Dividends receivable		8	—
		602	160
Share capital		400	100
Profit and loss account		172	52
Proposed dividend		30	8
		602	160

ANALYSIS OF EQUITY OF LOUGHRIGG

	Total	*Group share pre-acquisition*	*Group share post-acquisition*
	£	£	£
Ordinary share capital	100	100	—
P/L reserves at acquisition	49	49	—
P/L reserves since acquisition	3	—	3
	152	149	3
Cost in investment in S		169	
Goodwill on consolidation		20	
Reserves of Easedale			172
Goodwill w/o against reserves			(20)
Consolidated P/L reserves			155

NOTE 2: CALCULATION OF PRE-ACQUISITION RESERVES

	£	£
Balance at 1.1.X3		40
Profit after tax for year	20	
Attributable to period 1.1.X3 to 30.9.X3		
$\frac{9}{12} \times 20$	15	
Less pre-aquisition part of final dividend	6	
		9
Therefore, pre-acquisition reserves		49

NOTE 3

Goodwill on consolidation is the amount by which the purchase consideration exceeds the net assets acquired. If a company pays a dividend before the date of sale, this affects the size of the bank balance, the purchase consideration and, of course, the goodwill.

However, a proposed dividend at the end of the year, paid to the new owner, has no effect on either assets taken over or purchase consideration. It cannot affect goodwill.

In the above example, had no dividend been proposed at the year end, the purchase consideration would still have amounted to £175 and the goodwill calculated at £20 as follows:

		£
Cost of investment		175
Group share pre-aquistion		
OSC	100	
P/L (40 + 15)	55	155
		20

CONSOLIDATED BALANCE SHEET

at 31.12.X3

Fixed assets	£	£
Tangible assets		290
Current assets		
Stocks	150	
Cash	145	
	295	
Less creditors: amounts falling due within one year:		
Proposed dividend	30	
Net current assets		265
Total assets less current liabilities		555
Called up share capital		400
Profit and loss account		155
		555

Consolidated profit and loss procedures

The key point to remember is that in method 2 we include a proportionate share ($\frac{3}{12}$) of the results of Loughrigg.

The consolidated profit and loss account will appear as follows:

CONSOLIDATED PROFIT AND LOSS ACCOUNT

for the year ended 31 December 19X3

	£	Workings
Turnover	950	$900 + \frac{3}{12} \times 200$
Cost of sales	528	$500 + \frac{3}{12} \times 112$
Gross profit	422	
Distribution costs	(94)	$90 + \frac{3}{12} \times 16$
Administrative expenses	(158)	$150 + \frac{3}{12} \times 32$
Profit on ordinary activities before tax	170	
Taxation	85	$80 + \frac{3}{12} \times 20$
Profit on ordinary activities after tax	85	
Proposed dividends	30	
Retained profit	55	

Statement of reserves	
Balance brought forward	120
Retained profit	55
Goodwill written off	(20)
Balance carried forward	155

NOTE 4

The balance brought forward relates to the holding company only. If a subsidiary is acquired during the current year, all of its reserves brought forward are pre-acquisition and have no effect on consolidated profit and loss reserves brought forward.

(d) Illustration 4—acquisition of a partly owned subsidiary

This example introduces two further complications:

(1) the newly acquired subsidiary paid an interim dividend before the date of acquisition;

(2) the new subsidiary includes a minority interest.

The example is concerned solely with the profit and loss account.

(1) Basic information

The draft profit and loss accounts of Langdale Ltd and Elterwater Ltd were as follows:

	Langdale £	Elterwater £
Turnover	3,000	1,200
Selling and marketing expenses	(700)	(240)
Administrative expenses	(400)	(120)
Operating profit	1,900	840
Dividends receivable (note 2)	27	—
Profit before tax	1,927	840
Taxation	950	420
Profit after tax	977	420
Dividends—paid	(100)	(60)
—proposed	(300)	(120)
Retained profit	577	240
Balance b/fwd	1,000	700
Balance c/fwd	1,577	940

NOTES

(1) The cost of investment was £1,850 and relates to a 90% shareholding acquired two months before the year end.

(2) The proposed dividend of £120 has been correctly treated in the accounts of the holding company:

Holding company share of final dividend = 90% × £120 = £108.

Maximum amount which may be treated as post-acquisition

$= 90\% \times \frac{2}{12} \times (£60 + £120)$

$= £27$

(That is, pre-acquisition part of final dividend is £108 − £27 = £81 and has been deducted from cost of investment.)

(2) Procedures

(a) Consolidated profit and loss account should include $\frac{2}{12}$ of the following items:

Turnover	$\frac{2}{12} \times £1,200$ =	£200
Selling expenses	$\frac{2}{12} \times £240$ =	£40
Administrative expenses	$\frac{2}{12} \times £120$ =	£20
Taxation	$\frac{2}{12} \times £420$ =	£70

(b) Since the consolidated profit and loss account includes only two months' proportion of the respective revenue items, minority interest must be based on two months' profit after tax.

i e $MI = 10\% \times \frac{2}{12} \times £420$
$\qquad = £7$

(3) 　　　　　　CONSOLIDATED PROFIT AND LOSS ACCOUNT
　　　　　　　　for the year ended 31 December 19X3

	£
Turnover	3,200
Selling and marketing expenses	(740)
Administrative expenses	(420)
Profit on ordinary activities before tax	2,040
Taxation	1,020
Profit on ordinary activities after tax	1,020
Minority interest	7
Profit attributable to members of Langdale Ltd	1,013
Dividends—paid	(100)
—proposed	(300)
Retained profit (see note)	613

NOTE
It is good presentation (though not mandatory) to disclose the split of retained profit between:

	£
(a) profit retained by holding company, i e;	577
and	
(b) profit retained by subsidiary:	
$90\% \times \frac{2}{12} \times £240 =$	36
	613

14.2 PREFERENCE SHARES IN SUBSIDIARIES

(a) Introduction

Most types of preference shares entitle the holder to:

(1) dividend of fixed amounts, in priority to ordinary dividends;
(2) on liquidation, a return of capital of a fixed amount in priority to ordinary shareholders.

These preference shares have no effect whatsoever on the holding company subsidiary relationship as they are not equity shares as such. Participating preference shares are a special case. They are equity shares and thus may affect the holding company subsidiary relationship. Such shares are not dealt with below as they are of little practical importance.

(b) Approach to consolidation

(1) Consolidated balance sheet:

(i) the difference between the cost of the investment in preference shares and the nominal value held should be adjusted through the goodwill calculation.

(ii) the nominal value of preference shares held by outsiders should form part of minority interest (non-current part).

(iii) preference dividends payable to outsiders are included as current items.

(2) Consolidated profit and loss account.

The subsidiary should be consolidated in the usual way. However, the minority interest calculation requires particular care.

Example

H Ltd acquired the following shareholdings in S Ltd several years ago:

80% of the ordinary share capital.

10% of the preference share capital.

The draft profit and loss account of S Ltd for the current year is as follows:

		£
Turnover		7,000
Operating expenses		3,000
Profit on ordinary activities		4,000
Taxation		1,800
Profit after tax		2,200
Preference dividends	600	
Ordinary dividends	1,000	
		1,600
Retained profit		600
Balance brought forward		3,000
Balance carried forward		3,600

How should minority interest be determined for profit and loss account purposes?

(1) Minority interest

Ordinary shares   20%
Preference shares   90%

(2) The starting point is profit after tax (£2,200).

(a) Minority interest in preference shares—fixed amount of 90% × £600 = £540.

(b) Minority interest in ordinary shares—based on available profit (£2,200 − £600 = (£1,600) i e 20% × £1,600 = £320).

So total minority interest is £860.

(3) For exam purposes, it is convenient to set the calculation out as follows:

	100% £		MI £
Profit after tax	2,200		
Preference dividends	600	× 90% =	540
Available for ordinary shareholders	1,600	× 20% =	320
MI in consolidated profit and loss account			860

NOTE
Had the ordinary and preference shares been acquired three months before the end of the year, only three months' results would be consolidated (as discussed in section 14.1) and the minority interest would also be based on three months. Minority interest would then amount to $\frac{3}{12} \times £860$ i e £215.

(c) A further example

It is useful to bring together the above points. For the sake of compactness, the accounting information has been summarised. More information would be required for Companies Act 1985 purposes.

The draft profit and loss accounts of Hill Ltd and Side Ltd for the year ended 31 December 19X3 were as follows:

	Hill £	Side £
Turnover	11,000	5,000
Expenses	4,000	2,200
Operating profit	7,000	2,800
Taxation	3,500	1,400
Profit after tax	3,500	1,400
Proposed dividends		
Preference shares	—	(320)
Ordinary shares	(2,000)	(800)
	1,500	280
Balance brought forward	4,100	740
Balance carried forward	5,600	1,020

DRAFT BALANCE SHEETS

at 31 December 19X3

	Hill £	Side £
Fixed assets	21,660	13,590
Debtors	8,290	4,150
Cash	4,150	2,100
Creditors	(6,500)	(3,700)
Proposed dividends—ordinary	(2,000)	(800)
—preference	—	(320)
	25,600	15,020

	£	£
Ordinary share capital	20,000	10,000
Preference share capital (8% £1 shares)	—	4,000
Profit and loss account	5,600	1,020
	25,600	15,020

Additional information

(1) Fixed assets includes the cost of the following investments:

    (i)   70% of the ordinary share capital of Side Ltd, acquired when its reserves amounted to £300—cost of investment, £8,500.

    (ii) 20% of the preference share capital of Side Ltd—cost of investment, £830.

(2) Hill Ltd has not yet made an entry in its books in respect of dividends receivable from Side Ltd. (Contrast this with the situation in previous examples.)

CONSOLIDATED BALANCE SHEET WORKINGS

		£
Dividends receivable by Hill		
Ordinary 70% × £800	=	560
Preference 20% × £320	=	64
		—
Total		624

The reserves of Hill of £5,600 should thus be increased by £624 to £6,224.

ANALYSIS OF SHAREHOLDERS EQUITY OF SIDE

	Total £	Group share (70%) pre-acquisition £	Group share (70%) post-acquisition £	MI (30%) £
Ordinary shares				
Ordinary share capital	10,000	7,000		3,000
P/L reserves at acquisition	300	210		90
P/L reserves since acquisition	720		504	216
	11,020	7,210		
Cost of investment		8,500		
Goodwill on consolidation		1,290		

		Group share (20%) £		MI (80%) £
Preference shares				
Preference share capital	4,000	800		3,200
Cost of investment		830		
Consolidation difference		30		

Hill Ltd reserves				
Per draft B/S	5,600			
Div. receivable	624		6,224	
Goodwill w/o against reserves		(1,290 + 30)	(1,320)	
Consolidated B/S totals			5,408	6,506

TUTORIAL NOTES

(1) Minority interest in proposed dividends is as follows:

		£
Ordinary dividend	30% × £800	240
Preference dividend	80% × £320	256
		—
		496

This total should be included under creditors due within one year.

(2) It is usually acceptable to offset any difference on the purchase of preference shares (i e 830 – 800 = 30) against goodwill on consolidation relating to ordinary shares.

CONSOLIDATED BALANCE SHEET

at 31 December 19X3

	£	£	£
Fixed assets			
Tangible assets (W1)			25,920
Current assets			
Debtors		12,440	
Cash		6,250	
		18,690	
Less creditors: amounts falling due within one year:			
Creditors	10,200		
Proposed dividends:			
Holding company	2,000		
Minority	496		
		12,696	
Net current assets			5,994
Total assets less current liabilities			31,914
Called-up share capital			20,000
Profit and loss account			5,408
Minority interest			6,506
			31,914

W1			
Fixed assets—per draft a/cs (21,660 + 13,590)	=		35,250
Less investments in subsidiary (8,500 + 830)	=		9,330
Tangible assets			25,920

CONSOLIDATED PROFIT AND LOSS ACCOUNT WORKINGS

(1) *Minority interest*

	100% £		MI £
Profit after tax	1,400		
Preference dividend	320	(80%)	256
Available for ordinary shareholders	1,080	(30%)	324
MI in consolidated profit and loss account			580

(2) *Retained profit allocation*

	£
Holding company	
Per draft accounts	1,500
Dividends to be accrued	624
	2,124
Subsidiary	
70% × £280	196
	2,320

(3) *Consolidated P/L reserves brought forward*

	£	£
Holding company		4,100
Subsidiary		
At 1.1.X3	740	
At acquisition	300	
Post-acquisition	440 × 70%	308
		4,408
Less goodwill w/o		1,320
		3,088

CONSOLIDATED PROFIT AND LOSS ACCOUNT

for the year ended 31 December 19X3

	£	£
Turnover		16,000
Operating expenses		6,200
Profit on ordinary activities before tax		9,800
Taxation		4,900
Profit on ordinary activities after tax		4,900
Minority interest		580
Profit available for holding company shareholders		4,320
Proposed dividends		2,000
Retained profit		2,320
Retained by holding company	2,124	
Retained by subsidiary	196	
	2,320	
Balance brought forward		3,088
Balance carried forward		5,408

14.3 DEBENTURES IN SUBSIDIARIES

Mathematically, the approach is similar to that used for preference shares:

(a) Consolidated balance sheet:

  (1) The difference between the cost of the investment in debentures and the nominal value held should be adjusted through the goodwill calculation.
  (2) The nominal value of debentures held by outsiders should be presented as a non-current liability (i e under 'creditors amounts falling due after more than one year'). It should *not* be included under minority interest.

(b) Consolidated profit and loss account:

  Interest paid will include the outside share of debenture interest.

Example

A owns the entire share capital of B, but only owns 10% of the debenture stock. The abbreviated profit and loss acounts are as follows:

	A £	B £
Operating profit	200	200
Interest received	5	—
Interest paid	—	(50)
Retained profit	205	150

The inter-company interest amounting to £5 should be eliminated on consolidation. The effect of the above items on the consolidated profit and loss account would be:

	£
Operating profit	400
Interest paid (50 − 5)	45
Retained profit	355

Holding company	205
Subsidiary	150
	355

14.4   INTER-COMPANY ITEMS

(a) Cash-in-transit

Cash-in-transit may be the cause of inter-company accounts failing to agree.

Example

At the year end, the current accounts in the books of H and S respectively show the following:

Books of H Ltd—account with S Ltd	£8,000
Books of S Ltd—account with H Ltd	£6,000

The difference is due to a cheque of £2,000 in transit.

   Procedure—amend books of H Ltd to £6,000 (so that inter-company balances may be offset) and remember to increase cash at bank by £2,000. A useful rule of thumb is:

(1) Items-in-transit between holding company and subsidiary—put 'journal' through holding company books.
(2) Items-in-transit between subsidiaries—amend books of recipient company.

(b) Loans

Assuming both sets of books are up-to-date, the inter-company balances should cancel each other out. Ensure that any loan interest charged has been correctly treated in both sets of books and that the charge is fair as regards the borrowing company (which may be a partly owned subsidiary).

(c) Management charges

Again, inter-company balances should cancel out. Management charges should be realistic. For example, if a holding company makes a management charge to a partly owned subsidiary, the charges will reduce the subsidiary's reserves and affect the rights of outside shareholders.

(d) Inter-company sales of goods

In a group of trading companies, it is not uncommon for companies to sell goods from one to another. If these goods are sold at a profit to the selling company, this raises the problem of unrealised inter-company profits.

Example

Eskdale owns 80% of the ordinary share capital of Grange Ltd. During the current year, Grange sold to Eskdale goods costing £15,000 at a price which gives a profit of 25% on the selling price. By the year end, Eskdale had sold three-quarters of these goods to third parties.

(1) The draft acounts of the two companies showed the following:

	Eskdale £	Grange £
Turnover	200,000	85,000
Cost of sales	(130,000)	(60,000)
Other expenses	(25,000)	(9,000)
Profit on ordinary activities	45,000	16,000
Taxation	22,000	7,300
Profit after tax	23,000	8,700
Balance brought forward	50,000	20,000
Balance carried forward	73,000	28,700

(2) Stocks in the draft balance sheet amounted to:

	£
Eskdale	180,000
Grange	70,000

(3) Eskdale purchased its shares when the reserves of Grange amounted to £6,000.
(4) No goods were transferred between the two companies in previous years.

Points to consider

(1) Group turnover should include only sales to third parties. Inter-company turnover amounts to £20,000 ($\frac{100}{75} \times$ £15,000).
   This must be taken into acount in arriving at consolidated sales.
(2) The profit on the sale of the goods amounts to £5,000. Of this amount, 75% (i e £3,750) may be regarded as realised since this relates to the proportion of the goods which had been sold to third parties by the balance sheet date. Thus unrealised profits amount to £1,250. These should be eliminated before arriving at consolidated profit.
(3) How much of the £1,250 should be eliminated?
   There are several viewpoints which can be put forward.

   (i) Both reserves and stocks should be reduced by £1,250. This has the advantage that in the consolidated balance sheet, stock is stated at the lower of cost and net realisable value from the viewpoint of the group (as opposed to the viewpoint of individual companies!). This approach is widely followed in practice and is recommended for exam purposes. Note that the amount of profit eliminated is the same whether the subsidiary is wholly owned or partly owned.
   (ii) A second approach is to eliminate only that part of the profit relating to the group (i e 80% × £1,250 = £1,000) on the grounds that the profit attributable to outside shareholders is realised by sale outside that company. Under this approach, both consolidated reserves and consoli-

dated stock are reduced by £1,000. A major disadvantage of this method is that it produces an unsatisfactory stock figure.

(iii) A third possibility is to reduce consolidated stock by £1,250 but to reduce group reserves by £1,000 and minority interest by £250. This reflects the holding company's ownership in the subsidiary. The method has merit, but would be difficult to operate for goods transferred within complex group structures.

Following approach (i) the unrealised profit adjustment of £1,250 would be dealt with in the analysis schedule as follows:

ANALYSIS OF SHAREHOLDERS EQUITY OF GRANGE

	Total	Group share (80%) pre-acquisition	Group share (80%) post-acquisition	Minority interest (20%)
	£	£	£	£
Ordinary share capital	X	X		X
P/L reserves acquisition	6,000	4,800		1,200
P/L reserves since acquisition	22,700	—	18,160	4,540
	XX	XX		
Cost of investment in Grange		X		
Goodwill on consolidation		XX		
Reserves of Eskdale			73,000	
Unrealised profit in stock			(1,250)	
Goodwill w/o against reserves			(XX)	
Consolidated balance sheet totals			XXX	XXX

	£
Stock in consolidated balance sheet	
Eskdale	180,000
Grange	70,000
	250,000
Unrealised profit in stock	1,250
∴ Stock in consolidated B/S	248,750

CONSOLIDATED PROFIT AND LOSS ACCOUNT WORKINGS

		£
Turnover	200,000 + 85,000 − 20,000 =	265,000
Cost of sales	130,000 + 60,000 − 20,000 + 1,250 =	171,250
Profit on ordinary activities	45,000 + 16,000 − 1,250 =	59,750
Minority interest	20% × £8,700 =	1,740
Reserves brought forward	50,000 + 80% (20,000 − 6,000) =	61,200

CONSOLIDATED PROFIT AND LOSS ACCOUNT FOR ...

	£
Turnover	265,000
Cost of sales	(171,250)
Other expenses	(34,000)
Profit on ordinary activities before tax	59,750
Taxation	29,300
Profit on ordinary activities after tax	30,450
Minority interest	1,740
Profit attributable to members of holding company	28,710
Balance brought forward	61,200
Balance carried forward (ignoring goodwill w/o)	89,910

(e) Inter-company transfers of fixed assets

In a group which includes manufacturing companies, one company may manufacture and sell to another company assets which are retained by the transferee company as fixed assets.

From the group accounts viewpoint this poses two problems:

(1) The once and for all profit on the transfer of the asset:
(2) The effect each year on the depreciation charge.

The problem is solved by making consolidation adjustments in respect of unrealised profit.

Example

Oakfield Ltd and Woodlands Ltd are both partly owned subsidiaries of Cotham Ltd. Woodlands Ltd manufactures office furniture. During the year ended 30 September 19X2, furniture costing £2,000 to manufacture is transferred to Oakfield Ltd at a price of £2,400. The furniture is considered to have a useful life of ten years, with a nil residual value.

Contrasting the effect on the accounts of individual companies and those of the group:

(1) *Individual companies*

    (i) Woodlands Ltd—as a separate legal entity, the profit on sale to Oakfield is a realised profit.

    (ii) Oakfield Ltd—the annual depreciation charge of £240 is based on the cost to Oakfield as a separate legal entity.

(2) *Group accounts*

    (i) In 19X2, the transfer profit of £400 is unrealised. In the opposite direction, depreciation charge is £240 compared with £200 had the asset been transferred at cost. The net effect of these should be reflected as a consolidation adjustment.

    (ii) In 19X3 and subsequent years, if no consolidation adjustment were made, the depreciation charge each year would be overstated each year by £40.

    The effect may be summarised as follows:

		Profit	
Year	*Overstated*	*Understated*	*Net*
	£	£	£
19X2	400	40	360
19X3	—	40	(40)
19X4	—	40	(40)
19X5	—	40	(40)
19X6	—	40	(40)
19X7	—	40	(40)
19X8	—	40	(40)
19X9	—	40	(40)
19X10	—	40	(40)
19X11	—	40	(40)
Totals	400	400	—

The column entitled 'net' is the amount of the consolidation adjustment. For example, in 19X2 the net book value of the furniture in the books of Oakfield is £2,400 − £240 = £2,160. The consolidation adjustment is to reduce group profit and loss account by £360 and group fixed assets by £360. So in the group balance sheet, the furniture would be included at £2,160 − £360 = £1,800 (split cost £2,000 less depreciation £200) i e as if it had been transferred at cost.

NOTES
(1) The adjustments (Dr £360 in 19X2 and credit £40 in 19X3) would appear in consolidated profit and loss reserves (as for stock in (e) above).
(2) The consolidation adjustments have no effect on the accounts of the individual companies—they are separate legal entities in their own right.
(3) As indicated for stock, the adjustment for unrealised profit could take account of minority interests. The approach adopted above, however, is recommended for exam purposes.

14.5   RESERVES OF SUBSIDIARIES

So far we have assumed that reserves of subsidiaries consist solely of accumulated profit and loss account balances. It is, of course, possible to have several categories of reserves including revaluation surplus (as a result of revaluing fixed assets) and share premium accounts.

The principles are still the same—each category of reserve must be split between pre-acquisition and post-acquisition.

Example

Henley Ltd acquired 60% of the ordinary share capital of Apsley Ltd several years ago when Apsley's reserves were as follows:

	£
Profit and loss account	12,000
Revaluation reserve	3,000
Share premium account	5,000

At the most recent balance sheet date, the reserves of the two companies were as follows:

	Henley	Apsley
	£	£
Profit and loss account	102,000	19,000
Revaluation reserve	67,000	8,000
Share premium account	35,000	5,000

The effect on the consolidated balance sheet may be illustrated as follows.

ANALYSIS OF SHAREHOLDERS EQUITY OF APSLEY LTD

	Total £	Group share (60%) of pre-acquisition reserves £	Group share of post-acquisition P/L £	Group share of post-acquisition re-valuation reserve £	Group share of post-acquisition share premium £	MI (40%) £
Ordinary share capital	X	X				X
P/L reserves at acquisition	12,000	7,200				4,800
P/L reserves since acq.	7,000		4,200			2,800
Revaluation reserves at acquisition	3,000	1,800				1,200
Revaluation reserves since acquisition	5,000			3,000		2,000
Share premiun at acquisition	5,000	3,000				2,000
	XX	XX				
Cost of investment		X				
Goodwill on consolidation		XX				
Reserves of Henley			102,000	67,000	35,000	
Goodwill w/o against reserves			(XX)			
Consolidated B/S totals			XX	70,000	35,000	XX

14.6 SHARE PURCHASES SPREAD OVER A PERIOD OF TIME

Clearly there are several possibilities but two particular ones are worth considering:

(a) A series of purchases building up to a controlling interest (piecemeal acquisition).
(b) An acquisition of a controlling interest followed by further purchases increasing the group shareholding.

Each of these is illustrated by an example:

(a) Piecemeal acquisitions

The general principle is that until control is obtained, no profits can be regarded as post-acquisition. However, if earlier purchases were acquired with the express intention of ultimately obtaining control it may be possible to treat each purchase individually as regards the split between pre- and post-acquisition profits.

Example

H Ltd acquired the following shareholdings in S Ltd:

30.6.19X2	20% (when reserves were £12,000)
31.3.19X3	40% (when reserves were £17,000)

At 31.12.X3 (the date of the consolidated balance sheet) the reserves were £25,000.
    Without any assumptions of ultimate control, the reserves would be allocated as follows:

		£
Group pre-acquisition	60% × £17,000	10,200
Minority interest	40% × £25,000	10,000
Group post-acquisition	60% × £8,000	4,800
		25,000

However, if it is assumed that the earlier purchase of 20% was with the specific intention of ultimately obtaining control (and subsequent events suggest this is a reasonable assumption!) then the reserves would be allocated as follows:

	£	£
Group pre-acquisition:		
20% × £12,000	2,400	
40% × £17,000	6,800	9,200
Minority interest:		
40% × £25,000		10,000
Group post-acquisition:		
20% (25,000 − 12,000)	2,600	
40% (25,000 − 17,000)	3,200	5,800
		25,000

Clearly it is important that you state your assumptions!

(b) Controlling interest and subsequent purchases

With a subsequent purchase, the relevant proportion of reserves at the purchase date is the pre-acquisition reserves for that part of the group shareholding.

Example

H Ltd acquired the following shareholdings in S Ltd.

30.9.X2	70% (when reserves were £22,000)
30.4.X3	20% (when reserves were £32,000)

At date of consolidated balance sheet, the reserves of S Ltd amounted to £45,000.
    The reserves of £45,000 would be allocated as follows:

	£	£
Group pre-acquisition:		
70% × £22,000	15,400	
20% × £32,000	6,400	21,800
Minority interest:		
10% × £45,000		4,500
		26,300
Group post-acquisition:		
70% × (45,000 − 22,000)	16,100	
20% × (45,000 − 32,000)	2,600	18,700
		45,000

14.7   BONUS ISSUES

If a subsidiary company makes a bonus (or capitalisation) issue prior to acquisition, there are no problems since both share capital and reserves have been adjusted. If the bonus issue was shortly before the acquisition date but has not yet been reflected in the accounts, it is advisable to alter share capital and the relevant part of reserves, before proceeding with the consolidation adjustments.

However, bonus issues made after the acquisition date may present difficulties. The key point is to determine whether the bonus issue is made out of pre-acquisition reserves or post-acquisition reserves.

(a) Out of pre-acquisition reserves

If the bonus issue is made soon after acquisition, this must be the situation. The recommended procedure is to reduce subsidiary reserves and increase subsidiary share capital, then to proceed in the usual way.

(b) Out of post-acquisition reserves

It is important to determine whether the bonus issue is out of reserves of a capital nature (share premium account, capital redemption reserve etc) or out of profit and loss account.

In the former case, no adjustment is needed for group accounts purposes. In the latter case, group distributable reserves will be affected.

Example

The summarised balance sheets of H Ltd and S Ltd (a 90% owned subsidiary) are as follows:

	H Ltd £	S Ltd £
Net assets	84,000	42,000
Investment in S Ltd	16,000	—
	100,000	42,000
Share capital	30,000	10,000
Profit and loss account	70,000	32,000
	100,000	42,000

The investment in S Ltd was acquired when its reserves amounted to £2,000. S Ltd now proposes to make a 2 for 1 bonus issue out of post-acquisition reserves.

Considering the principal aspects of the consolidated balance sheet in turn:

(1) Consolidation goodwill is calculated as follows:

	£
Cost of investment	16,000
Group share of net assets (equal to share capital plus reserves) at acquisition 90% (10,000 + 2,000)	10,800
	5,200

A post-acquisition bonus issue cannot affect the goodwill figure.

(2) Minority interest is based on proportionate share of assets at balance sheet date i e 10% × £42,000 = £4,200.

(3) Consolidated profit and loss account reserves is calculated as follows:

	£
H Ltd	70,000
S Ltd 90% (32,000 − 2,000)	27,000
	97,000
Less goodwill written off	5,200
	91,800

However, the fact that S Ltd is declaring a bonus issue out of post-acquisition profits is effectively saying that £20,000 (2 for 1 on share capital of £10,000) of profits which were previously distributable are now no longer regarded as distributable. The group proportion of this is £18,000. In order to present a true and fair view, this figure should be disclosed as a memorandum note in the group accounts.

(4) From the above it is clear that for exam purposes it is better not to adjust for the bonus issue, otherwise there is a danger that goodwill whether written off or capitalised, will be incorrect.

(5) The consolidated balance sheet (in summarised form) will appear as follows:

	£
Net assets	126,000
Goodwill on consolidation	—
	126,000
Share capital	30,000
Profit and loss account (see note)	91,800
Minority interest	4,200
	126,000

Note: Profit and loss account includes £18,000 not available for distribution.

14.8   EXTRAORDINARY ITEMS

The subject of extraordinary items was dealt with in an earlier chapter. However, it is worth considering here the effect of extraordinary items in a partly owned subsidiary. Remember that extraordinary items are presented net of minority interest.

Example

S Ltd is a 70% owned subsidiary acquired when its reserves were £1,900. The draft profit and loss accounts of H Ltd and S Ltd are as follows:

	H Ltd £	S Ltd £
Operating profit	5,000	2,000
Profit on sale of property		500
Taxation	(2,500)	(1,000)
Balance brought forward	11,000	4,200
Balance carried forward	13,500	5,700
Share capital:	20,000	10,000

No tax is provided on the property sale as roll-over relief will be claimed. The important matter of whether the £500 should be classified as extraordinary or exceptional was considered earlier. For illustration purposes only, we will consider the effect on the consolidated profit and loss account of treating the £500 as:

(a) exceptional;
(b) extraordinary.

In the case of (a), minority interest is 30% (2,000 + 500 − 1,000) i e £450.
In the case of (b), minority interest is 30% (2,000 − 1,000) i e £300 and extraordinary item is 70% × £500 i e £350.

The consolidated profit and loss accounts under the two alternatives would appear as follows:

	(a)	(b)
Profit on ordinary activities before tax	7,500	7,000
Taxation	3,500	3,500
Profit on ordinary activities after tax	4,000	3,500
Minority interest	450	300
Profit before extraordinary items	3,550	3,200
Extraordinary items	—	350
Profit attributable to holding company shareholders	3,550	3,550
Balance brought forward	12,610	12,610
Balance carried forward	16,160	16,160

Working

Balance brought forward	
H Ltd	11,000
S Ltd	
70% (4,200 − 1,900)	1,610
	12,610

NOTE
Although the two possibilities give different presentations of minority interest in the profit and loss account, there will be no difference in the consolidated balance sheet. In either event, minority interest is £4,710 (i e 30% × (10,000 + 5,700)).

14.9 SEVERAL SUBSIDIARIES—THE PROBLEM OF GOODWILL

In all the examples considered so far, acquisitions have given rise to positive goodwill (cost of investment exceeding assets acquired).

It is possible that on certain occasions negative goodwill will arise in which case it should be kept separate and treated in accordance with SSAP 22 (see chapter 7).

15 VERTICAL AND MIXED GROUPS

15.1 INTRODUCTION

This chapter is concerned with the two special situations which were referred to in chapter 13 (see section 13.3(a)).

First of all the vertical group situation where company B is a subsidiary of company A, and company C is a subsidiary of company B.

Secondly, the mixed group situation where company A is a member of company B and controls the composition of the board of directors of company B.

Each of these situations will be covered in turn and will be illustrated by examples.

15.2 VERTICAL GROUPS—A WORKED EXAMPLE

The summarised draft final accounts of Holbrook, Sevier and Tipton for the year ended 31 December 19X9 were as follows:

Balance sheets	Holbrook Ltd £'000	Sevier Ltd £'000	Tipton Ltd £'000
Tangible fixed assets	500	300	150
Net current assets	220	130	60
Investment in Sevier	410	–	–
Investment in Tipton		110	–
	1,130	540	210
Called-up share capital (£1 ordinary shares)	700	300	100
Profit and loss account	330	200	95
Proposed dividends	100	40	15
	1,130	540	210

Profit and loss accounts	Holbrook Ltd £'000	Sevier Ltd £'000	Tipton Ltd £'000
Turnover	800	180	80
Operating costs	480	70	44
Operating profit	320	110	36
Taxation	140	50	16
	180	60	20
Proposed dividends	100	40	15
Retained profit	80	20	5
Balance at 1.1.X9	250	180	90
Balance at 31.12.X9	330	200	95

The following information is also relevant:

(1) Sevier acquired 60% of the ordinary share capital of Tipton in 19X2 when the reserves of Sevier were £125,000 and those of Tipton, £60,000.

(2) Holbrook acquired 80% of the ordinary share capital of Sevier in 19X4 when the reserves of Sevier were £165,000 and those of Tipton, £85,000.

(3) Neither Holbrook nor Sevier have yet accrued their shares of dividends receivable.

Required: A consolidated profit and loss account and consolidated balance sheet for 19X9.

15.3 SUMMARY OF SHAREHOLDINGS

The position as regards reserves and shareholdings may be illustrated as follows:

(a) Reserves at dates of acquisition of share purchases

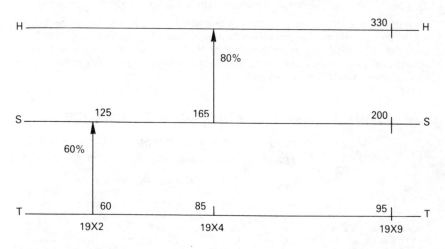

(b) Shareholdings

	Sevier	Tipton		
Holbrook	80%	80% × 60% =	48%	(I)
MI	20%	40% (D) =	52%	
		20% × 60% (I)		
	100%		100%	

NOTES

(1) T is a subsidiary of S. S is a subsidiary of H, therefore T is a subsidiary of H. This is so in spite of the fact that H's effective share of T is only 48% (80% × 60%).

(2) Group accounts are required dealing with H, S and T. 100% of the assets and liabilities of T should be consolidated. However, since H owns only 48% of T, minority interest should be based on 52%.

(3) In the shareholdings table, D refers to direct (ie a direct shareholding by H) while I refers to indirect (ie an indirect shareholding by H).

15.4 APPROACHES TO CONSOLIDATION

In principle, there are two possible methods:

(a) indirect (2-stage) consolidation;
(b) direct (1-stage) consolidation.

In practice, (a) is usually followed. For examinations, both methods should be known and will be illustrated below.

15.5　INDIRECT CONSOLIDATION

The group structure is:

```
H
↑   80%
S
↑   60%
T
```

Indirect consolidation involves two stages:

(a) Stage 1—consolidation of Sevier group (ie Sevier and Tipton)
(b) Stage 2—consolidation of Holbrook with the Sevier group.

Note that this is what would happen in practice. Under UK company law, Sevier would be required to prepare group accounts. The only exemption would be if Sevier was a wholly owned subsidiary of Holbrook (in which case the group accounts of Sevier would serve little purpose) when group accounts of Sevier and its subsidiary would not be required.

15.6　STAGE 1—CONSOLIDATION OF SEVIER GROUP

ANALYSIS OF EQUITY OF TIPTON

(Sevier share 60%, minority 40%)

	Total £	Group share pre-acquisition £	Group share post-acquisition £	Minority interest £
Ordinary share capital	100,000	60,000		40,000
Reserves at acquisition by Sevier	60,000	36,000		24,000
Reserves since acquisition	35,000		21,000	14,000
Total	195,000	96,000		
Cost of investment by Sevier		110,000		
Goodwill on consolidation written off against reserves		14,000	(14,000)	
Reserves of Sevier including dividends receivable from Tipton (200,000 + 60% × 15,000)			209,000	
Totals for Sevier group consolidated balance sheet			216,000	78,000

CONSOLIDATED BALANCE SHEET OF SEVIER GROUP AT 31 DECEMBER 19X9

	£	£	£
Fixed assets			
Tangible fixed assets			450,000
Net current assets		190,000	
Proposed dividends			
Holding company	40,000		
Minority (40% × 15,000)	6,000	46,000	
			144,000
Total assets less current liabilities			594,000

Capital reserves	
Called-up share capital	300,000
Profit and loss account	216,000
	516,000
Minority interest	78,000
	594,000

TUTORIAL NOTE
The reserves of £216,000 are all post-acquisition as regards the Sevier group but include £15,000 (ie 60% × (85,00 − 60,000) which are pre-acquisition as regards the Holbrook group).

15.7 STAGE 2—CONSOLIDATION OF HOLBROOK AND SEVIER GROUP

ANALYSIS OF EQUITY OF SEVIER

(Holbrook share 80%, minority 20%)

	Total £	Group share pre-acquisition £	Group share post-acquisition £	Minority interest £
Ordinary share capital	300,000	240,000		60,000
Reserves at acquisition of Holbrook (see note below)	180,000	144,000		36,000
Reserves since acquisition per analysis of Tipton (216,000 − 180,000)	36,000		28,800	7,200
	516,000	384,000		
Cost of investment by Holbrook		410,000		
Goodwill on consolidation w/o against reserves		26,000	(26,000)	
Reserves of Holbrook including dividends receivable from Sevier (330,000 + 80% × 40,000)			362,000	
Consolidated balance sheet totals			364,800	103,200

NOTE
The consolidated P/L reserves of Sevier group at date of acquisition by Holbrook is calculated as follows:

	£
P/L reserves of Sevier	165,000
Sevier's share of post-acquisition reserves of Tipton 60% (85 − 60)	15,000
	180,000

Note this calculation very carefully: the increase in reserves from 60 to 85 is post-acquisition as regards the Sevier group but pre-acquisition as regards the Holbrook group.

Other workings

		£
(1) Minority interest (non-current)		
	Tipton	78,000
	Sevier	103,200
		181,200
(2) Minority interest (current)		
	Tipton 40% × £15,000	6,000
	Sevier 20% × £40,000	8,000
		14,000

CONSOLIDATED BALANCE SHEET OF HOLBROOK GROUP AT 31 DECEMBER 19X9

	£	£	£
Fixed assets			
Tangible assets			950,000
Net current assets		410,000	
Proposed dividends:			
Holding company	100,000		
Minority	14,000	114,000	296,000
Total assets less current liabilities			1,246,000
Capital and reserves			
Called-up share capital			700,000
Profit and loss account			364,800
			1,064,800
Minority interest			181,200
			1,246,000

15.8 CONSOLIDATED PROFIT AND LOSS ACCOUNT—INDIRECT METHOD

S GROUP

Stage 1

	£	£
Turnover		260,000
Operating costs		114,000
Operating profit		146,000
Taxation		66,000
Profit after tax		80,000
Minority interest (40% × 20,000)		8,000
		72,000
Proposed dividends		40,000
Retained profit		32,000
Balance b/f		
S	180,000	
T 60%(90,000 − 60,000)	18,000	
	198,000	
Less goodwill w/o	14,000	
		184,000
		216,000

Stage 2

	£	£
Turnover		1,060,000
Operating costs		594,000
Operating profit		466,000
Tax		206,000
Profit after tax		260,000
Minority interest		
Per S group P/L	8,000	
Tipton 12% × 20,000	2,400	
Sevier 20% × 60,000	12,000	
	————	
		22,400
		237,600
Proposed dividends		100,000
Retained profit		137,600
Balance b/f		
Holbrook		250,000
S group	184,000	
Pre-acq S	(165,000)	
Pre-acq T 60% × (85 − 60)	(15,000)	
	————	
	4,000	
H's share 80%		3,200
		253,200
Less goodwill w/o (Holbrook in Sevier)		(26,000)
		227,200
Balance c/f		364,800

15.9 DIRECT CONSOLIDATION

(a) This method omits the intermediate stage of the construction of the consolidated accounts of the Sevier sub-group. (consisting of Sevier and its subsidiary, Tipton).

The equity of each subsidiary (ie Sevier and Tipton) is analysed using the *effective* group percentages:

	Group	MI
Sevier	80%	20%
Tipton	80% × 60% = 48%	52%

(b)   ANALYSIS OF EQUITY OF SEVIER

(Group holding 80%, MI 20%)

	Total £	Group share pre-acquisition £	Group share post-acquisition £	Minority interest £
Ordinary share capital	300,000	240,000		60,000
Reserves at acquisition (19X4)	165,000	132,000		33,000
Reserves since acquisition				
Per acs	35,000			
Share of div. receivable 60% × 15,000	9,000			
	44,000		35,200	8,800
	509,000	372,000		
Cost of investment		410,000		
Goodwill w/o against reserves (see below)		38,000		
Carried forward to summary			35,200	101,800

(c)   ANALYSIS OF EQUITY OF TIPTON

(Effective group holding 48%, MI 52%)

	Total £	Group share pre-acquisition £	Group share post-acquisition £	Minority interest £
Ordinary share capital	100,000	48,000		52,000
Reserves at acquisition (NB: 19X4)	85,000	40,800		44,200
Reserves since acquisition	10,000		4,800	5,200
	195,000	88,800		
Cost of investment (allocated 80%:20%)		(88,000)		(22,000)
Group share w/o against group reserves		(800)		
Carried forward to summary			4,800	79,400

(d) **Summary**

	£	Group P/L reserves £	MI (non-current) £	MI (current) £
Holbrook				
Per acs	330,000			
Div receivable 80% × 40,000	32,000			
		362,000	–	–
Equity of S		35,200	101,800	
Proposed dividend S 20% × 40,000				8,000
Equity of T		4,800	79,400	
Proposed dividend T 40% × 15,000				6,000
Goodwill adjustments (38,000 – 800)		(37,200)		
Consolidated B/S totals		364,800	181,200	14,000

(e)   CONSOLIDATED BALANCE SHEET OF HOLBROOK GROUP
AT 31 DECEMBER 19X9

	£	£	£
Fixed assets			
Tangible assets			950,000
Net current assets		410,000	
Proposed dividends:			
Holding company	100,000		
Minority	14,000	114,000	296,000
Total assets less current liabilities			1,246,000
Capital and reserves			
Called-up share capital			700,000
Profit and loss account			364,800
			1,064,800
Minority interest			181,200
			1,246,000

(f)   CONSOLIDATED PROFIT AND LOSS ACCOUNT OF HOLBROOK GROUP
USING DIRECT CONSOLIDATION

	£	£
Turnover		1,060,000
Operating costs		594,000
Profit on ordinary activities before tax		466,000
Tax on profit on ordinary activities		206,000
Profit on ordinary activities after tax		260,000
Minority interest		22,400
Profit attributable to members of Holbrook		237,600
Proposed dividends		100,000
		137,600
Retained profit		
Holding company	112,000	
Subsidiaries	25,600	
	137,600	
Balance at 1.1.X9		227,200
Balance at 31.12.X9		364,800

(g) **Workings—consolidated profit and loss account**

(1) Minority interest

	£
Tipton 52% × £20,000	10,400
Sevier 20% × £60,000	12,000
	22,400

(2) Retained profit allocation

(a) Holbrook

	£
Per draft accounts	80,000
Dividend receivable from Sevier	
80% × £40,000	32,000
	112,000

(b) Subsidiaries

	£
Sevier	
Per draft accounts	20,000
Dividend receivable Tipton	
60% × £15,000	9,000
	29,000

Group share 80% × £29,000	23,200
Tipton	
Group share 48% × £5,000	2,400
	25,600

(3) Balance at 1.1.X9

Holbrook	250,000
Sevier 80%(180,000 − 165,000)	12,000
Tipton 48%(90,000 − 85,000)	2,400
	264,400
Less goodwill written off	37,200
	227,200

15.10   MIXED GROUPS—A WORKED EXAMPLE

The summarised draft balance sheets of Hiland, Fresno and Stockton at 31 December 19X9 were as follows:

	Hiland Ltd £'000	Fresno Ltd £'000	Stockton Ltd £'000
Tangible fixed assets	500	200	100
Net current assets	213	88	66
Investment in Stockton		42	
Investment in Fresno	255		
Investment in Stockton	57		
	1,025	330	166
Called-up share capital (£1 ordinary shares)	600	200	100
Profit and loss account	425	130	66
	1,025	330	166

The following information is also relevant:

(1) Fresno acquired 30% of the ordinary share capital of Stockton in 19X1 when the reserves of Fresno were £47,000 and those of Stockton were £24,000.
(2) Hiland acquired 90% of the ordinary share capital of Fresno in 19X3 when the reserves of Fresno were £60,000 and those of Stockton were £36,000.
(3) Hiland acquired 25% of the ordinary share capital of Stockton 19X5 when the reserves of Fresno were £92,000 and those of Stockton were ££44,000.

Required: A consolidated balance sheet at 31 December 19X9.

15.11 SUMMARY OF SHAREHOLDINGS

(a) Reserves at dates of acquisition of share purchases

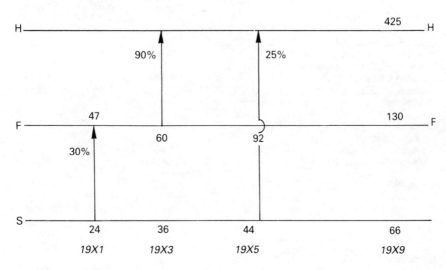

(b) Shareholdings

	Fresno	Stockton	
Hiland	90%	25% (D) 90% × 30% (I)	} 52%
MI	10%	45% (D) 10% × 30% (I)	} 48%
	100%	100%	

15.12 APPROACH TO CONSOLIDATION

In this situation, the best approach is direct consolidation. The mechanics of this is similar to that for vertical groups.

ANALYSIS OF EQUITY OF FRESNO

(Group holding 90%, MI 10%)

	Total £	Group share pre-acquisition £	Group share post-acquisition £	Minority interest £
Ordinary share capital	200,000	180,000		20,000
Reserves at acquisition	60,000	54,000		6,000
Reserves since acquisition	70,000		63,000	7,000
	330,000	234,000		
Cost of investment		255,000		
Goodwill on consolidation		21,000		
			63,000	33,000

ANALYSIS OF EQUITY OF STOCKTON

(Group holding 52%, MI 48%)

	Total £	Group share pre-acquisition £	Group share post-acquisition £	Minority interest £
Ordinary share capital	100,000	52,000		48,000
Reserves at acquisition (19X5 when Stockton becomes part of Hiland Group)	44,000	22,880		21,120
Reserves since acquisition	22,000		11,440	10,560
	166,000	74,880		
Cost of investment				
direct		(57,000)		
indirect (allocated 90%:10%)		(37,800)		(4,200)
Goodwill		19,920		
			11,440	75,480

Summary

	Group P/L reserves £	MI £
Hiland	425,000	
Equity of Fresno	63,000	33,000
Equity of Stockton	11,440	75,480
Goodwill adjustments (21,000 + 19,920)	(40,920)	
Consolidated B/S totals	458,520	108,480

CONSOLIDATED BALANCE SHEET OF HILAND GROUP

as at 31 December 19X9

	£
Fixed assets	
Tangible assets	800,000
Net current assets	367,000
	1,167,000
Capital and reserves	
Called-up share capital	600,000
Profit and loss account	458,520
	1,058,520
Minority interest	108,480
	1,167,000

16 ACQUISITIONS, MERGERS AND SSAP 14

16.1 SSAP 14 (GROUP ACCOUNTS)

SSAP 14 on group accounts deals with the following topics:

(a) the usual form of group accounts;
(b) uniform accounting policies;
(c) group accounting periods and dates;
(d) changes in the composition of the group—acquisitions;
(e) changes in the composition of the group—disposals;
(f) exclusion of subsidiaries from consolidation;
(g) minority interests;
(h) restrictions on distributions.

16.2 THE USUAL FORM OF GROUP ACCOUNTS

The Companies Act 1985 requires a holding company and its subsidiaries to present group accounts (see section 13.3(b)). These group accounts usually take the form of a single consolidated balance sheet, a consolidated profit and loss account and notes to the accounts which present the information as though it related to the financial statements of a single company.

Although the Companies Act 1985 permits group accounts to take alternative forms, this flexibility is limited by the requirement of SSAP 14 and the overriding true and fair view requirement. In practice, the alternative forms relate to special situations such as subsidiaries with activities different from the rest of the group (see section 16.9 below).

16.3 UNIFORM ACCOUNTING POLICIES

Wherever possible, all group companies should adopt the same accounting policies. However, there may be cases where certain subsidiary companies adopt policies which differ from the rest of the group. In this case, consolidation adjustments should be put through in order that the group accounts are presented on the basis of uniform accounting policies.

SSAP 14 refers to exceptional cases where consolidation adjustments are impractical, in which case the group accounts will not be based on uniform accounting policies. Disclosure is then required of:

(a) the different accounting policies used;
(b) an indication of the amounts of the assets and liabilities involved and where practicable, an indication of the effect on results and net assets of the adoption of policies different from those of the group;
(c) the reasons for the different treatment.

Such cases are likely to be rare and restricted to overseas subsidiaries.

16.4   GROUP ACCOUNTING PERIODS AND DATES

(a) The general rule

Wherever practicable, the financial statements of all subsidiaries should be made up to the same accounting date as the holding company and relate to identical accounting periods.

(b) Situations

Situations where financial statements are made up to a different date might include:

(1) Where the year end of the subsidiary is based on a convenient date corresponding with the natural trading cycle (for example a plantation company).
(2) Where the group accounts include subsidiaries' accounts made up to a date, say, three months earlier in order to avoid undue delay in the presentation of the group accounts.
(3) Other reasons may include local regulations concerning accounting dates or the possible tax consequences of changing dates.

(c) Two possible alternatives

In cases where it is *not* practicable for a subsidiary (or subsidiaries) to draw up its annual accounts to the same date as the holding company, SSAP 14 deals with two possible alternatives:

(1) the inclusion of special accounts prepared purely for the purposes of the consolidation;
(2) if (1) is not practicable, then the subsidiary accounts (made up to an earlier date) should be used but the group accounts should be adjusted for 'any abnormal transactions in the intervening period'.

(d) Special accounts

This alternative will require Department of Trade approval. Say, for example, that the consolidated accounts cover the year ended 31 December 19X4. The results of the subsidiary may be included as follows:

(1) nine months' proportion of the audited annual accounts to 30 September 19X4;
(2) three months' specially prepared accounts up to 31 December 19X4;
(3) it will also be necessary to prepare an interim balance sheet at 31 December 19X4.

(e) Accounts made up to different dates

Suppose that the 30 September 19X4 accounts of a subsidiary are to be consolidated with the accounts of the remainder of the group made up to 31 December 19X4. What adjustments should be made for 'abnormal transactions' arising in the three months to 31 December 19X4?

There are two categories of situations requiring adjustment:

(1) significant (but normal) transactions with other group companies, for example, in the situation referred to earlier, a significant remittance of cash on 30 November 19X4 to the holding company;
(2) events such as major changes in exchange rates, major trade losses, and significant fixed asset sales or discontinuance of business activities.

(f) Disclosure implications for (e)

(1) SSAP 14 requires the following disclosure information concerning any subsidiary with a different accounting date:

    (i)   its name;
    (ii) its accounting date;
    (iii) the reason for using a different accounting date.

    Similar information is also required by the Companies Act.

(2) Disclosure is also required of the accounting period involved where a principal subsidiary has an accounting period which differs in length from that of the holding company.

16.5 CHANGES IN THE COMPOSITION OF THE GROUP—GENERAL CONSIDERATIONS

(a) The term 'changes in the composition of the group' can refer to purchases or sales of shareholdings in subsidiary companies.

(b) A typical example of disclosure in the statement of accounting policies is:

> Where subsidiary companies are acquired or sold during the year, their results and turnover are included from the date of acquisition or excluded from the date of sale.

(c) A key factor is the effective date of acquisition or disposal. This is defined in SSAP 14 as the earlier of:

    (1) the date on which consideration passes; or
    (2) the date on which an offer becomes or is declared unconditional.

In some cases, consideration is by instalments over a period of time. Clearly (2), the date when the purchase or sale becomes binding on both parties, is then the effective date.

16.6 CHANGES IN THE COMPOSITION OF THE GROUP— ACQUISITIONS

(a) Introduction

SSAP 14 deals with two aspects of the topic—computational and disclosure.

(b) Computational aspects

Chapter 16 deals with the computational aspects of newly acquired subsidiaries. The results of new subsidiaries are included only from the date of acquisition. Unless there is evidence that business is seasonal, this may be determined by time apportionment. The date of acquisition is defined above.

The other computational aspect, referred to in previous chapters, is the calculation of goodwill (or capital reserve) on consolidation.

(c) Goodwill on consolidation

(1) Goodwill on consolidation (or discount on acquisition) is the difference between:

    (i)   the purchase consideration; and
    (ii) the fair value to the acquiring company of net tangible assets (including patents, trade marks, deferred development expenditure but not goodwill in the accounts of an individual company).

(2) Wherever possible, any adjustments to asset values should be put through the books of the acquired company. Failing this, consolidation adjustments should be put through the group accounts in order to ensure that goodwill on consolidation is a meaningful figure and does not partly reflect undervaluation of assets such as freehold property.

Illustration

The draft balance sheet of S Ltd at acquisition appears as follows:

Freehold property	150,000
Other assets	90,000
Liabilities	(60,000)
	180,000
Share capital	100,000
Profit and loss account	80,000
	180,000

H Ltd acquired the entire share capital. The purchase consideration was cash of £360,000. On the face of it, goodwill on consolidation is £180,000. But is this sensible? On closer inspection the freehold has an open market value of £250,000! Goodwill on consolidation is therefore more sensibly calculated as £80,000.

In the consolidation working papers, it would be necessary to create a revaluation surplus account amounting to £100,000 (ie £250,000 less £150,000). All of this is pre-acquisition.

Analysis of equity would appear as follows:

ANALYSIS OF EQUITY

	Total £	Group share pre- acquisition £	Group share of post- acquisition P/L £	Group share of post- acquisition revaluation reserve £
Ordinary share capital	100,000	100,000		
P/L reserve at acquisition	80,000	80,000		
P/L reserve since acquisition	N/A		N/A	
Revaluation reserve (consolidation adjustment)	100,000	100,000		N/A
	280,000	280,000		
Cost of investment		360,000		
Goodwill on consolidation		80,000		
Reserves of holding company			X	X
Goodwill w/o against reserves		(80,000)		
Consolidated B/S totals			XX	XX

(d) Disclosure

As regards disclosure, SSAP 14 simply requires the consolidated financial statements to contain 'sufficient information about the results of the subsidiaries acquired . . . to enable shareholders to appreciate the effect on the consolidated results'.

Some companies are able to quantify the effect of the new acquisition and disclose amounts. For example, in the example in section 14.1(c) we could say that the group results include the following amounts in respect of the newly acquired subsidiary:

	£
Turnover	50
Profit on ordinary activities before tax	10
Taxation	5

On the other hand some companies state that such amounts cannot meaningfully be identified owing to the degree of integration of the combining companies.

16.7 CHANGES IN THE COMPOSITION OF THE GROUP—DISPOSALS

(a) Computational aspects

The effective date of disposal is defined above. SSAP 14 requires the consolidated profit and loss account to include the results of the subsidiary up to the date of disposal, as well as the gain or loss on sale of the investment.

SSAP 14 describes the method of calculating the gain or loss. This is calculated by comparing:

(1) the proceeds of sale; and
(2) the holding company's share of its net assets together with any premium (less any amounts written off) or discount on acquisition. In many cases, goodwill will previously have been fully written off in accordance with SSAP 22.

This calculation is illustrated in the example below.

(b) Disclosure

SSAP 14 requires disclosure of 'sufficient information about the results of subsidiaries ... sold to enable shareholders to appreciate the effect on the consolidated results'.

16.8 DISPOSAL OF SHARES—A WORKED EXAMPLE

(a) Basic information

(1) Draft final accounts of Henry Ltd and Sidney Ltd

Profit and loss accounts, year end 31.12.X3	Henry £	Sidney £
Profit on ordinary activities	408,300	28,000
Dividends received—interim	3,000	–
—final	4,500	–
	415,800	28,000
Corporation tax	(204,150)	(14,000)
	211,650	14,000
Extraordinary gain (see note (2))	28,350	–
	240,000	14,000
Dividends—paid (August)	(80,000)	(3,000)
—proposed	–	(6,000)
Retained profit	160,000	5,000
Balance b/f	220,000	180,000
Balance c/f	380,000	185,000

Balance sheets at 31.12.X3	£	£
Cost of investment (75% × £230,000)	172,500	–
Other assets less liabilities	703,000	291,000
Dividends receivable	4,500	–
Proposed dividends	–	(6,000)
	880,000	285,000
Called-up share capital	500,000	100,000
Profit and loss account	380,000	185,000
	880,000	285,000

(2) Henry acquired 100% of the share capital of Sidney several years ago at a cost of £230,000. Goodwill on consolidation was originally calculated as follows:

	£	£
Cost of investment		230,000
OSC	100,000	
Reserves at acquisition	80,000	180,000
Goodwill on consolidation		50,000

(3) 25,000 shares were sold on 30.9.X3 giving Henry Ltd an extraordinary gain (after tax) of £28,350.

	£	£
Proceeds of sale		98,000
Cost of investment 25% × £230,000	57,500	
Taxation (assumed 30% of 98,000 − 57,500)	12,150	69,650
		28,350

(b) Consolidated balance sheet workings

ANALYSIS OF EQUITY
(reflecting ownership at the year-end)

	Total	Group share (75%) pre-acquisition	Group share (75%) post-acquisition	MI (95%)
	£	£	£	£
Ordinary share capital	100,000	75,000		25,000
P/L reserves at acquisition	80,000	60,000		20,000
P/L reserves since acquisition	105,000		78,750	26,250
	285,000	135,000		
Cost of investment (75% retained)		172,500		
Goodwill on consolidation		37,500		
Henry Ltd reserves (including dividend receivable from Sidney)			380,000	
Goodwill w/o against reserves			(37,500)	
Consolidated B/S totals			421,250	71,250
Minority interest				
non current				71,250
current (25% × 6,000)				1,500

Consolidated balance sheet at 31.12.X3

	£
Assets less liabilities	994,000
Less dividend payable to minority shareholders	1,500
	992,500
Called-up share capital	500,000
Profit and loss account	421,250
	921,250
Minority interest	71,250
	992,500

POINTS TO NOTE

The consolidated balance sheet should reflect ownership of the subsidiary at the balance sheet date:

(1) Goodwill w/o relates to the remaining 75% of shares still held.
(2) Minority interest should reflect 25% outside ownership at year end.
(3) Profit and loss account should include 75% of post-acquisition reserves of Sidney.

(c) Consolidated profit and loss account procedures

Key points to remember:

(1) The consolidated profit and loss account should include a full year's results of Sidney since the company was a subsidiary (with changing ownership) through the year.
(2) Minority interest should reflect the changing ownership during the year (see diagram).
(3) The allocation of profit after tax may be illustrated diagrammatically as follows:

	Minority interest	25%
100%	Holding company	75%

1.1.X3   30.9.X3   31.12.X3

Profits attributable to Henry are:

(i) 100% of profits from 1.1.X3 to 30.9.X3; *plus*
(ii) 75% of profits from 1.10.X3 to 31.12.X3.

This is achieved by consolidating a full year's profits and making a deduction for minority interest.

Minority interest is $25\% \times \frac{3}{12} \times £14,000 = £875$

(4) A particular complication is the calculation of the extraordinary gain or loss on disposal. Using the formula in SSAP 14:

	£	£
Proceeds of sale		98,000
Net assets of sale		
OSC	100,000	
P/L b/f	180,000	
PAT (9 m)	10,500	
Div paid	(3,000)	
	287,500	×25% (71,875)
Tax		(12,150)
Extraordinary gain (after tax)		13,975

NOTE
The net assets of the subsidiary at the date of disposal of the shares are estimated by time apportioning the shareholders' funds. This requires particular care as time apportioning retained profits may give the wrong result! The interim dividend of £3,000 paid in August reduces the bank balance taken over and so must be deducted to arrive at net assets. By contrast, the proposed dividend of £6,000 is irrelevant.

The extraordinary gain of £13,975 appears in the consolidated profit and loss account whereas the holding company profit and loss account includes £28,350. The relationship between these two figures is explained at the end of the example.

The consolidated profit and loss account may now be completed:

CONSOLIDATED PROFIT AND LOSS ACCOUNT

for the year ended 31 December 19X3

	£	£
Turnover		X
Cost of sales		(X)
Gross profit		X
Distribution costs	X	
Administrative expenses	—	(X)
Profit on ordinary activities before tax		436,300
Taxation		218,150
Profit on ordinary activities after tax		218,150
Minority interest		875
Profit before extraordinary items		217,275
Extraordinary income	26,125	
Taxation	12,150	13,975
		231,250
Dividend paid		80,000
Retained profit		151,250
Balance at 1.1.X3		270,000
Balance at 31.12.X3		421,250

Working—balance brought forward

	£
Henry	220,000
Sidney (100% × (180,000 − 80,000))	100,000
	320,000
Less goodwill w/o	50,000
	270,000

(*Note:* this must be the figure which appeared in last year's consolidated balance sheet when the subsidiary was wholly owned.)

NOTE: RELATIONSHIP BETWEEN EXTRAORDINARY GAIN FIGURES FOR THE GROUP AND FOR THE HOLDING COMPANY
The most important point to remember is that the holding company profit and loss account records only dividends received from subsidiaries. Retained profits of subsidiaries are ignored.

By contrast, the group profit and loss account includes all attributable profits of subsidiaries, whether they are paid out as dividends or whether they are ploughed back and retained.

The key to the different figures is therefore retained profits relating to the period when the shares were held.

Numerically, the reconciliation is:

	£	£
Extraordinary gains per group accounts		13,975
Attributable share of retained profits between date of acquisition and 1.1.X3		
25% (180,000 – 80,000)		25,000
Attributable share of profits from 1.1.X3 until 30.9.X3		
9 months' profit after tax $\frac{9}{12}$ × £14,000	10,500	
Less interim dividend paid	3,000	
	£7,500	
25% × £7,500		1,875
Goodwill applicable to shares sold,written off against group reserves		(12,500)
Extraordinary gain per holding company accounts		28,350

16.9 EXCLUSION OF SUBSIDIARIES FROM CONSOLIDATION

(a) Introduction

It is important to be clear about the distinction between exclusion from group accounts and exclusion from consolidation.

Exclusion from group accounts means that a particular subsidiary is omitted from the group accounts. Effectively, it is treated as a fixed asset investment. The Companies Act 1948 specified particular situations where group accounts need not deal with a particular subsidiary and sets out the information required (now to be found in CA 1985). However, SSAP 14 points out that 'consideration will need to be given to whether the resulting financial statements give a true and fair view of the position of the group as a whole'.

On the other hand exclusion from consolidation can mean that the group accounts are presented in a form other than a single consolidated balance sheet and a single consolidated profit and loss account (see for example, dissimilar activities).

(b) The four situations

SSAP 14 requires that a particular subsidiary *should* be excluded from consolidation if:

(1) its activities are so dissimilar from those of the group companies that a single set of consolidated financial statements would be misleading; or
(2) the holding company does not control the voting power or has restrictions imposed on its ability to appoint the majority of the board of directors; or
(3) the subsidiary operates under severe restrictions which significantly impair control by the holding company over the subsidiary's assets and operations for the foreseeable future; or
(4) control is intended to be temporary.

(c) Exclusion because of dissimilar activities

(1) *SSAP 14*

A subsidiary should be excluded from consolidation if 'its activities are so dissimilar from those of other companies within the group that consolidated financial statements would be misleading and that information for the holding company's shareholders and other users of the statements would be better provided by presenting separate financial statements for such a subsidiary'.

Examples of companies in this situation could include banking and insurance subsidiaries within non-financial groups.

(2) *Accounting treatment*

(i)   The subsidiary should be included in the consolidated financial statements on the basis of the equity method of accounting. This is defined in SSAP 14, para 14 on the basis of inclusion in the consolidated balance sheet at cost plus attributable post-acquisition reserves. (But note also comments in chapter 17.)

(ii) The group accounts should include separate financial statements for that subsidiary. (If other subsidiaries have similar operations, the respective financial statements may be combined.)

(iii) The separate financial statements should also give:

   (1) a note of the holding company's interest;
   (2) particulars of intra-group balances;
   (3) the nature of transactions with the rest of the group;
   (4) a reconciliation with the amount included in the consolidated financial statements for the group's investment in the subsidiary.

NOTE
The treatment of the equity method is dealt with in chapter 17.

(d) Exclusion because of lack of effective control

(1) *SSAP 14*
A subsidiary should be excluded from consolidation if

> ... the holding company, although owning directly or through other subsidiaries more than half of the equity share capital of the subsidiary, either:
>
> (i) does not own share capital carrying more than half the votes; or
> (ii) has contractual or other restrictions imposed on its ability to appoint the majority of the board of directors.

NOTE
It is important to appreciate that the term 'equity shares' includes certain non-voting shares such as 'A' ordinary shares and participating preference shares.

(2) *Accounting treatment*
The accounting treatment in the consolidated accounts will depend on whether or not the associated company conditions regarding significant influence can be satisfied:

(i) if they can, the investment will be treated under the equity method of accounting (cost plus post-acquisition reserves in the consolidated balance sheet);

(ii) if not, the investment should be stated in the consolidated balance sheet at cost or valuation less any provision required.

(For accounting treatment, see chapter 17.)

   Whichever situation applies, the group accounts should contain separate financial information concerning the excluded subsidiary in order to comply with Companies Act requirements.

(e) Exclusion because of severe restrictions over assets and operations

(1) *SSAP 14*
A subsidiary should be excluded from consolidation if 'the subsidiary operates under severe restrictions which significantly impair control by the holding company over the subsidiary's assets and operations for the foreseeable future'.

(2) *Accounting treatment*

(i) The investment in the subsidiary should be stated in the consolidated balance sheet at cost plus post-acquisition reserves up to the date the restrictions came into force. No further accruals should be made for profits or losses.
(ii) However, in these circumstances it may well be the case that the investment has been impaired by a permanent decline in value. If this is so, provision for the loss should be made through the consolidated profit and loss account.

(3) *Disclosure*

The following disclosure is required by SSAP 14:

(i)   the net assets of the subsidiary;
(ii) its profits or loss for the period;
(iii) any amounts included in the consolidated profit and loss account in respect of:

   (a) dividends received;
   (b) write-down of investment because of permanent fall in value.

(f) Exclusion because control is intended to be temporary

In this situation, the temporary investment in the subsidiary should be included in the consolidated balance sheet as a current asset at the lower of cost and net realisable value.

(g) Exclusion from consolidation—general disclosure requirements of SSAP 14

SSAP 14 requires the disclosure of certain information regarding excluded subsidiaries:

(1) the reasons for exclusion from consolidation;
(2) the names of principal subsidiaries excluded;
(3) any premium or discount on acquisition,to the extent not written off;
(4) any further detailed information required by the Companies Act.

16.10 MINORITY INTERESTS

(a) General requirements

SSAP 14 specifies several points of disclosure in the consolidated accounts:

(1) In the consolidated balance sheet, minority interest should be shown as a separate item and not treated as part of shareholders' funds.
(2) In the consolidated profit and loss account:

   (i) subsidiary company profits or losses (after tax but before extraordinary items) attributable to outside shareholders should be shown as a separate item positioned after group profit or loss after tax but before extraordinary items;
   (ii) extraordinary items should be stated net of minority interest (if applicable).

(b) Loss-making subsidiaries

In cases where the company is still in a satisfactory position, the effect on the minority interest is:

(1) In the consolidated profit and loss account, ignoring any other subsidiaries, the minority interest share of the loss will appear as a figure in brackets.

(2) In the consolidated balance sheet, the minority interest will be equivalent to a percentage of net assets of the subsidiary. However, if a company continues to lose money, the minority interest in successive consolidated balance sheets will become smaller and smaller!

(c) Insolvent subsidiaries

(1) Leaving for a moment the question of minority interest, the first point is whether a subsidiary with a negative equity interest (debit balance on reserves in excess of share capital) should be consolidated?

   (i)   If the going concern assumption can be justified, the subsidiary should be consolidated. To justify this, it will be necessary to demonstrate holding company guarantees, injections of fresh finance and so on.

  (ii) if the holding company intends to abandon the subsidiary and to allow it to go into liquidation, it would be misleading to consolidate. It would, of course, be important to ensure the holding company had made adequate provision for previous guarantees given in respect of the subsidiary.

(2) Suppose the going concern assumption is justified and the company is partly owned. How should minority interest be treated for consolidation purposes?

   (i)   SSAP 14 refers to the special case of debit balances on shareholders' funds and states that 'debit balances should be recognised only if there is a binding obligation on minority shareholders to make good losses incurred which they are able to meet'. It would be rare for these conditions to be present.

  (ii) IAS 3 (consolidated financial statements) is more explicit:

> The losses applicable to the minority interest in a consolidated subsidiary may exceed the minority interest in the shareholders' equity of the subsidiary. The excess and any further losses applicable to the minority interest are charged against the majority interest except to the extent that the minority interest has a binding obligation to make good the losses. If future profits are reported by the subsidiary, the majority interest is credited with all such profits until the minority's share of losses previously absorbed by the majority has been recovered.

Illustration

H Ltd has owned 80% of the ordinary share capital of S Ltd for several years. Recently the financial position of S Ltd has deteriorated. Drastic reorganisation of S Ltd has now taken place, and H Ltd has guaranteed the bank overdraft and made the necessary arrangements with suppliers.

H Ltd intends to work S Ltd back into a state of solvency and profitability. S Ltd is regarded as a going concern and will be consolidated in the usual way. No binding obligations to make good losses have been entered into by the minority shareholders.

The results, calculations and key figures in the consolidated accounts are set out below:

(a) Profit and loss account and balance sheet extracts

	Profit and loss accounts			Balance sheet of S Ltd		
	H Ltd	*S Ltd*	*Total*	*OSC*	*P/L*	*Total (= net assets)*
	£	£	£	£	£	£
19X3	600	(100)	500	1,000	(700)	300
19X4	750	(200)	550	1,000	(900)	100
19X5	700	(300)	400	1,000	(1,200)	(200)
19X6	800	(300)	500	1,000	(1,500)	(500)
19X7	850	100	950	1,000	(1,400)	(400)
19X8	800	450	1,250	1,000	(950)	50
19X9	1,000	600	1,600	1,000	(350)	650

(b) Allocation of profit (loss) each year between minority interest (MI) and H Ltd

	Profits (losses) of S	Allocation H	MI	Memo-MI share of loss absorbed by H (cumulative)
	£	£	£	£
19X3	(100)	(80)	(20)	N/A
19X4	(200)	(160)	(40)	N/A
19X5	(300)	(280)	(20)	(40)
19X6	(300)	(300)	Nil	(100)
19X7	100	100	Nil	(80)
19X8	450	440	10	N/A
19X9	600	480	120	N/A

Explanation of calculations

19X3 Shareholders' equity at year end is positive so loss is allocated 80%/20%.

19X4 As for 19X3.

19X5 Since minority shareholders have not entered into binding obligations to make good losses, MI in consolidated balance sheet cannot be negative. Since MI at beginning of year was £20, MI share of loss is restricted to £20. Loss borne by H is a balancing figure (300 − 20 = 280).

Loss which should have been borne by MI is 20% × £300 =	60
Less loss actually allocated	20
So MI share of loss suffered by H	40

19X6 H absorbs full amount of loss. So cumulative amount of MI share of loss absorbed by H is (40) + 20% × (300) = (100).

19X7 Although S has made profits, MI share of profits (£20) is exceeded by the memo share of losses brought forward (£100). Memorandum note is now 100 less 20 = 80.

19X8 MI share of profit is 20% × £450 = £90. However, £80 of this is required to clear the memorandum of share of loss brought forward. So MI share of profit is 10 (ie 90 − 80) and the balance of 440 (ie 450 − 10) is allocated to H.

19X9 Normal allocation of profit.

(c) Effect on consolidated accounts

(1) *Consolidated profit and loss accounts*

	Profit on ordinary activities	MI	Profit attributable to shareholders of H
	£	£	£
19X3	500	(20)	520
19X4	550	(40)	590
19X5	400	(20)	420
19X6	500	Nil	500
19X7	950	Nil	950
19X8	1,250	10	1,240
19X9	1,600	120	1,480

(2) *Consolidated balance sheet*

	MI b/f	MI in P/L	In c/f	*Check:* 20% × (shareholders' equity = net assets)
	£	£	£	£
19X3	80	(20)	60	20% × 300 = 60
19X4	60	(40)	20	20% × 100 = 20
19X5	20	(20)	Nil	20% × (200) ie Nil
19X6	Nil	Nil	Nil	20% × (500) ie Nil
19X7	Nil	Nil	Nil	20% × (400) ie Nil
19X8	Nil	10	10	20% × 50 = 10
19X9	10	120	130	20% × 650 = 130

16.11   RESTRICTIONS ON DISTRIBUTIONS

(a) Introduction

SSAP 14, para 36 states:

> If there are significant restrictions on the ability of the holding company to distribute the retained profits of the group (other than those shown as non-distributable) because of statutory, contractual or exchange control restrictions, the extent of the restrictions should be indicated.

(b) Situations

Most of the situations envisaged are likely to relate to overseas subsidiaries, although situations involving UK subsidiaries could include:

(1) profits capitalised by a subsidiary (for example, a bonus issue out of post-acquisition profits—see section 14.7);
(2) post-acquisition profits which have been applied by a subsidiary against its pre-acquisition losses (see below).

(c) Example

The balance sheets of H Ltd and its wholly owned subsidiary, S Ltd at 31.12.X2 are as follows:

	H Ltd £	S Ltd £
Investment in S Ltd	144	–
Net assets	1,156	340
	1,300	340
Called-up share capital	1,000	200
Profit and loss account	300	140
	1,300	340

At acquisition, the debt balance on S's reserves amounted to £32.
   The usual consolidation procedures would calculate group revenue reserves as follows:

	£
Reserves of H	300
Post-acquisition reserves of S (32 + 140)	172
	472

However, it would be misleading to include this amount without an accompanying note stating that of this amount,£32 was not available for distribution. This makes sense since the maximum dividend which S could pay would be £140 and this would have the effect of increasing H's reserves to £440.

16.12   ACCOUNTING FOR ACQUISITIONS AND MERGERS

(a) Acquisition accounting

In previous sections, subsidiary companies have been consolidated by a method referred to as acquisition (or purchase) accounting. One particular feature of this method is that pre-acquisition profits of subsidiaries are regarded as capital from the group viewpoint.

Acquisition accounting is used for the great majority of business combinations, and is a method which has been widely operated for many years.

However, certain business combinations have been accounted for by a radically different method referred to as merger accounting (or pooling of interests). The remainder of this chapter is concerned with merger accounting, the circumstances in which it may be used and its method of operation.

(b) Background to merger accounting

(1) Merger accounting was first introduced in an accounting statement by ED 3 in 1971. Some large groups (Cadbury Schweppes, Bass Charrington) used merger accounting in the late 1960s and early 1970s.
(2) The legality of merger accounting was always uncertain since no share premium account was created on the issue of shares. In 1980 it was decided in *Shearer v Bercain* [1980] 3 All ER 295, [1980] STC 359 that merger accounting was (and always had been) illegal.
(3) The accountancy bodies immediately asked the government to bring in legislation which would protect companies which had, in good faith, used merger accounting for past combinations and which would also permit the future use of merger accounting in certain specified situations. This has now been achieved by means of ss 130–134 of the Companies Act 1985.
(4) Following the Companies Act 1981, the Accounting Standards Committee published a new exposure draft (ED 31) to replace ED 3. An accounting standard, SSAP 23, was published in April 1985 and is referred to below.

16.13 AQUISITION ACCOUNTING AND MERGER ACCOUNTING CONTRASTED

(a) A simple illustration

Before considering the details of SSAP 23, it may be useful to contrast the two consolidation techniques using a very simple illustration.

The balance sheets of A and B at 31.12.X6 are as follows:

	A £	B £
Net assets	500	500
Ordinary share capital (£1 shares)	200	200
P/L	300	300
	500	500

A and B are identical in all respects. A makes an offer on 31.12.X6 for the entire share capital of B. The offer takes the form of an exchange of shares—A issues 200 shares to the shareholders of company B. B then becomes a subsidiary of A. Assume that A's shares have a value of £4 per share.

(b) Acquisition accounting

A's acquisition of shares in B must now be reflected in A's balance sheet. The following journal entry will be needed:

	£
Dr investment in B	
(200 shares issued at a value of £4 each)	800

Cr ordinary share capital of A
(nominal issued)   200

Cr merger reserve
(premium on issue—see 16.16 for explanation)   600
                                                                                              ———
                                                                                              800
                                                                                              ═══

The consolidated balance sheet of the A group will now appear as follows:

	£
Tangible net assets (500 + 500)	1,000
Goodwill on consolidation	300
	═══
	1,300
	═══

	£
Ordinary share capital	400
Merger reserve (non statutory share premium account)	600
Profit and loss account (note 2)	300
	═══
	1,300
	═══

NOTES
(1) Consolidation goodwill of £300 will usually be written off against reserves. The merger reserve would be available for this purpose (see section 16.16(b)).
(2) Under acquisition accounting, the pre-acquisition reserves of the acquired company are deemed to be capital. Group P/L reserves consist of:

	£
Holding company (A)	300
Post-acquisition reserves of subsidiary	Nil
	———
	300

(c) Merger accounting

Under merger accounting, it will be usual for company A to record investment in company B at nominal value issued by A, ie journal entry would be:

	£
Dr investment in B	200
	———
Cr share capital	200
	———

The consolidated balance sheet of the A group on a merger accounting basis would then be:

	£
Tangible net assets	1,000
	═══
Ordinary share capital	400
Profit and loss account	600
	═══
	1,000
	═══

(d) Comparison of the two approaches

Note that merger accounting takes the view that nothing has really changed. Both former groups of shareholders still own the shares of the two group companies. As the combination is on the basis of a share-for-share exchange, no resources have left the group.

Merger accounts treats the merging companies as if they had been linked from the very beginning of their respective existences. Had they operated quite separately each company would possess distributable reserves of £300 ie a combined total of £600. As nothing has really changed, the merger accounting group balance sheet should reflect this reality.

It would not, of course, be possible to employ the above arguments had A acquired shares in B by the use of cash. In that case there would have been no continuing ownership by the former shareholders of B. Additionally, resources would have left the group.

16.14 THE APPROACH OF SSAP 23

A business combination which satisfies the four conditions specified by SSAP 23 (see below) may be regarded as a merger. In this situation SSAP 23 would permit the group accounts to be drawn up *either* on an acquisition basis *or* on a merger basis. Combinations which did not satisfy the merger conditions would have to be drawn up on an acquisition basis only.

16.15 RELATIONSHIP TO SSAP 14

The principles and disclosures of acquisition accounting are contained in both SSAP 14 and SSAP 23. There is no inconsistency between these two statements.

Companies which can satisfy the merger conditions and which wish to prepare consolidated accounts on a merger accounting basis should refer to SSAP 23 only.

16.16 THE ACCOUNTS OF THE HOLDING COMPANY

SSAP 23 does not deal directly with the accounting treatment of investments in the books of the holding company although the matter is referred to in the non-mandatory appendix to SSAP 23.

However, the following provisions of the Companies Act 1985 are relevant:

(a) *Section* 130

If a company issues shares at a premium, whether for cash or otherwise, a sum equal to the aggregate amount or value of the premiums should be transferred to a share premium account.

(b) *Section* 131

This deals with the situation where the issuing company obtains at least 90% of the equity of another company. Section 130 does not apply to the premiums on any shares which are included in the consideration. Section 131 relief only applies to the issue of shares which take the holding to at least 90%. SSAP 23 appendix refers to a merger reserve.

Illustration

A already holds 15% of the share capital of company B. A issues 100,000 £1 ordinary shares (value £3) in order to obtain 80% of the share capital of B.

The journal entry in the books of company could be as follows:

Debit cost of investment in B   £300,000   *Credit* OSC   £100,000
                                             Merger reserve   £200,000

(c) *Section* 133

This refers to situations where the premium may be disregarded in determining the carrying amount.

Illustration

In the above example, A could record its investment in B as follows:

Debit cost of investment   £100,000   *Credit* OSC   £100,000

16.17   SSAP 23—CONDITIONS FOR A MERGER

The following four conditions must all be satisfied if it is required to account for a particular business combination on a merger basis:

(a) the business combination results from an offer to the holders of all equity shares and the holders of all voting shares which are not already held by the offeror; and

(b) the offeror has secured, as a result of the offer, a holding of (i) at least 90% of all equity shares (taking each class of equity separately) and (ii) the shares carrying at least 90% of the votes of the offeree; and

(c) immediately prior to the offer, the offeror does not hold (i) 20% or more of all equity shares of the offeree (taking each class of equity separately) or (ii) shares carrying 20% or more of the votes of the offeree; and

(d) not less than 90% of the fair value of the total consideration given for the equity share capital (including that given for shares already held) is in the form of equity share capital; not less than 90% of the fair value of the total consideration given for voting non-equity share capital (including that given for shares already held) is in the form of equity and/or voting non-equity share capital.

16.18   THE ACCOUNTS OF THE GROUP

Where the group can satisfy the four conditions referred to above and chooses to prepare consolidated accounts on a merger basis, the following principles apply:

(a) Where carrying value of investment in subsidiary (usually equivalent to nominal value of shares issued) is less than the nominal value of the shares received from the offeree, the difference should be treated as a reserve arising on consolidation.

(b) Where the carrying value of investment in subsidiary is greater than nominal value of the shares received, the difference should be treated on consolidation as a reduction of reserves.

(c) In the consolidated profit and loss account, the full year's profits of the offeree should be included (note carefully).

(d) As regards comparative figures, these should be presented as if the companies had been combined throughout the previous period and at the previous balance sheet date (note very carefully).

16.19 EXAMPLE ON ACQUISITION AND MERGER ACCOUNTING

(a) Basic information

Panna Ltd and Rama Ltd decide to merge. Panna Ltd will issue 6,000 £1 shares in exchange for the entire share capital of Rama Ltd. The date of the merger is 30 September 19X3. The merger satisfies the criteria specified in SSAP 23.

The draft financial statements of the two companies are as follows. No entries have yet been made in respect of the merger.

PROFIT AND LOSS ACCOUNT

for the year ended 31 December 19X3

	Panna £	Rama £
Turnover	22,000	20,000
Cost of sales	(8,000)	(6,000)
Distribution costs	(2,000)	(4,000)
Administrative expenses	(3,000)	(2,000)
Operating profit	9,000	8,000
Taxation	4,500	4,000
Profit after tax	4,500	4,000
Balance brought forward	8,000	5,500
Balances carried forward	12,500	9,500

Balance sheets at 31 December 19X3	Panna £	Rama £
Tangible fixed assets	16,000	11,000
Net current assets	13,500	9,500
	29,500	20,500
Called-up share capital (£1 shares)	8,000	8,500
Share premium	4,000	1,500
Revaluation reserve	5,000	1,000
Profit and loss account	12,500	9,500
	29,500	20,500

(b) Merger accounting procedures

(1) Carrying value in books of Panna Ltd of investment in Rama Ltd is £6,000 (ie nominal value of shares issued in exchange). Share capital of Panna Ltd is now increased to £14,000.

(2) Consolidated balance sheet workings:

	£	£	£
(i) Carrying value of investment			6,000
Nominal value received			8,500
Reserve arising on consolidation			2,500

(ii) Reserve balances

	P/L £	Share premium £	Revaluation Reserve £
Panna	12,500	4,000	5,000
Rama	9,500	1,500	1,000
	22,000	5,500	6,000

NOTES

(1) No distinction is made between pre-acquisition and post-acquisition reserves. The combining companies are treated as though they had operated as a combined unit since the date of incorporation.

(2) The fixed assets of the offeree company (Rama Ltd) are not revalued to determine fair value. This is not so with acquisition accounting.

The consolidated balance sheet under merger accounting principles is as follows:

	£
Tangible fixed assets	27,000
Net current assets	23,000
	50,000
Called-up share capital	14,000
Share premium account	5,500
Revaluation reserve	6,000
Capital reserve on merger	2,500
Profit and loss account	22,000
	50,000

(3) In preparing the consolidated profit and loss account, remember to bring in a full year's results for Rama Ltd even though the combination was on 30 September 19X3. Remember also that it is unnecessary (and inappropriate!) to adjust the reserves of Rama Ltd between pre- and post-merger.

CONSOLIDATED PROFIT AND LOSS ACCOUNT
(ON A MERGER ACCOUNTING BASIS)

for the year ended 31 December 19X3

	£
Turnover	42,000
Cost of sales	14,000
Gross profit	28,000
Distribution costs	(6,000)
Administrative expenses	(5,000)
Profit on ordinary activities before tax	17,000
Taxation	8,500
Profit on ordinary activities after tax	8,500
Balance brought forward	13,500
Balance carried forward	22,000

(c) Acquisition accounting procedures

A business combination capable of satisfying the four conditions could alternatively be accounted for on an acquisition basis.

For this purpose assume that the following additional information is provided:

(a) The shares in Panna Ltd are issued at £5 per share.
(b) At 30.9.X3, the fixed assets of Rama Ltd have a fair value of £15,000.
(c) The balances on share premium account and revaluation reserve are pre-acquisition.
(d) The balance on profit and loss account at 30.9.X3 was £8,500 (estimated by time apportionment).

(1) Consolidated balance sheet procedures

Before setting out the working papers, it is necessary to record the issue of 6,000 shares at an issue price of £30,000. The shares are issued at a premium of £2,400. The journal entry in the books of Panna Ltd is:

Debit cost of investment in		*Credit* ordinary share capital	6,000
Rama Ltd *(6,000 × £5)*	*30,000*	*Credit* merger reserve	24,000
		(see above)	

Remember also that the adjustment account must reflect the undervaluation of fixed assets of £4,000 (ie £15,000 – £11,000) — see (6) below.
Consolidated fixed assets are £16,000 + £15,000 ie £31,000.

(2) Analysis of equity

	Total £	Pre-acquisition £	Post-acquisition P/L £	Post-acquisition share premium £	Post-acquisition revaluation reserve £
Share capital	8,500	8,500			
P/L at acq.	8,500	8,500			
since acq.	1,000		1,000		
Share premium	1,500	1,500		–	
Revaluation					
per acs	1,000	1,000			–
consol. adj.	4,000	4,000			–
	24,500	23,500			
Cost of investment		30,000			
Goodwill on consolidation written off against merger reserve of Panna		6,500			
Panna's reserves			12,500	4,000	5,000
Consolidated B/S totals			13,500	4,000	5,000

(1) Consolidated balance sheet (acquisition accounting basis)

	£
Tangible fixed assets	31,000
Net current assets	23,000
	54,000
Called up share capital	14,000
Share premium account	4,000
Merger reserve (24,000 – 6,500)	17,500
Revaluation reserve	5,000
Profit and loss account	13,500
	54,000

(2) Consolidated profit and loss account procedures

The key point to remember is that under acquisition, only three months' results of Rama Ltd would be included.

The consolidated profit and loss account is as follows. No workings are provided since the figures are easy to derive.

CONSOLIDATED PROFIT AND LOSS ACCOUNT
(ACQUISITION ACCOUNTING BASIS)

for the year ended 31 December 19X3

	£
Turnover	27,000
Cost of sales	9,500
Gross profit	17,500
Distribution costs	(3,000)
Administrative expenses	(3,500)
Profit on ordinary activities before tax	11,000
Taxation	5,500
Profit on ordinary activities after tax	5,500
Balance brought forward	1,500
Balance carried forward	7,000

(d) Merger accounting—a complication

Referring back to section 16.18 there are two possibilities:

(1) Nominal value of shares issued by offeror is less than nominal value received from offeree. This was the case above, where Panna Ltd issued 6,000 shares of £1 in exchange for 8,500 shares of £1 in Rama Ltd. The difference of £2,500 was treated as an unrealised reserve.

(2) Nominal value issued exceeds nominal value received. This is illustrated in the example below.

Example

In the case of Panna Ltd, suppose 10,500 £1 shares were issued in exchange for 8,500 shares in Rama Ltd.

The excess of £2,000 should be treated as a reduction of reserves.

Under these circumstances, the consolidated balance sheet would appear as follows:

	£
Tangible fixed assets	27,000
Net current assets	23,000
	50,000
Called up share capital (8,000 + 10,500)	18,500
Share premium account (4,000 + 1,500)	5,500
Revaluation reserve (5,000 + 1,000)	6,000
Profit and loss account (12,500 + 9,500)	22,000
Consolidation difference on merger reserve	(2,000)
	50,000

Since the difference of £2,000 reflects the extent to which reserves have been capitalised as a result of the merger, the £2,000 could be adjusted against share premium of Rama (£1,500) the balance of £500 being adjusted against revaluation reserve of Rama.

(e) SSAP 23 disclosures

(1) The following information should be disclosed in respect of all material business combinations, whether accounted for as acquisitions or mergers, in the financial statements of the acquiring or issuing company which deal with the year in which the combination takes place:

(i)   the names of the combining companies;

(ii) the number and class of the securities issued in respect of the combination, and details of any other consideration given;

(iii) the accounting treatment adopted for the business combination (ie whether it has been accounted for as an acquisition or a merger); and

(iv) the nature and amount of significant accounting adjustments by the combining companies to achieve consistency of accounting policies.

(2) As required by SSAP 14, in respect of all material acquisitions during the year, the consolidated financial statements should contain sufficient information about the results of subsidiaries acquired to enable shareholders to appreciate the effect on the consolidated results. In addition, disclosure should be made of the date from which the results of major acquisitions have been brought into the accounts (that is, the effective date of those acquisitions).

(3) In respect of all material mergers, the following information should be disclosed in the financial statements of the issuing company for the year in which the merger takes place:

(i)   the fair value of the consideration given by the issuing company;

(ii) an analysis of the current year's attributable profit before extraordinary items between that of before and that of after the effective date of the merger;

(iii) an analysis of the attributable profit before extraordinary items of the current year up to the effective date of the merger and of the previous year between that of the issuing company and that of the subsidiary; and

(iv) an analysis of extraordinary items so as to indicate whether each individual extraordinary item relates to pre- or post-merger events, and to which party to the merger the item relates.

16.20   MAIN DIFFERENCES BETWEEN ACQUISITION ACCOUNTING AND MERGER ACCOUNTING

(a) Accounts of parent company

	Acquisition	*Merger*
(1) Carrying amount of investment	Fair value of consideration given	Nominal value of shares plus fair value of other consideration
(2) Excess of fair value of shares issued over nominal value	(i) merger reserve (if CA 85 s 131 applies) otherwise (ii) share premium account	N/A
(3) Distribution of pre-combination profits of acquiree company to acquiror	In either case these may be treated as realised profits in the hands of the recipient *unless* the payment of the dividend (reducing the assets of the acquiree) makes it necessary for the acquiror to provide for diminution in value of investment (see also appendix to SSAP 23 and section 16.22 below).	

(b) Consolidated accounts

(1) Difference between carrying value and fair value of assets of acquiree	Goodwill on consolidation (SSAP 22)	N/A
(2) Difference between carrying value and nominal value received	N/A	Either (i) reduction in reserves, or (ii) capital reserve on consolidation
(3) Assets of acquiree	At fair value to acquiror (note effect on dep. charge in consol. P/L)	At book value in accounts of acquiree
(4) Profits of acquiree in year of combination	Post-combination profits only	Full year profits may be included
(5) Comparatives in consol. P/L and B/S	No restatement	Restated as though combining companies had been merged throughout previous year

16.21 ADVANTAGES CLAIMED FOR MERGER ACCOUNTING

(a) No need to set up share premium account—but if CA 85 s 131 applies, a share premium account should not be set up.
(b) No need to record assets of acquired company at fair value and thus put higher depreciation charge through consolidated P/L.—this latter affects group reported profit only; it has no effect on distributable profits of individual companies.
(c) No need to account for consolidation goodwill—if consolidation goodwill is written off wholly or partly, distributable profits of individual companies are unaffected.
(d) No need to freeze pre-combination profits—this affects the appearance of the consolidated accounts (ie a lower consolidated P/L reserves in consolidated B/S) but does not necessarily affect the distributable profits of individual companies.
(e) No restrictions on inclusion of profits of acquired company in year of combination—consolidated profit and loss account will show higher group profit under merger accounting than acquisition accounting.
(f) Investment in subsidiary may be recorded at nominal value rather than fair value—this option may be available to the acquiror under CA 85 s 133 irrespective of consolidation method to be used.

16.22 THE PROBLEM OF PRE-ACQUISITION DIVIDENDS

Dividends paid out of pre-acquisition profits have in the past usually been treated as capital in the hands of the recipient company and not available for distribution to the recipient company's shareholders.

This view is still accepted where a subsidiary has been acquired other than by an issue of shares by the offeror. However, the view is now being challenged in the case of share for share issues. Consider the following illustration.

Illustration

A and B are two identical companies. Their respective balance sheets are set out below.

Suppose that A issues 300 shares (deemed to have a value of £5 each) in order to acquire the entire share capital of B.

Two points may be made:

(1) The issue of shares falls within s 131 of CA 85 so if the investment is recorded at fair value of £1,500 (ie 300 shares issued valued at £5 each), the premium of £1,200 must be taken to a merger reserve and not to a share premium account.

(2) Under s 133 of CA 85, the investment in B may be recorded at nominal value issued ie at £300.

Balance sheets

	A (before)	B (before)	A (after −s 131)	A (after −s 133)
Sundry assets	1,000	1,000	1,000	1,000
Investment in B	–	–	1,500	300
	1,000	1,000	2,500	1,300
OSC	300	300	600	600
P/L	700	700	700	700
Merger reserve	–	–	1,200	
	1,000	1,000	2,500	1,300

Now suppose B distributes its entire (and pre-acquisition) profit and loss account balance. How should this receipt be dealt with in the accounts of A?

(a) Where A's investment in B is recorded at £300 SSAP 23 appendix (accounts of the holding company) points out that '... where a dividend is paid to the acquiring or issuing company out of pre-combination profits, it would appear that it need not necessarily be applied as a reduction in the carrying value of the investment in the subsidiary'.

Such a dividend received should be applied to reduce the carrying value of the investment to the extent that it is necessary to provide for a diminution in value of the investment in the subsidiary as stated in the accounts of the issuing company. To the extent that this is not necessary, it appears that the amount received will be a realised profit in the hands of the issuing company.

If A credits the dividend to its P/L ac, investment in B will remain at £300. This will be matched by B's remaining asset of £300 after the dividend payments (ie 1,000 − £700 = £300).

It is not necessary to provide for diminution in value.

(b) Where A's investment in B is recorded at £1,500—SSAP 23 appendix, referring to situations where the holding company records the investment a fair value, points out:

it will in some cases ... be necessary for the holding company to credit to the investment the dividend paid out of the subsidiary's pre-combination profits.

Thus the dividend received of £700 should be credited to cost of investment of £1,500 leaving an adjusted carrying amount of £800.

The £800 is represented by:

Tangible assets of B	300
Non-purchased goodwill (1,500 − 1,000)	500
	£800

The two balance sheets for company A may be compared as follows:

	Situation (a)	Situation (b)
Sundry assets	1,700	1,700
Investment in B	300	800
	2,000	2,500
OSC	600	600
P/L	1,400	700
Merger reserve	–	1,200
	2,000	2,500

Given that s 133 offers A a free choice of recording its investment in B at either £1,500 (fair value issued) or £300 (nominal value issued), it seems inconsistent that on the face of it A's distributable profit can be either £1,400 or £700.

With regard to (b), SSAP 23 appendix goes on to say:

> In these circumstances, the question arises as to whether as a result of this treatment an equivalent amount of the merger reserve can legally be regarded as realised. No firm legal ruling on this is yet available.

Note the caution expressed by ASC. However, if this view can be confirmed at some future date, £700 of the merger reserve could be regarded as distributable.

Total distributable reserves would then amount to £1,400 ie the same as for situation (a).

17 ACCOUNTING FOR FIXED ASSET INVESTMENTS

17.1 INTRODUCTION

The term fixed asset investments covers a broad spectrum and includes:

(a) investments in subsidiary companies;
(b) investments in associated companies (as defined by SSAP 1);
(c) other fixed asset investments (this includes what used to be referred to as trade investments).

17.2 TREATMENT IN THE ACCOUNTS OF INDIVIDUAL COMPANIES

In the balance sheet the investment is usually included at cost, provided it has not suffered a permanent diminution in value.
    In the profit and loss account, dividend income should be included.

17.3 TREATMENT IN THE ACCOUNTS OF GROUPS

(a) Investments in subsidiary companies

These are usually consolidated in the normal way. However, SSAP 14 prescribes four situations where subsidiaries should not be consolidated and sets out the alternative accounting treatments. This was discussed in chapter 16.

(b) Investments in associated companies

These should be accounted for in the group accounts using the equity method of accounting. 'Equity method' is an important term and is discussed below.

(c) Other fixed asset investments

These are usually included in the consolidated balance sheet at cost. The consolidated profit and loss account includes dividend income.

17.4 ASSOCIATED COMPANIES

(a) Background

The original version of SSAP 1 (accounting for associated companies) was published in 1971. It is useful to consider briefly the background up to that date.
    Prior to 1971, a number of companies were conducting a substantial part of their business through other companies in which a substantial number of shares were held. As the proportion of shares held was 50% or less, such companies were not counted as subsidiaries. However, since the investing company was often in a position to exert significant influence over the activities of the investee company, it seemed sensible to distinguish them from trade investments in which a far smaller number of shares were held.
    This distinction was followed by SSAP 1 which introduced the concept of

equity accounting for certain types of investments. Under the equity method, the *consolidated* profit and loss account of the investor included a proportionate share of the profits of the investee rather than simply including dividend income.

Correspondingly, the reserves in the consolidated balance sheet included the group's share of post-acquisition retained profits of the investee.

These points are illustrated below.

(b) Illustration 1

The H group holds 30% of the share capital of Associate Ltd. The profit and loss account of A Ltd showed the following position:

	£
Turnover	8,000
Operating expenses	3,500
Profit on ordinary activities before tax	4,500
Taxation	2,000
	2,500
Dividends proposed	1,000
Retained profit	1,500

The balance sheet of A Ltd was as follows:

	£
Fixed assets	6,500
Net current assets	500
	7,000
Ordinary share capital	2,000
Profit and loss account	5,000
	7,000

The shares were purchased several years ago at a cost of £1,100 when A's reserves amounted to £1, 000.

(1) Consolidated profit and loss account

The consolidated profit and loss account is shown under the three following assumptions:

(a) H group has no investment in A Ltd;
(b) H group accounts for its investment in A Ltd using the cost method (the traditional method of accounting for fixed asset investments);
(c) H group accounts for its investment in A Ltd using the equity method.

For simplicity no information is given as regards subsidiary companies of company H. Assume, however, that H is required by law to prepare consolidated accounts.

	Consolidated profit and loss account		
	Situation	*Situation*	*Situation*
	(a)	(b)	(c)
Turnover	30,000	30,000	30,000
Operating expenses	(8,000)	(8,000)	(8,000)
Dividends receivable	–	300	–
Share of profit of investment	–	–	1,350
Profit on ordinary activities before tax	22,000	22,300	22,350
Tax			
Group	(11,000)	(11,000)	(11,000)
Share of investee's tax			(600)
Profit after tax	11,000	11,300	11,750
Dividends	5,000	5,000	5,000
Retained profit	6,000	6,300	6,750

NOTES
(1) Under the cost method, only the share of dividend receivable (30% × £1,000 = £300) is included.

Under the equity method, a proportionate share of profit before tax (30% × £4,500 = £1,350) and a proportionate share of tax (30% × £2,000 = £600) is included.

(2) The cost method does not include the group's proportion of the retained profits of the associate (30% × £1,500 = £450). This accounts for the difference between the two retained profit figures.

(3) The difference between the two approaches could have a significant effect on earnings per share (which is based on profit after tax).

(2) Consolidated balance sheet

(i) Reserves
The essential difference between the cost method and the equity method is that under the latter group reserves includes a proportionate share of post-acquisition retained profits of A.

	£
Reserves of A	
At year end	5,000
At acquisition	1,000
	4,000
Proportionate share 30% × £4,000	£1,200

Group reserves would therefore include an additional amount of £1,200 attributable to the associated company.

(ii) Fixed asset investment
Under the cost method, the investment would be included at £1,100.

Under the equity method, this would be increased by £1,200 (calculated above) to £2,300. However there are two ways of presenting the balance sheet figure of £2,300.

PRESENTATION 1 (PURE EQUITY APPROACH)	£
Cost of investment	1,100
Post-acquisition reserves	1,200
	2,300

PRESENTATION 2 (UNDERLYING NET ASSETS APPROACH)	£
Net assets (30% × £7,000)	2,100
Premium on acquisition (see below)	200
	2,300

WORKINGS—CALCULATION OF PREMIUM	£
Cost of investment	1,100
Proportion of net assets at acquisition	
30% (2,000 + 1,000)	900
	200

Presentation 1 was preferred in the original (1971) version of SSAP 1. Presentation 2 is required by the present version of the standard.

(c) Revision of SSAP 1

The original version of SSAP 1 was issued in 1971. The standard was reviewed in 1979 and an exposure draft (ED 25) was published in October 1979. The revised version of SSAP 1 was issued in April 1983. The notes below refer to the latest standard although occasional reference will be made to the previous version.

(d) Definition

The full definition of an associated company is as follows:

An associated company is a company not being a subsidiary of the investing group or company in which:

(1) the interest of the investing group or company is effectively that of a partner in a joint venture or consortium and the investing group or company is in a position to exercise a significant influence over the company in which the investment is made; or
(2) the interest of the investing group or company is for the long-term and is substantial, and, having regard to the disposition of the other shareholdings, the investing group or company is in a position to exercise a significant influence over the company in which the investment is made.

Significant influence over a company essentially involves participation in the financial and operating policy decisions of that company (including dividend policy) but not necessarily control of those policies.

Representation on the board of directors is indicative of such participation, but will neither necessarily give conclusive evidence of it nor be the only method by which the investing company may participate in policy decisions.

The following points should be noted:

(1) Holdings in associated companies are not restricted to group situations. The definition above envisages the two situations, illustrated below.

In the diagrams, H is the investing company, S is a subsidiary and A is an associated company.

Ⓐ

Investing
company
situation

H

|

A

Ⓑ

Investing
group
situation

H

S   A

in Ⓑ, group accounts are prepared and the accounting problems revolve around how to incorporate the associated company into the group accounts (ie consolidated balance sheet and consolidated profit and loss account).

Ⓐ is a comparatively uncommon situation—group accounts are not prepared.

The accounting treatment differs as between the two situations (this is dealt with later).

(2) There are two distinct strands to the definition (ie d(1) or d(2) above). The more usual situation (in practice as well as in exams!) is d(2) where the group's interest has three features; it is:

(a) long term;
(b) substantial; and
(c) in a position to exert significant influence.

Where the group's interest exceeds 20% or more of the equity voting rights of the investee, it is presumed that significant influence exists unless the contrary can be shown (eg where another party holds 77% of the shares).

Where the interest is under 20%, there is a presumption that the group or company is not in a position to exert significant influence. This presumption can be overturned if significant influence can be demonstrated. This will usually require a statement from the investee to the effect that it accepts that the investor is in a position to exert significant influence.

In calculating the percentage of voting shares, the only shares which may be included are those held by the investing company or any of its subsidiaries.

(3) The above references to 20% do not apply to the other strand of the definition which deals with an interest in a joint venture or partnership.

(e) Related company

The Companies Act 1985 uses the term 'related company' rather than the SSAP 1 term 'associated company'. The Act defines a related company as any body corporate (excluding a group company) in which the investing company holds on a long-term basis a qualifying capital interest for the purpose of securing a contribution to the investing company's own activities by the exercise of any control or influence arising from that interest. A qualifying capital interest is broadly a holding in excess of 20% of the voting equity share capital of the investee.

The two terms are thus broadly similar, although strictly the term 'related company' has a wider meaning than 'associated company'.

Many companies now use the term 'related company' in their annual accounts. If a company continues to use the term 'associated company' it must include a note to the effect that there are no other related companies apart from those shown as associated companies.

(f) Associated companies held in a group situation

(1) *Overall view*

	Holding company accounts	Group (consolidated) accounts
Balance sheet		
(i) *Fixed assets — shares in associated companies*	Usually at cost of investment less any amounts written off (in some cases shown at a valuation).	Total of: (i) group share of net assets (other than goodwill); (ii) group share of goodwill in associated companies' balance sheet; (iii) premium (discount) on acquisition of shares.
(ii) *Reserves* Profit and loss account	Dividends received and receivable by investing group.	Include also group share of retained post-acquisition profits.
Revaluation reserve	N/A	Include group share of post-acquisition revaluation reserve of associated companies.
Profit and loss account	Dividends received and receivable.	Group share of profits less losses of associated companies.

(2) *Consolidated balance sheet in detail (CBS)*
The consolidated balance sheet may include several items relating to associated companies.

Item in CBS	Comments
Fixed asset investments — shares in associated companies	Comprises: (i) group share of net assets (other than goodwill); (ii) group share of goodwill in associated companies b/s; (iii) premium (discount) on acquisition of shares. (i) must be disclosed separately but (ii) and (iii) may be disclosed as a single figure.
Fixed asset investments — loans to associated companies	
Debtors — amounts owed by associated companies	Disclose separately. Do not net off against other items.

Creditors — amounts owed to associated companies:
  Due within one year
  Due after more than one year	

Reserves: Profit and loss account	Disclose group share of post-acquisition retained profits.
Revaluation reserve	Disclose group share of post-acquisition revaluation reserve.

The above information is sufficient for the majority of associated company situations. However, if the associated company's profits/assets/scale of operations are material in relation to the group, further disclosure may be required in the interest of a true and fair view. This might cover more detailed information concerning the tangible and intangible assets of the associated company, as well as its liabilities.

(3) *Consolidated profit and loss account in detail (CPL)*

Item in CPL	Comments
Turnover	Investing group share of associated company turnover should *not* be disclosed (but separate disclosure may be required in certain situations — see below).
Cost of sales	
Distribution costs	
Administrative expenses	Share relating to associated companies not included.
Other operating income	
Share of profits (less losses) of associated companies	Include (and disclose as a separate item) the investing group's share of associated company profit before interest and tax.
Interest receivable Interest payable	Include investing group's share of these items.

Item in CPL	*Comments*
Taxation	Include (and disclose as separate item) the investing group's share of associated company tax on profit on ordinary activities.
Extraordinary items	Include (and, where material to group, disclose as a separate item) group share of extraordinary items.

SSAP 1 specifically states that the investing group should not include its share of 'associated companies' items such as turnover and depreciation in the aggregate amounts of these items disclosed in the consolidated financial statements.

However, SSAP 1 goes on to say that in some cases more detailed information would be required in the interest of a true and fair view. These cases are where the results of one or more associated companies are particularly significant in relation to the group, as regards profit and scale of operation. A separate note could then give more detailed profit and loss information, including turnover and other items.

(4) *Examples of inclusion of associated companies in group accounts*
The two examples below are intended to illustrate the principles and disclosures referred to above.

Illustration 2

Company	Cost of investment	Percentage of ordinary shares held	P/L reserves at date of acquisition (several years ago)
	£	%	£
S Ltd	7,000	80	3,000
A Ltd	550	30	400

The draft accounts for the year ended 31 December 19X4 are as follows:

Profit and loss account

	H Ltd	S Ltd	A Ltd
	£	£	£
Turnover	20,000	10,000	5,000
Cost of sales	5,000	3,000	2,000
Gross profit	15,000	7,000	3,000
Distribution costs	(2,000)	(500)	(600)
Administrative expenses	(1,000)	(600)	(700)
Operating profit	12,000	5,900	1,700
Dividends—S	800	–	–
—A	60	–	–
Profit on ordinary activities before tax	12,860	5,900	1,700
Taxation	5,000	2,200	800
Profit after tax	7,860	3,700	900
Dividends proposed	2,000	1,000	200
Retained profit	5,860	2,700	700
Balance at 1.1.X4	20,000	6,000	2,100
Balance at 31.12.X4	25,860	8,700	2,800

Balance sheets

	H Ltd	S Ltd	A Ltd
	£	£	£
Fixed assets			
Tangible	20,000	6,000	2,000
Investments—S	7,000	–	–
—A	550	–	–
Stock	7,000	8,100	800
Debtors	7,200	1,800	700
Dividends receivable	860	–	–
Cash at bank	1,750	800	1,050
Creditors (due within one year)	(6,500)	(3,000)	(550)
Proposed dividends	(2,000)	(1,000)	(200)
	35,860	12,700	3,800
Ordinary share capital	10,000	4,000	1,000
Profit and loss account	25,860	8,700	2,800
	35,860	12,700	3,800

Consolidated balance sheet

Key figures:

(1) *Goodwill on consolidation (re company S)*
7,000 – 80% (4,000 + 3,000) = £1,400

(2) *Minority interest*
(a) Non-current:
20% × £12,700 = £2,540
(b) Current:
20% × £1,000 = £ 200

(3) *Profit and loss account*	£
H	25,860
S 80% (8,700 – 3,000)	4,560
A 30% (2,800 – 400)	720
	31,140

(4) *Associated companies*

(a) Investment

	£
Proportion of net assets 30% × £3,800	1,140
Premium £550 − 30% (1,000 + 400)	130
	1,270

(b) Dividend receivable

30% × £200 ie	£60

(5) *Assets and liabilities*

These are arrived at by combining respective items for H and S.
The consolidated balance sheet may now be completed:

	£	£	£
Fixed assets:			
Tangible assets			26,000
Investments—shares in associated company			1,270
			27,270
Current assets:			
Stock		15,100	
Debtors		9,000	
Dividend receivable from associated company		60	
Cash at bank		2,550	
		26,710	
Creditors—amounts falling due within one year:			
Creditors	9,500		
Dividends due to members of holding company	2,000		
Dividends due to minority shareholders	200	11,700	
Net current assets			15,010
Total assets less current liabilities			42,280
Capital and reserves			
Called-up share capital			10,000
Profit and loss account			29,740
			39,740
Minority interest			2,540
			42,280

Consolidated profit and loss account

Many items are arrived at by combining respective items for H and S. Items for which separate calculations are required include

		£
(1) Associated company:		
Share of profit	30% × £1,700 =	510
Share of tax	30% × £800 =	240
(2) Minority interest	20% × £3,700 =	740

(3) Retained profit:

Holding company		5,860
Subsidiary	80% × £2,700 =	2,160
Associated company	30% × £700 =	210
		8,230

(4) Balance brought forward:

Holding company		20,000
Subsidiary	80% (6,000 – 3,000) =	2,400
Associated company	30% (2,100 – 400) =	510
		22,910
Less goodwill w/o		1,400
		21,510

The consolidated profit and loss account may now be completed:

	£	£
Turnover		30,000
Cost of sales		8,000
Gross profit		22,000
Distribution costs	2,500	
Administrative expenses	1,600	4,100
		17,900
Share of profits of associated companies		510
Profit on ordinary activities before tax		18,410
Tax on profit on ordinary activities:		
Investing group	7,200	
Associated company	240	7,440
Profit on ordinary activities after tax		10,970
Minority interest		740
Profit attributable to shareholders of H		10,230
Dividends proposed		2,000
Retained profit for year:		8,230
Holding company	5,860	
Subsidiary	2,160	
Associated company	210	
	8,230	
Balance at 1.1.X4		21,510
Balance at 12.12.X4		29,740

Illustration

Horton Ltd is the holding company of a small group of private companies. Some years ago, Horton Ltd purchased a 30% shareholding in Apsley Ltd at a cost of £160,000.

Charles, one of Horton's directors, was appointed to the board of directors of Apsley, and Apsley is regarded as an associated company.

The balance sheets of the associated company as at the date of purchase of the shares, and as at the consolidation date (31.12.X5) are shown below.

(1) Balance sheets

	At date of purchase of shares £	At 31.12.X5 £
Ordinary shares	200	200
Profit and loss account	120	380
Revaluation reserve	75	125
Loans from companies in Horton Group	–	100
Current liabilities	60	105
Proposed dividends	–	50
	455	960
Fixed assets	290	560
Purchased goodwill	–	85
Current account with companies in Horton Group	–	90
Current assets	165	225
	455	960

(2) Profit and loss account for YE 31.12.X5

	£
Profit on ordinary activities	230
Tax	(110)
Proposed dividends	(50)
Retained profit	70
Balance sheet at 1.1.X5	310
Balance sheet at 31.12.X5	380

Required: The relevant extracts from the group financial statements for the year ended 31 December 19X5.

Consolidated balance sheet at 31.12.X5

£

Workings will be required for:

(a) Premium on acquisition:

Cost of investment	160.0
Net assets at acquisition (fair value) —group proportion 30% (455 – 60)	118.5
Premium	41.5

(b) Proportion of net assets (other than goodwill) at 31.12.X5:
30% × (560 + 90 + 225 – 100 – 105 – 50)

186.0

(c) Proportion of goodwill:
30% × 85

25.5

(d) Attributable post-acquisition reserves at 31.12.X5:

Profit and loss account 30% × (380 – 120)	78.0
Revaluation reserve 30% (125 – 75)	15.0
	93.0

(e) Attributable post-acquisition reserves at 1.1.X5:

Profit and loss account	30% × (310 − 120)	57.0
Revaluation reserve (assume as for 31.12.X5)		15.0
		72.0

(f) Dividend receivable: 30% × 50   15.0

Relevant extracts are:

(a) Fixed assets—investments:

Shares in related companies (note 1)	253.0
Loans to related companies	100.0

NOTE 1

Group's share of net assets other than goodwill	186.0
Goodwill	25.5
Premium on acquisition	41.5
	253.0

(b) Debtors—amounts owed by related companies (dividend receivable)	15.0
(c) Creditors—amounts owed to related companies	90.0
(d) Revaluation reserve—total includes	15.0
(e) Profit and loss account—total includes	78.0

Additional disclosures:

Amounts in respect of related companies relating to (d) and (e) should be separately disclosed.

NOTE

It would have been acceptable to use the SSAP 1 term 'associated company' instead of the legal term 'related company'.

Consolidated profit and loss account   £

Workings will be required for:

Profit before tax	30% × 230	69.0
Tax	30% × 110	33.0
Retained by related companies	30% × 70	21.0

Relevant extracts are:

(a) Share of profits of related companies	69.0
(b) Tax on ordinary activities—related companies	33.0
(c) Profit retained by related companies	21.0

Statement of reserves

Amounts brought forward in respect of related companies will include:

Revaluation reserve	15.0
Profit and loss account	57.0

17.5 ASSOCIATED COMPANIES—A WORKED EXAMPLE

The summarised profit and loss accounts of Tinker plc, Tailor Ltd and Soldier Ltd for the year ended 31 December 19X8 were as follows:

	Tinker plc	Tailor Ltd	Soldier Ltd
	£	£	£
Turnover	1,560,000	960,000	420,000
Operating costs	775,400	532,000	312,000
Trading profit	784,600	428,000	108,000
Investment income	50,600	–	–
Profit before tax	835,200	428,000	108,000
Corporation tax	392,300	214,000	54,000
Profit after tax	442,900	214,000	54,000
Preference dividends:			
Paid (30.6.X8)	–	(12,000)	–
Proposed	–	(12,000)	–
Ordinary dividends			
Paid (17.8.X8)	(85,000)	(25,000)	–
Proposed	(115,000)	(45,000)	(36,000)
Retained profit	242,900	120,000	18,000
Balance at 1.1.X8	3,674,200	766,000	107,000
Balance at 31.12.X8	3,917,100	886,000	125,000

The following information is also relevant:

(1) Tinker plc acquired 40% of the ordinary share capital of Soldier Ltd on 30 September 19X8 at a cost of £86,500. Soldier Ltd is to be regarded as an associated company. Ordinary share capital of Soldier Ltd is £50,000.
(2) Tinker plc acquired 90% of the ordinary shares and 25% of the preference shares of Tailor Ltd on 1 September 19X8.
(3) Investment income of Tinker plc comprises:

	£
Tailor Ltd—preference dividend	3,000
—ordinary dividend	40,500
Spy Ltd —ordinary dividend	7,100
	50,600

(4) Income tax is to be taken as 30%.

Required:

(a) A consolidated profit and loss account for the year ended 31 December 19X8.
(b) The relevant balance sheet extracts as at 31 December 19X8 relating to reserves and associated company.
(c) The relevant extract from the statement of accounting policies.

Ignore the requirements of SSAP 22 concerning consolidation goodwill.

(a) CONSOLIDATED PROFIT AND LOSS ACCOUNT FOR THE TINKER PLC GROUP

for the year ended 31 December 19X8

	£	£
Turnover		1,880,000
Operating costs		952,733
Trading profit		927,267
Investment income		10,143
Share of profits of associated company		10,800
Profit on ordinary activities before tax		948,210
Taxation on profits on ordinary activities:		
UK corporation tax:		
Group	463,633	
Associated company	5,400	
Tax credit on dividends received on ordinary activities	3,043	
		472,076
Profit on ordinary activities after tax		476,134
Minority interest		12,334
		463,800
Profit attributable to the members of the holding company (of which £426,000 has been dealt with in the separate accounts of Tinker plc)		
Dividends—paid	85,000	
—proposed	115,000	
		200,000
Retained profit		263,800
Retained by:		
Holding company	226,000	
Subsidiary	36,000	
Associated company	1,800	
	263,800	
Balance at 1.1.19X8		3,674,200
Balance at 31.12.19X8		3,938,000

(b) Balance sheet extracts at 31 December 19X8

(i) Reserves
Reserves includes £1,800 in respect of an associated company.

(ii) Interest in associated company

Net assets	70,000
Premium on acquisition	7,500
	77,500

(iii) Current assets

Dividend receivable from associated company investment	£14,400

(c) Extract from statement of accounting policies

Profits of subsidiaries and associated companies acquired during the year are included as from the respective dates of acquisition.

Workings—Part (a)

(i)	Turnover $(1,560,000 + \frac{4}{12} \times 960,000)$	=	1,880,000
(ii)	Operating costs $(775,400 + \frac{4}{12} \times 532,000$	=	952,733
(iii)	Trading profit $(784,600 + \frac{4}{12} \times 428,000)$	=	927,267
(iv)	Investment income $(7,100 \times \frac{10}{7})$	=	10,143
(v)	Associated company = profit $40\% \times \frac{3}{12} \times 108,000$	=	10,800
	tax $\quad 40\% \times \frac{3}{12} \times \ 54,000$	=	5,400
(vi)	Corporation tax—investing company and subsidiary $(392,300 + \frac{4}{12} \times 214,000$	=	463,633

(vii) Minority interest in Tailor Ltd

	Total £	MI £
Profit after tax (4 months) $\frac{4}{12} \times 214,000$	71,333	
Preference dividend (4 months)	8,000 (75%)	6,000
Available for ordinary shareholders	63,333 (10%)	6,334
Total		12,334

(viii) Dividends receivable by Tinker plc

	£
Ordinary in Tailor $90\% \times 45,000$	40,500
Post-acquisition $90\% \times \frac{4}{12} \times 70,000$	21,000
$\therefore$ Pre-acquisition	19,500
Preference in Tailor $25\% \times 12,000$	3,000
Post-acquisition $\frac{4}{6} \times 3,000$	2,000
$\therefore$ Pre-acquisition	1,000
Ordinary in Soldier $40\% \times 36,000$	14,400
Post-acquisition $\quad 40\% \times \frac{3}{12} \times 36,000$	3,600
$\therefore$ Pre-acquisition	10,800

(ix) Retained profit allocation

	£	£
Holding company		
Pre-accounts		242,900
Post-acquisition dividend (Soldier)		3,600
		246,500
Less: Pre-acquisition dividend (Tailor)		
—ordinary	19,500	
—preference	1,000	20,500
		226,000
Subsidiary $\quad 90\% \times \frac{4}{12} \times 120,000$		36,000
Associated company $\quad 40\% \times \frac{3}{12} \times 18,000$		1,800

(x) Profit dealt with in separate accounts of Tinker plc

	£
Per accounts	442,900
Less: pre-acquisition dividend (Tailor)	20,500
	422,400
Add: post-acquisition dividends (Soldier)	3,600
	426,000

(xi) Interest in associated company

(1) Net assets at 31.12.X8 40% (50,000 + 125,000)		70,000
(2) Premium		
Net assets at acquisition		
OSC	50,000	
P/L 1.1.X8	107,000	
9 m PAT ($\frac{9}{12}$ × 54,000)	40,500	
	197,500	
40% × £197,500	79,000	
Cost of investment	86,500	
∴ Premium		7,500
		77,500

17.6 ASSOCIATED COMPANIES IN A NON-GROUP SITUATION

This is the investing company situation which was illustrated in 17.4(d), above, as follows:

The problem is that the Companies Act 1985 permits the equity method to be used in consolidated accounts only. So, in the above example, H may include only dividend income from A in its profit and loss account. The investment in A should be included at cost.

However, SSAP 1 requires the equivalent information regarding the associate to be included in memorandum form. This will include balance sheet and profit and loss information.

(a) Balance sheet information

SSAP 1 requires that an investing company which does not prepare consolidated accounts (except for the wholly owned subsidiary situation) should show the information referred to above either by:

(1) preparing a separate balance sheet; or
(2) adding the information in supplementary form to its own balance sheet.

(b) Profit and loss information

Similarly, such a company should either:

(1) prepare a separate profit and loss account; or
(2) add the information in supplementary form to its own profit and loss account. This should ensure that its share of associated company profits are *not* treated as realised for Companies Act purposes.

The ASC statement accompanying SSAP 1 included the following illustration:

Profit and loss account of investing company		£'000
Turnover		2,000
Cost of sales		1,400
Gross profit		600
Distribution costs	175	
Administrative expenses	125	300
Profit on ordinary activities before taxation		300
Tax on profit on ordinary activities		85
Profit on ordinary activities after taxation		215
Dividends—proposed		80
Amount set aside to reserves		135

Supplementary statement incorporating results of associated companies	
	£'000
Share of profits less losses of associated companies	50
Less tax	15
Share of profits after tax of associated companies	35
Profit on ordinary activities after taxation (as above)	215
Profit attributable to members of the investing company	250
Dividends—proposed	80
Net profit retained (£35,000 by associated companies)	170

Note: The earnings per share figure would be based on £250,000.

17.7   ACCOUNTING FOR INVESTMENTS—POSSIBLE METHODS

(a) Introduction

Having considered associated companies and the equity method of accounting, it would be useful to outline the methods which in theory could be used to account for fixed asset investments held by groups. In the following section, the possible uses of the various methods will be summarised.

(b) Methods theoretically possible

These include:

(1) cost method;
(2) equity method:

    (i)   pure approach (SSAP 14, para 14);
    (ii) net assets/premium approach;

(3) normal or conventional consolidation;
(4) pro rata or partial or proportional equity consolidation.

(c) Illustration

The H group acquired 70% of the ordinary share capital of S Ltd several years ago when the reserves of S Ltd amounted to £30.
    Summarised financial statements for 19X9 are set out below:

Balance sheets at 31.12.X9	H Group £	S Ltd £
Fixed assets	1,105	600
Investment in S	350	–
Dividend receivable	35	–
Current assets	505	220
Current liabilities	(205)	(90)
Dividend payable	–	(50)
	1,790	680
Ordinary share capital	1,000	400
Profit and loss account	790	280
	1,790	680

Profit and loss accounts year end 31.12.X9	£	£
Operating profit	485	250
Dividends receivable	35	–
	520	250
Corporation tax	(230)	(110)
	290	140
Dividends paid	(100)	–
Dividends payable	–	(50)
Retained profit	190	90
P/L at 1.1.X9	600	190
P/L at 31.12.X9	790	280

The consolidated balance sheets under the various methods are set out as follows:

	Cost method £	Equity method £	Normal consolidation £	Pro rata or partial consolidation £
Goodwill	–	–	49	49
Tangible fixed assets	1,105	1,105	1,705	1,525
Investments	350	525	–	–
Current assets	505	505	725	659
Current liabilities	(205)	(205)	(295)	(268)
MI—dividend	–	–	(15)	–
—OSC and reserves	–	–	(204)	–
Dividend receivable	35	35	–	–
	1,790	1,965	1,965	1,965
Called-up share capital	1,000	1,000	1,000	1,000
Profit and loss account	790	965	965	965
	1,790	1,965	1,965	1,965

Balance sheet note—equity method

	£	£
Investments—pure approach		
Cost of investment	350	
Reserves	175	
	525	
Investments—net assets/premium approach		
Net assets	476	
Premium	49	
	525	

Workings—equity method

	£		£
(1) Reserves 70% (280 − 30)		=	175
(2) Net assets 70% × £680		=	476
(3) Premium			
Cost of investment			350
OSC	400		
Reserves	30		
	430	× 70%	301
Premium			49
(4) Consolidated reserves			
H group			790
S (as above)			175
			965

Workings—normal consolidation

(5) Goodwill—as (3) above   49

Note: for illustration purposes, goodwill is presented as an intangible fixed asset (for an acceptable treatment, see chapter 7).

	£
(6) MI	
OSC and reserves 30% × £680	204
Dividend 30% × £50	15

Workings—pro rata (partial) consolidation

(7) Fixed assets   1,105 + (70% × 600)   1,525

(8) Current assets   505 + (70% × 200)   659

The consolidated profit and loss accounts are:

	Cost method £	Equity method £	Normal consolidation £	Pro rata or partial consolidation £
Profit of group	485	485	735	660
Share of profit of S	–	175	–	–
Dividends receivable	35	–	–	–
	520	660	735	660
Corporation tax	230	307	340	307
Profit after tax	290	353	395	353
Minority interest	–	–	42	–
	290	353	– 353	353
Dividends paid	100	100	100	100
Retained profit	190	253	253	253
Balance b/f	600	712	712	712
Balance c/f	790	965	965	965

Workings—equity method

		£		£
(1) Share of profit of 70% × £250			=	175
(2) Corporation tax				
H		230		
S 70% × £110		77		307
(3) Balance b/f				
H		600		
S 70% (190 – 30)		112		712

Workings—normal consolidation

			£
(4) MI 30% × £140		=	42

Workings—pro rata or partial consolidation

		£
(5) Profit of group		
H		485
S 70% × £250		175
		660

NOTE ON DISCLOSURE

In pro rata or partial consolidation, a possible variant would be to disclose separately the amounts in the consolidated balance sheet and profit and loss account relating to S. Such disclosure could either be on the face of the financial statements or in a separate note.

17.8 APPLICATIONS OF THE VARIOUS METHODS

Considering each method in turn, applications include:

(a) Cost method

(1) 'Trade' investments.
(2) Subsidiaries excluded from consolidation on the grounds of lack of effective control where significant influence cannot be demonstrated.
(3) Subsidiaries excluded from consolidation on the grounds that control is intended to be temporary.

(b) Equity method

(1) Associated companies.
(2) Subsidiaries excluded from consolidation on the grounds of lack of effective control *but* where significant influence *can* be demonstrated.
(3) Subsidiaries excluded on the grounds of dissimilar activities.

(c) Normal consolidation

All subsidiaries, except where SSAP 14 requires them to be excluded from consolidation.

(d) Pro rata or partial or proportional equity consolidation

Applications are rare but two examples are:

(1) RTZ which present two forms of consolidation—conventional and proportional equity.
　　The two forms are presented side by side and both are reported on by auditors. Proportional equity consolidation is applied to both subsidiaries and associated companies. It is unlikely that proportional equity by itself would be regarded as presenting a true and fair view of the group's activities.
(2) SSAP 1, para 10 which states:

> In some cases, partnerships or non-corporate joint ventures can have features which justify accounting for a proportionate share of individual assets and liabilities as well as profits or losses.

18 ACCOUNTING FOR OVERSEAS OPERATIONS

18.1 INTRODUCTION

Many UK companies at some stage become involved in transactions of an overseas nature. Involvement ranges from purchasing goods from an overseas supplier to conducting overseas operations through a subsidiary company or branch.

Clearly, the accounting problem is to find an acceptable approach to expressing the results of such operations in sterling so that they may be combined with those already expressed in sterling.

Put in these terms, the procedures seem routine and dull! Yet few topics, except for inflation accounting, have generated controversies to match those of foreign currency translation.

Previous attempts to produce an acceptable standard included ED 16 (1975), ED 21 (1977) and ED 27 (1981). It was only in 1983 that a definitive standard, SSAP 20 entitled 'Foreign currency translation' was finally issued.

18.2 APPROACH TO FOREIGN CURRENCY TRANSLATION

This chapter follows the approach of SSAP 20 in dealing separately with two aspects of the subject:

(a) Overseas business transactions entered into by individual companies. This includes overseas borrowings and purchases from overseas suppliers. This aspect is dealt with in section 18.3.
(b) The foreign operations of a UK company conducted through foreign enterprises, whether they be subsidiaries, associated companies or branches. This aspect is dealt with in the remaining parts of the chapter, and revolves around the preparation of consolidated financial statements.

18.3 ACCOUNTS OF INDIVIDUAL COMPANIES

(a) Objective

A company may enter into transactions which are denominated in a foreign currency. For example, a UK company may borrow $100,000 repayable in ten years' time. At each balance sheet date it will be necessary to express this in sterling for inclusion in the UK balance sheet expressed in sterling.

It is important to remember what we are trying to achieve. SSAP 20 states that 'the translation of foreign currency transactions . . . should produce results which are generally compatible with the effects of rate changes on a company's cash flows and its equity and should ensure that the financial statements present a true and fair view of the results of management actions . . .'.

(b) Basic rule

Assuming a UK company, the results of each transaction should normally be translated into £ sterling using the exchange rate in operation on the date on which the transaction occurred.

In certain circumstances, it may be acceptable to use an average rate for the period—this may be useful if there are a large number of transactions.

There are two important exceptions to this basic rule:

(1) where the transaction is to be settled at a contracted rate, the contracted rate should be used;
(2) where a trading transaction is covered by a related or matching forward contract, the rate of exchange specified in that contract may be used.

(c) Non-monetary assets

The term non-monetary assets includes plant and machinery, land and buildings, equity investments and stock.

As soon as non-monetary assets have been translated into sterling (normally using the rate at the transaction date per (b) above) and recorded in the books, they should not be retranslated at a later date.

Illustration 1

A UK company purchases plant and machinery for use in the UK from a Canadian company for $267,000. The exchange rate at the date of purchase was $1.8 = £1. So the company should record the fixed asset in its records at £148,333. The asset should not be translated again: subsequent changes in exchange rates will have no effect. The annual depreciation charge should be based on £148,333.

(d) Monetary assets and liabilities

The term includes debtors, cash, creditors and loans payable. Two possible situations may arise:

(1) the transaction has been settled by the balance sheet date eg the amount owing to an overseas supplier has been paid in full;
(2) the transaction is still outstanding at the balance sheet date.

In each case, exchange differences will arise. These will normally be included as part of the profit on ordinary activities for the year. The two examples immediately below illustrate the above points.

Illustration 2

A UK company purchased goods from a French company in May 19X4 for Fr 10,500 when the exchange rate was Fr 11.6 = £1. The account was paid on 15 July 19X4 when the exchange rate was Fr 11.9 = £1.

The supplier's account in the records of the UK company would appear as follows:

A SUPPLIER

19X4	£	19X4	£
15 July Cash (10,500 ÷ 11.9)	882	May Purchases (10,500 ÷ 11.6)	905
31 Dec P/L a/c	23		
	905		905

Illustration 3

A UK company purchased goods from a German supplier in November 19X4 for DM 4,500 when the exchange rate was DM 3.9 = £1. The account has not been settled by 31 December 19X4, the company's year end. At that date the exchange rate was DM 3.8 = £1.

The supplier's account would appear as follows:

B SUPPLIER

19X4	£	19X4	£
31 December Balance c/d		November Purchases	
(4,500 ÷ 3.8)	1,184	(4,500 ÷ 3.9)	1,154
		31 December P/L	30
	1,184		1,184

NOTE
(1) In each case, the exchange gain or loss would form part of the profit (or loss) on ordinary activities before taxation. In the Companies Act 1985 formats they would normally be grouped within other operating income or expense, but there is no specific requirement to disclose separately.
(2) The exchange gain in A Supplier of £23 has already been reflected in cash flows (ie the amount paid was £882 as opposed to £905). The exchange loss in B Supplier is reasonably certain to be reflected in cash flows (it is only a matter of time before the bill is paid!).

(e) Long-term monetary items

Exchange gains on short-term monetary items (considered in (d) above) are fairly straightforward to deal with as they are already (or soon will be) reflected in cash flows.

With long-term monetary assets, for example, a loan repayable in several years' time in a foreign currency, there are additional considerations. It will be difficult (if not impossible!) to predict the exchange rate when the loan comes up for repayment. The basic approach of SSAP 20 is:

(1) outstanding loans should be translated into sterling at each balance sheet date using the year end exchange rate;
(2) exchange differences arising between successive balance sheet dates should normally be reported as part of the profit or loss on ordinary activities.

Illustration 4

A UK company takes out a ten-year loan from an American bank in August 19X5 for US $800,000. The proceeds of the loan are converted to sterling and remitted to the UK when the exchange rate was 1.41 (so the proceeds amounted to £567,376).

At the company's year end at 31 December 19X5, the exchange rate was 1.42 and at 31 December 19X6 was 1.39.

The loan account in the books of the UK company would appear as follows:

US LOAN ACCOUNT

19X5	£	19X5	£
31 December Balance c/d		August Cash	567,376
(800,000 ÷ 1.42)	563,380		
P/L a/c	3,996		
	567,376		567,376
19X6		19X6	
31 December Balance c/d		1 January Balance b/d	563,380
(800,000 ÷ 1.39)	575,540		
		P/L a/c	12,160
	575,540		575,540

The exchange gain in 19X5 of £3,996 would be included within other interest receivable and similar income, while the exchange loss of £12,160 would be included within other interest payable and similar charges.

In 19X5, the company's profit and loss account is credited with an unrealised gain of £3,996. This treatment is justified by SSAP 20, paras 10 and 11 as follows:

Paragraph 10
In order to give a true and fair view of results, exchange gains and losses on long-term monetary items should normally be reported as part of the profit or loss for the period in accordance with the accruals concept of accounting; treatment of these items on a simple cash movements basis would be inconsistent with that concept. Exchange gains on unsettled transactions can be determined at the balance sheet date no less objectively than exchange losses; deferring the gains whilst recognising the losses would not only be illogical by denying in effect that any favourable movement in exchange rates had occurred, but would also inhibit fair measurement of the performance of the enterprise in the year. In particular, this symmetry of treatment recognises that there will probably be some interaction between currency movements and interest rates and reflects more accurately in the profit and loss account the true results of currency involvement.

Paragraph 11
For the special reasons outlined above, both exchange gains and losses on long-term monetary items should be recognised in the profit and loss account. However, it is necessary to consider on the grounds of prudence whether the amount of the gain, or the amount by which exchange gains exceed past exchange losses on the same items, to be recognised in the profit and loss account, should be restricted in the exceptional cases where there are doubts as to the convertibility or marketability of the currency in question.

(f) Equity investments financed by foreign borrowings

This special situation is dealt with in section 18.7.

18.4 CONSOLIDATION OF FOREIGN SUBSIDIARIES— AN INTRODUCTION

(a) Objectives

The objectives are set out in SSAP 20:

(1) Results should be produced which are compatible with the effects of exchange rates on a company's cash flows.
(2) The consolidated accounts should reflect the results and relationships which existed in the foreign currency statements (eg the relationship between profits earned and assets employed).

(b) Method

There are two main methods available for translating the results of an overseas operation into sterling—the closing rate method, and the temporal method. The two methods are not alternatives.

In any given situation, the method to be used will depend on the relationship between the holding company and the overseas entity (assumed, for the present, to be a subsidiary). This may be illustrated diagrammatically:

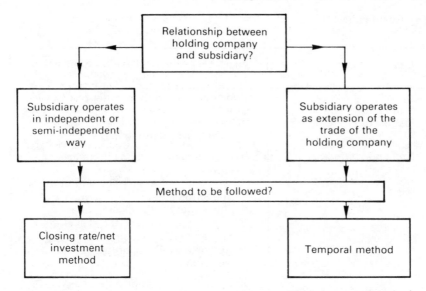

It is clear that SSAP 20 intends that the closing rate method will be appropriate in the vast majority of cases. This is confirmed by the English Institute's survey of published accounts of the leading UK companies.

(c) Foreign branches

Where a branch operates as a separate business with local finance, SSAP 20 states that the closing rate/net investment method should be used. If, however, the branch operates as an extension of the company's trade and its cash flows have a direct impact on those of the company, SSAP 20 requires the temporal method to be used.

The examples below relate to foreign subsidiaries but clearly the same principles should be applied to foreign branches. Foreign branches are considered further in section 18.8.

(d) Examinations

Knowledge of the situations when each method applies as well as the mechanics of each method are required for examination purposes.

18.5   CLOSING RATE/NET INVESTMENT METHOD

(a) When appropriate

In broad terms, the method is appropriate whenever the subsidiary is independent or autonomous. Such situations may show the following characteristics.

(1) The holding company's investment is in the net worth of the foreign enterprise (as opposed to a direct investment in its assets and liabilities).
(2) The foreign enterprise will normally have both fixed assets and working capital, and these may be part-financed by local currency borrowings (as opposed to being entirely financed by the holding company).
(3) In its day-to-day operations, the foreign enterprise is not usually dependent on the reporting currency of the investing company (ie £ sterling).
(4) The holding company will expect dividends to be paid out of future profits, but its investment will remain until such future time as the foreign enterprise is liquidated, or the investment disposed of.

(b) Basic rules

Balance sheet	All assets and liabilities translated at closing rate of exchange.
Profit and loss account	Two options permitted under SSAP 20 — either: (1) all items at closing rate; or (2) all items at average rate.
Exchange differences	Two types of translation differences may arise: (1) exchange differences arising from the retranslation of the opening net investment at the closing rate; (2) differences between P/L at average rate and P/L at closing rate (only applicable if P/L option (2) is adopted). Both types of exchange differences should be recorded as reserve movements with no entry in the profit and loss account.

(c) Worked example

Many years ago, a UK company called Panther plc purchased a 70% holding of an overseas company called Clouseau SA. The investment cost £2,600 and at the date of acquisition, the reserves of Clouseau were Fr 3,200.

The relevant exchange rates were as follows:

Date of acquisition	7.0 Fr to £1
31.12.X2	5.6 Fr to £1
Average for 19X3	5.1 Fr to £1
At payment of interim dividend	4.9 Fr to £1
31.12.X3	4.6 Fr to £1

The relevant final accounts are as follows:

	Panther plc £	Clouseau SA Fr
Balance sheet at 31.12.X3		
Tangible fixed assets—cost	92,000	56,000
—depreciation	(24,800)	(20,400)
Investment in Clouseau	2,600	–
Stock	19,600	14,120
Debtors	14,130	15,270
	103,530	64,990
Cash at bank	1,921	3,860
Dividends receivable	244	–
Loans	(10,000)	(6,000)
Creditors	(10,430)	(13,120)
Taxation	(10,400)	(6,800)
Proposed dividends	(7,000)	(1,600)
	67,865	41,330
Called-up share capital	30,000	15,000
Profit and loss account	37,865	26,330
	67,865	41,330

Profit and loss account for year end 31.12.X3

	£	Fr
Turnover	80,000	37,890
Cost of sales	(22,000)	(13,640)
Distribution costs	(16,500)	(2,090)
Administrative expenses	(14,600)	(7,200)
Dividends from Clouseau	415	–
Profit on ordinary activities before tax	27,315	14,960
Taxation	(10,400)	(6,880)
Profit on ordinary activities after tax	16,915	8,080
Extraordinary items	9,300	–
	26,215	8,080
Dividends—interim (paid)	(5,000)	(1,200)
—final (proposed)	(7,000)	(1,600)
Retained profit	14,215	5,280
P/L balance at 1.1.X3	23,650	21,050
P/L balance at 31.12.X3	37,865	26,330

(d) Workings

The recommended approach is to tackle the workings in the following sequence:

(1) Translation of subsidiary's balance sheet.
(2) Consolidated balance sheet workings.
(3) Consolidated balance sheet.
(4) Translation of subsidiary's profit and loss account.
(5) Calculation of total exchange difference.
(6) Analysis of total exchange difference.
(7) Consolidated profit and loss account workings.
(8) Consolidated profit and loss account.
(9) Statement of reserves.

(e) Translation of balance sheet

	Fr	Rate	£'000
Fixed assets—cost	56,000		12,174
—depreciation	(20,400)		(4,434)
Stock	14,120		3,070
Debtors	15,270		3,319
Cash at bank	3,860	4.6	839
Loans	(6,000)		(1,304)
Creditors	(13,120)		(2,852)
Taxation	(6,800)		(1,478)
Proposed dividends	(1,600)		(348)
	41,330		8,986
Ordinary share capital	15,000		2,143
Pre-acquisition reserves	3,200	7	457
Post acquisition reserves	23,130	Balancing	6,386
		figure	
	41,330		8,986

Explanatory notes
(1) All assets and liabilities are translated into £ sterling using the closing rate of exchange of 4.6.
(2) Shareholders' funds of £8,986 do not appear in the consolidated balance sheet as

such—they are subject to consolidation adjustments in order to arrive at goodwill on consolidation, minority interest and consolidated profit and loss reserves.

In order to make the subsequent calculations easier, it is convenient (although not absolutely necessary) to divide into the three parts shown above. Since reserves at acquisition are stated as Fr 3,200, the post-acquisitions reserves of Fr 23,130 are the carry forward of Fr 26,330 less Fr 3,200. Share capital and pre-acquisition reserves are translated at 7 (these two figures are taken into account in calculating goodwill) and the figure of £6,386 is a balancing item. Remember that the workings are set out this way in order to ease the calculations! Other possible ways of setting out workings would have exactly the same effect on the consolidated balance sheet.

(f) Consolidated balance sheet workings

Analysis of equity

	Total	Group share (75%) of pre-acquisition reserves	Group share (70%) of post-acquisition reserves	MI (30%)
	£	£	£	£
Ordinary share capital	2,143	1,500		643
P/L reserves at acquisition	457	320		137
P/L reserves since acquisition	6,386		4,470	1,916
	8,986	1,820		
Cost of investment		2,600		
Goodwill on consolidation w/o against reserves		780	(780)	
Reserves of Panther (including dividends received and receivable)			37,865	
Consolidated B/S totals			41,555	2,696
MI in proposed dividend (388 – 244)				104

CONSOLIDATED BALANCE SHEET

at 31 December 19X3

	£	£	£
Fixed assets			
Tangible assets			74,940
Current assets			
Stock		22,670	
Debtors		17,449	
Cash		2,760	
		42,879	
Less creditors: amounts falling due within one year			
Creditors	13,282		
Taxation	11,878		
Dividends payable:			
Holding company shareholders	7,000		
Minority shareholders	104		
		32,264	
Net current assets			10,615
Total assets less current liabilities			85,555
Creditors: amounts falling due after more than one year			(11,304)
			74,251
Called-up share capital			30,000
Profit and loss account			41,555
			71,555
Minority interest			2,696
			74,251

(g) Translation of subsidiary's profit and loss account

	Fr	Rate	£
Turnover	37,890		7,429
Cost of sales	(13,640)		(2,674)
Gross profit	24,250		4,755
Distribution costs	(2,090)	5.1	(410)
Administration expenses	(7,200)		(1,412)
Operating profit	14,960		2,933
Tax	6,880		1,349
	8,080		1,584
Dividends—paid	(1,200)	4.9	(245)
—proposed	(1,600)	4.6	(348)
Retained profit	5,280		991

Explanatory notes
(1) All profit and loss items have been translated at an average rate for the period. An acceptable alternative policy would have been to translate at closing rate.
(2) Dividends paid are translated at the rate of exchange at the date of payments, while dividends proposed are translated at the closing rate. This should correspond with the rates used by the holding company in its own separate accounts.

(h) Calculation of total exchange difference

So far we have:

(1) Split the closing reserves of the subsidiary between pre-acquisition and post-acquisition (see working (e)).
(2) Translated various profit and loss items (working (g)).

Before we can calculate the total exchange difference on translation for the year, we need to know the equivalent split of opening reserves between pre-acquisition and post-acquisition. In practice, this information would be available from the previous year working papers. As this information is not available, it is necessary to carry out a rather artificial exercise of reconstructing the previous year's closing balance sheet.

Net assets at 31 December 19X2 may be calculated as a global total by adding together share capital and reserves (Fr 15,000 + 21,050 = 36,050). Post-acquisition reserves (in francs) may again be calculated as a balancing figure.

	Fr	Rate	£
Sundry net assets	36,050	5.6	6,438
Ordinary share capital	15,000		2,143
Pre-acquisition reserves	3,200	7.0	457
Post-acquisition reserves	17,850	Balancing figure	3,838
	36,050		6,438

Explanatory notes
(1) First of all, the opening balance sheet in francs should be reconstructed. Although the breakdown of the net assets figure of Fr 36,050 is not known, this does not matter as all items included in this are translated at the same rate of exchange.
(2) The various items should be translated into £ sterling using the same procedures as in (e) above. The post-acquisition reserves of £3,838 are calculated as a balancing figure.

Calculation of total exchange difference

Post-acquisition reserves at 1.1.X3 (working (i))	3,838
Post-acquisition reserves at 31.12.X3 (working (e))	6,386
Increase	2,548
Retained profit (working (g))	991
Exchange difference (gain)	1,557

As the subsidiary is 70% owned, then 70% × £1,557, ie £1,089, will be shown as a movement on group reserves (with no entry in the consolidated profit and loss account for the year).

(i) Analysis of total exchange difference

Where the profit and loss account of the subsidiary is translated at the average rate of exchange, SSAP 20 distinguishes between two elements of the exchange difference:

(1) exchange differences arising from retranslation of the opening net investment at the closing rate; and
(2) the difference between the profit and loss account translated at an average rate and at the closing rate.

The total exchange difference of £1,557 above may be analysed as follows:

	Fr	Rate	£
Equity interest at 1.1.X3	36,050	5.6	6,438
Gain on retranslation at closing rate (bal figure)	–	–	1,399
Equity interest at 1.1.X3:			
Restated at closing exchange rate	36,050	4.6	7,837
Retained profit per p/1 workings	5,280	–	991
Exchange difference—p/1 at average rate compared with closing rate			

$$\frac{5,280}{4.6} - 991$$

	–	–	158
Equity interest at 31.12.X3	41,330	4.6	8,986

Total exchange difference = (1,399 + 158) = £1,557
   Group share treated as movement on reserves during the year 70% × £1,557 = £1,089.

COMMENT
As the above split between £1,399 and £158 has no effect on the published accounts, the above analysis need only be provided if requested by the examiner.

(j) Consolidated profit and loss account workings

For most items, it is simply a question of combining two sets of figures: those of the holding company, and the £ sterling figures for the subsidiary as calculated in (g) above.

   The only other calculation required is that for minority interest. From working (g), MI is calculated as follows:

30% × £1,584 = £475

(k)   CONSOLIDATED PROFIT AND LOSS ACCOUNT
for the year ended 31 December 19X3

	£	£
Turnover		87,429
Cost of sales		24,674
Gross profit		62,755
Distribution costs	16,910	
Administration expenses	16,012	32,922
Profits on ordinary activities before tax		29,833
Tax		11,749
Profit on ordinary activities after tax		18,084
Minority interest		475
		17,609
Extraordinary items		9,300
		26,909
Dividends—interim (paid)	5,000	
—final (proposed)	7,000	12,000
Retained profit		14,909
Retained by holding company		14,215
Retained by subsidiary		694
		14,909

Working: 70% × £991 (working (g)) = £694.

(l) Statement of reserves

This statement 'links in' the retained profit in the P/L and the group share of the exchange difference with the reserves in the consolidated balance sheet.

		£
So far we have calculated:		
(i) Retained profit (from consolidated P/L);		14,909
(ii) Group share of exchange difference (workings (h) and (i)).		1,089

We need to calculate the balance on consolidated P/L reserves at 1.1.X3 (this is the figure which appeared in last year's consolidated balance sheet).

	£
This is calculated as follows:	
Panther reserves at 1.1.X3	23,650
Panther's share of post-acquisition reserves at 1.1.X3 of Clouseau (working (h)):	
70% × £3,838	2,687
	26,337
Less goodwill w/o	780
	25,557

The statement of reserves which would be disclosed in the published accounts would be:

	£
Profit and loss account at 1.1.X3	25,557
Retained profit	14,909
Exchange differences	1,089
Profit and loss account at 31.12.X3	41,555

(Note that this last figure agrees with the consolidated balance sheet at 31 December 19X3.)

18.6   TEMPORAL METHOD

(a) When appropriate

The temporal method should be used in those relatively few cases where the foreign operations are carried out through foreign enterprises which operate as a direct extension of the trade of the investing company.

(b) Dominant currency

The temporal method should be used where it is considered overall that the currency of the investing company (ie holding company) is the dominant currency in the economic environment in which the subsidiary operates.

This assessment will require the following to be taken into account:

(1) the extent to which the subsidiary's cash flows have a direct impact on the cash flows of the investing company;
(2) the extent to which the functioning of the subsidiary depends directly on the holding company;
(3) the currency in which the majority of trading transactions are denominated;
(4) the major currency to which the operation is exposed in its financing structure.

(c) Possible situations

SSAP 20 gives the following as examples of situations where the temporal method may be appropriate:

(1) Where the foreign enterprise acts as a selling agency, receiving stocks of goods from the investing company and remitting the proceeds back to the company.

(2) Where the foreign enterprise produces a raw material or manufactures parts or sub-assemblies which are then shipped to the investing company for inclusion in its own product.

(3) Where the foreign enterprise is located overseas for tax, exchange control or similar reasons to act as a means of raising finance for other companies in the group.

(d) Basic rules

(1) *Balance sheet items*

Item	Examples	Exchange rate
Monetary assets and liabilities	Debtors cash Creditors Loans	closing rate
Non-monetary assets	Stock	Rate at date of acquisition of stock (but closing rate is usually acceptable)
	Fixed assets (cost less depreciation)	(1) Acquired before acquisition of subsidiary — rate at date of acquisition of subsidiary (2) Acquired after acquisition of subsidiary — rate at date of purchase of fixed assets

(2) *Profit and loss items*

Item	Exchange rate
Sales Expenses (excluding depreciation)	Average rate of exchange
Depreciation	Same rate as for fixed assets
Taxation	Closing rate (although some accountants consider that average rate should be used)
Dividends	Paid — rate at payment date Proposed — closing rate

(3) *Exchange differences*

These should be included in the profit and loss account and taken into account in arriving at profit on ordinary activities before taxation. They will normally be included under 'other operating income or expense'.

(e) Worked example

The previous example of Panther plc will be reworked using the temporal method. This is for purpose of illustration only, as the closing rate method would normally be appropriate for the circumstances of that company.

The 70% holding was acquired several years ago at a cost of £2,600 when the reserves of Clouseau amounted to Fr 3,200.

The relevant exchange rates were:

Acquisition of subsidiary	7.0 Fr to £1
Acquisition of fixed assets	6.1 Fr to £1
31.12.X2	5.6 Fr to £1
Average for 19X3	5.1 Fr to £1
Payment of dividend	4.9 Fr to £1
31.12.X3	4.6 Fr to £1

The relevant final accounts are as follows:

Balance sheets at 31.12.X3

	Panther plc £	Clouseau SA Fr
Tangible fixed assets—cost	92,000	56,000
—depreciation	(24,800	(20,400)
Investment in Clouseau	2,600	–
Stock	19,600	14,120
Debtors	14,130	15,270
Cash at bank	1,921	3,860
Dividends receivable	244	–
Loans	(10,000)	(6,000)
Creditors	(10,430)	(13,120)
Taxation	(10,400)	(6,800)
Proposed dividends	(7,000)	(1,600)
	67,865	41,330
Called-up share capital	30,000	15,000
Profit and loss account	37,865	26,330
	67,865	41,330

Profit and loss account for year end 31.12.X3

	Panther plc £	Clouseau SA Fr
Turnover	80,000	37,890
Cost of sales	(22,000)	(13,640)
Distribution costs	(16,500)	(2,090)
Administrative expenses	(14,600)	(7,200)
Dividends from Clouseau	415	–
Profit on ordinary activities before tax	27,315	14,960
Taxation	(10,400)	(6,880)
Profit on ordinary activities after tax	16,915	8,080
Extraordinary items	9,300	–
	26,215	8,080
Dividends—interim (paid)	(5,000)	(1,200)
—final (proposed)	(7,000)	(1,600)
Retained profit	14,215	5,280
P/L balance at 1.1.X3	23,650	21,050
P/L balance at 31.12.X3	37,865	26,330

NOTES
(1) Loan interest has been ignored for this example.
(2) Cost of sales includes depreciation of 5,600 francs. There is no other depreciation.

(f) Workings

The recommended approach is to tackle the workings in the following sequence:

(1) Translation of subsidiary's balance sheet.
(2) Consolidated balance sheet workings.
(3) Consolidated balance sheet.
(4) Translation of subsidiary's profit and loss account.
(5) Calculation of total exchange difference.
(6) Consolidated profit and loss account workings.
(7) Consolidated profit and loss account.

(g) Translation of balance sheet

	Fr	Rate	£'000
Fixed assets—cost	56,000	6.1	9,180
depreciation	(20,400)		(3,344)
Stock	14,120		3,070
Debtors	15,270		3,319
Cash at bank	3,860		839
Loan	(6,000)	4.6	(1,304)
Creditors	(13,120)		(2,852)
Taxation	(6,800)		(1,478)
Proposed dividends	(1,600)		(348)
	41,330		7,082
Ordinary share capital	15,000	7	2,143
Pre-acquisition reserves	3,200		457
Post-acquisition reserves	23,130	Balancing figure	4,482
	41,330		7,082

EXPLANATORY NOTE
As with the approach used for the closing rate method, the post acquisition reserves of £4,482 is calculated as a balancing figure.

(h) Consolidated balance sheet workings

Analysis of equity

	Total £	Group share (70%) of pre-acquisition reserves £	Group share (70%) of post-acquisition reserves £	MI (30%) £
Ordinary share capital	2,143	1,500		643
P/L reserves at acquisition	457	320		137
P/L reserves since acquisition	4,482		3,137	1,345
	7,082	1,820		
Cost of investment		2,600		
Goodwill on consolidation w/o against reserves		780	(780)	
Reserves of Panther			37,865	
Consolidated B/S totals			40,222	2,125
MI in proposed dividend (388 − 244)				104

(i)   CONSOLIDATED BALANCE SHEET
                         at 31 December 19X3

	£	£	£
Fixed assets			
Tangible assets			73,036
Current assets			
Stock		22,670	
Debtors		17,449	
Cash		2,760	
		42,879	
Less creditors: amounts falling due within one year			
Creditors	13,282		
Taxation	11,878		
Dividends payable:			
Holding company shareholders	7,000		
Minority shareholders	104	32,264	
Net current assets			10,615
Total assets less current liabilities			83,651
Creditors: amounts falling due after more than one year			(11,304)
			72,347
Called-up share capital			30,000
Profit and loss account			40,222
			70,222
Minority interest			2,125
			72,347

(j) Translation of subsidiary's profit and loss account

	Fr	Rate	£
Turnover	37,890	5.1	7,429
Cost of sales (excluding depreciation)	(8,040)	5.1	(1,576)
Depreciation	(5,600)	6.1	(918)
Gross profit	24,250		4,935
Distribution costs	(2,090)	5.1	(410)
Administrative expenses	(7,200)	5.1	(1,412)
Operating profit	14,960		3,113
Tax	(6,880)	4.6	(1,496)
	8,080		1,617
Dividends—paid	(1,200)	4.9	(245)
—proposed	(1,600)	4.6	(348)
Retained profit	5,280		1,024

(k) Calculation of total exchange differences

The approach adopted is similar to that for the closing rate method. Again, for reasons previously explained, it is necessary to reconstruct the opening balance sheet. The main point to note, however, is that opening net assets must be split between fixed assets and others, as different exchange rates are appropriate.

The calculations are set out below, followed by explanatory notes.

	Fr	Rate	£
Fixed assets			
(35,600 + 5,600)	41,200	6.1	6,754
Other assets less liabilities	(5,150)	5.6	(920)
	36,050		5,834
Ordinary share capital	15,000	7.0	2,143
Pre-acquisition reserves	3,200	7.0	457
Post-acquisition reserves	17,850	Balancing figure	3,234
	36,050		5,834

EXPLANATORY NOTES

(1) Assuming no acquisition or disposals of fixed assets during the year, it is possible to work back to the figure at the beginning of the year by adding back the depreciation charge.
(2) Post-acquisition reserves of Fr 17,850 is calculated as under the previous method (ie 21,050 − 3,200).
(3) Net liabilities of Fr 5,150 are calculated as a balancing figure.
(4) Amounts are translated into sterling using temporal principles.
(5) Post-acquisition reserves of £3,234 is calculated as a balancing figure.

Calculation of total exchange difference

	£
Post-acquisition reserves at 1.1.X3 (working (k))	3,234
Post-acquisition reserves at 31.12.X3 (working (g))	4,482
Increase	1,248
Retained profit (working (j))	1,024
Exchange difference (gain)	224

SSAP 20 does not attempt to analyse the component parts of the exchange gain—in fact such an analysis would have little meaning.

(l) Consolidated profit and loss account workings

Again for most items it is simply a question of combining two sets of figures.

(1) Minority interest

	£
Profit after tax (working (i))	1,617
Exchange gain taken to P/L	224
	1,841

MI: 30% × £1,841 = £552

(2) P/L balance as at 1.1.X3

	£
Panther reserves at 1.1.X3	23,650
Panther's share of post-acquisition reserves at 1.1.X3 of Clouseau (working (k)) 70% × £3,234	2,263
	25,913
Less goodwill w/o	780
	25,133

(m) CONSOLIDATED PROFIT AND LOSS ACCOUNT

for the year ended 31 December 19X3

	£	£
Turnover		87,429
Cost of sales		24,494
		———
Gross profit		62,935
Distribution costs	16,910	
Administration expenses	16,012	32,922
	———	———
		30,013
Other operating income (exchange gain)		224
		———
Profits on ordinary activities before tax		30,237
Tax		11,896
		———
Profit on ordinary activities after tax		18,341
Minority interest		552
		———
		17,789
Extraordinary items		9,300
		———
		27,089
Dividends—interim (paid)	5,000	
—final (proposed)	7,000	12,000
	———	———
		15,089
Retained by holding company	14,215	
Retained by subsidiary (working)	874	
	———	
	15,089	
	———	
Profit and loss account balance at 1.1.X3		25,133
		———
Profit and loss account balance at 31.12.X3		40,222
		———

Working
70% (1,024 (j) + 224 (k))

18.7 EQUITY INVESTMENTS FINANCED BY FOREIGN BORROWINGS

(a) Background

Exchange gains or losses on foreign currency borrowings would normally be reported as part of the company's or group's profit on ordinary activities.

However, where the purpose of such borrowings is to provide a hedge against the risks associated with foreign equity investments, an alternative may be available.

SSAP 20 deals with this in two parts:

(1) in the accounts of the investing company;
(2) in the group accounts.

(b) Accounts of the investing company

(1) *Situation*

Where an individual company has used borrowings in currencies other than its own, either:

(i)   to finance foreign equity; or
(ii) where the purpose of such borrowings is to provide a hedge against the exchange risk associated with existing (ie previously acquired) equity investments;

then the company may be covered in economic terms against any movements in exchange rates.

(2) *Options*

Provided the company can satisfy the conditions set out below, the company *may* denominate its foreign equity investments in the relevant foreign currency and translate the carrying amount at each balance sheet date at the closing rate of exchange.

Any resulting exchange differences *should* be taken direct to reserves. Against these exchange differences *should* then be offset against exchange gains or losses on related borrowings.

(3) *Conditions*

The three conditions to be satisfied are:

(i)   In any accounting period, exchange gains or losses arising on the borrowings may be offset only to the extent of exchange differences arising on the equity investments.
(ii) The foreign currency borrowings (whose exchange gains or losses are used in the offset process) should not exceed, in the aggregate, the total amount of cash that the investments are expected to be able to generate, whether from profits or otherwise.
(iii) The accounting treatment adopted should be applied consistently from period to period.

(4) *Illustration*

Suppose in the Panther example, the investment in Clouseau was part financed by a loan of 12,600 francs repayable in twenty years' time. Assume this loan is part of Panther's total borrowings.

(i) Ignoring SSAP 20 option

(a) The separate balance sheet of Panther will include:

Shares in group company	£2,600
Loan $\left(\dfrac{\text{Fr }12,600}{4.6}\right)$	£2,739

(£2,739 is part of a larger total of £10,000.)

(b) The loss on translation of the loan during the year is calculated as:

$\text{Fr}\dfrac{12,600}{5.6}$	2,250
$\text{Fr}\dfrac{12,600}{4.6}$	2,739
Translation loss, charged to profit and loss account	489

(ii) SSAP 20 option

As an alternative, provided the above three conditions are satisfied, the company may take advantage of the option in SSAP 20 as follows:

(a) Shares in group company. Instead of showing this each year at an unchanged amount of £2,600, this equity investment may be denominated in francs, ie 18,200 francs (investment cost £2,600) when exchange rate was 7.0. This will then be retranslated each year at the closing rate of exchange:

Balance sheet 31.12.X2 $\dfrac{\text{Fr }18,200}{5.6}$ 3,250

Balance sheet 31.12.X3 $\dfrac{\text{Fr }18,200}{4.6}$ 3,957

(b) Loan in foreign currency borrowing:

Balance sheet 31.12.X2 $\dfrac{\text{Fr }12,600}{5.6}$ 2,250

Balance sheet 31.12.X3 $\dfrac{\text{Fr }12,600}{4.6}$ 2,739

(c) Exchange differences arising during the year:

Exchange difference on investment
(3,957 – 3,250)   707 Cr

Exchange difference on loan
(2,739 – 2,250)   489 Dr

Net effect (credit)   218

If the company takes advantage of the option, £218 should be credited direct to reserves (with no entry in the profit and loss account).

(c) Group accounts

(1) *Situation*

Within a group, foreign borrowings may have been used to finance group investments in foreign enterprises (such as subsidiaries or associated companies) or to provide a hedge against the exchange risk associated with existing investments.

Any increase or decrease in the amount outstanding on the borrowings arising from exchange rate movements will probably be covered by corresponding changes in the carrying amount of the net assets underlying the net investments.

(2) *Option*

In the consolidated accounts, provided the conditions below are satisfied:

(i)   exchange gains or losses on such currency borrowings (which would otherwise be passed through the consolidated profit and loss account) *may* be offset as reserve movements against;
(ii)   exchange differences on retranslation of the net investments.

(3) *Conditions*

The four conditions to be satisfied are:

(i)   the relationship between the investing company and the foreign enterprises concerned should be such as to justify the use of the closing rate method for consolidation purposes;
(ii)   the other three conditions are those referred to on p. 397 except that 'net investments in foreign enterprises' applies instead of 'equity investments'.

(4) *Illustration*

Using the data from the Panther example:

(i) Ignoring SSAP 20 option

(a) Loss on translation of loan of £489 is debited to profit and loss account.
(b) Group share of exchange differences (70% × £1,557 = £1,089) to reserves.

(ii) SSAP 20 option

The difference on translation of the foreign currency borrowings may be offset against the difference on retranslation of the opening net investment:

	£
Gain on retranslation of opening net investment (see earlier workings)	
70% × 1,399	979
Loss on translation of foreign currency borrowings	489
Exchange gain after offset	490
Group share of exchange difference on P/L translation: 70% × £158	110
So movement on reserves (credit) during the year is (490 + 110) ie	600

18.8 FOREIGN BRANCHES

(a) Translation method

The relationship between the branch and the head office will determine the translation method to be used. It is likely that most branches will conduct their business as an extension of the trade of the head office in which case the temporal method will be applicable.

This will not always be the case, however, and it is necessary to consider the definition of 'foreign branch' provided by SSAP 20.

(b) Definition

A foreign branch is either:

(1) a legally constituted enterprise located overseas, or
(2) a group of assets and liabilities which are accounted for in foreign currencies.

(c) Special situations

The extension of the definition ((b)(2), above), to a 'group of assets and liabilities' effectively means that certain branches (as defined) should be translated using the closing rate method.

The statement which accompanied the issue of SSAP 20 gave the following as examples of situations where a group of assets and liabilities should be accounted for using the closing rate/net investment method:

(i) a hotel in France financed by borrowings in French francs;
(ii) a ship or aircraft purchased in US dollars—with an associated loan in US dollars—which earns revenue and incurs expenses in US dollars;
(iii) a foreign currency insurance operation where the liabilities are substantially covered by the holding of foreign currency assets.

Both assets and liabilities will be translated at the exchange rate at the balance sheet date. Gains and losses on retranslation of opening 'equity' will be taken direct to reserves.

18.9   FOREIGN ASSOCIATED COMPANIES

By definition an associated company is not 'controlled' by the investor. Consequently, the closing rate/net investment method will usually be appropriate.

18.10   DISCLOSURE IN FINANCIAL STATEMENTS

(a) Accounting policies

The statement of accounting policies should disclose the translation method and the treatment of exchange differences.

(b) Disclosure of exchange gains

The net amount of exchange gains or losses on foreign currency borrowings less deposits should be disclosed, showing separately:

(1) the amount offset in reserves as under SSAP 20, paras 51, 57 and 58 (ie the options referred to above); and
(2) the net amount charged or credited to the profit and loss account.

This is not required for exempt companies as defined by SSAP 20.

(c) Movement on reserves

Net movement on reserves arising from exchange differences should be disclosed.

(d) Unrealised profits included in profit and loss account

If unrealised profits on long-term foreign loans are included in the profit and loss account, the Companies Act 1985 require disclosure of:

(1) particulars of the departure (from the prudence concept);
(2) reasons for departure;
(3) effect of departure.

(You should refer back to section 18.3 (e) above.)

19 ACCOUNTING FOR PRICE CHANGES—1

19.1 BUSINESS PROFIT OR BUSINESS INCOME

An economist might refer to business profit or income as being the maximum a company could distribute during the year and still expect to be as well off at the end of the year as it was at the beginning of the year. Alternatively, this could be described in terms of the maximum which could be distributed and still keep the capital of the business intact.

Business capital may be measured in several ways, each of which can give rise to different profit figures, for example:

(a) money capital of shareholders funds (historical cost account);
(b) purchasing power of the money capital of shareholders funds (current purchasing power accounting);
(c) productive or operating capacity (current cost accounting).

The possible approaches are discussed later in this and the following chapter.

19.2 THE ACCRUALS CONCEPT

The accounting approach revolves around the accruals concept (SSAP 2, Disclosure of accounting policies). Under the accruals concept, revenues and costs are accrued and matched with one another. For example, in a manufacturing company, pre-tax profit is determined by matching cost of sales against sales to arrive at gross profit, and then deducting operating expenses such as distribution costs and administrative expenses.

SSAP 2, para 14(b) states:

> The accruals concept implies that the profit and loss account reflects changes in the amount of net assets that arise out of the transactions of the relevant period (other than distributions or subscriptions of capital and unrealised surpluses, arising on revaluation of fixed assets) ...Under the accruals concept, the balance sheet reflects the effect of transactions still to be completed, for example, amounts to be paid or collected, stock to be sold, or fixed assets with a remaining number of years' service potential.

19.3 WEAKNESSES OF THE HISTORICAL COST CONVENTION

The main weaknesses may be considered under the following headings:

(a) Profit and loss account

Historical cost accounting (HCA) matches current revenues (expressed in up-to-date prices) with historical costs. In some cases these costs will relate to price levels of previous accounting periods (for example, depreciation of fixed assets).

When prices rise, the matching process may result in inflated profits being reported. Unless some part of the historical cost-profit is retained within the business, business capital will not be maintained in real terms.

(b) Balance sheet

The historical cost of assets (depreciated where relevant) does not present a current measure (expressed in up-to-date prices) of resources employed in a business.

In the UK, some companies mitigate this weakness by incorporating revaluations of fixed assets (for example, freehold land and buildings) into the balance sheet. This practice is usually referred to as modified historical cost (MHC).

(c) Interpretation of accounts

Historical cost accounts can give misleading impressions of growth and profitability. This criticism is particularly apparent in the case of ten-year summaries included by listed companies in their annual reports. Statistics such as turnover, pre-tax profit, earnings per share and assets employed can give a distorted view of a company's performance and position. Clearly, much of this is due to the fact that money, the value of which changes over time, is an imperfect unit of measurement.

Following on from the above, the following specific comments can be made:

(1) Return on capital employed (ROCE) can be distorted as a result of profits being overstated in real terms and assets such as fixed assets being understated.
(2) Historical cost accounts may fail to show:

    (i) whether a company is earning sufficient funds to enable it to maintain its capital in real terms;
    (ii) the extent to which funds can prudently be distributed in the form of dividends.

It should be noted that many accountants consider that the above weaknesses apply when inflation rates are running at relatively low figures, say 5% per annum.

19.4 APPROACHES TO ACCOUNTING FOR PRICE CHANGES

(a) Introduction

The aim of this and the following chapters is to discuss some of the proposals put forward by the Accounting Standards Committee over the past twelve or so years.

In the UK, the search continues to find an alternative to historical cost accounting which will attract the widespread support of accountants and various user groups.

A summary of statements since 1973

Date	Reference and title of statement	Issued by
1973	ED 8—Accounting for changes in the purchasing power of money	ASC
1974	SSAP 7 (provisional)—same title as ED 8	ASC
1975	Report of the Sandilands Committee	Government
1976	ED 18—Current cost accounting	ASC
1977	Hyde guidelines on current cost accounting	ASC
1979	ED 24—Current cost accounting	ASC
1980	SSAP 16—Current cost accounting	ASC
1984	ED 35—Accounting for the effects of changing prices	ASC
1986	Accounting for the effects of changing prices: a Handbook	ASC

(*Note:* ED 35 and SSAP 16 have both been withdrawn.)

The following section discusses the current purchasing power approach set out in ED 8/SSAP 7.

19.5 CURRENT PURCHASING POWER (CPP) ACCOUNTING

(a) Background

In the UK, the first proposal for CPP accounting came in the form of ED 8 (accounting for changes in the purchasing power of money). A provisional accounting standard, SSAP 7, with the same title, was issued in May 1974. However CPP suffered a major blow in September 1975 as a result of the publication of the report of the Sandilands Committee which rejected CPP in favour of current cost accounting (CCA).

In spite of the ASC's subsequent preference for CCA, some accountants have argued forcibly in favour of the merits of CPP. In particular, Professor D R Myddelton of Cranfield School of Management has been a powerful advocate of current or constant purchasing power accounting.

(b) Capital maintenance concept

CPP is concerned with maintaining the purchasing power (measured in terms of the retail price index) of the shareholders' equity. Under CPP, no profits result until the shareholders' equity at the beginning of the year has been maintained in purchasing power terms.

The way in which CPP profit is determined is set out in a detailed example later in this section.

(c) Principal proposals of SSAP 7

Although SSAP 7 has been withdrawn, it is useful to consider briefly its main proposals:

(1) Annual accounts of listed companies were to be accompanied by a supplementary statement which showed in terms of pounds of purchasing power at the accounting year end:

    (i)   the financial position at the year end; and
    (ii) the results for the year.

(2) The conversion of the basic accounts used to provide the information for the supplementary statement was to be by means of a general index of prices i e the retail price index (RPI).

(d) Terminology

The standard used certain terms which included:

(1) *Monetary items:* assets, liabilities or capital, the amounts of which are fixed by contract or statute in terms of numbers of pounds regardless of changes in the purchasing power of money.

    Examples: debtors, cash, overdraft, creditors, long-term debt, preference share capital, investments in debentures or preference shares.

(2) *Non-monetary items:* all items which are not monetary items with the exception of the total equity interest which is neither monetary nor non-monetary.

    Examples: fixed assets, stocks, investments in ordinary shares.

(3) *Conversion:* the process of translating figures from historical pounds to pounds of current (constant) purchasing power.

(4) *Updating:* the process of translating figures of an earlier accounting period from pounds of current purchasing power at one date to pounds of current purchasing power at another, later, date.

(e) Conversion and updating

These terms may be illustrated as follows by considering successive balance sheets at 31.12.X8 and 31.12.X9.

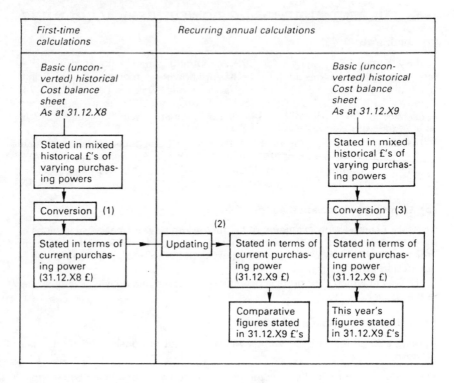

Comments

(1) This relates to the conversion of the 31.12.X8 balance sheet. Monetary items are automatically expressed in terms of purchasing power units at 31.12.X8. Non-monetary items need to be converted.

Illustration

A fixed asset was acquired three years ago on 1.1.X6 at a cost of £50,000. It is depreciated at a straight-line annual rate of 10% and so its NBV at 31.12.X8 is £35,000. Assumed that the RPI at 1.1.X6 and 31.12.X8 was 110 and 150.4 respectively.

The conversion from historical cost (£H) to current purchasing power units (31.12.X8 or £c) is as follows:

		Conversion factor	£31.12.X8
Cost	50,000	150.4	68,364
		――――	
		110.0	
Depreciation	15,000	150.4	20,509
		――――	
NBV	35,000	110.0	47,855

(2) A year later, the balance sheet in (1) above is required for the purpose of comparative figures. Since the CPP balance sheet at 31.12.X8 was prepared a year previously, all that is now required is for this to be updated to £s of purchasing power at 31.12.X9. This is a straightforward calculation requiring each balance sheet item to be multiplied by a factor of:

$$\frac{\text{RPI at } 31.12.X9}{\text{RPI at } 31.12.X8}$$

Note that since all items in the CPP balance sheet at 31.12.X8 were stated in terms of year-end purchasing power units, each asset and liability (whether monetary or non-monetary) is adjusted by the same conversion factor.

(3) The historical cost balance sheet at 31.12.X9 must be converted into a homogeneous balance sheet in which each item is expressed in purchasing power at 31.12.X9.

These stages are illustrated in the example below.

(f) Illustrative example

(1) Basic information

Westbury Traders plc is an established listed company involved in various wholesaling activities. The company has prepared its usual historical cost accounts, set out below. You have been asked to assist in the preparation of supplementary CPP information (including comparatives).

The profit and loss account for the year ended 31 December 19X9 is as follows:

	£'000	£'000
Sales		800,000
Opening stock	52,000	
Purchases	640,000	
	692,000	
Closing stock	72,000	
Cost of sales		620,000
Gross profit		180,000
Distribution costs	6,000	
Debenture interest (paid 31.12.X9)	10,000	
Administrative expenses (including £42m depreciation)	57,800	73,800
Profit on ordinary activities before tax		106,200
Taxation		51,000
Profit after tax		55,200
Interim dividend (paid 30.6.X9)	10,000	
Final dividend (proposed)	20,000	30,000
Retained profit		25,200
Profit and loss account balance at 1.1.X9		80,500
Profit and loss account balance at 31.12.X9		105,700

The respective historical cost balance sheets are as follows:

	19X9		19X8	
	£'000	£'000	£'000	£'000
Tangible fixed assets		358,000		320,000
Current assets:				
Stock	72,000		52,000	
Debtors	218,000		170,000	
Cash at bank	1,500		8,000	
	291,500		230,000	
Creditors—payable within a year:				
Trade creditors	122,800		63,500	
Dividends	20,000		15,000	
Taxation	51,000		41,000	
	193,800		119,500	
Net current assets		97,700		110,500
		455,700		430,500
Creditors payable in more than one year				
5% debenture stock		(200,000)		(200,000)
		255,700		230,500
Capital and reserves:				
Called-up capital		150,000		150,000
Profit and loss account		105,700		80,500
		255,700		230,500

Additional information:

(i) *Fixed assets*

	31.12.X9	31.12.X8
	£'000	£'000
Cost	480,000	400,000
Depreciation	122,000	80,000
	358,000	320,000

The company acquired additions to office machinery on 30.9.X9. No disposals took place during the year. The assets held at 31.12.X8 were acquired on 1.1.X7. The company's depreciation policy is to provide for depreciation on a straight-line basis at a rate of 10% per annum.

(ii) *Profit and loss account items*
Sales, purchases, distribution costs and administrative expenses occurred at an even rate during the year.

(iii) *Stock ageings*
In each of the two years, it is assumed that stock held at the balance sheet date was originally acquired three months before the end of the year.

(iv) *Retail price index information*
The following (fictitious) RPI index information is provided:

31.12.X5	100 (base year)
31.12.X6	105
31.12.X7	110
30.9.X8	114
1.1.X9	115
31.3.X9	117
30.6.X9	120
30.9.X9	122
31.12.X9	125

(2) Workings to suggested solution

For the purposes of clarity, the workings are set out in five stages. The symbols £31.12.X8 and £31.12.X9 refer to purchasing power units derived from changes in the retail price index.

Stage 1—conversion of HCA balance sheet at 31.12.X8 into £31.12.X8
As the principal objective is to prepare balance sheets and profit and loss accounts stated in terms of purchasing power units at the balance sheet date (ie in terms of £31.12.X9), this stage is not strictly necessary. It could have been combined with Stage 2. However, Stage 1 does illustrate the procedure which would have taken place one year previously.

   The key point is to distinguish between monetary items (which require no conversion as they are already expressed in year-end purchasing power units) and non-monetary items which do require conversion.

	£'000 H	Conversion factor	£'000 31.12.X8
Fixed assets—costs	400,000	115	438,095
		——	
		105	
Fixed assets—agg dep	(80,000)	115	(87,619)
		——	
		105	
Stock	52,000	115	52,456
		——	
		114	
Debtors	170,000	–	170,000
Cash	8,000	–	8,000
Creditors	(63,500)	–	(63,500)
Final dividend	(15,000)	–	(15,000)
Corporation tax	(41,000)	–	(41,000)
Debentures	(200,000)	–	(200,000)
Net assets = total equity	£230,500 H	–	£261,432 C

Note: £c (ie £s current) is a shorthand expression for £s of purchasing power at the balance sheet date.

Stage 2—update of 31.12.X8 balance sheet
One year later, the balance sheet at 31.12.X8 is required for comparative figure purposes. Since the 31.12.X8 HCA balance sheet has already been converted (from 'mixed' pounds to pounds of identical purchasing power), all that is required is an update from £31.12.X8 to £31.12.X9.

   Since all items are expressed in terms of the same measuring unit, each item is multiplied by a factor

$$\frac{\text{RPI } 31.12.X9}{\text{RPI } 31.12.X8}$$

	£'000 31.12.X8	Update factor	£'000 31.12.X9
Fixed assets—cost	438,095		476,190
Fixed assets—agg dep	(87,619)		(95,238)
Stock	52,456		57,017
Debtors	170,000	125	184,783
Cash	8,000	——	8,696
		115	
Creditors	(63,500)		(69,022)
Final dividend	(15,000)		(16,304)
Corporation tax	(41,000)		(44,565)
Debentures	(200,000)		(217,392)
Net assets = total equity	£261,432 C		£284,165 C

Stage 3—conversion of 31.12.X9 balance sheet

	£'000 H	Conversion factor	£'000 31.12.X9
Fixed assets—cost	480,000	(see note)	558,157
Fixed assets—agg dep	(122,000)	(see note)	(144,906)
Stock	72,000	125	73,770
		—	
		122	
Debtors	218,000	–	218,000
Cash	1,500	–	1,500
Creditors	(122,800)	–	(122,800)
Final dividend	(20,000)	–	(20,000)
Corporation tax	(51,000)	–	(51,000)
Debentures	(200,000)	–	(200,000)
Net assets = total equity	£255,700 H		£312,721 C

NOTE—FIXED ASSET CONVERSION

	COST			AGGREGATE DEPRECIATION		
Acquired	Cost £'000 H	Conversion factor	£ 31.12.X9	Agg dep £'000 H	Conversion factor	Agg dep £ 31.12.X9
1.1.X7	400,000	125	476,190	120,000	125	142,857
		—			—	
		105			105	
30.9.X9	80,000	125	81,967	2,000	125	2,049
		—			—	
		122			122	
	£480,000 H		£558,157 C	£122,000 H		£144,906 C

Stage 4—calculation of CPP profit

PART 1

Calculate *total* CPP profit as a balancing figure.

	£31.12.X9
Increase in shareholders' equity in purchasing power terms at 31.12.X9	
Equity at 31.12.X8	284,165
Equity at 31.12.X9	312,721
Increase	28,556

PART 2
Convert detailed profit and loss account.

	£'000 H	Conversion factor	£'000 31.12.X9
Sales	800,000	125	833,333
		$\frac{120}{}$	
Opening stock	52,000	$\frac{125}{114}$	57,017
Purchases	640,000	$\frac{125}{}$	666,667
		120	
	692,000		723,684
Closing stock	72,000	$\frac{125}{122}$	73,770
Cost of sales	620,000		649,914
Gross profit	180,000		183,419
Depreciation	(40,000)	× 125	(47,619)
		$\frac{105}{}$	
	(2,000)	× 125	(2,049)
		$\frac{122}{}$	
Debenture interest	(10,000)	–	(10,000)
Distribution costs	(6,000)	× 125	(6,250)
		$\frac{120}{}$	
Administrative expenses (57,800 – 42,000)	(15,800)	× 125	(16,458)
		$\frac{120}{}$	
Corporation tax (see note below)	(51,000)	–	(51,000)
Interim dividend	(10,000)	125	(10,417)
		$\frac{120}{}$	
Final dividend	(20,000)	125	(20,000)
		$\frac{125}{}$	
Retained profit for the year	£25,200 H		19,626
Gain on net monetary liabilities (inserted as balancing figures here, but calculated independently in Stage 5)			8,930
Retained 'CPP' profit for the year (calculated in Part 1, above)			£28,556 C

Note: Since the Inland Revenue did not accept CPP basis, no adjustment was required by SSAP 7 to be made to the HCA tax charge.

Stage 5—reconciliation of gain in purchasing power

The figure of £31.12.X9 8,930, calculated as a balancing figure in Stage 4, may be reconciled as follows. The key is to reconcile opening and closing net monetary liability figures.

PART 1
Calculate net monetary liabilities at 31.12.X8 and 31.12.X9 respectively:

	31.12.X8	31.12.X9
	£	£
	H	H
Debentures	200,000	200,000
Current liabilities	119,500	193,800
Debtors	(170,000)	(218,000)
Cash	(8,000)	(1,500)
	£141,500	£174,300

PART 2

	£'000	Conversion	£'000
	H	factor	31.12.X9
Net monetary liabilities at 1.1.X9	(141,500)	125	(153,804)
		115	
		125	
Sales	800,000	125	833,333
		120	
Purchases	(640,000)	125	(666,667)
		120	
Distribution costs	(6,000)	125	(6,250)
		120	
Administrative expenses	(15,800)	120	(16,458)
Debenture interest paid	(10,000)	125	(10,000)
		125	
Purchase of fixed assets	(80,000)	125	(81,967)
		122	
Dividends (interim and final)	(30,000)	Per P/L	(30,417)
Corporation tax	(51,000)	125	(51,000)
		125	
	£174,300		£183,230
	H		C
Net monetary liabilities at 31.12.X9	£174,300		£174,300
	H		C
Gain in purchasing power			£8,930
			C

(3) Presentation of CPP information

The presentation below is typical of that compatible with SSAP 7:

Analysis of gain in purchasing power

	£
	31.12.X9
Gain on long-term liabilities (debentures)	
217,392 – 200,000 (Stage 2)	17,392
Loss on short-term monetary items (balancing figure)	(8,462)
Overall gain	8,930

Information to be presented to the shareholders

(i) Summary of results and financial position, adjusted for changes in the purchasing power of money, of Westbury Traders plc

SUMMARY OF RESULTS

for the year ended 31 December 19X9

	Historical basis		Current purchasing power basis	
	19X8 £'000	19X9 £'000	19X8 £'000	19X9 £'000
Turnover		800,000		833,333
Profit before taxation		106,200		109,973
Taxation		51,000		51,000
Profit after taxation		55,200		58,973
Dividends		30,000		30,417
Retained profit for the year		25,200		28,556
Earnings per ordinary share		36.8 p		39.3 p
Dividend cover (times)		1.8		1.9

(ii) Summary of financial position as at the end of the year

	Historical basis		Current purchasing power basis	
19X8	19X9 £'000	19X8 £'000	19X9 £'000	£'000
Fixed assets less depreciation	320,000	358,000	380,952	413,251
Net current assets	110,500	97,700	120,605	99,470
	430,500	455,700	501,557	512,721
Less debenture capital	200,000	200,000	217,392	200,000
Total equity interest	230,500	255,700	284,165	312,721
Return on total equity interest (%)		21.6		18.9
Net assets per equity share (f)		1.7		2.1

(iii) Notes on the summary of results and financial position adjusted for changes in the purchasing power of money

For the sake of conciseness, this part of the information presented to shareholders has not been reproduced.

However, one important piece of information which should be disclosed is the analysis of the net gain resulting from changes in the purchasing power of money:

	£'000 31.12.X9
(a) on the company's net monetary assets excluding debenture capital	(8,462)
(b) on debenture capital	17,392
Net gain	8,930

(g) Monetary gains and losses

(1) *Monetary losses*

Funds held in the form of monetary assets, for example, cash or debtors, do not keep pace with inflation. Such funds will realise only the amount at which they are stated in the historical cost accounts.

Under CPP accounting, the notional amount by which the value of monetary assets should have to increase to keep pace with inflation is regarded as a monetary loss.

(2) *Monetary gains*

A house owner benefits during a period of inflation in that while the value of the house (a non-monetary asset) increases, the monetary amount of the loan is unaffected by inflation.

CPP regards as a monetary gain the notional amount by which the loan should have increased simply to protect the lender against inflation. This monetary gain is partially offset by the interest on borrowings.

(h) The nature of CPP profit

CPP effectively eliminates the impact of inflation and only includes in CPP profit the gain or loss on monetary items.

Non-monetary assets are assumed to keep pace with inflation and cannot contribute to CPP profit.

CPP profits can arise only from:

(1) trading; and
(2) gains/losses on monetary items.

(i) Advantages of the CPP approach

Professor Myddelton* has judged both CPP and CCA against eight criteria:

(1) Allows for inflation.
(2) Comparable over time.
(3) Objective.
(4) Comprehensive (industry).
(5) Comprehensive (size of firm).
(6) Consistent.
(7) Practically workable.
(8) Acceptable to businessmen.

Professor Myddelton has argued that CPP satisfies all eight criteria. CCA, on the other hand, it is argued, fails to satisfy any.

(j) Criticisms of the CPP approach

Criticisms which have been made include the following:

(1) Suppose a company, financed to a large extent by long-term borrowings, is in a highly illiquid situation. Under CPP, the monetary gains on the long-term borrowings could mean that the company shows a large CPP profit.
    SSAP 7 made the comment:

> ... it has to be appreciated that there may be circumstances in which it will be accompanied by a dangerously illiquid situation or by excessively high gearing, and for this reason any such gain should be shown as a separate figure

and continued:

> It has been argued that the gain on long-term borrowing should not be shown as profit in the supplementary statement because it might not be possible to distribute it without raising additional finance. This argument, however, confuses the measurement of profitability with the measurement of liquidity ...

> SSAP 7 also referred to the fact that it was inconsistent to exclude the gain while at the same time charging to profit and loss accounts the cost of borrowings.

*D R Myddelton *On a Cloth Untrue—Inflation Accounting: The Way Forward* (1984) Woodhead–Faulkner.

(2) Many accountants criticised the supplementary status of the CPP accounts arguing that the presence of two sets of accounts would devalue the impact of the CPP information. However, the same criticism could be made against current cost accounting (CCA) since several of the ASC statements permitted CCA to be presented in supplementary form.

Some proponents of CPP have argued that CPP accounts should form the main statutory accounts.

(3) CPP has been criticised on the grounds that CPP information is of little relevance to the management of the business. CPP converts non-monetary assets such as fixed assets and stock by an adjustment factor based on the retail price index.

Critics of CPP would argue that what is of relevance to management is specific price changes of these non-monetary assets.

(4) The Sandilands Committee report considered there were great conceptual difficulties in grasping the meaning of purchasing power units.

19.6 CURRENT VALUE SYSTEMS

The weaknesses of historical cost accounting were considered in section 19.3. Over the years, accountants have come up with various proposals aimed at overcoming these drawbacks (see 19.4). These proposals have fallen into two main groups:

(a) Current purchasing power accounting (ED 8, SSAP 7), considered in section 19.5.
(b) Current value systems (for example, current cost accounting as proposed by the Sandilands report: ED 18, Hyde Guidelines, ED 24, SSAP 16, ED 35).

Strictly speaking, the term 'current value systems' refers to a family of approaches which includes:

(1) current replacement cost (entry values);
(2) net realisable value (exit values);
(3) economic value;
(4) a mixed system which combines features of (1), (2) and (3).

Current cost accounting (CCA) is an example of a mixed system.

19.7 CURRENT REPLACEMENT COST (ENTRY VALUES)

(a) Main elements

The main elements of current replacement cost (CRC) are as follows:

(1) *Balance sheet*

(i)   Fixed assets—at net current replacement cost (NCRC).
(ii) Stocks—at current replacement cost (CRC).
(iii) Other items—at historical cost.

(2) *Profit and loss account*

(i)   Depreciation charge—based on current replacement cost.
(ii) Cost of sales—based on current replacement cost.
(iii) Other items—at historical cost.

Note: Mixed systems, such as CCA, cover aspects such as monetary working capital adjustment and gearing. These are dealt with in the following chapter, and are not further referred to here.

(b) Terminology

Current replacement cost of stock means the cost at which stock could have been replaced in the normal course of business at the balance sheet date or at the date of sale, whichever is relevant.

For fixed assets, net current replacement cost is calculated by determining gross replacement cost at the balance sheet date, less a proportionate deduction for accumulated depreciation.

(c) Illustration

Green Traders Ltd commenced business on 1.1.X2. On that date the company issued 1,000 shares of £1 each at par. The proceeds were applied as follows:

	£
Fixtures and equipment (estimated life, ten years)	600
Purchase of goods for resale 400 units at £1	400
	1,000

The goods were sold on 30.6.X2 for proceeds of £600. The goods were immediately replaced at a total cost of £480 (ie 400 units at £1.20). These goods were still in stock at the year end 31.12.X2 when their replacement cost was £1.30 per unit.

The gross replacement cost of equipment at the year end was £720. Equipment is depreciated on a straight-line basis assuming nil residual value.

Required: profit and loss account and balance sheets on a replacement cost (entry value) basis.

Calculations

	£
(1) *Goods sold*	
(i) Under HCA, profit is (600 – 400), ie:	200

(ii) Under RCA, the total gain of 200 is analysed between operating profit and *realised* holding gains:

	£
Operating profit = sales – replacement cost of sales = £600 – (400 × £1.20)	120
Realised holding gain = replacement cost at date of sale – historical cost = £480 – £400	80
	200

(2) *Goods unsold*
(i) Under HCA, no account is taken of the increase in replacement cost between 30.6.X2 and 31.12.X2 as the gain is unrealised.
(ii) Under RCA, the increase in replacement cost (400 × £1.30 less 400 × £1.20) ie £40 is classified as an *unrealised* holding gain.

(3) *Fixtures and equipment*
(i) Under HCA, depreciation charge in the profit and loss account is £60. Accounts net book value in the balance sheet £540.
(ii) Under RCA, depreciation charged in the profit and loss account may be based on either average values or year-end values. The average approach is generally to be preferred as the equipment is consumed over a period of one year. RCA depreciation on an average basis is 10% (600 + 720) ie £66.
(iii) Under RCA, net current replacement cost at the balance sheet date is calculated as follows:

	£
GRC	720
Accumulated depreciation (one year)	
$\frac{1}{10} \times 720$	72
NCRC	648

(4) *Replacement reserve*

The replacement reserve will include realised and unrealised holding gains. The movement on the account may be summarised as follows:

	Total	Realised holding gains	Unrealised holding gains
	£	£	£
Goods:			
Sold	80	80	–
Unsold	40		40
Fixed assets:			
Depreciation	6		
(66 – 60)		6	
Net book value at year end	108		
(648 – 540)			108
Totals at 31.12.X2	234	86	148

Replacement cost accounts

(1) PROFIT AND LOSS ACCOUNT

for the year ended 31 December 19X2

	£
Sales	600
Replacement cost of sales	480
Gross profit	120
Depreciation	66
Operating profit	54

(2) BALANCE SHEET

as at 31 December 19X2

	£
Fixtures and equipment	648
Stock	520
Cash	120
	1,288
Ordinary share capital	1,000
Profit and loss account	54
Replacement reserve	234
	1,288

Note: The replacement reserve includes realised holding gains of £86 and unrealised holding gains of £148.

(d) Advantages and disadvantages of the replacement cost approach

(1) *Advantages of RCA*

RCA focuses attention on the effect of price changes on the non-monetary assets of the business.

In the balance sheet, stock is stated at its replacement cost at the balance sheet date. Fixed assets are stated at net current replacement cost. This is effectively the remaining number of years' service potential of the asset measured in terms of current replacement price. The replacement cost balance sheet thus offers an up-to-date measure of resources employed in the business.

Replacement cost profit is arrived at by matching current cost of sales and depreciation against sales. Replacement cost profit offers a far better guide than historical cost profit of the amount a business can distribute to shareholders without impairing its productive capacity or ability to produce goods and services in the future.

The analysis of gains between operating profit and holding gains provides useful information for those who wish to assess the two aspects of a company's performance.

(2) *Disadvantages of RCA*

(i)   RCA does not take account of changes in the purchasing power of money. Unlike CPP, RCA is not a system of accounting for inflation.
(ii) Estimation of current replacement costs at particular dates can involve subjective judgements. It can be argued that this is a cost to be weighed against possible benefits deriving from more useful information than that contained in HCA.
(iii) By itself, RCA is not a comprehensive system of accounting for price changes. For example, it fails to take account of the effect of price changes on monetary items.

19.8   NET REALISABLE VALUE (EXIT VALUES)

(a) Basic approach

Under exit value accounting, balance sheet values are based on the prices which assets such as fixed assets and stocks could obtain if sold in an orderly manner at the balance sheet date. The illustration below sets out a simple approach to exit value accounting.

(b) Illustration

Suppose the following additional information relates to the accounts of Green Traders Ltd:
Net realisable value of fixed assets and stocks at 31.12.X2 were £550 and £700 respectively.
Summarised financial statements would appear as follows:

(1) Revenue statement

	£	£
Realised gross profit (per HCA) (600 – 400)		200
Less depreciation		
NRV at 31.12.X2	550	
Acquisition cost	600	(50)
Add unrealised gain on stock	700	
NRV at 31.12.X2	480	220
HC		
Increase in reserves		370

(2) Balance sheet

	£
Fixtures and equipment	550
Stock	700
Cash	120
	1,370
Ordinary share capital	1,000
Reserves	370
	1,370

(c) Advantages and disadvantages of exit value or net realisable value approach

(1) *Advantages of net realisable value (NRV)*

(i) Net realisable value is a concept which non-accountants find easy to understand.

(ii) If all businesses were to include assets in the balance sheet at net realisable value, accounts would become easier to compare.

(2) *Disadvantages of NRV*

(i) NRV is inconsistent with the going concern concept. For a going concern business, NRV of fixed assets is of little relevance.

(ii) NRV focuses on total gains. It makes no attempt to segregate operating gains (unlike RCA).

(iii) NRV is hardly a practicable concept for the majority of non-monetary assets, as it will often be difficult to determine.

As with RCA, NRV is, by itself, unsatisfactory. However, NRV may provide a useful element of a mixed value system such as that set out in SSAP 16.

19.9 ECONOMIC VALUE METHOD (EV)

(a) General approach

Under the economic value approach, the current value of an individual asset is based on the present value of the future cash flows that are expected to result from ownership of the asset.

To calculate this present value, it is necessary to know the following:

(1) the cash amount of the future benefits;

(2) the timing of these benefits;

(3) an appropriate discount factor, for example, the cost of capital to the company.

(b) Illustration

A company owns a particular item of machinery. At 31.12.X3, the asset is expected to generate the following cash flows (measured in terms of excess of sales over operating costs)

	£
19X4	8,000
19X5	11,000
19X6	12,000

Assuming a cost of capital of 14%, the economic value may be calculated using present value tables:

	Net inflow £	Present value factor	NPV £
19X4	8,000	0.877	7,016
19X5	11,000	0.769	8,459
19X6	12,000	0.675	8,100
Total			23,575

The asset would be stated in the balance sheet at 31.12.X3 as £23,575.

(c) Problems with the EV approach

The EV approach suffers from several practical drawbacks including the following:

(1) The calculations of EV are dependent on the reliability of estimated future cash flows. Estimation of these amounts would give rise to many practical difficulties, and the resulting information would be subjective to an unacceptable extent.
(2) EV can only be applied to the business as a whole. It would be difficult to provide a detailed analysis of profit. Profit would be determined by comparing EVs at successive balance sheet dates and adjusting for capital introduced and dividends.

(d) Relevance of EV approach

As with RCA and NRV, economic value may provide a useful component of a mixed value system.

19.10 MIXED SYSTEMS

(a) The concept of deprival value

The Sandilands Committee Report (1975) recommended an approach to asset valuation based on the concept of value to the business.

Value to the business is effectively the same as deprival value, a term used in earlier accounting literature. The deprival value of an asset is the minimum compensation a business would require if deprived of the use of an asset.

(b) Determination of deprival value

This may be illustrated diagrammatically as follows:

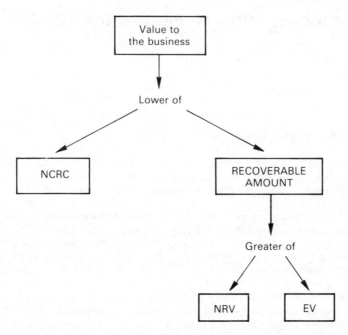

In the majority of cases, the future cash flows (EV) expected to be generated by a fixed asset will exceed its net current replacement cost. If deprived of the asset, the business would simply require sufficient compensation to replace with an equivalent asset (in terms of productive capacity, remaining years' service potential and so on). Value to the business would be NCRC.

However, in restricted cases the amount expected to be recoverable from an asset may be lower than its NCRC. In such a situation, the business would not wish to replace the asset. Minimum compensation required if deprived of the asset would be either expected sales proceeds (NRV) or cash flows that would otherwise have been earned (EV).

(c) Application to the UK

The deprival value concept is embodied in the Handbook of Accounting for the effects of changing prices which is dealt with in the following chapter.

20 ACCOUNTING FOR PRICE CHANGES—2

20.1 BACKGROUND

The term current cost accounting refers to a family of current value techniques which draw mainly upon replacement cost (or entry value) accounting techniques but also, to a lesser extent, net realisable values (exit values) and economic values.

The main pronouncements on CCA were listed in the previous chapter. Clearly there are variations between each, but the purpose of this chapter is to describe in broad terms the mechanics of CCA rather than to examine the various statements.

For this purpose, the discussion will centre around *Accounting for the effects of changing prices: a Handbook* (ASC, 1986) as this represents the current state of play as regards thoughts on CCA.

Readers will be only too aware of the controversies surrounding the subject of accounting for price changes and the failure of the main accountancy bodies to find a solution acceptable to the majority of accountants and key user groups.

20.2 FACTORS AFFECTING THE METHOD OF PROFIT DETERMINATION

The handbook identifies three key factors on which any accounting system is dependent. These are:

(a) the basis of asset valuation (i e historical cost or current cost);
(b) the capital maintenance concept (operating capital maintenance (OCM) or financial capital maintenance (FCM);
(c) unit of measurement (nominal £s or units of constant purchasing power (UCPP).

These three factors can be combined in a number of ways, the main ones of which are:

(1) HC + FCM + £s = historical cost accounting (HCA);
(2) HC + FCM + UCPP = current purchasing power (CPP);
(3) CC + OCM + £ = current cost accounting (CCA);
(4) CC + FCM + £ = real terms version of CCA.

20.3 RECOMMENDATIONS OF THE HANDBOOK

Historical cost accounting is rejected for the reasons stated earlier. Current purchasing power accounting (discussed in chapter 19) is rejected for the main reason that since input prices specific to a particular company may fluctuate independently of general prices indices, CPP asset figures may bear no relationship to current values.

The two methods considered acceptable are:

(a) current cost accounting—operating capital maintenance version;
(b) current cost accounting—real terms version.

Each of these are considered in turn.

20.4 OPERATING CAPITAL MAINTENANCE CONCEPT OF CCA

(a) Operating capability

This concept is based on the entity's operating capability. Operating capability means the amount of goods and services which the business is able to supply in the period with its existing resources. In accounting terms, operating capability is represented by net operating assets of fixed assets and working capital.

The term monetary working capital is defined below, but in broad terms it refers to debtors less creditors.

For a trading company, this may be expressed as follows:

Operating capability	Financing
Fixed assets	Shareholders' funds
Working capital (a) stock (b) monetary working capital	Borrowings

In broad terms, monetary working capital refers to trade debtors less trade creditors. Some accountants, however, do not consider monetary working capital to be part of net operating assets (this is further referred to below in section 20.8(e)).

(b) A key concern in the OCM concept is the effect of input price changes (raw materials, wages, overheads, plant and machinery etc) on the funds required to maintain entity's operating capability.

Input price increases do have funding implications. For example:

(1) A going-concern business will eventually have to replace its fixed assets, even if the form of the replacement assets bears little resemblance to the assets which are being replaced. Replacement costs will inevitably be much greater than historical costs. It is important that sufficient funds are retained within the business as opposed to being paid out as dividends. Historical cost profit is an unreliable measure of the entity's ability to pay out dividends.
(2) Stocks consumed or sold will eventually have to be replaced at prices considerably in excess of original cost.
(3) Entities in a net debtor position (debtors in excess of creditors) will find that an increasing amount of funds must be tied up in debtors simply to maintain in real terms the present level of business operations. Conversely, entities in a net creditor position (for example, supermarkets) may find that higher replacement costs of stock are financed by a semi-automatic increase in creditors.
(4) To the extent that part of the net operating assets are financed by share-holders, additional funds *will* be required. However, to the extent that lenders will fund part of the operating assets, additional replacement costs of fixed assets and stocks may be financed by additional borrowings.

The OCM version of CCA deals with each of the above points by means of a specific adjustment to historical cost profit:

(i) depreciation adjustment (DA);
(ii) cost of sales adjustment (COSA);
(iii) monetary working capital adjustment (MWCA);
(iv) gearing adjustment (GA).

These adjustments are described later in the chapter. Again note that some accountants are opposed to the inclusion of MWCA and GA in a current cost accounting system.

(c) Under some versions of OCM (such as that in SSAP 16), two separate current cost profit figures may be highlighted. The first profit figure considers the viewpoint of the entity, irrespective of how it is financed as between shareholders and lenders of funds. The second takes account of financing and considers the viewpoint of the shareholders.

(1) *Current cost operating profit*

This is the surplus arising from ordinary activities of the business after allowing for the impact of price changes on the funds needed to continue the business and maintain its operating capability. Note that this profit figure is determined before charging interest and tax and takes no account of the way in which operating capability is financed as between shareholders' funds and borrowings.

(2) *Current cost profit on ordinary activities before taxation*

This is the surplus arising after allowing for the impact of price changes on the funds needed to maintain the shareholders' proportion of operating capability. This profit figure is determined after interest and gearing adjustment.

   This may be expressed diagrammatically as follows:

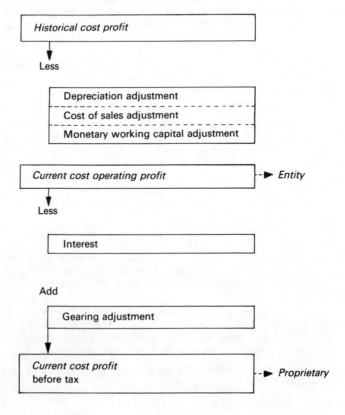

20.5 ILLUSTRATION—PREPARING CURRENT COST ACCOUNTS

The extracts below are taken from the historical cost financial statements of Lynton Traders plc. The current cost calculations will be set out in the following sections and the current cost financial statements summarised in section 20.10(a).

(a) Profit and loss account for the year ended 31 December 19X7

	£	£
Sales		16,500
Opening stock	2,200	
Purchases	12,100	
	14,300	
Closing stock	2,500	
Cost of sales		11,800
Gross profit		4,700
Depreciation		(340)
Operating expenses		(1,080)
Interest payable		(180)
Profit on ordinary activities		3,100
Tax		(1,200)
Profit after tax		1,900
Proposed dividends		(800)
Retained profit		1,100
Balance at 1.1.19X7		5,700
Balance at 31.12.19X7		6,800

(b) Balance sheet at 31 December 19X7

	31.12.X7 £	31.12.X6 £
Land and buildings—cost	7,000	7,000
—depreciation	(200)	(160)
Fixtures and equipment—cost	3,000	3,000
—depreciation	(1,050)	(750)
Stock	2,500	2,200
Debtors	2,900	2,700
Cash	1,700	160
Creditors	(2,050)	(1,800)
Taxation	(1,200)	(1,050)
Dividends	(800)	(600)
6% Loan Stock 19×24	(3,000)	(3,000)
	8,800	7,700
Ordinary share capital	2,000	2,000
Profit and loss account	6,800	5,700
	8,800	7,700

(c) Additional information

(1) Land and buildings were acquired on 1.1.19X3. The split of total cost is estimated as land, £5,000 and buildings, £2,000. Buildings are depreciated at 2% per annum on a straight-line basis.

Estimated open market values on existing use basis are as follows:

	31.12.X7	31.12.X6
	£	£
Land	16,000	14,000
Buildings	6,300	6,000
Total	22,300	20,000

(2) Equipment was acquired on 30.6.19X4 and is depreciated at 10% per annum on a straight-line basis. Suitable government-produced indices for CCA purposes are as follows:

30.6.19X4	122
31.12.19X6	153
Average 19X7	163
31.12.19X7	173

(3) Stock, debtors and creditors at each balance sheet date are estimated to have an age of two months. Suitable indices are:

31.10.19X6	132
31.12.19X6	134
Average 19X7	140
31.10.19X7	144
31.12.19X7	146

(4) During 19X7, the retail price index showed the following:

31.12.19X6	124
Average 19X7	131
31.12.19X7	138

(5) The company has produced supplementary current cost accounts since 19X3.

At 31.12.19X6, the balance on current cost reserve was £14,684 (£920 realised, £13,764 unrealised).

(6) Deferred tax and ACT on proposed dividends have been ignored.

Note: All individual calculations will be made to the nearest £. In practice, of course, it is important to avoid the impression of spurious accuracy when much of CCA relies on subjective judgement.

20.6 FIXED ASSETS AND DEPRECIATION

(a) Basic aims

The profit and loss account is charged with a current rate for services provided (i e use of asset) during the period. The balance sheet shows the current cost of purchasing the asset's remaining service potential (i e remaining number of years of useful life).

(b) CCA balance sheet

Fixed assets should be stated at value to the business (i e the deprival value concept referred to in the previous chapter).

Value to the business may usefully be described diagrammatically as follows:

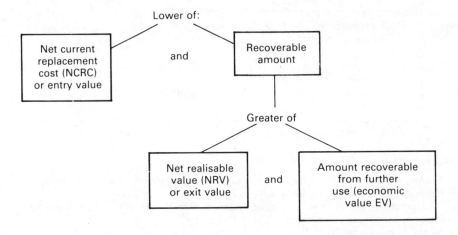

In most situations, value to the business will be represented by NCRC. Recoverable amount may be appropriate in restricted cases, e g:

(1) A group of assets is losing money i e operating costs exceed revenues. There is no prospect of improvement. The company's best option is to sell the assets as soon as possible. NRV is the appropriate basis.

(2) A group of assets is suffering from declining revenues. In two years' time, operating costs are expected to exceed operating revenues. The company has no intention of replacing the assets. However, at the present time, the company is better off continuing to use the assets (and earning cash flows i e economic value) rather than selling the assets immediately. Economic value is the appropriate basis.

(c) Calculating value to the business

Assume that net realisable value and economic value are not appropriate in any of the situations below.

(1) *Non-specialised land and buildings*

Value to the business can only be determined by specific valuation (i e open market value, existing use basis) as location is the main factor affecting valuation. Index numbers are inappropriate. Non-specialised land and buildings include shops, offices, showrooms and general purpose industrial units.

Illustration

The appropriate figures for Lynton at each year end would be as follows:

	£
31.12.X7	22,300
31.12.X6	20,000

(2) *Specialised land and buildings*

This would include specialised chemical factories, oil refineries, power stations and so on. Value to the business would be determined in two stages.

(i) Determine open market value of land using specific valuation techniques, and *add*:

(ii) depreciated replacement cost of buildings. The calculation is similar to that for plant and machinery (see below):

> (1) First calculate GRC using construction index numbers:
>
> $$HC \times \frac{\text{Index at B/S date}}{\text{Index at acquisition}} = GRC$$
>
> (2) Then deduct proportionate accumulated depreciation.

(3) *Plant and machinery*

Ideally, NCRC should be calculated using direct valuation techniques (specific valuation, quotation, supplier's price list).

In practice, government-produced index numbers (e g PINCCA, Price Index Number for Current Cost Accounting) are used.
NCRC is calculated as follows:

> | | £ |
> |---|---|
> | (1) Calculate GRC | |
> | *Historical cost* $\times \dfrac{\text{index at B/S date}}{\text{index at acquisition}}$ | A |
> | *(2) Deduct accumulated depreciation* | B |
> | | C |

Illustration

Using figures for Lynton, the respective CCA balance sheet figures would be calculated as follows:

	31.12.X7 £	31.12.X6 £
Gross replacement cost:		
$£3,000 \times \dfrac{153}{122}$		3,762
$£3,000 \times \dfrac{173}{122}$	4,254	
Accumulated depreciation:		
$£750 \times \dfrac{153}{122}$		941
$£1,050 \times \dfrac{173}{122}$	1,489	
	2,765	2,821

(d) Depreciation charge

The depreciation charge in the profit and loss account should be based on the value to the business of assets consumed during the year. This approach will be followed here. However it should be noted that some accountants regard a depreciation charge based on year end GRC as a reasonable approximation.

The depreciation adjustment (sometimes referred to as additional depreciation) is the difference between historical cost depreciation charge and the current cost depreciation charge.

The *amount* of the depreciation adjustment has no significance. For example, a company which adopts a modified historical cost convention may need only a relatively small depreciation adjustment. What *is* important is the size of the current cost operating profit after a full current cost depreciation charge has been allowed for.

Illustration

Using the information on Lynton, the calculation of the depreciation charge may be approached in two stages:

(1) Fixtures and equipment

The depreciation adjustment will be calculated using index numbers:

	£
Historical cost depreciation 10% × £3,000	300
Index number at acquisition 122	
Average index for 19X7 163	
Current cost depreciation	
$£300 \times \dfrac{163}{122}$	401
So depreciation adjustment is	101

(2) Land and buildings

As the land and buildings are non-specialised index numbers are inappropriate. Also depreciation relates to the buildings element only.

	£
Historical depreciation	
2% × £2,000	40

Current cost depreciation based on 31.12.X6 values

OMV at 31.12.X6

Remaining years' life i e $\dfrac{£6,000}{46 \text{ years}}$ =	130

Current cost depreciation based on 31.12.X7 values

OMV at 31.12.X7

Remaining years' life i e $\dfrac{£6,300}{45 \text{ years}}$ =	140

Current cost depreciation based on average values	
$\frac{1}{2}(130+140)$ i e	135
HC depreciation	40
Depreciation adjustment	95

(3) Summary

Depreciation adjustment:	
Fixtures and equipment	101
Land and buildings	95
Total	196

20.7 STOCKS AND THE COST OF SALES ADJUSTMENT

(a) Basic aims

The CCA profit should be determined by matching sales with cost of sales measured in current value terms and not historical cost terms. Stocks should usually be stated in the balance sheet at current replacement cost (entry value).

(b) CCA balance sheet

Stocks should be stated at the lower of:

Current replacement cost (entry value);
and
Net realisable value (exit value).

The term current replacement cost means the cost at which the stock item could have been replaced (either by purchase or by manufacture) in the normal course of business at the valuation date. Valuation date may, of course, refer either to the date of sale or the balance sheet date.

(c) Determination of CRC

CRC may be calculated by any of a number of methods. The method chosen will depend on the nature and size of the business and its accounting systems.
   Possible approaches include:

(1) suppliers' price list or quotation;
(2) stock or costing records;
(3) index numbers:

   (i) produced in-house;
   (ii) published by the government (PINCCA, Price Index Numbers for Current Cost Accounting).

Illustration

Assuming the index number approach is acceptable, CRC may be calculated as follows:

$$CRC = HC \times \frac{\text{index at valuation date}}{\text{index at acquisition}}$$

(d) CCA profit and loss account

A principal objective of CCA is to match sales revenue with the current (i e up-to-date) costs of earning that revenue.

Illustration

A wholesaler buys 100 Wods on 1 January 19X4 at a cost of 120p each. He sells the entire stock on 31 January for proceeds of 180p at which date the replacement cost of each Wod has risen to 135p.
   Historical cost profit is £180 − £120 = £60.
   Under CCA, this is analysed between:

		£
(1) Operating profit:		
Sales less current cost of sales		
i e (180 − 135)		45
(2) Holding gain (realised):		
Replacement cost at date		
of sale	135	
Historical cost	120	15
	——	——
		60
		==

In the terminology for SSAP 16, the realised holding gain of £15 is referred to as a cost of sales adjustment (COSA).

Supplementary CCA information could be presented as follows:

	£
Historical cost profit	60
Cost of sales adjustment	15
Current operating profit	45

The current cost operating profit offers a better guide to dividend policy than the equivalent historical cost profit. For example, if the business used £45 out of the proceeds of sale of £180, there would still be £135 left to finance replacement of 100 Wods at 135p. Capital (in terms of operating capability) would have been kept intact in real terms.

In principle, the cost of sales adjustment (COSA) should be calculated separately for each individual transaction and then aggregated to determine the COSA for the business as a whole. In practice, this approach is not necessarily feasible or necessary and a number of short-cut methods are available which offer reasonably acceptable approximations.

(e) Methods of calculating COSA

The following are examples of the main approaches:

(1) Determination of actual costs incurred at the valuation date (e g where a business possesses a computerised stock system).
(2) Suppliers' price lists—a time-consuming approach which might be practicable for high-value items.
(3) Indices applied to historical costs.
(4) Standard costs.
(5) Last-in-first-out—for the purposes of profit determination, LIFO may give a reasonable approximation to current costs. However, the LIFO balance sheet stock figure will need to be updated to current costs.
(6) Price indices used together with the averaging method (advocated by the Sandilands Committee Report).

(f) Averaging method

The averaging method assumes that purchases, sales and price increases occur evenly through the period. It is important that the prices indices selected for this method reflect the purchasing experience of the company. The method also requires that historical cost stock figures are determined on a FIFO or average cost basis.

The calculations are illustrated using the figures from Lynton Traders. It is assumed that the above assumptions are valid for the whole year.

Illustration

The relevant part of the HCA profit and loss account of Lynton Traders is:

	£	£
Sales		16,500
Opening stock	2,200	
Purchases	12,100	
	14,300	
Closing stock	2,500	
Cost of sales		11,800
Gross profit		4,700

A problem with HCA is that cost of sales do not reflect price levels ruling at the date of sale.
  Both sales and purchases are stated in prices which represent a spread throughout the
year. However, both opening and closing stock are stated in terms of prices which obtained
two months before each year end. If both opening and closing stocks are restated in terms of
average prices for the year, an approximate figure of current costs of sales may be calculated.

	HCA £	Adjustment factor	Adjusted for CCA £
Sales	16,500	—	16,500
Opening stock	2,200	140	2,333
		132	
Purchases	12,100	—	12,100
	14,300		14,433
Closing stock	2,500	140	2,430
		144	
Cost of sales	11,800		12,003
Gross profit/operating profit	4,700		4,497

Cost of sales adjustment = current cost of sales less historical cost of sales
$$= £12,003 - £11,800$$
$$= £203$$

Since neither sales nor purchases affect the calculation of COSA, COSA may be determined
in a more compact way:

	HCA £	Adjustment factor	Adjusted for CCA £
Opening stock	2,200	140	2,333
		132	
Closing stock	2,500	140	2,430
		144	
Increase (decrease) in stock	300		97

The amount by which closing stock exceeds opening stock (£300) could reflect either or
both of two factors—different physical quantities or the fact that the cost per unit of closing
stock is higher than the equivalent figure for opening stock.
  However, the comparison of £2,333 and £2,430 is in terms of price levels at the same date
(i e mid-year prices) and thus reflects different stock volumes in real terms.

COSA   = total stock – volume stock = 300 – 97 = 203
(price effect)   change   change

Two additional points may be noted:

(1) Neither of the adjusted stock figures may be used for CCA balance sheet purposes since
    they do not represent current costs ruling at the balance sheet dates.
(2) If the assumptions referred to earlier are not valid for the year as a whole, it may be
    possible to show they are valid for shorter periods. For example, suppose a company
    can satisfy the conditions for three-month periods, it could calculate four separate
    quarterly COSA calculations and then aggregate them for the year as a whole.

(g) CCA balance sheet

As explained in section (c), if the index number approach is adopted, CRC at the year end may be calculated as follows:

$$CRC = HC \times \frac{\text{Index at year end}}{\text{Index at acquisition}}$$

Illustration

For Lynton Traders the calculations are as follows:

	31.12.X7	31.12.X6
	£	£
HC	2,500	2,200
CRC		
£2,200 × 134/132		2,233
£2,500 × 146/144	2,535	

It is assumed that at both balance sheet dates, NRV is in excess of CRC.

20.8 MONETARY WORKING CAPITAL

(a) Basic aims

The term monetary working capital is defined in (b), below. In broad terms, monetary working capital (MWC) is the excess of trade debtors over trade creditors. Some businesses, for example, supermarkets, have an excess of creditors over debtors. Monetary working capital may thus represent net assets or net liabilities.

For businesses which buy and sell on credit terms, MWC is an important part of their operating capability. For businesses in a net debtor position, a rise in the price of inputs (wages, materials etc) during the year will mean that additional funds must be tied up in MWC if the business is not to reduce in size.

This is not simply a problem for manufacturing and trading companies. A service company, for example, an engineering consultancy firm, will have considerable funds tied up in debtors and unbilled work. If the payroll costs during the year increase by 10% and fees are accordingly increased, the level of year-end debtors will also need to be allowed to increase. The monetary increase in debtors does not represent an increase in real terms. However, the increase does place an imposition on funds which might otherwise have been used for an alternative purpose.

The monetary working capital adjustment (MWCA) represents the amount of additional (or reduced, in the case of a net creditor position) finance needed for monetary working capital as a result of changes in input prices of goods and services. It is important to appreciate that the MWCA is regarded as a funding adjustment.

(b) Definition of monetary working capital

Monetary working capital may be defined as the net aggregate of the following items:

(1) Trade debtors, prepayments and trade bills receivable.
(2) Certain special categories of stocks where a cost of sales adjustment is regarded as inappropriate.
(3) Trade creditors, accruals and trade bills payable.

NOTES
(1) In most cases, cash and overdrafts are classified as borrowings and taken into account in arriving at the gearing adjustment

(2) Hire-purchase and leasing obligations, ACT, MCT and deferred tax are regarded as borrowings and not monetary working capital

(c) Current cost profit and loss account

The MWCA must be taken into account in arriving at current cost operating profit. Any method of calculating MWCA which achieves the objectives referred to in (a) above is acceptable.

However, in practice the averaging method is usually adopted. The calculations for the averaging method are similar to those for the cost of sales adjustment (COSA). The price indices used to calculate COSA are normally used also to determine MWCA.

Illustration

In the case of Lynton Traders, MWC at each balance sheet date is as follows:

	31.12.X7 £	31.12.X6 £
Debtors	2,900	2,700
Creditors	(2,050)	(1,800)
MWC	850	900

Since both debtors and creditors have an average age of two months, the calculations may be based on net MWC. Where ageings of debtors and creditors differ significantly, separate calculations should be carried out and the results combined.

Using the averaging method, MWCA may be determined as follows:

	HCA £	Adjustment factor	Adjusted for CCA £
Opening MWC	900	140	954
		132	
Closing MWC	850	140	826
		144	
Increase (decrease) in MWC	(50)		(128)

MWCA (price effect) = total MWC change − volume MWC change
= −50 − (−128)
= £78

Since the company is in a net debtor position, MWCA of £78 is a deduction in arriving at current cost operating profit.

For companies in a net creditor position, assuming prices are rising throughout the year, MWCA is added in arriving at current cost operating profit.

(d) Current cost balance sheet

All monetary items are stated in the CCA balance sheet at the same amounts as in the HCA balance sheet.

(e) Criticisms of the MWCA

Paragraph 3.11 of the Handbook states that '... the treatment of monetary working capital remains the subject of much debate. This is because some commentators do not view the allowance as being consistent with the operating capital maintenance concept. Some do not consider monetary working capital to be part of net operating assets'.

20.9 GEARING ADJUSTMENT

(a) Basic aims

Part of the operating capability of a business is financed by borrowings. The interest cost of these borrowings is charged to profit and loss account.

During a period of rising prices, the non-monetary assets (fixed assets, stocks) financed by these borrowings increase in monetary amount, while the amount of the loans remains unchanged. The HCA profit and loss account fails to reflect the gains even though interest is charged.

Some accountants consider that in an OCM system, a gearing adjustment is required. However, the Handbook refers to two types of gearing adjustments and each of these will be discussed below. Note that as under MWCA, some accountants are opposed to any concept of gearing adjustment (see below).

(b) Type 1 gearing adjustment

This version of the gearing adjustment indicates the benefit (assuming rising prices) to shareholders which is realised in the period measured by the extent to which a proportion of net operating assets are financed by borrowings.

The overall effect of depreciation adjustment, COSA and MWCA is to recognise the funding implications of increased replacement costs. However, these adjustments are concerned with the entity as a whole and take no account of the way in which the operating capability (or net operating assets) is financed as between shareholders and borrowings.

To the extent that part is financed by borrowings, part of the above adjustments are not regarded as necessary in determining the position as regards the shareholders (the proprietary aspect).

(c) Type 2 gearing adjustment

This may be regarded as those parts of the total adjustments made to allow for the impact of price changes on the net operating assets, including the net surplus on the revaluations of assets arising during the period, that may be regarded as associated with items that are financed by borrowings.

(d) Definitions

For the purpose of measuring the two different gearing adjustments the definitions of borrowings and shareholders' funds are important.

These may be related to a current cost balance sheet as follows:

Operating capability	Financing
Fixed assets (Including trade investments, associated companies, intangibles)	*Shareholders' funds* • Ordinary share capital • Preference share capital • Reserves (adjusted to take account of restatement of fixed assets and stocks from HC to CC) • Proposed dividends • Minority interest
Working capital	
Stocks	*Net borrowings* • Loans and debentures • Overdraft (cash) (unless included within MWC) • Tax liabilities, deferred tax • Hire-purchase and leasing obligations • (Marketable securities)
Monetary working capital	

(e) Type 1 gearing adjustment calculation

There are three main stages to the calculation:

(1) Determine average gearing ratio:

$$\frac{\text{average net borrowings}}{\text{average net borrowings} + \text{average shareholders funds on CCA basis.}}$$

At this stage, a detailed analysis of shareholders' funds is not yet possible as the CCA profit and loss account has not been completed.

(2) Summarise current cost operating adjustments.

```
COSA
MWCA
DA
```

(3) Apply average gearing ratio to current cost operating adjustments.

Illustration

Using information from Lynton Traders:

	19X7 £	19X6 £
Net borrowings		
Loan stock	3,000	3,000
Taxation	1,200	1,050
Cash	(1,700)	(160)
Totals	2,500	3,890

Shareholders' funds
Per HCA B/S

OSC	2,000	2,000
P/L	6,800	5,700

Restatement of non-monetary
assets from HC to CC:

Stock

(2,535 – 2,500)	35	
(2,233 – 2,200)		33

Land and buildings

(22,300 – 6,800)	15,500	
(20,000 – 6,840)		13,160

Fixtures and equipment

(2,765 – 1,950)	815	
(2,821 – 2,250)		571
	25,150	21,464

Average net borrowings $= \frac{1}{2}(2,500 + 3,890)$
$\qquad\qquad\qquad = 3,195$

Average shareholders' funds $= \frac{1}{2}(25,150 + 21,464)$
$\qquad\qquad\qquad\qquad = £23,307$

Average gearing ratio $= \dfrac{3,195}{3,195 + 23,307} \times 100$

	12.1%

Current cost operating adjustments

Depreciation adjustment	196
Cost of sales adjustment	203
Monetary working capital adjustment	78
	477

$\therefore$ Gearing adjustment
$\quad = 12.1\% \times £477 = £58$

20.10 CURRENT COST FINANCIAL STATEMENTS

The information below is presented in summarised form. For the purposes of illustration a current cost balance sheet has been presented although this is not strictly necessary for presentation purposes.

(a) Current cost profit and loss account for the year ended 31 December 19X7

	£	£
Turnover		16,500
Profit before interest and taxation		
on the historical cost basis		3,280
Current cost operating adjustments		
Depreciation adjustment	196	
Cost of sales adjustment	203	
Monetary working capital adjustment	78	
		477
Current cost operating profit		2,803
Gearing adjustment	(58)	
Interest payable	180	122

Current cost profit before tax	2,681
Taxation	1,200
Current cost profit for the financial year	1,481
Dividends	800
Retained current cost profit for the year	681
Retained current cost profit B/F	4,780
Retained current cost profit C/F	5,461
Retained current cost profit of the year	681
Retained current cost profit B/F	4,780
Retained current cost profit C/F	5,461

(b) Current cost balance sheet at 31 December 19X7

	£	£
Fixed assets		
Land and buildings		22,300
Fixtures and equipment		2,765
		25,065
Current assets		
Stock	2,535	
Debtors	2,900	
Cash	1,700	
	7,135	
Current liabilities		
Creditors	2,050	
Taxation	1,200	
Dividends	800	
	4,050	
Net current assets		3,085
Total assets less current liabilities		28,150
Loan stock 19X24		(3,000)
		25,150
Ordinary share capital		2,000
Profit and loss account		5,461
Current cost reserve		17,689
		25,150

(c) Movement on current cost reserve

	Total £	Unrealised £	Realised £
Balance at 1.1.X7	14,684	13,764	920
Depreciation adjustment	—	(196)	196
Cost of sales adjustment	—	(203)	203
Monetary working capital adjustment	78		78
Gearing adjustment	(58)		(58)
Revaluation surpluses reflecting price changes:			
Fixed assets	2,780	2,780	—
Stock	205	205	
Balance at 31.12.X7	17,689	16,350	1,339

Workings

(1) *Retained current cost profit brought forward*

	£
Per historical cost accounts	5,700
Less current cost adjustments charged to CCA profit and loss a/cs of previous years (= realised element of opening balance on CCR)	920
	4,780

(2) *Reconciliation of unrealised element of opening balance on current cost reserve*

(i) Restatement of opening fixed assets from HC to CC:

	Fixtures and equipment £	Land and buildings £	Total £
HCA	2,250	6,840	9,090
CCA	2,821	20,000	22,821
Restatement	571	13,160	13,731

(ii) Restatement of opening stocks from HC to CC:

HCA		2,200	
CCA		2,233	
Restatement			33
Total			13,764

(3) *Reconciliation of unrealised element of closing balance on current cost reserve*

(i) Restatement of closing fixed assets from HC to CC:

	Fixtures and equipment £	Land and buildings £	Total £
HCA	1,950	6,800	8,750
CCA	2,765	22,300	25,065
Restatement	815	15,500	16,315

(ii) Restatement of closing stock from HC to CC:

HCA	2,500	
CCA	2,535	
		35
Total		16,350

(4) *Revaluation surpluses reflecting price changes*

	Fixed assets £	Stock £	Total £
Opening assets	13,731	33	13,764
Closing assets	16,315	35	16,350
Increase (decrease)	2,584	2	2,586
DA/COSA	196	203	399
Movement during year	2,780	205	2,985

(d) Type 2 gearing adjustment

Under this alternative, the gearing adjustment is defined as those parts of the total adjustments made to allow for the impact of price changes on the net operating assets, including the net surplus on the revaluation of assets arising during the period, that may be regarded as associated with items that are financed by net borrowings.

Illustration

Using the figures from Lynton Traders:
Gearing ratio: 12.1%

	£
Total adjustments:	
Net surplus on revaluation of:	
Fixed assets (see 20.10(c))	2,780
Stocks (see 20.10(c))	205
MWCA	78
	3,063

Gearing adjustment
= 12.1% × £3,061
= £370

Note that the difference between the two measurements of gearing adjustment is one of timing. The type 1 adjustment follows the prudence concept and only counts realised gains. By contrast, the type 2 adjustment applies the gearing adjustment to all gains arising during the period whether realised or unrealised.

Eventually all unrealised gains become realised as an asset is depreciated or sold.

20.11   OCM—FURTHER CONSIDERATIONS

(a) Current cost balance sheet

SSAP 16 and previous statements required the presentation of a current cost balance sheet. Some users apparently took the view that a CCA balance sheet represented the value of the business. For this reason a current cost balance sheet is no longer required. Selected information, however, regarding the value to the business of year end stocks and fixed assets may assist analysts.

(b) Criticisms of the gearing adjustment

Criticisms fall into two groups:

(1) Those accountants who disagreed with the gearing adjustment required by SSAP 16 (the type 1 adjustment). They considered that the type 1 adjustment failed to bring into the profit and loss account all the benefits of gearing even though interest was charged in full. This criticism related to the timing of the recognition of gearing benefits. All benefits would eventually be recognised under a type 1 gearing adjustment once an asset was sold or depreciated.

This criticism was essentially answered by the type 2 gearing adjustment outlined in the Handbook.

(2) Those accountants who rejected altogether the concept of a gearing adjustment (and presumably the MWCA as well!). In their view the correct response to the problem of monetary items was to deal with the matter under the concept of financial capital maintenance (the real terms system). This is considered in section 20.12.

20.12   THE REAL TERMS VERSION OF CCA

(a) Introduction

This version of CCA refers to a system of accounting for the effects of changing prices which measures whether a company's financial capital (shareholders' funds) is maintained in real terms. Assets are measured at current cost.

(b) Real terms profit

The measurement of real terms profit involves the following four stages:

(1) calculate shareholders' funds at the beginning of the period (based on current cost asset values);
(2) restate (1) in terms of £s of the reporting date (i e multiply by factor RPI at end of period divided by RPI at beginning);
(3) calculate shareholders' funds at the end of the period (again based on current cost asset values);
(4) compare (3) with (2) to determine whether a real term profit has been made (allow for capital introduced, capital withdrawn and dividends).

(c) A simple layout

The calculation of total real gains is illustrated by reference to Lynton Traders (see section 20.5). Assume additionally that the increase in the Retail Price Index during the year amounted to 5%.

Unrealised holding gains during the year were calculated in section 20.10(c) (4) and amounted to:

	£
Stock	2
Fixed assets	2,584
	2,586

The inflation adjustment to shareholders' funds is 5% of £21,464 (see section 20.9 (e) (3)) i e £1,073. Total real gains may be calculated as follows:

	£	£
Historical cost profit (before tax)		3,100
Add: unrealised holding gains during the year	2,586	
Less: inflation adjustment to shareholders' funds	1,073	
Real holding gains		1,513
Total real gains		4,613

(d) A more comprehensive layout

This layout has the advantage of presenting within the same statement both current cost operating profit (which is useful where the concept of operating capital maintenance *is* relevant to a particular company) and total real gains.

Using the data from Lynton Traders the comprehensive layout of real terms system profit and loss would be as follows:

	£	£
Sales		16,500
Less: Cost of goods sold	11,800	
Cost of sales adjustment	203	
Depreciation	340	
Depreciation adjustment	196	
Other expenses	1,080	(13,619)
Current cost operating profit		2,881
Less: Loan interest		(180)
Current cost profit		2,701
Add: Realised holding gains		
Cost of sales adjustment	203	
Depreciation adjustment	196	
	399	
Unrealised holding gains	2,586	2,985
Total gains		5,686
Less: inflation adjustment to shareholders' funds		1,073
Total real gains		4,613

Note: Unlike the OCM version of this example, no adjustments for MWCA and gearing adjustment have been made. The Handbook states that both these adjustments are inconsistent with the approach to monetary items implicit in the financial capital maintenance concept.

20.13   CHOOSING A CAPITAL MAINTENANCE CONCEPT

In general terms the Handbook regards both the OCM and real terms version of CCA as generally acceptable. However, for particular types of companies and particular users, one approach may be preferable to the other.

The table below sets out some general pointers. Note that in situations where the OCM concept may be appropriate, the equivalent information (except for gearing adjustment and MWCA) may be available in the comprehensive layout of the real terms system.

Criteria	OCM concept of CCA	Real terms version of CCA
TYPE OF BUSINESS	OCM is appropriate to companies with an easily definable operating capability.	(1) Real-terms is also appropriate to this type of company provided comprehensive layout used. (2) Useful for businesses without an easily definable operating capability – value based companies (e g investment companies) – commodity traders – construction companies (unique contracts)
USER GROUP (a) shareholders (b) management (c) employees	OCM may be relevant to users who are concerned with the ability of the business to produce similar quantities of goods and services in the future	Real terms version may be more appropriate (purchasing power of equity) Real terms may also be useful provided comprehensive layout used.

20.14   CRITICISMS OF CCA

Many of the earlier criticisms of CCA were aimed at specific statements such as SSAP 16 and ED 35. ASC attempted to defuse the situation by the publication in 1986 of the Handbook on Accounting for the effects of changing prices pending the issue of a new exposure draft (which so far has not yet appeared).

Subject to this some of the criticisms made, (including those referring to practical considerations) included:

(a) the failure of any CCA system to attract widespread support from industrial and commercial accountants, auditors and businessmen;
(b) the fact that many accountants considered CCA systems to rely to an unreasonable extent on subjective judgements;
(c) the problems experienced by particular industries, such as shipping and commodity brokers and the failure to extend CCA to value-based companies (note the real terms system above);
(d) the fact that CCA is not a system of accounting for inflation. Under CCA, successive balance sheets are stated in terms of £s of different purchasing powers and are thus not directly comparable;
(e) many accountants never really accepted the theoretical basis of the MWCA and gearing adjustments (again note the real terms system);
(f) many accountants were unconvinced that any benefits claimed for CCA were more than outweighted by preparation and audit costs.

In the light of the reactions to SSAP 16 and ED 35, the ASC clearly has a difficult task ahead in formulating an exposure draft which is both seen to be generally acceptable and at the same time worthwhile in terms of usefulness of information to users.

The ASC's task has not been made any easier by the lower levels of inflation experienced in the mid-1980's. To some accountants this in itself is sufficient reason for 'shelving' the issue of price change accounting. It should be pointed out that many experts take strong issue with this viewpoint!

21 ANALYSIS OF ACCOUNTS—1: FUNDS FLOW STATEMENTS

21.1 FUNDS FLOW CONCEPTS

(a) Terminology

Funds statements may be referred to by the following terms:

(1) funds flow statements;
(2) source and application of funds statements;
(3) movement of funds statements;
(4) statement of changes in financial position.

(b) The need for funds statements

The profit and loss account shows the amount of profit during the year and the way in which it arose. The balance sheets at the beginning and end of the year show the disposition of the company's resources at those dates. However, the balance sheet and profit and loss account do not identify the movements in assets and liabilities during the year, and the effect on net liquid funds. By providing an overall picture of the changes in a company's financial position over the year, a funds statement gives a fuller understanding of a company's affairs.

The funds statement is essentially a selection reclassification and summarisation of information contained in the profit and loss account and the balance sheet(s). The funds statement is not intended as a substitute for those financial statements. Instead the funds statement provides an important link between the balance sheet at the beginning of the period, the profit and loss account for the period and the balance sheet at the end of the period. This link is illustrated in the diagram below which summarises some of the main changes in financial position.

CHANGES IN FINANCIAL POSITION DURING THE YEAR

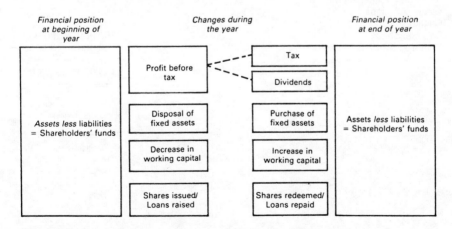

The principal objectives of the various financial statements are summarised in chapter 6 (section 6.7(k)).

(c) What are funds?

There is no single unique definition of funds. Possible funds concepts include:

(1) the cash concept—where the term is restricted to cash and bank balances;
(2) net liquid funds—which includes cash and cash equivalents (see section 21.2(b), below);
(3) working capital concept—which includes cash, debtors, stock less creditors.

Funds statements of UK companies tend to emphasise either (2) or (3). For certain users however, a concept based on (1) may be useful.

(d) Funds statement formats

In theory, formats chosen may relate to a direct or indirect approach. Under a direct approach, sales income and related expenses are separately identified.

Under an indirect approach, the statement usually commences with net profit or net income. Three possible layouts under the indirect approach include:

(1) balanced form layout;
(2) remainder type layout;
(3) reconciling type layout.

Each of these is illustrated using the example below:

Illustration 1

The balance sheets of Bamford Ltd at 31.12.X3 and 31.12.X2 were as follows:

	31.12.X3	31.12.X2
	£	£
Tangible fixed assets—freehold property	301,000	391,000
Tangible fixed assets—plant and machinery	225,600	160,200
Stock	520,000	440,000
Debtors	83,100	53,100
Cash	70,300	1,700
Investment in Upton Ltd	200,000	–
	1,400,000	1,046,000
Called-up share capital	150,000	100,000
Profit and loss account	615,000	405,000
Share premium account	100,000	–
Long-term loans	–	170,000
Creditors	65,000	51,000
Corporation tax	350,000	230,000
Proposed dividends	120,000	90,000
	1,400,000	1,046,000

Additional information

(1) *Extracts from profit and loss account for year ended 31 December 19X3*

	£	£
Profit on ordinary activities before tax		760,000
Corporation tax		350,000
Profit on ordinary activities after tax		410,000
Dividends on ordinary shares		
Interim (paid)	80,000	
Final (proposed)	120,000	200,000
Retained profit		210,000
Balance at 1.1.X3		405,000
Balance at 31.12.X3		615,000

(2) During the year, depreciation charged on plant and machinery amounted to £16,400. There were no disposals of plant and machinery.

(2) Freehold property with a net book value at sale of £90,000 was sold for net book value.

(4) The investment in Upton Ltd is held as a fixed asset investment.

(e) Balanced form layout

Sources of funds	£
Profit before tax	760,000
Depreciation	16,400
Sales of fixed assets	90,000
Issue of shares	150,000
Increase in creditors	14,000
	1,030,400

Application of funds	
Purchase of fixed assets	81,800
Loans repaid	170,000
Purchase of investments	200,000
Tax paid	230,000
Dividends paid	170,000
Increase in stocks	80,000
Increase in debtors	30,000
Increase in cash	68,600
	1,030,400

Workings

(1) Purchase of plant

NBV B/F	160,200
Additions (balancing figure)	81,800
Depreciation	(16,400)
NBV C/F	225,600

(2) *Dividends paid*

Proposed 19X2	90,000
Interim 19X3	80,000
	170,000

(f) Remainder type

	£	£
Profit before tax		760,000
Depreciation		16,400
		776,400
Issue of shares	150,000	
Sale of fixed assets	90,000	240,000
		1,016,400
Purchase of fixed assets	81,800	
Purchase of investment	200,000	
Loans repaid	170,000	
Tax paid	230,000	
Dividends paid	170,000	(851,800)
Increase in working capital		164,600
Increase in stocks	80,000	
Increase in debtors	30,000	
(Increase) in creditors	(14,000)	
Increase in cash	68,600	164,600

This type of layout is preferred by SSAP 10 (see section 21.2).

(g) Reconciling type format

Suppose the aim is to emphasise changes in the cash balance:

		£
Cash at 1.1.X3		1,700
Add sources of funds		
Profit before tax	760,000	
Depreciation	16,400	
	776,400	
Issue of shares	150,000	
Sale of fixed assets	90,000	1,016,400
Less applications of funds		1,018,100
Purchase of fixed assets	81,800	
Purchase of investments	200,000	
Loans repaid	170,000	
Tax paid	230,000	
Dividends paid	170,000	

Stocks	80,000		
Debtors	30,000		
Creditors	(14,000)	96,000	947,800
Cash at 31.12.X3			70,300

21.2   REQUIREMENTS OF SSAP 10

(a) General objectives

A funds statement (or statement of source and application of funds) should show the sources from which funds have flowed into the company and the way in which they have been used.

The following additional considerations should also be noted:

(1) the statement should distinguish between long-term and short-term items;
(2) the statement should distinguish between funds used to acquire fixed assets and those used to increase the working capital of the company;
(3) there should be a minimum of netting off, eg purchases and sales of fixed assets should be disclosed in separate parts of the funds statement.
(4) figures in the funds statement should be capable of reconciliation with related items in the balance sheet or profit and loss account. Where adjustments to published figures are necessary, details should be given by way of note to the funds statement.

(b) Terminology

SSAP 10 provides only one definition, namely net liquid funds. These are defined as: cash at bank and in hand and cash equivalents (eg investments held as current assets) less bank overdrafts and other borrowings repayable within one year of the accounting date.

(c) Standard accounting practice

(1) SSAP 10 is applicable to all financial statements intended to give a true and fair view of financial position and profit or loss. SSAP 10 is not mandatory for enterprises with an annual turnover below £25,000.
(2) Audited financial statements should include a funds statement with current period and comparative figures.
(3) The statement should disclose:

    (i)   profit or loss for the period;
    (ii) adjustments required for items which did not use (or provide) funds in the period;
    (iii) dividends paid;
    (iv) acquisitions and disposals of fixed and other non-current assets;
    (v) funds raised by increasing, or expended in repaying or redeeming, medium or long-term loans or the issued capital of the company;
    (vi) increase or decrease in working capital sub-divided into its components, and movements in net liquid funds.

(4) In the case of groups, the funds statements should be framed so as to reflect the operations of the group. (See section 21.3.)

Note: SSAP 10 does not specify a particular layout.

(d) Approach to the preparation of funds statements

For examination purposes, the best approach is to use a method that requires the minimum amount of workings. For this reason, the extended worksheet approach which is frequently used in practical situations is not followed here.

The recommended approach may be illustrated diagrammatically as follows:

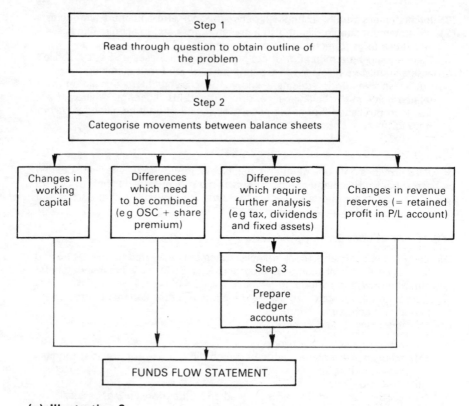

(e) Illustration 2

The summarised balance sheets of Waddev plc are as follows. A working notes column is provided to assist with the preparation of the funds statement:

	31.12.X7 £'000	31.12.X8 £'000	Working notes
Capital employed:			
£1 ordinary shares	800	1,000	200(3)
Revenue reserves	619	929	310(4)
Share premium account	300	400	100(3)
Bank loan	250	–	(250)(1)
Trade creditors	183	219	36(1)
Corporation tax	243	395	(6)
Proposed dividend	45	60	(6)
Bank overdraft	15	–	(15)(2)
	2,455	3,003	
Represented by:			
Freehold property	1,100	1,096	(5)
Plant and machinery (cost less aggregate depreciation)	732	726	(6)
Stock	365	537	172(1)
Debtors	258	432	174(1)
Cash at bank	–	212	212(2)
	2,455	3,003	

The following details are extracted from the profit and loss account for the year ended on 31.12.X8

	£'000	£'000
Profit before depreciation		862
Depreciation—buildings	4	
—plant	65	
—unprovided on disposals of plant	(7)	62
Profit before tax		800
Corporation tax		395
Profit after tax		405
Dividends—paid	35	
—proposed	60	95
Retained profit added to reserves		310

The net book values of disposals amounted to £121,000. Required: a statement of source and application of funds for the year ended December 31 19X8. There is no deferred tax account. ACT may be ignored, and comparative figures are not required.

(f) Approach to workings

Referring to the number key in the working notes column in the previous section:

(1) Items marked (1) in the working notes column are taken direct to the funds statement.
(2) The turnaround in the bank balance is shown as a single item.
(3) The proceeds of the rights issue are shown as a single item.
(4) This difference is the retained profit for the year.
(5) The reduction in the book value of the freehold property is accounted for by buildings depreciation as shown in the profit and loss account.
(6) These items provide opening and closing balances in the ledger accounts. The relevant items are then transferred from profit and loss account. The balancing figures in the ledger accounts, representing the cash transactions, are then transferred to the funds statement.

(i) PLANT AND MACHINERY ACCOUNT (NBV)

	£'000		£'000
NBV b/d	732	P/L a/c depreciation	65
Additions (balancing figure)	180	Disposals a/c	121
		NBV c/d	726
	912		912

(ii) PLANT AND MACHINERY DISPOSALS ACCOUNT

	£'000		£'000
Plant and machinery a/c	121	Proceeds of sale (balancing figure)	128
P/L a/c depreciation overprovided	7		
	128		128

(iii) TAXATION ACCOUNT

	£'000		£'000
Cash paid (balancing figure)	243	Balance b/d	243
Balance c/d	395	P/L a/c	395
	638		638

(iv) ORDINARY DIVIDENDS ACCOUNT

	£'000		£'000
Cash paid (balancing figure =		Balance b/d	45
45 + 35)	80	P/L a/c—interim (19X8)	35
Balance c/d	60	—final (19X8)	60
	140		140

The following points should be noted:

(1) The depreciation charge is added back since it is simply a book entry and does not involve a movement of funds during the year.
(2) Additions to and disposals of fixed assets are shown separately and not netted-off.
(3) Figures in the statement (for example, profit) may be reconciled with the final accounts.

(g) Presentation of the funds statement

The appendix to SSAP 10 includes illustrations of funds statements which comply with the minimum requirements of SSAP 10. The appendix is not mandatory and some companies present funds statements using a different format.

In this and the following section, the statements given are based on the appendix to SSAP 10.

The funds statement for Waddev plc may be presented as follows:

WADDEV PLC: STATEMENT OF SOURCE AND APPLICATION OF FUNDS

for the year ended December 31 19X8

Source of funds	£'000	£'000
Profit on ordinary activities before tax		800
Adjustments for items not involving the movement of funds: depreciation		62
Total generated from operations		862
Funds from other sources		
Issue of ordinary shares	300	
Proceeds of sale of fixed assets	128	428
		1,290
Total sources		
Application of funds		
Dividends paid	80	
Tax paid	243	
Repayment of bank loan	250	
Purchase of fixed assets	180	753
Increase in working capital		537

Components of increase in working capital

Increase in stocks	172
Increase in debtors	174
Increase in creditors falling due within one	
year (excluding tax and dividends)	(36)
Movement in net liquid funds:	
Increase in cash at bank	227
	537

(h) Extraordinary items

The main body of SSAP 10 does not refer to extraordinary items. However, the non-binding appendix to SSAP 10 includes two examples which show extraordinary income as a separate source of funds immediately following profit before tax.

An acceptable approach to the treatment of extraordinary items would appear to be as follows:

(1) Extraordinary income or charges which are unrelated to fixed asset disposals: show as a separate component part of source of funds or application of funds, as applicable.

(2) Extraordinary items which relate to fixed asset disposals: include as part of the proceeds of sale of tangible fixed assets (see (i) below). In these situations, extraordinary items would not feature as separate items on the face of the funds statement.

(i) Disposal of tangible fixed assets

Proceeds of sale of such assets should be included under 'funds from other sources'.

According to the treatment in the profit and loss account, the profit or loss on disposal may be dealt with as follows:

(1) Profit or loss treated as depreciation over or underprovided: profit or loss netted-off against depreciation charge (on grounds of immateriality) and included as part of the adjustment for items not involving the movement of funds. This was the situation in the illustration in (e) above.

(2) Profit or loss treated as an exceptional item: assuming funds statement commences with profit on ordinary activities before tax, treat surplus (or loss) on sale of tangible fixed assets as a deduction (or addition) under the heading adjustment for items not involving the movement of funds.

(3) Profit or loss treated as extraordinary: if the funds statement commences with profit on ordinary activities before tax, no further adjustment is necessary. The only reference to the transaction will be under funds from other sources—proceeds of sale of tangible fixed assets.

(j) Revaluation of tangible fixed assets

A revaluation of fixed assets during the year which is reflected in the financial statements has no effect on funds and its effect should thus be entirely excluded from the funds statement. The increase in the fixed asset figure should be offset against the increase in revaluation reserve for funds statement calculation purposes.

(k) Acquisition of fixed assets for non-cash consideration

Suppose a company acquires a freehold building by issuing 100,000 £1 shares at a premium of 50p per share.

Proceeds of share issue of £150,000 should be included as a source of funds, while purchase of fixed assets £150,000 should be included as an application of funds.

(I) Conversion into ordinary shares of convertible loan stock

Where, in accordance with the terms of a trust deed, convertible loan stock is converted into ordinary shares, the transaction should be reflected in the funds statements.

Although no cash is involved, the transaction does involve a change in the company's financial position (eg its gearing ratio). The same argument is true for (k) but not for (j).

The reduction in nominal value of the loan stock should be treated as an application while the increase in ordinary share capital/premium should be regarded as a source of funds.

21.3   FUNDS FLOW STATEMENTS FOR GROUPS

(a) Possible approaches

Where companies have subsidiaries, the fund statement should be based on the accounts of the group. Acquisitions and disposals of subsidiaries should be reflected in one of two ways:

(1) by reflecting the effect on the separate assets and liabilities dealt with in the group funds statement (the 'detailed breakdown' approach per example 2 of the appendix to SSAP 10); or

(2) by reflecting the effect as a separate item (the 'net outlay' approach in example 3 of the appendix to SSAP 10).

(b) Illustration—acquisition during the year

The consolidated balance sheets of Southdale plc at 31.12.X3 and 31.12.X2 were as follows:

	31.12.X3 £	31.12.X2 £
Tangible fixed assets	1,068,900	640,600
Goodwill on consolidation	300,000	250,000
Shares in associated company	245,000	206,000
Stock	586,000	492,000
Debtors	307,000	164,000
Cash	91,100	32,100
	2,598,000	1,784,700
Called-up share capital	210,000	50,000
Profit and loss account	701,000	580,000
Revaluation reserve	320,000	100,000
Share premium account	160,000	–
Minority interest:		
Ordinary share capital and reserves	325,000	295,000
Dividends payable	16,000	13,700
Corporation tax	380,000	360,000
Proposed dividends	190,000	165,000
Creditors	296,000	221,000
	2,598,000	1,784,700

Additional information

(1) Extracts from consolidated profit and loss account for year ended 31 December 19X3

	£	£
Profit on ordinary activities before tax		970,000
Corporation tax		430,000
Profit on ordinary activities after tax		540,000
Minority interest		69,000
		471,000
Dividends on ordinary shares		
Interim (paid)	160,000	
Final (proposed)	190,000	350,000
Retained profit		121,000
Balance at 1.1.X3		580,000
Balance at 31.12.X3		701,000

Profit on ordinary activities before tax and corporation tax include £120,000 and £50,000 respectively, in respect of associated companies.

(2) During the year, the group acquired a wholly-owned subsidiary, Dunster Ltd. The details of the acquisition were:

	£
Purchase consideration:	
160,000 £1 ordinary shares issued at £2	320,000
Tangible fixed assets	140,000
Goodwill on consolidation	50,000
Stock	70,000
Debtors	90,000
Creditors	(30,000)
	320,000

(3) Details of tangible fixed assets:

	Freehold property £	Machinery and vehicles £	Total £
NBV at 1.1.X3	410,000	230,600	640,600
Additions	55,000	195,000	250,000
Revaluation	220,000	–	220,000
Depreciation	(10,000)	(31,700)	(41,700)
	675,000	393,900	1,068,900

Required: a group funds statement for the year ended 31.12.X3. Ignore ACT.

(c) Workings: detailed breakdown approach

(i) Dividends paid to holding company shareholders

	£
Last year proposed final	165,000
This year interim paid	160,000
	325,000

(ii) Taxation paid (holding company and subsidiaries)

	£
Last year tax liability	360,000

(iii) Minority interest
To the extent that a partly-owned subsidiary pays dividends to its minority shareholders, there is an outflow of funds from the group. Although there is no single approach to the problem, many companies show dividends paid to minority shareholders as an application of funds. This approach will be adopted here.

Dividends paid to minority shareholders may be calculated as a balancing item by reconstructing a minority interest account as follows:

MINORITY INTEREST ACCOUNT

	£		£
Cash paid (balancing figure)	36,700	Balances at 1.1.X3	
Balances at 31.12.X3		OSC + reserves	295,000
OSC + reserves	325,000	Dividends	13,700
Dividends	16,000	P/L	69,000
	377,700		377,700

(iv) Associated company
The relevant information may be summarised as follows:

	£	£
Investment (shares)		
31.12.X3		245,000
31.12.X2		206,000
Increase (= retained profit)		39,000
Share of profits	120,000	
Share of tax	50,000	70,000
Dividends received		31,000

One possible solution would be to show £31,000 as a separate source of funds.
However this approach is not generally preferred for two reasons:

(1) It fails to make the distinction (which SSAP 1 and the Companies Act 1985 make) between associated (related) companies and trade (fixed asset) investments.
(2) The usual starting figure in a group funds statement is profit on ordinary activities before tax, and this includes the share of profit of associated (related) companies.

Consequently, an adjusting item (usually described as share of profits of associates less dividends received) is made under 'adjustments for items not involving the movement of funds'. This adjusting item is £89,000 (ie £120,000 less £31,000). The overall effect on the group funds statement is as follows:

	£
Profit on ordinary activities before tax includes share of profit of:	120,000
Adjustment for items effectively deducts	89,000
So overall effect on statement is (ie dividends received)	31,000

Note that the £89,000 is simply a balancing figure which enables the starting figure of group profit to agree with an item in consolidated profit and loss account, as well as to recognise that overall benefit to group funds is £31,000. Note that associated company share of tax is excluded from group tax for funds statement purposes.

(v) Preparation of group funds statement
Using the detailed breakdown approach, most of the items (other than those above) are calculated from a comparison of opening and closing balance sheet figures.

SSAP 10 recommends (but does not make mandatory) that in the year of an acquisition or disposal, a separate summary appears at the foot of the funds statement. This is illustrated below:

(d) Funds Statement: detailed breakdown approach

Southdale Group: Statement of source and application of funds for the year ended 31.12.19X3

(Based on the accounts of the group and showing the effects of acquiring Dunster Ltd on the separate assets and liabilities of the group.)

	£	£
Source of funds		
Profit on ordinary activities before tax		970,000
Adjustment for items not involving the movement of funds:		
Depreciation	41,700	
Profits of associates less		
dividends received	(89,000)	(47,300)
		922,700
Funds from other sources		
Issue of ordinary shares		320,000
		1,242,700
Application of funds		
Purchase of tangible fixed assets	250,000	
Purchase of goodwill	50,000	
Dividends paid:		
Holding company shareholders	325,000	
Minority shareholders	36,700	
Tax paid	360,000	1,021,700
		221,000
Increase (decrease) in working capital		
Increase in stock	94,000	
Increase in debtors	143,000	
(Increase) in creditors	(75,000)	
Movement in net liquid funds:	59,000	
Increase in cash balance		221,000

Summary of the effects of the acquisition of Dunster Ltd.

Net assets acquired	£	*Discharged by*	£
Tangible fixed assets	140,000	shares issued	320,000
Goodwill	50,000		
Stock	70,000		
Debtors	90,000		
Creditors	(30,000)		
	320,000		320,000

(e) Workings: net outlay approach

The main change compared with the detailed breakdown approach is that the purchase of Dunster Ltd (£320,000) is shown as a separate application.

In order to achieve this, funds statement items for fixed assets, goodwill, stock, debtors and creditors must be reduced, as follows:

	Detailed breakdown items	Adjustment	Net outlay items
	£	£	£
Fixed assets	250,000	(140,000)	110,000
Goodwill	50,000	(50,000)	–
Stock	94,000	(70,000)	24,000
Debtors	143,000	(90,000)	53,000
Creditors	(75,000)	30,000	(45,000)
Purchase of subsidiary		(320,000)	320,000

The funds statement then appears as follows:

(f) Funds statement: net outlay approach

Southdale group: Statement of source and application of funds for the year ended 31.12.X2

(Based on the accounts of the group and showing the acquisition of a subsidiary as a separate item.)

	£	£
Source of funds		
Profit on ordinary activities before tax		970,000
Adjustment for items not involving the movement of funds:		
Depreciation	41,700	
Profits of associates less dividends received	(89,000)	(47,300)
Total generated from other operations		922,700
Funds from other sources		
Issue of ordinary shares		320,000
		1,242,700
Application of funds		
Purchase of tangible fixed assets	110,000	
Purchase of Dunster Ltd	320,000	
Dividends paid:		
Holding company shareholders	325,000	
Minority shareholders	36,700	
Tax paid	360,000	1,151,700
		91,000
Increase (decrease) in working capital		
Increase in stock	24,000	
Increase in debtors	53,000	
(Increase) in creditors	(45,000)	
Movement in net liquid funds:	59,000	
Increase in cash balance		91,000

Analysis of the effects of the acquisition of Dunster Ltd

Net assets required	£	Discharged by	£
Tangible fixed assets	140,000	shares issued	320,000
Goodwill	50,000		
Stock	70,000		
Debtors	90,000		
Creditors	(30,000)		
	320,000		320,000

(g) Acquisition of a partly-owned subsidiary

Suppose in the previous illustration, £320,000 had been the cost of a 90% interest in Dunster Ltd.
  Goodwill would have amounted to:

	£
Cost of investment	320,000
Net assets at acquisition	
(140,000 + 70,000 + 90,000 − 30,000)	
ie £270,000	
Group share 90% × 270,000	243,000
Goodwill	77,000

In the group balance sheet, goodwill would have been £27,000 greater and minority interest would have been greater by the same amount. The treatment of minority interest depends on the approach adopted:

(1) Directed breakdown:
    Other sources would include a separate item 'minority interest in new subsidiary' £27,000 (ie 10% × 270,000)
(2) Net outlay:
    Figures would be identical to those in (f).

In either case, the separate statement at the foot of the group funds statement would appear as follows:

Net assets acquired	£	Discharged by	£
Fixed assets	140,000	Share issued	320,000
Goodwill	77,000	Minority interest	27,000
Stock	70,000		
Debtors	90,000		
Creditors	(30,000)		
	347,000		347,000

(h) Illustration—disposal during the year

The following summarised accounts relate to Dorset plc and its subsidiaries, Wiltshire Ltd and Hampshire Ltd.

CONSOLIDATED BALANCE SHEET

	31.12.X5 £'000	31.12.X6 £'000
Fixed assets—cost	3,050.0	2,550.0
—depreciation	(1,062.0)	(1,019.0)
Goodwill on consolidation	149.0	78.0
Stock	618.0	661.0
Debtors	949.0	859.0
Cash at bank	72.0	210.0
	3,776.0	3,339.0
Ordinary share capital	800.0	800.0
Revenue reserves	1,115.7	1,321.4
Dividends payable—holding company	105.0	120.0
—minority shareholders	15.0	18.0
Creditors	451.0	463.0
Minority interest	372.3	264.6
Bank overdraft	411.0	–
Corporation tax	506.0	352.0
	3,776.0	3,339.0

CONSOLIDATED PROFIT AND LOSS ACCOUNT
for the year ended 31 December 19X6

	£'000
Profit on ordinary activities before tax	781.5
Corporation tax	412.8
	368.7
Minority shareholders' interest	67.8
	300.9
Extraordinary item—gain on disposal of shares in subsidiary	24.8
	325.7
Proposed ordinary dividend	120.0
Retained profit	205.7
Balance at 1.1.X5	1,115.7
Balance at 31.12.X6	1,321.4

Additional information

(1) Dorset plc has for several years held 70% of the ordinary share capital of Wiltshire Ltd and 60% of the ordinary share capital of Hampshire Ltd.

(2) Dorset plc sold its entire shareholding in Hampshire Ltd on 30 September 19X6. The details are as follows:

	£'000	£'000
Proceeds of sale		320.0
Net assets:		
Fixed assets—cost	500	
—depreciation	(207)	
	293	
Stock	41	
Debtors	132.8	
Cash	26.7	
	493.5	
Creditors	(59.0)	
Taxation $\frac{9}{12} \times 81$	(60.8)	
	373.7	
Group share 60%	224.2	
Goodwill	71.0	295.2
Extraordinary gain		24.8

Note: MI at disposal (for detailed breakdown approach) is 40% × 373.7 = 149.5

(i) Workings: detailed breakdown approach

(i) FIXED ASSETS—COST

	£'000		£'000
Balance b/f	3,050	Disposals	500
		Balance c/d	2,550
	3,050		3,050

(ii) FIXED ASSETS—DEPRECIATION

	£'000		£'000
Disposals	207	Balance b/d	1,062
Balance c/d	1,019	P/L account:	
		Depreciation charge	164
	1,226		1,226

(iii) MINORITY INTEREST

	£'000		£'000
Minority interest at disposal	149.5	Balance b/d:	
Dividend paid:		SC & res	372.3
Wiltshire	15.0	Dividend	15.0
Hampshire	8.0	P/L	67.8
Balance c/d:			
SC & res	264.6		
Dividend	18.0		
	455.1		455.1

(iv) CORPORATION TAX ACCOUNT

	£'000		£'000
Cash	506.0	Balance b/d	506.0
Disposal of subsidiary	60.8	P/L account (inc 60.8 in respect	
Balance c/d	352.0	of Hampshire)	412.8
	918.8		918.8

Note: ACT and tax on disposal of share in subsidiary have been ignored.

(j) Funds statement—detailed breakdown approach

Dorset plc: Source and application of funds statement for the year ended 31 December 19X6

(Based on the accounts of the Group and showing the effects of disposing of a subsidiary on the separate assets and liabilities of the group.)

	£	£
Profit before tax		781.5
Adjustment for items not involving the movement of funds:		
Depreciation	164.0	
Surplus on sale of subsidiary company	24.8	188.8
		970.3
Total generated from operations		
Funds from other sources:		
Sale of fixed assets*	293.0	
Sale of goodwill*	71.0	364.0
		1334.3
Application of funds:		
Dividends paid—holding company	105.0	
—minority shareholders	23.0	
Minority interest on disposal of subsidiary*	149.5	
Tax relating to disposal of subsidiary	60.8	
Tax paid	506.0	844.3
		490.0
Increase in working capital:		
Increase in stock*	43.0	
(Decrease) in debtors*	(90.0)	
(Increase) in creditors*	(12.0)	
	(59.0)	
Movement in liquid funds:		
Increase in cash balance*	549.0	490.0

*Summary of the effects of the disposal of Hampshire Ltd

Net assets disposed of	£'000	Discharged by	£'000
Fixed assets	293.0	Cash received	320.0
Goodwill	71.0	Minority interest	149.5
Surplus on sale	24.8		
Stock	41.0		
Debtors	132.8		
Cash	26.7		
Creditors	(59.0)		
Taxation	(60.8)		
	469.5		469.5

(k) Funds statement—net outlay approach

Statement of source and application of funds

(Based on the accounts of the Group and showing the disposal of the subsidiary as a separate item.)

	£'000	£'000
Profit before tax		781.5
Adjustment for items not involving the movement of funds—depreciation		164.0
		945.5
Funds from other sources:		
Proceeds of sale of subsidiary*		320.0
		1,265.5
Application of funds:		
Dividends paid—holding company	105.0	
—minority shareholders	23.0	
Tax paid	506.0	634.0
		631.5
Increase in working capital:		
Increase in stocks	84.0	
Increase in debtors	42.8	
(Decrease) in creditors	(71.0)	
Movement in liquid funds:		
Cash at bank	575.7	631.5

Analysis of the effects of the disposal of Hampshire Ltd

Net assets disposed of	£'000	Discharged by	£'000
Fixed assets	293.0	Cash received	320.0
Goodwill	71.0	Minority interest	149.5
Surplus on sale	24.8		
Stock	41.0		
Debtors	132.8		
Cash	26.7		
Creditors	(59.0)		
Taxation	(60.8)		
	469.5		469.5

21.4 VALUE ADDED STATEMENTS

(a) Introduction

The recommendations of the ASC discussion paper, 'The Corporate Report', were discussed in chapter 6. One of the additional statements recommended was a statement of value added.

The main purpose of the statement is to show how the benefits of the efforts of an enterprise are shared between:

(1) employees;
(2) providers of capital;
(3) the state;
(4) reinvestment.

(b) Value added

Value added is basically sales income less materials and services purchased. Value added is the wealth which the reporting entity has been able to create by its own and its employees' efforts.

(c) The value added statement

The statement should show how value added has been used to pay those who have contributed to its creation.

The discussion paper recommended that the value added statement should contain the following minimum information:

(1) turnover;
(2) bought in materials and services;
(3) employees' wages and benefits;
(4) dividends and interest payable;
(5) tax payable;
(6) amount retained for re-investment.

Illustration

The Corporate Report included the following illustration of a typical value added statement.

		Year to 31 Dec 19X4		Preceding year
		£m		£m
Turnover		103.9		102.3
Bought-in materials and services		67.6		72.1
Value added		£36.3		£30.2
Applied the following way				
To pay employees				
wages, pensions and fringe benefits		25.9		17.3
To pay providers of capital				
interest on loans	0.8		0.6	
dividends to shareholders	0.9		0.9	
	—	1.7	—	1.5
To pay government				
corporation tax payable		3.9		3.1
To provide for maintenance and expansion of assets				
depreciation	2.0		1.8	
retained profits	2.8		6.5	
	—	4.8	—	8.3
Value added		£36.3		£30.2

NOTE
Bought-in materials and services would include cost of sales and overheads other than those separately referred to elsewhere in the statement.

(d) Some problem areas

(1) *Depreciation*

The majority of companies producing value added statements include depreciation under 'provide for maintenance and expansion of assets'.

However it can be argued that the use of an asset during the year, whether owned or hired, should be reflected in bought-in materials and services.

Illustration

Using the information above and making use of an additional column for percentages, the value added statements may alternatively be set out as follows. For brevity comparative figures have been excluded although they clearly offer a useful basis of comparison:

	£m	£m	%
Turnover		103.9	
Bought in materials and services	67.6		
Depreciation	2.0	69.6	
Net value added		34.3	100.0
Applied as follows:			
To pay employees—wages, pensions and fringe benefits		25.9	75.5
To pay providers of capital			
interest on loans	0.8		
dividends to shareholders	0.9	1.7	5.0
To pay government corporation tax payable		3.9	11.4
To provide for expansion retained profits		2.8	8.1
		34.3	100.0

(2) *Payments to employees*

Some commentators take the view that it is more relevant to employees to emphasise net take-home pay as opposed to gross pay. If this approach is adopted the section 'to pay employees . . .' must be clearly labelled. The section 'to pay government . . .' should include a separate heading in respect of deductions for income tax and national insurance.

(3) *Sources of income other than trading income*

These could include:

(i)   investment income—interest receivable and dividends from fixed asset investments (other than associated companies);

(ii) extraordinary income.

An acceptable way of including these would be as follows:

	£	£
Sales		X
Bought in materials and services	X	
Depreciation	X	
Net value added by company (group)		X
Investment income	X	
Extraordinary income	X	
		X
Value added available for sharing		
or retention		X

(iii) Income from associated companies: This could be treated in the same way as investment income (above). Alternatively the value added statement could include associated company profits as follows:

Illustration

Group share of associated company income is as follows:

	£'000
Share of profit	40
Share of tax	20
Share of profit after tax	20
Share of dividend	8
Share of retentions	12

The two possible formats may be presented as follows:

	(a) Dividends only £'000	(b) Share of profits £'000
Turnover	500	500
Bought in materials and services	330	330
Value added by group	170	170
Share of income of associated company	8	40
Value added available for sharing or retention	178	210
Wages	105	105
Interest and dividends	15	15
Tax	20	40
Retentions	38	50
	178	210

Approach (2) is preferred on the grounds that it is consistent with the equity method of accounting. Approach (1) fails to distinguish between the treatment of trade investments and that of associated companies.

(4) *Group statements and the treatment of minority interests*

The illustration below presents two alternative presentations of minority interest both of which are used in published statements. The illustration is derived from the following data:

The individual profit and loss accounts of H and S, and the consolidated profit and loss account are set out below. H acquired 80% of the ordinary share capital of S several years ago.

	H £'000	S £'000	Consolidated £'000
Sales	5,000	1,000	6,000
Goods and services	2,500	500	3,000
Wages and salaries	500	100	600
Depreciation	500	100	600
Interest	500	100	600
	4,000	800	4,800
Profit before tax	1,000	200	1,200
Dividend received	32	–	–
	1,032	200	1,200
Corporation tax	500	100	600
Profit after tax	532	100	600
Minority interest	–	–	(20% × 100) 20
	532	100	580
Dividends paid	250	40	250
Retained profit	282	60	330
Retained by:			
Holding company			282
Subsidiary (80% × 60)			48
			330

The alternative presentations are set out below. For the reasons referred to earlier, both presentations treat depreciation on a net value added basis.

	(a) Minority interest as single item		(b) Minority interest split between dividends and retentions	
	£'000	£'000	£'000	£'000
Sales		6,000		6,000
Less: bought-in materials and services	3,000		3,000	
depreciation	600		600	
	——	3,600	——	3,600
Net value added		2,400		2,400
Applied as follows:				
Employees—wages and salaries		600		600
Providers of capital:				
Interest on borrowings	600		600	
Dividends to holding company shareholders	250		250	
Dividends to minority shareholders in subsidiary	–		8	
Minority interest in subsidiary (20% × 100)	20		–	
	——	870	——	858
Government—UK taxation		600		600
Retained profits:				
Attributable to minority shareholders in subsidiary	–		12	
Attributable to shareholders of holding co.	330		330	
	——	330	——	342
Net value added		2,400		2,400

The second approach has the advantage of distinguishing between dividends paid to minority shareholders and retentions. In the first approach it is hardly realistic to regard 20 as being distributed to providers of capital!

(e) Statement of value added and source and use of funds combined

The illustration below is taken from the published accounts of Scottish and Newcastle Breweries plc.

STATEMENT OF VALUE ADDED AND SOURCE AND USE OF FUNDS
53 weeks ended 3 May 1987

	1987		1986	
	£m	£m	£m	£m
Turnover		827.5		773.6
Less: Customs and excise duties	196.8		204.2	
Bought-in materials and services	355.6		320.8	
	——	552.4	——	525.0
VALUE ADDED		275.1		248.6
Less: Payable in respect of:				
Staff costs	145.3		135.9	
Interest on borrowed money less income from investments	12.8		13.8	
Taxation on profit on ordinary activities	29.3		23.9	
Allocation to profit sharing scheme after taxation	2.1			
Extraordinary items	8.9		3.0	
Dividends	27.9		21.1	
	——	226.3	——	199.1
FUNDS AVAILABLE FROM TRADING		48.8		49.5
Issue of shares				
—ordinary	31.1		2.0	
—convertible cumulative preference	67.7		–	
Asset disposals	21.9		15.2	
	——	120.7	——	17.2
		169.5		66.7
FUNDS WERE USED FOR				
Purchase of tangible assets and investments		76.3		96.2
Acquisition of subsidiaries		123.5		–
Increase in loans to customers		9.2		10.3
Increase (decrease) in working capital and provisions		(17.7)		6.8
Expenses of bond issue		–		1.0
		191.3		114.3
NET INCREASE IN BORROWINGS				
Increase in overdrafts and short term borrowings, net of cash and short term deposits	15.9		0.2	
Increase in loan capital	4.7		47.4	
	——		——	
	20.6		47.6	
Add: Relating to acquisition of subsidiaries	1.2		–	
	——	21.8	——	47.6

NOTES

		1987 £m	1986 £m
1	Funds available from trading comprise:		
	Profit retained	22.1	19.8
	Depreciation and assets scrapped	26.7	29.7
		48.8	49.5
2	Increase (decrease) in working capital and provisions comprises:		
	Stocks	(5.0)	(15.7)
	Debtors	–	16.7
		(5.0)	1.0
	Creditors taxation, deferred taxation and dividends	(12.7)	5.8
		(17.7)	6.8
3	Acquisition of subsidiaries		
	Net assets acquired:		
	Tangible fixed assets	128.8	
	Loans to customers	2.4	
	Stocks	6.1	
	Debtors	4.9	
	Cash and short term deposits	1.2	
		143.4	
	Less:		
	Creditors, taxation and deferred taxation	19.4	
		124.0	
	Less:		
	Surplus arising on acquisitions	0.5	
		123.5	
	Discharged by:		
	Issue of ordinary shares	28.1	
	Issue of convertible cumulative preference shares	67.7	
	Cash	27.7	
		123.5	

21.5 FURTHER EXTENSIONS TO CORPORATE REPORTING

Chapter 6 also referred to certain further statements recommended by the Corporate Report. These are dealt with below.

(a) Employment report

This should show the size and composition of the workforce which relies on the enterprise, as well as work contribution of employees and benefits earned.

The Corporate Report recommended that information regarding the following should be included:

(1) details of numbers employed and broad reasons for changes therein;
(2) age distribution and sex of employees;

(3) functions of employees;
(4) geographical locations;
(5) closures, disposals and acquisitions;
(6) hours worked;
(7) employment costs;
(8) pension scheme costs;
(9) time and cost of training;
(10) trade unions;
(11) health and safety;
(12) employment ratios.

Illustration

EMPLOYMENT REPORT OF CROWN HOUSE PLC FOR 1986

for the year ended 31 March 1986

Number employed	*31 March 1986*		*1 April 1985*	
Total employees	*Male*	*Female*	*Male*	*Female*
Full time	4,627	1,158	4,946	1,003
Part time	39	439	35	408
	4,666	1,597	4,981	1,411
Functions of employees				
Engineering, production and service	4,065	479	4,377	388
Distribution, selling and marketing	278	574	249	496
Administration	323	544	355	527
	4,666	1,597	4,981	1,411

Remuneration

	1986 *£m*
Gross pay	57

Education and training

	Hours
Total employee time spent in training during the year within the company (excluding on-the-job training)	142,183
External training courses	19,955
	162,138

	£'000
Cost of training	
Training department	122
Wages paid during training	156
Training Board levy	148
External courses	116
	542
Less: Training Board grant	110
	432

Trade unions

At 31 March 1986 the principal trade unions recognised by member companies of the group were:

Ceramic and Allied Trades Union; Electrical and Engineering Staff Association; Electrical, Electronics, Telecommunications and Plumbing Trades Union; National Union of Sheet Metal Workers, Coppersmiths, Heating and Domestic Engineers; General, Municipal, Boilermakers and Allied Trades Union; National Union of Flint Glassworkers; Transport and General Workers Union; Union of Construction Allied Trades and Technicians; Amalgamated Union of Engineering Workers; Association of Scientific, Technical and Managerial Staff; National Society of Metal Mechanics.

Accidents

In the year there were 93 reportable accidents which represented a frequency of 0.0075 accidents per 1000 hours worked.

Disabled persons

There were 46 registered disabled persons employed by the group at 31 March 1986.

(b) Statement of money exchanges with government

The statement should show the financial relationship between the enterprise and the state, and could include the following information:

(1) PAYE collected and paid over;
(2) VAT collected and paid over;
(3) corporation and similar taxes;
(4) rates and similar levies;
(5) other sums paid to government departments;
(6) money receipts from government.

A distinction should be made between amounts collected and paid over in the capacity of agent, and those directly borne by or benefiting the entity.

(c) Statement of transactions in foreign currency

This should show the direct cash dealings of the reporting entity between this country and abroad. The following information should be included:

(1) UK cash receipts for direct exports of goods and services;
(2) cash payments from the UK to overseas concerns for direct imports, distinguishing between imports of a capital nature and those of a revenue nature;
(3) overseas borrowings remitted to or repaid from the UK;
(4) overseas investments and loans made from or repaid to the UK;
(5) overseas dividends, interest or similar payments received in the UK or UK dividends, interest or similar payments remitted overseas.

	19X2 £'000	19X1 £'000
Receipts:		
Exports from the UK	71,857	46,884
Dividends, interest and fees remitted by overseas subsidiaries	411	1,240
Repayment of loans by overseas subsidiaries	200	1,007
	72,468	49,131

Payments:

Imports into the UK	28,026	4,327
Investment in overseas subsidiaries	8,230	1,574
	36,256	5,901
Net inflow to the UK	36,212	43,230

(d) Statement of future prospects

This should show the likely future profit, employment and investment levels. This type of information is more likely to be covered by the chairman's or chief executive's statement rather than in a separate statement.

(e) Statement of corporate objectives

This should show management policy and medium-term strategic targets. Areas covered could include:

(1) sales;
(2) added value;
(3) profitability;
(4) investment and finance;
(5) dividends;
(6) employment;
(7) consumer issues;
(8) environmental matters;
(9) other relevant social issues.

(f) General comment

With the exceptions of the value added statement and the employment report, the other statements referred to above are met only rarely.

22 ANALYSIS OF ACCOUNTS—2: EARNINGS PER SHARE

22.1 BASIC CONSIDERATIONS

(a) Importance of earnings per share

From the viewpoint of a shareholder, earnings per share offers a basis of comparability of after-tax profits attributable to each share from one year to the next.

Investment analysts are also interested in earnings per share and use EPS to calculate the price/earnings ratio (PER). The price/earnings ratio (quoted price per share as a multiple of earnings per share) offers a useful basis for comparing companies within particular industrial and commercial sectors.

(b) SSAP 3

SSAP 3 requires listed companies to publish earnings per share statistics on the face of the profit and loss account. The basis of calculation of EPS should be disclosed in a note to the accounts.

In certain circumstances, companies are required to display the fully diluted earnings per share in addition to the basic earnings per share. This is explained below.

(c) Definition

Earnings per share is defined by SSAP 3 as the profit in pence attributable to each equity share based on the consolidated profit of the period after tax after deducting minority interests and preference dividends but before taking into account extraordinary items, divided by the number of equity shares in issue and ranking for dividend in respect of the period.

Illustration 1

The following extract is taken from the consolidated profit and loss account of CJ plc for the year ended 31 December 19X4. The company has 3m 25p ordinary shares in issue and which rank for dividend for the period:

		£
Profit on ordinary activities after tax		1,826,000
Minority interest		(70,000)
		1,756,000
Extraordinary charges		(200,000)
		1,556,000
Preference dividend	300,000	
Ordinary dividend	700,000	
		1,000,000
Retained profit		556,000

(1) Calculations

Earnings = £1,756,000 less £300,000
= £1,456,000

Earnings per share = $\dfrac{£1,456,000}{3\,\text{million}}$ = 48.5p

(2) Disclosures

(i) On face of consolidated profit and loss account.

	Year ended 31 December	
	19X4	19X3
Earnings per ordinary share of 25p	48.5p	X

(ii) Notes to the accounts.
The calculation of earnings per share is based on earnings of £1,456,000 (19X3 £-----)
and 3m shares in issue throughout the two years 31 December 19X4.

22.2 NET AND NIL BASIS

The tax charge of a company may contain some elements which are fixed
(irrespective of the level of the dividends paid) and some which vary according to
the level of dividend.

This gives rise to two possible measurements of EPS:

(1) The net basis, where the tax charge used to calculate the EPS includes
irrecoverable ACT and any unrelieved overseas tax arising from the payment
or proposed payment of dividends.
(2) The nil basis which excludes the above two items from the tax charge used as
the basis of the EPS calculation.

SSAP 3 requires that earnings per share is determined on a net basis ie taking
account of both fixed and variable elements of the tax charge.

However, where the nil basis calculation would differ significantly from the net
basis, the nil basis should also be disclosed.

Illustration 2

**Extract from the consolidated profit and loss account of Unrelieved plc for
the year ended 31 December 19X6**

The company had shares in issue throughout the year.

		£
Profit on ordinary activities before tax		1,200
Taxation		
Corporation tax	480	
Unrelieved advance corporation tax	105	595
Profit on ordinary activities after tax		605

Calculations

(1) Basic EPS net basis $\dfrac{(1200-595)}{2,000,000}$ = 30.2p per share.

(2) Basic EPS nil basis $\dfrac{(1200-480)}{2,000,000}$ = 36p per share.

As the nil basis differs significantly from the net basis, the nil basis should be disclosed in
addition to the net basis.

22.3 LOSSES

Where a loss is incurred or where the amount earned for equity (ie after deducting preference dividends) is a negative figure, EPS should be calculated in the usual way and the result described as a loss per share.

22.4 BASIC EPS CHANGES IN THE CAPITAL STRUCTURE DURING THE YEAR

Possible situations include:

(a) bonus issue;
(b) issue for full consideration;
(c) rights issue.

(a) *Bonus issue during the year*

Where new equity shares have been issued by way of capitalisation of reserves during the financial year, the earnings per share should be based on the increased number of shares ranking for dividend after the capitalisation issue.

The corresponding earnings per share disclosed in respect of all earlier periods should be adjusted proportionately in respect of the capitalisation issue.

Illustration 3

In 19X4, the earnings of A plc amounted to £2,400,000 and the number of ordinary shares in issue and ranking for dividend amounted to 6m. EPS disclosed was therefore 40 pence per share.

Halfway through 19X5, the company made a bonus issue of 1 for 2. Earnings amounted to £2,700,000 and the number of shares, 9m.

In the accounts for 19X5, earnings per share would be disclosed as 30p per share. In order to achieve comparability with the previous year, the EPS of 19X4 should be restated to take account of the increased level of share capital.

That is, $\dfrac{£2,400,000}{9m} = 26.7p$

Figures disclosed in the 19X5 accounts would therefore be:

	19X5	19X4
Earnings per ordinary share of	30p	26.7p

(b) *Issue of shares for full consideration*

Where there has been an issue of shares for cash or other full consideration, ranking for dividend during the year, earnings per share on the weighted average share capital are shown.

Illustration 4

During the year ended 31 December 19X9, X plc earned £24,000. On 1 January 19X9, the ordinary share capital was 100,000 shares of 50p each. On 30 September 19X9, a further 200,000 ordinary shares of 50p each were issued.

Earnings per share: $\dfrac{£24,000 \times 100}{150,000\,(100,000 + \frac{1}{4} \times 200,000)} = 16p$

Note: The calculation of earnings per share is based on earnings of £24,000 and on the weighted average of 150,000 ordinary shares in issue during the year.

(c) *Rights issue*

An issue of shares to an existing shareholder at a price below the current market price is equivalent to an issue of shares at full market price plus a bonus issue. Previous years' earnings per share must be adjusted for the bonus element in the rights issue. Calculations should be based on the official middle price of the closing price on the last day of the quotation cum-rights. The calculation will be as follows:

$$\text{Earnings per share for previous years} \times \frac{\text{Theoretical ex-rights price}}{\text{Actual cum-rights price}}$$

To avoid splitting the earnings during the current year between the periods before and after the rights issue, the share capital before the rights issue should be adjusted by the reciprocal of the factor used for calculating the previous years' earnings per share, viz:

$$\frac{\text{Actual cum-rights price}}{\text{Theoretical ex-rights price}}$$

Illustration 5

Y plc share capital of £2m all in ordinary shares of 25p each was increased on 1 July 19X9 to £3m by a rights issue of ordinary shares in the proportion of 1 for 4 at 50p per share = 2m shares for £1m. The middle market price of the ordinary shares on the last day of quotation cum-rights was 200p. Profits after tax were:

	£
Year ended 31 December 19X9	850,000
Year ended 31 December 19X8	800,000

Calculation of earnings per share
The holder of 100 ordinary shares would on taking up his entitlement subscribe for 25 new shares costing £12.50. His total holding of 125 shares would, assuming no other change in circumstances, be worth £212.50 or 170p per share.
   The factor for adjusting past earnings per share is therefore:

$$\frac{\text{Ex-rights price}}{\text{Cum-rights price}} = \frac{£1.70}{£2.00} \text{ or } \frac{85}{100}$$

Previous year's earnings per share
As previously calculated:

$$\frac{£800,000}{8,000,000} \times 100 = 10p$$

Adjusted for bonus element in rights issue.

$$10p \times \frac{85}{100} = 8.5p$$

Earnings per share for current year (19X9)
Number of shares:

$$8 \text{ million} \times \frac{6}{12} \times \frac{\text{Cum-rights price}}{\text{Ex-rights price}}$$

$$(\text{period})$$

$$8,000,000 \times \frac{6}{12} \times \frac{100}{85} = 4,705,880$$

Number of shares after rights issue

$$10,000,000 \times \frac{6}{12} = 5,000,000$$

	(period)	
Weighted average number of shares		9,705,880

Earnings per share:

$$\frac{£850,000}{9,705,880} \times 100 = 8.8p$$

Profit and loss account presentation

	Year ended 31 December 19X9	Year ended 31 December 19X8
Earnings per ordinary share of 25p	8.8p	8.5p

Note: The calculation of earnings per share is based on earnings of £850,000 (19X8 £800,000) and on the weighted average of 9,705,880 ordinary shares after adjustment of the number of shares in issue prior to the rights issue on 1 July 19X9 by the factor:

$$\frac{100p}{85} \quad \frac{\text{Cum-rights}}{\text{Ex-rights}}$$

The earnings per share for 19X8 have been adjusted accordingly.

(d) *Acquisitions of subsidiaries for cash*
The acquisition should be accounted for in the consolidated accounts on the basis of SSAP 14 (Group accounts). This will usually mean that profits are included from the date of acquisition. The earnings per share will be based on reported earnings and ordinary shares in issue throughout the year.

(e) *Business combinations—share for share basis*
The business combination should be accounted for on the basis of SSAP 23 (Accounting for acquisitions and mergers). This means that the consolidated accounts may be accounted for either on the basis of acquisition accounting or merger accounting (assuming the necessary conditions are satisfied).

In the case of a share for share exchange, the appendix to SSAP 3 states that for the purpose of calculating the earnings per share it should be assumed that the securities were issued on the first day of the period for which the profits of the new subsidiary are included in the earnings of the group.

SSAP 14 and SSAP 23 were issued some years after SSAP 3 (revised) and group accounts reporting practices have changed as a result. In addition the appendix to SSAP 3 is not mandatory. The following alternative treatment is therefore suggested:

(1) Group accounts prepared on an acquisition basis:

    (i)   Current year EPS should be calculated by dividing reported earnings by weighted number of equity shares in issue throughout the year. This ensures consistency between numerator and denominator, ie after the acquisition date group earnings reflect post-acquisition results of new subsidiary. This is matched in the denominator by a proportionate amount of increased shares as a result of the acquisition.

    (ii) Comparative EPS—no restatement is required.

(2) Group accounts prepared on a merger basis:

    (i)   Current year EPS reflect a full year's earnings in respect of the new subsidiary. This should therefore be divided by the new number of shares (a weighted average would be inconsistent).

    (ii) Comparative EPS—this should be restated. Restated comparative earnings (inclusive of a full year comparative earnings of the new subsidiary) should be divided by the new number of shares in issue as a result of the combination.

The method of group accounting will thus affect the EPS figure. The basis of calculation should thus be clearly stated.

22.5 FULLY DILUTED EARNINGS PER SHARE

(a) Possible situations

At the balance sheet date a company may have previously entered into commitments which could result in the issue at some future date of further ordinary shares.

Such an issue could adversely affect the interests of existing shareholders in terms of a reduction (or dilution) in earnings per share.

For this reason, SSAP 3 requires that in certain specified situations, a listed company should be required to publish its fully diluted earnings per share (based on certain hypothetical assumptions) in addition to its basic earnings per share (on the net basis as described above).

The situations where fully diluted earnings per share (FDEPS) are required to be shown are as follows:

(1) where the company has issued a separate class of equity shares which do not rank for any dividend in the period under review but which will do so in the future;
(2) where the company has issued debentures or loan stock (or preference shares) convertible into equity shares of the company;
(3) where the company has granted options or issued warrants to subscribe for equity shares of the company.

(b) FDEPS—additional considerations

(1) FDEPS need only be disclosed if the effect of the dilution is material (a reduction of more than 5% compared with basic EPS).
(2) Basis of calculation of FDEPS should be disclosed.
(3) FDEPS and basic EPS should be given equal prominence.
(4) FDEPS for the comparative period should not be given unless the assumptions on which the previous year's calculations were based still apply this year.

(c) FDEPS—calculations

(1) *Issue of shares ranking for dividend in a future period*
FDEPS is calculated by dividing actual earnings by the total equity shares in issue, whether or not they ranked for dividend this year.

(2) *Convertible stocks or shares*
FDEPS is calculated by adjusting:

(i) earnings for any savings of interest (net of corporation tax) or preference dividend as a result of conversion to ordinary shares;
(ii) maximum number of ordinary shares that could be in issue at a future date. (Clearly a hypothetical calculation, since present loan stock holders may or may not exercise their right to convert into ordinary shares.)

Illustration 6

Z plc share capital was £2m in ordinary shares of 25p each ie 8m shares. Some years previously the company had issued £2,500,00 8% convertible unsecured shares. Each £100 nominal of the stock will be convertible as follows:

On December 31   19X11   125 shares
                 19X12   118 shares
                 19X13   115 shares
                 19X14   108 shares

Results

	Year ended 31 December 19X9 £	Year ended 31 December 19X8 £
Profits before tax and interest	2,200,000	1,800,000
Interest on 8% convertible unsecured stock loan	200,000	200,000
Profits before tax	2,000,000	1,600,000
Corporation tax, say	1,000,000	800,000
Profits after tax	£1,000,000	£800,000
Number of shares	8,000,000	8,000,000
Earnings per share	12.5p	10p

Fully diluted earnings per share		
Earnings as above		£1,000,000
Add Loan interest	200,000	
Less Corporation tax, say	100,000	100,000
Adjusted earnings		£1,100,000

Number of shares:

Up to 19X10, the maximum number of shares issuable after the end of the financial year will be at the rate of 125 shares per £100, viz: 3,125,000 shares, making a total of 11,125,000.

Fully diluted earnings per share 9.9p.

Profit and loss account presentation

	Year ended 31 December 19X9	Year ended 31 December 19X8
Basic earnings per ordinary share of 25p	12.5p	10p
Fully diluted earnings per ordinary share of 25p	9.9p	–

NOTE
The basic earnings per share is calculated on earnings of £1,000,000 (19X8 £800,000) and 8m ordinary shares in issue throughout the two years ended 31 December 19X9.

The fully diluted earnings per share is based on adjusted earnings of £1,100,000 after adding back interest net of corporation tax on the 8% convertible unsecured loan stock. The maximum number of shares into which this stock becomes convertible on 31 December 19X11 is 3,125,000, making a total of 11,125,000 shares issued and issuable.

(3) *Options and warrants*
In order to calculate FDEPS, SSAP 3 requires two sets of assumptions to be made:

(i)   That the maximum number of new ordinary shares had been issued under the terms of the options or warrants. It is also assumed that these are exercised on the first day of the period (or date of issue of options or warrants if this is later).

(ii) That the earnings are adjusted for notional interest on the cash proceeds which would be received by the company if the options or warrants were to be taken up. SSAP 3 requires the calculation to be based on the assumption that the proceeds of subscription had been invested in $2\frac{1}{2}$% consolidated stock on the first day of the period (using the quoted price of the previous day).

22.6 PROBLEMS OF COMPARABILITY

When comparing two companies, care should be taken to ensure that EPS has been calculated on a consistent basis as between the two companies.

The following are possible reasons why two identical companies might come up with different EPS figures:

(a) inconsistent treatment of extraordinary and exceptional items (SSAP 6);
(b) depreciation charges based on historical cost, valuation or some combination of the two (SSAP 12);
(c) goodwill amortised through profit and loss account over a number of years, or written off immediately against reserves (SSAP 22);
(d) finance leases capitalised or not capitalised (SSAP 21);
(e) profit and loss accounts of foreign subsidiaries translated at average or closing rate (SSAP 20);
(f) business combinations satisfying merger conditions being treated as acquisitions or as mergers (SSAP 23);
(g) post-balance sheet events involving closure decisions taken after the balance sheet date where different interpretations may be placed on the prudence concept.

The above are simply intended as examples of situations which show how important it is to scrutinise accounting policies and notes to accounts before making a final comparison of two or more companies.

23 ANALYSIS OF ACCOUNTS—3: INTERPRETATION OF ACCOUNTS

23.1 INTRODUCTION

(a) Purpose of analysis

The process of interpreting accounts is essentially the art and science of translating figures in financial statements so as to reveal financial strengths and weaknesses. The analysis should hopefully help to identify the underlying causes which have contributed to these strengths and weaknesses.

Analysis is not necessarily restricted to historical cost based financial statements. It may also be applied to interim statements (see chapter 26) and forecast statements.

(b) Interested persons

The following users may have a particular interest in interpreting particular aspects of financial statements:

(1) the owners or, in the case of a limited company, the shareholders;
(2) debenture holders, or the holders of any other form of long-term loan capital;
(3) bank managers, financial institutions etc;
(4) investors and their professional advisers;
(5) financial journalists and commentators;
(6) creditors;
(7) HM Inspectors of Taxes.

(c) Areas of interest

These include:

(1) profitability trends, scope for improvement;
(2) solvency;
(3) ownership and control;
(4) financial strength;
(5) borrowing potential;
(6) gearing and interest cover;
(7) dividend cover.

(d) Profit and loss account

Analysts are likely to be concerned with:

(1) turnover:

    (i) variations in volume and price;
    (ii) sales mix changes (eg larger proportion of sales of higher-priced goods);

(2) gross profit ratios (gross profit as a percentage of sales);
(3) ratios of purchases and sales to creditors and debtors;
(4) ratios of stocks to cost of sales;
(5) fluctuations in expense elements (selling, distribution, administration, finance).

Comparisons may be made with figures of previous periods, with previously established budgets for the current period or with yardsticks for similar businesses.

(e) Balance sheet

(1) share capital including potential for future share issues;
(2) debentures—whether secured by fixed or floating charges;
(3) amount and adequacy of working capital;
(4) nature, purpose and limitations on use of reserves;
(5) valuations of property assets;
(6) goodwill—if it appears in a company balance sheet it is usually disregarded by analysts as the figure shown usually has little meaning.

23.2   RATIO ANALYSIS TECHNIQUES

(a) Introduction

Ratio analysis techniques help compare and interpret significant features in financial statements. Salient features may be brought into focus and areas requiring further investigations highlighted. Analysis helps to evaluate how we did last year, where we are now and possibly how we will fare in the future. Analysis may be concerned therefore with both control and prediction.

(b) Basis of comparison

Ratios calculated may be compared with:

(1) previous years (intra-firm comparisons);
(2) similar businesses (inter-firm comparisons).

Additionally ratios actually achieved for the current period may be compared with planned ratios established by management.

(c) Ratios in perspective

Ratio analysis should be regarded as an important part of an overall exercise involving interpretative techniques, including analysis of funds flow statements, scrutiny of accounting policies and so on. An analyst requires an overall picture of a business and should always avoid the danger of viewing ratios in isolation (refer also to section 23.4).

   Auditors, for example, use ratio analysis techniques to provide corroborative evidence of the reasonableness of the view presented by the financial statements.

(d) Return on capital employed (ROCE)

Return on capital employed is often referred to as the primary ratio. The ratio comments on the efficiency of the management by contrasting the profit made by the business with the funds utilised to make that profit. It may be used to show the relative efficiency of the business as compared with the return on capital employed in other companies in the same industry, or in different industries, or in another country, or for the same concern in earlier years. The maintenance of the same ratio of profit to capital employed should be the lowest aim of every board of directors or proprietor: its improvement is probably a necessity in the face of mounting competition at home and abroad.

   ROCE essentially expresses profit as a percentage return on net assets.

   More specifically, profit is usually taken to refer to profit before deducting interest on long-term loans and tax. Net assets are fixed assets plus working capital (which is the same as shareholders' funds plus long-term liabilities).

   There are several variants of ROCE, but the above is often regarded as the most useful and is the definition which will be adopted here.

(e) Secondary ratios

Closely allied to the primary ratio are (1) the profitability of sales disclosed by the ratio or percentage of net profit to sales, and (2) the intensity with which the capital is employed in the business as shown by the ratio of sales to capital employed. These ratios will support any conclusions drawn from the primary ratio and may indicate the reason for an unsatisfactory return on capital employed.

The relationship between the primary and secondary ratios may be illustrated as follows:

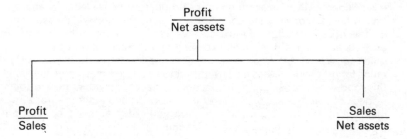

$$\frac{\text{Profit}}{\text{Sales}} \text{ is effectively a profit margin on sales.}$$

$$\frac{\text{Sales}}{\text{Net assets}} \text{ is sometimes referred to as asset turnover.}$$

(f) Pyramid of ratios

The above analysis can be taken further:

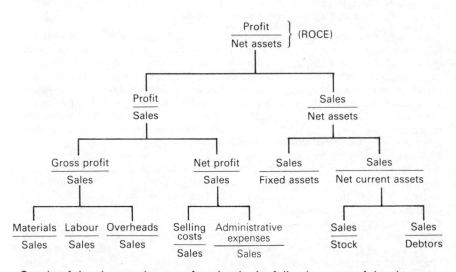

Certain of the above ratios are referred to in the following parts of the chapter.

(g) Ratio of profit to sales

(1) *The ratio of gross profit to sales* serves as an overall guide to the efficiency of production in a manufacturing business while, in non-manufacturing

businesses it should correspond with the trade mark-up, which may be constant in respect of the whole of the sales, or variable in respect of known proportions of total turnover; in this type of business this ratio also serves as a valuable check upon the accuracy of the closing stock figure. Its limitations lie in the fact that as no account is taken of selling and distribution expenses it may be misleading; a product which is costly to produce, or purchase (in the case of a non-manufacturing concern), may incur very little in the way of selling and distribution expenses and vice versa.

(2) *The ratio of net profit to sales* discloses the ultimate proportion of sales and miscellaneous revenue accruing to the proprietors, or available for appropriation in the case of a limited company. Probably the most widely used ratio of all, this does not suffer from the disadvantages inherent in the ratio of gross profit to sales since it takes all expenditure into account and can serve as a guide to overall performance, when compared with previous years and the ratios for other businesses e g HM Inspectors of Taxes may, inter alia, employ this ratio when considering the accuracy of accounts submitted to them in respect of sole traders or firms. Where miscellaneous income from investments, rents etc forms a significant proportion of total revenue, appropriate adjustments should be made to expenditure and net profit to determine the net profit attributable to sales.

(3) *The ratio of bad debts to sales* discloses whether sales are being made to creditworthy customers. A high ratio may indicate reckless selling and/or the need for more efficient credit control, by checking the creditworthiness of new and existing customers and by the collection of outstanding debts before the affairs of customers get out of hand.

(4) *Production ratios*
These include:

(i)   factory costs to sales;
(ii) administration costs to sales;
(iii) selling costs to sales;
(iv) distribution costs to sales;
(v)   research and development costs to sales.

Although the above could be expressed as ratios of total cost (being an equally important factor) it is considered that it is more advantageous to use sales since these ratios are probably best expressed as percentages, when the residual percentage will, after taking into account miscellaneous income, represent net profit; the relative effect upon net profits of trends or proposals will then be readily seen. To enhance their value, each of these would need to be broken down under the main items contained in each category e g it would be vital to analyse factory costs into materials, direct labour and factory overheads. Trends in the ratios over a number of years or periods would need to be studied, while the relative size of each heading and/or item should govern the extent of the investigations undertaken. It will be immediately apparent that if one item amounts to 1% of sales, while another accounts for 40%, greater potential savings are likely to result from a close scrutiny of the latter item. Some effort should be made by the analyst to distinguish between controllable costs and uncontrollable costs, which are due to external factors, such as a general increase in the price of certain raw materials, while it should be possible to correlate the behaviour of various costs, with a view to reducing total costs. This might apply where, for example, a reduction in direct labour has been achieved, or is proposed, by purchasing components and/or increasing the degree of mechanisation. The degree of correlation found from experience, or from one budget may provide a collateral check upon a number of flexible budgets.

The use of historical costs is implicit in the foregoing; however, trends based upon past performance are of limited value only in assessing efficiency due to the absence of an absolute or realistic yardstick. Comparison with carefully prepared budgeted or standard costs can, on the other hand, enhance the value of production and cost ratios immensely.

(h) Ratio of sales to net assets (capital employed)

The ratio of sales to capital employed discloses the 'rate of turnover' of the capital employed in the business. Unless overtrading is prevalent, a high ratio is a healthy sign, for the more times capital is turned over, the greater will be the opportunities for making profits. A low ratio, on the other hand, may be indicative of unused capacity, or undertaking, especially if this is accompanied by a high ratio of fixed factory overhead expenditure to sales. It may be advantageous to subdivide this ratio between fixed and working capital to discover whether fixed capital is overemployed, whilst the working capital ratio remains dormant, or vice versa: for this reason capital employed should, in this context, be taken to mean net assets. However, it will be necessary to study the behaviour of the constituent elements of working capital before reaching a decision, for a constant ratio may merely mask fluctuations of cash, stock, debtors and creditors. Attempts should be made to minimise the level of working capital by, for example, reducing the period of credit extended to debtors as sales increase.

Quoted investments should be excluded from working capital, since sales will not be directly influenced by these. Similarly, it may be advisable to exclude trade investments and shares in subsidiary companies from fixed capital, where the return on these is competitive, on the grounds that sales may have been unaffected by the employment of such funds. Much, however, will depend upon the circumstances in each case, which will need to be treated on its merits, for connections with associated and subsidiary companies will often provide outlets for additional sales. A more realistic picture may emerge by basing this ratio upon the average of fixed and working capital employed throughout the year, derived from interim accounts (if any) prepared at monthly or quarterly intervals.

(i) Stock ratios

These ratios indicate efficiency in the control of stocks of raw materials, work-in-progress and finished goods. Excessive stocks are to be avoided since, apart from incidental costs e g storage, insurance etc, working capital will be tied up which could perhaps be invested in securities or otherwise profitably employed. Where, moreover, superfluous stocks are in effect financed by an overdraft, the cost of such facilities is wasteful.

The ratios computed will be governed by the type of business; where, for instance, goods are produced for stock, there may be little or no work-in-progress, ratios being confined to raw materials and finished stock; where, however, the business is engaged upon job production, there should be no stocks of finished goods, but levels of raw material stocks and work-in-progress will need to be controlled.

It should be stressed that calculation of ratios is no substitute for efficient storekeeping, a perpetual inventory system and the objective calculation of minimum and maximum stocks for each item of raw material and components.

(1) *Raw material stock to purchases* shows the rate of stock turnover. The ratio of closing stock to purchases indicates the number of days' (weeks' or months') purchases held in stock and can act as a guide to excessive stockholdings. A high ratio may signify the presence of obsolescent stocks, or inefficiency on the part of the buying department by purchasing too far in advance of requirements: if, however, such purchases were made at favourable prices prior to impending price increases, this may, on the contrary, denote efficiency on the part of the buyer. The ratio may be analysed between raw materials and components, and indeed different classes of raw materials, in order to pinpoint obsolescent items and forward purchases.

(2) *Work-in-progress to cost of production* indicates the length of the production cycle where a uniform product is manufactured. Comparison with earlier
periods can provide a measure of efficiency or otherwise of the production
department. In a medium-sized or large plant, figures would be available for
each direct department, thus enabling the ratio for each department to be
ascertained; bottlenecks indicated by these ratios can result in action being
taken to expedite the production cycle in particular departments, resulting in
a quicker overall production cycle, since this is clearly dependent upon the
weakest link in the chain. Ratios based upon monthly figures may be even
more enlightening since seasonal variations due, for example, to holidays and
sickness, may come to light, both on a global and departmental basis, which,
if capable of remedial action, may speed the production cycle still further.
Where production is carried out in accordance with customer's specifications
(i e job production) the production cycle will vary widely from one job to
another, when the time taken to complete each job, and the level of work-in-
progress, will need to be considererd on its merits.

(3) *Finished stock to total turnover* shows how long finished goods are kept in
store before being sold. Needless to say, stock should be held for as short a
time as possible if profits are to be maximised. This ratio is best calculated by
dividing annual turnover by the average of the stock figures at the close of
each month, as ratios based upon opening or closing stock for the year, or the
average of these, may be misleading, unless stocks are constant throughout
the year. The question arises as to whether turnover and stock should be at
selling price or cost price; however, provided both elements are either at cost
or selling price, a realistic ratio should emerge. When the ratio increases, steps
should be taken either to increase sales or to curtail output, if overproduction
has occurred. In any event, sales and production will need to be co-
ordinated. Care should be taken to ensure that turnover of stock does not
increase too much, signified by a very low ratio, otherwise it may prove
difficult to meet customers' demands promptly. It should be noted that this
ratio is sometimes expressed as a single figure, turnover being divided by
stock.

(j) Ratio of credit sales to debtors

This shows the rate at which customers are paying for credit sales. This ratio
should approximate to the credit terms allowed by the business and is, therefore, a
comment on the efficiency of credit control. If three months' credit is extended to
customers, then the normal ratio should be 4 to 1 (365 divided by 91). Thus, if
annual turnover is £24,000, debtors should be approximately £6,000. This will,
however, only apply if sales in terms of sterling are spread evenly over the year,
since seasonal sales will give rise to variance; e g if the above turnover comprised
sales of £5,000 for the first three-quarters of the year and £9,000 for the last
quarter, then debtors at the year end should be in the region of £9,000. The higher
the ratio, the more favourable the effect upon working capital, because outsiders
are being financed to a lesser extent while liquid resources will, other things being
equal, increase.

(k) the solvency ratios

Although not referred to under the pyramid of ratios, these ratios are particularly
important.

(1) *The current (or working capital) ratio*

This is determined by calculating the ratio of current assets to current liabilities. It
shows whether there is an adequate amount of working capital to meet running
expenses and service fixed assets. Movements will indicate how much of the

concern's own resources are being utilised to finance current assets, as opposed to funds raised from current liabilities, e g an upward movement in stocks may be accompanied by a corresponding increase in creditors, rather than a decrease in cash. It should be remembered that the level of debtors and creditors represents the extent to which the business is financing, or is being financed by, respectively, outsiders. The extent of any unused overdraft facilities is important for, if the company has reached the limit of its short-term borrowing powers, difficulties will arise in times of emergency and expansion will be inhibited unless further long-term capital is raised.

Although it is desirable that current assets should exceed current liabilities, if only to provide ample coverage in the event of a liquidation, no two businesses are alike, and indeed it may be perfectly healthy for many businesses to work on a negative ratio. General criteria, such as the 'two to one' ratio should, therefore, be viewed with some scepticism. Again, due to seasonal idiosyncrasies the working capital position at the date of a balance sheet may represent maximum or minimum liquidity, not to mention 'window dressing', when an average over the year may provide a truer picture.

The principal factors which determine the optimum level of working capital may be summarised as follows:

(i) The extent to which the business is subject to seasonal fluctuations and the vagaries of taste and fashion.
(ii) The amount of working capital required to finance any plans for expansion.
(iii) Terms of trade extended by suppliers and allowed to customers.
(iv) Bank overdraft facilities.
(v) The length of the business cycle i e the finance tied up in production, or a specific order, from the time work commences until the receipt of cash. Much will obviously depend upon the nature of the product e g ocean-going liners or safety pins, while the level of work-in-progress will indicate the length of the cycle.
(vi) The amount of working capital required to service fixed assets, which will be governed largely by the amount of capital sunk in these.
(vii) The extent to which speculative activities are undertaken in the purchase of stock.

Attempts to expand turnover to a point when the working capital becomes inadequate to finance day-to-day operations produces a malady known as 'overtrading'. Symptoms of overtrading may take the following forms:

(i) creditors will tend to increase in relation to debtors;
(ii) a growth in the rate of long and/or short-term borrowing;
(iii) minimal cash resources;
(iv) an increase in stocks unaccompanied by an increase in turnover;
(v) a diminution of gross and/or net profit;
(vi) heavy expenditure on fixed assets.

A long production cycle will inevitably aggravate the shortage of liquid resources where this situation prevails.

An inadequate volume of business leads, on the other hand, to 'undertrading'. When trade diminishes beyond a certain point, a business will suffer the embarrassment of meeting its fixed and reduced variable costs from current assets which remain relatively static. The situation will be aggravated when the amount of fixed assets is large, since these will still have to be serviced, probably to a greater extent, due to underemployment.

(2) *Liquid (or quick) ratio*

The ratio, sometimes referred to as the acid test, is defined as:

$$\frac{\text{Current assets excluding stock}}{\text{Current liabilities}}$$

The ratio attempts to gauge the ability of a business to meet all its creditors from liquid resources, should they demand payment simultaneously. Although a useful guide to the solvency position of a business, it is somewhat unreal since many of the creditors are unlikely to demand payment at once. Quick assets comprise cash, quoted investments and bills receivable (as these may be discounted); in addition, an analysis of debtors may warrant the inclusion of some, considered to be readily realisable, but this is, however, a refinement. Businesses may be loath to realise investments where such action would result in a loss, while corporation tax payable on a chargeable gain may inhibit the realisation of investments where the reverse applies.

(l) The capital ratios

(1) *The capital gearing ratio* discloses the relationship between the ordinary share capital of a company and fixed interest capital, in the form of preference shares and debentures. A company with a preponderance of ordinary share (or equity) capital is said to be 'low-geared', while a company with a capital structure in which fixed interest capital is the higher, is said to be 'high-geared'. Gearing is neutral when ordinary and fixed interest capital are equal, resulting in a ratio of 1 to 1.

Reserves should be included as part of the equity of the company. Where a company's capital structure is low-geared, preference shareholders and debenture holders enjoy greater security, while the potential dividends payable to ordinary shareholders will not be subject to violent fluctuation with variations in profit. On the other hand, in a highly-geared company variations in profit will tend to produce disproportionate changes in equity earnings, due to the burden of interest payable on fixed interest capital; in fact if profits fall too low, no dividend may be payable on the ordinary shares. Furthermore, where the structure is highly-geared, a higher rate of interest would probably be offered to holders of prior charge capital to compensate for the greater risk attaching to their investment, both as regards security and income thereon.

(2) *The ratio of fixed assets to capital employed* reveals the disposition of funds between fixed and working capital: for the purposes of this ratio, fixed assets should be restricted to those of a tangible nature, while capital employed may be based on either gross or net assets, provided either basis is used consistently. Used in conjunction with the working capital ratio, this ratio may indicate the adequacy or otherwise of working capital to service fixed assets or an excess or deficiency of fixed assets, from which earnings can be generated. Comparison of the ratio for the current year with earlier years, against the background of the ratios of sales to working capital and sales to fixed capital, may indicate the optimum disposition of available funds. Comparison with ratios disclosed by the accounts of other businesses of a comparable type and scale may serve to support any conclusions drawn from study of internal ratios.

(m) The earnings or investment ratios

These relate to earnings on shares as opposed to earnings of the company itself and provide valuable information to actual or potential shareholders: they are also of great interest to higher management since a company depends upon its shareholders and would-be shareholders for its capital, and further funds for expansion. The following ratios are, therefore, closely associated with the capital ratios.

(1) *The ratio of net profit after corporation tax and preference dividend to equity capital* (ordinary shares plus reserves) shows the return on capital invested in the business by the ordinary shareholders regardless of the dividends paid or proposed on these shares. A more realistic and, invariably, conservative rate of earnings may be obtained by employing the real value of equity capital employed (i e the current value of the assets, less preference shares and liabilities) as the denominator. However, as mentioned earlier, assessment of the current value of the assets of a concern is no easy matter, and for this reason will not generally be available.

(2) *Earnings per share* representing net profit after corporation tax and preference dividend per ordinary share is closely allied to the above ratio and was recognised as a vital indicator by the Accounting Standards Committee in SSAP 3, under which such information must be appended to the published accounts of companies. (See chapter 22.)

(3) *The ratio of profit available for dividend to dividend paid,* or dividend cover, reveals the distribution and 'plough-back' policies of the directors. The ratio of retained earnings to net profit i e the complementary ratio, may also be computed to show the potential of an ordinary share for capital growth, while the margin of profit above that which is required to pay the expected dividend can be used to estimate the security of the share so far as dividend payments are concerned. Investors and would-be investors may use these ratios as criteria for decisions, so that they may have a direct effect on the demand for, and market price (in the case of a quoted company) of the shares.

The board of directors of a company should, therefore, always endeavour to maintain a careful balance between their dividend and 'plough-back' policies, for if dividends are too restricted, the market price of the shares may fall and a take-over bid ensue. On the other hand distribution of dividends on too generous a scale may inhibit the ability of a company to expand without resort to fresh capital or loans, besides depleting its current liquid resources.

Care should be taken to deduct preference dividends from net profit when comparing the cover on ordinary shares.

(4) *The ratio of profit available for dividend to preference dividend* will reveal the number of times the preference divided is covered by earnings and thus indicate the preference shareholders' security, so far as income is concerned.

(5) *The dividend yield ratio* is the ratio of dividend received to the price paid for a share, or the current market price thereof. The yield acceptable to an investor will depend upon the risk attaching to the investment and the potential for capital growth; generally speaking, the greater the yield the greater the risk. Investors may be induced to accept a low yield where the market price of shares has fallen and the company is ripe for a take-over bid, or where the prospects are outstanding.

(6) *The price/earnings ratio* from an individual investor's viewpoint is ascertained by comparing the market price of an ordinary share with the earnings, or net profit per share, after deduction of corporation tax and preference dividends; this may be expressed as so many years' purchase of the profits: in other words, assuming stability of market price and ignoring the incidence of taxation of dividends, an investor's capital outlay will, at the present level of earnings, be recouped after so many years, either in the form of dividends received, or capital growth by virtue of retained profits. This ratio may provide a collateral check upon conclusions drawn from other earnings ratios, while calculations may be based upon forecast profits to provide a prospective price/earnings ratio.

This ratio may also be computed by comparing the Stock Exchange value of the ordinary shares of a company, i e price per ordinary share times the number of ordinary shares, with net profit after corporation tax and preference dividends, thus enabling the large investor and board of directors alike to compare the overall efficiency of a particular company with similar, or indeed, dissimilar companies (if the company in question is potentially adaptable): such comparisons will, however, only be valid if a reasonable degree of parity prevails between market prices, bearing in mind that these are subject to external influences e g government measures or the world economic climate, and/or domestic influences e g restrictive or overgenerous dividend policies.

Mention may be made, in passing, that the Stock Exchange value of a company is, in itself, of immense interest to financiers in connection with prospective take-overs bids and mergers.

23.3   RATIO ANALYSIS ILLUSTRATION

The ratios are set out in the order in which they were discussed earlier in the chapter. Reference should be made to the comments made in respect of each ratio.

Return on capital employed
  (PBIT/FA+WC)
$$\frac{133,600+6,000}{924,300} \times 100 \qquad 15.1$$

$\dfrac{\text{Gross profit}}{\text{Sales}}$
$$\frac{284,000}{791,000} \times 100 \qquad 35.9$$

$\dfrac{\text{PBIT}}{\text{Sales}}$
$$\frac{133,600+6,000}{791,000} \times 100 \qquad 17.6$$

$\dfrac{\text{Materials}}{\text{Sales}}$
$$\frac{352,400}{791,000} \times 100 \qquad 44.5$$

$\dfrac{\text{Labour}}{\text{Sales}}$
$$\frac{137,900}{791,000} \times 100 \qquad 17.4$$

$\dfrac{\text{Factory overheads}}{\text{Sales}}$
$$\frac{47,700}{791,000} \times 100 \qquad 6.0$$

$\dfrac{\text{Administrative expenses}}{\text{Sales}}$
$$\frac{74,200}{791,000} \times 100 \qquad 9.4$$

$\dfrac{\text{Selling and distribution expenses}}{\text{Sales}}$
$$\frac{107,300}{791,000} \times 100 \qquad 13.6$$

$\dfrac{\text{Bad debts}}{\text{Sales}}$
$$\frac{2,500}{791,000} \times 100 \qquad 0.3$$

$\dfrac{\text{Sales}}{\text{Capital employed}}$
$$\frac{791,000}{924,300} \qquad \frac{0.8}{1}$$

$\dfrac{\text{Raw material stocks}}{\text{Purchases}}$
$$\frac{76,400}{319,000} \qquad \frac{0.24}{1}$$

Alternatively, raw material stocks could be described as 88 days' purchases (0.24 × 365).

Work-in-progress
Cost of production
$$\frac{12,800}{538,000} \qquad \frac{0.02}{1}$$

(That is, WIP is equivalent to eight days' production.)

Finished stock
Turnover
$$\frac{40,100}{1,791,000} \qquad \frac{0.05}{1}$$

(That is, finished stock is equivalent to 18 days' sales.)

Current sales
Debtors
$$\frac{791,000}{116,870} \qquad \frac{6.8}{1}$$

(That is, debtors are equivalent to 54 days' sales.)

Current assets
Current liabilities
$$\frac{489,290}{147,690} \qquad \frac{3.3}{1}$$

Liquid assets
Current liabilities
$$\frac{489,290 - 129,300}{147,690} \qquad \frac{2.4}{1}$$

Debt
Equity
$$\frac{150,000}{709,400} \qquad \frac{0.2}{1}$$

Fixed assets
Capital employed
$$\frac{582,700}{924,300} \qquad \frac{0.63}{1}$$

Net profit after tax and
preference dividend
Shareholders' equity
$$\frac{67,700 - 5,600}{709,400} \times 100 = \qquad 8.7\%$$

Earnings per share
$$\frac{67,700 - 5,600}{400,000} = \qquad 15.5\text{p per share}$$

Dividend cover (ordinaries)
$$\frac{67,700 - 5,600}{20,000} = \qquad 3.1 \text{ times}$$

Dividend cover (preference)
$$\frac{67,700}{5,600} = \qquad 12.1 \text{ times}$$

NOTE
In the absence of a quoted share price, neither dividend yield nor earnings per share can be calculated.

23.4   INFORMATION AVAILABLE FROM PUBLISHED REPORTS

(a) Introduction

Some people appear to take the view that a company's position, performance and prospects can only be assessed by reference to information contained in the balance sheet, profit and loss account and related notes. This is often hardly the case! Useful information may be contained elsewhere in a company's annual report. Possible sources include:

(1) chairman's (or chief executive's) statement;
(2) divisional review;
(3) financial summaries and highlights;
(4) segmental analysis;
(5) funds flow statements;
(6) ratio analysis information including earnings per share;
(7) value added statements;
(8) comparison of profits with those measured under United States generally accepted accounting principles (GAAPs).

(b) Chairman's statement

The statement of the chairman or chief executive often includeds a concise review of the company's or group's progress. The statement may well give some indication of likely prospects for the forthcoming year. Such information, however, is not subject to minimum legal requirements regarding content nor is it technically within the scope of the auditor's report. Additionally the statement is likely to emphasise matters which the board wish to emphasise! Nevertheless to the average reader the statement is likely to be of significant interest.

(c) Divisional review

This may provide an informative perspective of business activities possibly with an indication of their relative importance in relation to sales and profits.

(d) Financial summaries and highlights

These are clearly aimed at the non-technical reader and aim to give a simple overview of financial highlights.

(e) Segmental analysis

Reporting requirements and the need for segmental analysis were referred to in chapter 5. As groups become larger and larger segmental analysis should take on an increasingly important role. Group accounts, after all, consolidate many different activities (except for those activities which are 'so dissimilar from those of other companies within the group that consolidated financial statements would be misleading . . .', see chapter 16). Information about performance and contribution of segments becomes crucial in providing a counter-balance to the broad-brush approach of consolidation.

In practice, the amount and quality of segmental information varies from group to group. Some groups provide information over and above the mandatory minimum. Useful illustrations of segmental disclosures are given below:

Illustration 1

CADBURY SCHWEPPES PLC 1986 ACCOUNTS

Sales trading profit and operating assets analysis

£ million	Total	United Kingdom	Europe	North America	Rest of the World
1986					
Sales					
Confectionery	841.9	411.1	56.9	192.7	181.2
Drinks	813.0	245.0	221.5	222.3	124.2
Beverages and Foods	185.0	110.0	14.7	—	60.3
	1,839.9	766.1	293.1	415.0	365.7
Trading profit					
Confectionery	65.6	46.0	2.9	(2.1)	18.8
Drinks	66.5	27.9	19.7	8.1	10.8
Beverages and Foods	8.3	2.3	0.8	—	5.2
	140.4	76.2	23.4	6.0	34.8
Operating assets					
Confectionery	389.7	166.8	25.1	120.2	77.6
Drinks	252.3	97.3	57.0	55.1	42.9
Beverages and Foods	23.8	—	—	—	23.8
	665.8	264.1	82.1	175.3	144.3
1985					
Sales					
Confectionery	769.6	375.3	53.4	189.1	151.8
Drinks	668.8	231.9	166.0	168.8	102.1
Beverages and Foods	377.5	286.1	33.8	—	57.6
Health and Hygiene	57.9	57.9	—	—	—
	1,873.8	951.2	253.2	357.9	311.5
Trading profit					
Confectionery	55.6	40.9	4.3	(6.8)	17.2
Drinks	42.8	16.9	14.0	1.2	10.7
Beverages and Foods	13.7	6.9	2.3	—	4.5
Health and Hygiene	0.9	0.9	—	—	—
	113.0	65.6	20.6	(5.6)	32.4
Operating assets					
Confectionery	387.1	166.2	19.5	138.6	62.8
Drinks	276.2	103.4	47.8	84.3	40.7
Beverages and Foods	94.4	69.7	7.5	—	17.2
Health and Hygiene	17.3	17.3	—	—	—
	775.0	356.6	74.8	222.9	120.7

TRADING PROFIT TO OPERATING ASSETS

	%	%	%	%	%
1986	21.1	28.9	28.5	3.4	24.1
1985	14.6	18.4	27.5	(2.5)	26.8

The geographical analysis is based on the location of the operating companies. Operating assets represent tangible fixed assets, stock, debtors and creditors after excluding borrowings, taxation and dividends.

Illustration 2

BEECHAM GROUP PLC 1987 ACCOUNTS

NOTES TO THE ACCOUNTS

Year Ended 31 March 1987

1 SEGMENT INFORMATION

The analysis of sales and trading profit by business sector and by the geographical area in which each company is located as follows:

	Sales		Trading profit	
	1986/87	*1985/86*	*1986/87*	*1985/86*
Business sector	*£m*	*£m*	*£m*	*£m*
Continuing operations				
Prescription and over the counter medicines				
Prescription medicines	770.3	699.3	249.4	218.4
Over the counter medicines	229.1	154.7	63.6	39.4
	999.4	854.0	313.0	257.8
Consumer products				
Toiletries, drinks and other consumer products	799.8	772.8	128.8	113.7
Cosmetics	477.4	438.0	41.7	31.5
	1,277.2	1,210.8	170.5	145.2
	2,276.6	2,064.8	483.5	403.0
Research and development expenditure	—	—	(99.4)	(88.3)
Total continuing operations	2,276.6	2,064.8	384.1	314.7
Discontinued operations	453.5	537.9	10.3	20.7
	2,730.1	2,602.7	394.4	335.4

	Sales		Trading profit	
	1986/87	*1985/86*	*1986/87*	*1985/86*
Geographical area	*£m*	*£m*	*£m*	*£m*
Continuing operations				
United Kingdom				
Home sales	392.8	381.7		
Export sales	216.7	190.7		
	609.5	572.4	179.2	153.8
Rest of Europe	930.5	765.3	143.0	112.0
The Americas	645.0	621.0	127.5	97.9
Rest of the World	244.6	232.6	33.8	39.3
Intra-group sales	(153.0)	(126.5)	—	—
	2,276.6	2,064.8	483.5	403.0
Research and development expenditure	—	—	(99.4)	(88.3)
Total continuing operations	2,276.6	2,064.8	384.1	314.7
Discontinued operations	453.5	537.9	10.3	20.7
	2,730.1	2,602.7	394.4	335.4

The Group's results for 1986/87 from continuing operations include those of Norcliff Thayer for a full year as compared with only a three month period in 1985/86. The incremental effect was to increase sales by £74.7m and trading profit by £24.5m.

The analysis of sales by location of customer is as follows:

	1986/87 £m	1985/86 £m
Continuing operations		
United Kingdom	409.5	392.9
Rest of Europe	910.0	745.7
The Americas	648.4	618.4
Rest of the World	308.7	307.8
Total continuing operations	2,276.6	2,064.8
Discontinued operations	453.5	537.9
	2,730.1	2,602.7

Group policy is that sales between Group companies are made at prices which ensure a fair profit to each company involved.

Discontinued operations

The analysis of sales and trading profit by business sector and geographical area of the businesses sold during the year, or in course of disposal at the year end, is as follows:

	Sales 1986/87 £m	Sales 1985/86 £m	Trading profit 1986/87 £m	Trading profit 1985/86 £m
Business sector				
Prescription medicines	6.9	8.0	—	—
Consumer products				
Drinks and Foods	236.8	295.6	12.3	12.4
Cosmetics	32.3	58.0	(12.8)	(8.1)
Home improvement products	177.5	176.3	10.8	16.4
Total	453.5	537.9	10.3	20.7
Geographical area				
United Kingdom	248.2	276.6	8.9	17.4
Rest of Europe	54.4	62.6	1.6	3.8
The Americas	141.2	175.6	(0.4)	2.3
Rest of the World	11.4	25.1	0.2	(2.8)
Intra-group sales	(1.7)	(2.0)	—	—
Total	453.5	537.9	10.3	20.7

(f) Funds flow statements

All companies and groups with an annual turnover in excess of £25,000 are required by SSAP 10 to present a funds flow statement as part of their financial statements (see chapter 21).

Funds flow statements should help to provide a 'fuller understanding' of a company's affairs. Nevertheless it should be appreciated that funds flow information by itself may be of limited value. For example, the statement may indicate a significant increase in working capital consisting mainly of increases in stocks and debtors. What the statement usually fails to indicate is whether such an increase is a good thing (e g planned expansion) or a bad thing (e g poor stock control and credit control). Other questions must therefore be raised if a realistic appraisal is to be obtained.

(g) Ratio analysis information including earnings per share

All listed companies are required by SSAP 3 to present earnings per share information on the face of the profit and loss account (see chapter 22). It is evident that many financial analysts and commentators place great importance on this statistic notwithstanding some of the important limitations placed on its usefulness (see 22.6).

Some companies present key ratios although such information is not mandatory. These ratios may be presented in the form of five-year (or even longer) summaries. A useful illustration, relating to the 1986 report of Cadbury Schweppes, is included below:

Illustration 3

CADBURY SCHWEPPES PLC

Financial ratios

			1986	1985	1984	1983	1982
PROFITABILITY							
Margin	*Trading profit* / *Sales*	%	7.6	6.0	7.7	7.4	7.0
Return on assets	*Trading profit* / *Operating assets**	%	21.1	14.6	18.5	17.5	16.1
INTEREST AND DIVIDEND COVER							
Interest cover	*Trading profit* / *Net interest charge*	times	9.8	4.1	4.1	4.9	5.0
Dividend cover	*Earnings per ordinary share* / *Dividend per ordinary share*	times	2.1	1.6	2.7	2.5	2.2
GEARING RATIOS							
	Net borrowings / *Shareholders' funds*	%	19.0	46.4	43.6	61.1	48.5
	Net borrowings / *Shareholders' funds plus minority interests*	%	17.1	42.6	39.9	55.3	44.2
LIQUIDITY RATIOS							
Quick ratio	*Current assets less stock* / *Current liabilities*	%	90.6	75.6	74.2	73.2	78.7
Current ratio	*Current assets* / *Current liabilities*	%	134.8	129.2	133.8	130.2	142.3
ASSET RATIOS							
Operating asset turnover	*Sales* / *Operating assets**	times	2.8	2.4	2.4	2.4	2.3
Working capital turnover	*Sales* / *Working capital*	times	14.6	9.2	8.6	8.0	7.0

PER SHARE

	1986	1985	1984	1983	1982
Earnings per share — pre-tax basis	p 21.34	15.56	23.62	21.25	17.96
— net basis	p 14.28	9.31	15.65	13.60	10.98
— net of extraordinary items basis	p 19.14	8.16	14.05	9.52	8.82
Dividends per share	p 6.70	5.90	5.90	5.40	4.90
Net assets per share	p 82.36	90.18	102.1	89.22	86.95

*Operating assets represent tangible fixed assets, stock, debtors and creditors after excluding borrowings, taxation and dividends.

(h) Value added statements

A small minority of listed companies present value added statements (see chapter 21). Such information may be of particular interest to specific user groups, for example, employees. Some of these companies present also certain ratios or statistics derived from value added statements, for example:

(1) sales per employee;
(2) value added per employee;
(3) value added as percentage of sales;
(4) wages as percentage of value added;
(5) value added as percentage of capital employed.

(i) Comparison with profits measured under United States generally accepted accounting principles (GAAPs)

Companies whose shares are traded in the US may present additional information which compare UK reported profits with those which would be reported under US GAAPs. Where such information is available it may give analysts a useful appreciation of the financial implications for the company's or group's results of using different accounting policies.

Illustration 4

ANNUAL REPORT OF CADBURY SCHWEPPES PLC FOR 1986

Additional information for US investors

Cadbury Schweppes American Depositary shares are traded over the counter and quoted on the NASDAO system. The ticker symbol is CADBY.

The group prepares its consolidated accounts in accordance with generally accepted accounting principles ('GAAP') applicable in the U.K.

The terms and principles used are explained on pages 31 to 33 and differ from those applicable in the US. The effect of such differences and an explanation of the accounting terms and principles are set out below.

Effect of differences

	Per UK GAAP		Per US GAAP	
	1985	*1986*	*1985*	*1986*
	£m	*£m*	*£m*	*£m*
Operating income	113.0	140.4	102.4	153.3
Income before tax	93.3	130.7	89.6	147.8
Net income (as below)	47.8	76.1	34.8	89.4
Shareholders' equity	471.0	463.2	467.0	573.1

	1985	*1986*	*1986*
	£m	*£m*	*$m**
Net income before extraordinary items per UK GAAP	47.8	76.1	113.4
US GAAP adjustments (net of tax):			
Goodwill	(1.3)	(3.0)	(4.5)
Capitalisation of interest	0.9	0.4	0.6
Elimination of revaluation surplus	0.7	0.3	0.4
Foreign currency translation	(1.0)	(0.3)	(0.4)
One-time credits/(charges)	(8.2)	22.0	32.8
Deferred taxation	(4.6)	(6.1)	(9.1)
Elimination of discontinued operations	0.5	—	—
Net Income per US GAAP	34.8	89.4	133.2

* At year-end exchange rate: £1 = US$1.49

Discontinued operations:

Net loss on operations	(0.5)	—	—
Loss on disposal	(5.8)	—	—

Financial ratios per US GAAP:

		1985	1986	
Operating income: net sales	%	5.5	8.3	
Operating income: operating assets	%	13.0	21.7	
Operating income: net equity	%	22.0	26.7	
Gross borrowings: net equity and gross borrowings	%	36.3	31.7	
Net income per ADS	£	0.68	1.68	$2.50
Net income per ADS adjusted for one-time credits/(charges)	£	0.84	1.27	$1.89
Net assets per ADS	£	8.94	10.21	$15.21

The net income per ADS figures are based on the weighted average number of ordinary shares in issue during the year as shown in note 12 on page 37.

ACCOUNTING TERMS AND PRINCIPLES

(a) Terms

Trading profit = operating income

Associated companies = investees accounted for under the equity method

Share premium = premium received on issue of stock in excess of par value which is not available for distribution

Advance corporation tax = tax due on payment of UK dividends which is treated as an advance in respect of taxes on corporate income

Capital allowances = accelerated depreciation allowed for tax purpose

(b) Goodwill

Under US GAAP goodwill is amortised by charges against income over the period which it is estimated will be benefited and, accordingly, goodwill has been amortised over a 40-year period which is its estimated useful life.

(c) Capitalisation of interest

Under UK GAAP the capitalisation of interest is not required and the group does not capitalise interest in its financial statements. US GAAP require interest incurred as part of the cost of acquiring fixed assets to be capitalised and amortised over the life of the asset.

(d) Deferred tax

Under UK GAAP no provision is made for deferred taxation if there is reasonable evidence that such deferred taxation will not be payable in the foreseeable future. In the US, Accounting Principles Board Opinion No. 11 requires deferred tax to be provided on the full deferral basis.

(e) Extraordinary items

Under UK GAAP the costs or credits associated with major restructuring programmes or the disposal of operations may be classified as extraodinary items. Such treatment is not necessarily permitted under US GAAP.

(f) Revaluation of properties

Under US GAAP the re-statement of properties on the basis of appraised values is eliminated.

(g) Foreign currency translation

Under UK GAAP the consolidated income statements may include the results of foreign subsidiaries translated at the year-end rates. The requirements under US GAAP for foreign currency translation require the use of a weighted average rate for the period in translating the results of foreign subsidiaries.

(h) Ordinary dividends

Under UK GAAP final ordinary dividends are provided in the financial statements on the basis of the recommendations by the directors which require subsequent approval by the shareholders. Under US GAAP dividends are provided when declared by the directors.

DIVIDENDS

The final dividend recommended for the year 1986 (if approved at the Annual General Meeting) will be payable on 10 June 1987 to the holders of American Depositary Receipts whose names are registered with Morgan Guaranty Trust Company of New York on 2 April 1987.

For US residents the gross final dividend per ADS (as recommended) will amount to 67.1p (1985–60.6p) on the basis of the UK tax proposals announced on 17 March 1987. On payment a withholding tax of 15% will be deducted. In the case of individuals this tax will normally be eligible for a credit against US federal income taxes obtained by filing Form 1116 'Computation of Foreign Tax Credit' with the Federal income tax return.

SEC FILINGS

In accordance with US legislation Cadbury Schweppes plc makes various filings including an annual report on Form 20-F with the Securities and Exchange Commission in Washington DC These filings are available for public inspection and ADR holders may obtain a copy of Form 20-F from Morgan Guaranty Trust Company of New York. Other shareholders wishing to see a copy of Form 20-F should apply to the Company Secretary in London.

23.5 INTERPRETATION OF ACCOUNTS—POSSIBLE LIMITATIONS ON THE USEFULNESS OF INTER-COMPANY COMPARISONS

(a) Introduction

It may be difficult to make a valid comparison between two companies if they adopt significantly different policies regarding the treatment, for example, of leasing, goodwill, foreign currency translation and fixed asset revaluations. Some of the main areas of difficulty are referred to below. Further reference should be made to the relevant section covered earlier in the book.

(b) Historical cost accounts

Weaknesses and criticisms of accounts drawn up on a historical cost basis were referred to in chapter 19. These weaknesses clearly have implications for the validity of comparisons between companies, hence the attempts of ASC to produce an acceptable standard dealing with accounting for price changes.

(c) Leasing

During the transitional period (capitalisation of finance leases becomes mandatory for accounts periods beginning on or after 1 July 1987) companies have a choice of capitalisation or of leaving the finance lease 'off-balance sheet'.

(d) Goodwill

Companies may either eliminate goodwill against reserves as soon as it arises (without any effect on reported profit) or amortise over a number of years (thus reducing annual reported profit).

(e) Foreign currency translation

Groups which adopt a policy of translating financial statements of foreign subsidiaries using the closing rate/net investment method may translate the subsidiary's profit and loss account at either average for the year rates or year-end rates (see chapter 18).

(f) Implications of modified historical cost

Whether and to what extent a company adopts modified historical cost can affect reported profits (the computations of depreciation charge and profit on sale of revalued assets were dealt with in chapter 7).

(g) Exceptional and extraordinary items

ASC's review of the operation of the original version of SSAP 6 identified some significant variations as between different companies of the treatment of exceptional and extraordinary items (frequent examples of problem areas included profits on sale of property assets and redundancy and reorganisation costs).

(h) Post-balance sheet events

A post-balance sheet event may be identified technically as being non-adjusting but a particular company may wish nevertheless to reflect it in current year accounts on prudence grounds. An example could relate to a closure decision taken shortly after the balance sheet date. Another company may reflect this transaction in the financial statements of the following year. Again this sometimes makes difficult valid inter-company comparisons.

(i) Exclusion of subsidiaries from consolidation

The criteria for deciding whether or not a particular subsidiary should be excluded from consolidated accounts were referred to in chapter 16. A particular example is 'dissimilar' activities. The decision whether or not to consolidate (which in some situations may be borderline) may have an important bearing on the complexion of the group financial statements.

Key ratios such as the debt/equity ratio could be affected. In the case of debt capital of a subsidiary, if the subsidiary is consolidated in the usual way, the subsidiary's debt capital will form part of non-current creditors in the group balance sheet. If the subsidiary is excluded, the group balance sheet will contain a one-line, net assets of excluded subsidiary, under the fixed asset investment heading. The net asset figure will be arrived at after deducting the subsidiary's debt capital.

(j) Off-balance sheet finance

This topic was referred to in 6.13. One particular matter of concern was potential distortion of the debt/equity ratio.

(k) Business combinations satisfying the merger conditions of SSAP 23

In these circumstances group accounts may be prepared on either an acquisition basis or a merger basis. This again can cause problems when making inter-company comparisons. Earnings per share aspects of this were referred to in 22.4(e).

24 INTERNATIONAL ACCOUNTING STANDARDS

24.1 INTRODUCTION

(a) The International Accounting Standards Committee (IASC)

IASC is referred to in section 6.5 of chapter 6 which includes a list of current international accounting standards.

IASC was founded in 1973 and is the only independent body charged by its member organisations to issue international accounting standards. In early 1985, IASC represented some 90 accountancy bodies in nearly 70 countries.

(b) Objectives of IASC

The main objectives are twofold:

(1) to develop, publish and promote international accounting standards for financial statements;
(2) to work generally for the improvement and harmonisation of accounting practices.

(c) Obligations of members of IASC

Each member undertook to support the work of IASC by publishing in their respective country every IAS.

Each member also undertook to use their best endeavours:

(1) to ensure that published finanical statements comply with IASs in all material respects and to disclose the fact of such compliance;
(2) to persuade governments and standard-setting bodies that published financial statements should comply with IASs in all material respects;
(3) to persuade authorities controlling securities markets and the industrial and business community that published financial statements should comply with IASs in all material respects and disclose the fact of such compliance;
(4) to ensure that the auditors satisfy themselves that the financial statements comply with IASs in all material respects;
(5) to foster acceptance and observance of IASs internationally.

(d) Relationship with national accounting standards

A principal object of IASC is to harmonise as far as is possible the diverse accounting standards and accounting policies of different countries. IASs do not override the local regulations governing the issue of financial statements in a particular country.

Where IASs are complied with in all material respects, this fact should be disclosed. An appropriate wording would be 'The financial statements are prepared in accordance with accounting principles generally accepted in the UK and conform in all material respects with International Accounting Standards'. Any difference between international and national standards, provided the effect is material, should be specified.

(e) Effect on UK standards

To date, no conflict between UK and international standards has arisen. This is due mainly to two factors:

(1) IASs are not applicable in the UK until specifically adopted by the CCAB.
(2) IASs are generally less restrictive than their UK counterparts.

Compliance with UK standards issued to date automatically ensures compliance with the respective IAS. Most UK standards incorporate a paragraph with words to the effect that compliance with the particular SSAP automatically ensures compliance with a specific international accounting standard.

(f) The importance of international accounting standards

If IASs are generally accepted, then investors, bankers, creditors, managers, employees and governments have less difficulty understanding and analysing annual and interim reports prepared in countries other than their own, and can have confidence in those reports.

IASs should help improve the quality, reliability and comparability of worldwide financial reporting.

Clearly international standards are particularly important to countries which do not have their own standard-setting bodies.

24.2   CURRENT ACCOUNTING STANDARDS

(a) IAS 1 Disclosure of accounting policies

In broad terms, IAS 1 follows SSAP 2 (see chapter 6) very closely.
   Points of difference worth noting are:

(1) Fundamental accounting assumptions are:
   going concern; consistency; accrual.
(2) Selection and application of accounting policies should be governed by:
   prudence; substance over form; materiality.
      The concept of substance over form is defined as: 'transactions and other events should be accounted for and presented in accordance with their substance and financial reality and not merely with their legal form'.

(b) IAS 2 Valuation and presentation of inventories in the context of the historical cost system

IAS 2 follows SSAP 9 (see chapter 8) fairly closely, except that IAS 2 does not deal with long-term contracts (see IAS 11, below).
   The main point of difference is that IAS 2 allows LIFO or base stock to be used provided that disclosure is made of the difference between:

(1) the amount of the inventories as shown in the balance sheet; and
(2) either:

   (i)   the lower of the FIFO/average cost and net realisable value (NRV); or
   (ii) the lower of current cost and NRV.

(c) IAS 3 Consolidated financial statements

The subject matter of IAS 3 overlaps with both SSAP 14 (see chapter 16) and SSAP 1 (see chapter 17).
   Main points of difference are:

(1) *Form of group accounts*

(i)   Where the activities of a subsidiary are so dissimilar from those of other group companies that better information would be provided by presenting separate financial statements, IAS 3 permits the subsidiary to be excluded from consolidation, whereas SSAP 14 makes such exclusion mandatory.

(ii) Where a group does not have control of a particular company but either:

    (a) owns more than half the equity capital but less than half the voting power; or

    (b) has the power to control (by statute or by agreement) the financial and operating policies of the management of the company

then the company concerned may be treated as a subsidiary and consolidated, with reasons for consolidation disclosed.

(2) *Definition of equity method of accounting*

IAS 3 defines the equity method as a method of accounting for certain types of long-term investments in associated companies and for certain unconsolidated subsidiaries (e g on grounds of dissimilarity of activities).

Under the equity method, the investment account of the investor is adjusted in the consolidated financial statements for the changes in the investor's share of the net assets of the investee. The income statement reflects the investor's share of the results of operations of the investee.

This definition may be regarded as considerably more helpful than that set out in para 14 of SSAP 14.

(d) IAS 4 Depreciation accounting

IAS 4 is similar in effect to SSAP 12 (see chapter 7). However IAS 4 does not deal with the depreciation problems which arise when revaluations are substituted for historical cost (i e the modified historical cost convention) which are covered by SSAP 12. It is important to note that IAS 16, Accounting for property, plant and equipment, does deal with modified historical cost.

(e) IAS 5 Information to be disclosed in financial statements

There is no UK equivalent of IAS 5, since company disclosure requirements are adequately covered by the provisions of the Companies Act 1985. Consequently, the requirements of IAS 5 will not be referred to.

(f) IAS 7 Statement of changes in financial position

IAS 7 deals with statements of source and applications of funds and is in many respects similar in effect to SSAP 10 (see chapter 21). Like SSAP 10, IAS 7 does not attempt to require a particular format.

IAS 7 does refer to alternative layouts of funds statements. It also refers to alternative treatments of particular accounting matters, and to this extent is more informative than SSAP 10. However, IAS 7 is unlikely to be any more successful than SSAP 10 in standardising funds statements.

(g) IAS 8 Unusual and prior period items and changes in accounting policies

IAS 8 is similar in effect to SSAP 6, dealing with extraordinary items and prior year adjustments, allowing for differences in terminology (unusual items as opposed to extraordinary items).

Main points of difference of treatment of items are:

(1) Treatment of prior period items (fundamental errors) and changes in accounting policies where IAS 8 offers two alternatives:

    (i) restatement of opening retained reserves (SSAP 6 approach); or

    (ii) separate disclosure in the profit and loss account as part of profit for the year (not acceptable under SSAP 6).

(2) Treatment of changes in accounting estimates, where IAS 8 requires that a

change in an accounting estimate should be accounted for as part of profit from ordinary activities of the enterprise in:

(i) the period of change if the change affects the period only; or

(ii) the period of change and future periods if the changes affects both.

The second possibility is not acceptable under SSAP 6.

(h) IAS 9 Accounting for research and development activities

Much of IAS 9 is similar to SSAP 13 (see chapter 7).

IAS 9 requires that research and development costs should be charged to profit and loss account as incurred except to the extent that development costs are capitalised and amortised in accordance with criteria similar to those in SSAP 9.

IAS 9 provides a list of expense categories that should be included in research and development costs. These include:

(1) the salaries, wages and other related costs of personnel engaged in research and development activities;

(2) the costs of materials and services consumed in research and development activities;

(3) the depreciation of equipment and facilities to the extent that they are used for research and development activities;

(4) overhead costs related to research and development activities;

(5) other costs related to research and development activities, such as the amortisation of patents and licences.

(i) IAS 10 Contingencies and events occurring after the balance sheet date

IAS 10 is covered by two separate UK accounting standards, SSAP 17 and SSAP 18 (see chapter 5).

Unlike SSAP 17, IAS 10 does not refer to window-dressing transactions. Nor does IAS 10 include an appendix giving details of events which would normally be regarded as adjusting or non-adjusting.

(j) IAS 11 Accounting for construction contracts

IAS 2 (see above) is concerned with stock and work-in-progress other than construction contracts. IAS 2 and IAS 11 taken together correspond with SSAP 9 (see chapter 8). Main points of difference between IAS 11 and SSAP 9 are:

(1) *Definitions*

Construction contracts (IAS 11)	Long-term contract (SSAP 9)
A contract for the construction of an asset or a combination of assets which together constitute a single project. Criteria: date at which contract activity is entered into and the date when the contract activity is completed fall into different accounting periods.	A contract entered into for manufacture or building of a single substantial entity or the provision of a service where the time taken to manufacture, build or provide is such that a substantial proportion of all such contract work will extend for a period exceeding one year.

Note that IAS 11 does not regard the specific duration of the contract performance as a distinguishing feature of a construction contract.

(2) *Accounting methods*

IAS 11 permits the use of either the percentage of completion method or the completed contract method. However, the percentage of completion method may only be used if specified conditions can be satisfied. All contracts meeting similar criteria should be accounted for by the same method.

In essence SSAP 9 follows the percentage of completion method.

(3) *Disclosures*

Where a company uses both the above methods for different contracts, the amount of construction work in progress should be analysed as between amounts under the two methods.

(k) IAS 12 Accounting for taxes on income

IAS 12 is concerned essentially with accounting for deferred tax, a topic covered by SSAP 15 (see chapter 9). The main differences between IAS 12 and SSAP 15 are:

(1) *Approach to deferred tax*

SSAP 15 requires a partial provision approach to be used provided certain criteria can be satisfied.

IAS 12 normally requires a full provision approach to be adopted. However, IAS 12 permits a partial provision approach to be adopted provided that certain criteria can be satisfied and that unprovided deferred tax is disclosed by way of memorandum note. The criteria are similar to those in SSAP 15.

(2) *Basis of evaluation of timing differences*

SSAP 15 effectively requires the liability method to be used. IAS 12 requires the use of either the deferral or the liability method.

(l) IAS 13 Presentation of current assets and current liabilities

There is no UK equivalent of IAS 13. However most of the content of IAS 13 is covered by the detailed requirements of the Companies Act 1985 and development of accounting practice in the UK, so no further reference will be made.

(m) IAS 14 Reporting financial information by segments

There is no UK equivalent of IAS 14. However, the Companies Act 1985 does specify disclosure of segmental information (see chapter 5, section 5.11).

The principal requirements of IAS 14 are as follows:

(1) Listed and other economically significant entities should give the segmental information specified below for:

    (i) significant industry segments (e g business activities);
    (ii) significant geographical segments (e g markets supplied).

(2) The enterprise should describe the activities of each reported industry segment and indicate the composition of each reported geographical area.
(3) The following financial information should be disclosed for each reported industry and geographical segment:

    (i) sales or other operating revenues, distinguishing between:

        (a) revenue derived from customers outside the enterprise; and
        (b) revenue derived from other segments;

    (ii) segment result;

(iii) segment assets employed, expressed either in money amounts or as percentages of the consolidated totals; and

(iv) the basis of inter-segment pricing.

(4) The enterprise should provide reconciliations between the sum of the information on individual segments and the aggregate information in the financial statements.

(5) Information should be given of changes in identification of segments and changes in accounting practices used in reporting segment information.

(n) IAS 15 Information reflecting the effect of changing prices

(1) *General considerations*

IAS 15 supersedes IAS 6. Unlike the previous UK standard SSAP 16, IAS 15 sets out extremely general requirements.

IAS 15 discusses the following broad approaches:

(i) a general purchasing power approach (as advocated by the former UK standard SSAP 7, see chapter 19);

(ii) a current cost approach;

(iii) a current cost approach, adjusted in particular respects for changes in the purchasing power of money.

IAS 15 was published in November 1981. IASC expressed the view that '... further experimentation is necessary before consideration can be given to requiring enterprises to prepare primary financial statements using a comprehensive and uniform system for reflecting changing prices. Meanwhile, evolution of the subject would be assisted if enterprises that present primary financial statements on the historical cost basis also provide supplementary information reflecting the effects of price changes'.

(2) *Requirements of IAS 15*

(i) APPROACH AND STATUS OF INFORMATION

Enterprises within the scope of the standard should present information disclosing the items below using an accounting method which reflects the effect of changing prices. Note that IAS 14 does not specify a particular approach.

The information required should be presented in supplementary form unless it is presented in the primary financial statements.

(ii) PROFIT AND LOSS INFORMATION

Items to be presented are:

(a) the amount of the adjustment to (or the adjusted amount of) depreciation of property, plant and equipment;

(b) the amount of the adjustment to (or the adjusted amount of) cost of sales;

(c) the adjustments relating to monetary items, the effect of borrowing, or equity interests when such adjustments have been taken into account in determining profit under the accounting method adopted;

(d) the overall effect on results of the adjustments in (a) and (b) and, where appropriate (c), as well as any other items reflecting the effects of changing prices that are reported under the accounting method adopted.

(iii) BALANCE SHEET INFORMATION

Where a current cost method is adopted, disclosure is required of the current cost of property, plant and equipment, and of stocks.

(iv) ACCOUNTING POLICIES

Enterprises should describe methods adopted to complete the information including the nature of indices used.

(o) IAS 16 Accounting for property, plant and equipment

(1) *General considerations*

No single UK accounting standard deals specifically with accounting for fixed assets. However, many of the requirements of IAS 16 are to be found in SSAP 12 (see chapter 7).

IAS 6 requires that the gross carrying amount of an asset included in property, plant and equipment should be either historical cost or a revaluation (i e modified historical cost).

The points below refer to matters not directly dealt with by SSAP 12.

(2) *Assets carried at historical cost*

(i)   Self-constructed property, plant and equipment: costs should include direct costs as well as costs relating to construction activity in general which can be allocated to the particular asset.

(ii) Property, plant and equipment acquired in part exchange for another asset: the cost of the asset acquired should be recorded at either:

    (a) fair value; or
    (b) the net carrying amount of the asset given up adjusted for any balancing payment or receipt of cash or other consideration.

(iii) Subsequent expenditures on fixed assets: should only be capitalised if they increase the future benefits from the existing asset beyond its previously assessed standard of performance.

(3) *Assets carried at revalued amounts*

(i)   Incorporation of property, plant and equipment revaluations in the financial statements: either an entire class of assets should be revalued or the selection of assets for revaluation should be made on a systematic basis.

(ii) Disclosures required:

    (a) basis of selection of assets for revaluation (if applicable);
    (b) method adopted to compute revalued amounts;
    (c) policy relating to frequency of revaluations;
    (d) nature of any indices used;
    (e) year of any appraisal made;
    (f) whether external valuer involved.

(p) IAS 17 Accounting for leases

In the UK, accounting for leases and hire-purchase is dealt with by SSAP 21 (see chapter 10). IAS 17 and SSAP 21 are very similar in overall affect. IAS 17 was published some two years prior to SSAP 21 and undoubtedly had an important influence on SSAP 21.

As regards lessee accounting, the requirements of IAS 17 and SSAP 21 are very similar.

As regards lessor accounting, IAS 17 offers a broader range of acceptable methods as compared with SSAP 21. IAS 17 requires that the recognition of finance income should be based on a pattern reflecting a constant periodic rate of return on either:

(1) the lessor's net investment outstanding; or
(2) the net cash investment outstanding in respect of the finance lease.

SSAP 21 normally requires alternative (2) and does not offer the option of lessor's net investment outstanding.

(q) IAS 18 Revenue recognition

There is no UK equivalent of IAS 18. The main requirements of the standard are as follows:

(1) *General principles*

Revenue from sales or service transactions should be recognised when the requirements as to performance set out below are satisfied. This is subject to the proviso that at the time of performance it is not unreasonable to expect ultimate collection. If at the time of sale or the rendering of the service it is unreasonable to expect ultimate collection, revenue should be postponed.

(2) *Transactions involving the sale of goods*

Performance should be regarded as being achieved when the following conditions have been fulfilled:

(i)   Seller of the goods has transferred to the buyer the significant risks and rewards of ownership, in that all significant acts have been completed and the seller retains no continuing managerial involvement in, or effective control of, the goods transferred to a degree usually associated with ownership.

(ii) No significant uncertainty exists regarding

    (a) the consideration that will be derived from the sale of the goods;
    (b) the associated costs incurred or to be incurred in producing or purchasing the goods;
    (c) the extent to which goods may be returned.

(3) *Transactions involving the rendering of services*

Performance should be measured either under the completed contract method or under the percentage of completion method, whichever method relates the revenue to the work accomplished.

Performance should be regarded as being achieved when no significant uncertainty exists regarding both of:

(i)   the consideration that will be derived from rendering the service; and
(ii) the associated costs incurred or to be incurred in rendering the service.

(4) *Interest, royalties and dividends*

Revenues should only be recognised when no significant uncertainty as to measurability or collectability exists.

Revenues should be recognised on the following bases:

(i)   interest—on a time proportion basis taking account of outstanding principal and interest rate.
(ii) Royalties—on an accruals basis in accordance with the terms of the relevant agreement.
(iii) Dividends from investments not accounted for under the equity method of accounting—when the shareholders' right to receive payment is established.

(r) IAS 18 Accounting for retirement benefits in the financial statements of employers

No UK exposure draft or standard has yet been issued on this subject. In view of differences in terminology and approaches, this international standard is not further referred to.

(s) IAS 20 Accounting for government grants and disclosure of government assistance

IAS 20 deals with the same ground as SSAP 4 (see chapter 7). Like SSAP 4, IAS 20 offers two alternative ways of treating capital-based grants, namely:

(1) setting up a deferred income account; or
(2) deducted in arriving at the carrying amount of the asset.

(t) IAS 21 Accounting for the effects of changes in foreign exchange rates

IAS 21 is a very detailed standard which deals with much the same matters as SSAP 20 (see chapter 18). However, IAS 21 deals with several specific matters that are not directly referred to in SSAP 20. The comments below refer to some of the more general matters.

(1) *Accounting for foreign currency transactions*

(i) Exchange differences arising on the retranslation of long-term foreign currency loans should normally be recognised in profit for the period. However, unlike SSAP 20, IAS 21 offers an alternative treatment and permits such exchange differences to be deferred and recognised in profits of current and future periods on a systematic basis, over the remaining lives of the monetary items to which they relate.

However, exchange losses on an item should not be deferred for recognition in future periods if it is reasonable to expect that recurring exchange losses will arise on that item in the future.

(ii) If foreign currency loans are designated as, and provide, an effective hedge against a net investment in a foreign entity, exchange differences arising on the loans should be taken to shareholders' interests to the extent that they are covered by exchange differences arising on the net investment (a similar provision to that in SSAP 20).

(2) *Translation of the financial statements of a foreign entity*

(i) The requirements are similar to those of SSAP 20. Except for foreign operations that are integral to the operations of the parent, foreign entity financial statements should be translated using the closing rate method.
(ii) Profit and loss items may be translated at either closing rate or exchange rates at transaction dates (for which average rate is an approximation).
(iii) Exchange differences should be taken direct to shareholders' interests.
(iv) Financial statements of foreign operations that are integral to the operations of the parent should be translated using the temporal method.

(u) IAS 22 Accounting for business combinations

IAS 22 is equivalent to UK statement SSAP 23, Accounting for acquisitions and mergers (see chapter 16).

(1) *Basic approach*

(i) Except for rare circumstances where there is deemed to be a uniting of interests, a business combination should be accounted for under the purchase method (i e acquisition accounting).
(ii) A business combination is deemed to be a uniting of interests only if:

(a) the shareholders of the combining enterprises achieve a continuing mutual sharing in the risks and benefits attaching to the combined enterprise; and

(b) the basis of the transaction is principally an exchange of voting equity shares of the enterprises involved; and

(c) the whole, or effectively the whole, of the net assets and operations of the combining enterprises are combined in one entity.

(iii) Where a business combination is deemed to be a uniting of interests, the pooling of interests method (i e merger accounting) may be used. Note that, in this standard, the use of merger accounting is not mandatory.

(2) *Purchase method (acquisition accounting)*

Much of this corresponds with SSAP 23 and SSAP 14. However IAS 22 deals also with the treatment of goodwill on consolidation. The treatment specified is in line with SSAP 22 (see chapter 7).

A further point is the situation where the acquisition agreement provides for an adjustment to the purchase consideration contingent on one or more future events. In this situation, the amount should be included in the cost of acquisition if payment is probable and a reasonable estimate of the amount can be made.

(3) *Pooling of interests method (merger accounting)*

This is very similar to the provisions of SSAP 23.

(4) *Disclosures*

The disclosure requirements of SSAP 22 are not as detailed as those of SSAP 23, and are not referred to here.

(v) IAS 23 Capitalisation of borrowing costs

(1) *Background*

No UK standard deals specifically with capitalisation of borrowing costs. The only reference is to be found in para 21, appendix 1 of SSAP 9 which states:

In ascertaining cost of long-term contract work in progress it is not normally appropriate to include interest payable on borrowed money. However, in those infrequent circumstances where sums borrowed can be identified as financing specific long-term contracts it may be appropriate to include such related interest in cost, in which circumstances the fact should be stated.

Capitalisation of borrowing costs is permitted by the Companies Act 1985 subject to certain conditions (see chapter 7, section 7.1 (p)).

(2) *General requirements of IAS 23*

An enterprise that has incurred borrowing costs and incurred expenditures on assets that take a substantial period of time to get them ready for their intended use or sale should adopt a policy of either capitalising borrowing costs or not capitalising borrowing costs.

(3) *Capitalisation of borrowing costs*

(i) Borrowing costs should be capitalised as part of the cost of an asset by applying a capitalisation rate to expenditures (i e acquisition, construction or production) on assets that require a substantial period of time to get them ready for their use or sale.

(ii) The capitalisation rate should be calculated by relating the borrowing costs incurred during a period to the borrowings outstanding during that period.

Where a new borrowing can be related to expenditures on the acquisition, construction or production of specific assets, the capitalisation rate may be

determined on the basis of actual borrowing costs incurred on that borrowing.
(iii) Commencement of capitalisation:

(a) For assets other than investments when the following three conditions are satisfied:

(1) expenditures for the asset are being incurred;
(2) activities that are necessary to prepare the asset for its intended use or sale are in progess;
(3) borrowing costs are being incurred.

(b) For investments, conditions (1) and (2) above must be satisfied. In addition, the investee should have activities in progress necessary to commence the asset's planned principal operations.

(iv) Cessation of capitalisation: capitalisation of borrowing costs should cease when the asset is ready for its intended use or sale.
(v) Overriding restriction on capitalisation: amount of borrowing costs capitalised during a period should not exceed the total amount of borrowings incurred by the enterprise in that period.

(w) IAS 24 Related party disclosures

So far, no UK accounting or auditing statement has been issued on this topic. The principal requirements of IAS 24 are referred to below.

(1) *Terminology*

(i) *Related party.* Parties are considered to be related if one party has the ability to control the other party or exercise significant influence over the other party in making financial and operating decisions.
(ii) *Related party transaction.* A transfer of resources or obligations between related parties, regardless of whether a price is charged.
(iii) *Control.* Ownership, directly, or indirectly through subsidiaries, of more than one-half of the voting power of an enterprise, or a substantial interest in voting power and the power to direct, by statute or agreement, the financial and operating policies of the management of the enterprise.
(iv) *Significant influence* (for the purpose of this statement). Participation in the financial and operating policy decisions of an enterprise, but not control of those policies.

Significant influence may be exercised in several ways, usually by representation on the board of directors but also by, for example, participation in the policy making process, material intercompany transactions, interchange of managerial personnel or dependence on technical information. Significant influence may be gained by share ownership, statute or agreement. With share ownership, significant influence is presumed in accordance with the definition contained in IAS 3, Consolidation financial statements.

(2) *Related party relationships included*

(i) Enterprises that directly, or indirectly through one or more intermediaries, control, or are controlled by, or are under common control with, the reporting enterprise. (This includes holding companies, subsidiaries and fellow subsidiaries.);
(ii) Associated enterprises (see IAS 3, Consolidation financial statements);
(iii) Individuals owning, directly, or indirectly, an interest in the voting power of the reporting enterprise that gives them significant influence over the enterprise, and close members of the family of any such individual.
(iv) Key management personnel, that is, those persons having authority and responsibility for planning, directing and controlling the activities of the

reporting enterprise, including directors and officers of companies and close members of the families of such individuals.

(v) Enterprises in which a substantial interest in the voting power is owned directly or indirectly, by any person described in (iii) or (iv) or over which such a person is able to exercise significant influence. This includes enterprises owned by directors or major shareholders of the reporting enterprise and enterprises that have a member of key management in common with the reporting enterprise.

(3) *Related party relationships excluded*

(i) Two companies whose only connection is a director in common (assuming the director is unable to affect the policies of both companies in their mutual dealings).

(ii) Normal dealings with providers of finance, trade unions, public utilities and government departments and agencies.

(iii) A single customer, supplier, franchisor, distributor or general agent with whom a significant volume of business is transacted.

(4) *Matters to be disclosed*

(i) Related party relationships where control exists irrespective of whether there have been transactions between the related parties.

(ii) Where there have been transactions between related parties, the nature of the related party relationships as well as the types of transactions and the elements of the transactions necessary for an understanding of the financial statements.

The standard permits items of similar nature to be disclosed in aggregate except when separate disclosure is necessary for an understanding of the effects of related party transactions on the financial statements of the reporting enterprise.

(x) IAS 25 Accounting for investments

There is no UK equivalent of IAS 25. In the UK the basic rules concerning accounting for and disclosure of investments are contained in the Companies Act 1985. In view of this IAS 25 is not considered further in this chapter.

(y) IAS 26 Accounting and reporting by retirement benefit plans

The subject of retirement benefit plans is covered in the UK by Statement of recommended practice No. 1 on Pension scheme accounts. These are regulated by the occupational Pension Schemes (Disclosure of Information) Regulations 1986. This topic was covered in chapter 12 and no further reference is made here.

25 CAPITAL REORGANISATIONS AND RECONSTRUCTIONS

25.1 CAPITAL REORGANISATIONS

(a) Introduction

The term capital reorganisation may refer to a wide range of rather diverse situations.

These may include:

(1) increasing the company's authorised share capital;
(2) bonus shares, scrip or captialisation issues (see (b) below);
(3) consolidating shares into shares of larger amounts;
(4) splitting shares into shares of smaller amounts;
(5) purchase and redemption of shares where a company has power to issue and redeem redeemable ordinary or preference shares, or alternatively to purchase its own shares even if these were not originally issued as redeemable (see section 25.2);
(6) reductions of capital (see section 25.3);
(7) amalgamations (see section 25.4);
(8) reconstructions (see section 25.5).

(b) Bonus shares, scrip or capitalisation issues

(1) *Introduction*

When a company has substantial undistributed profits on profit and loss account or other reserve account, the total capital employed in the business tends to be obscured. Such accumulations are usually represented by fixed assets or permanent working capital.

To bring the issued share capital into proper relationship with the capital employed in the business, the accumulations can be capitalised and applied in paying up the amounts due on shares to be issued to the members as bonus shares.

Cash is not involved in a bonus issue and a bonus issue of shares adds nothing to the net assets of the company; it divides the capital employed in the business into a larger number of shares. This can be explained by an illustration.

Illustration 1

A company's summarised balance sheet is as follows:

Share capital in £1 shares	£100,000	Sundry assets less creditors	£150,000
Reserves	50,000		

If the assets and goodwill are fully valued, each £1 share is worth £1.50. On the profits being capitalised, if the bonus shares are issued at par, the share capital becomes £150,000 in £1 shares. Each share is now worth £1, but each shareholder has 50 per cent more shares. The shareholders are no better off.

(2) *Implications*

On The Stock Exchange a bonus issue is often considered a bull point and it is common for a bonus issue to be followed by an increased dividend. A bonus issue attracts attention to the company's shares and often increases dealings in the shares which forces up the market value and enables shareholders who wish to do so to realise an immediate profit.

Seldom will the net assets as shown in the balance sheet reflect the true market value of the shares, which will depend primarily on the income they yield and growth prospects. The company may have paid a dividend of 12% and if a reasonable yield were 6% the shares would possibly be quoted round about £2 each, and the total value of the capital would be £200,000. The real value of the shares after the bonus issue would still be £200,000, or 133p each, if it is anticipated that the company will only distribute the same amount of profits as before and will reduce the rate of dividend proprotionately, i e to 8%. The market, however, will usually gamble on the dividend not being reduced so much and may quote the shares at, say, £1.50 or £1.75 in the expectation of 9% or more being paid. A member who shares in this expectation might then sell part of his shares, while retaining the anticipation of the same income.

(3) *Accounting entries*

Consider a company having a reserve of £25,000 and a paid-up capital of £100,000 in £1 shares, which resolves to pay a bonus of 20% out of its reserve by the issue of one fully-paid share for each five shares held.

The journal entries would be as follows:

Reserve account	20,000	
Bonus account		20,000
Bonus of 20% payable out of the reserve account in fully-paid shares as per resolution dated ...		
Bonus account	20,000	
Share capital account		20,000
Issue of 20,000 shares of £1 each fully paid in satisfaction of bonus at the rate of one share for every five held		

25.2   PURCHASE AND REDEMPTION OF SHARES

(a) Redeemable shares

A company limited by shares or a company limited by guarantee and having a share capital may issue redeemable shares (ordinary or preference) provided it is authorised to do so by its articles.

The Companies Act 1985, ss 159–161 specify the following additional conditions:

(1) redeemable shares may not be issued unless at the time of issue there are issued shares of the company which are not redeemable;
(2) redeemable shares may not be redeemed unless they are fully-paid;
(3) the terms of redemption must provide for payment on redemption.

(b) Financing the redemption

The method of redemption is restricted to the following three possibilities:

(1) by the proceeds of a new issue of shares of any class; or
(2) out of distributable profits; or
(3) by a combination of (1) and (2).

Where shares are redeemed wholly out of profit, an amount equivalent to the nominal value of shares redeemed is to be transferred from distributable profits to a capital redemption reserve.

Where shares are redeemed wholly or partly out of the proceeds of a fresh issue of shares, a transfer to capital redemption reserve is required to the extent that the proceeds of the issue fall short of the nominal value redeemed (Companies Act 1985, s 170).

> CRR transfer = nominal value redeemed — proceeds of new issue of shares

(c) Capital redemption reserve (CRR)

For the purposes of reduction of capital, the capital redemption reserve is treated as though it were paid-up share capital. However, the CRR may be applied in making a bonus issue of fully-paid shares.

(d) Premium on redemption of redeemable shares

The basic rule is that any premium payable on redemption must be paid out of distributable profits of the company.

There is an exception to this rule, but it only applies if two conditions can both be satisfied:

(1) the shares to be redeemed were originally issued at a premium; and
(2) the redemption is to be financed by a fresh issue of shares.

In this situation, the premium or redemption may come out of share premium account (rather than distributable profit) but the amount of share premium account which may be used for this purpose is restricted to the lower of:

(i)   the aggregate of premiums received on the original issue of the shares to be redeemed; and
(ii) the present balance on share premium account taking into account any premium relating to the fresh issue of shares.

(e) Cancellation of shares

Shares redeemed under the Companies Act 1985, ss 159–161 are to be treated as cancelled on redemption, and the company's issued share capital reduced accordingly.

However, the redemption of share capital is not to be taken as reducing the company's authorised share capital.

Illustration 2

The summarised balance sheet of Trym Traders plc at 31 December 19X4 was as follows:

	£
Sundry assets	840,000
Cash at bank	300,000
	1,140,000
Less liabilities	210,000
	930,000
	£
Authorised, called-up and fully-paid capital:	
200,000 £1 ordinary shares	200,000
400,000 £1 6% redeemable preference shares	400,000
	600,000
Profit and loss account	330,000
	930,000

By the terms of their issue the preference shares were redeemable at a premium of 5% on 1 January 19X5 and it was decided to arrange this as far as possible out of the company's resources subject to leaving a balance of £100,000 to the credit of the profit and loss account. It was also decided to raise the balance of money required by the issue of a sufficient number of ordinary shares at a premium of 25p per share.

Required: Journal entries and ledger account entries to reflect the above transactions, and a summarised balance sheet thereafter. Ignore taxation.

Workings

As redeemable shares were originally issued at par, the premium on redemption must come out of distributable profits. A further consideration is that the amount by which the nominal value redeemed exceeds the proceeds of the new issue should be transferred to capital redemption reserve.

	£
Existing balance on P/L	330,000
Required for premium on redemption	
5% × 400,000	20,000
	310,000
Final balance on P/L is required to be	100,000
∴ 'Available' for transfer to CRR	210,000

Proceeds of new issue

= nominal value redeemed − 210,000
= £400,000 − £210,000
= £190,000

So nominal value of shares to be issued at a premium of 25p per share

$$\frac{£190,000}{125p} = £152,000$$

Journal entries

	£	£
6% redeemable preference share capital	400,000	
Premium on redemption of preferences shares	20,000	
Preference shares redemption account		420,000
Transferring 400,000 £1 redeemable preference shares redeemable at a premium of 5%		
Application and allotment (ordinary shares)	190,000	
Ordinary share capital		152,000
Share premium account		38,000
Issue of 152,000 ordinary shares at premium of 25p per share		
Cash	190,000	
Application and allotment		190,000
Cash received on issue on 152,000 ordinary shares		
Preference share redemption account	420,000	
Cash		420,000
Redemption of 400,000 6% redeemable preference shares at a premium of 5%		
Profit and loss account	210,000	
Capital redemption reserve		210,000
Transfer out of profit of amount equal to nominal amount of shares redeemed otherwise that out of the proceeds of a new issue		
Share premium account	20,000	
Profit and loss account		20,000
Providing for premium on redemption out of share premium account		

Ledger accounts

6% REDEEMABLE PREFERENCE SHARE CAPITAL

		£			£
Jan 1	Preference share redemption account	400,000	Jan 1	Balance b/f	400,000

PREMIUM ON REDEMPTION OF PREFERENCE SHARES

		£			£
Jan 1	Preference share redemption account	20,000	Jan 1	Profit and loss account	20,000

PREFERENCE SHARE REDEMPTION ACCOUNT

		£			£
Jan 1	Cash	420,000	Jan 1	6% redeemable preference shares	400,000
				Premium on redemption	20,000

ORDINARY SHARE CAPITAL

		£			£
Jan 1	Balance c/f	352,000	Dec 31	Balance b/f	200,000
			Jan 1	Application and allotment	152,000
		352,000			352,000

SHARE PREMIUM ACCOUNT

		£			£
Jan 1	Balance c/f	38,000	Jan 1	Application and allotment	38,000

APPLICATION AND ALLOTMENT (ORDINARY SHARES)

		£			£
Jan 1	Share capital	152,000	Jan 1	Cash	190,000
	Share premium	38,000			
		190,000			190,000

PROFIT AND LOSS ACCOUNT

		£			£
Jan 1	Premium on redemption of preference shares account	20,000	Dec 31	Balance b/f	330,000
	Capital redemption reserve	210,000			
	Balance c/f	100,000			
		330,000			330,000

CAPITAL REDEMPTION RESERVE

					£
			Jan 1	Profit and loss account	210,000

CASH BOOK

		£			£
Dec 31	Balance b/f	300,000	Jan 1	Preference share redemption account	420,000
	Application and allotment account (ordinary shares)	190,000		Balance c/f	70,000
		490,000			490,000

SUMMARISED BALANCE SHEET OF TRYM TRADERS PLC AFTER THE REDEMPTION OF PREFERENCE SHARES

	£
Sundry assets	840,000
Cash at bank	70,000
	910,000
Less liabilities	210,000
	700,000

	£
Authorised, called-up and fully-paid capital:	
352,000 £1 ordinary shares	352,000
Capital redemption reserve	210,000
Share premium account	38,000
Profit and loss account	100,000
	700,000

Note that share capital and non-distributable reserves are maintained as a comparison of the position pre- and post-redemption shows:

	Pre-redemption £	Post-redemption £
Ordinary share capital	200,000	352,000
Preference share capital	400,000	—
Capital redemption reserve	—	210,000
Share premium	—	38,000
Total share capital and non-distributable reserves	600,000	600,000

(f) A problem area

The legislation may give rise to problems of interpretation in certain situations where the shares to be redeemed were themselves issued at a premium. It is possible that a literal interpretation of the legislation may result in a reduction in the total of share capital and non-distributable reserves.

Illustration 3

Several years ago, Redeemables plc issued 100,000 £1 redeemable preference shares at a premium of 8p per share. These shares are now due to be redeemed at a premium of 25p per share. The redemption is to be part-financed by a fresh issue of 80,000 £1 shares at a premium of 12.5p per share.

The balance on a share premium account prior to the fresh issue of shares was £12,000. Ignore other share capital of the company.

(1) Basic calculations

	£
(i) Transfer to CCR	
Nominal value of shares to be redeemed	100,000
Proceeds of new issue	90,000
Transfer to CRR	10,000

(ii) Premium on redemption of shares (£25,000)

Since shares to be redeemed were originally issued at a premium, share premium account may be used to extent of lower of:

(a)	premium on original issue	8,000
(b)	balance on share premium account (including premium on fresh issue of shares) = £12,000 + £10,000	22,000
	i e lower amount is	8,000

(2) Journal entries

	£	£
Cash	90,000	
Share capital		80,000
Premium		10,000
Cash		125,000
Share capital	100,000	
Share premium	8,000	
Distributable profits	17,000	
Distributable profits	10,000	
Capital redemption reserve		10,000

(3) Comparisons of share capital and non-distributable reserves

	Pre-redemption £	Post-redemption £
Share capital	100,000	80,000
Share premium	12,000	14,000
Capital redemption reserve	—	10,000
Share capital and non-distributable reserves	112,000	104,000

There is some disagreement over the interpretation of the legislation. Some commentators have concluded that the legislation is deficient in that it may result in a reduction of capital and non-distributable reserves, as in the above example.

Others have commented that where part of the premium on redemption comes out of the proceeds of a fresh issue (i e £8,000 in the example above) it should reduce the aggregate proceeds available in determining the transfer to capital redemption reserve. Accordingly, a further £8,000 should be transferred out of distributable profit and into capital redemption reserve in order to maintain the total of share capital and non-distributable reserves.

This latter approach may be defended on prudence grounds even though the relevant sections of the Companies Act 1985 may be open to more than one interpretation.

(g) Purchase of own shares

A company limited by shares or a company limited by guarantee and having a share capital may purchase its own shares (including only redeemable shares) provided it is authorised to do so by its articles (Companies Act 1985, s 162).

However, a company may not purchase any of its shares if as a result of the share purchase there would be no member of the company holding shares other than redeemable shares.

There are three prescribed procedures for the purchase of shares by a company:

(1) off-market purchase;
(2) contingent purchase contracts;
(3) market purchase.

A detailed consideration of these, including necessary authorisations, is outside the scope of a financial accounting textbook.

All of the matters considered earlier relating to redeemable shares apply also to the purchase of own shares, except the terms and manner of purchase need not be determined by the articles.

(h) Purchase of redemption out of capital

(1) *Introduction*

This power is available to private companies only. Under no circumstances is it available to public limited companies.

The Companies Act 1985, ss 171–173 allow a private company limited by shares, or a private company limited by guarantee and having share capital, to make a payment out of capital provided it is permitted to do so by its articles.

The term 'payment out of capital' essentially means a redemption or purchase of shares other than out of the company's distributable profit, or out of the proceeds of a fresh issue of shares.

(2) *Conditions*

(i) The Act refers to the term *permissible capital payment* (PCP). This is the amount by which the purchase or redemption cost exceeds the total of available (i e distributable) profits, plus the proceeds of a fresh issue of shares made for the purpose of the redemption or purchase.

(ii) The difference between the PCP and the nominal value of shares redeemed or purchased is to be dealt with as follows:

    (a) If the total of PCP, plus the proceeds of a fresh issue of shares, is less than the nominal value of shares redeemed or purchased, the amount of the difference is to be transferred to capital redemption reserve.

    (b) If the total of PCP, plus the proceeds of a fresh issue of shares, is more than the nominal value, the excess may be used to reduce any of the following:

        (a) capital redemption reserve;
        (b) share premium account;
        (c) fully paid share capital;
        (d) revaluation reserve.

(iii) The Companies Act 1985 specifies stringent legal conditions in connection with purchase or redemption out of capital. While the Act attempts to offer private companies greater flexibility than public companies, it is particularly concerned with the protection of creditors.

    The legal conditions, a detailed consideration of which is outside the scope of this book, include:

    (a) the approval by the members of the company by means of a special resolution;

    (b) a statutory declaration of solvency by the directors with prescribed form and content and having annexed to it a special auditors' report;

    (c) publicity for proposed payment out of capital; and

    (d) rights of members or creditors to object.

Illustration 4

Private Ltd issued 1,000 £1 ordinary shares several years ago at par. Following the death of one of the major shareholders, the company now wishes to purchase 300 shares at a cost of £350. Distributable reserves amount to £270.

(1) Basic calculations

(i) Permissible capital payment (PCP)

	£
Purchase cost	350
Distributable profits	270
	——
PCP	80
	≡≡

(ii) CRR calculation

	£
Nominal value purchased	300
PCP	80
	——
	220
	≡≡

(2) Journal entries

	£	£
Cash		350
Share capital	300	
Distributable profits	50	
Distributable profits	220	
CRR		220

Note that share capital and non-distributable reserves have been reduced by £80 i e the amount of the permissible share capital payment.

	Pre-purchase £	Post-purchase £
Share capital	1,000	700
CRR	—	220
	——	——
Share capital and non-distributable reserves	1,000	920
	≡≡	≡≡

25.3 REDUCTION OF CAPITAL

(a) Introduction

The Companies Act 1985, ss 135–141 deals with reduction of capital. The term may apply to any of the following three situations, namely where a company wishes to:

(1) extinguish or reduce the liability in respect of share capital not fully paid up; or

(2) cancel any share capital which is lost or unrepresented by available assets; or

(3) pay off any paid-up share capital which is in excess of the company's requirements.

(b) Legal considerations

Section 135 sets out three conditions, all of which must be satisfied:

(1) The company must have the necessary authority under its articles.

(2) A special resolution for reducing share capital must be passed.

(3) The confirmation of the court must be obtained.

The following additional comments may be made:

(1) Where the proposed reduction involves either diminution of liability on unpaid share capital, or the payment to shareholders of any paid-up share capital, creditors are entitled to object and may require to be paid off or to have their liability secured.

(2) The court will take particular account of the rights of creditors and the equitable adjustment of any loss between the various classes of shareholders according to their capital and dividend rights.

(3) Once the company's special resolution has been confirmed by the court, it is binding on all members of the company. Members who did not vote in favour of the resolution cannot demand to be bought out. However, a company could not carry through a scheme which provided for the reduction of fully-paid shares to partly-paid shares and then for a further call to be made on shareholders unless the written consent of every member was obtained.

It would be possible to effect such an arrangement under s 582 whereby the company could be wound up voluntarily and its business or property transferred to another company in exchange for partly-paid shares therein. Under s 582, any member who did not vote in favour of the scheme could demand to be bought out.

(c) Writing off capital unrepresented by available assets

The procedures are as follows:

(1) Set up the fund for the capital reduction by debiting the various share capital accounts and crediting capital redemption account with the amounts by which the capital is to be reduced.

(2) Apply the fund in eliminating a debit balance on profit and loss account and in writing off or writing down assets.

Note that where drastic alterations in capital are involved, it is preferable to close the old capital accounts by:

(i) crediting all the capital to the capital reduction account; and

(ii) debiting the capital reduction account and crediting the new share capital accounts with the new shares issued.

Illustration 5

The summarised balance sheet of Moorhead Ltd at 31 March 19X8 was as follows:

	£	£
Fixed assets		
Goodwill		25,000
Patents and trade marks		10,000
Deferred advertising expenditure		25,000
		60,000
Land and buildings	88,000	
Plant and machinery	86,000	
		174,000
Investments—shares in Saltash Ltd		30,000
		264,000
Current assets		
Stock	73,000	
Debtors	98,500	
		171,500

Current liabilities	£	£
Creditors	85,000	
Bank overdraft	60,000	
Debenture interest	2,500	
	147,500	
Net current assets		24,000
		288,000

	£	£
5% debenture stock (secured on land and buildings)		50,000
Directors' loans		23,000
Authorised, issued and called-up share capital:		
200,000 £1 ordinary shares	200,000	
100,000 £1 6% preference shares	100,000	
	300,000	
Profit and loss account	(85,000)	
		215,000
		288,000

Additional information

(1) Preference share dividends are three years in arrears.
(2) There is a contingent liability for damages amounting to £10,000.
(3) A capital reduction scheme, duly approved, settled the following terms:

    (i) The preference shares to be reduced to 80p each and the ordinary shares to 25p each, and the resulting shares then to be converted into preference and ordinary stock respectively and consolidated into units of £1. The authorised capital to be restored to £100,000 6% cumulative preference stock and £200,000 ordinary stock. The preference shareholders waive two-thirds of the dividend arrears and receive ordinary stock for the balance.

    (ii) All tangible assets to be eliminated, and bad debts of £7,500 and obsolete stock of £10,000 to be written off.

    (iii) The shares in Saltash Ltd are sold for £60,000.

    (iv) The debenture holder agreed to take over one of the company's properties (book value £18,000) at a price of £25,000 in part satisfaction of the debenture and to provide further cash of £15,000 on a floating charge. The arrears of interest are paid.

    (v) The contingent liability materialised but the company recovered £5,000 of these damages in an action against one of its directors. This was debited to his loan account of £8,000, the balance of which was repaid in cash on his resignation.

    (vi) The remaining directors agree to take ordinary stock in satisfaction of their loans.

Required:

(1) Journal entries to record the above, including the cash transactions;
(2) Capital reduction account;
(3) The revised balance sheet after giving effect to the entries in (1).

Ignore taxation.

Suggested solution

(1) *Journal entries*

	£	£
Preference share capital account	20,000	
Ordinary share capital account	150,000	
Capital reduction account		170,000

20p per share written off 100,000 6% cumulative preference shares of £1 each and 75p per share written off 200,000 ordinary shares of £1 each in accordance with capital reduction scheme.

Preference share capital account	80,000	
Ordinary share capital account	50,000	
6% cumulative preference stock account		80,000
Ordinary stock account		50,000

Conversion of 100,000 preference shares of 80p each
and 200,000 ordinary shares of 25p each into stock and
consolidation into 80,000 £1 units of 6% cumulative preference
stock and £50,000 £1 units of ordinary stock respectively.

Capital reduction account	6,000	
Ordinary stock account		6,000

Allotment of 6,000 £1 ordinary stock units in satisfaction of
one-third of the arrears of preference dividend, the other
two-thirds being waived.

Capital reduction account	162,500	
Goodwill		25,000
Patents and trade marks		10,000
Deferred expenditure—advertising		25,000
Profit and loss account		85,000
Debtors		7,500
Stock		10,000

Writing off of intangible assets, bad debts and obsolete stock.

Cash	60,000	
Shares in Saltash Ltd		30,000
Capital reduction account		30,000

Sale of shares in Saltash Ltd for £60,000 and
transfer of profit (£30,000) to capital reduction
account.

5% debenture	25,000	
Land and buildings		18,000
Capital reduction account		7,000

Transfer to debenture holder at a valuation of £25,000 in part
satisfaction of debenture for £50,000 of property of book value
of £18,000 and transfer of profit to capital reduction account.

Debenture interest	2,500	
Cash		2,500

Payment of accrued interest on £50,000 5% debenture.

Cash	15,000	
Second debenture		15,000

Cash received for a new debenture carrying a floating charge
over the assets of the company.

Capital reduction account	5,000	
Directors' loan account	5,000	
Cash		10,000

Payment of £10,000 in settlement of contingent liability and
recovery of £5,000 thereof by set-off against director's loan.

Directors' loans	18,000	
Cash		3,000
Ordinary stock account		15,000

Repayment to former director of balance of loan and allotment
of ordinary stock in satisfaction of other directors' loans.

Capital reduction account	33,500	
Capital reserve account		33,500

Balance on capital reduction account transferred to capital
reserve.

(2) *Capital reduction account*

	£		£
Ordinary stock account allotment of ordinary stock in satisfaction of arrears of preference divided	6,000	Preference share capital —reduction of 20p per share on 100,000 shares	20,000
Cash—discharge of contingent liability	10,000	Ordinary share capital— reduction of 75p per share on 200,000 shares	150,000
Amounts written off:		Shares in subsidiary company:	
Goodwill	25,000	Profit on sale	30,000
Patents and trade marks	10,000	Property—profit on sale	7,000
Deferred expenditure	25,000	Cash—recovery of	
Profit and loss account	85,000	damages from director	5,000
Debtors	7,500		
Stock	10,000		
Capital reserve—balance transferred	33,500		
	212,000		212,000

(3) *Balance sheet—after reduction of capital*

	£	£
Tangible fixed assets:		
Land and buildings		70,000
Plant and machinery		86,000
		156,000
Current assets:		
Stocks	63,000	
Debtors	91,000	
	154,000	
Creditors—amounts falling due within one year;		
Bank overdraft	500	
Trade creditors	85,000	
	85,500	
Net current assets		68,500
Total assets less current liabilities		224,500
Creditors—amounts falling due after more than one year:		
5% debenture (secured)	25,000	
Second debenture (secured)	15,000	
		(40,000)
		184,500
Capital and reserves:		
Called-up share capital:		
71,000 £1 ordinary stock units		71,000
80,000 £1 6% cumulative preference stock		80,000
Capital reserve		151,000
		33,500
		184,500

NOTE

	£
Authorised share capital consists of:	
200,000 £1 ordinary stock units	200,000
100,000 £1 6% cumulative preference stock	100,000
	300,000

(d) Repayment of share capital in excess of company's requirements

An illustration of this was the capital reconstruction of the General Electric Company Ltd in 1977.

The overall effect of the reconstruction was that £178.3m standing to the credit of share premium account and resulting from the earlier acquisitions of Associated Electrical Industries Ltd in 1967 and English Electric Company Ltd in 1968 was converted to £178.3m of floating rate unsecured capital notes 1986. It was considered that the total of shareholders' funds was excessive in relation to the total capital of the company.

Part of the floating rate capital notes could be:

(1) redeemed by the company over the period 1979–1985;
(2) purchased by the company on the open market and handed over to trustees for cancellation;
(3) redeemed at the option of loan stockholders after 1982.

In any event, all the loan stock was to be redeemed by November 1986.

(e) Capital reductions involving compromises or arrangements with creditors

These should be carried out under the terms of ss 425–427 of the Companies Act 1985 (see section 25.5 below).

25.4 AMALGAMATIONS

(a) Introduction

The term 'amalgamation' is not defined in law, but is usually taken to refer to the merging of two or more companies. One possibility is that, for example, company A absorbs company B. An alternative would be for a new company, C, to be formed to absorb companies A and B.

The companies to be absorbed will go into voluntary liquidation and the purchasing company will usually take over the whole of the assets and assume the ordinary trade liabilities of the other(s), any debentures being either paid off in cash or exchanged for debentures or other interests in the purchasing company.

An amalgamation may be brought about under two possible schemes under the Companies Act 1985:

(1) s 582; or
(2) ss 425–427.

(b) Amalgamations under s 582

The essential feature of a s 582 amalgamation is that one company (the transferor company) is either in voluntary liquidation or is about to go into liquidation and transfers the whole or part of its undertaking to another company (the transferee company). The consideration for the transfer consists wholly or partly of shares in the transferee company which are to be distributed amongst members of the transferor company.

The scheme will usually require the passing of two special resolutions:

(1) approval of the scheme for the sale of the undertaking in exchange for shares in the transferee company;

(2) putting the company into members' voluntary liquidation.

The scheme must not involve a compromise or arrangement with creditors. Shareholders of the transferor company who did not vote in favour of the scheme may require the liquidator to purchase their interest for cash.

(c) Amalgamations under ss 425–427

This may be appropriate where it is thought necessary to alter the rights of the creditors or members. The scheme requires the sanction of the court, for example to:

(1) transfer to the transferee company the whole or part of the undertaking of the transferor company;

(2) allot shares or debentures to shareholders or debenture holders of the transferor company;

(3) dissolve the transferor company without winding it up.

(d) Accounting entries for closing the books of the transferor

The entries in the books will be similar to those required for the purpose of closing the books of a partnership on dissolution, i e:

Debit	Credit	With
Realisation account	Asset accounts	Book value of assets taken over by the purchasing company
Cash	Asset accounts	Proceeds of assets not taken over by purchasing company
Asset accounts	Realisation account *or*	Profit on disposal of assets *not* taken over by the purchasing company
Realisation account	Asset account	Loss on disposal of assets *not* taken over by the purchasing company
Share capital reserve account	Sundry members account	Balances attributable to sundry members
Sundry members account	Profit and loss account	Debit balances attributable to sundry members
Purchasing company	Realisation account	Total purchase consideration (including agreed amounts payable to creditors, debenture holders etc taken over)
Sundry members account Sundry debenture holders etc Cash Creditors	Purchasing company	Allocation of purchase consideration (e g shares, debentures, cash) Discharge of creditors etc taken over

Debit	Credit	With
Sundry debenture holders	Realisation account *or*	Remaining credit balance
Realisation account	Sundry debenture holders	Remaining debit balance
Realisation account	Cash	Realisation expenses
Realisation account	Sundry members account *or*	Balance on realisation account
Sundry members account Liability accounts	Cash	Closure of cash book by payment to members of residual cash and/or settlement of liabilities deferred until receipt of cash from the purchasing company

NOTE

In some examples, liabilities taken over by the purchasing company are credited to the realisation account and the purchase consideration excludes the amounts the purchasing company has agreed to pay in settlement of the liabilities. It is, however, considered easier to adopt the above method because no difficulties will arise when the liabilities are not taken over at book values.

A provision for bad and doubtful debts must be dealt with on its merits. If the debts are taken over by the absorbing company at their book value, the provision for doubtful debts account should be transferred to the credit of realisation account; if the debts are taken over at their full value, the provision, since it is being ignored, must be transferred to the credit of sundry members account. If book debts are not taken over any bad debts incurred can be charged to the provision account, and the balance, if a debit, taken to realisation account, or if a credit, to sundry members account.

(e) Accounting entries for the books of the transferee company

Debit	Credit	Notes
(1) Asset accounts Goodwill	Liabilities Vendor account Capital reserve	Assets and liabilities at acquisition values; the vendor account is credited with the purchase consideration. Goodwill is debited with the excess of the purchase consideration over the net assets acquired; capital reserve is credited if the net assets acquired exceed the purchase consideration.
(2) Vendor account	Share capital Cash etc	Discharge of purchase consideration by issue of shares, paying cash etc

(f) Illustration 6

The Associated Engineering Co plc is absorbed by the United Engineering Co plc, the consideration being the assumption of the liabilities, the discharge of the debentures at a premium of 5%, by the issue of 5% debentures in the United Co, a payment in cash of £3 per share, and the exchange of three £1 shares in the United Co, at an agreed value of 150p per share, for every share in the Associated Co.

The summarised balance sheet of the Associated Co at the date of transfer was as follows:

	£	£
Fixed assets:		
Goodwill		25,000
Land and buildings		76,500
Plant and machinery		220,000
Patents		7,500
		329,000
Investments on compensation fund account		5,000
Current assets:		
Stock	106,000	
Debtors	45,000	
Cash at bank and in hand	35,000	
	186,000	
Less creditors	30,000	
Net current assets		156,000
		490,000
5% debentures		(150,000)
		340,000
60,000 £5 ordinary shares		300,000
General reserve		32,000
Profit and loss account		3,000
		335,000
Accident insurance fund		5,000
		340,000

Required:
(1) Close off the books of the Associated Co giving journal entries.
(2) Show the opening journal entries in the books of the United Co.

Suggested solution

(1) *Journal of the Associated Co*

	£	£
Realisation account	520,000	
Sundry assets		520,000
Assets sold to the United Engineering Co as per balance sheet		
Creditors	30,000	
Realisation account		30,000
Liabilities taken over by the United Engineering Co		
Realisation account	7,500	
Debentures account		7,500
Premium of 5% new provided for		

United Engineering Co plc	607,500	
Realisation account		607,500
Purchase price as per agreement		

Cash	180,000	
Shares (United Engineering Co):		
180,000 shares of £1 each fully paid at £1.50 per share	270,000	
Debentures account—5% debentures exchanged	157,500	
United Engineering Co plc		607,500
Discharge of purchase consideration		

Accident insurance fund	5,000	
General reserve account	32,000	
Profit and loss account	3,000	
Realisation account—profit on transfer	110,000	
Share capital account	300,000	
Sundry members account		450,000
Balances transferred		

Sundry members account	450,000	
Cash		180,000
United Engineering Co shares account		270,000
3 shares of £1 each valued at £1.50 per share, and £3 per share in cash for each of 60,000 shares distributed to shareholders		

(2) *Ledger accounts (for additional explanation only)*

REALISATION ACCOUNT

	£		£
Sundry assets	520,000	Creditors	30,000
Premium on debentures	7,500	United Engineering Co plc	
Sundry members account		—purchase consideration	607,500
profit on absorption	110,000		
	637,500		637,500

SUNDRY LIABILITIES

	£		£
Realisation account	30,000	Creditors	30,000
	30,000		30,000

DEBENTURES

	£		£
United Engineering Co plc	157,500	Balance b/f	150,000
		Realisation account—premium	7,500
	157,500		157,500

SUNDRY MEMBERS

	£		£
Cash	180,000	Share capital	300,000
Shares in United Engineering		Accident insurance fund	5,000
Co plc	270,000	General reserve	32,000
		Profit and loss account	3,000
		Realisation account—profit	110,000
	450,000		450,000

SHARES IN UNITED ENGINEERING CO PLC

	£		£
United Engineering Co plc	270,000	Sundry members account	270,000
	270,000		270,000

ACCIDENT INSURANCE FUND

	£		£
Sundry members	32,000	Balance b/f	32,000
	32,000		32,000

GENERAL RESERVE

	£		£
Sundry members	3,000	Balance b/f	3,000
	3,000		3,000

PROFIT AND LOSS ACCOUNT

	£		£
Sundry members	3,000	Balance b/f	3,000
	3,000		3,000

UNITED ENGINEERING CO PLC

	£		£
Realisation account—		Cash	180,000
purchase consideration	607,500	Shares	270,000
		Debentures	157,500
	607,500		607,500

(3) *Journal for opening entries in books of United Engineering Co plc*

UNITED ENGINEERING COMPANY'S JOURNAL

	£	£
Land and buildings	76,500	
Plant and machinery	220,000	
Patents	7,500	
Stocks	106,000	
Debtors	45,000	
Investments	5,000	
Cash at bank and in hand	35,000	
Goodwill	142,500	
Associated Engineering Company plc		607,500
Creditors		30,000
	637,500	637,500

Assets and liabilities taken over as per purchase agreement.

	£	£
Associated Engineering Company plc	607,500	
Cash		180,000
5% debentures account		157,500
Share capital account—180,000 shares of £1 each		180,000
Share premium account		90,000
	607,500	607,500

Discharge of purchase consideration, the shares being taken
as issued at £1.50 per share.

Notes to illustration

(1) ACCIDENT INSURANCE FUND

The fund has been raised by the Associated Engineering Co out of profits and is represented
by specific investments. Since there remains a credit balance on the fund account at the date
of the sale of the undertaking, the Associated Co has made a profit of £5,000 by undertaking
its own risks, instead of insuring outside.

Therefore, although the United Engineering Co takes over the investments representing
such insurance profit, it only buys them as investments, and should not bring the fund
account into its books. In the vendor company's books the balance of this fund account will
be transferred to the sundry members account in common with the other accumulated profit
balances.

(2) GOODWILL

The final figure of goodwill, £142,500, shown in the United Engineering Co's books is
arrived at by taking the difference between the valuation of the assets acquired and the
purchase consideration plus liabilities taken over.

	£
The amount can be proved as follows:	
Goodwill as per vendor company's books	25,000
Profit on absorption	110,000
Premium on debentures unrepresented by assets	7,500
	142,500

(3) PREMIUM ON SHARES

In the vendor company's books the premium forms part of the cost of the shares in the
purchasing company acquired; it forms part of the price received for goodwill, since it
increases the profit on realisation disclosed by the realisation account. In the purchasing
company's books, the share premium increases the cost of goodwill; it must be credited to
share premium account and can only be dealt with in accordance with the provisions of
s 130 of the Companies Act 1985.

25.5   RECONSTRUCTIONS

(a) Possible situations

The term 'reconstruction' may refer to any of the following:

(1) The alteration of the capital structure of a single company, e g a company in
    severe financial difficulties which needs to reach a compromise with its
    creditors;
(2) a demerger, where the various activities of a single company are to be
    transferred to separate companies under separate management following
    liquidation of the first company;
(3) the transfer of the undertaking of one company to another company owned
    by substantially the same shareholders.

Reconstructions may be effected under either s 582 or ss 425–427 of the
Companies Act 1985.

(b) Reconstructions under s 582

Section 582 was referred to in section 25.4(b) above. Under s 582 it is not possible to reach a compromise with creditors—that is possible only under s 425. Section 582 protects the rights of creditors and offers dissentient shareholders the right to demand to be bought out at a fair price.

Section 582 may be used to transfer the undertaking of one company to another company owned by substantially the same shareholders. The section may also be used for demerger situations.

(c) Reconstructions under ss 425–427

These sections may be required if on a reconstruction the company proposes a compromise or arrangement between itself and its creditors. Reconstructions under these sections require the sanction of the court.

Illustrations of situations affecting rights of creditors are given below.

(d) Compromise with creditors

When a company has sustained a considerable loss of capital and is unable to satisfy its creditors in full, the reconstruction scheme commonly provides for a reduction of the original capital, a compromise with the creditors either for cash or for the issue of fully-paid shares or debentures and the provision of new working capital by the issue to the existing shareholders of partly-paid up shares, in exchange for shares held in the old company.

Illustration 7

The final trial balance of the Patent Bottle Company plc was as follows:

	£	£
Share capital:		
50,000 shares of £1 each fully paid		50,000
Creditors		26,500
Patent rights	48,000	
Debtors	4,500	
Stock	10,000	
Profit and loss account	13,850	
Cash	150	
	76,500	76,500

Further information

Efforts to secure sufficient new capital to pay off the liabilities and place the concern on a sound basis having proved unsuccessful, it was decided to reconstruct, and the following scheme was submitted to, and approved by, the shareholders and creditors:

(1) The company to go into voluntary liquidation, and a new company having a nominal capital of £100,000 to be formed, called the New Patent Bottle Co plc, to take over the assets and liabilities of the old company.

(2) The assets to be taken over at book value, with the exception of the patent rights, which were to be subject to adjustment.

(3) The creditors to be discharged by the new company on the following basis:

	£
Preferential creditors to be paid in full	500
Unsecured creditors to be discharged by paid composition of 50p in the £	13,400
Unsecured creditors to be discharged by the issue of 6% debentures fully paid at a bonus of 10%	12,600
	26,500

(4) 50,000 shares of £1 each, 50p paid up, to be issued to the shareholders in the old
      company, payable 25p on application and 25p on allotment.
(5) The costs of liquidation amounting to £250 to be paid by the new company as part
      of the purchase consideration.

Required:
(1) Close off the books of Patent Bottle Co plc;
(2) Show opening entries in books of New Patent Bottle Co plc;
(3) Prepare a balance sheet of New Patent Bottle Co plc, assuming all the shares and
      debentures have been allotted, and all the cash for the shares has been received.

Suggested solution

(1) *Closing off books of old company*

	£	£
Realisation account	62,650	
Patent rights		48,000
Debtors		4,500
Stock		10,000
Cash		150
Sundry assets transferred		

	£	£
Realisation account	1,260	
Creditors		1,260
Bonus of 10% of £12,600 payable in 6%		
debentures fully paid as per agreement		

		£	£
Purchasing company		46,310	
Realisation account			46,310
Purchase consideration payable under scheme as follows:			
50,000 shares of £1 each, 50p paid up to be issued to shareholders	25,000		
£13,860 6% debentures fully paid to be issued to creditors in part payment	13,860		
Cash to creditors in part payment of unsecured creditors and in full discharge of preferential creditors	7,200		
Cash for liquidation expenses	250		
	46,310		

	£	£
Realisation account	250	
Cash		250
Payment of liquidation expenses		

	£	£
Shares account—50,000 shares of £1 each, 50p paid up	25,000	
Debentures account—£13,860 6% debentures	13,860	
Cash	7,450	
Purchasing company		46,310
Assets handed over by New Co to liquidator in settlement of purchase consideration		

	£	£
Creditors	27,760	
Debentures		13,860
Cash		7,200
Realisation account		6,700
Discharge of amounts due to creditors as per agreement and		
Transfer of balance to realisation account		

Sundry members	11,150	
Realisation		11,150
Loss on realisation		

Sundry members	13,850	
Profit and loss account		13,850
Balance transferred		

Share capital	50,000	
Sundry members account		50,000
Share capital transferred		

Sundry members	25,000	
Shares in New Co		25,000
Issue of 50,000 shares £1 each, 50p paid up in		
New Co in exchange for shares in old		

REALISATION ACCOUNT

	£		£
Patent rights	48,000	Purchasing company—	
Debtors	4,500	purchase consideration	46,310
Stock	10,000	Creditors, rebate allowed	6,700
Cash	150	Sundry members account, loss	11,150
Creditors—10% bonus	1,260		
Cash—expenses	250		
	64,160		64,160

PURCHASING COMPANY

	£		£
Realisation account—		Shares in purchasing company	25,000
purchase consideration	46,310	Debentures in purchasing	
		company	13,860
		Cash	7,450
	46,310		46,310

SUNDRY CREDITORS

	£		£
Debentures in New Co	13,860	Balance b/f	26,500
Cash	7,200	Realisation account	1,260
Realisation account	6,700		
	27,760		27,760

SUNDRY MEMBERS

	£		£
Realisation account, loss	11,150	Share capital account	50,000
Profit and loss account	13,850		
Shares in New Co	25,000		
	50,000		50,000

CASH BOOK

	£		£
Purchasing company	7,450	Creditors	7,200
		Liquidation expenses	250
	7,450		7,450

(2) *Opening entries in the books of new company*

JOURNAL

	£	£
Patent rights	31,660	
Debtors	4,500	
Stock	10,000	
Cash	150	
Vendor		46,310
Asset taken over per scheme of reconstruction		
Vendor	46,310	
Share capital account—50,000 shares of £1 each, 50p paid up		25,000
6% debentures		13,860
Cash		7,450
Shares and debentures issued and cash paid in settlement of purchase consideration		
Application and allotment account	25,000	
Share capital		25,000
25p per share payable on application and 25p on allotment of 50,000 shares issued		

CASH BOOK

	£		£
Vendor	150	Vendor	7,450
Application	12,500	Balance c/f	17,700
Allotment	12,500		
	25,150		25,150

(3) *Balance sheet of New Patent Bottle Co plc*

	£	£
Fixed assets:		
Patent rights at costs		31,660
Current assets:		
Stock	10,000	
Debtors	4,500	
Cash	17,700	
		32,200
		63,860
6% debenture stock		(13,860)
		50,000
Called-up share capital:		
50,000 £1 ordinary shares fully paid		50,000

Note to balance sheet—authorised share capital is 100,000 £1 shares.

Notes
(i) PAYMENT OF CREDITORS
As the liquidator is responsible to the creditors of the old company to see that the conditions of the scheme of reconstruction are carried out, the liabilities will be discharged through him, and the transactions will consequently be recorded in the books of the old company.
(ii) THE ADJUSTED VALUE OF THE PATENT RIGHTS
The value placed upon the patent rights is the difference between the purchase price payable to vendor and the assets taken over upon which an agreed value was placed.

(e) Capital reduction schemes involving compromise or arrangement with creditors

(1) *Introduction*

Section 135 of the Companies Act 1985 is only available for straightforward reductions which do not affect the rights of creditors. Reductions affecting rights of creditors should be carried out under the terms of the Companies Act 1985, s 425.

(2) *Basic approach*

Capital reduction schemes are only worth considering if the company has recovery prospects; the rights of the various classes of persons interested must be considered. The object of the scheme is the resumption of dividend payments.

The first step is to determine the amount required to eliminate any fictitious assets, and write down overvalued assets; overvaluation of assets may result in excessive charges to profit and loss account for depreciation, causing profits to be understated or losses overstated.

Debit balances on profit and loss account should be written off; goodwill, patents, trade marks, patterns etc should be written down to their book values.

(3) *Rights of creditors and shareholders*

Having determined the total amount to be written off, the rights of the debenture holders, creditors and various classes of shareholders must be considered. The following factors are relevant:

(i) DEBENTURE HOLDERS
They can sometimes be persuaded to make sacrifices to give the company a new lease of life.

If it can be proved that on a forced realisation of assets such as would ensue if the company were driven into liquidation, the assets, after providing for preferential creditors and the costs, would not realise sufficient to repay the debentures in full, but that there is every prospect of the security being enhanced in the future if the company is reorganised, then the debenture holders may consent to co-operate by sacrificing some of their capital.

Some recompense is usually required e g an increased rate of interest, and/or an interest in the equity by the issue to them of fully-paid ordinary shares for a proportion of their capital contribution to the amount required for writing off assets.

(ii) OTHER CREDITORS
Creditors other than preferential creditors in a winding up, may agree to a share in a reduction, particularly if the debenture holders have agreed to a sacrifice, since in a liquidation they would obtain little or nothing. It must be proved to creditors that they will obtain more by accepting a reduction than by forcing the company into liquidation.

Usually, neither debenture holders nor creditors can be expected to share in the reduction, the amount required being provided by writing down share capital alone.

(iii) ORDINARY SHAREHOLDERS

The bulk of the loss, usually the whole of it, must fall upon the shareholders. If creditors are to come into the scheme, the shareholders must surrender something to them e g a share in the equity that will enable the creditors to reap some reward in future years for their immediate sacrifice.

As regards the position of the various classes of shareholders, where capital has been lost then the brunt of the loss must fall on the *ordinary* shareholders. However, if this meant the loss of their entire interest in the company, they would not agree to the scheme. The company may have retained in the past profits which could have been distributed as dividends in order to strengthen the company's finances. As the company fell on lean times, such reserves may have been drawn upon to pay prefererence dividends, with the result that the ordinary shareholders may have already made a sacrifice for the benefit of the preference shareholders.

(iv) EFFECTS OF WRITING DOWN CAPITAL

It is essential to appreciate the effect of writing down capital. For example, suppose the capital of a company is £100,000 divided into 60,000 6% preference shares of £1 each, and 40,000 £1 ordinary shares. Profits, after the preference dividend of £3,600 has been paid, are divisible among the ordinary shareholders. It does not matter to what nominal value the ordinary shares are written down; the amount of the dividend per share remains the same, and the market value of the shares will not be affected by the reduction in nominal value. Writing down ordinary shares therefore entails no real sacrifice so long as the shareholders' interest in the divisible profits is not reduced.

A reduction in the nominal value of the preference shares, however, or in their rate of dividend, will reduce the value of their shares.

Again, if the preference shareholders have the right to preferential repayment of capital, but are entitled to no right to share in a surplus on a winding up, the ordinary shareholders will receive all the assets remaining after repaying the preference capital, no matter what the nominal value of the ordinary shares may be. Writing down ordinary shares imposes only a nominal sacrifice upon the holders of such shares.

Where preference shareholders are entitled to share in a surplus, the writing down of the ordinary shares does involve a sacrifice of rights, since a bigger proportion of any surplus would then go to the preference shareholders. The ultimate winding up rights, however, are not so immediately important as the dividend i e going concern rights, and therefore, where preference shareholders are called upon to share in a reduction of capital, it is only equitable that ordinary shareholders should surrender part of their rights to the preference shareholders.

(v) PREFERENCE SHAREHOLDERS

Preference shareholders should only be asked to share in a reduction if the amount to be written off exceeds the ordinary share capital. Either their capital and/or their rate of dividend may be reduced. They should be compensated by a share in the equity, so that they may recoup their losses should the company's fortunes improve.

Arrears of cumulative preference dividends must be dealt with on their merits. If they are cancelled, the preference shareholders should be compensated by the issue of shares or other consideration for the whole or part of the arrears, the cancellation of which will benefit the ordinary shareholders.

(vi) FAIRNESS OF THE SCHEME

The test of whether the scheme is reasonably equitable is to compute how the estimated future income will be divisible under the new share capital holdings compared with the old, bearing in mind that all classes of shares can anticipate immediate dividends instead of waiting until the debit balance on profit and loss account is eliminated by profits. The benefit of immediate dividends is greater, the lower the priority the class of shares has. Deferred shares, as a rule, will have to be cancelled, or given a very minute interest in the reorganised company. If, however, they hold valuable rights pari passu with the ordinary shares, they will have to rank equitably with the latter.

(4) *Illustration* 8

The following is the summarised balance sheet of Sea Mills plc as at 31 December 19X6:

	£	£
Fixed assets:		
Goodwill		100,000
Patents and trade marks		80,000
		180,000
Freehold land and buildings	135,000	
Plant and machinery	85,000	
		220,000
		400,000
Current assets:		
Stock	79,900	
Debtors	110,000	
Cash in hand	100	
	190,000	
Current liabilities:		
Creditors	64,000	
Bank overdraft	24,000	
Debenture interest	12,000	
	100,000	
Net current assets		90,000
		490,000

	£	£
6% debentures (secured by a floating charge)		100,000
Authorised, issued and called-up shared capital:		
250,000 £1 ordinary shares	250,000	
250,000 £1 6% cumulative preference shares	250,000	
	500,000	
Profit and loss account	(110,000)	
		390,000
		490,000

Additional information

(1) The dividends on the preference shares are five years in arrear.
(2) The directors state that the current trading results show a marked improvement, and that they anticipate a net profit of £20,000 per annum will be maintained in future years.
(3) The directors desire to resume the payment of dividends as soon as possible and are accordingly considering the reduction of the company's capital.
(4) The debenture holders, to assist in the revival of the company, have expressed their willingness to exchange their arrears of interest for an interest in the equity of the business of one-half of the nominal value of the arrears, and to provide £25,000 further cash (on a floating charge) to repay the bank overdraft and to provide working capital of £1,000.

(5) The preference shares are described by the articles as not preferential to capital, but any arrears of dividends are to form a first charge upon any surplus on winding up. The preference shareholders have expressed their willingness to a reduction in the rate of dividend to 5% and to forego two-thirds of their arrears, provided that they receive an interest on the equity equal in nominal value to the remaining third.

Required:
(1) To draft a suggested scheme for the reduction of capital which should include the elimination of goodwill (acquired from James Mills on the formation of the company in exchange for 100,000 ordinary shares which he still holds) and the profit and loss account balance, the reduction of the value of patents and trade marks by £50,000, and the provision of a capital reserve through which any adjustments arising out of the capital rearrangements etc may be dealt with. After reduction, the ordinary shares are to be converted into 5p shares.
(2) To redraft the balance sheet, giving effect to the scheme you suggest.

Suggested solution

(1) *Suggested scheme*

(i) *Elimination of capital*

The capital must be reduced by £285,000, made up as follows:

	£
To eliminate goodwill	100,000
To eliminate profit and loss account balance	110,000
To write down patents and trade marks	50,000
To provide for one-third of arrears of preference dividend	25,000
	285,000

(ii) *Reorganisation of capital*
Since the preference shares are not entitled to a prior return of capital at first sight the loss of capital should be borne equally between the ordinary and preference shareholders. It makes no difference that the preference shareholders are to receive a share in the equity of £25,000 for the cancellation of £75,000 dividend arrears. But since the preference shareholders have consented to a reduction in their rate of cumulative dividend to 5%, which, of itself, will reduce the value of their shares, they should be required to suffer a correspondingly smaller reduction in their nominal capital.
   The capital should be reorganised as follows:

(a) The 250,000 6% cumulative preference shares of £1 each to be reduced to shares of 67½p each and sub-divided into:

	£
250,000 5% cumulative preference shares of 50p each	125,000
875,000 ordinary shares of 5p each	43,750
	168,750

	£
This represents a reduction in capital of	81,250

In addition, the preference shareholders to receive 500,000 ordinary shares of 5p each = £25,000, in satisfaction of one-third of their arrears of dividend, the balance to be cancelled.
(b) The 250,000 ordinary shares of £1 each to be reduced to shares of 20p each and converted into 1,000,000 ordinary shares of 5p each.
   This represents a reduction in capital of   200,000
(c) The debenture holders to be allotted 120,000 ordinary shares of 5p each in satisfaction of half their arrears of interest, the balance to be cancelled.
   This represents a reduction of   6,000

Total reduction   287,250

Of this amount, £285,000 will be applied in writing down the assets and providing for the £25,000 arrears of preference dividend as shown above. The balance of £2,250 may be applied in meeting the costs of the reduction scheme and any adjustments arising out of it, and in reducing the book value of such other of the assets as may be determined by the directors.

The paid-up capital of the company will now consist of:

	£
250,000 5% cumulative preference shares of 50p each	125,000
2,495,000 ordinary shares of 5p each	124,750
	249,750

The resolution for reduction of capital should at the same time provide for the restoration of the authorised capital to £500,000, leaving £250,250 unissued capital, which would be available for issue at some future date, if required.

(iii) Effect on security holder's income

The effect of the above reorganisation of capital, assuming an annual profit of £20,000 to be maintained, will be to cause the profits to be divided between the existing preference and ordinary shareholders in approximately the following proportions. Although on a profit of £20,000, the preference shareholders will receive a little less than previously, their holding of ordinary shares will give them the control of the company, and they will take a major share in any increase in distributable profits over £20,000.

	£	£
Existing preference shareholders will receive:		
Dividend of 5% on £125,000 new preference shares	6,250	
Dividend of, say, 10% on £68,750 new ordinary shares	6,875	
		13,125
Existing ordinary shareholders will receive:		
Dividend of, say, 10% on 50,000 new ordinary shares		5,000
Debenture holders will receive:		
Dividend, of say, 10% on £6,000 new ordinary shares		600
		18,725
Carry forward		1,275
		20,000

Note: It is assumed that the debenture interest would already have been provided for before arriving at the profit of £20,000.

(2) *Sea Mills plc—redrafted balance sheet at 31 December 19X6*

	£	£
Fixed assets:		
Intangible fixed assets:		
Patents and trade marks		30,000
Tangible fixed assets:		
Freehold land and buildings	135,000	
Plant and machinery	85,000	
		220,000
		250,000
Current assets:		
Stock	79,900	
Debtors	110,000	
Cash	1,100	
	191,000	
Creditors—amounts falling due within one year		
Creditors	64,000	

Net current assets	127,000
Total assets less current liabilities	377,000
Creditors—amounts falling due after more than one year:	
6% debentures (secured by floating charge)	(125,000)
	252,000

Capital and reserves:		
Called-up share capital:		
2,495,000 5p ordinary shares		124,750
250,000 50p 5% cumulative preference shares		125,000
		249,750
Capital reserve		2,250
		252,000

NOTE
Authorised share capital is £500,000.

26 SPECIAL REPORTS INCLUDING STOCK EXCHANGE SITUATIONS

26.1 OUTLINE OF PRINCIPAL REPORTING REQUIREMENTS

(a) Introduction

This chapter considers the main reporting requirements applicable in specified situations to companies listed on The Stock Exchange.

The majority of the regulations derive from The Stock Exchange (Listing) Regulations 1984 set out in The Stock Exchange's 'Yellow Book' (Admission of Securities to Listing). The new regulations came into force on 1 January 1985.

(b) The main situations

These are set out in the diagram below and discussed briefly in the remainder of this section.

MAIN REPORTS AND DOCUMENTS

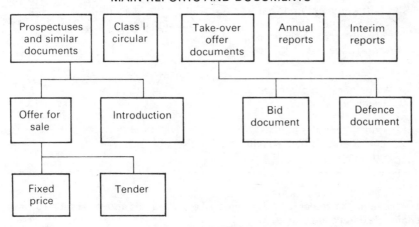

Private reports, such as 'background' reports for merchant banks, are not referred to above.

(c) Prospectuses and similar documents

The most common such situations are offers for sale where the company's shares are offered by a merchant bank.

Some offers for sale are at fixed price. Others are by tender where individual applicants choose the price per share at which they wish to apply subject to the stated minimum price. After applications have been received, the bank will fix a 'striking price'. Applicants tendering at or above the striking price may receive an allotment.

An introduction covers a situation of a company coming to the market for the first time and does not involve the issue of shares. What an introduction does achieve is to convert an unlisted company into a listed company. In most respects, reporting formalities are similar to those for an offer for sale.

In prospectuses, the accountants' report deals essentially with a five-year historical summary (discussed a detail in section 26.2). However, should the document concerned include a profit forecast, a separate accountant's report is required. (See section 26.3).

Reporting requirements for prospectuses are set out in the 'Yellow Book' and in the Companies Act 1985. However, no further reference is made to the Companies Act 1985 as the Yellow Book requirements overlap and extend the legal requirements.

Finally, the Auditing Practices Committee have issued an auditing guideline entitled 'Prospectuses and the Reporting Accountant'.

(d) Class 1 circulars

These are concerned with transactions which are considered sufficiently material as to require listing particulars to be published or a circular to be sent to shareholders.

A Class 1 transaction is defined as one where a comparison on any one of the four bases referred to below amounts to 15% or more:

Basis	Comparison with
(1) Value of assets acquired or disposed of	Assets of the acquiring or disposing company
(2) Net profits before tax and extraordinary items attributable to assets acquired or disposed of	Net profits of acquiring or disposing company
(3) Aggregate value of consideration given or received	Assets of the acquiring or disposing company
(4) Equity capital issued as consideration by the acquiring company	Equity capital previously in issue

In broad terms, a circular will be required where *any* of the above exceeds 15% but certain relaxations are permitted.

The content of a Class 1 circular is specified by the Yellow Book. In addition, an accountants' report is required in the case of an acquisition of an unlisted company.

(e) Take-over offer documents

A take-over bid may result in the issue of one or more documents, each of which is considered by Stock Exchange regulations, e g:

(1) An offer document sent by the offeror company (or a merchant bank acting on its behalf) to the shareholders of the offeree company.
(2) A document responding to the above sent by the directors of the offeree company of the shareholders of the offeree company and recommending rejection of the offer.
(3) Listing particulars where application has been made to the Council of The Stock Exchange for the securities to be issued as consideration for the proposed acquisition to be admitted to the Official List. The listing particulars

give extensive financial and other information regarding the companies concerned.

Where (1) and (2) contains a profit forecast, an accountants' report is required. This is covered in section 26.3.

(f) Annual reports and interim reports

The Stock Exchange disclosure requirements for annual reports of listed companies were outlined in chapter 5.

Interim reports covering the first six months of the year are discussed below, in section 26.4.

26.2 ACCOUNTANTS' REPORT—FIVE-YEAR HISTORICAL SUMMARIES

(a) General requirements

Information given should refer to all group companies including companies which will become part of the group as a result of agreements made since the last balance sheet date.

(b) Principal contents covering a five-year period

(1) *Profit and loss information*

(i)   Turnover,
(ii)   Cost of sales:

    (a) showing separately distribution and administration expenses;
    (b) noting amortisation and depreciation; leasing and hire charges; directors' remuneration; auditors' remuneration.

(iii)   Investment and other income.
(iv)   Interest payable.
(v)   Exceptional items.
(vi)   Share of profits and losses of related companies.
(vii)   Profit or loss before tax and extraordinary items.
(viii) Tax on profits (UK; overseas; related companies).
(ix)   Minority interests.
(x)   Preference dividends.
(xi)   Profit or loss attributable to equity shareholders before extraordinary items.
(xii)   Extraordinary items (disclosing attributable taxation).
(xiii) Profit or loss attributable to equity shareholders.
(xiv)   Dividends on each class of shares (disclosing dividend rates and waivers).
(xv)   Any other items warranting separate disclosure.
(xvi)   Increase (or decrease) for the year in retained profits shown in the balance sheet.

(2) *Per share information*

(i)   Amount of profit or loss after tax per share (earnings per share).
(ii)   Dividends per share.

(3) *Reserves*

Movements on reserves not reflected in the statement of profits and losses.

(4) *Balance sheet information*

(i)   Company or group balance sheets; *or*

(ii) Statements of assets and liabilities of the business.

(5) *Source and application of funds information*

Company or group statements.

(6) *Borrowings analysis*

An analysis for the latest balance sheet date showing for:

(i)   bank loans and overdrafts;
(ii) other borrowings.

the aggregate amounts repayable:

(i)   in one year or less or on demand;
(ii) between one and two years;
(iii) between two and five years; and
(iv) in five years or more.

(7) *Interest capitalised*

Statement of interest capitalised by the company with an indication of the amount and treatment of any related tax relief.

(8) *Accounting policies*

Accounting policies followed in dealing with items which are judged material in determining profits of losses and net assets reported on.

(9) *Other matters*

Any other matters which appear to be relevant for the purposes of the report.

(c) Adjustments for the purposes of the report

(1) *Main criteria*

The reporting accountants should make any adjustments to previously audited accounts for the purpose of the five-year summary.
   The reporting accountants should state either that they have made all adjustments considered necessary or alternatively that no adjustments were necessary.
   The statement of adjustments should reconcile the figures in the report with the corresponding figures in the audited accounts. The statement of adjustments should be signed by the reporting accountants and be made available for inspection by the public. The statement does not have to follow a standard format.

(2) *Adjustment situations*

Where the effect is material, adjustments may be required in the case of:

(i)   changes in accounting policies;
(ii) correction of fundamental errors;
(iii) reclassification of extraordinary and exceptional items;
(iv) adjusting post-balance sheet events.

(3) *Disclosures*

In order to ensure that the accountants' report gives a true and fair view, it may be necessary to disclose (rather than adjust for) the following matters:

(i)   effect of significant changes in the composition of the group (unless merger accounting has been adopted, in which case the previous year's figures should be restated);

(ii) effect of loss-making subsidiaries;
(iii) effect of discontinued activities.

(d) Accounting standards

Accountants' reports for companies incorporated in the UK or the Republic of Ireland should be drawn up in accordance with statements of Standard Accounting Practice.

Significant departures from accounting standards should be disclosed and explained, and the financial effects of such departures quantified.

The standards to be followed will usually be those applicable for the last period reported on. Whenever possible, results and financial positions of earlier years should be restated in accordance with current standards.

(e) Age of figures

The date of the report should normally be within six months of the end of the last period reported on.

(f) Reporting requirements

The reporting accountants should express an opinion whether or not a true and fair view is given of the state of affairs, of the profits or losses and the source and application of funds for the periods reported on.

Illustration of wording

We have examined the financial information presented below for Dalehead plc and its subsidiaries for the five years to 31 December 19X8 in accordance with approved auditing standards. The company and its subsidiaries are referred to as the Group. Dunbar, Sandon, Blundell and Co have acted as the company's auditors throughout the relevant period. The financial information set out below is based on the audited financial statements of the company and the group after making such adjustments as we consider appropriate.

In our opinion the financial information shown below gives, under the historical cost convention (which has been modified by the revaluation of certain assets), a true and fair view of the results and source and application of funds of the group for the five years ended 31 December 19X8 and of the state of affairs of the company and the group at that date.

26.3 ACCOUNTANTS' REPORTS—PROFIT FORECASTS

(a) Situations

The directors, if they so choose, may include profit forecasts in the following documents:

(1) Prospectuses and similar documents.
(2) Take-over offer documents.

Where a profit forecast is included, it must be accompanied by an accountants' report. Guidance is given in a CCAB statement entitled 'Accountants' Reports on Profit Forecasts'.

(b) Reporting requirements

The reporting accountants should:

(1) examine and report on the accounting policies and calculations for the forecast;

(2) satisfy themselves that the profit forecast, so far as the accounting policies and calculations are concerned, have been properly compiled on the footing of the assumptions made.

(c) Illustration 1

The illustration below is taken from the listing particulars produced by P & O in connection with the proposed merger with Sterling Guarantee Trust plc.

Part V Profit forecast of the SGT Group

1. Profit forecast

The Directors of SGT forecast that the profit on ordinary activities before taxation of the SGT Group for the year ending 24th March, 1985 will amount to not less than £24.0 million (1983/4 £16.5 million). Included in the forecast profit on ordinary activities before taxation is revenue derived from SGT's holding of Deferred Stock in P & O totalling £4.3 million (1983/4 £0.3 million), net of financing costs of £4.7 million (1983/4 £0.4 million), as if the holding of the Deferred Stock in P & O were held to 24th March, 1985.

2. Bases and assumptions

The profit forecast of the SGT Group for the year ending 24th March, 1985 takes account of the unaudited interim accounts for the half year ended 28th September, 1984, updated by later management accounts where available and a forecast for the remaining period to 24th March, 1985. The forecast includes the appropriate share of profits of P & O on an equity accounting basis from 28th September, 1984, has been prepared in accordance with the accounting policies normally adopted by SGT and is based on the following principal assumptions:

(a) the present management and accounting policies of SGT and its subsidiaries will not be changed;

(b) there will be no material disruptions to the business of SGT and its subsidiaries owing to industrial disputes or business failures of any of their principal customers or suppliers;

(c) there will be no material change in interest rates during the remainder of the forecast period; and

(d) there will be no material change in exchange rates during the remainder of the forecast period.

3. Letters

The Directors of SGT have received the following letters from Peat, Marwick, Mitchell & Co., SGT's auditors, and from Hambros and Barclays Merchant Bank in connection with the profit forecast for the year ending 24th March, 1985.

"The Directors   1 Puddle Dock
Sterling Guarantee Trust PLC   London EC4V 3PD
4 Carlton Gardens
Pall Mall
London SW1Y 5AB

1st February, 1985

Dear Sirs,

We have reviewed the accounting policies and calculations for the profit forecast of Sterling Guarantee Trust PLC and its subsidiaries (for which the Directors are solely responsible) for the year ending 24th March, 1985 set out in Part V of the Listing Particulars of The Peninsular and Oriental Steam Navigation Company to be dated 1st February, 1985. This profit forecast takes account of the results shown by the unaudited interim accounts for the half year ended 28th September, 1984, updated by later management accounts where available.

In our opinion, the profit forecast, so far as the accounting policies and calculations are concerned, has been properly compiled on the basis of the assumptions made by the Directors set out in Part V of the Listing Particulars and is presented on a basis consistent with the accounting policies normally adopted by Sterling Guarantee Trust PLC.

Yours faithfully,
PEAT, MARWICK, MITCHELL & CO.
Chartered Accountants"

"The Directors 15/16 Gracechurch Street
Sterling Guarantee Trust PLC London EC3V 0BA
4 Carlton Gardens
Pall Mall 41 Bishopsgate
London SW1Y 5AB London EC2P 2AA

1st February, 1985

Dear Sirs,

We refer to the profit forecast of Sterling Guarantee Trust PLC and its subsidiaries for the year ending 24th March, 1985 contained in Part V of the Listing Particulars of The Peninsular and Oriental Steam Navigation Company to be dated 1st February, 1985.

We have discussed with you this forecast and the bases and assumptions on which it is made and we have considered the letter to be dated 1st February, 1985 addressed to yourselves from Peat, Marwick, Mitchell & Co. regarding the accounting policies and calculations for this forecast.

On the basis of the assumptions used by you and relying on the accounting policies and calculations reviewed by Peat, Marwick, Mitchell & Co., we have formed the opinion that the profit forecast referred to above (for which you as Directors are solely responsible) has been made after due and careful enquiry.

Yours faithfully, Yours faithfully,
for *for and on behalf of*
BARCLAYS MERCHANT BANK LIMITED HAMBROS BANK LIMITED

I.J. SCOTT C.H. SPORBORG

Director *Deputy Chairman"*

26.4 INTERIM REPORTS TO SHAREHOLDERS

(a) Introduction

Once a company's securities have been admitted to listing on The Stock Exchange, that company is obliged to follow specified continuing obligations.

One such continuing obligation is that a company must prepare a half-yearly report on its activities and profit or loss during the first six months of each financial year. This report should either be sent to shareholders or inserted in two national daily newspapers.

(b) Accounting and audit requirements

The figures in the half-yearly or interim reports are the sole responsibility of the directors.

The accounting policies applied to the interim figures should be consistent with those for the annual accounts. Where a change in policy is proposed, the Quotations Department of The Stock Exchange should be consulted as regards periods to be coverd by the interim report. The figures in the interim report are unaudited.

(c) Minimum contents of an interim report

(1) *Figures in table form*

The following figures in table form for the interim period and for the corresponding previous period should be included:

(i)   turnover;
(ii)   profit or loss before taxation and extraordinary items;
(iii)   tax on profits (showing separately UK tax; overseas tax; related companies tax);
(iv)   minority interests;
(v)   profit or loss attributable to shareholders before extraordinary items;
(vi)   extraordinary items (net of taxation);
(vii)   profit or loss attributable to shareholders;
(viii) rates and amounts of dividends paid and proposed;
(ix)   earnings per share.

(2) *Explanatory statement*

The report should include an explanatory statement relating to the group's activities and profit or loss during the relevant period. This must include any significant information enabling investors to make an informed assessment of the trend of the group's activities and profit or loss together with an indication of any special factor which has influenced those activities and the profit or loss during the period in question. The statement should enable a comparison to be made with the corresponding period of the preceding financial year.

As far as possible, the statement should refer to the group's prospects in the current financial year.

(3) *Audit status*

The report must state the fact that the accounting information given in the half-yearly report has not been audited.

26.5   SHARE VALUATION REPORTS

(a) Share valuation situations

The range of situations where share valuations may be required is diverse and could include the following:

(1) share valuations in an unquoted company for the requirements of a prospective buyer or seller;
(2) share valuations in an unquoted company for tax purposes (for example, capital gains tax or capital transfer tax);
(3) valuation of shares for an offer for sale document, where the offer price must appear attractive to prospective purchasers in terms of dividend yield and price/earnings ratio;
(4) valuation of shares in quoted companies for the purpose of determining share exchange terms.

The main purpose of this chapter is to refer to some of the more important considerations to be taken into account in share valuation situations such as (1) above. Detailed consideration of share valuations for tax purposes is outside the scope of this book. Situations (3) and (4) will be referred to later in the chapter.

(b) Form and content of report

Form and content will clearly vary as between the different share valuation situations. For simplicity, only reports of share valuations in unlisted companies will be considered.

The report should be set out under main headings. For the purpose of clarity, detailed information should be relegated to appendices.

For most purposes, the following headings would be adequate:

(1) *Introduction*

This should set out the terms of reference including the main purpose for which the valuation is required.

(2) *Conclusions*

Some accountants consider that a summary of the principal conclusions should appear at the beginning of the report.

(3) *General Background*

Not all readers of the report will be aware of the background of the company and the industry. Any relevant information should be included.

(4) *Information used*

Much of the information and calculations will be based on audited accounts of previous years. However, unaudited financial statements of the current period may also be useful, as may profit forecasts. Thus, the sources of the relevant information should be clearly described so that readers are aware of any limitations relating to information used.

(5) *Assumptions*

Any underlying assumption which may not be readily apparent to readers should be clearly set out in a similar way to published profit forecasts.

(6) *Shareholdings*

A breakdown of present and possible future shareholdings is likely to be particularly relevant. Any special circumstances, e g the possible sale of shares to a special buyer such as a key shareholder, should be referred to.

(7) *Financial position of the company*

It may be useful to refer to the following:

(i) profitability (past and future);
(ii) liquidity;
(iii) asset backing;
(iv) key ratios.

(8) *Specific considerations*

The following may also be relevant:

(i) future plans, including expansion and diversification into new products and markets;
(ii) management record;
(iii) key personnel.

(9) *Basis of valuation*

The valuation basis should be stated together with reasons for adopting this approach.

(10) *Detailed conclusions and recommendations*

Appendices
(a) Valuations.
(b) Summary of asset and liabilities (e g five years).
(c) Summary of profit and loss accounts (e g five years).

(d) Extracts from memorandum and articles.
(e) Service contracts of key executives.

(c) Some basic considerations

The following points are worth noting:

(1) *Preference shares*

Most share valuation situations relate to ordinary shares. Preference shares may be valued by capitalising prospective (fixed) dividends at an appropriate yield.

Suppose a valuation is required of £1 8% preference shares. Dividend per share is 8p, or $8 \times \frac{10}{7}$ i e 11.43 p in gross terms. If 12% is regarded as an appropriate yield, the shares may be valued at

$$\frac{11.43}{0.12} = 95.2p$$

(2) *Main differences between quoted and unquoted shares*

The three main differences are:

(i)   shareholdings in quoted companies are more widely dispersed than for unquoted companies;
(ii) in quoted companies, management and shareholdings tend to be separated, whereas in many unquoted companies the directors and shareholders are one and the same;
(iii) shares in quoted companies are easy to sell. By comparison, it is often difficult to sell shares in private unquoted companies because of restrictions in the articles of association.

(3) *Relevance of future benefits*

A share valuation at a particular date should reflect the future benefits expected to be derived from the holding of the shares.

These will include:

(i)   expected dividends;
(ii) expected capital gains;
(iii) voting power.

While historical data is clearly important, expected future benefits should not be ignored.

For example, suppose a company formed five years ago showed the following results:

Year		
19X1	Loss	£30,000
19X2	Loss	£45,000
19X3	Loss	£12,000
19X4	Loss	£22,000
19X5	Profit	£1,000

If future years were expected to show a profit, a share valuation based on the average results of the last five years would be misleading. This is particularly important for start-up companies.

(4) *Rights attaching to shares*

It is important to establish rights in relation to matters such as voting, dividends, sale of shares and liquidation.

(d) Size of shareholding

The choice of valuation approach depends to a large extent on the size of shareholding to be valued in relation to other shareholdings in the company. For example, in some companies, a shareholding of 30% may be the largest single shareholding in the company and thus carry effective day-to-day control. On the other hand, a 30% shareholding may carry little influence in a company where one other person holds 70% of the shares.

Certain key levels of shareholding are critical in share valuations.

Shareholding	Comments
75% or more	Ability to pass a special resolution (could alter articles, liquidate company etc)
More than 50% but less than 75%	(1) Day-to-day control of the company (2) Control composition of board of directors (3) Control level of directors' remuneration (4) Control of dividend policy
More than 25% but not more than 50%	Ability to prevent a special resolution being passed
25% or less	Statutory remedies: (1) petition court for an order for the compulsory winding-up of the company on the just and equitable ground (2) apply to Department of Trade for appointment of inspectors to investigate the affairs of the company (3) petition court for relief on the ground of unfair prejudice to the interests of members (In practice, holdings of around 20% may be capable of allowing the owner of the shares to exert significant influence over the affairs of the company.)

Finally, it is important to remember the position of the 'special buyer'. For example, a sale of a small parcel of shares amounting to 2% of the share capital of the company would be extremely attractive to a person holding at present 49% of the share capital of the company.

(e) Share valuation methods

(1) Introduction

The principal approaches may be summarised diagrammatically as follows:

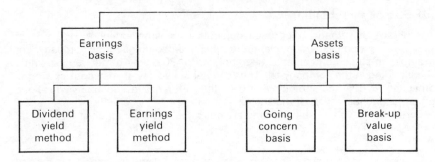

It should be appreciated that a comprehensive approach to the theory of share valuation is covered by financial management textbooks.

This section attempts only to give an outline of some of the main considerations. Each of the possible approaches is covered in turn.

(2) *Dividend yield method*

This method attempts to value shares by reference to prospective future dividends. The method is useful for valuing small parcels of shares in unquoted companies where the size of the holding is not large enough to have a significant influence on dividend policy. The method may also be useful in offer for sale situations, since quoted shares must offer an attractive yield as compared with similar companies.

The value per share on a dividend yield basis is given by the formula:

$$\text{Value per share} = \frac{\text{expected future}}{\text{dividend (grossed up)}} \times \frac{100}{\text{required dividend yield}}$$

This formula ignores growth in dividends. The value per share should reflect future benefits and thus prospective dividends are more important than historical dividends. The required dividend yield is the yield which will satisfy an investor. Generally speaking, a higher dividend yield is required on unquoted shares as compared with quoted shares.

Illustration 3

Cuttings Ltd is a small private company.
Expected future dividends per share are 12p (cash) or $(12 \times \frac{10}{7})$ i e 17.1p when grossed up at 30%.

The average yield for quoted companies in the same industrial sector is currently 11.4%. However, as this company is unquoted, it is considered that the shares should offer a significantly higher yield. One possible approach is to increase 11.4% by an arbitrary uplift of 25%–30% to allow for unmarketability. On the basis, the required yield would be between 14.25% and 14.8%, say, 14.5%

$$\text{Value per share} = 17.1 \times \frac{100}{14.5}, \text{ i e 117.9 pence per share.}$$

In view of the subjective nature of the share valuation calculations, it may be sensible to express the result in terms of a range (say, between 115p and 120p) which would then offer a basis for subsequent negotiation.

(3) *Earnings yield method*

Where the size of the shareholding is such that a holder would have either significant influence or control over dividend policy, it makes sense to consider earnings (i e profit available for dividends) rather than solely dividends. This approach may be appropriate, therefore, for substantial minority holdings as well as majority holdings.

The basic approach is to capitalise prospective future earnings by means of a suitable price/earnings ratio. If the valuation relates to an unlisted company, it may be necessary to use price/earnings ratios applicable to quoted companies in the same industrial sector.

Illustration 4

Prospective future earnings per share of Prospects Ltd is 28.9p. Quoted companies in the same industrial sector stand on a price/earnings multiple of 12.2. As Prospects Ltd is unquoted, it is decided that a price/earnings ratio of 10.0 would be suitable. An earnings basis valuation might therefore come up with a value per share in the region of 289p.

(4) *Assets basis*

If a company is viewed as a going concern, an attempt should be made to appraise the fair value of the assets. This would give a net asset per share based on realistic values although this would not include goodwill. The absence of a realistic figure for goodwill reduces the relevance of this approach other than as possibly a cross-check on the earnings basis method.

Alternatively, if a prospective buyer intends to acquire over 75% of the share capital and subsequently put the company into liquidation, it may be more relevant to consider break-up values rather than going concern values.

(f) Special factors

In a particular situation, some of the following factors may be relevant:

(1) Restrictions in the articles of association regarding share transfers; for small shareholdings, excessive restrictions are likely to depress the value per share. For example, the required dividend yield of a private company with severe share transfer restrictions may need to be 50% above the level for a comparable quoted company. However, it is important not to lose sight of the reasons for the purchase of the shares which could include a possible future seat on the board of directors. This prospect may be just as important as future dividends and may more than compensate for excessive restrictions in the articles!

(2) Excessive directors' remuneration paid in previous years: this may be purely for tax reasons. It is important to consider future remuneration policy taking account of changes in the membership of the board and future intentions.

(3) Little or no dividend paid in the past for tax reasons: historical dividend policy may be of little relevance if future policy will show significant changes.

(4) Loans to the company at low interest rates: these loans may not continue in the future. It would be wise to compute prospective future earnings on the basis of commercial interest rates.

(5) The special buyer: this has been referred to previously. One example would be the holder of 49% of the share capital who would be prepared to pay an extremely high price per share in order to obtain a further holding of 2%. A strong bargaining position could be an important factor in share valuations!

(g) Illustration 5

The directors of New Products plc are considering a possible future offer for sale of shares of the company.

Summarised accounts for the last five years show the following position:

	19X6 £'000	19X5 £'000	19X4 £'000	19X3 £'000	19X2 £'000
Tangible fixed assets	2,920	2,230	2,100	1,790	1,660
Trade investments	430	320	290	130	120
Net current assets	570	590	320	260	170
Loans and provisions	(1,740)	(1,180)	(900)	(570)	(560)
	2,180	1,960	1,810	1,610	1,390
Called-up capital (25p shares)	340	340	340	340	340
Profit and loss account	1,840	1,620	1,470	1,270	1,050
	2,180	1,960	1,810	1,610	1,390
Results:					
Turnover	9,560	8,070	7,390	5,980	4,730
Cost of sales	8,000	6,630	5,880	4,660	3,780
Gross profit	1,560	1,440	1,510	1,320	950
Operating expenses	890	910	920	740	440
Profit before tax	670	530	590	580	510
Taxation	368	298	320	300	280
Profit after tax	302	232	270	280	230
Dividends	82	82	70	60	50
Retained profit	220	150	200	220	180
Balance B/F	1,620	1,470	1,270	1,050	870
Balance C/F	1,840	1,620	1,470	1,270	1,050

Two companies which are considered competitors in the major markets are already quoted and the most recent data from the Financial Times relating to them is shown below:

19X6		Company	+ or Div				Yield	
High	Low		Price	−	Net	Cover	Gross	P/E
277	201	A plc 50p	202	−4	6.23	3.5	4.7	9.3
168	132	B plc 25p	132	−3	3.27	5.6	3.8	7.2

Required: advise the directors on the possible range that might be obtained showing clearly the alternative methods of calculation you have used.

Possible solution

Consider three possible valuation approaches:

(1) *Dividend yield approach*
A company coming to the market for the first time must offer a dividend yield which compares favourably with those of its main competitors.
  Dividend yields of competitors:

A plc   4.7%
B plc   3.8%

Dividend cover of New Products for 19X6 is 3.7 × (302 ÷ 82). As company A is closer to this figure than company B, the valuation will be based on a yield of 4.7%.

Dividend per share share (gross) of New Products $= \dfrac{(82,000)}{(340,000 \times 4)} \times \dfrac{100}{70} = 8.6\text{p}.$

So dividend yield valuation $= \dfrac{8.6\text{p}}{0.047} = 183\text{p}.$

(2) *Earnings yield approach*
Earnings per share based on most recent set of accounts (19X6)

$$= \frac{£302,000}{4 \times 340,000} \times 100 = 22.2\text{p per share.}$$

Using the P/E ratio applicable to company A, value per share = 9.3 × 22.2p = 206p.

(3) *Assets basis*
It is impossible to arrive at a meaningful figure since goodwill is excluded from the balance sheet, and tangible fixed assets have not been revalued.

On present figures, net assets per share $= \dfrac{£2,180,000}{4 \times 340,000} \times 100 = 160\text{p.}$

Conclusions
As the assets basis does not provide a meaningful figure, it is suggested that the other approaches offer a range of 183p to 206p within which a suitable figure may be arrived at. Remember that share valuations are an art and not a science!

(h) Share exchange terms

(1) *Introduction*

This section attempts to outline some of the more important considerations relevant in determining share exchange terms.

Consider the example of A plc which wishes to acquire B plc. The overall situation may be illustrated as follows:

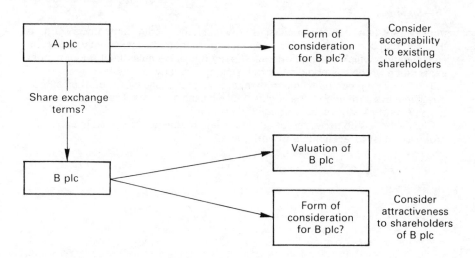

(2) *Shareholders of A plc*

Once A has decided what company B is worth, the question arises as to what form the purchase consideration should take, e g the split between cash, share, debentures and convertible loan stock.

A's shareholders will wish to appraise the effect of the purchase consideration split in terms of effect on:

(i) voting power;
(ii) earnings per share;
(iii) dividend cover;

(iv) debt/equity ratio;
(v) liquidity;
(vi) borrowing power.

(3) *Valuation of B plc*

A key consideration in the valuation of company B would be in terms of prospective future earnings.

In assessing future profit levels, account should be taken of the following:

(i)   profit forecasts of previous periods, compared with actual results;
(ii) quality of earnings, particularly as regards earnings from speculative activities or activities with a limited number of years' earning power;
(iii) economies in future costs, particularly with regard to realism of anticipated cost savings;
(iv) directors' emoluments, particularly having regard to changes in the size of the board of directors.

(4) *Shareholders of B plc*

In assessing the attractiveness of the offer, the following considerations are relevant:

(i)   effect on income;
(ii) effect on capital (these are usually set out in the takeover document);
(iii) equity participation—either immediately in the form of shares or at some future date in the form of convertible loan stock;
(iv) taxation considerations (income tax, capital gains tax).

(5) *Summary*

Initially the crucial point to establish is how much the 'victim' company is worth to the acquiring company. This sets a ceiling equivalent to the maximum value of the consideration which must be offered. Clearly this value must meet the minimum expectation of the shareholders of the 'victim' company.

The acquiring company must then assess the implications of the various possible ways of financing the acquisition, e g cash or shares. The factors referred to in (2) and (4) above are particularly relevant.

Clearly there is no perfect solution. At the end of the day, however, the package proposed must be acceptable to both parties.

INDEX